Ethical Problems
In Federal
Tax Practice

ASPEN PUBLISHERS

Ethical Problems In Federal Tax Practice

Fourth Edition

Bernard Wolfman
Fessenden Professor of Law Emeritus
Harvard Law School

Deborah H. Schenk
Marilynn and Ronald Grossman Professor of Law
NYU Law School

Diane Ring
Professor of Law
Boston College Law School

Wolters Kluwer
Law & Business

AUSTIN   BOSTON   CHICAGO   NEW YORK   THE NETHERLANDS

Aspen Publishers
Attn: Permissions Department
76 Ninth Avenue, 7th Floor
New York, NY 10011-5201

To contact Customer Care, e-mail customer.care@aspenpublishers.com, call 1-800-234-1660, fax 1-800-901-9075, or mail correspondence to:

Aspen Publishers
Attn: Order Department
PO Box 990
Frederick, MD 21705

Printed in the United States of America.

1 2 3 4 5 6 7 8 9 0

ISBN 978-0-7355-7634-6

Library of Congress Cataloging-in-Publication Data

Wolfman, Bernard, 1924-
  Ethical problems in federal tax practice / Bernard Wolfman, Deborah H. Schenk, Diane Ring — 4th ed.
    p. cm.
  Includes bibliographical references and index.
  ISBN 978-0-7355-7634-6
1. Taxation — Law and legislation — United States. 2. Legal ethics — United States. 3. Tax consultants — Legal status, laws, etc. — United States. I. Schenk, Deborah H., 1947- II. Ring, Diane M. III. Title.

KF6289.W64 2008
343.7304 — dc22

2008010430

About Wolters Kluwer Law & Business

Wolters Kluwer Law & Business is a leading provider of research information and workflow solutions in key specialty areas. The strengths of the individual brands of Aspen Publishers, CCH, Kluwer Law International, and Loislaw are aligned within Wolters Kluwer Law & Business to provide comprehensive, in-depth solutions and expert-authored content for the legal, professional, and education markets.

CCH was founded in 1913 and has served more than four generations of business professionals and their clients. The CCH products in the Wolters Kluwer Law & Business group are highly regarded electronic and print resources for legal, securities, antitrust and trade regulation, government contracting, banking, pension, payroll, employment and labor, and health care reimbursement and compliance professionals.

Aspen Publishers is a leading information provider for attorneys, business professionals, and law students. Written by preeminent authorities, Aspen products offer analytical and practical information in a range of specialty practice areas from securities law and intellectual property to mergers and acquisitions and pension/benefits. Aspen's trusted legal education resources provide professors and students with high-quality, up-to-date, and effective resources for successful instruction and study in all areas of the law.

Kluwer Law International supplies the global business community with comprehensive English-language international legal information. Legal practitioners, corporate counsel, and business executives around the world rely on the Kluwer Law International journals, loose-leafs, books, and electronic products for authoritative information in many areas of international legal practice.

Loislaw is a premier provider of digitized legal content to small law firm practitioners of various specializations. Loislaw provides attorneys with the ability to quickly and efficiently find the necessary legal information they need, when and where they need it, by facilitating access to primary law as well as state-specific law, records, forms, and treatises.

Wolters Kluwer Law & Business, a unit of Wolters Kluwer, is headquartered in New York and Riverwoods, Illinois. Wolters Kluwer is a leading multinational publisher and information services company.

To my wife, Toni G. Wolfman
B.W.

To Proctor, Bebeth, and Courtney
D.H.S.

To Liam, Caroline, and Anna
D.M.R.

Summary of Contents

Table of Contents

Preface

The "old authors," Bernard Wolfman and Deborah Schenk, are delighted to welcome Diane Ring as a co-author, not only because of her acumen and writing skills but also because she pulled the laboring oar on this edition. This is also an appropriate time to acknowledge our deep gratitude to Jim Holden, who was a co-author of the first three editions. Jim is a towering member of the tax bar and an expert in professional responsibility issues as they arise in tax practice. He is widely viewed as a conscience of the practicing tax bar. This edition draws heavily on the prior editions and Jim's contributions to those earlier editions have continued to shape our work.

It has been over a decade since the last edition and much has happened since then. The ABA's Model Rules of Professional Conduct have been adopted by most states as the basis for regulating lawyer conduct within their borders and have been amended several times. As law firms have expanded and become global entities, the ethical problems faced by lawyers have taken on new dimensions and become ever more complex. After a relative period of quiet, tax shelters, particularly those used by corporations, have become a significant issue again. It has become increasingly apparent that lawyers have played an important role in designing and marketing shelters, as well as issuing opinion letters designed to protect clients from penalties. As a result the Internal Revenue Service has shifted its focus somewhat to target attorneys. The Treasury Department's efforts to regulate tax practice through Circular 230 were met with a storm of criticism and many disagreements continue. Finally, the last decade has seen a large number of accounting and financial scandals, as well as the implosion of major corporations and accounting firms. Repeatedly commentators have asked, "Where were the lawyers?"

We have designed this book to provide a framework and a source of materials for the study of the ethical problems that a lawyer faces in federal tax practice. It has evolved from our experience in teaching this subject and in our tax practice activity as well. We are convinced that that the prism of tax practice is a useful one through which to explore the most practical as well as the most abstract and philosophical of ethical concerns. We find that a professional responsibility course taught from this focus can provide insights and principles that are applicable in virtually any area of law practice as well as insights that are peculiar to tax practice. Two of us have offered a course in Ethical Problems in Tax Practice that satisfies the ABA mandate that all law students take a course in professional responsibility. One of us has taught a more specialized course to those pursuing an LLM in tax.

Those who have taught from the book before will find that the basic structure of this edition follows the earlier editions, although much material is new, and there has been some reorganization.

Throughout the book we have maintained the underlying theme of role differentiation that brings to the fore the somewhat differing standards that govern the tax lawyer as *advocate* from those that govern the tax lawyer as *advisor*. This reflects the approach taken by the Model Rules, which has standards of conduct that are not quite the same for advisor and advocate. Following an introductory chapter that provides a general professional and philosophical perspective, there are four chapters that study the tax lawyer in his performance of the four overlapping roles that he commonly plays. The next chapter examines the special issues the tax lawyer confronts in government and as the lawyer for an entity. The final chapter turns to the business of the profession.

The materials that we have included are not exhaustive. Every student should acquire a copy of the Model Rules of Professional Conduct (and perhaps the ethical rules that are effective in the state in which he or she will practice). Students will find other helpful materials in the Appendix. A useful reference work is Standards of Tax Practice (Wolfman, Holden and Harris 6th ed.), published by Tax Analysts.

Bernard Wolfman
Deborah Schenk
Diane Ring

April 2008

Ethical Problems
In Federal
Tax Practice

Chapter 1

A Perspective

A. The Tax Lawyer's Roles and Responsibilities

Although the demand for tax advice is met by a professional mix of lawyers and nonlawyers, the roles and responsibilities of the tax lawyer are the main concerns of this book. From time to time we will advert to accountants and others in the field and to points of cooperation and abrasion between the lawyer and other professionals, but we will focus primarily on the ethical problems and professional obligations of the lawyer who practices tax law.

1. The Tax Lawyer's Duties

The layman and the legal novice usually think of the lawyer as the client's champion, fighting the client's every battle before administrative agencies and judges. The role of legal fighter is an important one. Many statements on the profession's ethical standards emerge from the picture that portrays the lawyer as a knight in armor (whether or not shining), but you will see that the fight in which he engages is one with some holds barred. Furthermore, the fighter role is not his only one, and certainly not the tax lawyer's exclusive role.

It is generally agreed that every lawyer, in private or government practice, owes his client the duty of competence, loyalty, and confidentiality. While the three prongs of that duty lie at the foundation of the lawyer-client relationship, the lawyer has other duties, and they too affect the framework of the relationship.

A second duty of pervasive importance is the one the lawyer owes to "the system," an imprecise concept blending together notions of society, the profession, and the law. Ordinarily, in performing his duty to the client, the lawyer carries out his duty to the system as well. There are times, however, when the lawyer, while pursuing his client's interests competently, loyally, and discreetly, must hold himself and his client's interests in check in order to perform the less defined, seemingly contradictory duty that he owes to the system as a whole.

You will also see that the functioning of the system in a complex society does not always permit easy identification of the lawyer's "client." Sometimes the system compels the lawyer to take into account the private interests of people whom he must treat as clients, although their interests may be antagonistic to those of the person who actually retains him. These system-created "clients" may be those on the opposite side of the nominal client's business deal, or they may be individual public investors, with the nominal client a promoter or corporation.

To this point we have mentioned only the duties of the lawyer, those he owes to the client, to the system, and to others. The client, however, also will have duties to honor, and the lawyer must advise him as to both the existence of a legal obligation and the performance required of him. For the tax lawyer, this will usually involve the duty that the client as taxpayer owes to the tax collector.

In advising a client to pay a tax, the lawyer may be carrying out an obligation that he owes equally to his client and to the government; that is, to the system that creates and administers the tax laws. There will be times, however, when the tax lawyer's fidelity to the system may require that he terminate a long-standing relationship with a client, this typically in a situation in which the client refuses to discharge an obligation that the lawyer told him was due.

The lawyer's duties to client and system as well as his duties to other clients are often complementary, but sometimes they conflict. A large part of your study of professional responsibility in the tax field will deal with the tension between the lawyer's basic duty to his client in dynamic relationship to his other duties, which may give texture to, and impinge upon, the duty he owes to his client. The breadth, difficulty, and subtlety of the tax lawyer's responsibilities will become clearer when you see them in context as the tax lawyer performs the variety of roles he must play. A number of high-profile tax and accounting scandals in this first decade of the twenty-first century, combined with continuing concern over the "tax gap" (taxes due but not reported or paid), have placed the role of the tax lawyer in high relief. Decisions on matters of tax ethics and professional responsibility are critical not just for tax lawyers and their clients, but also for the government and society.

2. *The Tax Lawyer's Roles*

When representing a client, the tax lawyer usually serves as adviser or advocate and sometimes as both. On occasion, the tax lawyer may act exclusively as citizen, speaking in her own right on an issue of tax policy, but a concurrent or prior relationship with a client may impose a constraint on the lawyer that does not restrict other citizens, one that grows out of a duty of loyalty or confidentiality owed to the client. The constraint may operate whether the lawyer serves the client as adviser or advocate.

You will see that sometimes the lawyer's responsibilities as adviser differ from those she bears as advocate. The lawyer's obligation to represent her client "zeal-ously" may dominate when she serves as an advocate in the courtroom. In the role of adviser, the lawyer's duty to the system may require that she repress her zeal for her client's cause, at least to a degree. Despite the usefulness of the adviser-advocate dichotomy as an analytic tool, however, it is inadequate by itself. You must examine the performance of the lawyer within the particular setting in which she is acting and inquire into her responsibilities in light of her role in that setting.

The tax lawyer works in four principal areas: compliance, controversy, planning, and tax policy. In each of the four settings, the lawyer will be adviser or advocate, and sometimes both.

Compliance finds the lawyer preparing or guiding the preparation of her client's tax return. In this role, the lawyer is primarily a legal adviser, although if she anticipates controversy, the advice she gives may reflect the advocate's strategy. Advice designed to avoid controversy, to avoid even an audit, raises some of the most difficult ethical questions with which she will deal.

Controversy usually begins when the government disputes a position taken on the client's return. In this context, the tax lawyer serves as advocate before the Internal Revenue Service or in court. She seeks to sustain her client's position or to better it. The controversy that begins with a revenue agent's simple inquiry may end with a decision of the Supreme Court. As you will see, because the government tends to be represented by professional people, often lawyers, when the matter is in controversy, the private lawyer's duty to her client is paramount. She tends to see her obligation that way, and so does the professional world in which she operates.

The third setting involves *planning* in which the lawyer helps her client arrange his affairs so as to minimize tax liabilities while maximizing the total return from his business and financial transactions. In planning, the tax lawyer may be only a counselor or she may be a negotiator as well. The planner's role may be only expositive, informing her client as to the state of the law. Or she may go well beyond, explaining how to select among various alternative approaches to a business or family objective, each of which has more or less tax exposure than another. To help the client achieve his objective after he has opted for a particular course of action, the lawyer may negotiate the business transaction, becoming an advocate while continuing to advise.

The government has an obvious interest in any transaction designed to minimize tax liabilities. Yet the government is not represented when the planning occurs. For that reason or perhaps for others, the zealousness of a tax lawyer's representation of her client's interests in the planning stage may disserve the system if it is too extreme. The system may therefore impose a restraint on the lawyer's conduct in the planning stage even though similar conduct, virtually unrestrained and aggressive, might be viewed quite favorably, as evidence of her loyalty and competence, if she were representing her client in the courtroom.

The fourth area in which to view the tax lawyer's performance is that of *tax policy.* Here the lawyer may serve as a paid lobbyist, seeking the adoption or repeal of particular tax legislation, or urging the Treasury Department to adopt or modify regulations. She may also speak in public forums, expressing her own view or the view of a client as to what the law ought to be, or she may write articles or books expressing her own views or those of the clients who retain her. A government lawyer working in the Treasury Department or on the staff of the Joint Committee on Taxation may be involved full-time in the preparation of legislative programs and the drafting of statutes.

When the private lawyer enters the realm of tax policy formulation, her professional responsibilities are poorly defined. Speaking out for herself or for a client, paid or unpaid, she is in an amorphous and ambiguous state. Sometimes her duty of client loyalty may seem to recede almost to the vanishing point. This is permitted, even encouraged at times, because the lawyer's deference to her conscience or the needs of the body politic for the views of experts untainted by economic interests are thought more important. Yet, at times, the interests of a present or former client will be allowed to silence a lawyer whose freedom to speak in the political arena would be uninhibited were she a citizen only.

B.   The Ethical Framework Surrounding Tax Practice

Examining the subject of professional responsibility through the window of tax practice should help you confront ethical problems with sophistication. Our hope is that you will find principles and standards to guide you in every field of practice. As a vehicle for the study of ethical standards, the tax field is special because it illuminates the importance of role differentiation. No other field so well crystallizes the almost ever-present conflict between the lawyer's duty to her client and her responsibility to the system. With the anchor and concreteness provided by the single body of substantive tax law, you are able to study problems of professional responsibility and ethics that may face every lawyer.

Perhaps because it constantly confronts this tension between duty to system and duty to client, the tax bar, as a group, has shown unusual interest in formulating and evaluating standards of practice. You should consider the opportunity that you as a tax lawyer will have to participate in this process.

1.   Ethical Regulation of the Tax Lawyer Through Professional Organizations

The American Bar Association, a national voluntary organization of lawyers, has assumed the primary responsibility for promulgating national ethical standards for the legal profession. In 1969, it adopted a Model Code of Professional Responsibility, which was superseded in 1983 by the Model Rules of Professional Conduct. The 1983 rules have been amended 28 times.

All lawyers are, of course, subject to ethical regulation by the authorities that admit them to practice, usually including the highest court of at least one state, as well as any federal courts before which the lawyer is admitted to practice, such as the United States Tax Court. Since most state and federal courts have adopted some version of the ABA Model Rules (some continue to follow the Model Code), we use the Model Rules and the ABA interpretations of them as a proxy for the rules and interpretations in any jurisdiction. You should recognize, however, that both the rules and their interpretation may differ in any particular jurisdiction, and there is no substitute for study of the local rules.

The ABA has a standing Committee on Ethics and Professional Responsibility that is charged with initiating amendments to the Model Rules and with issuing opinions interpreting the application of the rules to particular factual situations. Most jurisdictions maintain committees that are a counterpart to the ABA committee, initiating changes in the local rules and issuing opinions interpreting them. Some of these opinions deal expressly with tax practice matters, and we will refer to them in subsequent chapters. It is important to recognize that the ABA Model Rules and opinions are only advisory because the ABA does not exercise disciplinary authority over its members — that is instead a function of the admitting courts. The ABA pronouncements nonetheless are authoritative primarily because of their widespread acceptance by the courts. Beyond that, they are important because most lawyers voluntarily accept them as articulating appropriate practice standards.

In addition to the ABA standing committee, the ABA Section of Taxation has a Committee on Standards of Tax Practice whose forums and meetings have created a stimulating and provocative intellectual environment for those interested in the ethics of the profession. This committee has been actively involved in promulgating and promoting a draft set of ethics guidelines for law firms. These guidelines are largely the work of the late Frederic Corneel, a Boston tax lawyer, and they provide a valuable reference as to how ethics issues might be anticipated and resolved in a law firm.

The tax lawyer's conduct is thus subject to regulation by the courts before which she is admitted to practice, and those courts are likely to be influenced by the ABA standards. The Tax Court Rules of Practice expressly adopt the ABA Model Rules as the standard that governs practice before the court. See, e.g., Fu Investment Co., Ltd. v. Commissioner, 104 T.C. 408 (1995), infra p. 196. Tax Court Rules 200, 201, and 202 deal with the subjects of admission, professional conduct, and disbarment. These rules are reprinted in Appendix D.

In fact, it is seldom that disciplinary activity for violations of specific tax practice standards occurs in courts other than the Tax Court. Most of the activity specifically related to enforcement of tax practice standards occurs in the two other arenas that we will discuss, the civil penalty provisions and Circular 230. The ABA is influential in these arenas as well, because it, like other professional organizations, works actively to influence the content and administration of the penalty provisions and Circular 230.

In assessing standards for tax practice, it is important to recognize that the professional tax marketplace is occupied by many professionals other than lawyers. While lawyers, with a few exceptions, enjoy the exclusive right to represent clients before the courts,* other professionals represent clients before the Internal Revenue

---

*Although any lawyer may be admitted to practice before the Tax Court, §7452, the Tax Court rules require that nonlawyer applicants successfully complete an examination that is administered by the Tax Court. Tax Court Rules §200(a)(3). In fact, very few nonlawyers have been admitted to practice under this provision. An interesting question is whether lawyers who are employed by accounting firms or other nonlaw professional service firms may represent clients before the Tax Court. Should they be entitled to do so? For that matter, should lawyers employed by commercial organizations, such

Service, give advice on the tax law, prepare returns, and engage in a host of other activities related to the tax law. One type of professional, a certified public accountant, is assured the right to practice before the IRS by federal statute, 5 U.S.C. §500(c) (reprinted in Appendix A). This statute generally provides that all lawyers may, without additional qualification, practice before federal agencies. However, it singles out practice before the IRS and, in this one forum, expressly assures CPAs the same status as lawyers. Why do you suppose that Congress, in enacting 5 U.S.C. §500, decided to extend this particular entitlement to CPAs?

Some of the other professional groups active in tax practice have their own professional standards that are applicable to their members active in tax practice. Notable among these are the Statements on Standards for Tax Service issued by the American Institute of Certified Public Accountants. These are thoughtful expressions of practice standards that are useful in developing this subject. We will refer to some of the AICPA statements in subsequent chapters, and they are reprinted in Appendix G.

Because tax practice takes place in a mixed-profession setting, there is a clear need for some form of ethical regulation beyond that provided by the individual professional organizations. It is important that there be uniform standards for the various professionals to the extent that they perform identical services in the tax market. These are found in the civil penalty provisions of the Code and regulations, and in the set of Treasury regulations known as Circular 230 (the terms of which extend beyond lawyers to all tax practitioners). We now turn to those standards.

2.   *Ethical Regulation of the Tax Lawyer Through the Civil Penalty Provisions*

The civil penalty provisions of the Internal Revenue Code, and the regulations issued under them, constitute a set of minimum standards of conduct for taxpayers, practitioners, and others. Some of those provisions are aimed directly at tax practitioners, the most important being the income tax preparer penalty under §6694 and the aiding and abetting penalty under §6701. We will explore these two penalties and their application to tax practitioners in the next chapter. Changes to §6694 in 2007 pose interesting questions about penalties and the dynamics between the tax practitioner and the client.

3.   *Ethical Regulation of the Tax Lawyer Through the Circular 230 Standards*

The Secretary of the Treasury is authorized to regulate practice before the department and to suspend or disbar any representative found to be incompetent or

---

as a department store, be entitled to represent tax clients before the courts? We will return to this subject later in this chapter.

disreputable or who violates regulations. 31 U.S.C. §330(b) (reprinted in Appendix B). Under this authority, the Treasury Department has issued a set of regulations that specifically govern practice before the Internal Revenue Service. 31 C.F.R. Part 10 (reprinted in Appendix C). These regulations are referred to popularly as "Circular 230," the name associated with an earlier directive. They are administered by an IRS Director of Practice, who reports to the Treasury general counsel.

Circular 230 §10.2(e) defines the term "practitioner" to include attorneys, CPAs, and "enrolled agents."* Attorneys and CPAs are, as noted previously, eligible to practice before the IRS by reason of their professional status by virtue of 5 U.S.C. §500(b), (c). Enrolled agents are individuals who either successfully complete an examination or establish that their prior IRS experience qualifies them for enrollment. §10.4. In this book, we use the term "practitioner" to refer to lawyers, CPAs, and enrolled agents involved in tax practice.

Circular 230 establishes standards in various areas, including minimum levels of accuracy for tax return advice given to clients, §10.34; the diligence required of practitioners, §10.22; limitations on fee arrangements, §10.27; limitations on former government employees who enter into private practice, §10.25; prohibition on representation of conflicting interests, §10.29; minimum quality standards for tax shelter opinions, §10.35; and numerous other aspects of tax practice.

To provide teeth for these standards, Circular 230 establishes disciplinary machinery under which sanctions such as disbarment, suspension, or reprimand may be imposed for violation of the standards. §§10.50-10.52. Proceedings are initiated by the Director of Practice, who may arrive at an administrative disposition of a matter. If the matter is contested, it is tried before an Administrative Law Judge, whose decision may be reviewed in a federal district court and in turn appealed to higher courts. §§10.6-10.72. In order to ensure that violations of the Circular 230 standards will not go unnoticed, IRS personnel who have reason to believe that a practitioner has violated Circular 230, or who receive information to that effect, are obligated to refer that information to the Director of Practice. §10.53. Moreover, as you will see in the next chapter, the fact that a civil penalty has been imposed on a practitioner may sometimes require a referral to the Director of Practice.

Washburn v. Shapiro

409 F. Supp. 3 (S.D. Fla. 1976)

FULTON, District Judge. On April 16, 1975, plaintiff, Paul C. Washburn, an accountant, filed his complaint in this Court seeking review of the administrative

---

*Circular 230 actually includes another professional group, enrolled actuaries, in the term "practitioner." Enrolled actuaries are actuaries who qualify under 29 U.S.C. §1242, and their practice before the IRS is limited to certain employee benefit matters. We do not deal in this book with practice standards for enrolled actuaries.

proceedings which resulted in his disbarment from practicing before the Internal Revenue Service.

On July 12, 1973, in this Court, Paul C. Washburn was convicted of violating 26 U.S.C. §7206(2) which prohibits willfully and knowingly aiding, assisting, counseling, procuring or advising the preparation or presentation to the Internal Revenue Service of a tax return which is fraudulent or false as to any material matter. This conviction arose from Washburn's having prepared a joint return for Edward B. McLean, which return Washburn signed for both Mr. McLean and his wife. Washburn, however, had no power of attorney to sign on Mrs. McLean's behalf, and knew that she had filed a separate return.

On October 10, 1973, the Director of Practice, United States Department of the Treasury, notified plaintiff that he was considering the institution of disbarment proceedings against the plaintiff. These proceedings were instituted on February 14, 1974. In his decision Judge Travis concluded that Washburn's conviction of an offense under 26 U.S.C. §7206(2) constituted a conviction of a criminal offense under the revenue laws of the United States for which he might be disbarred or suspended from practice before the Internal Revenue Service. He held that Washburn had been shown to be disreputable within the meaning of 31 C.F.R. §10.50 in view of his criminal conviction and the conduct supporting it. He ordered the respondent disbarred from further practice before the Internal Revenue Service subject only to the condition that if his conviction were nullified the disbarment would be terminated. The plaintiff appealed that decision and on February 24, 1975, the General Counsel of the Treasury Department issued his decision affirming the initial decision of the administrative law judge. The General Counsel's decision constitutes the final administrative action in the matter.

Considering the complaint on the merits, defendants contend that the administrative proceedings which resulted in plaintiff's disbarment were entirely proper, both substantively and procedurally. The Court agrees.

The substantive law governing plaintiff's disbarment is Section 1026 of Title 31 of the United States Code which provides:

> The Secretary of the Treasury may prescribe rules and regulations governing the recognition of agents, attorneys, or other persons representing claimants before his department, and may require of such persons, agents and attorneys, before being recognized as representatives of claimants, that they shall show that they are of good character and in good repute, possessed of the necessary qualifications to enable them to render such claimants valuable service, and otherwise competent to advise and assist such claimants in the presentation of their cases. And such Secretary may after due notice and opportunity for hearing suspend, and disbar from further practice before his department any such person, agent, or attorney shown to be incompetent, disreputable, or who refuses to comply with the said rules and regulations, or who shall with intent to defraud, in any manner willfully and knowingly deceive, mislead, or threaten any claimant or prospective claimant, by word, circular, letter, or by advertisement.

Plaintiff does not challenge the validity of this statute or of the regulations promulgated pursuant thereto as set forth in 31 C.F.R. §10.50 *a et seq.*

The evidentiary criterion for judicial review of a final decision of an administrative agency is whether there is substantial evidence in the record to support the challenged administrative determination.

It is a matter of record that Paul C. Washburn was convicted of a felony under 26 U.S.C. §7206(2), that all appeals are exhausted and that the conviction is final.

The complaint filed by the Director of Practice alleged that the respondent was enrolled to practice and has engaged in practice before the IRS; and that the respondent was subject to disbarment from practice before the IRS (1) by reason of his having been convicted of violating 26 U.S.C. §7206(2), pursuant to 31 C.F.R. §10.51(a), and (2) by reason of his having given false or misleading information to the IRS or an officer or an employee thereof in connection with a matter pending before them, knowing such information to be false or misleading, pursuant to 31 C.F.R §10.51(b). The respondent filed no answer to the complaint filed by the Director of Practice. 31 C.F.R. §10.58(c) provides that every allegation in the complaint which is not denied in the answer shall be deemed to be admitted and may be considered as proved. It also provides that failure to file an answer shall constitute an admission of the allegations of the complaint, a waiver of hearing, and the Examiner may make his decision by default.

At the hearing, exhibits were introduced into evidence by the complainant, Director of Practice. No testimony was offered by the complainant or the respondent.

PROCEDURAL DUE PROCESS

Plaintiff has raised the following arguments in support of his contention that the administrative proceedings violated his right to procedural due process of law:

1. Defendants provided him with inadequate notice of the administrative disbarment proceedings;
2. Defendants failed to give him knowledge of the specific allegations made against him;
3. Plaintiff was denied the right to confront adverse witnesses;
4. Plaintiff was denied the right to question the admissibility of documents submitted by the government at the hearing;
5. Plaintiff's attorney was compelled to make admissions and statements regarding his client which violated the attorney-client privilege;
6. The burden of proof was unconstitutionally shifted from the prosecuting authority to plaintiff at the hearing;

7. The documents relied on at the hearing were not properly received in evidence;
8. Testimony was received at the hearing by one or more witnesses who were not sworn and or who were not subject to cross examination;
9. There was lack of separation of prosecuting authority and judicial authority;
10. The initial decision was written by a different judge than the judge who presided over the hearing;
11. Plaintiff was required to bear the burden of proving his "innocence" rather than requiring the government to prove his "guilt";
12. The administrative proceedings should have been stayed pending plaintiff's appeals of his conviction;
13. The complainant failed to identify plaintiff as the same person as the person convicted under 26 U.S.C. §7206(2); and
14. It was improper for the Treasury Department's general counsel to act on behalf of the Secretary of the Treasury in rendering the appellate decision affirming the initial decision of the administrative law judge.

Defendants contend that the procedural standards required in a "full-blown" hearing set forth in the Administrative Procedure Act, 5 U.S.C. §§556 and 557, are not applicable here because 5 U.S.C. §554 provides that the standards apply only when required by statute. With respect to plaintiff's disbarment, no such statutory requirement exists. Plaintiff does not contest this. The applicable statute, 31 U.S.C. §1026, states that the Secretary is required to provide "due notice and an opportunity for hearing." Thus although a respondent in a disbarment proceeding is not entitled to a "full-blown" hearing, he is entitled to the requisites of elementary fairness — due notice and the opportunity to be heard. The Court has carefully considered each of plaintiff's allegations of procedural violations and finds them all to be without merit.

. . . Upon review of the record, the Court concludes that there was substantial evidence to support Washburn's disbarment, and that there was no violation of plaintiff's right to substantive due process of law.

NOTE

Mr. Washburn argued that he was denied procedural due process because there was a "lack of separation of prosecuting authority and judicial authority," but the court apparently was not impressed. How troubling is it that the IRS or the Treasury Department may hold most of the cards in this kind of disciplinary forum? Is it troubling that a practitioner who is aggressively representing her client, by irritating the IRS personnel on the other side, could risk referral to the Director of Practice, another official, who has the power to initiate some rather awesome disciplinary machinery?

Owrutsky v. Brady

Unpublished Opinion Available at 91 TNT 49-46, LEXIS, FEDTAX Library,
TNT File (March 4, 1991)*

WILKINS, Circuit Judge. The Secretary of the Treasury appeals an order of the district court reversing the Secretary's decision to disbar Morton J. Owrutsky from practice before the Internal Revenue Service for failure to timely file income tax returns. We reverse.

Owrutsky is an attorney admitted to practice law in the state of Maryland. He had sufficient income to require him to file personal federal income tax returns for the tax years 1974 through 1979. He received an extension to August 25, 1975 for filing his 1974 tax return, but did not file it until May 4, 1976. He filed his 1975 tax return, due April 15, 1976, more than two years late on April 24, 1978. Although he was granted an extension to June 15, 1977 for his 1976 return, he did not file it until September 18, 1978. His 1977 return, due April 15, 1978, was not filed until June 4, 1980. He filed his 1978 return on July 12, 1980, which was more than one year after the extended deadline of April 30, 1979. After receiving an extension to June 15, 1980 for filing his 1979 tax return, he finally filed that return on June 26, 1981. Owrutsky received refunds for the years 1974, 1975, and 1976 and reported no tax liability for 1977, 1978, and 1979. During these years he represented clients in both civil and criminal tax matters in Internal Revenue Service proceedings.

On February 23, 1984, the Director of Practice for the Department of the Treasury initiated proceedings to have Owrutsky disbarred from practice before the Internal Revenue Service for willfully failing to file timely returns for the tax years 1974 through 1979. At a hearing before an administrative law judge, Owrutsky stated that he had not timely filed his tax returns because a partner in a real estate venture did not maintain adequate records to provide him the information needed to complete the returns in a timely manner. Rejecting this explanation, the ALJ found that the specific testimony given by Owrutsky and other witnesses who testified on his behalf concerning the partnership was not truthful and that in general Owrutsky's testimony was not worthy of belief.

The ALJ concluded that Owrutsky knew he was required to file returns, knew when they were required to be filed, and knew they were required to be timely filed. He held that Owrutsky's failure to timely file tax returns for six consecutive years was "clearly a voluntary, intentional violation of a known legal duty." Accordingly, he ordered Owrutsky disbarred from further practice before the Internal Revenue Service. In affirming the decision of the ALJ, the Secretary concluded that Owrutsky was aware of his obligations to timely file and "consciously, intentionally, and voluntarily chose not to file his returns when they were due."

The Secretary of the Treasury is authorized to "disbar from practice before the Internal Revenue Service any attorney . . . shown to be . . . disreputable." 31 C.F.R.

---

* Reprinted with permission by Tax Analysts.

section 10.50 (1990). Disreputable conduct includes "willfully failing to make Federal tax returns in violation of the revenue laws of the United States." 31 C.F.R. section 10.51(d) (1990). The Internal Revenue Code provides that individuals are required to file income tax returns before the April 15 deadline or within a period of time granted by an extension. See I.R.C. sections 6012(a), 6072(a), 6081(a) (West 1989). In the context of the felony and misdemeanor sections of the Revenue Code, the term "willfully" is defined as "a voluntary, intentional violation of a known legal duty." United States v. Pomponio, 429 U.S. 10, 12 (1976).

The district court held that Owrutsky's eligibility for refunds and his lack of any tax liability precluded a willful motive. The court overlooked the important finding by the ALJ that Owrutsky, an experienced practicing attorney, was fully aware that he had a legal duty to timely file returns regardless of his tax liability. See Spies v. United States, 317 U.S. 492 (1943). Under the *Pomponio* standard, willfulness does not require proof of any motive other than an intentional violation of a known legal duty. Cheek v. United States, 59 U.S.L.W. 4049 (U.S. Jan. 8, 1991); see also United States v. Sullivan, 369 F. Supp. 568, 569 (D. Mont. 1974) ("If by congressional fiat it is bad to fail to file an income tax return," then willfulness may be found when "the obligation to act is fully known and consciously disregarded.").

We hold that these facts, coupled with the ALJ's findings of the lack of credibility on the part of Owrutsky and his witnesses, provide substantial evidence to support a determination of willfulness.

NOTES

1.   Circular 230 mandates that no practitioner may employ or accept assistance from a disbarred or suspended person or be employed by or assist such a person. §10.24. It also prohibits aiding a disbarred or suspended person in practicing before the IRS, and the maintaining of a partnership with such a person is presumed to be a violation. §10.51(j). If Mr. Owrutsky was a member of a law firm or an employee of such a firm, would that firm be required to expel him in order to avoid further violations of Circular 230? This ripple effect of a violation can have serious consequences.

For a detailed consideration of Circular 230 and related issues (including administrative law jurisprudence of the Supreme Court, accuracy related penalties, and reportable transaction rules), see Practicing Law Institute's *Circular 230 Deskbook* by Jonathan G. Blattmachr, Mitchell M. Gans, & Damien Rios (2006).

2.   In connection with the prior problem, assume that no other member or employee of the firm engages in practice before the IRS. Could the firm employ Mr. Owrutsky on the ground that no violation would occur? Consider that all lawyers are, per se, "practitioners" subject to Circular 230. Does it matter if the other members of the firm, though not practicing before the IRS, do represent clients in tax matters, for example in tax planning?

3.   For that matter, what is "practice before the IRS"? Originally the definition in §10.2(d) appeared to require presentations to or communications with the IRS. Amendments to §10.2(d), finalized on September 26, 2007, clarify that practice

before the IRS includes the "rendering written advice with respect to any entity, transaction, plan or arrangement, or other plan or arrangement having a potential for tax avoidance or evasion." This clarification eliminates the question that had been raised as to what was the basis for §10.35, which sets minimum standards for tax shelter opinions, documents that seldom involve any direct presentation to or communication with the IRS. Is there any rational limit on what constitutes practice before the IRS?

4.   The status of a practitioner who is under suspension from practice became a significant matter of concern after the IRS announced its nonfiler initiative in 1993. In order to encourage nonfilers to come forward, the IRS announced that it would not prosecute those nonfilers who voluntarily came forward to disclose their situations. It turned out that many of the nonfilers were practitioners. For them, the question became one not only of prosecution but also of suspension from practice, carrying with it the necessity for expulsion from their firms. In order to overcome the deterring effect of that result, the Director of Practice issued a policy statement indicating that disciplinary action in his office, in nonegregious cases, would be so formulated so as not to require expulsion. 94 TNT 94-17, LEXIS, FEDTAX Library, TNT File (May 16, 1994).

4.   *The Interplay of Professional Self-Regulation and Government Regulation of Tax Practice Standards*

As you have seen, the rules and regulations that affect and often govern the professional conduct of tax lawyers emanate from both the government and the organized bar. The tension between the legal profession and government is an unresolved one. It is one that occurs between government and professions other than the law as well. Often a profession will claim a right to self-regulation to the exclusion of any role for government. It will argue that its unique expertise is needed to fashion and enforce sensible and fair rules, that without that expertise at the regulatory helm, society as a whole will suffer from the misguided directives of government bureaucrats. On the other hand, people outside the profession, government officials and others, frequently insist that if left entirely to itself, the profession will be self-serving. See Rhode, Why the ABA Bothers: A Functional Perspective on Professional Codes, 59 Tex. L. Rev. 689 (1981); Green, Whose Rules of Professional Conduct Should Govern Lawyers in Federal Court and How Should the Rules Be Created?, 64 Geo. Wash. L. Rev. 460 (1996). They believe that the public interest requires a public overseer to assure it its due.

In our country in which both the public and the profession play regulatory roles, it may well be that the performance of each is stimulated and energized by the other. It is possible that if one or the other were the sole player, neither would contribute as effectively as each does now. This speculation poses an empirical question for which there is no body of data to help provide an answer.

The past two decades have been notable because the dynamic interaction of government and the legal profession has resulted in heightened activity by both, more regulation than before, and a wider-spread interest in the regulation of the profession than one could observe in the preceding years.

For example, in 1980, government officials challenged the tax bar to modify its standards of conduct so that lawyers would play less of a role in fostering "abusive" tax shelters. The Treasury Department laid down the gauntlet by proposing new, strict standards for practice before the Internal Revenue Service. The government's announced plans for revision of Circular 230 led leaders of the tax bar, within the framework of the ABA, to leap-frog the government by promulgating ABA Formal Opinion 346. Less restrictive than the proposed amendments to Circular 230, Opinion 346 nevertheless imposed new rules on the tax lawyer with the goal of denying his aid and comfort to the promoter of publicly offered "abusive" tax shelter investments.

After the bar acted, the Treasury accepted the standards of Opinion 346 as essentially its own, largely incorporating them in Circular 230 in place of its earlier proposals. §10.33 (in 1984). Would the bar have acted if the government had not threatened to do so? Should the government have acquiesced in the bar's standards, less strict than those it had proposed? Would the Treasury's stricter standards, had they been adopted, have been effective if they lacked wide support among the bar? Would they have been preferable standards for society and its tax system? Did the bar's action in publishing Opinion 346 help to validate §10.33 (1984) against the challenge that it did not properly reflect professional standards?

In 1982, 1984, and 1989, Congress enacted amendments to the Internal Revenue Code, imposing new and stricter penalties on taxpayers whose tax returns, though not fraudulent or even negligent, claim deductions or exclusions that result in a substantial understatement of their tax liability. In the case of tax shelters, the penalty attaches to the understatement of tax liability unless, when the return was filed, "the taxpayer reasonably believed that the tax treatment of such item . . . was more likely than not the proper treatment." It is the lawyer, and sometimes the accountant, who will generally advise the taxpayer as to the likelihood that his tax return position will be accepted as "proper treatment." Even more directly implicated, the tax lawyer himself will be subject to direct penalties if he participates in the promotion of an "abusive tax shelter" or "aids" or "advises" with respect to a tax return knowing that it understates the taxpayer's liability.

The 1982 penalty provisions were enacted after the ABA issued Opinion 346, but before the Treasury incorporated its standards in Circular 230. Did the congressional action suggest that the government was unpersuaded that self-regulation of the tax bar had gone far enough? Would the Treasury have accepted the Opinion 346 standards in place of its own more stringent proposals if Congress had not entered the fray?

After the bar issued Opinion 346 and the government modified Circular 230 accordingly, the bar took a step not pressed by the government. The ABA's Section of Taxation proceeded to consider a revision of ABA Formal Opinion 314 that set the standards of conduct for a lawyer advising a client with respect to a position he might take on his tax return. The revision established a higher standard governing such conduct. Would the government have moved if the bar had not? Would the bar have taken its initiative with respect to Opinion 314 if the Treasury had not pointed its finger earlier with respect to tax shelter activity and if Congress had not enacted the penalties it did?

As tax shelters, particularly corporate tax shelters, continued to be a pressing concern in the 1990s, both Congress and the IRS acted again. In 2004, Congress implemented a stiffer regime of "reportable" transactions with increased penalties. Concerned that the opinion letters issued by lawyers with respect to tax shelters played a large role in fueling demand, Circular 230 was amended to impose very stringent guidelines on opinion letters. §§6662A, 6664(d). These developments and their direct effect on tax advisors and on tax opinions are considered extensively in Chapter 4.

NOTES

1. Professor Richard Abel has argued that the ABA's guidelines for professional responsibility "can only fail in the hopeless effort to mediate the contradictions inherent in the capitalist commodification of legal services, the differentiation of professional roles, and liberal agnosticism about truth." The following excerpt sets forth his argument:

> The Rules of Professional Conduct purport to resolve the ethical dilemmas of lawyers. They do so in order that those who draft, discuss, and consult them may be reassured that their conduct is morally correct. But the Rules do not resolve those dilemmas; they merely restate them in mystifying language that obscures the issues through ambiguity, vagueness, qualification, and hypocrisy. The capacity of these precepts to legitimate is constantly being eroded as internal inconsistencies, the meaninglessness of the language, and the empirical falsity and impossibility of their claims and prescriptions become apparent or are exposed by criticism. Hence, the Rules must constantly be rewritten in a vain effort to renew their legitimating force.
>
> The Rules cannot resolve the ethical dilemmas of lawyers because those dilemmas are inherent in the structure of the lawyer's role. First, legal representation, like all other goods and services under capitalism, has become a commodity. This means that clients *can* buy loyalty, which should be given freely out of a sense of social and political commitment. It means that clients *must* buy justice, which should be theirs by right, and will obtain only as much justice as they can afford. And it means that lawyers *must* seek to maximize their profits (especially as competition within the market for legal services intensifies), with the result that they must sell their services to the highest bidder and withhold them from those who cannot pay the price. In a capitalist society, the highest bidders will necessarily be those who own large amounts of capital and, within that group, those who wield monopoly power. Lawyers are, therefore, partisans in the class conflict that capitalism generates and cannot resolve, and virtually all lawyers are enlisted on the side of capital and against the numerous groups it oppresses, disenfranchises, and exploits — workers, the nonworking poor, women, minorities, citizens of the Third World, and all those who must live in a polluted environment and suffer the depletion of its resources.
>
> Nor can the Rules resolve the contradictions that arise from the fact that roles in large complex societies are differentiated but not dissociated. Lawyers and clients remain people. Although the lawyer claims to be amoral in agreeing to represent a client, and,

thus, refuses to accept ethical responsibility, lawyer, client, and society all persist in viewing the lawyer as implicated in the client's ends and accountable for the means used to pursue them. The client is usually also a responsible adult and cannot help but resent being dependent on the lawyer, especially when the legal profession has deliberately sought to foster this dependence by monopolizing expertise. For client, lawyer, and society all know that such one-sided dependence inevitably leads to exploitation.

Finally, the Rules cannot resolve the contradictions inherent in liberalism, which denies the existence of any truth other than the process of pursuing truth. This denial is essential if lawyers are to claim to be morally unaccountable for their clients' aims. But it requires a faith in process — judicial, legislative, electoral, administrative, even market — that few, if any, honestly maintain. Clients know they are interested in outcome, not process. Lawyers know they are striving to manipulate the process instrumentally. And society sees case after case in which it knows that the process is corrupt and the result is wrong.

Richard Abel, Why Does the ABA Promulgate Ethical Rules? 59 Tex. L. Rev. 639, 686-688 (1981).*

Is Professor Abel right? As to everything he says? As to anything? Former Judge Marvin E. Frankel thinks otherwise. See Marvin E. Frankel, Why Does Professor Abel Work at a Useless Task?, 59 Tex. L. Rev. 723 (1981).

2.   Practice standards for lawyers historically have evolved from the machinery of self-regulation. This process could be overtaken by legislative prescription of practice standards, with the result that such standards would be (as are penalties today) a matter of statutory interpretation rather than ethical reasoning. Would that result be satisfactory?

3.   Does that result exist today to the extent that tax practice standards are established by federal regulation, for instance, in Circular 230? Consider that many of the standards reflected in Circular 230 correspond to those prevailing in the professional marketplace. Can the 2004 changes be seen in that light? Would it be appropriate for Treasury to announce standards in Circular 230 that were markedly more restrictive than professional practice? Would such standards be observed? Could they be enforced?

C.   Ethics and Profession

Ethics is a branch of philosophy with a very rich literature that subsumes but does not often explicate the obligations of the lawyer. Let us begin therefore with a look at some of the writing that connects the responsibilities of the lawyer with the very broadest precepts of moral duty.

Charles Fried, The Lawyer as Friend: The Moral Foundations of the Lawyer-Client Relations

85 Yale L. J. 1060 (1976)*

Can a good lawyer be a good person? The question troubles lawyers and law students alike. They are troubled by the demands of loyalty to one's client and by the fact that one can win approval as a good, maybe even great, lawyer even though that loyalty is engrossed by over-privileged or positively distasteful clients. How, they ask, is such loyalty compatible with that devotion to the common good characteristic of high moral principles? And whatever their views of the common good, they are troubled because the willingness of lawyers to help their clients use the law to the prejudice of the weak or the innocent seems morally corrupt. The lawyer is conventionally seen as a professional devoted to his client's interests and as authorized, if not in fact required, to do some things (though not anything) for that client which he would not do for himself. In this essay I consider the compatibility between this traditional conception of the lawyer's role and the ideal of moral purity — the idea that one's life should be lived in fulfillment of the most demanding moral principles, and not just barely within the law. So I shall not be particularly concerned with the precise limits imposed on the lawyer's conduct by the positive rules of law and by the American Bar Association's Code of Professional Responsibility except as these provide a background. I assume that the lawyer observes these scrupulously. My inquiry is one of morals: Does the lawyer whose conduct and choices are governed only by the traditional conception of the lawyer's role, which these positive rules reflect, lead a professional life worthy of moral approbation, worthy of respect — ours and his own?

I will argue in this essay that it is not only legally but also morally right that a lawyer adopt as his dominant purpose the furthering of his client's interests — that it is right that a professional put the interests of his client above some idea, however valid, of the collective interest. I maintain that the traditional conception of the professional role expresses a morally valid conception of human conduct and human relationships, that one who acts according to that conception is to that extent a good person. Indeed, it is my view that, far from being a mere creature of positive law, the traditional conception is so far mandated by moral right that any advanced legal system which did not sanction this conception would be unjust.

In explicating the lawyer's relation to his client, my analogy shall be to friendship, where the freedom to choose and to be chosen expresses our freedom to hold something of ourselves in reserve, in reserve even from the universalizing claims of morality. These personal ties and the claims they engender may be all-consuming, as with a close friend or family member, or they may be limited, special-purpose claims, as in the case of the client or patient. The special-purpose claim is one in which the

*Reprinted by permission of the Yale Law Journal Company, Inc. and The William S. Hein Company, Volume 85, page 1060-1089. Citations omitted. This article appears in an expanded version as chapter seven of Right and Wrong, by Charles Fried (Harvard University Press 1978).

beneficiary, the client, is entitled to all the special consideration *within* the limits of the relationship which we accord to a friend or a loved one. It is not that the claims of the client are less intense or demanding; they are only more limited in their scope. After all, the ordinary concept of friendship provides only an analogy, and it is to the development of that analogy that I turn.

How does a professional fit into the concept of personal relations at all? He is, I have suggested, a limited-purpose friend. A lawyer is a friend in regard to the legal system. He is someone who enters into a personal relation with you — not an abstract relation as under the concept of justice. That means that like a friend he acts in your interests, not his own; or rather he adopts your interests as his own. I would call that the classic definition of friendship. To be sure, the lawyer's range of concern is sharply limited. But within that limited domain the intensity of identification with the client's interests is the same. It is not the specialized focus of the relationship which may make the metaphor inapposite, but the way in which the relation of legal friendship comes about and the one-sided nature of the ensuing "friendship." But I do insist upon the analogy, for in overcoming the arguments that the analogy is false, I think the true moral foundations of the lawyer's special role are illuminated and the utilitarian objections to the traditional conception of that role overthrown.

I come to what seems to me one of the most difficult dilemmas of the lawyer's role. It is illustrated by the lawyer who is asked to press the unfair claim, to humiliate a witness, to participate in a distasteful or dishonorable scheme. I am assuming that in none of these situations does the lawyer do anything which is illegal or which violates the ethical canons of his profession; the dilemma arises if he acts in a way which seems to him personally dishonorable, but there are no sanctions — legal or professional — which he need fear.

This set of issues is difficult because it calls on the same principles which provide the justification for the lawyer's or the friend's exertions on behalf of the person with whom he maintains a personal relation. Only now the personal relation is one not of benefit but of harm. In meeting the first criticism, I was able to insist on the right of the lawyer as friend to give this extra weight to the interests of his client when the only competing claims were the general claims of the abstract collectivity. But here we have a specific victim as well as a specific beneficiary. The relation to the person whom we deceive or abuse is just as concrete and human, just as personal, as to the friend whom we help.

It is not open to us to justify this kind of harm by claiming that personal relations must be chosen, not thrust upon us. Personal relations are indeed typically chosen. If mere proximity could place on us the obligations of friendship, then there would soon be nothing left of our freedom to bestow an extra measure of care over and above what humanity can justly claim. But there is a personal relation when we inflict intentional harm; the fact that it is intentional reaches out and particularizes the victim. "Who is my neighbor?" is a legitimate question when affirmative aid is in question; it is quite out of order in respect to the injunction "Do not harm your neighbor." Lying, stealing, degrading, inflicting pain and injury are personal relations too. They are not like failing to benefit, and for that reason they are laid under a correspondingly stricter regime than abstract harms to the collectivity. If I claim respect for my own concrete particularity, I must accord that respect to others. Therefore, what pinches here is the fact that the lawyer's personal engagement with the client is urging him to do that to his adversary which the very principles of personal engagement urge that he not do to anyone.

It is not wrong but somewhat lame to argue that the lawyer like the client has autonomy. From this argument it follows that the lawyer who is asked to do something personally distasteful or immoral (though perfectly legal) should be free either to decline to enter into the relationship of "legal friendship" or to terminate it. And if the client can find a lawyer to do the morally nasty but legally permissible thing for him, then all is well — the complexities of the law have not succeeded in thwarting an exercise of autonomy which the law was not entitled to thwart. So long as the first lawyer is reasonably convinced that another lawyer can be found, I cannot see why he is less free to decline the morally repugnant case than he is the boring or poorly paid case. True, but lame, for one wants to know not whether one *may* refuse to do the dirty deed, but whether one is morally *bound* to refuse — bound to refuse even if he is the last lawyer in town and no one else will bail him out of his moral conundrum.

If personal integrity lies at the foundation of the lawyer's right to treat his client as a friend, then surely consideration for personal integrity — his own and others' — must limit what he can do in friendship. Consideration for personal integrity forbids me to lie, cheat, or humiliate, whether in my own interests or those of a friend, so surely they prohibit such conduct on behalf of a client, one's legal friend. This is the general truth, but it must be made more particular if it is to do service here. For there is an opposing consideration. Remember, the lawyer's special kind of friendship is occasioned by the right of the client to exercise his full measure of autonomy within the law. This suggests that one must not transfer uncritically the whole range of personal moral scruples into the arena of legal friendship. After all, not only would I not lie or steal for myself or my friends, I probably also would not pursue socially noxious schemes, foreclose on widows or orphans, or assist in the avoidance of just punishment. So we must be careful lest the whole argument unravel on us at this point.

Balance and structure are restored if we distinguish between kinds of moral scruples. Think of the soldier. If he is a citizen of a just state, where foreign policy decisions are made in a democratic way, he may well believe that it is not up to him to question whether the war he fights is a just war. But he is personally bound not to fire dum-dum bullets, not to inflict intentional injury on civilians, and not to abuse prisoners. These are personal wrongs, wrongs done by his person to the person of the victim. So also, the lawyer must distinguish between wrongs that a reasonably just legal system permits to be worked by its rules and wrongs which the lawyer personally commits. Now I do not offer this as a rule which is tight enough to resolve all borderline questions of judgment. We must recognize that the border is precisely the place of friction between competing moral principles. Indeed, it is unreasonable to expect moral arguments to dispense wholly with the need for prudence and judgment.

Consider the difference between humiliating a witness or lying to the judge on one hand, and, on the other hand, asserting the statute of limitations or the lack of a written memorandum to defeat what you know to be a just claim against your client. In the latter case, if an injustice is worked, it is worked because the legal system not only permits it, but also defines the terms and modes of operation. Legal institutions have created the occasion for your act. What you do is not personal; it is a formal, legally-defined act. But the moral quality of lying or abuse obtains both without and within the context of the law. Therefore, my general notion is that a lawyer is morally entitled to act in this formal, representative way even if the result is an injustice, because the legal system which authorizes both the injustice (e.g., the result following the plea of the statute of limitations) and the formal gesture for working it insulates him from personal moral responsibility. I would distinguish between the lawyer's own wrong and the wrong of the system used to advantage by the client.

The clearest case is a lawyer who calls to the attention of the court a controlling legal precedent or statute which establishes his client's position even though that position is an unjust one. (I assume throughout, however, that this unjust law is part of a generally just and decent system. I am not considering at all the moral dilemmas of a lawyer in Nazi Germany or Soviet Russia.) Why are we inclined to absolve him of personal moral responsibility for the result he accomplishes? I assert it is because the wrong is wholly institutional; it is a wrong which does not exist and has no meaning outside the legal framework. The only thing preventing the client from doing this for himself is his lack of knowledge of the law or his lack of authority to operate the levers of the law in official proceedings. It is to supply that lack of knowledge or of formal capacity that the lawyer is in general authorized to act; and the levers he pulls are all legal levers.

Now contrast this to the lawyer who lies to an opposing party in a negotiation. I assume that (except in extreme cases akin to self-defense) an important lie with harmful consequences is an offense to the victim's integrity as a rational moral being, and thus the liar affirms a principle which denigrates his own moral status. Every speech act invites belief, and so every lie is a betrayal. However, may a lawyer lie in his representative capacity? It is precisely my point that a man cannot lie just in his representative capacity; it is like stabbing someone in the back "just" in a representative capacity. The injury and betrayal are not worked by the legal process, but by an act which is generally harmful quite apart from the legal context in which it occurs.

There is an important class of cases which might be termed "lying in a representative capacity." An example is the lawyer presenting to the court a statement by another that he knows to be a lie, as when he puts a perjurious client-defendant on the stand. There is dispute as to whether and when the positive law of professional responsibility permits this, but clearly in such instances it is not the lawyer who is lying. He is like a letter carrier who delivers the falsehood. Whether he is free to do that is more a matter of legal than personal ethics.

A test that might make the distinction I offer more palpable is this: How would it be if it were known in advance that lawyers would balk at the practice under consideration? Would it not be intolerable if it were known that lawyers would not plead the defense of the Statute of Frauds or of the statute of limitations? And would it not be quite all right if it were known in advance that you cannot get a lawyer to lie for you, though he may perhaps put you on the stand to lie in your own defense?

A more difficult case to locate in the moral landscape is abusive and demeaning cross-examination of a complaining witness. Presumably, positive law and the canons of ethics restrict this type of conduct, but enforcement may be lax or interpretation by a trial judge permissive. So the question arises: What is the lawyer morally free to do? Here again I urge the distinction between exposing a witness to the skepticism and scrutiny envisaged by the law and engaging in a personal attack on the witness. The latter is a harm which the lawyer happens to inflict in court, but it is a harm quite apart from the institutional legal context. It is perhaps just a matter of style or tone, but the crucial point is that the probing must not imply that the lawyer believes the witness is unworthy of respect.

The lawyer is not morally entitled, therefore, to engage his own person in doing personal harm to another, though he may exploit the system for his client even if the system consequently works injustice. He may, but must he? This is the final issue to confront. Since he may, he also need not if there is anyone else who will do it. Only if there is no one else does the agony become acute. If there is an obligation in that case, it is an institutional obligation that has devolved upon him to take up a case, to make arguments when it is morally permissible but personally repugnant to him to do so. Once again, the inquiry is moral, for if the law enjoins an obligation against conscience, a lawyer, like any conscientious person, must refuse and pay the price.

The obligation of an available lawyer to accept appointment to defend an accused is clear. Any moral scruples about the proposition that no man should be accused and punished without counsel are not morally well-founded. The proposition is intended to enhance the autonomy of individuals within the law. But if you are the last lawyer in town, is there a moral obligation to help the finance company foreclose on the widow's refrigerator? If the client pursues the foreclosure in order to establish a legal right of some significance, I do not flinch from the conclusion that the lawyer is bound to urge this right. So also if the finance company cannot foreclose because of an ideological boycott by the local bar. But if all the other lawyers happen to be on vacation and the case means no more to the finance company than the resale value of one more used refrigerator, common sense says the lawyer can say no. One should be able to distinguish between establishing a legal right and being a cog in a routine, repetitive business operation, part of which just happens to play itself out in court.

CONCLUSION

I do not imagine that what I have said provides an algorithm for resolving some of these perennial difficulties. Rather, what I am proposing is a general way of looking at the problem, a way of understanding not so much the difficult borderline cases as the central and clear ones, in the hope that the principles we can there discern will illuminate our necessarily approximate and prudential quest for resolution on the borderline. The notion of the lawyer as the client's legal friend, whatever its limitations and difficulties, does account for a kind of callousness toward society and exclusivity in the service of the client which otherwise seem quite mysterious. It justifies a kind of scheming which we would deplore on the part of a lay person dealing with another lay person — even if he were acting on behalf of a friend.

But these special indulgences apply only as a lawyer assists his client in his legal business. I do not owe my client my political assistance. I do not have to espouse his cause when I act as a citizen. Indeed, it is one of the most repellent features of the American legal profession — one against which the barrister-solicitor split has to some extent guarded the English profession — that many lawyers really feel that they are totally bought by their clients, that they must identify with their clients' interests far beyond the special purpose of advising them and operating the legal system for them. The defendants' antitrust lawyer or defendants' food and drug lawyer who writes articles, gives speeches, and pontificates generally about the evils of regulation may believe these things, but too often he does so because it is good for business or because he thinks that such conduct is what good representation requires. In general, I think it deplorable that lawyers have specialized not only in terms of subject matter — that may or may not be a good thing — but in terms of plaintiffs or defendants, in terms of the position that they represent.

There is a related point which cuts very much in the opposite direction. It is no part of my thesis that the *client* is not morally bound to avoid lying to the court, to pay a just debt even though it is barred by the statute of limitations, to treat an opposite party in a negotiation with humanity and consideration for his needs and vulnerability, or to help the effectuation of policies aimed at the common good. Further, it is no part of my argument to hold that a lawyer must assume that the client is not a decent, moral person, has no desire to fulfill his moral obligations, and is asking only what is the minimum that he must do to stay within the law. On the contrary, to assume this about anyone is itself a form of immorality because it is a form of disrespect between persons. Thus in very many situations a lawyer will be advising a client who wants to effectuate his purposes within the law, to be sure, but who also wants to behave as a decent, moral person. It would be absurd to contend that the lawyer must abstain from giving advice that takes account of the client's moral duties and his presumed desire to fulfill them. Indeed, in these situations the lawyer experiences the very special satisfaction of assisting the client not only to realize his autonomy within the law, but also to realize his status as a moral being. I want to make very clear that my conception of the lawyer's role in no way disentitles the lawyer from experiencing this satisfaction. Rather, it has been my purpose to explicate the less obvious point that there is a vocation and a satisfaction even in helping Shylock obtain his pound of flesh or in bringing about the acquittal of a guilty man.

Finally, I would like to return to the charge that the morality of role and personal relationship I offer here is almost certain to lead to the diversion of legal services from areas of greatest need. It is just my point, of course, that when we fulfill the office of friend—legal, medical, or friend *tout court*—we do right, and thus it would be a great wrong to place us under a general regime of always doing what will "do the most good." What I affirm, therefore, is the moral liberty of a lawyer to make his life out of what personal scraps and shards of motivation his inclination and character suggest: idealism, greed, curiosity, love of luxury, love of travel, a need for adventure or repose; only so long as these lead him to give wise and faithful counsel. It is the task of the social system as a whole, and of all its citizens, to work for the conditions under which everyone will benefit in fair measure from the performance of doctors, lawyers, teachers, and musicians. But I would not see the integrity of these roles undermined in order that the millennium might come sooner. After all, it may never come, and then what would we be left with?

NOTE

Professor Fried, in his lawyer-as-special-purpose-friend analogy, is able to conclude that the lawyer is morally entitled to act in a representative way even if the client wins a result that is unjust. He suggests that we must distinguish between "wrongs that a reasonably just system permits to be worked by its rules and wrongs which the lawyer personally commits." Does this mean that the lawyer may always escape moral responsibility for actions taken on behalf of his client as long as they are lawful? If not, what are the limitations?

Murray Schwartz, The Professionalism and Accountability of Lawyers*

66 Cal. L. Rev. 669 (1978)

The lack of definite answers to professional questions can in large part be explained by the absence of a general, coherent theory of professional behavior for lawyers. Indeed, given the persistent and pervasive nature of the dilemmas, it is surprising that such a theory has only recently received systematic consideration. The American Bar Association's Code of Professional Responsibility is the most prominent attempt to provide a guide for professional conduct. It has serious limitations, however, and it highlights the need for a general theory of professional behavior without satisfying it. One consequence of the absence of any general theory is that lawyers often respond to professional problems in ad hoc, pragmatic ways, redefining the issues to avoid reaching the ethical question. Such an approach, while not manifestly illegitimate, is a very limited and intellectually unsatisfactory way of responding to professional problems.

   This Article represents a step toward the development of a comprehensive analytical framework for considering questions of professional behavior and responsibility. It addresses primarily situations where in the course of a lawyer's representation of a client the conduct of either will affect a third party, and examines principles that might properly govern the lawyer's actions in such situations when the ends sought or the means used, though not illegal, could be described as unfair, unjust, or unconscionable.

   In considering these principles, it is necessary to distinguish between the lawyer acting as an *advocate* within the adversary system and the lawyer acting as *nonadvocate* (e.g., as negotiator or counselor) outside that system. For the advocate, two principles are posited as necessary to the effective working of the adversary system: a Principle of Professionalism, which obliges the lawyer within professional constraints to maximize the likelihood that the client will prevail, and a Principle of Nonaccountability, which relieves the advocate of legal, professional, and moral accountability for proceeding according to the first principle. This Article suggests that these principles cannot be transferred automatically to the nonadvocate, because the absence of a third-party arbiter in the negotiating/counseling situation fundamentally changes the lawyer's role. This discrepancy calls for a different professional rule for the nonadvocate which would require that as a matter of professionalism the nonadvocate lawyer refrain from assisting a client by "unconscionable" means or from aiming to achieve "unconscionable" ends, with the term "unconscionable" drawing its meaning largely from the substantive law of rescission, reformation, and torts. Furthermore, while the advocate may claim to be insulated from moral accountability because of the necessary implications of the adversary system, the nonadvocate may not make that claim — the nonadvocate lawyer should be held morally accountable for assistance rendered the client even though the lawyer is neither legally nor professionally accountable.

   [T]his Article proceeds on the assumption that the Advocate's Principle of Nonaccountability in all of its dimensions is necessary for the effective operation of the adversary system. If advocates could be called personally to account for representing clients fully within established professional restraints, they might give less than full commitment to their clients. Such a result would undercut the very assumptions of the adversary system. This Article proceeds on the hypothesis that in order to provide maximum opportunity to resolve disputes fairly, correctly, efficiently, and promptly, the adjudicatory system requires a corps of professionals committed to giving their best efforts to represent their clients.

   This Article adopts this hypothesis as applied to advocates, without attempting to prove it, in order to distinguish and consider the professionalism and accountability of lawyers functioning in a nonadvocate capacity. It is argued that whatever the validity of the Principle of Nonaccountability for advocates, its legitimacy rests on the particular structures and functions of the adversary system, and that the circumstances of nonadvocate lawyers require a different predicate for analysis of their professionalism and accountability. If the arguments justifying advocates' non-accountability fall short, and the distinction between the advocate and the nonadvocate proves insufficient to warrant different analysis, the moral problems that inhere in the adversary system would have to be confronted for both the advocate and the nonadvocate. It may also be that the following discussion of the nonadvocate's principles will raise doubts about the advocate's principles. In that case, an important issue would be whether, in the procedural language used earlier, the advocate should be entitled to file a demurrer in response to an attempt to impose moral accountability for professional behavior. The approach of this Article precludes treating these issues here. . . .

In the adversary system, the presence of the impartial arbiter has two important effects. First, it assures that there is one — and only one — part of the system charged with the responsibility of reaching the correct decision under the law (here the impartiality is non-partisanship and freedom from bias). Second, it makes it possible to entrust the parties with the presentation of issues, evidence, and arguments and with the challenges to them (here the impartiality is non-participation). The arbiter sees to it that the rules of the contest are followed, and then decides who has prevailed. Putting one's best foot forward by stepping on the feet of the other side makes sense because of the presence of an impartial arbiter. That presence legitimates the zealous advocate model of the lawyer and all that it entails. Lawyers are justified in using methods and seeking results with which they may personally disagree because of faith in the ability of the arbiter to reach a correct decision. . . .

Lawyers outside the adversary system face different environments and different expectations. It is therefore necessary to consider, independently of the parallel issues within the adversary system, what principles of professionalism and accountability should apply to the lawyer representing clients in a nonadvocate role.

Whatever other differences in role there may be for the lawyer serving in a nonadvocate capacity, the client's expectations of the lawyer would no doubt be the same as for the advocate. These expectations might warrant a Principle of Professionalism for the nonadvocate which would track closely the advocate's Principle of Professionalism. For example:

> When acting in a nonadvocate capacity on behalf of a client, a lawyer must, within the established constraints upon professional behavior, attempt to achieve the client's objectives.

It must be stressed that such a principle need not be derived solely from the advocate's principle proposed earlier, nor from the advocate's role. It could be derived independently from the nature of the lawyer-client relationship, which may present a set of general expectations regardless of context. But the problem nonetheless remains: since the advocate's principle was validated by the adversary system in which the advocate functions, the absence of that system may mean that a parallel principle for the nonadvocate, however derived, is not as readily or completely validated. The adversary system obliges the advocate to assist the client even though the means used or the ends sought may be unjust. Is the same obligation properly applied to the nonadvocate's professional conduct?

Two considerations suggest a negative answer. First, the basic difference between the environment of the adversary system on the one hand, and the range of nonadversary environments on the other, indicates that identical professional requirements might be inappropriate. Second, while the "established constraints upon professional behavior" for the advocate are specific and extensive, for the nonadvocate they are neither. The two general professional principles might, therefore, have to differ in order to compensate for the difference in the extent to which lawyers in the two roles are subject to special rules of professional behavior.

. . . . In the earlier discussion of the advocate's role, it was argued that the effective operation of the adversary system required a Principle of Professionalism which obliges the advocate to proceed in ways and toward ends that might be morally questionable. A second principle was, therefore, appropriate to provide that the advocate who adheres to the Principle of Professionalism is neither legally, professionally, nor morally accountable for the means used or the ends achieved. Should there be a similar principle for the nonadvocate who adheres to the limitations imposed by the proposed Professional Rule? In other words, may the nonadvocate demur to a charge of accountability, particularly *moral* accountability, for assisting a client in immoral conduct which is not prohibited by substantive law nor by a professional rule?

The issue is highlighted by comparing the moral accountability of the lawyer under the current ABA Code of Professional Responsibility with that of the nonlawyer representative. Generally, the nonlawyer representative is viewed as an agent of the principal, and thus is held morally accountable for any result to which the representative substantially contributes. A defense of duress may be available to the representative where the principal has threatened to subject the agent to pain, punishment, or other sanction sufficient to overcome the fortitude of a reasonable person in those circumstances. The representative might also claim a defense of "replacement" — that nothing would have been gained by refusing the principal since the agent would have been easily replaced with a willing substitute — though this argument is singularly unpersuasive in moral terms.

In contrast, Ethical Considerations 7-8 and 7-9 of the Code of Professional Responsibility appear to claim immunity from moral accountability for all lawyers. The key language in Ethical Consideration 7-8 is the admonition that "the decision whether to forego legally available objectives or methods . . . is ultimately for the client. . . ." Ethical Consideration 7-9 recognizes that actions "in the best interest of the client" may seem to the lawyer "to be unjust." Both ethical considerations permit but do not require the lawyer to withdraw in these circumstances.

The provision that the lawyer may but need not withdraw necessarily implies that either decision is correct as a matter of professional as well as legal accountability. With respect to moral accountability, if the provision may be read as taking any position at all on the issue, it is that as long as neither lawyer nor client does anything illegal, there is no moral accountability for the lawyer.

The stated purpose of the ethical considerations is to set forth principles that are "aspirational in character and represent the objectives toward which every member of the profession should strive." Use of the word "unjust" in the Code suggests an implicit recognition that there are problems of moral accountability. Thus, it is probably accurate to infer that by allowing the lawyer some latitude in deciding whether to withdraw, the Code is attempting to provide the nonadvocate with the same immunity from moral accountability that it accords the advocate. At the very least, there is something odd about a code of professional behavior which admonishes lawyers to attempt to prevent their clients from engaging in "unjust" conduct (impliedly conceding that this is an identifiable genus), and yet permits them to go forward without fear of reproach if the client is adamant.

Is there any reason why lawyers who have a right to withdraw should not be personally accountable for their conduct if they continue to pursue their clients' ends, merely because those ends are not proscribed by professional rule? For the advocate, the demands of the adversary system were sufficient to justify moral nonaccountability. It is now necessary to consider whether in the absence of that system there are attributes inherent in the nonadvocate role that independently justify an immunity for the lawyer which is not granted to lay representatives.

Much of the earlier discussion of the nonadvocate's Professional Rule is relevant to this question, particularly the implications of the first alternative version of the rule which, like the Code of Professional Responsibility, would allow the lawyer either to withdraw or to continue. It will be recalled that the objections surveyed earlier fell into three categories: unfairness to the lawyer, damage to the integrity of the lawyer-client relationship, and unfairness to the client.

The objection of unfairness to the lawyer rested on grounds of vagueness and unenforceability. Such considerations are not germane to questions of moral accountability. Since neither formal sanctions nor external enforcement agencies are involved, issues of fair notice and arbitrary enforcement simply do not arise.

The second objection, that the integrity of the lawyer-client relationship would be impaired, was based on two independent concerns. The first was that the client would resent the lawyer's presenting himself as a moral rather than purely legal advisor. Yet, as was previously noted, the Code of Professional Responsibility already encourages lawyers to tell their clients when they think their proposals are unjust. Recognition that lawyers have a moral obligation to do so, and will be held morally accountable for their own conduct or the achievement of their clients' goals, is not likely to have any further significant impact upon the lawyer-client relationship.

Another concern about the integrity of the lawyer-client relationship was that the client might make insufficient disclosure out of fear that the lawyer would conclude that the proposal was unjust and withhold assistance. But since the proposed Professional Rule does not oblige the nonadvocate to withdraw when the proposals are unjust (rather than unenforceable or substantively unconscionable), the impact of accountability is no more than this: lawyers must be prepared to defend, if they choose to do so, the morality of their own behavior and of their clients' objectives.

The final objection was that it would be unfair to the client to allow or oblige the lawyer to refrain from activity that the lawyer thought unconscionable, since the effect might be to deny legal assistance to clients whose sense of justness did not conform to the legal profession's arguably limited norm. That objection is just as valid here. Lawyers might hesitate to represent such clients *if* they could be held morally accountable even for ends which are neither criminal, fraudulent, nor unconscionable in the sense of the Professional Rule.

It is, of course, precisely this fear which in the context of the adversary system justifies obliging advocates to proceed without regard to the morality of the client's ends or the lawyer's means even when they believe that what they are doing is unjust. To justify the same immunity for the nonadvocate, we would have to find a social need for the technical assistance of nonadvocates that would take priority over moral considerations — a special need of men and women to have available persons in whom they may freely confide and who are professionally obliged to put their clients' interests above their own scruples.

Such a need, and such a justification, have recently been claimed by Professor Charles Fried. He argues that the moral justification for a lawyer's seemingly immoral behavior is analogous to the moral justification for one friend's behavior on behalf of another. Although the aptness of the analogy has been questioned, the core of the argument remains: the continued societal protection of the nonadvocate functions of the legal profession may depend in significant part upon the need for a morally insulated body of professionals who perform the social function of acting for others in this confidential, committed way. Professor Fried attempts further to justify nonaccountability by arguing that the lawyer's principal social function is to preserve the client's autonomy under the law. Without the lawyer's technical assistance, the argument goes, the client would suffer unjustified loss of autonomy since the client would no longer obtain all that the law allows. Practically all of Professor Fried's illustrations, however, especially of this second argument, are drawn from the context of litigation. The moral justification for enabling a client to obtain an immoral or unjust advantage when no third-party tribunal is available to review the transaction is far less clear.

From the standpoint of moral accountability, when a client seeks to retain a lawyer for help with a transaction, the lawyer may or may not believe that what is sought is immoral or unjust. A lawyer who does not believe that what is sought is immoral has no problem about proceeding one who believes that what is sought is immoral still has a choice of whether to assist or not. The lawyer is not prohibited legally or professionally from assisting. The assignment of moral accountability means only that the lawyer who proceeds must answer to the charge of immoral behavior. That lawyer may not demur. . . .

A compromise may be possible. Assume that all available lawyers refuse to assist in an undertaking because each has concluded that the proposed course of action is immoral or unjust and none wishes to assume moral accountability for immoral or unjust conduct. In that situation, there could be a group obligation to provide assistance, with the individual lawyer selected by lot, rotation, or special qualification, as is done in appointing counsel for an unpopular criminal defendant. The lawyer should then properly be able to claim immunity from moral accountability.

On the other hand, if it is clear from the outset that the client ultimately *will* be able to obtain the professional assistance needed to achieve the immoral end, there is little to be gained from holding lawyers morally accountable for voluntarily agreeing to assist. This could indeed argue for a general principle of moral nonaccountability for the nonadvocate similar to that which has been hypothesized for the advocate.

An ultimate resolution must turn on the balance to be struck between the social value of requiring nonadvocate lawyers to bear moral responsibility for their professional behavior and the political value of preventing government from exercising its licensing power in a way that frustrates citizens in the realization of their legal rights. In this light, the initial question of whether a nonadvocate should be granted the extraordinary insulation from moral accountability provided the advocate becomes clearer. The analysis outlined in this Article suggests that the answer to the question should be negative, so long as it is recognized that the answer is based on an essentially political judgment that lawyers outside the adversary system should not be obliged to assist all clients as a condition of being licensed to practice law. Furthermore, this conclusion is conditioned upon the validity of the basic assumptions which have informed this discussion that every client is entitled to be told whether a proposed course of action is or is not unlawful (lawyers may properly claim immunity from moral accountability if that is all they do); that clients may proceed to undertake the proposed course of action without the professional assistance of lawyers; and that all that is required of lawyers is that they be prepared to justify their conduct in moral terms — they may not demur to a charge of immorality in their professional behavior as nonadvocates.

NOTES

1.   For purposes of discussion, Professor Schwartz accepts the principle that a lawyer advocate may escape moral accountability for his lawful acts on behalf of a client, but he rejects the notion that such a principle protects the lawyer in a nonadvocate role. Does the lawyer act as advocate only when he appears in a representative capacity before courts or agencies? Or does he act as advocate whenever he represents his client in negotiation with third parties? Is nonadvocate activity essentially limited to counseling the client in a one-on-one environment? If so, is Professor Schwartz's position anything more than a conclusion that the lawyer may not, without becoming morally accountable, counsel his client to engage in unjust activity? If the client nevertheless elects to proceed with the unjust (though lawful) activity and directs the lawyer to sally forth and accomplish the deed, has counseling ended and advocacy begun? May the lawyer, having counseled against the unjust activity, become an advocate to effectuate it, free of moral accountability?

2.   Model Rule 1.2(b) states that "A lawyer's representation of a client, including representation by [judicial] appointment, does not constitute an endorsement of the client's political, economic, social or moral views or activities." No counterpart to this rule existed in the Model Code. Why did the authors of the Model Rules

include this statement as a rule? Will it have any impact on the public perception of a lawyer's association with a particular client? Might it also encourage lawyers to accept the representation of unpopular clients that they might have otherwise declined?

3.   What is the difference between tax fraud and an "ethical conflict"? Is the tax lawyer's primary duty to the client or to the government fisc? How would the answer to that question impact a lawyer's decision to handle the following issues on a tax return: ambiguity, mathematical error, change of facts, or mistake of law? To explore these questions, see Camilla E. Watson, Tax Lawyers' Ethical Obligations, and the Duty to the System, 47 Kan. L. Rev. 847 (1999).

D.   Members of the "Profession"

This chapter focuses on the duties, responsibilities, and ethical regulations applicable to tax lawyers. However, these discussions beg the question of who is a tax lawyer, and what constitutes the boundaries of legal practice. Tax lawyers, like all lawyers, are part of an organized profession. The license granted to lawyers to practice law confers on the holder both rights and responsibilities. This section deals with some of these limitations, especially as they impact tax lawyers.

States and the federal courts generally exclude nonlawyers from "the practice of law," presumably to protect the public from incompetence and to maintain standards. Nonlawyers can be penalized for the "unauthorized practice of law." What constitutes the practice of law, however, is a difficult question. This section tackles that issue, particularly as it relates to accountants whose practice increasingly is similar to that of lawyers.

1.   Unauthorized Practice — Lawyers vs. Nonlawyers

The tax field is a mixed professional market in which lawyers, accountants, employee benefit counselors, realtors, bankers, insurance salesmen, and others are all active to one degree or another. The established precept is that only lawyers may practice law. Model Rule 5.5 provides:

Rule 5.5 Unauthorized Practice of Law
(a) A lawyer shall not practice law in a jurisdiction in violation of the regulation of the legal profession in that jurisdiction, or assist another in doing so.

The official comment to the rule unduly minimizes the definitional difficulties. Seldom do unauthorized practice cases present anything other than a struggle over the definitional content and boundaries of "law practice," and the resolution is far from established.

In the tax area, however, despite the fact that the practitioners are mainly from two professions, law and accounting — or perhaps because of it — relatively few pending jurisdictional disputes occur between them. In a rather thorough review of unauthorized practice activity, tax practice is not even mentioned in the list of the most common areas of unauthorized practice. See Deborah Rhode, Policing the Professional Monopoly: A Constitutional and Empirical Analysis of Unauthorized Practice Prohibitions, 34 Stan. L. Rev. 1, 30 (1981). This does not mean that tax practitioners have generally adjusted to the tensions and that all accept the idea and reality of an interdisciplinary world of tax practice. In fact, tax practitioners, particularly lawyers, seem unable to let the matter rest. They address it with sufficient frequency that the intellectual pot keeps simmering, and sometimes it boils.

When actual disputes arise (as distinguished from mere dialogue), they seldom involve direct interdisciplinary challenges between lawyer and accountant. Instead, they most often involve a client who has been well served by a nonlawyer but seeks to avoid paying a fee on the ground that the services rendered constituted the unauthorized practice of law.

a.   The Authorized Practice of Tax Law by Nonlawyers — Federal Preemption

The primary reason for the relatively settled state of affairs is that a large part of tax practice is formally open to nonlawyers. Thus, to the extent that this practice is *law* practice, those nonlawyers who engage in it are pursuing the *authorized* practice of law.

Under 5 U.S.C. §500 (1982), reproduced in Appendix A, lawyers, by virtue of their status as such, are automatically entitled to practice before federal agencies, and the agencies may not impose added requirements for admission. However, §500(c) specifies that an individual who is a CPA may, by virtue of that status, represent a person before the IRS. Thus, CPAs are provided status equivalent to lawyers insofar as admission to practice before the Service is concerned, although Circular 230 makes reasonably clear that it is not authorizing "practice of law" for those whom state law does not authorize. See Agran v. Shapiro, infra. Moreover, in Circular 230, infra Appendix C, the Treasury Department establishes rules under which individuals who are neither lawyers nor CPAs may be admitted to practice before the Service.

As noted above, the September 26, 2007 changes to Circular 230 clarified that the term "practice before the Service" is very broad, touching upon most areas of tax practice other than litigation. It expressly includes the preparation of tax returns (Circular 230, §10.7, as amended February 23, 1984); it certainly includes rulings practice; and it includes the furnishing of tax opinions and written advice (Circular 230, §10.2(a)(4) amended 2007).

Under Rule 200 of the Rules of Practice of the United States Tax Court, reprinted in Appendix D, lawyers are automatically eligible to practice before the court, but nonlawyers who pass an admission examination may also be admitted to practice.

The question arises whether and to what extent this federally prescribed system of regulating both lawyers and accountants preempts the application of state limitations on the unauthorized practice of tax law. The following case is very important to the resolution of that question.

Sperry v. Florida
373 U.S. 379 (1963)

Mr. Chief Justice WARREN delivered the opinion of the Court.

Petitioner is a practitioner registered to practice before the United States Patent Office. He has not been admitted to practice law before the Florida or any other bar. Alleging, among other things, that petitioner "is engaged in the unauthorized practice of law, in that although he is not a member of the Florida Bar, he nevertheless maintains an office . . . in Tampa, Florida, . . . holds himself out to the public as a Patent Attorney . . . represents Florida clients before the United States Patent Office, . . . has rendered opinions as to patentability, and . . . has prepared various legal instruments, including . . . applications and amendments to applications for letters patent, and filed same in the United States Patent Office in Washington, D.C.," the Florida Bar instituted these proceedings in the Supreme Court of Florida to enjoin the performance of these and other specified acts within the State. Petitioner filed an answer in which he admitted the above allegations but pleaded as a defense "that the work performed by him for Florida citizens is solely that work which is presented to the United States Patent Office and that he charges fees solely for his work of preparing and prosecuting patent applications and patent assignments and determinations incident to preparing and prosecuting patent applications and assignments."

We do not question the determination that under Florida law the preparation and prosecution of patent applications for others constitutes the practice of law. Greenough v. Tax Assessors, 331 U.S. 486; Murdock v. Memphis, 20 Wall. 590. Such conduct inevitably requires the practitioner to consider and advise his clients as to the patentability of their inventions under the statutory criteria, as well as to consider the advisability of relying upon alternative forms of protection which may be available under state law. It also involves his participation in the drafting of the specification and claims of the patent application, which this Court long ago noted "constitute[s] one of the most difficult legal instruments to draw with accuracy," Topliff v. Topliff, 145 U.S. 156, 171. And upon rejection of the application, the practitioner may also assist in the preparation of amendments, which frequently requires written argument to establish the patentability of the claimed invention under the applicable rules of law and in light of the prior art. Nor do we doubt that Florida has a substantial interest in regulating the practice of law within the State and that, in the absence of federal legislation, it could validly prohibit nonlawyers from engaging in this circumscribed form of patent practice.

But "the law of the State, though enacted in the exercise of powers not contraverted, must yield" when incompatible with federal legislation. Gibbons v. Ogden, 9 Wheat. 1, 211. Congress has provided that the Commissioner of Patents "may prescribe regulations governing the *recognition* and conduct *of agents,* attorneys, *or other persons* representing applicants or other parties before the Patent Office," and the Commissioner has provided by regulation that "[a]n applicant for patent . . . *may be represented by an attorney* or *agent* authorized to practice before the Patent Office in patent cases." [Emphasis added.] The current regulations establish two separate registers "on which are entered the names of all persons recognized as *entitled to represent applicants* before the Patent Office in the preparation and prosecution of applications for patent." [Emphasis added.] One register is for attorneys at law, and the other is for nonlawyer "agents." A person may be admitted under either category only by establishing "that he is of good moral character and of good repute and possessed of the legal and scientific and technical qualifications necessary to enable him to render applicants for patents valuable service, and is otherwise competent to advise and assist them in the presentation and prosecution of their applications before the Patent Office."

The statute thus expressly permits the Commissioner to authorize practice before the Patent Office by nonlawyers, and the Commissioner has explicitly granted such authority. If the authorization is unqualified, then, by virtue of the Supremacy Clause, Florida may not deny to those failing to meet its own qualifications the right to perform the functions within the scope of the federal authority. A State may not enforce licensing requirements which, though valid in the absence of federal regulation, give "the State's licensing board a virtual power of review over the federal determination" that a person or agency is qualified and entitled to perform certain functions, or which impose upon the performance of activity sanctioned by federal license additional conditions not contemplated by Congress. "No State law can hinder or obstruct the free use of a license granted under an act of Congress." Pennsylvania v. Wheeling & B. Bridge Co., 13 How. 518, 566.

b. Window onto What It Means to Practice Law: Cases Involving Client-Nonlawyer Fee Disputes

As indicated above, most unauthorized practice cases in the tax field involve the client's use of the practice barrier as a sword to defeat the otherwise just claim of a nonlawyer practitioner to his fee for services rendered. The following cases illustrate the principle. *The Matter of New York County Lawyers' Assn.* and *Gardner* cases, discussed in Agran v. Shapiro, are examples of tax cases that did not involve a fee dispute.

Agran v. Shapiro

127 Cal. App. 2d Supp. 807, 273 P.2d 619 (1954)

PATROSSO, Judge. [Plaintiff recovered a $2,000 judgment from defendants for "accounting services" rendered. Defendants appeal, arguing that the services in question constitute the practice of law for which plaintiff is not entitled to recover.

Plaintiff, a CPA admitted to practice before the Treasury but not a member of the bar, had prepared defendants' federal income tax returns for the years 1947 through 1950 and their estimated 1951 returns. Defendants had leased a building to Pritchard, a used car dealer, for a fixed rental and a percentage of his profits. As part of the arrangement, defendants agreed to guarantee the Bank of America against loss in financing Pritchard's operations and deposited $115,000 to secure the guarantee. Subsequently, the bank foreclosed against Pritchard and $43,260.56 of defendants' deposit was forfeited. Plaintiff claimed that amount as a loss on defendants' 1948 return and filed an application for tentative carry back adjustment to the preceding two years. The applications were apparently granted and defendants received a refund.

For the preparation of the 1947 return, plaintiff charged and was paid the sum of $30. Plaintiff submitted no statement for the preparation of returns for subsequent years, explaining to the defendants that the IRS normally audited all tentative tax refund claims and therefore he could not fix his fee until after discussing the problem of the net operating business loss with the revenue agent. He added that his fee would be based on any tax savings accomplished.

No problem arose until August 1951. Then plaintiff received a call from Mr. Manson, a treasury agent, who stated that the Pritchard loss did not qualify as a "net operating loss" and that defendants were subject to an additional assessment of $15,000 for the years 1946 through 1949. Plaintiff disputed this contention and in the course of several meetings with Mr. Manson "cited him numerous cases." Plaintiff "spent five days in the county law library and in his office reading tax services, cases, reports and decisions," and "spent approximately four days in reading and reviewing over one hundred cases on the proposition of law involved."

As a result of these conferences, Mr. Manson submitted a report recommending an additional assessment of $6,280. Subsequently, another treasury agent, Mr. Stewart, was assigned to the case. After one meeting and two telephone conferences, Mr. Stewart expressed agreement with plaintiff's contention but "wanted to talk to the defendant once more." Early in 1952, defendant advised plaintiff that his services were no longer needed and that an agreement had been signed with Mr. Stewart closing the matter. On March 31, 1952 plaintiff submitted the following bill to defendants:]

To Professional Services Rendered:
Conferences with revenue agent Edgar Manson re his examination of the income tax returns of Morris and Helen Shapiro for the years 1946, 1947, 1948, and 1949.

Research of the problems involved and preparation of arguments to overcome the following proposed assessments of income tax:

Conference with conferee James A. Stewart and subsequent discussion of the questions involved by telephone, resulting in a reversal of all disputed items contained in revenue agent Manson's report.

Report submitted by conferee James A. Stewart resulted in a tax saving in excess of $6,000.00

Total due for services to date $2,000.00.

While courts have experienced difficulty in formulating a precise and all-embracing definition as to what constitutes the practice of law, the one generally accepted is that announced in Eley v. Miller, 7 Ind. App. 529, 535, and adopted by our Supreme Court in People v. Merchants' Protective Corp., 1922, 189 Cal. 531, 535, as follows: "'As the term is generally understood, the practice of the law is the doing and performing services in a court of justice, in any matter depending therein, throughout its various stages, and in conformity to the adopted rules of procedure. But *in a larger sense it includes legal advice and counsel, and the preparation of legal instruments and contracts by which legal rights are secured although such matter may or may not be depending in court.*'" [Emphasis added.] However, whether a particular activity falls within this general definition is frequently a question of considerable difficulty, and particularly is this true in the field of taxation where questions of law and accounting are frequently inextricably intermingled as a result of which doubt arises as to where the functions of one profession end and those of the other begin. Specifically, whether practice before an administrative tribunal in tax matters constitutes the practice of law has been the subject of decisions elsewhere which appear to be in some conflict.

It appears to be generally conceded that it is within the proper function of a public accountant, although not a member of the bar, to prepare federal income tax returns, except perhaps in those instances where substantial questions of law arise which may competently be determined only by a lawyer. In the case at hand we find no real difficulty in concluding that in the preparation of the income tax returns in question plaintiff did not engage in the practice of law. They are of such a simple character that an ordinary layman without legal or accounting training might have prepared them in the first instance. An inspection thereof discloses that the defendants had but three sources of taxable income: Mr. Shapiro's salary, the rental received from the building leased to Mr. Pritchard, and the rental from a two-flat building, one-half of which was occupied by the defendants as their residence, with the exception of the year 1950 in which the defendants in addition received interest from savings and loan associations in the total sum of $612.68. Likewise the deductions claimed therein, other than the portion of the Pritchard loss carried forward into the 1949 return were usual and ordinary expenses incident to the ownership and operation of income producing real property, the determination of the propriety of which required no particular legal knowledge.

A different and more serious question arises, however, with respect to the services rendered by the plaintiff in preparing the applications for a carry back adjustment and refund of taxes paid for the previous two years, and the preparation of the 1949 return wherein a deduction was claimed for a portion of the Pritchard loss, as well as his subsequent services in resisting the additional assessment proposed by the Treasury Department upon the ground that the Pritchard loss did not constitute a "net operating loss" within the meaning of the "carry back" provisions of the statute. At this stage no question of accounting was involved. Neither the fact that the loss had been sustained nor the manner in which it arose was questioned. The only question was whether, under the admitted facts, the loss was one which could be "carried back," the answer to which depended upon whether or not it was a loss "attributable to the operation of a trade or business regularly carried on by the taxpayer" within the meaning of that phrase as used in the Internal Revenue Code. We see no escape from the conclusion that under the circumstances this question was purely one of law. . . .

Not only was the question which arose here one of law but a difficult and doubtful one as well. Moreover, it is evident that the plaintiff himself fully appreciated this. He not only testified that "in his opinion it was a tough case because it was an isolated one" but he detailed at length the extensive research of the legal authorities which he was required to make in order to support his position that the loss was one which qualified as a "net operating loss" under a proper interpretation of the statutory definition.

Both parties place reliance upon the decision in the Matter of New York County Lawyers Ass'n, 1948, 273 App. Div. 524, affirmed without opinion in 299 N.Y. 728.

There one Bercu, an accountant, not a member of the bar, was consulted by a corporation [which kept its books upon an accrual basis] as to whether or not certain sales taxes accrued but not paid in a preceding year could be deducted in the income tax return for a subsequent year. Thereafter he rendered an opinion to the effect that such taxes might be deducted in the year of their payment, for which services he submitted a bill for $500. This not being paid, he instituted suit in the municipal court and was denied recovery upon the ground that the services for which he sought payment constituted the practice of law. Thereafter the reported proceeding was instituted by the Lawyers' Association to have him adjudged guilty of contempt of court and to enjoin him from similar activities in the future. The court held that in undertaking to render an opinion upon the point in question Mr. Bercu was unlawfully undertaking to practice law. However, the court seems to have been influenced in reaching the conclusion which it did largely by reason of the fact that Mr. Bercu had not previously performed any accounting work for the corporation, nor was the advice given in connection with the preparation by him of an income tax return for the corporation. It must be admitted that, as contended by plaintiff here, the language of the opinion suggests that if Bercu had been the accountant of the corporation or engaged to prepare its income tax return, he might have advised it as he did in his opinion without subjecting himself to the charge of practicing law in so doing. In the course of the opinion it said

> Respondent is most persuasive when he challenges the consistency of recognizing an accountant's right to prepare income tax returns while denying him the right to give income tax advice. As respondent says, precisely the same question may at one time arise during the preparation of an income tax return and at another time serve as the subject of a request for advice by a client. The difference is that in the one case the accountant is dealing with a question of law which is only incidental to preparing a tax return and in the other case he is addressing himself to a question of law alone.

Thus it would appear that the New York court adopts, as the criterion for determining whether advice relative to tax matters constitutes the practice of law, whether or not it is given as an incident to accounting work or in the preparation of tax returns. While for reasons hereinafter stated we are not prepared to accept the view to its fullest extent, we do not believe that the court necessarily entertained the view that, as plaintiff here contends, having prepared the return, an accountant who is not a member of the bar may thereafter undertake to advise his client with respect to difficult or doubtful legal questions arising therefrom or undertake to seek a refund, the right to which depends wholly upon the interpretation of the taxing statutes. No such question was there presented, and we are not prepared to accept the decision as holding that a nonlawyer may properly perform services such as those last enumerated.

We believe, however, that the criterion formulated by the New York court for determining whether a particular activity does or does not constitute the practice of law is unsatisfactory for the reasons well stated by the Supreme Court of Minnesota in Gardner v. Conway, 1951, 234 Minn. 468. There a nonlawyer had undertaken to prepare a federal income tax return which necessarily involved the determination by him of various questions of law. By reason of this a proceeding in contempt and to restrain him from similar practice in the future was instituted against him, and he defended upon the ground that, while the preparation of the tax return involved the determination of legal questions, this did not constitute the practice of law because the resolving of such questions was but incidental to the preparation of the return which was an act that any layman might perform. In the course of an elaborate opinion, the court said

> If we bear in mind that any choice of criterion must find its ultimate justification in the interest of the public and not in that of advantage for either lawyer or nonlawyer, we soon cease to look for an answer in any rule of thumb such as that based upon a distinction between the incidental and the primary. Any rule which holds that a layman who prepares legal papers or furnishes other services of a legal nature is not practicing law when such services are incidental to another business or profession completely ignores the public welfare. A service performed by one individual for

another, even though it be incidental to some other occupation, may entail a difficult question of law which requires a determination by a trained legal mind. Are we to say that a real estate broker who examines an abstract of title and furnishes an opinion thereon may not be held to practice law merely because the examination of a title is ancillary to a sale and purchase of real estate? . . . The incidental test has no value except in the negative sense that if the furnishing of the legal service is the primary business of the actor such activity is the practice of law, even though such service is of an elementary nature. In other words, a layman's legal service activities are the practice of law unless they are incidental to his regular calling; but the mere fact that they are incidental is by no means decisive. In a positive sense, the incidental test ignores the interest of the public as the controlling determinant.

In rejecting the incidental test, it follows that the distinction between law practice and that which is not may be determined only from a consideration of the nature of the acts of service performed in each case. No difficulty arises where such service is the primary business of the actor. We then have law practice. Difficulty comes, however, when the service furnished is incidental to the performance of other service of a nonlegal character in the pursuit of another calling such as that of accounting. In the field of income taxation, as in the instant case, we have an overlapping of both law and accounting. An accountant must adapt his accounting skill to the requirements of tax law, and therefore he must have a workable knowledge of law as applied to his field. By the same token, a lawyer must have some understanding of accounting. In the income tax area, they occupy much common ground where the skills of both professions may be required and where it is difficult to draw a precise line to separate their respective functions. The public interest does not permit an obliteration of all lines of demarcation. We cannot escape reality by hiding behind a facade of nomenclature and assume that "taxation," though composed of both law and accounting, is something *sui generis* and apart from the law. If taxation is a hybrid of law and accounting, it does not follow that it is so wholly without the law that its legal activities may be pursued without proper qualifications and without court supervision. The interest of the public is not protected by the narrow specialization of an individual who lacks the perspective and the orientation which comes only from a thorough knowledge and understanding of basic legal concepts, of legal processes, and of the interrelation of the law in all its branches. Generally speaking, whenever, as incidental to another transaction or calling, a layman, as part of his regular course of conduct, resolves legal questions for another — at the latter's request and for a consideration — by giving him advice or by taking action for and in his behalf, he is practicing law if difficult or doubtful legal questions are involved which, to safeguard the public, reasonably demand the application of a trained legal mind. What is a difficult or doubtful question of law is not to be measured by the comprehension of a trained legal mind, but by the understanding thereof which is possessed by a reasonably intelligent layman who is reasonably familiar with similar transactions. A criterion which designates the determination of a difficult or complex question of law as law practice, and the application of an elementary or simple legal principle as not, may indeed be criticized for uncertainty if a rule of thumb is sought which can be applied with mechanical precision to all cases. Any rule of law which purports to reflect the needs of the public welfare in a changing society, by reason of its essential and inherent flexibility, will, however, be as variable in operation as the particular facts to which it is applied.

We are confirmed in our conclusion that the activities of the plaintiff which we have detailed fall within the domain of the lawyer by a consideration of The Statement of Principles Relating to Practice in the Field of Federal Income Taxation, which was recommended by the National Conference of Lawyers and Certified Public Accountants and approved by the Council of the American Institute of Accountants, May 8, 1951, wherein it is stated:

> *3. Ascertainment of Probable Tax Effects of Transactions.* . . . The ascertainment of probable tax effects of transactions frequently is within the function of either a certified public accountant or a lawyer. However, in many instances, problems arise which require the attention of a member of one or the other profession, or members of both. When such ascertainment raises uncertainties as to the interpretation of law (both tax law and general law), or uncertainties as to the application of law to the transaction involved, the certified public accountant should advise the taxpayer to enlist the services of a lawyer. When such ascertainment involves difficult questions of classifying and summarizing the transaction in a significant manner and in terms of money, or interpreting the financial results thereof, the lawyer should advise the taxpayer to enlist the services of a certified public accountant. . . .
>
> *6. Representation of Taxpayers before Treasury Department.* Under Treasury Department regulations lawyers and certified public accountants are authorized, upon a showing of their professional status, and subject to certain limitations as defined in the Treasury Rules, to represent taxpayers in proceedings before that Department. If, in the course of such proceedings, questions arise involving the application of legal principles, a lawyer should be retained, and if, in the course of such proceedings accounting questions arise, a certified public accountant should be retained. . . .
>
> *8. Claims for Refund.* Claims for refund may be prepared by lawyers or certified public accountants, provided, however, that where a controversial legal issue is involved or where the claim is to be made the basis of litigation, the services of a lawyer should be obtained.

From what has been said, it appears that plaintiff undertook to determine the "tax effect" of defendant's transaction with Pritchard, the ascertainment of which involved uncertainties both as to the interpretation of the taxing statute as well as the application thereof to the transaction in question. It is likewise evident from the plaintiff's testimony that at the time of preparing the application for carry back adjustment and refund he realized that a "controversial legal issue" was involved with respect to which the Treasury Department might take a contrary view, for he assigned this as a reason why he could not then advise defendants as to what his fee in the matter would be. And when he finally submits his bill we find that, in detailing therein the services covered thereby, no mention is made of accounting work or that involved in the preparation of the returns, but rather he describes the same as consisting of "conferences with revenue agent(s)" and "*research of the problems involved and preparation of arguments to overcome*" the proposed additional assessments, the only basis for which could be the Treasury Department's claim that the

Pritchard loss did not constitute a "net operating loss" under section 122. Surely the solution of this "problem" did not involve or depend upon the application of accounting principles or procedure, but of legal principles and precedents. These were the subject of plaintiff's "research" and these alone could serve as the foundation for his "arguments" addressed to the representatives of the Treasury Department in resisting the "proposed assessments."

From what has been said, we would have but little hesitancy in concluding that the services rendered by plaintiff other than those involved in the preparation of the income tax returns and possibly others of an accounting character constitute the practice of law as that term has been judicially defined in this State. The more serious questions which present themselves, however, are (1) whether the controlling test of what constitutes the practice of law in the field of federal income taxation is dictated by federal legislation, congressional or administrative, and (2) the effect of the federal regulations which have been adopted in this field. Upon behalf of the plaintiff, it is urged by *amicus curiae* that an affirmative answer is required to the first inquiry and that, inasmuch as plaintiff was enrolled as an agent in the Treasury Department, and by virtue thereof licensed to practice before that Department, all of his activities in the instant case were within the scope of such license, and any action by a state court which would interfere with or curtail the right so granted is not only unwarranted but unconstitutional.

[T]he Secretary of the Treasury is authorized to prescribe "regulations governing the recognition of agents representing claimants before his departments." Pursuant to this statutory authority, the Secretary issued Circular 230, which insofar as material here reads as follows:

> An agent enrolled before the Treasury Department shall have the same rights, powers and privileges and be subject to the same duties as an enrolled attorney: *Provided,* that an enrolled agent shall not have the privilege of drafting or preparing any written instrument by which title to real or personal property may be conveyed or transferred for the purpose of affecting Federal taxes, nor shall such enrolled agent advise a client as to the legal sufficiency of such an instrument or its legal effect upon the Federal taxes of such client; *And provided further,* That nothing in the regulations in this part shall be construed as authorizing persons not members of the bar to practice law.
>
> Practice before the Treasury Department shall be deemed to comprehend all matters connected with the presentation of a client's interests to the Treasury Department, including the preparation and filing of necessary written documents, and correspondence with the Treasury Department relative to such interests.

No case which we have been able to discover has undertaken to directly decide the precise question with which we are confronted, namely, whether the Treasury Regulations referred to have the effect of declaring that services performed by an enrolled agent in connection with federal income tax matters do not constitute the practice of law in the sense that such practice is prohibited, by state law, when engaged in by other than members of the bar. . . .

We do not believe that the regulations in question were intended to or have the effect contended for on behalf of plaintiff. We regard as highly significant the concluding clause in section 10.2(f) "that nothing in the regulations in this part shall be construed as authorizing persons not members of the Bar to practice law." This statement must be read in context with the opening sentence of the section providing that "An agent enrolled before the Treasury Department shall have the same rights, powers and privileges ... as an enrolled attorney" and as qualifying the same. As admittedly the Treasury Department is without authority to prescribe the rights and privileges to be exercised by persons except those appearing before it upon behalf of others, this provision could only have been intended as a disavowal of any intent upon the part of the Secretary of the Treasury to confer authority upon enrolled agents, not members of the bar, to perform acts upon behalf of others in connection with matters before the department which would otherwise constitute the practice of law. We cannot subscribe to the argument advanced upon behalf of the plaintiff that this provision was merely "a catch-all clause designed to prevent enrolled agents from holding themselves out as general attorneys" and "to limit the authority granted an enrolled agent to the precise field of Federal income taxation." Rather it suggests a recognition that "practice before the Treasury Department," while it may include acts which do not constitute the practice of law, and hence within the authority of enrolled agents, though not lawyers, to perform, also comprehends others of such character as to bring them within this classification.

In essence plaintiff's contention is that the effect of the Treasury Regulations is to declare that an enrolled agent, though not a lawyer, may, in the representation of others in tax matters before the Treasury Department, lawfully perform all of the services which a member of the bar is authorized to perform except "the privilege of drafting or preparing any written instrument by which title to real or personal property may be conveyed or transferred for the purpose of affecting Federal taxes" or advising "a client as to the legal sufficiency of such an instrument or its legal effect upon the Federal taxes of such client." If this be true, we see no reason for the concluding proviso in 10.2(f), disavowing any intent to thereby authorize non-lawyers to perform acts in connection with tax matters before the department which would constitute the practice of law.

Yet another consideration confirms us in the conclusion we have reached. We refer to the Statement of Principles previously adverted to, wherein it is recognized that representation before the Treasury Department may involve the "application of legal principles" necessitating the retention of a lawyer. We can hardly believe that, if the conferees representing the certified public accountants who joined in recommending the adoption of the Statement and the Members of the Council of the American Institute of Accountants who approved it, were of the view that the effect of the Treasury Regulations authorized an enrolled agent who was not a lawyer to perform any and all services on behalf of others before the Treasury Department that might be performed by a lawyer, they would have given their adherence thereto.

Thus we conclude that, as indicated, the judgment in favor of plaintiff includes an award for services which constituted the practice of law, for which, not being a member of the bar he was not entitled to recover.

———————

The court in *Agran* was troubled by the proviso in Circular 230 that none of its provisions should be "construed as authorizing persons not members of the bar to practice law." This provision survives as §10.32 of the current version of Circular 230. To what extent did it contribute to the court's decision in *Agran?* What is the purpose of §10.32?

The Treasury Department responded to cases like *Agran* by issuing the following interpretation.

21 Federal Register 833

(February 7, 1956)

For some months the Treasury Department has had under consideration the revision of Treasury Department Circular 230 relating to practice before the department. Congress has given the Treasury Department the responsibility of regulating practice before the department. It is in the exercise of this responsibility that the department has issued the rules and regulations set forth in Circular 230, taking into consideration, among other things, the need of taxpayers for tax advice and assistance, the number of tax returns filed each year, the volume and complexity of problems relating thereto, the skills and training required for proper representation of taxpayers' interests and the availability of people who can provide such service.

The department believes the standards prescribed in Circular 230 have generally operated in a highly satisfactory manner, have made available to taxpayers representatives to assist them in presenting their interests to the department, and have facilitated fair and orderly administration of the tax laws.

It is the intention of the department that all persons enrolled to practice before it be permitted to fully represent their clients before the department, in the manner hereinafter indicated. This is apparent from §10.2(b), which states that the scope of practice (of agents as well as attorneys) before the department comprehends "all matters connected with the presentation of a client's interest to the Treasury Department." Enrollees, whether agents or attorneys, have been satisfactorily fully representing clients before the department for many years. The department believes this has been beneficial to the taxpayers and to the government and that there presently appears no reason why the present scope and type of practice should not continue as it has in the past.

The department's attention has been called to the decisions of certain state courts and to statements which suggest varying interpretations of §10.2(f) of the circular. This subsection makes it clear that an enrolled agent shall have the same rights, powers, and privileges and be subject to the same duties as an enrolled attorney, except that an enrolled agent may not prepare and interpret certain written instruments. The second proviso of the subsection states that nothing in the regulations is to be construed as authorizing persons not members of the bar to practice law. The uniform interpretation and administration of this and other sections of Circular 230 by the department are essential to the proper discharge of the above responsibility imposed on it by the Congress.

It is not the intention of the department that this second proviso should be interpreted as an election by the department not to exercise fully its responsibility to determine the proper scope of practice by enrolled agents and attorneys before the department. It should be equally clear that the department does not have the responsibility nor the authority to regulate the professional activities of lawyers and accountants beyond the scope of their practice before the department as defined in §10.2(b) and nothing in Circular 230 is so intended.

The Department has properly placed on its enrolled agents and its enrolled attorneys the responsibility of determining when the assistance of a member of the other profession is required. This follows from the provision in §10.2(z) that enrolled attorneys must observe the canons of ethics of the American Bar Association and enrolled agents must observe the ethical standards of the accounting profession. The department has been gratified to note the extent to which the two professions over the years have made progress toward mutual understanding of the proper sphere of each, as for example in the Joint Statements on Practice in the Field of Federal Income Taxation and Estate Planning.*

The question of Treasury practice will be kept under surveillance so that if at any time the department finds that the professional responsibility of its enrolled agents and enrolled attorneys is not being properly carried out or understood, or that enrolled agents and attorneys are not respecting the appropriate fields of each in accordance with that Joint Statement, it can review the matter to determine whether it is necessary to amend these provisions of the circular to take other appropriate action.

NOTES

1. *Agran* was decided before *Sperry*. Would *Sperry* have changed the view of the California court? Can the court's conclusion stand after *Sperry*? In Grace v. Allen, 407 S.W.2d 321 (Tex. Civ. App. 1966), the court held that the *Sperry* rationale applied to practice before the IRS. The court permitted a CPA to sue for his fee for resolving a client's case in an IRS administrative appeal.

2. Eligibility to practice before state agencies is governed by state law. The New York Court of Appeals upheld the constitutionality of a state provision that limited the right to represent clients in state tax appeals to attorneys and CPAs, but not IRS-enrolled agents. New York State Society of Enrolled Agents v. New York

---

* Reprinted in its 1981 form, infra p. 48.

State Division of Tax Appeals, 559 N.Y.S.2d 906 (2d Dept. 1990). See also Kentucky State Bar Assn. v. Bailey, 409 S.W.2d 530 (Ky. 1966) (determining that accountant who had been hired to file for review of adverse rulings by the state revenue department had engaged in the unauthorized practice of law).

3. Is an accountant who provides advice about the tax consequences of a contemplated transaction engaged in the unauthorized practice of law? Suppose the accountant issues an opinion letter relating to the tax consequences of an investment in a tax shelter. Does the fact that Circular 230 provides standards of conduct for the issuance of such opinions authorize nonlawyers to issue an opinion? For an argument that accountants are engaged in the "authorized practice of federal tax law," see William Raby, Chairman's column, AICPA Fed. Tax Div. News. (Fall, 1983).

Joffe v. Wilson

381 Mass. 47, 407 N.E.2d 342 (1980)

KAPLAN, Judge. In 1965 the plaintiff Freda Joffe and her husband John J. Joffe incorporated under the name Joffe Oil Co., Inc., an oil business which they had owned and operated as individuals. A rather intricate tax problem arose from the assumption by the corporation of liabilities of the individuals. On December 12, 1967, the Internal Revenue Service (IRS) assessed a deficiency of $83,399.70 against them on their joint income tax return for the tax year 1965. The public (not "certified") accountant who represented them, feeling beyond his depth, asked Saul Wilson, defendant in the main action, a certified public accountant, to look into the case. Wilson had experience in tax matters and in negotiating for clients with the IRS. He concluded that the deficiency assessment was according to the letter of the code, but that it was inequitable, and he thought there was a chance the authorities could be induced to settle on a basis favorable to the taxpayers. Wilson had a talk with John Joffe and in early 1968 Freda and John gave Wilson a power of attorney to proceed on their behalf with the IRS. No arrangement was made at this time about a fee.

Wilson, after conferring unsuccessfully with a conferee in the IRS office in Springfield, took an administrative appeal to the Appellate Division of the IRS in Boston. He prepared himself with care on the facts and the law, and appeared in Boston perhaps four times to press the case. The division did not yield, and in late 1969 a "ninety-day letter" issued. Wilson advised the son, Herbert Joffe, who was acting for the family (John having died), to continue the struggle by bringing an action in the United States District Court, but he pointed out that this would mean retaining an attorney to handle the action and also paying in, provisionally, a substantial part of the assessment. Herbert was willing to have the lawsuit go forward, but he did not want to incur any substantial additional expense, especially as the prospects of success did not appear bright.

Accordingly, a contingent arrangement was made, embodied in Wilson's letter to Herbert dated March 19, 1970. Wilson was to be paid $1,000, stated to be "payment for all expense and services that have been performed to date"; and there was to be no charge "for any further expenses or any services performed by me or others," except that Wilson would be entitled to 25% of any saving that came about, that is, "25% of the difference between $83,399.70 (1965) deficiency plus interest and the amount that is finally determined as due, plus interest. . . ."

Wilson had had earlier professional dealings with Mr. Irving D. Labovitz, an associate of a law firm in Springfield, and he went to that firm to handle the contemplated action. The record does not indicate that any definite arrangement was then made about a fee for the firm. After payment-in, action was brought in the United States District Court for Massachusetts in November, 1970, and trial occurred in October, 1972. Wilson worked cooperatively with Labovitz. He supplied the attorney with the substance of the material used in the Appellate Division and helped him to organize the facts. Wilson testified as an expert witness for the plaintiff at the trial which was attended also by Herbert Joffe. The judge held for the government in January, 1973.

Then arose the question of appealing to the Court of Appeals. Herbert was consulted and agreed to the appeal. It was taken in March, 1973, and a brief was prepared, with Wilson reading and criticizing Labovitz's draft. Around this time, apparently, it appears Wilson came upon a recent decision supporting the result he had been urging. Negotiations with the government were resumed, evidently by Labovitz, with the happy result that the deficiency assessment was completely withdrawn, and by October, 1973, a government check was in hand for the amount paid in with accumulations.

At a meeting attended by Herbert and Freda the check was indorsed to Wilson, and Wilson returned his check in lesser amount with a receipt by him dated October 25, 1973, noting payment in full for accounting and legal services. Wilson's fee was $38,022, one-third of the savings calculated as $114,070. He paid the law firm a fee of about $6,500.

The increase of Wilson's contingent fee from a fourth to a third of the savings was explained by him in his testimony in the present case as being in accordance with an oral agreement made with Herbert at the time it was decided to take an appeal to the Court of Appeals, and reflecting, according to Wilson, the added work involved in a matter that had already run some five years. Herbert, however, denied that there was such an agreement, and this difference presumably led to the present action. Herbert wrote to Wilson on November 29, 1974, referring to and insisting on the terms of the agreement of March 19, 1970.

This brings us to the present action by Freda, individually and as executrix of John's estate. She sought to rescind the fee agreement with Wilson on grounds of illegality—that as a nonlawyer he had engaged in the practice of law—and to recapture the $38,022 paid to him. Wilson denied that liability. . . .

The issues to be discussed are how to characterize or appreciate Wilson's activities in respect to the assessment and what consequences may follow.

There was nothing unlawful or questionable about Wilson's work as an advocate and negotiator through the Appellate Division, including not only the element of auditing involved but also the work of analyzing the statute and decided cases, and then arguing the matter on both phases. Wilson was entitled to and did "practice before the Internal Revenue Service" pursuant to Treasury Department Circular No. 230 (revised through 1966). When the time came to commence an action in the District Court, Wilson acknowledged that he was not qualified to appear, and that an attorney must be retained to handle the proceedings. This was also under-stood by Herbert Joffe. In the actual cooperative work of Wilson, as accountant, and Labovitz, as lawyer, there was no irregularity. It was right, and useful, for Wilson to impart to Labovitz what he had gathered in his previous representation. It was for Labovitz to use this material to enhance his preparations for trial and then for appeal. He properly put Wilson forward as an expert witness. It is certainly possible for an accountant to offend by taking on the distinctive role of lawyer, but that did not occur here.

We agree . . . that in another aspect there was a relationship here against the policy of the law. This lay in the fact that the client took no part in selecting the attorney who would conduct the litigation, the choice being made by Wilson, and that the usual direct personal connection did not exist between client and attorney. Wilson was an "intermediary" and the law firm presumably looked to Wilson for its fee, although that may have been understood as emanating from the savings to the client.

A policy against intermediation is subsumed by the general terms of Canon 5 of S.J.C. Rule 3:22, 359 Mass. 814 (1972), Canons of Ethics and Disciplinary Rules Regulating the Practice of Law: "A Lawyer Should Exercise Independent Professional Judgment on Behalf of a Client." This indicates that the lawyer should be free of direction by a third person. [DR 5-107] In our decided cases, the problem has arisen typically in the context of an organization furnishing some service to subscribers for a price — say road service to motorists, or collection service to mem-bers of an industry, or service in preparing tax returns — to which is added the making available to subscribers of attorneys, if needed, in connection with that service — say to defend the motorists in court in certain events, or to bring suit for the companies on unpaid accounts, or to carry through tax litigation. These organizations have been held to be engaged in the "purchase and sale of legal services" and thus illegally practicing law where the control of the attorneys rested with the organizations rather than with the subscribers who were the true clients.

There was no irregularity where, despite payment by the organization, the ultimate control lay with the subscribers. The propriety of particular arrangements may be a matter of degree. We should add that a concern with the intermediary problem is manifest in the recent legislation regarding "legal services plans."

Although there was intermediation in the situation at bar, the vice was not extreme. This was a single transaction, not a holding out to numerous persons. Here was not an offer by a layman to provide miscellaneous future legal services as part of a merchandising package, but a specific retainer of a lawyer for the purpose of taking a matter to court after efforts by another professional on the administrative level were exhausted. The client was a man of business, fully informed and agreeing — and very willing not to involve himself and to let the accountant see to the arrangements. While a direct relationship between attorney and client would have been desirable, consultation with the client did not have the usual importance because the facts and the issue were technical. In the event, there was no need to consult the client about the acceptability of the settlement because the recovery was complete. The interests of the accountant did not diverge from those of the client. The judge noted, incidentally, that the settlement was won, in the end, on the administrative, not the court level, and on that level the accountant was competent to practice.

In these circumstances, the judge below had to decide whether Wilson should forfeit compensation for services rendered, with the plaintiff correspondingly gaining a windfall. He answered that question in the negative. . . .

The judge in the present case, considering the illegality serious, but not so serious as to forfeit recovery, thought Wilson's compensation should be on the basis of reasonable value. The jury fixed that value, not unreasonably, in the terms originally thought suitable by the parties themselves, and the judge accepted the result.

Judgments affirmed.

NOTES

1.   Suppose an action had been brought to enjoin Wilson from "practicing law." How would the Massachusetts Supreme Judicial Court have responded? How should that or any other court respond? The unauthorized practice of law is a criminal offense in some jurisdictions. Should Wilson be convicted of a crime for his conduct?

2.   Does the *Sperry* principle apply where, as in *Joffe*, federal court, not Tax Court, proceedings are involved? Would it have relevance if a federal district court were to amend its rules to permit nonlawyers to appear in tax cases? If Congress created an Article III court (federal court of tax appeals) would *Sperry* permit the court to admit nonlawyer practitioners?

c.   Treaties and Tensions Between Lawyers and Accountants

As indicated earlier, there is little litigation about practice jurisdiction between lawyers and accountants. This may in part be attributable to the work of the American Bar Association and the American Institute of Certified Public Accountants, organizations that have joined together in a National Conference of Lawyers and Certified Public Accountants. This conference has published a series of accords designed to facilitate harmonious relationships, the most recent of which is set forth next.

National Conference of Lawyers and Certified Public
Accountants: A Study of Interprofessional Relationships*

36 Tax Law. 26 (1981)

STATEMENTS ON PRACTICE IN THE FIELD OF FEDERAL
INCOME TAXATION AND ESTATE PLANNING

I.   PREFACE

This document is respectfully dedicated to all lawyers and all certified public accountants with the hope that it will help them to work together with mutual understanding in the service of their clients and in the public interest.

It is published jointly by the American Institute of Certified Public Accountants and the American Bar Association, through the agency of the National Conference of Lawyers and Certified Public Accountants. The conference consists of representatives appointed by the two national organizations. For more than thirty-five years it has engaged in meetings and in continuous communication for the purpose of promoting understanding between the two professional groups.

The objective of the document is to tell lawyers something about the professional responsibilities of CPAs — and to tell CPAs something about the professional responsibilities of lawyers.

Many members of both professions already know much about each other from day-to-day working relationships. They know the kinds of contributions they can make on their own to further the public interest. They also know how — and when — by working together they can better accomplish their objectives.

There are, at present and on the horizon, new developments such as continuing education, advertising, and the specialization of practice. The efforts of this conference and similar efforts on the state level between state and local bar associations and state societies of CPAs should ensure the continuation of the high level of understanding between the two professions and the realization of our ultimate objective — the best possible service to our clients and the public.

It is hoped that both groups will find this document useful in pointing up ways of promoting greater understanding among all lawyers and CPAs.

II.   THE NATIONAL CONFERENCE

More than thirty-five years ago the American Bar Association and the American Institute of Certified Public Accountants established the National Conference of Lawyers and Certified Public Accountants to promote understanding between the professions in the interests of their clients and the general public. The recommendations of the conference are only advisory, since lawyers and CPAs must ultimately look to the laws and governmental regulations in force where they practice. In order to serve better those of the American public who are clients of persons practicing in

---

*© 1981 by the American Bar Association. Reprinted with permission.

the professions of law and public accounting, and to promote greater understanding of their respective skills and cooperation in serving their clients, the National Conference of Lawyers and CPAs offers the views expressed in this publication.

In 1951, through the efforts of the National Conference, the ABA and the AICPA adopted an advisory Statement of Principles Relating to Practice in the Field of Federal Income Taxation for reference by members of each profession. The Statement was rewritten in 1981 and entitled Statement on Practice in the Field of Federal Income Taxation.

Without presuming to define the practice of law or accounting, the Statement contains suggested guides regarding the respective roles of lawyers and CPAs in the area of taxation. It urges cooperation between the two professions in the highest public interest; it recommends that services and assistance in federal income tax matters be rendered by qualified lawyers and CPAs; it counsels them to avoid unnecessary conflict; and it highlights the beneficial effects of education and discussion. The Statement, as rewritten in 1981, is reproduced in part V.

In 1975 the ABA and the AICPA approved the advisory Statement of Principles in Estate Planning promulgated by the National Conference of Lawyers and Certified Public Accountants. The Statement was rewritten in 1981 and entitled Statement on Estate Planning. Its principal purpose is to indicate the importance of education and cooperation between the legal and accounting professions, whose members should use their knowledge and skills to the best advantage of the public. It urges cooperation between the two professions in estate planning; it counsels CPAs becoming involved in this area permeated by legal problems to advise clients that ordinarily it is in the client's best interest to engage the services of an attorney at an early stage; it counsels lawyers to recognize that a CPA may play an important role in the planning process and, in such event, it recommends that he or she be engaged at an early stage. The Statement, as rewritten in 1981, is reproduced in part VI.

Educational efforts and discussions have also been undertaken at the state and local levels. The results of surveys undertaken by the conference reveal that there are joint conferences of lawyers and CPAs in a number of states and in some cities. Where such conferences exist, meetings to discuss programs and progress have contributed to educational efforts and awareness of developments of concern to members of both professions.

Clients of lawyers and CPAs are best served when they understand the expertise that members of each profession can apply to clients' problems.

III.   PROFESSIONAL SERVICES OF LAWYERS AND CPAS

Some understanding of another's professional work and an appreciation of his or her competence in the particular discipline are vital to good business and personal relations. Lawyers and CPAs are members of learned professions. Each discipline requires long periods of general education and professional study, culminating in qualifying examinations. Each is subject in the various jurisdictions to specific codes of ethics and disciplinary procedures to enforce the codes. Each demands high integrity and competence.

A.   What Is a CPA?

The CPA members of the National Conference endeavor to answer the question, "What is a CPA?"

A certified public accountant is a person trained and expert in accounting who has passed a uniform examination and, by this demonstration of competency and by meeting other requirements, has been certified by a state board to express professional opinions on financial statements.

There are approximately 192,000 CPAs in the United States, 173,000 of whom are members of the American Institute of Certified Public Accountants. In addition to certified public accountants who engage in public practice, there are many in corporate employment, government, and teaching.

The services of most CPAs can be classified broadly as accounting, auditing, tax services, and management advisory services. The increasing public interest in the professional practice of certified public accountants has pointed up the need for a conceptual description of the nature of CPA services. Recognizing this, the Council of the American Institute of Certified Public Accountants, its governing body, has approved A Description of the Professional Practice of Certified Public Accountants, which is summarized in the next several paragraphs.

Accounting is a discipline which provides financial and other information essential to the efficient conduct and evaluation of the activities of any organization.

The information which accounting provides is essential for: (1) effective planning, control, and decision making by management, and (2) discharging the accountability of organizations to investors, creditors, government agencies, taxing authorities, association members, contributors to welfare institutions, and others.

Accounting includes the development and analysis of data, the testing of their validity and relevance, and the interpretation and communication of the resulting information to intended users. The data may be expressed in monetary or other quantitative terms, or in symbolic or verbal forms.

Often the data with which accounting is concerned are not precisely measurable, but necessarily involve assumptions and estimates as to the present effect of future events and other uncertainties. Accordingly, accounting requires not only technical knowledge and skill but, even more important, disciplined judgment, perception, and objectivity.

CPAs have a distinctive skill in examining financial statements submitted to investors, creditors, and other interested parties, and in expressing independent opinions on the fairness of such statements. This distinctive skill has inevitably encouraged a demand for the accounting opinions of CPAs on a wide variety of other representations, such as compliance with rules and regulations of government agencies, sales statistics under lease and royalty agreements, and adherence to covenants in indentures.

The examination of financial statements requires CPAs to review many aspects of an organization's activities and procedures. Consequently, they advise clients of needed improvements in internal financial and accounting controls and make constructive suggestions on financial, tax, and other operating matters. An important part of the CPA's service to clients includes tax planning, preparation of tax returns and appearances before the Internal Revenue Service.

In addition to furnishing advice in conjunction with independent examinations of financial statements, CPAs provide objective advice and consultation on various management problems. Many of these involve information and control systems and techniques, such as budgeting, cost control, profit planning, internal reporting, automatic data processing, and quantitative analysis. CPAs also assist in the development and implementation of programs approved by management.

The complexities of an industrial society make demands upon all professions. The accounting profession is no exception. These demands are so wide and varied that many individual CPAs choose to limit their practice to particular types of service.

B.   What Is a Lawyer?

The lawyer members of the National Conference endeavor to answer the question, "What is a lawyer?"

A lawyer is a person trained and expert in law who has passed the bar examination [1] and has, by this demonstration of competency and by meeting other requirements, been admitted to the bar. Once admitted to the bar, the lawyer becomes an officer of the court subject to the disciplinary powers of the court.

There are approximately 565,000 lawyers in this country. Most of them are members of state and local bar associations and approximately half of them are members of the American Bar Association. In addition to lawyers who engage in public practice, there are many in corporate employment, government, and teaching.

A lawyer is trained and experienced in the rules regulating relationships of people with each other and with all kinds of property. Organized society, whether it be a family, a tribe, a village, a city, a state or nation, and now even the world, must have rules by which people individually and collectively can try to live harmoniously with each other.

People own and drive automobiles, acquire and dispose of houses, furnishings, and physical assets, deal with pieces of paper such as corporate stock, get married and divorced, enter into all kinds of contracts, sign deeds and wills and agreements, sue and get sued, are arrested or fear arrest, join organizations and become involved with meetings and bylaws, and hundreds of other things, all of which involve these rules of law. In many of these situations there are also economic and financial

---

1. In Wisconsin graduates of the two ABA-approved law schools located in that state are admitted without taking the bar examination. [Effective for the law school class graduating in 2008, New Hampshire has instituted a limited "diploma privilege" for a select group of students at Pierce Law School, which deems them to have passed the bar exam upon graduation from law school (with only the MPRE and character and fitness requirements remaining). — EDS.]

considerations and rules which concern the lawyer, and may also concern the certified public accountant.

There are some legal situations in which a lawyer is usually not needed, such as the simple cash purchase of merchandise or the routine disposition of a ticket for overtime parking. But sometimes the very simple and innocent written contract, such as the purchase of personal property on the installment plan, may become a very complicated legal matter, even though most people have no legal advice when they sign on the dotted line. Many people who need legal services do not seek them, or cannot obtain them. Bar associations through lawyer-referral services, legal aid societies, government agencies, and others are trying to fill this need, especially for the poor.

Many people think of the lawyer only as the person who represents others in court. This is probably the smallest part of the activity of most lawyers. Even those whose principal work is involved in litigation generally spend much more time negotiating settlements than they do trying cases. Through the centuries the lawyer has been the business and personal adviser to many people, not only when they are already in trouble, but much more often when they seek guidance to handle transactions properly and to keep out of trouble. Most lawyers spend much more time and effort *keeping* people out of court than *getting* them out of court. The scope of the law is so wide and varied that many lawyers choose to specialize in particular areas of the law.

Traditionally the lawyer has been the long-time family and business friend to whom clients turn for advice and help with their problems and troubles, some of which have little to do with the strict rules of law. In recent years this function of the lawyer as the personal adviser, especially in business situations, is often paralleled by a similar function of the CPA.

Law is the sometimes imperfect tool developed by an organized society of imperfect people who frequently do not agree on what constitutes justice. The lawyer often deals in broad concepts that are sometimes full of doubt and uncertainty and are not susceptible of precise definition. The practice of law has sometimes been called the pursuit of justice. In some ways this is like the "pursuit of happiness," a continuing quest.

C. Dual Practice of Law and Accounting

In some cases members of the bar are employees of or partners in accounting firms. Likewise there are CPAs who are members of the bar and are associates of or partners in law firms.

It is altogether appropriate for a lawyer with accounting training to use that skill to be a better lawyer, or for a CPA who has legal training to use that training to be a better accountant.

While it is proper for an individual to engage in practice simultaneously as a lawyer and as a CPA, that person is subject to all applicable laws, rules, and regulations that are in effect in each jurisdiction in which the individual practices.

D. Lawyers and CPAs Working Together

Collectively, lawyers and CPAs provide services which cut across almost every facet of human endeavor. It is no accident, then, considering the interrelationship of financial and legal aspects of our society, that lawyers and CPAs are often concerned with similar problems, although perhaps viewed from different perspectives.

We believe there are opportunities for lawyers and CPAs to pool their knowledge in the best interests of their clients. Examples of the areas in which these efforts are likely to be fruitful would include the following: estate planning, tax matters, business insolvency matters, bankruptcy proceedings, legal actions involving accounting matters, establishing and terminating a business, business corporations and liquidations, mergers, reorganizations, sales and purchases of a business, personal financial management, compensation planning, labor matters, insurance losses, and SEC registration.

IV. MAINTAINING GOOD INTERPROFESSIONAL RELATIONS

As stated earlier, this document is intended to help lawyers understand better what the accounting profession is and what CPAs do, and to help CPAs understand better the profession of law and what lawyers do. Obviously, the reader can further that purpose by direct personal contact and discussion with members of the other profession. We believe that all CPAs and all lawyers will be better able to serve their own clients if they make an affirmative effort to obtain information and education from their friends in the other profession.

This can be especially useful if it occurs in situations in which both professions are already involved; or ought to be involved. While lawyers and CPAs often work together, too often they work separately when they ought to share their expertise. Failure to do so is often a matter of inertia or lack of time, even though the wisdom of seeking help from the other profession may be obvious.

Every lawyer or CPA brought into a matter should determine at an early stage whether the talent and training of a member of the other profession are needed and should make appropriate recommendations to his or her client. At the beginning of any such engagement, we recommend strongly that lawyers and CPAs discuss with each other and the client what each will be expected to do and be responsible for, and how each will report to and confer with the client and the other. An analysis of things to be done and who will do them should produce better results for the client and avoid misunderstandings. If specific problems arise with incipient or actual misunderstandings, the lawyer and CPA involved should confer with the client and resolve them promptly.

The National Conference of Lawyers and Certified Public Accountants encourages more active discussion and communication between state and local bar associations and state societies of CPAs and their local counterparts. The Conference stands ready to counsel with or otherwise assist state and local groups to initiate such discussions. They are urged to initiate or increase efforts for organized group education, discussion of professional problems, and generally intensified interprofessional communication.

In an increasingly complex world, it is imperative that practitioners not only endeavor to keep abreast of developments in their own profession but also make use of the talents of members of the other profession in matters which require the best that well-qualified CPAs and lawyers can provide.

V.   STATEMENT ON PRACTICE IN THE FIELD OF FEDERAL INCOME TAXATION

A.   Preamble

This document addresses issues that relate to practice in the field of federal income taxation. It has been prepared by the National Conference of Lawyers and Certified Public Accountants, drawing upon the experience and expertise of the participants in their own fields. The Statement offers a suggested way of dealing with various problems affecting the public that relate to practice in the field of federal income taxation. The suggestions in this Statement are advisory and voluntary, and readers are cautioned that there may well be other responsible ways of handling the issues that are raised. The only limitations and restrictions that can be binding or governing are those imposed by applicable statutes, court decisions, and other lawful rules and regulations.

In our present complex society, the average citizen conducting a business is confronted with a myriad of governmental laws and regulations which cover almost every phase of human endeavor and raise intricate and perplexing problems. These are further complicated by the tax incidents attendant upon all business transactions. As a result, citizens in increasing numbers have sought the professional services of lawyers and certified public accountants. Each of these groups is well qualified to serve the public. The lawyer ordinarily advises a client with respect to the legal implications involved in such problems, whereas the certified public accountant advises with respect to the accounting aspects thereof. Frequently the legal and accounting phases are so interrelated, interdependent, and overlapping that they are difficult to distinguish. Particularly this is true in the field of income taxation where questions of law and accounting are often inextricably intertwined. This Statement discusses some general problems relating to practice in the field of federal income taxation.

B.   Utilization of Skills of Lawyers and Certified Public Accountants Desirable

It is in the public interest that lawyers and certified public accountants render services and assistance in federal income tax matters. They are trained in their respective fields by education and experience, and must meet requirements as to education, citizenship, and high moral character for admission to professional standing. They are required to pass written examinations and are subject to rules of professional ethics that set a high standard of professional practice and conduct. Many problems connected with business require the skills of both lawyers and certified public accountants and there is every reason for a close and friendly cooperation between the two professions. It is in the best interests of their clients that lawyers encourage them to seek the advice of certified public accountants whenever accounting problems arise and that certified public accountants encourage them to seek the advice of lawyers whenever legal questions are presented.

C.   Preparation of Federal Income Tax Returns

It is a proper function of a lawyer or a certified public accountant to prepare federal income tax returns.

When a lawyer prepares a return in which questions of accounting arise, he should advise the taxpayer to enlist the assistance of a certified public accountant.

When a certified public accountant prepares a return in which questions of law arise, he should advise the taxpayer to enlist the assistance of a lawyer.

D.   Ascertainment of Probable Tax Effects of Transactions

In the course of the practice of law and in the course of the practice of accounting, lawyers and certified public accountants are often asked about the probable tax effects of transactions.

The ascertainment of probable tax effects of transactions frequently is performed by either a certified public accountant or a lawyer. However, in many instances, problems arise which require the attention of a member of one or the other profession, or members of both. When such problems raise uncertainties as to the interpretation of law, or uncertainties as to the application of law to the transaction involved, it may be in the interest of the client for the certified public accountant to advise the taxpayer to enlist the services of a lawyer. When such problems involve difficult questions of classifying and summarizing the transaction in a significant manner and in terms of money, or interpreting the financial results thereof, it may be in the interest of the client for the lawyer to advise the client to enlist the services of a certified public accountant.

In many cases, therefore, the public will be best served by utilizing the combined skills of both professions.

E.   Preparation of Legal and Accounting Documents

It is part of the special training and experience of a lawyer to prepare legal documents such as agreements, conveyances, trust instruments or wills, or give advice as to the legal sufficiency or effect thereof, or take the necessary steps to create, amend, or dissolve a partnership, corporation, trust, or other legal entity.

Similarly, it is part of the special training and experience of a certified public accountant to advise as to the preparation of financial statements included in reports or submitted with tax returns, or as to accounting methods and procedures.

F. Representation of Taxpayers Before Treasury Department

Under Treasury Department regulations lawyers and certified public accountants are authorized, upon a showing of their professional status, and subject to certain limitations as defined in the Treasury rules, [2] to represent taxpayers in proceedings before that Department. If, in the course of such proceedings, questions arise involving the application of legal principles, it may be advisable for the taxpayer to retain a lawyer and if, in the course of such proceedings, accounting questions arise, it may be advisable for the taxpayer to retain a certified public accountant.

G. Practice Before the United States Tax Court

Under the Tax Court rules nonlawyers may be admitted to practice.

However, since upon issuance of a formal notice of deficiency by the Commissioner of Internal Revenue a choice of legal remedies is afforded the taxpayer under existing law (either before the United States Tax Court, a United States District Court, or the Court of Claims), it may be in the best interests of the taxpayer that the advice of a lawyer be sought if further proceedings are contemplated. It is not intended hereby to foreclose the right of nonlawyers to practice before the United States Tax Court pursuant to its rules.

Here also, as in proceedings before the Treasury Department, the taxpayer, in many cases, is best served by the combined skills of both lawyers and certified public accountants, and the taxpayers, in such cases, should be advised accordingly.

H. Claims for Refund

Claims for refund may be prepared by lawyers or certified public accountants. Where a legal issue is involved or where the claim is to be made the basis of litigation, it may be advisable for the client to obtain the services of a lawyer.

I. Criminal Tax Investigations

When a certified public accountant learns that his client is being specially investigated for possible criminal violation of the income tax laws, he should promptly advise his client to seek the advice of a lawyer as to his legal and constitutional rights.

---

2. See Treasury Circular 230 and Pub. L. No. 89-332 (November 8, 1965).

J. Conclusion

This Statement is subject to revision and amplification in the light of future experience. Cooperation between the two professions is in the interest of the public, and members should use their knowledge and skills to the best advantage of the public. It is recommended that joint committees representing the local societies of both professions be established. Such committees might well take permanent form as local conferences of lawyers and certified public accountants patterned after this conference, or could take the form of special committees to handle a specific situation.

VI. STATEMENT ON ESTATE PLANNING

A. Preamble

Lawyers engage in all aspects of estate planning and certified public accountants also participate in various aspects of estate planning. This document addresses issues that relate to estate planning. It has been prepared by the National Conference of Lawyers and Certified Public Accountants, drawing upon the experience and expertise of the participants in their own fields. Without presuming to define or expand upon the meaning of the terms "the practice of law" or "the practice of accountancy," the Statement offers a suggested way of dealing with various problems affecting the public that relate to estate planning. The suggestions in this Statement are advisory and voluntary, and readers are cautioned that there may well be other responsible ways of handling the issues that are raised. The only limitations and restrictions that can be binding or governing are those imposed by applicable statutes, court decisions, and other lawful rules and regulations. Therefore, the National Conference has adopted the following Statement on Estate Planning.

B. Statement

1. When a client is served by both a lawyer and a certified public accountant, a good working relationship between both professionals should be established at the earliest time practicable in order to provide the client with the best possible service at a fair cost.
2. When a certified public accountant becomes involved in estate planning, the client should be advised that it may be desirable to engage the services of a lawyer at an early stage, since legal problems permeate the entire estate planning process and it is the lawyer who has the legal skills needed to advise his clients properly on those legal issues and to prepare the legal documents for implementing an estate plan.
3. When a lawyer becomes involved in estate planning, he should recognize that a certified public accountant often plays an important role in the planning process, and that it may be desirable so to advise the client at an early stage.

C.   Conclusion

This Statement is not intended to change the activities of either lawyers or CPAs in tax matters as authorized under applicable law. It should be regarded as subject to revision and amplification in light of future experience. Cooperation between the legal and accounting professions is in the interest of the public, and members of the two professions should use their knowledge and skills to the best advantage of the public.

NOTE

One long-standing advantage that tax lawyers traditionally possessed was the attorney-client privilege. However, in 1998, Congress enacted §7525, which grants a limited privilege for "federally authorized tax practitioners" and their clients. As enacted, the privilege did not apply to certain communications regarding corporate tax shelters. In 2004, that limitation was expanded beyond corporate tax shelters to cover any tax shelter in §6662(d)(2)(C)(ii).

The 1981 statement of the National Conference addresses the respective roles of lawyers and accountants, and it seeks in a conciliatory fashion to smooth out disagreements over those roles. The statement does not deal, however, with one issue that has attracted recent attention — the application of the unauthorized practice and ethical rules to lawyers who are employed by accounting firms. Generally speaking, state unauthorized practice statutes do not directly address the question whether a lawyer may be employed by a nonlawyer, although by implication they suggest that a nonlawyer may not engage vicariously in the practice of law by employing a lawyer to service clients of the nonlawyer.

To the extent that the activities of lawyers employed by accounting firms have come under ethical scrutiny, the attention has focused on the ABA Model Rules and Code. Three rules are implicated. A lawyer is not permitted to share fees with a nonlawyer. Model Rule 5.4(a); DR 3-102. A lawyer is prohibited from permitting a third party, such as an employer, to direct or regulate the lawyer's independent professional judgment in rendering legal services. Model Rule 5.4(c); DR 5-107(B). A lawyer may not form a partnership with a nonlawyer if any of the activities of the partnership consist of the practice of law. Model Rule 5.4(b); DR 3-103.

In considering the permissible activities of a lawyer employed by an accounting firm, it is appropriate to consider three different forms of activity: first, consulting with clients of the firm to perform such activities as tax planning and the issuance of tax opinions; second, representing clients of the firm before the IRS in such activities as obtaining a private letter ruling or resolving a tax controversy; and, third, representing firm clients in cases before the U.S. Tax Court.

A number of ABA ethics opinions deal with the general subject matter. ABA Opinion 239 (1942) holds that a lawyer may enter into a partnership with an accountant to "carry on any activity which does not constitute the practice of law by a layman." ABA Opinion 272 (1946) holds that an attorney may not be employed by an accounting firm to render legal services to its clients. ABA Inf. Opinions 1032 (1968) and 1241 (1975) conclude that a lawyer employed by an accounting firm may not ethically represent clients of that firm before either the IRS or the Tax Court. The ABA lead in this area has been followed in some states. Illinois Opinion 760 (1982) prohibits a lawyer employee or partner of an accounting firm from representing clients before the Tax Court. N.Y. State 557 (1984) prohibits a lawyer and an accountant from forming a firm to provide "tax-related legal and accounting services." In the last opinion, the committee reasoned that, "While there are many services that may properly be undertaken by lawyers and non-lawyers alike, especially in the fields of taxation and tax planning, when such services are performed by a lawyer who holds himself out as a lawyer, they constitute the practice of law."

The Justice Department issued a report in 1976 that was sharply critical of the position taken in ABA Inf. Opinion 1032 that a lawyer employed by an accounting firm may not represent clients of the firm before the IRS. The department also responded critically to a 1976 report of an advisory panel to the IRS Chief Counsel that had endorsed the results reached in ABA Inf. Opinion 1032. See Justice Department Comments on Report of IRS Chief Counsel's Advisory Committee on Rules of Professional Conduct in Representation to Taxpayers Before IRS, reprinted in 241 BNA Daily Tax Report at J-1 (Dec. 14, 1976). The comments clearly reflect the view that this is essentially a turf battle. The report emphasized, however, that competition was desirable:

> The recent decision of the Supreme Court in Goldfarb v. Virginia State Bar, 421 U.S. 773 (1975), makes clear that competition must have increasing importance in the professions and in the service sector generally, as in other areas of the economy. In *Goldfarb*, the Court indicated that lawyers, and presumably other professionals, play an important part in commercial intercourse, and that anticompetitive activities of professionals may restrain free market mechanisms unlawfully. Unreasonable commercial restraints deprive consumers of the benefits of competition and make it unnecessarily difficult to select professional services in an informed manner.

The Justice Department noted that "tacit federal approval of ABA Opinion 1032 may suggest inaccurately that a private association of competitors may legitimately limit the competitive ability of some of those who compete in a particular market."

The Justice Department report also rejected the logic of ABA Opinion 1032:

> We recognize that unauthorized practice statutes might be in issue when lawyers enter into partnership with non-lawyers for the practice of law or when non-lawyers, including CPAs, provide services that state law legitimately restricts to lawyers. Such statutes, however, should not be permitted to interfere with a federally-conferred right to

appear in a representative capacity before a specified federal agency and, therefore, should not be construed categorically to disqualify from IRS practice non-CPA lawyers employed by CPA firms, nor CPAs and enrolled agents employed by law firms.

In Sperry v. Florida, 373 U.S. 379 (1963), the Court stated that "registration in the Patent Office confers a right to practice before the Office without regard to whether the State within which the practice is conducted would otherwise prohibit such conduct." The same rationale appears fully applicable to IRS practice by either CPAs or enrolled agents. It would seem clear that an enrolled agent cannot be engaged in the unauthorized practice of law when carrying on activities permitted by federal law. It would also seem clear, then, that law firms could properly employ CPAs or enrolled agents to represent the firm's clients before the IRS, so long as non-lawyers are not permitted to hold themselves out as lawyers.

As noted, the restriction imposed in ABA Opinion 1032 on non-CPA lawyers employed by CPA firms was not predicated on rules concerning unauthorized practice of law. Rather, the ABA articulated the need for a flat prohibition against IRS appearance based on the legal profession's duty to ensure that lawyers exercise independent professional judgment. According to ABA Opinion 1032, the judgment of a lawyer so employed would be controlled by a "lay" intermediary, the CPA firm. Because that lawyer's judgment would be subject to exploitation, clients and society would be disserved if lawyers employed by CPA firms were permitted, in their capacity as lawyers, to represent CPA firms' clients before the IRS.

A stipulation that CPAs are laymen in the IRS practice market, however, clearly contradicts the design of 5 U.S.C. §500. It is true that a lawyer employed by a law firm would not be subject to control and exploitation by "laymen"; however, in a mixed-profession market, such logic, designed to bolster traditional purity of legal service delivery teams, should be unpersuasive. Furthermore, it seems unsound to assume, as the writers of ABA Opinion 1032 apparently did, that tax firm employers who are lawyers will be more sensitive to the value of independence than will tax firm employers who are CPAs. Because CPAs are enjoined from subordinating their professional judgment to others, AICPA Code of Professional Ethics ET §102 (1976), it would seem reasonable to expect CPA-employers to appreciate fully the value of independent judgment.

In addition, both lawyers and CPAs, irrespective of the professional context in which they are employed, are obligated to exercise independent professional judgment and must render services competently. If firms misrepresent particular practitioners' credentials, or if mixed-firms exhibit professional incompetence, specific misconduct can be punished by various state disciplinary boards and by the IRS. See, e.g., 31 C.F.R. §§10.50, 10.51, which authorize the Secretary of the Treasury to suspend or disbar IRS practitioners who are incompetent or disreputable or who intentionally deceive claimants.

By statute and long-standing custom, practitioners with varying professional experiences have been declared competent to appear in a representative capacity before the IRS. As indicated, 5 U.S.C. §500 authorizes licensed attorneys and certified public accountants to practice before the IRS; and for many years, the Service has permitted laypersons to practice before the IRS as enrolled agents if they were formerly employed by the IRS or if they successfully complete the written enrollment examination. 31 C.F.R. §10.3(c), 10.4. Thus, as a matter of policy and tradition, practice before the

IRS appears to be a special, unitary service market, in which persons with differing professional training have similar, if not identical, professional abilities and in which development of mixed-profession service teams should be encouraged.

In such a mixed-profession market, particularly one declared mixed by Congress, it seems uniquely inappropriate for the IRS to permit the imposition of artificial limitations on the competitive ability of a particular class of IRS practitioners. A restriction on mixed-profession service teams, like that contained in ABA Opinion 1032, however, creates just such a limitation. CPA firms are limited in their ability to hire and use non-CPA lawyers, and non-CPA lawyers who wish to practice before the IRS may be effectively dissuaded from seeking employment with nonlaw tax firms. In addition, such a restriction stifles the development of innovative, efficient, mixed-profession business entities and limits the design of specific federal legislation. In a federally defined mixed-profession market, we believe the IRS should promote, not discourage, competition and should eliminate, not support, unreasonable artificial restrictions.

Note that the Justice Department relied on *Sperry* and the design of 5 U.S.C. §500 to reject the conclusion of ABA Opinion 1032 that accounting firm lawyers may not appear before the IRS. However, the Justice Department did not comment on the other holding of ABA Opinion 1032, that such lawyers may not represent firm clients before the U.S. Tax Court. Why do you suppose the department opted for silence on this equally important holding?

After these 1975 and 1976 pronouncements, there was a period of silence on the issue of accounting firm lawyers, except as broken by the Illinois and New York opinions cited above. During this period, lawyers employed by accounting firms engaged widely in the representation of their firm clients within their offices and before the IRS, and it would appear that the rationale of ABA Opinion 1032, insofar as it related to such activities, effectively has been rejected by the marketplace, and, given the rationale of the Justice Department comments, it is difficult to see how the matter could have developed differently. During this same post-1976 period, there was no rush by accounting firm lawyers to appear in the Tax Court, and it might be that the marketplace concluded that this is not an appropriate role for these lawyers.

In 1994, however, there was a flurry of activity that raised the Tax Court issue. There was publicity that lawyers employed by at least one of the major accounting firms were appearing in the Tax Court on behalf of firm clients and that the particular firm planned to continue this practice. Sarah M. Hodder, Accounting Firms Eye Lawyer's Turf, Legal Times (Feb. 7, 1994). At the May 1994 meeting of the ABA Tax Section, the plenary session included a panel presentation on "Accounting Firm Practice in Tax Court," at which these issues were discussed. N.C. Ethics Decision 250 (1994) held that an attorney could not ethically appear before the Tax Court on behalf of an accounting firm client. Since that time, however, lawyers who are employed by accounting firms generally have refrained from appearing in Tax Court.

How should this question be resolved? Is there any reason to view the Tax Court differently from any other court? A lawyer who is employed by an accounting firm obtains admission to the bar of the Tax Court, like any other court, by virtue of her status as a lawyer. The Tax Court, in admitting lawyers to practice, apparently does not inquire into their employment relationships. If a lawyer is admitted to practice before the Tax Court and may represent her accounting firm's clients in that forum, is she equally entitled to practice in other courts, as, for example, in appealing an adverse Tax Court decision to the courts of appeals and the Supreme Court? Or by choosing a refund route and bringing suit in a district court or the Court of Federal Claims?

If a lawyer employed by an accounting firm may not do these things, why not? Are the principles underlying the ethical rules cited previously (primarily fee sharing and independence) important enough in this context to rule out the form of practice in question? Are the principles underlying the unauthorized practice statutes (primarily client protection) important enough to rule it out? Are there valid client protection concerns merely because a lawyer is employed by an accounting firm? Note that the Supreme Court previously has held that unauthorized practice statutes do not preclude lawyers employed by unions and organizations such as the NAACP from representing individuals who turn to those organizations for particular forms of legal assistance. See NAACP v. Button, 371 U.S. 415 (1963); Brotherhood of RR Trainmen v. Virginia, 377 U.S. 1 (1964); United Mine Workers v. Illinois State Bar Assn., 389 U.S. 217 (1967); United Transp. Union v. State Bar of Michigan, 401 U.S. 576 (1971). In these cases, the Supreme Court held that the regulatory objective of the state could not stand against a First Amendment challenge. Would a state restriction imposed on the ability of an accounting firm lawyer to represent a taxpayer in court violate the First Amendment rights of either the lawyer or the accounting firm? If an accounting firm may employ lawyers to represent its clients in court, may a department store hire lawyers and through them engage in the business of representing taxpayers in the courts? Could a tax return preparation firm offer the same kind of service?

These questions were considered with renewed vigor in the late 1990s, and in 1998 the ABA appointed a Commission on Multidisciplinary Practice ("MDP") to review the professional conduct rules as they related to MDPs (entities with both lawyers and nonlawyers that provide both legal and nonlegal services). The Commission ultimately recommended revising the professional responsibility rules to permit the activities of MDPs (by allowing lawyers to practice law in that setting — i.e., partnership with nonlawyers, and fee sharing with nonlawyers). However, the ABA delegates did not accept those recommendations. ABA Commn. on Multidisciplinary Practice, MDP Final Report (1999). Following the ABA's consideration of the MDP issue, many of the state bar associations established committees to examine the MDPs, with an outcome that was generally negative (or resulted in postponement of the question).

To what extent do MDPs actually exist today despite restrictions on fee sharing or partnership with nonlawyers (Model Rule 5.4)? What about the current Big Four Accounting firms? How is the situation different outside the United States? See Kathryn Yarbrough, Multidisciplinary Practices: Are They Already Among Us? 53 Ala. L. Rev. 639 (2002).

If accounting firm lawyers are eligible to represent firm clients in the courts, are the clients of those lawyers entitled to the protection of the attorney-client privilege and the work product doctrine? Are communications between the accounting firm lawyer and her clients made in confidence, or is there an imputed further communication by the lawyer to nonlawyer personnel of the accounting firm? If such imputation exists, is it sufficient to destroy the privilege? What is the impact of §7525 (added to the Code in 1998 to extend a limited privilege to federally authorized tax practitioners and their clients) to these questions of privilege? Chapter 3 examines issues of confidentiality, privilege, and work product doctrine in greater detail.

It should be evident that the question of the proper role of accounting firm lawyers raises very broad and very difficult questions. The rules that evolve here could significantly affect the underlying concepts of unauthorized practice and ethical limitations on forming relationships by lawyers with nonlawyers. The resolution of these questions could extend well beyond tax practice and could affect the whole fabric of the attorney-client relationship.

NOTE

As we know from the above cases, it is not "the unauthorized practice of law" to represent tax clients as permitted by the IRS. (Of course, that protection does not permit the tax practitioner to *claim* to be a lawyer). However, what if a lawyer works for an accounting firm in a state in which he is not authorized to practice law? What kinds of rules apply? Consider the analysis of the court in Palmer v. Ernst & Young LLP et al., 22 Mass. L. Rptr. 277 (2007):

> [T]his Court must grapple with the question of whether a tax attorney [working for Ernst & Young, who was] authorized to practice law in another state is prohibited from offering legal advice in Massachusetts to a Massachusetts resident regarding federal income tax issues without either being admitted to the Massachusetts Bar or obtaining admission pro hac vice. This Court finds that he is not so prohibited. . . . Therefore, this Court finds that [the defendant] was engaged in the practice of law when he offered the legal advice summarized in the Engagement Letter [with the caption: Privileged Opinion and Advice of Counsel] . . . [and the defendant's activities did not constitute] the unauthorized practice of law.
>
> Having so found, this Court must confront the defendants' third argument [as to why the Engagement Letter, which contained language limiting Ernst & Young's liability did not violate Massachusetts Disciplinary Rules that bar a lawyer from seeking to limited liability for personal malpractice]. . . .
>
> The bottom line is that attorneys and law firms engaged in the practice of law in Massachusetts, regardless of whether or not they are members of the Massachusetts Bar, cannot contractually limit their liability to their Massachusetts clients for legal malpractice. . . .
>
> This prohibition against limiting liability, however, does not generally extend to accounting firms or consulting firms or even tax planning firms, who, like other

commercial entities, are free to negotiate limitation of liability provisions with their clients, provided they are clearly stated and not oppressive. . . . Since [the defendant] was acting on behalf of Ernst & Young, not a law firm, when he provided . . . the Engagement Letter, this Court does not find that the limitation of liability provision violates the public policy [in the Massachusetts Bar rules on limiting liability].

Is the court correct? Is there a contradiction where a lawyer's actions constitute the practice of law — and are permissible because he is a lawyer *somewhere* — and yet his contract with the client for these services is not subject to the rules governing contracts for legal fees? Is it clear what would have been the outcome had the Ernst & Young lawyer been licensed in Massachusetts instead of out of state?

E. Professional Liability

For tax lawyers, who are members of the profession, there are constraints imposed beyond bar sanctions (discipline may be imposed under the disciplinary mechanism the state has established) and government sanctions (e.g., discipline may be imposed by the Treasury if his conduct violates the standards imposed by Circular 230). In fact, perhaps the more powerful enforcement weapon lies with a client who can bring a malpractice action if the attorney has been negligent. Attorneys increasingly must be conscious of professional liability standards. Are the liability and measure of damages simply a matter of general tort and contract law, or does the concept of "professional or specialist" introduce new elements? Might a breach of a standard imposed by Circular 230 give rise to civil liability?

When a lawyer breaches his duty of competence, the consequence may be a liability to the client. Problems in this area involve the determination of the requisite level of competence and whether the lawyer's performance in a particular case fell below it.

Horne v. Peckham

97 Cal. App. 3d 404 (1979)

PARAS, Acting Presiding Justice. Defendant, an attorney, appeals from a judgment entered after a jury awarded damages of $64,983.31 against him for legal malpractice in connection with the drafting of a "Clifford Trust" for plaintiffs Roy C. Horne (Horne) and Doris G. Horne, husband and wife. He contends that the judgment should be reversed or in the alternative that another attorney, Thomas J. McIntosh, upon whom he relied for advice, should indemnify him.

In 1960, Horne obtained a patent for processing low grade wood into defect-free material known as "Perfect Plank Plus." In 1962, he founded a business called "Perfect Plank," and in 1967 began to produce the patented product. The business was incorporated in 1965, with the Hornes as sole shareholders. Horne anticipated that production of the product might generate substantial income, so he became interested when he read in a newsletter of the tax advantages of a so-called "Clifford Trust." On July 18, 1967, on the recommendation of Herbert McClanahan, his accountant, he went to defendant and asked him to prepare such a trust, Horne's three sons to be its beneficiaries.

Defendant testified he told Horne ". . . that I had no knowledge of tax matters. I had no expertise in tax matters; that if somebody else could figure out what needed to be done, I could draft the documents." He said that McClanahan had provided him with ". . . a couple of pages of translucencies . . . governing Clifford Trusts," and he also consulted the two-volume annual set of American Jurisprudence on federal taxation, which included a discussion of Clifford Trusts; he otherwise relied on McClanahan's judgment.

The original plan was to put the patent, which had 10 more years of life, into the trust. However, on October 11, 1967, Horne told defendant he no longer desired this and asked ". . . if it wouldn't be just as good to put in a [nonexclusive] [l]icense . . ." of the patent rights. Horne testified that he preferred not to put the patent itself into the trust, because the substantial royalties from it would result in more money than should properly be given to his sons.

Defendant testified he told Horne that ". . . I didn't know whether . . . [a license] would be just as good or not, but that we were having a high-priced tax expert come up here — like the following day — who was undoubtedly going to charge plenty of money for the consultation, and that we should ask him on that point." The tax expert to whom defendant referred was McIntosh, an attorney from Albany, California, who had been recommended by McClanahan as an expert in deferred compensation and profit-sharing plans. Such plans for Horne's company were to be discussed at a meeting with McIntosh arranged by McClanahan and scheduled for the next day, October 12. Unknown to defendant, McIntosh had been licensed to practice law less than a year, although he was also a certified public accountant and had worked for two and one-half or three years as a tax accountant.

The meeting of October 12 was attended by Horne, his wife, one son, McClanahan, defendant, and McIntosh. Defendant testified that he asked McIntosh whether it would be just as effective to transfer a license agreement into the contemplated trust as the patent itself, and received an affirmative answer. He further testified that Horne had been talking of a nonexclusive license during the meeting, thus McIntosh should have been aware that such a license was contemplated. However, defendant also testified that no one told McIntosh that the contemplated license would have a five-year duration.

Horne testified that he thought the subject of license versus patent arose at that meeting, but he had no independent recollection of it. McIntosh testified that even though at his deposition he thought he recalled such a discussion, he did not recall it at trial.

Sometime after the meeting, defendant drafted the final documents and sent them to McClanahan for approval. He had no further discussions or correspondence with McIntosh. The documents were signed in November 1967, although dated February 1, 1967, the date production of the product began. The first document was an irrevocable trust agreement between the Hornes as trustors and McClanahan, defendant, and one Bill Ryan as trustees for the Hornes' three sons, to terminate in twelve years (1979). The second was a license agreement between Horne and Perfect Plank, granting the corporation a license to produce the patented product for two years with an option to renew for an additional three years, in return for royalty payments determined by production; *inter alia*, the agreement stated "This license is not exclusive. Licensor retains the right to issue other licenses of the same patent to any other parties whatsoever." The third document was an assignment to the trustees by Horne of Horne's rights under the license agreement thus furnishing the trust with a corpus.

. . . In August 1970, the I.R.S. assessed a deficiency on the ground that the trust did not transfer tax liability for the licensor's income to the beneficiaries. . . .

Defendant's first argument on appeal is that "It is not legal malpractice (negligence) on the part of an attorney general practitioner to draw documents without doing research on a point of law on which there is no appellate decision or statute in point."

The argument has two parts; first, that the trust documents were in fact valid as a tax shelter, second, that even if invalid, their invalidity is so debatable that he should not be liable for making an error regarding a matter about which reasonable attorneys can disagree. He is wrong on both points. The documents are invalid for their intended purpose, and the invalidity is rather obvious. To demonstrate this, one need go no further than the original *Clifford* case, from which the name "Clifford Trust" is derived, and the legislation it brought about. . . .

[The court discusses the Supreme Court's decision in Helvering v. Clifford, 309 U.S. 331 (1940) and subsequent amendments to the Internal Revenue Code, specifically §675, which results in the income being taxed to the grantor. It also discusses Commissioner v. Sunnen, 333 U.S. 591 (1948), a case cited by the defendant, which provided further authority to establish the trust's invalidity as a Clifford trust.]

In light of the foregoing, it is apparent that there is no merit to defendant's contention that there was "no appellate decision or statute in point." Internal Revenue Code section 675 and the *Sunnen* case were very much in point.

Defendant's second contention is that "An attorney in general practice does not have a duty to refer his client to a 'specialist' or to recommend the assistance of a specialist' or be guilty of malpractice."

The court gave a jury instruction which states:

> It is the duty of an attorney who is a general practitioner to refer his client to a specialist or recommend the assistance of a specialist if under the circumstances a reasonably careful and skillful practitioner would do so.
>
> If he fails to perform that duty and undertakes to perform professional services without the aid of a specialist, it is his further duty to have the knowledge and skill ordinarily possessed, and exercise the care and skill ordinarily used by specialists in good standing in the same or similar locality and under the same circumstances.
>
> A failure to perform any such duty is negligence.

This instruction is based upon California's Book of Approved Jury Instructions (BAJI), Instruction No. 6.04, which is found in that work's section on medical malpractice. Its applicability to legal malpractice presents an issue of first impression. Defendant points out that legal specialties were not officially recognized in California until 1973, and therefore contends that he could not have had a duty in 1967 to refer his client to a specialist or to meet the standard of care of a specialist.

We cannot accept this contention. A California survey in 1968 revealed that two-thirds of the attorneys in the state at that time limited their practice to a very few areas, frequently to one only. Thus, in the words of a leading treatise, the recent debate over *official* recognition of specialists must be considered "academic," for "[t]he reality is that many attorneys have become specialists." Mallen and Levitt, Legal Malpractice (1977), §114, p.172. Moreover, "[I]n those jurisdictions which recognize specialties or permit the attorney to make such a designation, taxation is one of the areas of law most commonly acknowledged." (Id., §268, p.368.) Taxation also was one of the three specialties initially recognized in California.

Defendant himself recognized the existence of tax specialists in 1967 when he advised Horne in 1967 that he was not a tax expert, and that such experts existed. Of course, the fact that the specialty exists does not mean that every tax case must be referred to a specialist. Many tax matters are so generally known that they can well be handled by general practitioners. (See Bucquet v. Livingston (1976) 57 Cal. App. 3d 914. [)] But defendant himself acknowledged his need for expert assistance throughout his testimony, insisting he had no opinion of his own as to the tax consequences of the trust. Under the circumstances he cannot argue persuasively that it was error for the court to give the above quoted instruction.

Defendant's next contention is that the question of law involved here was one upon which reasonable doubt may be entertained by well-informed lawyers, and therefore he should not be found liable for committing error. He relies upon Lucas v. Hamm (1961) 56 Cal. 2d 583, which held (as restated in Smith v. Lewis (1975) 13 Cal. 3d 349), that "the rule against perpetuities poses such complex and difficult problems for the draftsman that even careful and competent attorneys occasionally fall prey to its traps."

But Lucas v. Hamm did not condone failure to do research, and Smith v. Lewis makes it clear that an attorney's obligation is not satisfied by simply determining that the law on a particular subject is doubtful or debatable: "[E]ven with respect to an unsettled area of the law, . . . an attorney assumes an obligation to his client to undertake reasonable research in an effort to ascertain relevant legal principles and to make an informed decision as to a course of conduct based upon an intelligent assessment of the problem." (Id., at p. 359.) In other words, an attorney has a duty to *avoid* involving his client in murky areas of the law if research reveals alternative courses of conduct. At least he should inform his client of uncertainties and let the client make the decision.

In any event, as stated above, there was nothing sufficiently doubtful or difficult about the invalidity of the trust documents in this case to permit invocation of Lucas v. Hamm as controlling precedent.

Professional Competence: How to Measure It, What to Do About It*

63 A.B.A. J. 1647 (1977)

Canon 6 of the Code of Professional Responsibility for the first time imposes on lawyers, as an ethical requirement, the obligation to be competent with respect to the client's affairs. But the code provides little guidance to determine what standards should measure the lawyer's competence and leaves those standards to be worked out by the judicial or disciplinary authorities who may deal with specific cases. The only background of comparison and measurement is that derived from malpractice litigation, in which the performance is measured for the purposes of civil liability rather than professional discipline.

Since the adoption of the code in 1970, little enlightenment has been provided either by judicial opinion, academic writing, or the published opinions of bar association ethics committees. An unreported decision in 1975 of the California District Court of Appeal, Long v. Diversified Securities, Inc., was the model from which the facts for this installment of Legal Ethics Forum were taken.

As you read the responses of the two opposing commentators, keep in mind these relevant questions:

1. Is competence genuinely a matter of ethics in the same way as fidelity to the client's interest is an ethical obligation, or is competence a different kind of duty or responsibility?
2. What standards should be used in determining a lawyer's competence?
3. Would it be desirable for bar association authorities to attempt to prepare and promulgate more detailed standards concerning competence than the broad injunction of the code?
4. In connection with this specific case, what more should the lawyer have done than to express his incompetence in the tax area about which he was consulted?
5. Should the lawyer refuse to continue to represent a client who wishes to take the risk of closing a transaction without adequate information? What kinds of risks, if any, should a lawyer refuse to allow his client to take?
6. Should competence for purposes of the code be measured by different standards than proper performance of services for purposes of determining civil liability?
7. Would it be sufficient for the lawyer to associate himself with an accountant expert in tax matters, or must he associate himself with another lawyer?

S.A.K.

(The editor-in-charge of Legal Ethics Forum is Stanley A. Kaplan.)

STATEMENT OF THE CASE

A client informs his lawyer that he is about to receive a distribution in 1975 under a testamentary trust created in 1940. The client has dissipated a previous bequest and wishes to avoid a repetition. Therefore, he tells his lawyer that he wishes to sell the securities he will receive in the distribution and put the proceeds into some kind of an arrangement that will be more stable and provide him a fixed income. He asks the lawyer about a suitable mutual fund that may achieve this end.

The lawyer tells him that he has to be concerned with the tax resulting from the sale of the securities because it will be very different and much higher if the tax base is the value of the securities in 1940 as contrasted with the value of the securities in 1975. The lawyer acknowledges that he has very little knowledge or experience in tax matters and strongly urges the client to seek the advice of a tax accountant.

The lawyer and the client visit a broker's office and discuss mutual funds. They arrange to return ten days later to consummate the sale of securities and the purchase of mutual funds. At the time of the second appointment, the lawyer asks the client whether he had obtained the tax information yet. The client replies that he hadn't gotten around to it yet but that he would do so the following week. The client then executes the necessary papers to sell the securities and purchase the mutual fund shares.

The following week the client goes to a tax accountant and finds out that the applicable tax base is the value as of 1940, thereby causing the capital gains tax to be very large, a fact which, had it been known to the client, he says would have prevented him from making the sale.

Has the lawyer violated any requirements of the Code of Professional Responsibility with respect to competence? Has the lawyer failed properly to represent his client by allowing the transaction to be closed in his presence when he was aware of the fact that the client lacked essential information that should have been obtained before the transaction was consummated? Is the lawyer subject to any disciplinary action?

YES, DISCIPLINE AND LIABILITY, BY JAMES DEVINE

The lawyer deserves to be disciplined and may be civilly liable for failing to represent his client competently.

A.   Disciplinary Action

Dealing with incompetent practitioners is a constant problem for any profession committed to high standards. Gross negligence in the form of habitual disregard of the interests of a client has been a basis for discipline for years. California Business and Professions Code, Section 6067; Sanchez v. State Bar, 555 P.2d 889 (Calif. 1976); Simmons v. State Bar, 470 P.2d 352 (Calif. 1970); Grove v. State Bar, 427

P.2d 164 (Calif. 1967); Bruns v. State Bar, 117 P.2d 327 (Calif. 1941); Waterman v. State Bar, 63 P.2d 1133 (Calif. 1936).

Rarely, if ever, has an attorney been disciplined solely for ordinary carelessness, lack of adequate preparation, or attempting to handle matters beyond his professional abilities. Any sanctions for these actions have come in the form of damages for malpractice.

The Code of Professional Responsibility now has provided a basis for discipline under Canon 6, which states that "A lawyer should represent a client competently."

Disciplinary Rule 6-101(A) provides that a lawyer shall not "(1) Handle a legal matter which he knows or should know that he is not competent to handle, without associating with him a lawyer who is competent to handle it. (2) Handle a legal matter without preparation adequate in the circumstances. (3) Neglect a matter entrusted to him."

Disciplinary rules state the minimum level of conduct below which no lawyer can fall without being subject to disciplinary action. It has been suggested that D.R. 6-101(A)(2) and (3) taken together would impose disciplinary sanctions for the same conduct which would give rise to a cause of action for malpractice. Outcault and Peterson, Lawyer Discipline and Professional Standards in California: Progress and Problem, 24 Hastings L. J. 691 (1973). It should be noted, however, that the word "neglect" as used in D.R. 6-101(A)(3) has been interpreted to mean indifference and consistent failure to carry out the obligations the lawyer has assumed to his client or a conscious disregard for the responsibility owed to the client. Neglect in this sense is usually evidenced by more than a single act or omission and is different from the concept of negligence. (American Bar Association Informal Opinion 1273.) This interpretation appears to adopt the gross negligence concept that appeared in the older disciplinary authorities cited above. Therefore, if the attorney is to be disciplined under the facts stated, that discipline must be based on a failure to observe the requirements of D.R. 6-101(A)(1) or D.R. 6-101(A)(2).

Unlike the disciplinary rules, which are mandatory, the ethical considerations are aspirational and "represent the objectives toward which every member of the profession should strive." The preliminary statement to the code declares, however, that an "enforcing agency, in applying the disciplinary rules, may find interpretive guidance in the basic principles embodied in the canons and in the objectives reflected in the ethical considerations." Therefore, certain ethical considerations are cited in the discussion, and their applicable provisions are set forth separately.

Applying the pertinent standards to the facts stated it seems clear that the attorney has not met the minimum standards imposed by D.R. 6-101(A)(1) and (2). The client has consulted with the attorney regarding a proposed transaction. The lawyer's function is that of an adviser. The lawyer has told his client that the client must be concerned with the tax resulting from the sales, that the tax will be higher if the securities have as their basis 1940 values rather than 1975 values, that the lawyer has little knowledge or experience in tax matters, and that the client should consult with a tax accountant to determine the tax consequences of the sales.

Notwithstanding his lack of experience or knowledge in tax matters, the lawyer has accepted the employment and has not associated with him anyone competent to give tax advice. Nor has the attorney made any effort to educate himself so as to advise the client of the consequences of his proposed action.

If the attorney lacked the required knowledge he should not have accepted the employment unless he intended to educate himself or to associate with a lawyer who had the necessary knowledge. E.C. 6-1, 6-3, and 6-4. Degen v. Stenbrink, 195 N.Y.S. 810, 814 (App. Div. 1922), affirmed, 142 N.E. 328 (N.Y. 1923). Having accepted the employment, it was improper to place the burden on the client to determine for himself the consequences of the proposed transaction. That is what the attorney was employed to do. If the client simply wanted to know how to execute a sale and purchase order or to identify the proper mutual fund to meet his needs, there are stockbrokers and others with whom he can consult. When the client consulted the lawyer it was with the implicit understanding that he was seeking advice as to the legal consequences of what he proposed to do as well as an explanation of possible alternatives to best meet his needs should the legal consequences of what he proposed be unsatisfactory. E.C. 7-3 and 7-8.

The tax consequences are an integral part, perhaps the most important aspect, of the entire transaction. The lawyer might have associated another lawyer competent to handle the matter, or he might have consulted with a qualified attorney or accountant as a part of the process of educating himself to become competent to handle the matter. (E.C. 6-3.) He did neither.

The attorney was sufficiently familiar with the tax law to recognize a potential problem, and he did take the first step of alerting the client to the problem. This alone, however, is not sufficient. In addition to having the duty either to associate a competent attorney or to ascertain for himself and to advise the client of the consequences of the transaction, the obligation to represent a client competently and to safeguard the client's interests requires that every effort be made to dissuade the client from completing the transaction before its consequences are known. E.C. 7-8. At the time of the sales, the lawyer learned that the client had not yet determined the tax consequences of the proposed sales. The attorney failed to fulfill his obligation to his client when he made no attempt to dissuade his client from making the sales until all the consequences were known and evaluated.

B. Civil Liability

The Code of Professional Responsibility does not undertake to define standards for civil liability of lawyers for professional conduct. In general, legal malpractice consists of the failure of an attorney to use such skill, care, prudence, judgment, and diligence as lawyers of ordinary skill and capacity possess and exercise in the performance of tasks which they undertake. Smith v. Lewis, 530 P.2d 589 (Calif. 1975); Goodley v. Wank and Wank, Inc., 133 Cal. Rptr. 83 (1976); Ventura County Humane Society v. Holloway, 115 Cal. Rptr. 464 (1974). When he breaches this duty and damage results to one to whom the duty is owed, a cause of action for professional negligence arises.

As pointed out in Smith v. Lewis, an attorney is expected to possess knowledge of those plain and elementary principles of law commonly known by well-informed lawyers and to discover those additional rules of law that, although not commonly known, may readily be found by standard research techniques. The attorney "assumes an obligation to his client to undertake reasonable research in an effort to ascertain relevant legal principles and to make an informed decision as to a course of conduct based upon an intelligent assessment of the problem." The court concluded that there was evidence to support a finding that the lawyer failed to perform adequate research and thus was unable to exercise the informed judgment to which his client was entitled.

In Bucquet v. Livingston, 129 Cal. Rptr. 514 (1976), the court, while declining to require that an attorney engaged in estate planning consult with a tax specialist, did hold that the potential tax problem of including general powers of appointment in instruments establishing trusts was within the ambit of a reasonably competent and diligent practitioner. The court found that a cause of action existed against an attorney whose draftsmanship did not accomplish the desired tax savings objectives.

Thus there is judicial recognition that at least some knowledge of tax law is within the ordinary competence of lawyers. A general knowledge of the capital gains tax is possessed by many persons not professionally trained in the law. It would appear to be sufficiently understood by so many that a generalized understanding of these principles should be held to be within the ordinary competence of lawyers. Through adequate research of the law applicable to tax basis, the obtaining of the necessary facts, and the application of the law to those facts, the attorney could have advised his client properly regarding the consequences of the proposed transaction.

Notwithstanding the failure to meet the standard of performance imposed by law, the attorney probably could have avoided liability had he attempted to dissuade his client from completing the transaction without the necessary information regarding its tax consequences. He should have called to his client's attention the relationship between basis and the amount of capital gains taxes payable. He should have emphasized that it is essential to have a reasonably accurate estimate of the capital gains taxes in order to know the amount of funds available for reinvestment. He should have made it clear that it was his professional advice that the transaction not be completed until these facts were known, and that if the client insisted on ignoring this advice it would be necessary for him to withdraw from the employment. This he failed to do. The transaction was completed, and the client suffered a loss in the form of a high tax liability.

Was the client contributorily negligent so as to bar or reduce his recovery for damages? The defense of contributory negligence is available in actions against attorneys for malpractice. Theobald v. Byers, 13 Cal. Rptr. 864 (1961). Whether it would be available to the attorney in the facts stated is an open question. In the Theobald case the attorney prepared a chattel mortgage to secure a loan made by his client but sent it to the client without recording it, so that the client's security was not perfected against subsequent creditors. The trial judge concluded that the attorney was negligent but that the client was contributorily negligent when he did not give any direction or make any inquiry as to recordation.

The appellate court declared that the facts, as a matter of law, did not establish the defense. It declared that the purpose of consulting a lawyer was to gain his superior knowledge of the proper legal formalities to secure the desired result. The plaintiffs could not be considered negligent in failing to perform the very acts for which they employed the attorney.

While contributory negligence is a question of fact, the reasoning of the court in Theobald might apply to the present facts. In the facts stated, unlike Theobald, the client was specifically alerted to the possibility of negative tax consequences. He may have been justified, however, in making the sale when it was done in the presence of his attorney, who made no effort to prevent it. The client might be determined to have relied on the superior knowledge of his attorney in completing the sale.

Absent a finding of contributory negligence, the attorney under the principles applicable to negligence should be civilly liable for the damage caused his client.

C.   Comparison of Disciplinary Standards and Standards for the Imposition of Civil Liability

The Code of Professional Responsibility does not establish a standard by which competence may be measured. The ethical considerations emphasizing the duty of the bar to protect the public and elevate the competence of lawyers to the highest level (E.C. 1-1, 1-2, 6-2, and 6-5) suggest that the disciplinary standards of competence should be at least as high as the standard that would impose liability for malpractice. The fact that no harm or damage has resulted to the client should not be a bar to disciplinary action as it would be to civil liability. It is the function of the bar to protect the public, and the imposition of high standards will best serve that function.

NO DISCIPLINE OR LIABILITY, BY DEY WATTS

It would be difficult to conclude that any lawyer should be subject to discipline or be civilly liable for negligence under the facts of this situation.

A.   Disciplinary Action

In the practical application of the relatively new Code of Professional Responsibility care must be taken in some areas to avoid interpretations which could result in impossible, idealistic standards of professional excellence that lawyers generally, being ordinary persons, do not possess. The new Canon 6, with its D.R. 6-101, is a prime example of a rule of conduct with which few would quarrel but which can paralyze the average practitioner and the administration of justice unless it is interpreted with a certain amount of understanding of the almost daily challenge faced by lawyers with varied practices.

D.R. 6-101 states that a lawyer should not "handle a legal matter which he knows, or should know, that he is not competent to handle, without associating with him a lawyer who is competent to handle it." What do we mean by competence? What degree of skill, knowledge, or experience is necessary before a lawyer is competent to handle a matter? How is a lawyer to know if he is competent? How can a disciplinary tribunal deal in fairness with a test that must be made subjectively by a lawyer at the outset without having its judgment affected by hindsight if the result of the advice (or lack of it) turns out to be unfortunate? Even in hindsight, what are the tests to be?

In dealing with Canon 6 and D.R. 6-101, we have an imprecise (and probably changing) standard involving the question of what degree of competence is intended, and in the application of the disciplinary rule in almost every case, we deal with the 20-20 vision of hindsight. Accordingly, fairness to the practicing lawyer requires a much greater degree of understanding and care than in many other areas of the code.

Canon 6 states simply that "A lawyer should represent a client competently." The preamble and preliminary statement to the code tells us that the canons embody the general concepts from which the disciplinary rules are derived.

It seems helpful to break down the present case into two inquiries:

First, did the lawyer handle the matter with competence?

Second, even assuming incompetence in handling the matter, did the lawyer discharge his obligation to his client sufficiently under Canon 6 to escape the potential threat of being disciplined?

My sympathies are all with the lawyer. I believe he represented his client competently. Even in an area where he professed to have no special knowledge, he spotted the problem and gave adequate advice to have enabled his client to have avoided the tax problem that ultimately developed. He told his client he did not know the answer to the question of the cost basis and told him how to find this out.

There is no requirement in the code that a lawyer attempt to prevent his client from completing a legitimate transaction contrary to his advice or to resign his representation if the client proceeds with the transaction. Clients do this every day after assessing the risks, and this client knew he was risking a potential liability for capital gains taxes. It is interesting to conjecture about the liability of the lawyer had he insisted in delaying the transaction in the face of a falling market price for the securities his client wanted to sell.

Does it follow from an admission of lack of knowledge of the law about an isolated problem involved in a particular transaction that a lawyer knew, or should have known, that he was not competent to handle the matter in the first instance? Of course not! Few lawyers have at their finger tips the answers to every question involved in every matter they are handling. The fact that the lawyer felt inexperienced in tax matters does not mean he was not competent to handle the matter. He was sufficiently knowledgeable and experienced to recognize the problem and advise his client to determine the facts. He declined to pass on the isolated question of tax basis or assume responsibility.

At this point he had three options open to him under D.R. 6101(A)(1). He could have terminated his relationship with the client, he could have undertaken the study necessary to qualify himself, or he could have associated with him a lawyer who was competent to handle the tax question. In essence, the attorney and client chose a perfectly acceptable alternative course by agreeing that the client would take it upon himself to consult an expert (in this case, a tax accountant).

The client apparently assumed responsibility for obtaining the tax advice and, while the lawyer may well have fallen short of certain "ethical aspirations" stated in E.C. 7-8 in permitting the transaction to close when he knew his client was not fully informed of all relevant considerations, the ethical considerations are not in themselves a basis for disciplinary action.

It seems unfortunate that the concept of "competence" can form the basis of disciplinary action against a lawyer. It makes the practice of law a very hazardous occupation, indeed. I doubt if very many lawyers appreciate that the "ethics" of the profession now seem to involve an element that requires a self-evaluation of ability, background, available time, and prior experience before every undertaking on behalf of a client. This is a far different thing from the usual understanding that ethics involve deviations from what is generally recognized as "moral character."

If it is not wisely administered, D.R. 6-101 can lead lawyers into becoming insurers of results, and I would hope that some element of good faith on the part of the lawyer will be read into this rule. It is interesting to note that at least one state bar association, in fact, has added just such a thought to the end of D.R. 6-101. For instance Rule 6-101 of the California Rules of Professional Conduct requires that the good faith of the attorney be considered in determining whether or not acts done through ignorance or mistake warrant the imposition of discipline under Rule 6-101.

In the present case there is no evidence whatsoever of any bad faith on the part of the lawyer. In view of his admitted lack of knowledge and skill it would seem that he acted with a good deal of competence under the circumstances. He should not be disciplined for the failure of his client to take his advice.

B. Civil Liability

A cause of action for professional negligence must contain each of the following four ingredients: (1) the professional's duty to use such skill as is commonly possessed by other members of the profession; (2) a breach of that duty; (3) a proximate causal connection between the negligent conduct and the resulting injury; and (4) actual loss or damage resulting from the professional negligence. Budd v. Nixen, 491 P.2d 433, 436 (1971); Prosser, Law of Torts, §§30, 32 (4th ed. 1971); 45 A.L.R.2d 11. The absence of any of the four elements is fatal to the action. Ventura County Humane Society v. Holloway, 115 Cal. Rptr. 464, 467 (1974).

In the present situation questions may be raised concerning both the duty assumed by the attorney and the proximate cause of the client's injuries.

Whether detailed knowledge of capital gains taxation is within the skills commonly possessed by attorneys is debatable, and it is clear that knowledge of certain specialized areas may be beyond the skills of the ordinary practitioner. Lucas v. Hamm, 364 P.2d 685 (1961). On the other hand, all attorneys are responsible for plain and elementary principles of law commonly known to all lawyers. Smith v. Lewis, 530 P.2d 589 (1975). When an attorney accepts employment on a certain matter, he impliedly agrees to undertake a reasonable amount of research in the law relating to the matter.

In this case, it seems clear, the attorney limited the scope of his employment by expressly disclaiming his ability to handle the incidental tax question. He did, however, possess sufficient knowledge and skill to recognize the problem and advise his client to seek specialized advice. He placed the responsibility of obtaining a tax opinion on the client, and the client raised no objection to this allocation of responsibilities. Since the parties had circumscribed the scope of the attorney's employment so as to exclude the tax question, the attorney had no duty with respect to it. Without a duty, the client loses his negligence claim.

Even assuming that the attorney's responsibilities extended to all matters incidental to the investment scheme, the client's informed decision to forgo the recommended expert opinion should insulate his attorney from liability for the proximate results of the omission. There are at least three reasons for this result.

First, the client's omission to obtain the needed opinion is an intervening cause of the economic harm he suffered. Prosser, Law of Torts 417 (4th ed. 1971).

Second, the client's failure to act should be an affirmative defense to the attorney's liability. If the course of conduct knowingly pursued by the client created an undue risk of harm to the client, this constitutes contributory negligence under the circumstances described and should be a defense in a malpractice action against the attorney. Prosser, at 418. Theobald v. Byers, 13 Cal. Rptr. 864 (1961).

Finally, the client assumed the risk of unfavorable tax consequences, since he knew and understood the risk he took but nevertheless voluntarily undertook to run that risk. He should not now be permitted to shift the loss resulting from that assumption of risk to the attorney. Prosser, at 497.

NOTES

1.   A lawyer must use such skill as is commonly possessed by other members of the profession. An initial issue is whether the basis for comparison should be the profession at large (see Myers v. Beem, 712 P.2d 1092, 1094 (Colo. App. 1985), the jurisdiction (see Russo v. Griffin, 510 A.2d 436 (Vt. 1986), or the particular locality (see Gifford v. New England Reinsurance Corp., 488 So. 2d 736 (La. App. 2d Cir. 1986)). Which standard is more appropriate in federal tax cases? This and other elements of a malpractice claim are discussed in some detail in Developments in the Law — Lawyers' Responsibilities and Lawyers' Responses, 107 Harv. L. Rev. 1551, 1557-1580 (1994).

2.   As Horne v. Peckham indicates, if a professional represents himself as possessing expertise in a field recognized as requiring special skills beyond those

of an ordinary member of the profession, he generally is held to a higher standard of care. Taxation is the classic example of such a field. See, for instance, Bent v. Green, 466 A.2d 322 (Conn. Sup. Ct. 1983). If an attorney advertised that his practice was limited to the taxation of corporate reorganizations, would he be held to yet a higher standard? Questions of advertising and expertise are considered in more detail in Chapter 7.

3.   Where are tax lawyers most likely to face malpractice claims? For a nuanced look at this question, see Jacob Todres, Malpractice and the Tax Practitioner: An Analysis of the Areas in Which Malpractice Occurs, 48 Emory L. J. 547 (1999); Jacob Todres, Malpractice and the Tax Practitioner: An Analysis of the Areas in Which Malpractice Occurs — An Update, 78 St. John's L. Rev. 1011 (2004). Although a simple answer is not possible, Todres views tax shelters and gift and estate tax as generating the most litigation.

4.   A "mere error in judgment" in a case involving uncertain law does not constitute malpractice. Thus, if the advice is incorrect, but was reasonable based on what was known at the time, the lawyer is not liable for negligence. On the other hand, the lawyer is required to exercise ordinary skill and care in forming a judgment as to the proper course of action. Bancroft v. Indemnity Insurance Co. of North America, 203 F. Supp. 49 (W.D. La. 1962). Suppose an attorney advised a client that there was a one-in-three likelihood of success if a matter was litigated, and, based on that advice, the client took a position on his return. He litigated the matter and lost, and, ultimately, the client was subject to a tax penalty because the argument was deemed "frivolous." Is the attorney liable for malpractice?

5.   To what extent is a violation of the Model Rules or the Code of Professional Responsibility evidence of malpractice? Both the Model Rules and the Model Code have disclaimers that they are to be used as the appropriate standard of care in determining malpractice. Some courts have taken the position that a violation of an ethical rule represents "rebuttal evidence." See, for example, Lipton v. Boesky, 313 N.W.2d 163 (Mich. 1981). How should a violation of Circular 230 be treated?

For example, if a tax lawyer issues a tax shelter opinion that violates the standards established in §10.35 or §10.37, should that violation be conclusive that the lawyer has violated a duty to client? Should it be only evidence of a violation? Should it be relevant at all to the issue of professional liability? Is it important to ask for whose protection the standards of Circular 230 and the Model Rules are established? See Forston v. Winstead, 961 F.2d 469 (1992), which suggests that a lawyer's violation of Circular 230 and ABA Opinion 346 would not establish actionable rights in third parties.

6.   The plaintiff in a professional malpractice case must prove that the defendant's negligence was the proximate cause of the plaintiff's injury. Thus, even if the plaintiff suffers adverse tax consequences as a result of the defendant's tax advice, the defendant will not be held liable if the plaintiff would have entered into the transaction in any event. For example, in Rockier & Co. v. Glickman, Isenberg, Lurie & Co., 273 N.W.2d 647 (Minn. 1978), the plaintiff, a broker-dealer in securities, kept two accounts, one for investment securities and an inventory account that included short sales. Since the plaintiff was in danger of losing a significant amount on the

short sales, he decided to transfer securities from his investment account to his inventory account. The defendant accountant erroneously told the taxpayer that subsequent sales would produce capital gain. The court refused to hold the defendant liable because his advice was not the cause of the plaintiff's loss.

7. The plaintiff can collect only for actual, rather than speculative, damages. Even if the tax lawyer's advice was incorrect, if the taxpayer would have paid the same taxes in any event, there are no damages. Conversely, a failure to provide adequate advice resulting in taxes that otherwise would not have been owed gives rise to actual damages. See, for instance, Linck v. Barokas & Martin, 667 P.2d 171 (Ak. 1983) (surviving spouse collected damages when law firm failed to advise her of option to renounce interest in her husband's estate, which resulted in gift taxes and a second tax on the death of the surviving spouse). Where there is intentional wrongdoing or fraud, the plaintiff may be able to recover punitive damages as well. See, for example, Midwest Supply, Inc. v. Waters, 510 P.2d 876 (Nev. 1970) (punitive damages where return preparer willfully and wantonly made false and fraudulent representations of tax expertise and caused plaintiffs erroneously to file claims for refund).

Many malpractice cases involve the practitioner's failure to file the client's tax return on a timely basis. Generally, the taxpayer may recover any interest and penalties assessed by the IRS, as well as legal and accounting fees incurred in an effort to avoid payment of the late filing charges. See Sorenson v. Fio Rito, 413 N.E.2d 47 (Ill. App. 1980). Where the defendant's negligence relates to an overpayment of tax, the plaintiff has a duty to mitigate any injury, for example, by filing an amended return.

Suppose the lawyer provides erroneous tax planning advice and the taxpayer follows it. Does the plaintiff have to show that the transaction could have been structured in such a way as to obtain the desired results? See, for instance, Whitney v. Buttrick, 376 N.W.2d 274 (Minn. App. 1985) (taxpayer who was advised that his majority corporate interest could be sold tax-free to the minority shareholder was required to show that the transaction could have been structured so as to reduce all or part of the tax liability). Suppose the transaction could not have been accomplished in a favorable way, but the taxpayer enters into the transaction solely because of the proffered tax benefits?

———

The following case discusses some of these issues and also raises the question of whether a lawyer has a continuing duty to advise a client.

Lama v. Shearman & Sterling

758 F. Supp. 159; (S.D.N.Y. 1991)

DUFFY, United States District Judge. Lama, Rana, and Rasha were formed in 1982 to facilitate a group of foreign investors' purchase of 24.9% of Smith Barney stock. Shearman & Sterling, a partnership organized under the laws of New York, created

Lama, a domestic United States corporation, and Rana and Rasha, its foreign parents, as a "General Utilities Structure" (the "Structure") whereby the foreign investors would be able to take advantage of the then-existing tax code. Lama is a Delaware corporation with no actual place of business in the United States. Rana is a corporation organized under the laws of the British Virgin Islands and also has no place of business in the United States. Rasha is a Netherlands Antilles corporation with no place of business in the United States. Lama was owned 33⅓% by Rasha and 66⅔% by Rana. Rasha in turn was owned in whole by Rana. This Structure eliminated United States withholding taxes on Smith Barney dividends issued to the foreign investors by paying them to Lama, a domestic corporation, in accordance with the General Utilities Doctrine. I.R.C. §337 (1954). In 1982, when the Structure was organized, payment of United States' taxes on any profit from the resale of the stock would also be eliminated by liquidating Lama and distributing the proceeds to its foreign parents, as also allowed under the General Utilities Doctrine. Id. . . .

Without first consulting . . . Shearman & Sterling . . . , on May 19, 1987 Lama, Rana, and Rasha executed an agreement with Smith Barney which required the plaintiffs to sell their Smith Barney shares to Primerica. This was done in the manner originally contemplated by the Structure, but the law had been changed and the desired benefits were no longer available. Although Lama, Rana, and Rasha realized a profit of approximately one hundred million dollars on the sale, they were also required to pay in excess of thirty-three million dollars in taxes. . . .

Lama, Rana, and Rasha allege that Shearman & Sterling . . . had a duty to inform of changes in the law and did not do so, thereby causing Lama, Rana, and Rasha to incur an unduly burdensome tax liability.

Shearman & Sterling moves to dismiss this action for failure to state a claim upon which relief can be granted and for a judgment on the pleadings. Shearman & Sterling claims that Lama, Rana, and Rasha plead insufficient facts to state a claim. I disagree. The complaint must be viewed in the light most favorable to the complainant and the factual allegations of the complaint taken as true. Miree v. DeKalb County, 433 U.S. 25, 53 L. Ed. 2d 557, 97 S. Ct. 2490 (1977). These pleadings are replete with facts sufficient to withstand this motion to dismiss.

For example, Lama, Rana, and Rasha allege that a specific inquiry was made of Shearman & Sterling in August or September of 1986 as to the possible effects on plaintiffs' interests of a tax bill then under consideration by Congress. A partner at Shearman & Sterling allegedly replied that there were no significant tax changes enacted as of that time, "but that the firm would inform Plaintiffs if any significant amendments to the United States tax laws were enacted." Id. If in fact such a specific commitment was made which was later handled in a negligent manner, liability may arise on that basis. In attorney-client agreements there may be liability "when there [is] a promise to perform and no subsequent performance, or when the attorney has explicitly undertaken to discharge a specific task and then failed to do so." Saveca v. Reilly, 111 A.D.2d 493, 494-495, 488 N.Y.S.2d 876, 878 (3d Dept. 1985). I find the pleadings sufficient on claims for breach and that questions of what, if anything, was said, and the extent to which injury was suffered thereby are questions to be resolved by a jury.

Shearman & Sterling also contends that there was no breach of a duty to Lama, Rana, and Rasha because the 1986 amendments had no impact on the Smith Barney investment. Shearman & Sterling believes that it can show that the Structure was intended solely to avoid taxes on dividends. This contention plainly raises issues of fact of the matter. Lama, Rana, and Rasha explicitly allege in the complaint that the investment was structured to minimize tax liability for dividend payments and for subsequent resale. Taking the allegations of the complaint as true, the change in law restricted the manner in which their stocks could be disposed of. This obviously did have an impact on the investment. Thus, the pleadings are sufficient to state the causes of action for negligent misrepresentation, breach of fiduciary duty, and professional malpractice.

Shearman & Sterling also contends, that as a matter of law, it cannot be held accountable for proximately causing the losses incurred by Lama, Rana, and Rasha. In order to establish that Shearman & Sterling's acts and omissions were the proximate cause of the alleged damages, Lama, Rana, and Rasha must establish that they would not have entered into the transaction but for Shearman & Sterling's negligent failure to reveal changes in the tax laws, and that this failure proximately caused damage to the plaintiffs. See Quintel Corp. v. Citibank, 606 F. Supp. 898, 912 (S.D.N.Y. 1945) (to establish proximate cause, client must show that he would not have entered into the transaction if attorney had properly investigated the transaction and that this failure damaged the client). In this case, Lama, Rana, and Rasha allege that had they known of the tax law change, they would not have structured the sale of their Smith Barney holdings in the manner which they did. They further allege that the structure of the deal caused them to incur tax liability in excess of $33 million when taxes could have been avoided entirely. These allegations are sufficient to withstand the instant motion.

Shearman & Sterling next maintains that even if there was a duty to keep Lama, Rana, and Rasha informed, their independent undertakings along with actions taken by Smith Barney and Bankers Trust constituted intervening events which were the proximate cause of injuries. When the acts of a third person intervene between defendant's conduct and plaintiffs' injury, the causal connection is not automatically severed. Derdiarian v. Felix Contracting Corp., 51 N.Y.2d 308, 315, 414 N.E.2d 666, 670, 434 N.Y.S.2d 166, 169 (1980). Liability then turns on whether the intervening act is a normal or foreseeable consequence of the situation created by defendant's negligence. An unforeseeable or extraordinary intervening act may well break the causal nexus. Questions as to what is normal and foreseeable are generally for the finder of fact to resolve. Id. Even if a subsequent act was either tortious or criminal, a negligent defendant can be insulated from liability only if that act was not reasonably foreseeable. Cullen v. BMW of N. Am., 691 F.2d 1097, 1101 (2d Cir. 1982), cert. denied 460 U.S. 1070, 75 L. Ed. 2d 948, 103 S. Ct. 1525 (1983).

Therefore, I need not address the merits at this juncture because sufficient facts were alleged to withstand this motion.

Although Lama, Rana, and Rasha may have acted hastily in committing to the sale of the stock, that does not defeat their claim at this stage. Merced v. AutoPak Co., 533 F.2d 71, 80 (2d Cir. 1976) (issue of contributory negligence is almost exclusively for the jury). Lama, Rana, and Rasha allegedly suffered a harm. That harm was a foreseeable consequence of Shearman & Sterling's alleged acts and omissions, namely, committing themselves to a sale which would be subject to tax. That a future sale of stock of this size may require secrecy and fast decision-making is obviously foreseeable. . . .

Shearman & Sterling sets forth the proposition that, where the actual cause of injury is not in dispute, the issue of proximate cause is for the court to determine, relying on Caraballo v. United States, 830 F.2d 19 (2d Cir. 1987). In that case, a thirty-nine year old plaintiff's reckless conduct in diving off a rotten pier into two to three feet of water was held as a matter of law the sole proximate cause of his broken neck. In stating that it was not the government's failure to post signs or its failure to adequately patrol the area that caused plaintiff's injury, the court emphasized the age and swimming experience of the plaintiff as well as the obviousness of the risks.

An analogy of this case with the suit at hand could not be more misplaced. I will not hold as a matter of law that relying on the advice of a professional law firm is comparable to diving from a rotten pier into shallow water. The case at bar involves numerous parties and complex issues of tax law. The pleading requirements were adequately met and the action cannot be disposed of as expeditiously as where the cause of a physical injury is clearly known.

Finally, Shearman & Sterling argues that because Lama, Rana and Rasha could have arranged a tax-free sale of their stock within the Structure established by Shearman & Sterling even after the tax law changed, no liability should attach. This argument is nonsensical. Lama, Rana, and Rasha's suit seeks liability for an alleged failure to inform, not for misfeasance in the creation of the structure. The fact that options existed under the Structure which would allow an avoidance of tax exposure upon a sale of the stock does not exculpate Shearman & Sterling. . . .

NOTES

1.   An attorney prepares an estate plan for a client that includes a trust. The trust is drafted in such a way as to qualify for the estate tax marital deduction. Several years after the engagement, and after the client has paid the lawyer, Congress amends the estate tax laws to provide that a marital deduction may not be taken for property poured into this type of trust. Does the lawyer have an obligation to contact the client?

2.   Suppose a law firm is not on retainer, but regularly provides corporate and tax advice to a corporation. Several years ago the corporation was advised to issue

a certain type of financial instrument that resulted in capital gains to the holder upon disposition. Congress adopts a new provision that results in a portion of the gain on the instruments being taxed as ordinary income, resulting in a decline in the value of the instrument. If the law firm fails to notify the corporation, does the corporation have a malpractice claim? Does it matter that the taxpayer most affected by the change is the holder of the instrument rather than the corporation?

3.   When does a law firm cease to have an obligation to advise of a change in the law? Frederic Corneel, Guidelines to Practice Second, 43 Tax Law. 297 (1990), includes the following:

> The desirability of assuring proper implementation of a plan that we helped create is very different from assuming any obligation to advise with respect to future changes in the law that may have a bearing on plans we have devised or on the repetition in future years of acts that we have previously approved. Most clients understand that nothing is less constant than the tax law and that what is right today may be wrong tomorrow. But it is a truth worth repeating both to our clients and ourselves.

One of the issues in this area is to identify the parties to whom the lawyer may be liable. Is he liable only to his client, or may he also be liable to third parties adversely affected by his advice to the client?

Bucquet v. Livingston
57 Cal. App. 3d 914 (1976)

TAYLOR, Presiding Justice. In July 1961, the settlor employed the attorney to perform the services necessary for the review and planning of his estate, and that of his wife, with the object of minimizing and avoiding federal estate taxes and California inheritance taxes otherwise payable at the death of each of them. Thereafter, the attorney prepared a revocable inter vivos trust specifically designating the beneficiaries, and George paid the attorney his fees. Both George and the attorney intended that the trust would accomplish the following: 1) on George's death, one-half of the principal would be available to Ruby, and would qualify the marital half for the marital deduction, pursuant to the federal estate tax; 2) the other (or nonmarital) one-half would be available to Ruby during her lifetime but would not be subject to any federal estate tax or state inheritance tax at her death, and would pass ultimately to the beneficiaries. . . .

The trust included the following language in Article IX: "George, or after his death or adjudicated incompetency, Ruby, if she is living, shall have the power at any time, by an instrument in writing delivered to the Trustees, to modify, alter, revoke, or terminate this agreement in whole or in part. . . ." Thus, the entire trust was made revocable by George, or after his death, by Ruby.

George died on July 27, 1964. After George's death, Ruby as a coexecutrix of the estate employed the attorney to probate George's estate and to represent her in tax matters related to the probate of George's estate. The attorney was paid additional fees for these services. The attorney also failed to advise Ruby of the tax effect of the general power of appointment in her estate and of her ability to disclaim the power under the applicable federal and state laws. The attorney's professional relationship with Ruby continued until her death in September 1969.

After George's death, Ruby incurred California inheritance taxes on the non-marital one-half as a consequence of her power of revocation. For tax purposes, she was treated as the owner of the nonmarital one-half of George's trust and not as a life tenant. The determination of the appropriate amount of California inheritance tax owed by Ruby also raised questions concerning the legal effect that the power of revocation would have upon Ruby's estate when she died. It became evident that the power of revocation in Ruby rendered the nonmarital one-half of the trust includable in her estate for both federal estate and California inheritance tax purposes. The record clearly indicates that George did not understand the tax consequences of the power of appointment and that the attorney corresponded with the state inheritance tax attorney as to the problems created by the power of appointment.

On March 21, 1969, Ruby executed a renunciation or disclaimer of the power of revocation in an attempt to prevent the nonmarital one-half from being included in her taxable estate. Ruby also assigned her life estate in the nonmarital one-half on the same date to make certain that none of the property in the nonmarital half of the trust would be included in her taxable estate for federal estate or California inheritance tax purposes. . . .

In addition to California inheritance taxes incurred by Ruby as the owner of the nonmarital one-half of the trust upon the death of George, Ruby incurred both federal and state gift taxes, allegedly a total sum of about $50,000, as a result of her renunciation of her power of revocation over the nonmarital one-half of the trust and the assignment of her life estate in the nonmarital one-half of the trust. Ruby also incurred attorney's fees in the alleged amount of $3,750 to effect the renunciation and the assignment. The gift taxes and attorney's fees were paid after Ruby's death.

. . . [A] major contention is that even assuming payment of the taxes and the attorney's fees from the trust assets, he had no duty to the beneficiaries sufficient to establish liability and that the judgment on the pleadings was properly granted on the basis of our opinion in Ventura v. Holloway, 40 Cal. App. 3d 897. As we said in *Ventura:* "The elements of a cause of action for professional negligence are, of course, well defined. These ingredients are: (1) the *duty* of the professional to use such skill, prudence and diligence as other members of his profession commonly possess and exercise; (2) *breach of that duty;* (3) *a proximate causal connection* between the negligent conduct and the resulting injury; and (4) actual loss or *damage* resulting from the professional negligence [citations]. When these elements coexist, they constitute actionable negligence. On the other hand, absence of, or failure to prove, any of them is fatal to recovery. This applies especially to the all important element of duty."

We also indicated that an attorney, by accepting employment to give legal advice or to render legal services impliedly agrees to use ordinary judgment, care, skill and diligence in the performance of the tasks he undertakes. This duty extends not only to the client, but also to the intended beneficiaries; a lack of privity does not preclude the testamentary beneficiary from maintaining an action against the attorney on either a contractual theory of third party beneficiary or a tort theory of negligence. Liability to testamentary beneficiaries not in privity is not, however, automatic. All of the authorities indicate that a determination whether liability exists in a specific case is a matter of policy and involves the balancing of various factors, including: 1) the extent to which the transaction was intended to affect the plaintiff; 2) the foreseeability of harm to him; 3) the degree of certainty that the plaintiff suffered injury; 4) the closeness of the connection between the defendant's conduct and the injury suffered; 5) the moral blame attached to the defendant's conduct; and 6) the policy of preventing future harm.

An attorney may be liable to testamentary beneficiaries only if the stated test is fully met, that is, if due to the attorney's professional negligence the testamentary intent in a legal instrument is frustrated and the beneficiaries clearly designated by the testator lose their legacy as a direct result of such negligence.

In Lucas v. Hamm, 56 Cal. 2d 583, 597, our Supreme Court concluded that "intended beneficiaries of a will who lose their testamentary rights because of failure of the attorney who drew the will to properly fulfill his obligations under his contract with the testator may recover. . . ."

Arguably, the provisions of the Internal Revenue Code and applicable regulations on the subject are as much of a "technicality-ridden legal nightmare" as the California law on perpetuities, involved in Lucas v. Hamm. However, the marital deduction trust, such as the one drafted in the instant case, is one of the best known estate planning devices. Its details and tax consequences are all the more significant for a California attorney since it is well known that the original Internal Revenue Code amendments permitting marital deduction trusts were enacted to make available to residents of noncommunity property states certain tax benefits enjoyed by residents of community property states, such as California. Further, the pertinent provisions of Internal Revenue Code section 2041 making taxable for federal estate tax purposes a general power of appointment created after October 21, 1942, were first enacted in 1951, ten years before the trust instrument here in issue was drafted. The potential consequences of the retention of a general power of appointment are a matter within the reasonable competence of an attorney. Although the question of whether the precise language creates a general power is a matter of federal law, the creation of general and special powers of appointment is also a significant aspect of the law of trusts and estates, apart from any tax considerations. Further, as indicated above, the complaint alleged that the beneficiaries here also incurred federal and state gift taxes, as well as California inheritance tax consequences that could have been avoided by proper draftsmanship.

While the record indicates that the attorney was acquainted with certain provisions of the Internal Revenue Code, it also shows that he apparently overlooked the potential interpretation of the language of Article IX as a general power of appointment. His letter to George dated January 16, 1962, specifically referred to "certain assets over which Ruby retained full control and are not in the trust." He admitted that he could not remember whether at the time of his correspondence with the state inheritance tax attorney after George's death, he was aware of the position of the state agency as to the tax consequences of Article IX.

Here, it is alleged that the attorney was employed to plan George's estate and attempted to carry out George's intent that the nonmarital one-half of the inter vivos trust principal would ultimately pass to the beneficiaries, free of the burden of federal estate tax and California inheritance tax after Ruby's death. The attorney did so by applying a well established tax saving device, the marital deduction trust. Thus, the 1961 transaction between George and the attorney was directly intended to affect the beneficiaries and the avoidance of federal estate tax and state inheritance tax was directly related to the amounts that George intended the beneficiaries to receive after Ruby's death.

The inclusion of Article IX with language that could be interpreted as a general power of appointment necessitated Ruby's renunciation and transfer of her life estate that led to the reduced beneficial attributes of the marital deduction device. Thus, the damage to the beneficiaries in the event that the power continued after George's death was clearly foreseeable and became certain after he died. Without these necessary remedial steps, the entire value of the nonmarital one-half of the trust would have been included in Ruby's estate and would have been subject to federal estate and California inheritance taxes. As the complaint alleged that the trust corpus, as well as the estate of Ruby, was reduced by the error in draftsmanship, we must assume, for the purposes of this appeal in its present posture, that the beneficiaries lost an ascertainable portion of their testamentary rights because of the attorney's failure to advise either George before his death or Ruby after, that a general power of appointment was created by Article IX. We think under the above cited authorities, the beneficiaries have stated a cause of action.

Any reliance on *Ventura* is misplaced as that case is readily distinguishable on its facts. There, the alleged error was an ambiguous designation of the beneficiaries. The beneficiaries, however, were designated exactly in the manner specified by the testator. We held that the attorney had no duty to investigate and make specific the ambiguous designation of the charitable organization supplied to him by his client. We noted that imposing such a burden on the legal profession would amount to a requirement that an attorney draft litigation-proof documents. (*Ventura*, supra, 40 Cal. App. 3d, at p.905, 115 Cal. Rptr. 464.) Aside from this consideration, we also held, as a matter of law, that the beneficiary organization was precluded from recovery as: 1) the trust purpose was clear and could be fully implemented since the testamentary intent was carried out and the beneficiaries under the residuary clause got their full share; and 2) the complaint was "utterly devoid of any indication as to what the true intention of the testator . . . was . . . [so that] it cannot be determined with any degree of certainty that appellants suffered harm or injury at all."

In the instant case, of course, there was no ambiguity, either as to the tax saving intent of George or of the identity of the beneficiaries. Since in the instant case the intent and beneficiaries were specified and the beneficiaries were to receive certain assets, it can be determined to what extent they were damaged, if the allegations of the complaint can be proved.

Of course, here, no less than in *Ventura*, can we demand of attorneys an impossible duty and a standard of care that requires litigation-proof documents. Nor, despite the recent recognition by our State Bar of taxation as a certifiable specialty, are we prepared to hold that an attorney engaged in estate planning has a duty to seek the advice of a certified tax specialist. As we have indicated in *Ventura*, balancing of all of the relevant factors is essential. Here, we may take judicial notice of the outstanding reputation for integrity and competence during the long career of the sole practitioner (now retired) who was the attorney for George and Ruby in the instant case, and the amendment to the complaint alleges no conduct to which any moral blame can be attached. We are not aware of any cases or guidelines establishing in a civil case a standard for the reasonable, diligent and competent assistance of an attorney engaged in estate planning and preparing a trust with a marital deduction provision. We merely hold that the potential tax problem of general powers of appointment in inter vivos or testamentary marital deduction trusts were within the ambit of a reasonably competent and diligent practitioner from 1961 to the present. Our recognition of the existence of a cause of action in the instant case also advances the judicially approved policy of pre- venting future harm and the standards of the legal profession, a matter that has been of great concern in recent years, both to the general public and to the profession, as well as the courts. Arguably, the interests of a beneficiary are even greater than those of the testator or settlor. After the death of the testator or settlor, a failure in the scheme of disposition works no practical effect except to deprive his intended beneficiaries of the intended bequest. The executor of an estate has no standing to bring an action for the amount of the bequest against an attorney who negligently prepared the estate plan since, in the normal case, the estate is not injured by such negligence, except to the extent of fees paid; only the beneficiaries suffer the real loss. Thus, the fact that Ruby's estate was not a party is of no significance here. Unless the beneficiaries can recover against the attorney, no one could do so and the social policy of preventing future harm would be frustrated.

Reversed.

KANE and ROUSE, JJ., concur.

In Chapter 4 we explore in greater detail some of the ethical problems that have grown out of the tax lawyer's opinion letter. See infra pp. 267-288. The case that follows involves the civil liability of one of the then "big six" accounting firms as a result of its opinion letter in connection with an oil drilling tax shelter.

Sharp v. Coopers & Lybrand

457 E Supp. 879 (E.D. Pa. 1978), aff'd in part,
649 F.2d 175 (3d Cir. 1981), cert. denied, 445 U.S. 938 (1982)

JOSEPH S. LORD, III, Chief Judge.

I. FACTS AT TRIAL

Plaintiffs are persons who purchased limited partnership interests in oil wells to be drilled in Kansas and Ohio, of which Westland Minerals Corporation (WMC) was general partner and promoter. As a result of criminal fraud by WMC, many of these wells were never drilled and much of the invested money was diverted to WMC's own use. Economic Concepts, Inc. (ECI), the selling agent for these limited partnerships, and WMC sought to engage in April 1971 the services of defendant in rendering opinions as to the federal income tax consequences of these limited partnerships. In July the defendant decided to write such opinion letters, and on July 22, 1971, an opinion letter signed by a Coopers & Lybrand partner in its name was sent to Charles Raymond, president of WMC, stating that "based solely on the facts contained [in the WMC Limited Partnership Agreement] and without verification by us" a limited partner who contributed $65,000 in cash could deduct approximately $128,000 on his 1971 tax return. That letter was drafted by defendant's employee Herman Higgins, who was at that time a tax supervisor working directly under the supervision of four partners of defendant. The letter was written specifically for the use of one Muhammed Ali, a potential WMC investor, with regard to reducing the amount of taxes that would be withheld from a fight purse. In early October 1971 Higgins told David Wright, a partner in the defendant firm, that copies of the July 22 letter had been shown to individual investors besides Ali, and Wright determined that a letter which would be seen by other investors should be more complete. Higgins redrafted the opinion letter, and on October 11, 1971, defendant sent another opinion letter, signed in defendant's name by Wright, and a covering letter to Raymond.

The jury found that the October 11 letter contained both material misrepresentations and material omissions, and that Higgins acted either recklessly or with intent to defraud in preparing the letters. Much of the evidence concerning those misrepresentations and omissions and their recklessness came from plaintiffs' expert witness, Professor Bernard Wolfman of the Harvard Law School, a specialist in federal income taxation. Most of his testimony was not rebutted by the defendant. Professor Wolfman explained the principles behind this tax shelter: a taxpayer who in 1971 contributed $25,000 to a partnership involved in a bona fide oil drilling venture, which then obtained for each $25,000 contribution an additional $25,000 bona fide bank loan that was fully secured by partnership property (the as yet undrilled wells) and then expended all of that $50,000 for drilling, could under the law applicable in 1971 deduct the full $50,000 from his taxable income.

The effect would be to accelerate the tax deduction available to the investor in 1971. Professor Wolfman's expert testimony in concert with other evidence provided the basis for the jury's findings that the October 11 letter misrepresented or omitted to state material facts in at least three ways.

First, Professor Wolfman testified that writing such a letter was reckless on its face in that it omitted to state that the non-recourse loan which the letter assumed lending institutions would make to WMC, the value of which loan would be deductible by the taxpayer according to the opinion letter, would have to be secured by collateral (i.e., the oil wells) whose value was equal to or greater than the amount of that loan. Non-recourse loans of the type contemplated by the opinion letter (i.e., with no personal liability to the limited partners) are very rarely entered into by banks for oil drilling ventures, according to Professor Wolfman, because it is hard to secure them fully by undrilled wells, whose value is not known. Unless the value of the property used by the partnership to secure the loan were equal to the amount of the loan, Professor Wolfman explained, the amount of the loan would not be deductible to the limited partner under §752(c) of the Internal Revenue Code. To assume this unlikely fact that the loans would be thus secured without stating the assumption was itself reckless, he said.

Second, the plaintiffs introduced evidence, principally through Higgins' testimony before a grand jury, that at the time Higgins drafted the October 11 letter he was aware of a number of facts because of his close relationship with ECI and WMC. In particular, this evidence suggested that Higgins as of October 11: (a) had recommended to WMC that it take the bank loans through mere bookkeeping transactions "without having to make a bank loan in the normal sense that we think of," (b) knew that WMC had acquired a bank, International Bank & Trust of the Bahamas (IBT), (c) knew that IBT was insolvent, or at least unable to make the loans necessary to fund the oil drilling ventures contemplated by the WMC limited partnership agreements and (d) knew that the actual drilling costs for each limited partnership would be less than $140,000. Higgins testified at his deposition that, while under the transaction contemplated by this "paper loan" WMC would not have access to the money it would "borrow" from IBT, that was "not a difference . . . that in my opinion would be that critical from the tax point of view." As it turned out, many of these facts were untrue as a result of WMC's fraud.

Professor Wolfman stated that if the writer had made such a recommendation and was aware of these facts, the October 11 letter contained a number of misstatements: that the driller would receive $140,000 in cash, that there would be partnership borrowing and that such borrowing would be from a suitable bank or other lending agency. These misrepresentations, which the jury could have found were intentional or at least reckless, in turn rendered the opinion as to tax consequences a misrepresentation, again at best recklessly made, because it was based on assumptions known to be false.

Third, the plaintiffs established that as of October 11 Higgins had decided to leave defendant's employ and that he had as of October 8 taken a leave of absence and was remaining there only to finish the opinion letter. There was evidence that by October 6 Higgins was working closely with ECI, WMC's selling agent, and on October 16 he got powers of attorney from Raymond to execute and file papers for WMC, of which Raymond was president, and for IBT, of which he was board chairman. Professor Wolfman testified that it was improper for an employee of an accounting firm who was employed by ECI to write a tax opinion letter and that the failure to disclose his relationship with the selling agent would be a material omission which would appear to have been intentional or reckless.

The jury concluded that, while Higgins caused the material misrepresentations and omissions in the October 11 letter recklessly or with an intent to defraud, no partner of the defendant firm caused any misstatements with such scienter. It also found no misrepresentations or omissions in the July 22 letter, so that liability is limited to those relying on the October 11 letter. With respect to the plaintiffs' negligence claim, the jury determined that defendant failed to exercise reasonable care but said that it was not foreseeable to the defendant that plaintiffs would be injured as a result of its negligent misrepresentations. With respect to common law fraud, the jury determined there was clear and convincing proof that the misrepresentations and omissions were made recklessly but not that they were made with knowledge and intent to deceive. Again, liability can arise only from reliance on the October 11 letter. The responses to interrogatories under §20(a) of the Securities Exchange Act were that the defendant had the power to control Higgins' wrongful activities and that its good-faith defense of reasonably adequate supervision of Higgins had not been made out.

II.   COMMON LAW NEGLIGENCE

After considerable dubitation as to whether the defendant could owe a duty to the plaintiff investors to exercise reasonable care in writing its opinion letters, we charged the jury and included interrogatories as to negligence. The questions we deemed common to the class were the existence of a duty to the plaintiffs and the defendant's standard of care. After the jury found that the defendant was negligent but that the named plaintiff's injury was not foreseeable to it, we entered judgment for the defendant on Count Three on the ground that defendant owed no duty of reasonable care to plaintiffs whose injury was not foreseeable. Plaintiffs have moved for judgment n.o.v. on the foreseeability issue and assert they should be allowed to pursue individual damage claims on a negligence theory.

[The court declined to consider individual damage claims until it could determine what state law to apply with respect to each plaintiff under choice of law rules. The court then denied plaintiffs' motion for judgment n.o.v. on Count Three as to foreseeability because (1) the motion was based on a ground not raised in plaintiffs' motion for a directed verdict as required by Fed. R. Civ. P 50(b), and (2) the entertainment of the motion might deprive defendant of its Seventh Amendment rights to trial by jury on Count Three. Finally, despite denying plaintiffs' motion, the court did vacate its judgment for defendant on Count Three on the ground that the uncertainty as to what state law applies should have precluded judgment being entered as to any plaintiff.]

III.   COMMON LAW FRAUD AND FORESEEABILITY

[The court denied defendant's motion for judgment n.o.v. on Count Two because of the choice of law problem.]

IV.   HIGGINS' RULE 10B-5 VIOLATIONS

A.   Foreseeability and Rule 10b-5

The jury determined that Herman Higgins made material misrepresentations and omissions in the October 11 opinion letter either recklessly or with intent to defraud. The defendant advances several grounds why it is entitled nonetheless either to a verdict in its favor on Count One, alleging violation of Rule 10b-5 under §10(b) of the Securities Exchange Act, or to a new trial on that count. Among these is the contention that the jury's finding of non-foreseeability of injury compels such a judgment in order to make the verdict on all counts consistent with the jury's answers to interrogatories, and that we must take the view of the case that renders these answers consistent. Underpinning this argument is a failure to ask the crucial question, "foreseeability of *what?*" and to make distinctions among the various possible answers. The foreseeability which is required under Rule 10b-5 is not foreseeability that a plaintiff might be injured, but merely that the defendant knew or should have known the opinion letter would be promulgated to investors.

The defendant is correct, however, in stating that the Third Circuit requires foreseeability as an element of a 10b-5 claim. In Landy v. Federal Deposit Insurance Corp., 486 F.2d 139, 168 (3d Cir. 1973), cert. denied, 416 U.S. 960 (1974), the court held that an accountant's alleged misstatements in reports could not be the basis of a 10b-5 action because

> None of the directors' reports was made in a manner reasonably calculated to influence the investing public [and there] is no proof that any were disseminated to the public or that any investor saw them except for Landy, a director and counsel for the bank.

As we concluded in SEC v. Penn Central Co., 450 F. Supp. 908, 912-13 (E.D. Pa. 1978), the "in connection with" requirement of Rule 10b-5 imposes in these cases the limitation that defendants can be liable for misrepresentations and omissions only if the defendants reasonably could foresee that these misstatements would be used in connection with the purchase or sale of a security — i.e., would go to a class of persons (including the plaintiff or plaintiffs in a private damage action) for their consideration in deciding whether to purchase or whether to sell securities. Defendant points to no evidence, nor could it, suggesting non-foreseeability in this sense. We hold as a matter of law that the defendant foresaw and reasonably could foresee that the October 11 opinion letter would be shown to potential investors in WMC limited partnerships, and we therefore conclude that this letter was used in connection with the purchase of those partnership interests.

In so holding, we conclude that an accounting firm's rendering of opinions to a client as to the tax consequences of purchases and sales of the client's securities, where the firm is or should be aware the opinion will be disseminated to potential purchasers and sellers of those securities, is analogous for Rule 10b-5 purposes to preparing or certifying financial statements which it actually or constructively knows will be used in the same way.

The other cases from this circuit cited by defendant for the proposition that foreseeability of loss is necessary in a 10b-5 case are not relevant to this motion. In our case the causal nexus takes a classic form, between an accountant's misrepresentation and purchases of securities, and causation follows from objective materiality, which has been proven, and subjective reliance, which has not been at issue in the trial thus far.

The other main line of authority invoked by the defendant involves the limitation of damages recoverable in a Rule 10b-5 action to those proximately caused by defendants' fraud. To the extent that the jury's finding of nonforeseeability would be relevant to that issue, it cannot be deemed competent because the damages issue has not yet been tried and hence the plaintiffs were not required at the trial of common issues to prove proximately caused damages. What role, if any, foreseeability will play in that determination cannot be ascertained until a later date.

Defendant also relies heavily on Ernst & Ernst v. Hochfelder, 425 U.S. 185 (1976), to impose a foreseeability requirement, mainly on the bases of (1) the Securities and Exchange Commission's proposed standard for recovery for negligent violations of Rule 10b-5, which the Court rejected in holding scienter is required, and (2) the Court's citation of Ultramares v. Touche, Niven & Co., 255 N.Y. 170 (1931). The SEC proposed that a defendant's liability for negligence be limited to those persons whose *reliance* could be foreseen by the defendant, which requirement has been met here in any case. Moreover, there is no reason to expect that the Court, in rejecting the sufficiency of negligence for 10b5 liability, in any sense adopted this limitation.[4] Nor should the citation of Ultramares v. Touche, Niven & Co., in *Ernst & Ernst* and in Blue Chip Stamps v. Manor Drug Stores, 421 U.S. 723, 747-748 (1975), suggest endorsement of a foreseeability rule. In both cases the Court echoed Chief Judge Cardozo's concern about the overbreadth of the class of plaintiffs to whom persons doing business might be liable, but neither opinion

4. Indeed, the plaintiffs point out, it is unlikely that *Hochfelder* imposes any foreseeability requirement since the Seventh Circuit had concluded in the decision below that harm to persons in the plaintiffs' limited class was not an actually foreseen result of the accountants' negligence. 425 U.S., at 192 n.9 (7th Cir. 1974). The Court equated that finding with *non foreseeability of use* of the accountant's audit by the client. Id., at 215 n.33. Had the Court deemed foreseeability of either sort necessary for liability under Rule 10b-5, its absence would have determined the case or at least ought to have been mentioned by the Court to support its holding.

suggests limiting an accountant's liability to purchasers and sellers for *fraudulent*, as opposed to negligent conduct. Thus once there is a breach of a duty extending to persons beyond those in privity with an accountant, i.e., once there is fraud and not mere failure to exercise reasonable care,

> If the certified financial statements [or opinions] are intended to be used and are used, to the knowledge of the accountants, in the sale of securities by the company or someone else to the public, there would seem to be little question that the purchasers are persons entitled to complaint of that breach of duty, even under Cardozo's opinion in the *Ultramares case* which is discussed in *Ernst & Ernst*.

B.   Recklessness and Rule 10b-5

In moving for judgment n.o.v. and for a new trial, defendant takes the alternative positions that it is entitled to judgment because reckless conduct is not grounds for 10b-5 liability and that our charge as to recklessness erroneously defined that legal standard. The former position was rejected expressly by the Third Circuit in Coleco Industries, Inc. v. Berman, 567 F.2d 569 (3d Cir. 1977), where it held in accordance with other courts which had decided the issue, explicitly unresolved in *Hochfelder*, that recklessness is sufficient to impose such liability. Concluding that the defendant's conduct was not reckless under any of the judicial standards of recklessness, the Third Circuit in *Coleco* did not expound upon the precise standard defining the lower boundary of 10b-5 scienter. We derived our charge to the jury from the following definition of recklessness formulated in Franke v. Midwestern Oklahoma Development Authority, 428 F. Supp. 719, 725 (W.D. Okl. 1976), and adopted by the Seventh Circuit in three of the recklessness cases cited in *Coleco*,

> [R]eckless conduct may be defined as a highly unreasonable omission [or misrepresentation], involving not merely simple, or even inexcusable, negligence, but an extreme departure from the standards of ordinary care, and which presents a danger of misleading buyers or sellers that is either known to the defendant or is so obvious that the actor must have been aware of it. [Citations omitted.]

We do not believe this formulation to differ fundamentally from the standard adopted by the district court in *Coleco*, 423 F. Supp. 275, 296 (E.D. Pa. 1976), "a misrepresentation so recklessly made that the culpability attaching to such reckless-conduct closely approaches that which attaches to conscious deception," and we originally attempted to incorporate the latter in our charge. We ultimately decided, however, that the *Coleco* language added little and that because of its legal rather than factual orientation (i.e., degree of culpability) would have been more confusing than helpful to the jury. We believe that our charge correctly reflected the meaning of "recklessness" and that the record amply supported the jury's finding that Higgins made misrepresentations or omissions either with that mental state or with intent to defraud.

C.   WMC Partnerships as Securities

Advancing the contention that the WMC limited partnership interests were securities within the meaning of the Securities Exchange Act only if the purchasers of them intended to profit from the actions of others and not if they purchased them merely for tax shelters, defendant argues that we erred in holding these interests were securities as a matter of law. Cf. §3(a)(10) of the Securities Exchange Act, 15 U.S.C. §78c(a)(10). But the very cases cited by the defendant tend to refute the proposition that there is an equation between securities and defendant's narrow definition of profit motivation. Rather, the meaning of securities under this legislation should be and has been interpreted like that under the Securities Act of 1933, which the Supreme Court has held to embody a flexible rather than a static principle, one that is capable of adaptation to meet the countless and variable schemes devised by those who seek the use of the money of others on the promise of profits.

SEC v. Howey Co., 328 U.S. 293, 299 (1946). The record clearly establishes that WMC partnership shares promised to investors "profits" in the broad sense meant by the Court, based on, *inter alia;* the tax consequences forecast by defendant. Moreover, courts have more recently reinforced and indeed broadened the doctrine that the definition of a security is "to be liberally construed under the federal securities laws," Ballard & Cordell Corp. v. Zoller & Danneberg Exploration, Ltd., 544 F.2d 1059, 1063 (10th Cir. 1976), cert. denied, 431 U.S. 965 (1977), in view of the fact that remedial legislation such as these laws should be broadly construed. Tcherepnin v. Knight, 389 U.S. 332, 336 (1967). See also Nor-Tex Agencies, Inc. v. Jones, 482 F.2d 1093, 1098 (5th Cir. 1973), cert. denied, 415 U.S. 977 (1974).

V.   LIABILITY OF DEFENDANT FOR HIGGINS' RULE 10B-5 VIOLATIONS

Even assuming Higgins violated Rule 10b-5 by misrepresenting and omitting to state material facts in the October 11 opinion letter, the defendant says it cannot be liable for those acts, particularly in light of the jury's finding that no partner in the defendant firm caused the misrepresentations or omissions to be made. We concluded as a matter of law that the defendant should be held liable on the basis of *respondeat superior* for acts of Higgins committed in the scope of his employment with Coopers & Lybrand, and we framed interrogatories to the jury concerning defendant's secondary liability under §20(a) of the Securities Exchange Act, the "controlling persons" provision. The defendant argues that it is entitled to judgment on Count One due to the inapplicability of agency principles to it and the lack of evidence to sustain a §20(a) violation, and alternatively that there should be a new trial because our charge was erroneous as to these issues.

A.   Respondeat Superior

[The court found that although the imposition of vicarious liability on the principal in a securities violation case is normally appropriate, the Third Circuit in Rochez Brothers, Inc. v. Rhoades created a "special duty" exception applicable to broker-dealers on the basis of their position of public trust.]

While we know of no case discussing the applicability of *respondeat superior* to accounting firms, we believe the "special duty" exception applies to them because their roles in securities transactions resemble more closely those of broker-dealers than those of corporations generally. We conclude that defendant here is liable for any conduct of Higgins which violated Rule 10b-5 occurring in the scope of his employment. While it is true that the defendant (like accountants generally) did not deal with purchasers as directly as broker-dealers do, its task in writing over its signature on the October 11 opinion letter, which it delegated in large part to Higgins, was to render an independent opinion which would influence potential investors in WMC. Moreover, Judge Newman's observation in Plunkett v. Dominick & Dominick, Inc., that "[h]olding the broker-dealer liable [for an employee's 10b-5 violation] allocates the risk of loss to the entity best able to prevent a loss and most able to sustain the monetary repercussions of the illegal act," 414 F. Supp., at 889, applies with equal force to accounting firms in situations such as this.

Higgins' misrepresentations were in a letter signed by a partner on defendant's behalf and came in the course of conduct for which the defendant was compensated. Professor Wolfman testified as to the high degree of care owed by accountants in such undertakings. Judge Frankel has noted, in holding an accounting firm had no duty to disclose material facts where it had not itself made any representations or certification, that

> Where it gives an opinion or certifies statements, an auditing firm publicly assumes a role that carries a special relationship of trust vis-à-vis the public. The auditor in such a case holds itself out as an independent professional source of assurance that the audited company's financial presentations are accurate and reliable. [citations omitted].

Gold v. DCL Inc., 399 F. Supp., at 1127. This special relationship and duty seem to us to justify under the *Rochez* rationale imposition of *respondeat superior* liability on an accounting firm for misrepresentations of an employee which, like those here, were expressed in a firm opinion. We note, finally, that a number of courts, including the Third Circuit, have discussed the liability of accounting firms under Rule 10b-5 for conduct (which of course can only be done by natural persons), apparently assuming the applicability of *respondeat superior*.

B.   §20 Liability

Section 20 of the Securities Exchange Act provides:

Liability of controlling persons.
(a) Every person who, directly or indirectly, controls any person liable under any provision of this chapter or of any rule or regulation thereunder shall also be liable

jointly and severally with and to the same extent as such controlled person to any person to whom such controlled person is liable, unless the controlling person acted in good faith and did not directly or indirectly induce the act or acts constituting the violation or cause of action.

On its face, the statute seems to make the existence of a controlling person-controlled person relationship sufficient to make out a prima facie case of liability, with a defense of good faith and non-inducement available to controlling persons.

Accordingly, we charged the jury first as to the law concerning whether defendant was a controlling person with respect to Higgins and framed the question as to whether Coopers & Lybrand "had the power or potential power to influence and control the activities" of Higgins. The jury decided it had that power. The courts have not stated explicitly whether the existence of this relationship *vel non* is a question of fact, as we believe it is, or of law. If it is the former, we believe we properly instructed and formulated the interrogatory to the jury under *Rochez,* and that its answer to the interrogatory was amply supported by the evidence. It stands as a finding that Coopers & Lybrand was a controlling person of Higgins with regard to the drafting of the WMC opinion letter. The project of writing that letter was, after all, firm business which was done under the direction of partners and for which the defendant was compensated. If this is a question of law, we hold likewise that defendant was a controlling person under the SEC's and this circuit's liberal construction of "control."

We next asked the jury whether the defendant exercised reasonably adequate and sufficient supervision over Higgins, on the premises that a showing of such supervision by defendant would make out the good faith aspect of the two-part §20 defense just as it would for broker-dealers and that this was the only basis on the record for a good faith defense. The jury concluded defendant did not. Again we find this determination was supported by the evidence that, *inter alia,* David Wright (the partner who most directly was charged with supervising Higgins), never read the WMC limited partnership agreements or asked Higgins whether he had read them. Particularly in light of the fact that defendant bears the burden under *Gould* of making out this defense, we are unable to conclude that the jury simply made a mistake, as the defendant contends, and to hold as a matter of law that the defendant exercised reasonably adequate supervision.

Defendant argues that we erred in not submitting to the jury the second half of a §20(a) defense, i.e., whether the defendant directly or indirectly induced Higgins' Rule 10b-5 violations.

. . . It is the *defendant* who must make out both elements of the *defense,* and the failure here to establish good faith precludes any need for inquiry into non-inducement, either by a jury or (as would be appropriate here) by a court in determining whether the undisputed facts amount to non-inducement. Where the resolution of an issue cannot affect the outcome of the case, a party has no "right" to have it determined. Hence the jury's findings are sufficient to impose §20(a) liability on the defendant for Higgins' acts.

A more substantial challenge by defendant arises from a point in the Third Circuit case law construing §20(a) which is at best ambiguous and at worst a mess. The defendant argues that our interpretation of the statute is inconsistent with that of the Third Circuit in *Rochez,* where it held "that secondary liability cannot be found under Section 20(a) unless it can be shown that the defendant was a culpable participant in the fraud." 527 F.2d, at 890.

This requirement appears to combine the statutory criteria of bad faith and inducement. In so doing, *Rochez* seems to create a new requisite for §20(a) liability and to suggest, contrary to the statute on its face, that plaintiff bears the burden of demonstrating aspects of both bad faith and inducement to make out a prima facie case. This position was squarely rejected six months later by the *Gould* court, which did not overrule *Rochez* and indeed cited it approvingly. This conflict, or at best lack of clarity, within the Third Circuit leaves us somewhat confused as to the necessary elements of §20(a) and as to burden of proof. We believe that we must resolve that problem by giving primacy to *Gould,* the most recent pronouncement of that court as to these issues under §20(a).

Even under *Rochez,* however, we believe that our charge and interrogatories were correct. Even if "culpable participation" is required to make a prima facie case, we cannot agree with the defendant that the issue of its presence was properly a question for the jury.

In *Rochez,* the court found a lack of culpable participation by the corporation where the violator, its president, acted for himself and traded the corporation's securities on his own account, where the corporation did not benefit from his conduct and where its other employees all were purely ministerial. 527 F.2d, at 891. Similarly, one of the Second Circuit cases from which *Rochez* gleaned the culpable participation requirement, Gordon v. Burr, was an instance in which the controlling person was far removed from the violation. There, a broker-dealer was deemed not to be a "culpably participating" controlling person of a salesman who violated the securities laws in sales which were not managed by the firm to a purchaser who was not a regular customer of the firm.

While we therefore have some idea of what constitutes a lack of culpable participation under *Rochez,* we are less informed as to what amounts to its presence. In Straub v. Vaisman & Co., where the Third Circuit upheld a district court holding that a corporate broker-dealer was liable under §20(a) as well as under *respondeat superior,* the court said only that such liability attached where the corporation's "role was not merely that of a facade for fraud, but rather one of a culpable confederate." 540 F.2d, at 596. There the broker-dealer's "participation" in its president's fraud with respect to another company's securities consisted in its being a market-maker in those securities, a financial consultant to the other company and the employer of the salesman who advised the purchase of these securities to plaintiff in a telex signed in the name of the corporation. The court's analysis is brief and does not in any sense define the lower threshold of culpable participation. Surely defendant is incorrect, however, when it argues that it cannot be found to have been a culpable participant because the jury found that no partner (whose acts defendant seems to equate legally with its own) made misstatements recklessly or with an intent to defraud. To hold that such a finding bars §20(a) liability would mean the section applies only where the controlling person's primary liability can be made out and thus would render §20(a) a nullity. We reject the idea that Congress intended §20(a) liability to be so narrow as to be virtually meaningless.

The facts in this case are clearly distinguishable from the "no culpable participation" cases decided by and endorsed by the Third Circuit and amount in our judgment to significant involvement by the defendant in the fraud. It may be, first of all, that the defendant's failure to sustain its burden as to good faith is itself sufficient to reach the legal conclusion of culpable participation, where the employee who was inadequately supervised committed the primary violation.

In this case, moreover, at least three factors demonstrate defendant's culpable participation: (1) the misrepresentations and omissions were made by an employee in the scope of his work for the defendant partnership's rendering of professional services for which it was compensated, and were expressed in an opinion letter signed by a partner for the partnership; (2) that work was supposed to be supervised by partners, and the jury expressly found defendant failed to supervise it adequately; and (3) as a result of this inadequacy the defendant failed to make out its §20(a) good faith defense. We concede that the defendant's involvement in the fraud, while significant and much closer than that in *Rochez* or *Gordon*, was somewhat less intimate than that of the defendant in *Straub*. We believe nevertheless that broker-dealers, accounting firms or other controlling persons with special relationships to the investing public are to be judged under more stringent standards in §20(a) cases than corporations generally. For such controlling persons, at least, these facts are sufficient to constitute "culpable participation" under *Rochez*.

VI.   OTHER GROUNDS FOR NEW TRIAL

Defendant also argued that we erred in admitting evidence that Coopers & Lybrand (Bahamas), an affiliate of defendant, knew of the insolvency of IBT, and that we erred in bifurcating the trial between the issues common to the class and the issues relating to individual damage claims.

[The court concludes that even if the Bahamian evidence were irrelevant, its admission was not error because no substantial right of the defendant was adversely affected by its admission].

NOTES

1.   Although the Third Circuit affirmed the trial court on the basic issues respecting liability, it reversed on the issue of damages. The trial court concluded that the investors were damaged to the extent that the price paid by them exceeded the *actual* value of the investment. 675 F.2d 175 (3d Cir. 1981). The defendant accounting firm argued that this improperly made it an insurer of the speculative

investment. The appeals court agreed, holding that the damage to the investors consisted of the amount of money paid by them less the amount that they would have paid had all facts wrongfully withheld by the defendants been made available to the investors at the time of investment. The appeals court rejected an argument that the lost tax benefits constituted the measure of damages.

2.   What is the federal income tax consequence of the recovery to the investors and, to the extent not insured, to the defendant? Should professional malpractice insurance premiums be deductible?

When a tax lawyer (or law professor) testifies for one of the parties as an expert, what is a proper method for determining his compensation? Would it be acceptable for an expert witness for the plaintiffs in a case like *Sharp* to receive a fee contingent on the outcome or a share of the plaintiff's attorney's fee, whether or not that is contingent?

Many courts require that a plaintiff use testimony from a qualified expert on the standard of care. Is there anything unusual about having tax law and tax shelters explained from the witness stand? Is it appropriate to have the accountant's standard of professional conduct the subject of expert testimony? What is the best way for tax law and professional standards to be conveyed to a jury in a civil suit for malpractice or securities fraud — by expert testimony, argument of counsel, judge's charge, or a combination? For an important contribution to the solution of these and other related questions, see Note, Expert Legal Testimony, 97 Harv. L. Rev. 797 (1984).

3.   In Croy v. Campbell, 624 F.2d 709 (5th Cir. 1980), investors in an unsuccessful tax shelter sued their counsel, a tax lawyer who had recommended the shelter to them. The action was brought under the federal securities laws, and the court denied recovery because (1) the tax lawyer was not a "seller" of a security, and (2) the evidence did not show deception on his part. The evidence did, however, indicate (1) that the lawyer looked to the promoter of the shelter for his fee and that the fee varied with the level of plaintiffs' investment, and (2) that the defendant made substantial errors in the computation of depreciation deductions available to plaintiffs. The court noted that the "complaint" does not include any counts alleging negligence or malpractice "on the part of the defendant." 624 F.2d, at 716 n.7. Is this a hint that plaintiffs might have enjoyed recovery had they pleaded on a different basis?

4.   For a useful source of current developments in professional malpractice, see Professional Liability Reporter.

Chapter 2

Tax Return Preparation and Advice

A tax practitioner's duties in either preparing a client's tax return or advising a taxpayer are derivative. They are defined by the client's duties. Thus, it is important to understand the taxpayer's duty with respect to filing a tax return and the standard of care that the taxpayer must use.

The various provisions of law that require taxpayers to file returns and keep records are set forth in §§6001-6115 of the Internal Revenue Code. Section 6012 requires individuals to file annual income tax returns. Other provisions require returns of corporations, partnerships, trusts, and estates.

Section 6011(a) gives the Treasury broad regulatory authority to prescribe the form and contents of a return. Reg. §1.6012-1 prescribes the form on which an individual must file an income tax return and specifies some of the information such a return must contain.

The legal duty of a person with the requisite minimum income to complete, sign, and file an income tax return on the form prescribed is unambiguous. The heart of the income tax system lies in the obligation of each taxpayer to declare what he owes. Because the taxpayer's obligation is a legal one, it is misleading to describe our tax system as "voluntary," although the system clearly depends to a very high degree on taxpayer compliance with the duty to self-assess by filing a timely and accurate return.

If the tax law were free of ambiguity, and if there were no unforeseen situations when Congress drafted the law, the scope of the tax lawyer's work would be considerably narrower than it is. Although the opportunity for tax planning would remain as long as the law allowed tax consequences to vary with a taxpayer's choice among alternative courses of conduct or with the form of a transaction, the role of a preparer in connection with the preparation of a client's return would be little more than ministerial. Notwithstanding its considerable ambiguity, the tax law imposes on taxpayers minimum standards of accuracy for tax return reporting. These taxpayer accuracy standards are reflected in the various civil and criminal penalties of the Internal Revenue Code, and lawyers who either advise clients with respect to tax return positions or prepare tax returns must be aware of the taxpayer standards in order to assess whether their clients are operating within the bounds of the law.

A. Tax Return Accuracy and the Taxpayer

Taxpayers who circumvent their tax obligations with criminal intent are, of course, subject to prosecution under various criminal provisions of the Internal Revenue Code. Section 7201 *et seq.* In addition, if any portion of an underpayment of tax is attributable to "fraud," the Code provides a civil penalty equal to 75 percent of the portion of the underpayment that is due to fraud. §6663. A lawyer may not assist a client in conduct that is criminal or fraudulent, see Model Rule 1.2(d), and thus we do not dwell on these extreme forms of taxpayer conduct. Instead, we limit our concern to the more typical situation of client conduct that, while legal, may or may not satisfy the accuracy obligation of the taxpayer.

The taxpayer's tax return accuracy obligation is set forth in §6662 of the Code, which imposes a single 20 percent accuracy penalty on any portion of an underpayment of tax that is attributable to (1) negligence or disregard of rules or regulations, (2) substantial understatement of income tax liability, or (3) valuation misstatement. §6662(b). However, no penalty may be imposed with respect to any portion of an underpayment if the taxpayer establishes that there was reasonable cause for that portion of the underpayment and that the taxpayer acted in good faith. §6664(c).

1. Negligence or Disregard of Rules or Regulations

The Code defines "negligence" to include any failure to make a reasonable attempt to comply with the tax laws. The regulations indicate that negligence also includes a failure to exercise ordinary and reasonable care in the preparation of a return and that a position lacking a "reasonable basis" is presumed attributable to negligence. Reg. §1.6662-3(b)(1). The regulations give as an example a failure to investigate the correctness of a deduction, credit, or exclusion on a return that would seem "to a reasonable and prudent person to be 'too good to be true.'" Reg. §1.6662-3(b)(1)(ii). Although in some instances, disclosure protects the taxpayer from penalty, the disclosure option is not available where negligence is involved. Legislative history indicates that disclosure is not relevant "because a taxpayer generally is not considered to have been negligent with respect to a return position, whether or not it was disclosed, if the position has a reasonable basis." More recently, Rev. Proc. 2005-75, 2005-50 I.R.B. 1137 affirms that the disclosure exception does not apply to the negligence provision of §6662.

The term "disregard" of rules or regulations includes any careless, reckless, or intentional disregard. §6662(c). "Rules or regulations" include the Code, temporary or final regulations, revenue rulings, and notices (other than proposed rulemaking) published in the Internal Revenue Bulletin. A taxpayer is not considered to have disregarded a revenue ruling or notice if the position adopted by the taxpayer has a realistic possibility of being sustained on its merits.*

A taxpayer can avoid the penalty for disregarding rules or regulations if he discloses his position on the return *and* the position has a reasonable basis. In the case of a regulation, the position also must represent a good faith challenge to the validity of the regulation. Reg. §1.6662-3(c)(1). As with negligence, if the taxpayer acted in good faith and with reasonable cause, the penalty is not imposed. §6664(c).

2. Substantial Understatement of Income Tax

An understatement of income tax occurs if the tax required to be shown on the return exceeds the tax actually shown on the return. The understatement is substantial if it exceeds the greater of 10 percent of the correct tax liability or $5,000 ($10,000 in the case of a corporation). §6662(d)(1)(A), (B). No penalty is imposed on an understatement to the extent that it is attributable to a position with respect to which (1) "substantial authority" exists, or (2) the relevant facts concerning tax treatment are "adequately disclosed" on the return or an attached statement and there is a reasonable basis for the position. If the position is contrary to a regulation, the position must represent "a good faith challenge to the validity of the regulation." Reg. §1.6662-3(c)(1).

The substantial authority standard is less stringent than a "more likely than not" standard (where there is a greater than 50 percent chance that the position will be upheld), but more stringent than a reasonable basis standard. Reg. §1.6662-4(d)(2). The regulations define authority to include the Internal Revenue Code and other statutes; proposed, temporary, and final regulations; tax treaties and their official explanations; court cases; committee reports and certain other legislative history, including "Blue Book" explanations; private letter rulings; technical advice memoranda; IRS information and press releases; and IRS notices and other announcements published in the Internal Revenue Bulletin. Conclusions reached in treatises, legal periodicals, legal opinions, or opinions rendered by tax professionals are not authority. Reg. §1.6662-4(d)(3)(iii).

Authority for a position is substantial if the weight of authorities supporting it is substantial in relation to the weight of authorities supporting a contrary position. Reg. §1.6662-4(d)(3)(i). A taxpayer may have substantial authority for a position that is supported only by a well-reasoned construction of the applicable statutory provision. Reg. §1.6662-4(d)(3)(ii).

Disclosure is adequate if made on the return or on a Form 8275 (Form 8275R if the position is contrary to a regulation) attached to the return. Reg. §1.6662-4(f)(1).

---

*The "realistic possibility" standard has been understood in related contexts to describe a position that has an approximately one-in-three chance (or greater) of success on the merits. Cf. Reg. §1.6694-2(b). Does this formulation suggest that a position contrary to a regulation can never meet the realistic possibility standard?

The penalty also may be avoided if the taxpayer acts in good faith and with reasonable cause. §6664(c).

3. Valuation Misstatement

The taxpayer accuracy penalty may also be triggered by substantial income tax valuation misstatements, substantial overstatements of pension liabilities, and substantial estate or gift tax valuation understatements. See §6662(e), (f), and (g). A substantial income tax valuation misstatement occurs if the value or adjusted basis of any property claimed on the return is 150 percent or more of the correct amount, or if a §482 transfer price is 200 percent or more (or 50 percent or less) of the correct price, or if the net adjustment is under §482 and exceeds the lesser of $5,000,000 or 10 percent of the taxpayer's gross receipts. §6662(e). An overstatement of pension liability occurs if the claimed liability is 200 percent or more of the correct liability. §6662(f). A substantial estate or gift tax valuation understatement occurs if the value claimed is 65 percent or less of the correct value. §6662(g). A *gross* misstatement occurs if: (1) the claimed value exceeds 200 percent (not 150 percent); (2) the transfer price is 400 percent or more (not 200 percent), or 25 percent or less (not 50 percent) of the correct price; (3) the transfer pricing adjustment exceeds the lesser of $20,000,000 (not $5,000,000) or 20 percent (not 10 percent); (4) pension liability overstatement of 400 percent (not 200 percent); or (5) gift or estate valuation understatement claiming value 40 percent (not 65 percent) or less of the correct value. In any of these cases of gross misstatements, the penalty rate becomes 40 percent rather than 20 percent. §6662(h).

   Understatements attributable to these causes are not reduced by the existence of substantial authority or adequate disclosure. The penalty is not imposed, however, if the taxpayer establishes good faith and reasonable cause. §6664(c).

NOTES

   1.   The substantial understatement penalty arose from proposals for the establishment of a "no-fault" penalty, the application of which would not carry any connotation of misconduct on the part of the taxpayer. Jerome Kurtz, Remarks to the American Institute of Certified Public Accountants, 103 Daily Tax Rep. (BNA), May 26, 1973, at J-3; Jerome Kurtz, Discussion on "Questionable Positions," 32 Tax Law. 13 (1978); Bernard Wolfman, Letter to IRS Director of Practice, reprinted in 34 Tax Notes 832 (1987). This was a tacit recognition that, in a world where only 1 or 2 percent of all income tax returns are examined by the IRS, a no-fault penalty offers some economic inducement to taxpayers either to report conservatively or, alternatively, to disclose questionable positions. Failure to do either exposes the taxpayer to risk of the penalty.

   2.   Section 6664(c) offers an escape route for a taxpayer who can establish reasonable cause for an understatement and that the taxpayer acted in good faith.

Does this concept turn what originated as a "no-fault" penalty into a fault-based penalty?

3.   Can a taxpayer avoid penalties because of the advice of a professional tax advisor? Regulations state that reliance on the advice of a professional tax advisor is not per se reasonable cause and good faith. Reg. §1.6664-4(b)(1). The determination of "good faith" and "reasonable cause" is based on the facts and circumstances. Such advice must be based on all material facts, including the taxpayer's motive for entering into the transactions. The advice cannot be based on unreasonable factual or legal assumptions and cannot unreasonably rely on statements, representations, findings, or agreements by the taxpayer or anyone else. Finally, the advice must be based on the law as it relates to the actual facts. Reg. §1.6664-4(c)(1).

4.   As noted above, a taxpayer also can avoid the disregard or substantial understatement elements of the accuracy penalty by disclosure so long as there is a reasonable basis for the reported position. The choice of "reasonable basis" as the minimum standard is somewhat unfortunate since that term has a long and somewhat confusing history in the rules governing the conduct of lawyers. In any event, Congress did not define the term statutorily but did say in legislative history that it was to be a "relatively high standard of tax reporting, that is, significantly higher than 'not patently improper.'" The Conference Report also notes that this standard "is not satisfied by a return position that is merely arguable or that is merely a colorable claim."

The regulations repeat the idea that reasonable basis is a "relatively high standard of tax reporting" noting that it is "significantly higher than not frivolous or patently improper." Specifically, the reasonable basis threshold is satisfied if the "return position is reasonably based on one or more of the authorities set forth in §1.6662-4(d)(3)(iii) (taking into account the relevance and persuasiveness of the authorities, and subsequent developments)." Reg. §1.6662-3(b)(3). The regulations observe that a return position might meet this reasonable basis standard and yet not satisfy the "substantial authority standard" of §1.6662-4(d)(2).

5.   Taxpayers are entitled to litigate tax disputes in the Tax Court before the IRS assesses the tax liability that would result from a decision in the government's favor. §6213. A taxpayer is entitled to present to the court any position that is "not frivolous," that is, any position for which there is a good faith argument for modification, extension, or reversal of existing law. Tax Court Rule 33; see ABA Model Rule 3.1. If the taxpayer is to exercise this right to preassessment litigation in the Tax Court, must we conclude that she is entitled to adopt on her return any nonfrivolous return position? To what extent has Congress circumscribed this right by limiting the disclosure option to positions that have a reasonable basis? Must the taxpayer risk a §6662 penalty in order to secure a Tax Court hearing on a nonfrivolous position that lacks reasonable basis? See Richard C. Stark, Let's Reconsider the Reasonable Basis Standard, 59 Tax Notes 1845 (June 28, 1993).

6.   A prior version of the substantial understatement penalty most closely resembled a no-fault penalty. Because disclosure of any nonfrivolous position vitiated the

penalty and there was no counterpart to §6664(c),* a taxpayer could evaluate the risk associated with a questionable position and disclose the position if the risk was too high. The attorney's role in this process was to inform the taxpayer whether there was substantial authority. Under current law, however, the attorney will be called upon to opine as to whether the taxpayer would be acting in good faith and whether he has reasonable cause. In James P. Holden, Practitioners' Standard of Practice and the Taxpayer's Reporting Standard, 20 Cap. U.L. Rev. 327, 341 (1991), the author notes: "The new law is likely to move us away from an atmosphere in which the taxpayer is motivated to disclose questionable positions as a matter of self-interest and toward an atmosphere in which the taxpayer will instead seek the practitioner's opinion as a key dispensational element needed to establish reasonable cause and good faith." Should §6664(c) be repealed? Should the level of the penalty be raised to 30 percent or higher?

Can the taxpayer be disadvantaged by seeking professional tax advice? If a taxpayer's position would meet the reasonable basis standard, but the "taxpayer chooses not to disclose contrary to the advice of the attorney-advisor, the taxpayer will no longer have a reasonable cause and good faith defense to the understatement penalty because the failure to disclose was contrary to the advice of the advisor." Camilla E. Watson, Tax Lawyers, Ethical Obligations, and the Duty to the System, 47 Kan. L. Rev. 847 (1999).

7.   Different penalty rules and standards apply in the context of tax shelters and reportable transactions. §§6662(b), (d)(1)(C); 6662A; 6664(d). These issues are taken up in Chapter 4.

B.   Tax Return Accuracy and the Lawyer

The tax lawyer's accuracy standards must be gleaned from a combination of the penalty provisions of the Code, the general ethical rules for lawyers, and the practice standards established by the Treasury Department for all persons who engage in practice before the Internal Revenue Service, whether they are lawyers or not. It is important to note that, in general, these standards define minimum acceptable conduct. They are disciplinary rules, not aspirational goals. We now turn to consideration of the standards applicable to lawyers.

1.   Tax Return Accuracy Under the Income Tax Return Preparer Penalty

a.   The Concept of Preparer

The conduct of all those who prepare income tax returns for compensation, regardless of their professional standing, is subject to regulation under the preparer

---

*Actually, the IRS was given authority to waive the penalty on the taxpayer's showing of reasonable cause and good faith, but this discretion seldom was exercised.

penalty provisions of the Internal Revenue Code. These provisions are very broad in their coverage, relating to lawyers, accountants, and all others who prepare income tax returns for compensation.

Any person who prepares a substantial portion of an income tax return for compensation is a "preparer" of that return, as is the employer of such a person. §7701(a)(36). A person who provides advice with respect to "the existence, characterization or amount" of an entry on a return is a preparer if the entry constitutes a substantial portion of the return. However, in order for a person to be a preparer, the advice must relate to events that have already occurred, and thus tax planning advice concerning contemplated activity does not make the advisor a preparer. Reg.§301.7701-15(a)(2). A preparer who signs the return is referred to as a "signing preparer." One who does not is a "nonsigning preparer."

For purposes of the income tax return preparer penalty, only one individual per firm is treated as a preparer with respect to the same return. If an individual associated with a firm signs the return, that individual is the firm's only preparer. If no individual associated with the firm signs the return, but multiple individuals so associated do perform preparer activity, the individual having overall supervisory responsibility for the firm's advice is the firm's only preparer. Reg. §1.6694-1(b). Although only one individual associated with a firm carries risk of a preparer penalty for any single return, both that individual and the firm may be penalized as preparers of the same return. See Reg. §§1.6694-2(a)(2) and 6694-3(a)(2).

An individual who prepares a return or claim for refund of a person by whom the individual is regularly and continuously employed is not a preparer. Reg. §301.7701-15(d). Thus, this penalty does not apply to "in-house" tax practitioners.

b. The §6694(a) Preparer Penalty

Under §6694(a), as amended in 2007, a tax return preparer is subject to a penalty equal to the greater of $1,000 or 50 percent of the income earned by the preparer with respect to the return, if any part of an understatement of liability on a return or claim for refund is due to a position for which: (1) "there was not a reasonable belief that the position would more likely than not be sustained on its merits," and (2) the position was not disclosed or "there was not reasonable basis for the position." §6694(a). Imposition of the penalty is subject to several limitations. First, it applies only if the preparer knew or reasonably should have known that the position was adopted on the return. Second, it does not apply if the preparer establishes that there was reasonable cause for the understatement and that the preparer acted in good faith. In Notice 2008-13, 2008-3 I.R.B. 282, the Service and the Treasury responded to concerns about the application of new §6694 with interim guidance. Regulations revising the regulatory framework applicable to return preparers is anticipated during 2008. Among is various temporary implementation provisions, the Notice states that the "more likely than not standard" faced by preparers is satisfied if the preparer "reasonably concludes in good faith that there is a greater than fifty percent likelihood that the tax treatment of the item will be upheld if challenged by the IRS."

The 2007 changes to §6694 sought to raise both the threshold and the penalty applicable to tax return preparers. Usually, a signing preparer has the opportunity to review the return and thus must assess whether the position in question has been disclosed in a manner adequate for the taxpayer to avoid the taxpayer accuracy penalty. A nonsigning preparer who provides advice to a taxpayer may not have the same access to the return, but this preparer is deemed to have made adequate disclosure (and has thus avoided risk of the preparer penalty) if the advice to the taxpayer includes a statement that the position lacks substantial authority and may subject the taxpayer to penalty under §6662 unless adequately disclosed. If the nonsigning preparer furnishes advice to another preparer rather than to the taxpayer, the nonsigning preparer is deemed to have made adequate disclosure by advising the other preparer that disclosure under §6694(a) is required. Reg. §1.6694-2(c).

The exception to the §6694(a) penalty for reasonable cause and good faith permits the preparer the same kind of latitude as is extended to taxpayers under §6664(c). Reliance on another competent professional is sufficient for a preparer to establish reasonable cause and good faith. Note, however, that the person relied upon must be a preparer (or a person who would be a preparer if the advice were substantial). Thus, the one-preparer per-firm rule precludes that preparer from pleading reliance upon the advice of other firm personnel. Reg. §1.6694-1(b)(3).

The following case illustrates the application of the preparer penalty. Although the case arises prior to the current language in §6694, it addresses an issue relevant both before and after 2007 — who is a return preparer?

Goulding v. United States

957 F.2d 1420 (7th Cir. 1992)

RIPPLE, Circuit Judge. Randall Goulding was retained to act as the attorney for several limited partnerships. Mr. Goulding prepared the partnership returns and the Schedules K-1 for each partnership. Under Treasury Regulation §301.7701-15(b)(3), the IRS deemed Mr. Goulding the preparer of the returns of the limited partners and assessed penalties against Mr. Goulding under 26 U.S.C. §6694 for the negligent preparation of those returns. . . .

For the years 1979 through 1981, Mr. Goulding prepared each partnership's 1065 form, reporting gains and losses, the Schedule K for each partnership, computing the partnership profits and losses, and Schedules K-1, allocating to each limited partner his share of the partnership's profits and losses. The general partner provided each limited partner with a copy of the Schedule K-1, and the limited partners (or their tax return preparers) used the numbers on it in filling out their returns. Mr. Goulding had no contact with the limited partners other than through his preparation of partnership tax returns and the Schedules K-1. He gave them no advice regarding the use of the information on the Schedules K-1, and he did not prepare their individual returns.

In preparing the partnership tax returns, Mr. Goulding listed what the district court later found to be non-deductible start-up costs as expenses/losses and depreciated the entire purchase price of the technologies, including the contingent portion. In computing the basis of each limited partner in his partnership interest, Mr. Goulding used the debt guaranteed by each to increase his basis and thus increase the allowable deductions. . . .

Mr. Goulding challenges both the validity of the Regulation under which he was deemed the preparer of the partners' returns, and the district court's determination that he was negligent in preparing those returns.

[R]egulation [1.301.7701-15] defines the circumstances in which the preparer of one return may be deemed the preparer of another which directly reflects an entry (or entries) of the return actually prepared:

> A preparer of a return is not considered a preparer of another return merely because an entry or entries reported on the return may affect an entry reported on the other return, unless the entry or entries reported on the prepared return are directly reflected on the other return and constitute a substantial portion of the other return.

The subparagraph gives the example of the preparer of a partnership return:

> For example, the sole preparer of a partnership return of income or a small business corporation income tax return is considered a preparer of a partner's or a shareholder's return if the entry or entries on the partnership or small business corporation return reportable on the partner's or shareholder's return constitutes a substantial portion of the partner's or shareholder's return.

Both the regulation quoted above and the statutory definition of preparer state that a person is not the preparer of a return unless one is responsible for a "substantial portion" of it. Treasury Regulation 301.7701-15(b)(1) sets forth what constitutes substantial preparation:

> *(b) Substantial Preparation.* — **(1)** Only a person (or persons acting in concert) who prepares all or a substantial portion of a return or claim for refund shall be considered to be a preparer (or preparers) of the return or claim for refund. A person who renders advice which is directly relevant to the determination of the existence, characterization, or amount of an entry on a return or claim for refund, will be regarded as having prepared that entry. Whether a schedule, entry, or other portion of a return or claim for refund is a substantial portion is determined by comparing the length and complexity of, and the tax liability or refund involved in, that portion to the length and complexity of, and tax liability or refund involved in, the return or claim for refund as a whole.

Subparagraph (2) of section 301.7701(b) establishes minimum amounts required for a schedule, entry or other part of a return to be considered a substantial portion of the return:

> For purposes of applying the rule of paragraph (b)(1) of this section, if the schedule, entry, or other portion of the return or claim for refund involves amounts of gross income, amounts of deductions, or amounts on the basis of which credits are determined which are —
>
> (i) Less than $2,000; or
> (ii) Less than $100,000, and also less than 20 percent of the gross income (or adjusted gross income if the taxpayer is an individual) as shown on the return or claim for refund,
>
> then the schedule or other portion is not considered to be a substantial portion. If more than one schedule, entry or other portion is involved, they shall be aggregated in applying the rule of this subparagraph (2). . . .

Mr. Goulding challenges the validity of Treasury Regulation §301.7701-15(b)(3), in accordance with which he was deemed the preparer of the partners' returns and penalized for the understatements in them. As the sole preparer of the partnership return, Mr. Goulding provided copies of the partnership K-1 forms to the individual partners, who then entered (or whose own return preparers then entered) a single number (a deduction) on their own tax returns. Mr. Goulding argues that he cannot have "prepared" returns he never saw or touched, that he did not give advice to partners he never met or spoke with, and that in any case, he cannot be considered as having prepared a "substantial portion" of returns on which he is responsible for a single entry. Mr. Goulding also argues that he was not "compensated" by the partners, as required by the statutory definition of preparer.

True, Mr. Goulding's work boiled down to one entry on each partner's return, but it represented a far more complicated analysis of partnership earnings — an analysis upon which the limited partners necessarily relied. Thus, Mr. Goulding's comparison of the Schedules K-1 to other informational forms is unconvincing. As appellee points out, normally it is "just a question of fact how much a taxpayer has earned from wages or interest; a bookkeeper can prepare a Form W-2 or 1099 and the taxpayer who receives the form can check it against his own records." Appellee's Br. at 31. This is not true of Schedules K-1; because of the often complicated nature of a partnership return and partnership transactions, a partner cannot readily verify the information and calculations on the partnership return. Moreover, the Internal Revenue Code requires, as a general rule, that tax treatment of partnership items be determined at the partnership level, see 26 U.S.C. §6221, and that an individual partner, on his own return, treat a partnership item in a manner which is consistent with the treatment of the item on the partnership return. See 26 U.S.C. §6222.

Because appellant's analysis of the partnership's financial operations was in essence an analysis of income directly taxable to the partners, and losses directly deductible by them, the regulation making him the preparer of their returns reflects the real relationship between Mr. Goulding and the partners. The compensation Mr. Goulding received for his legal service to the partnership is, given the relationship of the partners to the partnership, really from the partners. His relationship to the partnership and its members was very much the one Congress had in mind in its regulation of income tax return preparers.

Finally, we cannot accept Mr. Goulding's contention that, by deeming him the preparer of the partners' returns, the regulation is inconsistent with other uses of the term "income tax return preparer" in the Internal Revenue Code. None of the other statutory provisions governing the conduct of income tax return preparers applies in blanket fashion to all preparers. Rather, in each case application is expressly limited to those specified in regulations prescribed by the Secretary. See 26 U.S.C. §6107(c); §6109(a); §6695(a), (b), (c), & (d). Thus, the statutory scheme reflects recognition of the fact that more than one person may be a preparer in respect to one return, and that not all provisions imposing duties on preparers will apply to all preparers.

In short, we conclude that the regulation "harmonizes with the plain language of the statute, its origin, and its purpose." National Muffler Dealers Ass'n v. United States, 440 U.S. 472, 477, 99 S. Ct. 1304, 1307, 59 L. Ed. 2d 519 (1979). It was well within the Commissioner's authority to promulgate the regulation in question, and under the terms of that regulation, Mr. Goulding is properly considered the preparer of the limited partners' returns.

NOTES

1. In Schneider v. U.S., 257 F. Supp. 2d 1154 (S.D. Ind. 2003), the plaintiff Schneider, an attorney and CPA who owned and operated an accounting firm, was assessed a §6694 return preparer penalty on a client's return. Schneider challenged the penalty on the grounds that he was not the "preparer" because an employee (Rhea) of Schneider's accounting firm prepared a substantial portion of the return (although Schneider signed the return and employed Rhea). Schneider, in claiming that *he* was not the "preparer," relied on Goulding and its statement that "where more than one person makes substantial contributions to the return the definition of preparer limits the liability to those who prepare a 'substantial portion' of the return." The court rejected Schneider's argument noting that Goulding involved a person who prepared the partnership returns but did not sign the individual partners' returns, not an employer/employee case.

2. In the light of the relatively small penalty ($250) under §6694(a) before 2007, why would a large preparer (one of the "big four" accounting firms, for example) care if it incurred one? How much impact will the new penalty provisions have?

3. Prior to 2007, the preparer rules applied only to the preparation of income tax returns and income tax claims for refund. Is not the accurate preparation of estate, gift, excise, and employment tax returns and claims also a matter of

importance? Note that the 2007 changes to §6694 eliminate the reference to "income tax" and the legislative history indicates that the provision now covers estate and gift tax, employment tax, excise tax, and exempt organizations.

4.   If a tax lawyer incorrectly advises, on the basis of events that have already occurred, that an income tax return is not required to be filed, is she a "preparer" subject to penalty under §6694(a)? Assume that, in arriving at her opinion, she took an unreasonable position, for instance, one that does not meet the "reasonable belief that the position would more likely than not be sustained on its merits" standard.

5.   If a particular preparer is suspected of widespread noncompliance, the Service may institute "program action" under which all returns prepared by him are identified for examination. See Internal Revenue Manual — 4.1.5.1.11(6)

6.   One implication of the 2007 changes to §6694 concerns the disparity it creates between the taxpayer's and the tax preparer's standards on filing, and the likely impact that will have on the dynamic between taxpayers and tax preparers. See infra note 4 on page 124.

c.   The §6694(b) Preparer Penalty

Section 6694(b) imposes on the preparer a separate penalty of $5,000 (or 50 percent of the income earned by the preparer on the return, whichever is greater) if any part of an understatement of liability on a return or claim for refund is due to a "willful attempt" to understate liability or is due to a "reckless or intentional disregard of rules and regulations." (This penalty was increased in 2007. Previously the penalty was $1,000.) A preparer willfully understates liability, for example, if he reports six dependents on a return after being advised by the taxpayer that the proper number is two dependents. Reg. §1.6694-3(b). This penalty may not be avoided by disclosure.

Although the regulations have not been revised to reflect the 2007 changes to §6694, it would be likely that the preparer penalty for disregarding rules or regulations, like the comparable taxpayer penalty discussed above, would not apply to a position taken in disregard of a rule or notice if that position satisfies the standard of a reasonable belief that success on the merits is more likely than not. Similarly, the preparer penalty for disregarding rules would not apply if the position contrary to a rule or regulation is adequately disclosed and meets some threshold (probably beyond "not frivolous"; however, in the case of a regulation, the position must also represent a good faith challenge to the validity of the regulation. (Note the regulations under pre-2007 §6694: Reg. §1.6694-3(c).)

No exception to the penalty under §6694(b) is available upon a showing of reasonable cause and good faith.

Both the §6694(a) penalty for an unreasonable position and the §6694(b) penalty for willful, reckless, or intentional disregard may be imposed on the same transaction, but, in that instance, the $5,000 or greater penalty under §6694(b) is reduced by the amount assessed under §6694(a). The burden of proof rests on the preparer for essentially everything related to the preparer penalty, except that the government bears the burden of proving that the preparer willfully attempted to understate the liability for tax. Reg. §§1.6694-2(e); 1.6694-3(h).

Section 6694(c) permits a preparer against whom a penalty has been assessed to pay an amount not less than 15 percent of the total assessment and to test the validity of the assessment by bringing a suit for refund in a federal district court. If a penalty is assessed against a preparer, but it is later determined in a proceeding involving the taxpayer that there was no understatement, the penalty assessment must be abated and any amounts collected refunded. §6694(e).

Section 6695 provides penalties for various specific forms of preparer misconduct, including failure to furnish the taxpayer with a copy of the return, failure to sign the return, failure to retain a copy of the return or list of returns prepared, failure to file correct information returns, and negotiation by a preparer of a refund check issued to a taxpayer.

Pickering v. United States

691 F.2d 853 (8th Cir. 1982)

PER CURIAM. Pickering is a certified public accountant. For several years until 1978, he prepared the federal corporate tax returns for A.P.T.'s shareholders. In 1978 A.P.T.'s returns and those of A.P.T.'s shareholders were audited by the Internal Revenue Service (IRS). The audit revealed that A.P.T. had paid, and improperly taken deductions for, a number of personal expenses of A.P.T. shareholders, including personal telephone service and gasoline and repairs for personal cars. The IRS assessed penalties against Pickering for willfully understating the federal income tax liability of A.P.T. and its shareholders in 1976 and 1977 pursuant to §6694(b).

A.P.T. employed a bookkeeper, Vinetta Smith, who paid the corporation's bills and kept its records. Pickering's obligation was to prepare A.P.T.'s tax returns. Each year Pickering would go through A.P.T.'s books and conduct a spot-check audit. This involved in part checking random invoices of bills the corporation had paid. Pickering then relied solely on the corporation's books, rather than the underlying documentation, to prepare the returns. Pickering testified that his spot-check audit did not turn up evidence indicating that corporate funds were being used to pay personal expenses of shareholders.

Mrs. Smith, the bookkeeper, testified that she was aware that the corporation paid many personal bills for its shareholders. She stated that on one occasion she asked Pickering "what [the] IRS was going to say about some of our personal expenses if they ever came to audit," and that Pickering responded, "don't worry about it."

The court noted that while Pickering had a right to rely upon the taxpayer and the information furnished by the taxpayer, he could not "ignore information which is called to his attention or inferences which are plainly available to him." Reg. §1.6694-1(2)(ii). Mrs. Smith's statement "called for further investigation and inquiry on [Pickering's] part," and his failure to so investigate, the district court concluded, constituted willfulness. . . .

The question of Pickering's willfulness turns on whether he had been put on notice of possible inaccuracies in A.RT.'s books, and whether he had a duty to further investigate. See Reg. §1.6694-1(b)(2). First, there was Mrs. Smith's testimony that she spoke to Pickering about the number of personal expenses paid for by A.P.T. Next, there are ledger sheets from A.P.T.'s books. The sheets contained "employee account" information, and indicate that as early as 1976 Pickering was aware that the corporation paid personal expenses. The ledger sheets show that A.P.T. paid various personal bills, then, at Pickering's direction, gave its employees bonuses — on paper — which were used to cancel out these payments. While there is nothing wrong with this, it does demonstrate that Pickering was aware that A.P.T. often paid personal shareholder expenses. A factfinder could determine that this knowledge placed Pickering on notice that A.P.T.'s books may have been incomplete or incorrect.

We have held, in cases interpreting another provision of the Code assessing civil penalties, that willfulness does not require fraudulent intent or an evil motive; it merely requires a conscious act or omission made in the knowledge that a duty is therefore not being met. Anderson v. United States, 561 F.2d 162 (8th Cir. 1977); see Emschwiller v. United States, 565 F.2d 1042 (8th Cir. 1977). While the evidence submitted at trial was weak, it was sufficient to support a finding that Pickering's act of deducting as business expenses items which were in fact personal expenses of the shareholders was a willful understatement of A.P.T.'s liability.

d.   Other Aspects of the Preparer Penalty Provisions

A preparer generally may rely in good faith without verification upon information furnished by a taxpayer, but the preparer may not ignore the implications of information furnished or otherwise known to her and must make reasonable inquiries if the information appears to be incorrect or incomplete. In those instances where the Code or regulations require that specific facts exist as a condition to a tax return position (for instance, travel and entertainment expenses), the preparer must make appropriate inquiries to determine the existence of those facts. Reg. §1.6694-1(e)(1).

The Service attempts to separate the preparer penalty determination from the examination of the taxpayer's return, and penalties are not to be proposed in the presence of the taxpayer. Internal Revenue Manual — Administration (CCH) §(20)(11)13.2. Generally, no penalty is proposed until the taxpayer's examination is completed at the group level. Internal Revenue Manual — §20.1.6.1.2(4). Although deficiency procedures do not apply to preparer penalties, §6696(b), the Service extends administratively to preparers the right to preassessment review in the Appeals Office. Reg. §1.6694-4(a)(1); Internal Revenue Manual — §20.1.6.1.3(2)b. Consider whether, when a preparer penalty is proposed, there arises a possible conflict of interest between preparer and taxpayer. Is the preparer's innate desire to avoid a penalty assessment at odds with her duty of loyalty to client?

The statute of limitations for the §6694(a) preparer penalty is three years from the date of filing of the taxpayer's return and is not extended by the taxpayer's own consent to extension. There is no statute of limitations on assessment of the §6694(b) preparer penalty. §6696(d); Internal Revenue Manual — §20.1.6.1.8(1).

Section 6694(a) provides a reasonable cause exception, but §6694(b) does not. Similarly, §6694(a) provides a limited disclosure option, but §6694(b) does not. As noted above, the regulations do create a disclosure option for the "disregard" portion of the §6694(b) penalty. This is important to preparers because the taxpayer may desire to take a position directly challenging the validity of a rule or regulation. Such a position would constitute "intentional disregard" and, without a disclosure option, would subject the preparer to penalty. The disclosure option is available with respect to a regulation only if the position represents a good faith challenge to the regulation. Reg. §1.6694-3(c).

In assessing the presence of reasonable cause under §6694(a), the regulations look to the nature of the error, whether the error was isolated or part of a pattern of errors, the materiality of the error, and the preparer's normal office practice concerning the minimization of errors. Reg. §1.6694-2(d).

If a preparer penalty is imposed against a "practitioner" (that is, a person admitted to practice before the IRS, generally a lawyer, CPA, or enrolled agent), the office imposing the penalty must refer the practitioner to the IRS Director of Practice. Internal Revenue Manual — §20.1.6.2.1.(1). This means that the Director of Practice will review the case to determine if disciplinary action under Circular 230 against the practitioner is warranted. Additional Circular 230 issues are taken up in Chapter 4.

The 2007 amendments to §6694 not only increased preparer penalties but they have also created conflicting standards for taxpayers and preparers in terms of what level of certainty they must achieve to avoid a penalty (without relying on disclosure — which many taxpayers seek to do. Recall that under §6662, taxpayers face no penalty if they have "substantial authority" for their position (not as stringent as "more likely than not"). However, for preparers to avoid penalty (where there is no disclosure) §6694 now requires a "reasonable belief" that it is "more likely than not" that the position will be sustained on its merits. What will this difference in standards mean for tax advice? Clients can avoid disclosing at a lower threshold than their preparers. What will they do? What can, and will, their tax preparers advise them? The New York State Bar Association has been an outspoken critic of the creation of this conflict between preparer and taxpayer standards. See Letter from New York State Bar Association to the House Committee on Ways and Means and to the Senate Committee on Finance, January 28, 2008.

e. Injunction Proceedings Against Preparers

Section 7407 permits the government to seek injunctive relief against preparers. The Internal Revenue Manual notes that the injunctive relief sought should be "commensurate with the conduct" of the preparer that led to the injunction. §20.1.6.8(5).

Section 7408 permits the government to seek an injunction against any person who engages in conduct subject to penalty under §6700, relating to the promotion of "abusive tax shelters." See, for instance, United States v. Buttorff, 563 F.Supp. 450 (N.D. Tex. 1983); United States v. Campbell, 897 F.2d 1317 (5th Cir. 1990). The Securities and Exchange Commission also has authority under the federal securities laws to seek an injunction. See, for instance, SEC v. Holschuh, 694 F.2d 130 (7th Cir. 1982) (injunction entered against tax shelter promoter).

2.   Tax Return Accuracy Penalty for Aiding and Abetting an Understatement

Section 6701 imposes a penalty of $1,000 ($10,000 if the liability of a corporation is involved) on any person who aids another in preparing or presenting any return or other document if he knows (or has reason to believe) that the return or other document will be used for tax purposes and knows that, if used, it will result in the understatement of the tax liability of another person. This penalty is effectively the civil counterpart of the criminal penalty for aiding and abetting under §7206(2). It is also the preparer counterpart of the taxpayer civil fraud penalty under §6663. As with the civil fraud penalty, there is no statute of limitations on assessment of this penalty. Lamb v. United States, 977 F.2d 1296 (8th Cir. 1992).

Note the breadth of this penalty as contrasted to the preparer penalty. It applies to volunteers as well as to paid personnel. In contrast to the preparer penalty, it applies to individuals who prepare documents on behalf of their regular employers. Consequently, sizeable categories of persons not subject to the preparer penalty may be subject to the aiding and abetting penalty. Moreover, there is no reasonable cause and good faith exception to this penalty.

According to the Internal Revenue Manual, targets of the penalty include tax counselors who advise clients to take unsupported positions. Internal Revenue Manual — §20.1.6.6.1(2)a. Legal opinions made available to promoters of tax shelters are another target. The penalty may be imposed even if the opinion does not contain any false advice if the writer knows that the opinion is based on inaccurate assumptions and/ or knows of other facts that render the legal advice false. Internal Revenue Manual — §20.1.6.6.1(2)b. A tax advisor would not incur the penalty for advising an aggressive but supportable filing position, but if the advisor suggested a position that he or she, knew could not be supported on any reasonable basis under the law, the penalty would apply. Internal Revenue Manual — §20.1.6.6.1(5)a. If an accountant overstates the value of depreciable property on an estate tax return, knowing that the overstatement will have no effect on estate tax liability because of the unified credit, but that it will provide an inflated basis for depreciation in the hands of the distributee beneficiary, the penalty applies. Internal Revenue Manual — §20.1.6.6.5(7).

The aiding and abetting penalty may not be assessed against any person with respect to whom a preparer penalty has been assessed in respect of the same document.

§6701(f)(2). If a penalty has been imposed under §6701 against a person relating to a document of a taxpayer, no additional penalty under that section may be imposed against the same person relating to another document of that taxpayer. §6701(b)(3).

PROBLEM

Assume that you have negotiated a settlement in the Appeals Office on behalf of a client. The appeals officer has prepared a computation. She sends it to you and asks that you review it. You note an error in the computation that favors your client by understating the correct liability under the settlement. If you fail to disclose this error, have you exposed yourself to a penalty under §6701? In the next chapter, we will take up the question of disclosure in greater detail, but you should be aware of the reach of §6701 in such situations.

3. Tax Return Accuracy Under the Ethical Rules of the Legal Profession

For many years, the most important authority outlining the tax lawyer's ethical obligations concerning tax return accuracy was ABA Opinion 314. It provided in part that a lawyer may advise a client to take a position on a tax return so long as there was a "reasonable basis" for that opinion. In 1985, the ABA abandoned that standard and adopted in its place a standard that permitted lawyers to advise tax return positions only if those positions had a "realistic possibility of success if litigated." ABA Opinion 85-352. Opinion 314 still retains some validity in other areas, particularly in tax controversy matters (as discussed in Chapter 3). Both opinions are reproduced below.

ABA Formal Opinion 314

(1965)

In practice before the Internal Revenue Service, which is itself an adversary party rather than a judicial tribunal, the lawyer is under a duty not to mislead the Service, either by misstatement, silence, or through his client, but is under no duty to disclose the weaknesses of his client's case. He must be candid and fair, and his defense of his client must be exercised within the bounds of the law and without resort to any manner of fraud or chicane.

CANONS INTERPRETED: PROFESSIONAL ETHICS 15,
22, 26, 29, 37, 41

The Committee has received a number of specific inquiries regarding the ethical relationship between the Internal Revenue Service and lawyers practicing before it. Rather than answer each of these separately, the Committee believing this to be a matter of general interest, has formulated the following general principles governing this relationship.

Canon 1 says: "It is the duty of the lawyer to maintain towards the Courts a respectful attitude." Canon 15 says that the lawyer owes "warm zeal" to his client and that "The office of attorney does not permit, much less does it demand of him for any client, violation of law or any manner of fraud or chicane." Canon 16 says: "A lawyer should use his best efforts to prevent his clients from doing those things which the lawyer himself ought not to do, particularly with reference to their conduct towards Courts . . ." Canon 22 says: "The conduct of the lawyer before the Court and with other lawyers should be characterized by candor and fairness."

All of these canons are pertinent to the subject here under consideration, for Canon 26 provides: "A lawyer openly, and in his true character, may render professional services . . . in advocacy of claims before departments of government, upon the same principles of ethics which justify his appearance before the Courts. . . ."

Certainly a lawyer's advocacy before the Internal Revenue Service must be governed by "the same principles of ethics which justify his appearance before the Courts." But since the service, however fair and impartial it may try to be, is the representative of one of the parties, does the lawyer owe it the same duty of disclosure which is owed to the courts? Or is his duty to it more nearly analogous to that which he owes his brother attorneys in the conduct of cases which should be conducted in an atmosphere of candor and fairness but are admittedly adversary in nature? An analysis of the nature of the Internal Revenue Service will serve to throw some light upon the answer to these questions.

The Internal Revenue Service is neither a true tribunal, nor even a quasi-judicial institution. It has no machinery or procedure for adversary proceedings before impartial judges or arbiters, involving the weighing of conflicting testimony of witnesses examined and cross-examined by opposing counsel and the consideration of arguments of counsel for both sides of a dispute. While its procedures provide for "fresh looks" through departmental reviews and informal and formal conferences procedures, few will contend that the service provides any truly dispassionate and unbiased consideration to the taxpayer. Although willing to listen to taxpayers and their representatives and obviously intending to be fair, the service is not designed and does not purport to be unprejudiced and unbiased in the judicial sense.

It by no means follows that a lawyer is relieved of all ethical responsibility when he practices before this agency. There are certain things which he clearly cannot do, and they are set forth explicitly in the canons of ethics.

Canon 15 scorns the false claim that it is the duty of the lawyer to do whatever may enable him to succeed in winning his client's cause no matter how unscrupulous, and after making it clear that the lawyer owes entire devotion to the interest of his client, Canon 15 concludes as follows:

> . . . But it is steadfastly to be borne in mind that the great trust of the lawyer is to be performed within and not without the bounds of the law. The office of attorney *does not permit*, much less does it *demand* of him for any client, violation of law or any

manner of fraud or chicane. He must obey his own conscience and not that of his client [emphasis supplied].

Canon 22 relating to candor and fairness, states that

It is unprofessional and dishonorable to deal other than candidly with the facts . . . in the presentation of causes.

These and all kindred practices are unprofessional and unworthy of an officer of the law charged, as is the lawyer, with the duty of aiding in the administration of justice.

Canon 29 provides in part that a lawyer

should strive at all times to uphold the honor and to maintain the dignity of the profession and to improve not only the law but the administration of justice.

Canon 32 states that

No client . . . is entitled to receive nor should any lawyer render . . . any advice involving disloyalty to the law whose ministers we are. . . . [He] advances the honor of his profession and the best interests of his client when he . . . gives advice tending to impress upon the client and his undertaking exact compliance with the strictest principles of moral law. . . . [A] lawyer will find his highest honor in a deserved reputation for fidelity to private trust and to public duty, as an honest man and as a patriotic and loyal citizen.

In addition, the preamble to the canons concludes as follows:

No code or set of rules can be framed which will particularize all the duties of the lawyer . . . in all the relations of professional life. The following canons of ethics are adopted by the American Bar Association as a general guide, yet the enumeration of particular duties should not be construed as a denial of the existence of others equally imperative, though not specifically mentioned.

The problem arises when, in the course of his professional employment, the attorney acquires information bearing upon the strength of his client's claim. Although a number of canons have general bearing on the problem (Canons 15, 16, 22 and 26), Canon 37 regarding client confidences and Canons 29, 41 and 44 regarding perjury, fraud and deception and the withdrawal of an attorney are most relevant.

For example, what is the duty of a lawyer in regard to disclosure of the weaknesses in his client's case in the course of negotiations for the settlement of a tax case?

Negotiation and settlement procedures of the tax system do not carry with them the guarantee that a correct tax result necessarily occurs. The latter happens, if at all, solely by reason of chance in settlement of tax controversies just as it might happen with regard to other civil disputes. In the absence of either judicial determination or of a hypothetical exchange of files by adversaries, counsel will always urge in aid of settlement of a controversy the strong points of his case and minimize the weak; this is in keeping with Canon 15, which does require "warm zeal" on behalf of the client. Nor does the absolute duty not to make false assertions of fact require the disclosure of weaknesses in the client's case and in no event does it require the disclosure of his confidences, unless the facts in the attorney's possession indicate beyond reasonable doubt that a crime will be committed. A wrong, or indeed sometimes an unjust, tax result in the settlement of a controversy is, not a crime.

Similarly, a lawyer who is asked to advise his client in the course of the preparation of the client's tax returns may freely urge the statement of positions most favorable to the client just as long as there is reasonable basis for those positions. Thus where the lawyer believes there is a reasonable basis for a position that a particular transaction does not result in taxable income, or that certain expenditures are properly deductible as expenses, the lawyer has no duty to advise that riders be attached to the client's tax return explaining the circumstances surrounding the transaction or the expenditures.

The foregoing principle necessarily relates to the lawyer's ethical obligations — what he is *required* to do. Prudence may recommend procedures not required by ethical considerations. Thus, even where the lawyer believes that there is no obligation to reflect a transaction in or with his client's return, nevertheless he *may*, as a tactical matter, advise his client to disclose the transaction in reasonable detail by way of a rider to the return. This occurs when it is to the client's advantage to be free from either a *claim* of fraud (albeit unfounded) or to have the protection of a shorter statute of limitations (which might be available by the full disclosure of such a transaction in detail by way of a rider to the return).

In all cases, with regard both to the preparation of returns and negotiating administrative settlements, the lawyer is under a duty not to mislead the Internal Revenue Service deliberately and affirmatively, either by misstatements or by silence or by permitting his client to mislead. The difficult problem arises where the client has in fact misled but without the lawyer's knowledge or participation. In that situation, upon discovery of the misrepresentation, the lawyer must advise the client to correct the statement; if the client refuses, the lawyer's obligation depends on all the circumstances.

Fundamentally, subject to the restrictions of the attorney-client privilege imposed by Canon 37, the lawyer may have the duty to withdraw from the matter. If for example, under all the circumstances, the lawyer believes that the service relies on him as corroborating statements of his client which he knows to be false, then he is under a duty to disassociate himself from any such reliance unless it is obvious that the very act of disassociation would have the effect of violating Canon 37. Even then, however, if a direct question is put to the lawyer, he must at least advise the service that he is not in a position to answer.

But as an advocate before a service which itself represents the adversary point of view, where his client's case is fairly arguable, a lawyer is under no duty to disclose its weaknesses, any more than he would be to make such a disclosure to a brother lawyer. The limitations within which he must operate are best expressed in Canon 22:

> It is not candid or fair for the lawyer knowingly to misquote the contents of a paper, the testimony of a witness, the language or the argument of opposing counsel, or the language of a decision or a textbook; or with knowledge of its invalidity, to cite as authority a decision that has been overruled, or a statute that has been repealed; or in argument to assert as a fact that which has not been proved, or in those jurisdictions where a side has the opening and closing arguments to mislead his opponent by concealing or withholding positions in his opening argument upon which his side then intends to rely.
>
> It is unprofessional and dishonorable to deal other than candidly with the facts in taking the statements of witnesses, in drawing affidavits and other documents, and in the presentation of causes.

So long as a lawyer remains within these limitations, and so long as his duty is "performed within and not without the bounds of the law," he "owes 'entire devotion to the interest of the client, warm zeal in the maintenance and defense of his rights and the exertion of his utmost learning and ability,' to the end that nothing be taken or be withheld from him, save by the rules of law, legally applied" in his practice before the Internal Revenue Service, as elsewhere (Canon 15).

ABA Formal Opinion 85-352

(1985)

TAX RETURN ADVICE; RECONSIDERATION OF FORMAL OPINION 314

A lawyer may advise reporting a position on a tax return so long as the lawyer believes in good faith that the position is warranted in existing law or can be supported by a good faith argument for an extension, modification or reversal of existing law and there is some realistic possibility of success if the matter is litigated.

The Committee has been requested by the Section of Taxation of the American Bar Association to reconsider the "reasonable basis" standard in the Committee's Formal Opinion 314 governing the position a lawyer may advise a client to take on a tax return.

Opinion 314 (April 27, 1965) was issued in response to a number of specific inquiries regarding the ethical relationship between the Internal Revenue Service and lawyers practicing before it. The opinion formulated general principles governing this relationship, including the following:

> [A] lawyer who is asked to advise his client in the course of the preparation of the client's tax returns may freely urge the statement of positions most favorable to the client just as long as there is a *reasonable basis* for this position. (Emphasis supplied.)

The Committee is informed that the standard of "reasonable basis" has been construed by many lawyers to support the use of any colorable claim on a tax return to justify exploitation of the lottery of the tax return audit selection process. [1] This view is not universally held, and the Committee does not believe that the reasonable basis standard, properly interpreted and applied, permits this construction.

However, the Committee is persuaded that as a result of serious controversy over this standard and its persistent criticism by distinguished members of the tax bar, IRS officials and members of Congress, sufficient doubt has been created regarding the validity of the standard so as to erode its effectiveness as an ethical guideline. For this reason, the Committee has concluded that it should be restated. Another reason for restating the standard is that since publication of Opinion 314, the ABA has adopted in succession the Model Code of Professional Responsibility (1969, revised 1980) and the Model Rules of Professional Conduct (1983). Both the Model Code and the Model Rules directly address the duty of a lawyer in presenting or arguing positions for a client in language that does not refer to "reasonable basis." It is therefore appropriate to conform the standard of Opinion 314 to the language of the new rules.

This opinion reconsiders and revises only that part of Opinion 314 that relates to the lawyer's duty in advising a client of positions that can be taken on a tax return. It does not deal with a lawyer's opinion on tax shelter investment offerings, which is specifically addressed by this Committee's Formal Opinion 346 (Revised), and which involves very different considerations, including third party reliance.

The ethical standards governing the conduct of a lawyer in advising a client on positions that can be taken in a tax return are no different from those governing a lawyer's conduct in advising or taking positions for a client in other civil matters. Although the Model Rules distinguish between the roles of advisor and advocate, [2] both roles are involved here, and the ethical standards applicable to them provide relevant guidance. In many cases a lawyer must realistically anticipate that the filing of the tax return may be the first step in a process that may result in an adversary relationship between the client and the IRS. This normally occurs in situations when a lawyer advises an aggressive position on a tax return, not when the position taken is a safe or conservative one that is unlikely to be challenged by the IRS.

1. This criticism has been expressed by the Section of Taxation and also by the U.S. Department of the Treasury and some legal writers. See, for instance, Robert H. Mundheim, Speech as General Counsel to Treasury Department, reprinted in How to Prepare and Defend Tax Shelter Opinions: Risks and Realities for Lawyers and Accountants (Law and Business, Inc. 1981); Rowen, When May a Lawyer Advise a Client That He May Take a Position on a Tax Return? 29 Tax Lawyer 237 (1976).

2. See, e.g., Model Rules 2.1 and 3.1.

Rule 3.1 of the Model Rules, which is in essence a restatement of DR 7-102(A)(2) of the Model Code, [3] states in pertinent part:

> A lawyer shall not bring or defend a proceeding, or assert or controvert an issue therein, unless there is a basis for doing so that is not frivolous, which includes a good faith argument for an extension, modification or reversal of existing law.

Rule 1.2(d), which applies to representation generally, states:

> A lawyer shall not counsel a client to engage, or assist a client, in conduct that the lawyer knows is criminal or fraudulent, but a lawyer may discuss the legal consequences of any proposed course of conduct with a client and may counsel or assist a client to make a good faith effort to determine the validity, scope, meaning or application of the law.

On the basis of these rules and analogous provisions of the Model Code, a lawyer, in representing a client in the course of the preparation of the client's tax return, may advise the statement of positions most favorable to the client if the lawyer has a good faith belief that those positions are warranted in existing law or can be supported by a good faith argument for an extension, modification or reversal of existing law. A lawyer can have a good faith belief in this context even if the lawyer believes the client's position probably will not prevail. [4] However, good faith requires that there be some realistic possibility of success if the matter is litigated.

This formulation of the lawyer's duty in the situation addressed by this opinion is consistent with the basic duty of the lawyer to a client, recognized in ethical standards since the ABA Canons of Professional Ethics, and in the opinions of this Committee: zealously and loyally to represent the interests of the client within the bounds of the law.

Thus, where a lawyer has a good faith belief in the validity of a position in accordance with the standard stated above that a particular transaction does not result in taxable income or that certain expenditures are properly deductible as expenses, the lawyer has no duty to require as a condition of his or her continued representation that riders be attached to the client's tax return explaining the circumstances surrounding the transaction or the expenditures.

In the role of advisor, the lawyer should counsel the client as to whether the position is likely to be sustained by a court if challenged by the IRS, as well as of the

---

3. DR 7-102(A)(2) states:

In his representation of a client, a lawyer shall not:
   (2) Knowingly advance a claim or defense that is unwarranted under existing law, except that he may advance such claim or defense if it can be supported by good faith argument for an extension, modification or reversal of existing law.

4. Comment to Rule 3.11; see also Model Code EC 7-4.

potential penalty consequences to the client if the position is taken on the tax return without disclosure. Section 6661 of the Internal Revenue Code imposes a penalty for substantial understatement of tax liability which can be avoided if the facts are adequately disclosed or if there is or was substantial authority for the position taken by the taxpayer.* Competent representation of the client would require the lawyer to advise the client fully as to whether there is or was substantial authority for the position taken in the tax return. If the lawyer is unable to conclude that the position is supported by substantial authority, the lawyer should advise the client of the penalty the client may suffer and of the opportunity to avoid such penalty by adequately disclosing the facts in the return or in a statement attached to the return. If after receiving such advice the client decides to risk the penalty by making no disclosure and to take the position initially advised by the lawyer in accordance with the standard stated above, the lawyer has met his or her ethical responsibility with respect to the advice.

In all cases, however, with regard both to the preparation of returns and negotiating administrative settlements, the lawyer is under a duty not to mislead the Internal Revenue Service deliberately, either by misstatements or by silence or by permitting the client to mislead. Rules 4.1 and 8.4(c); DRs 1-102(A)(4), 7-102(A)(3) and (5).

In summary, a lawyer may advise reporting a position on a return even where the lawyer believes the position probably will not prevail, there is no "substantial authority" in support of the position, and there will be no disclosure of the position in the return. However, the position to be asserted must be one which the lawyer in good faith believes is warranted in existing law or can be supported by a good faith argument for an extension, modification or reversal of existing law. This requires that there is some realistic possibility of success if the matter is litigated. In addition, in his role as advisor, the lawyer should refer to potential penalties and other legal consequences should the client take the position advised.

NOTES

1.   Opinion 85-352 does not attempt to designate a numerical value that would identify a probability of success that can be viewed as "realistic," but a task force of the ABA Tax Section, appointed to review and comment on the new standard, did venture the view that a position "having a 5 percent or 10 percent likelihood of success, if litigated, should not meet the new standard. A position having a likelihood of success closely approaching one-third should meet the standard." Paul Sax, James P. Holden, Theodore Tannenwald Jr., David Watts & Bernard Wolfman,

---

*[This penalty is now imposed by §6662. The penalty can be avoided by disclosure only if the taxpayer has a reasonable basis for the position taken. — Ed.]

Report of the Special Task Force on Formal Opinion 85-352, reprinted in 39 Tax Law. 635, 638-639 (1986).

Can a lawyer actually quantify the likelihood of success? Is it possible to differentiate between a one-third chance and a 10 percent chance? Although the process may not be a precise one, it is not uncommon for taxpayers to request and tax lawyers to provide, percentage estimates of success.

2. Prior to 1988, the American Institute of Certified Public Accountants advised its members that they could advise a tax return position where it had a "reasonable support." See AICPA Statements on Responsibilities in Tax Practice No. 10 (April 1977). In August 1988, the AICPA issued a new Statement on Responsibilities in Tax Practice No. 1 in which it adopted the realistic possibility standard. The realistic possibility standard was retained when the AICPA issued their "Statement on Standards for Tax Services" in 2000 (reprinted in Appendix H), which replaced the earlier statement on responsibilities. The AICPA, unlike the ABA Tax Section task force referred to above, does not define the realistic possibility standard by reference to percentage odds. Rather standard is expected to reflect "a good-faith argument for an extension, modification, or reversal of the existing law through the administrative or judicial process." Statement on Standards for Tax Services (2000) No. 1(4). In addition, the realistic possibility standard is described as "less stringent than the substantial authority standard and the more likely than not standard that apply under the Internal Revenue Code (IRC) to substantial understatements of liability by the taxpayers. The realistic possibility standard is stricter than the reasonable basis standard that is in the IRC." Id. at (5).

Accordingly, both the legal and the accounting professions have provided guidance to their members under which a tax professional is warranted in providing tax advice or tax return services only where the realistic possibility standard is satisfied, although there does not appear to be agreement among professionals on the ability to quantify that standard.

3. The issue of disclosure plays an interesting role in the interpretation of the accuracy standard for practitioners. A taxpayer escapes risk of penalty by adequately disclosing a position, for which there is a reasonable basis. If, however, that position fails to meet the realistic possibility standard, does Opinion 85-352 permit a lawyer ethically to advise it? Can the lawyer sign a return adopting it? The ABA Tax Section task force referred to above concluded that there was no disclosure option. However, the Section later abandoned that view in commenting on the amendments to Circular 230 that resulted in the adoption of the realistic possibility standard in that regulation.

On the accounting side, AICPA Statement from 2000 expressly adopts a disclosure option. Both professions thus appear to permit a disclosure option for non-frivolous positions. What does the tax law now say about disclosure, and how does that fit with the professional standards? Recall that with the 2007 changes to §6694, the preparer's penalty permits a disclosure option where there is a reasonable basis, similar to the taxpayer's disclosure option.

    4.   What happens if the taxpayer does not intend to disclose? What does the tax law provide? As previously noted, if the client does not want to disclose, the client can sign a return that satisfies the "substantial authority standard," whereas a tax adviser can "prepare" such a return only if it meets the higher, "more likely than not" standard. §6694. If that is the case, there is a clear discontinuity between the lesser taxpayer standard and the stricter preparer standard in §6694 (and in Opinion 85-352 and the AICPA standards which both require a "realistic possibility" for undisclosed positions). If a taxpayer proposed to adopt, but not disclose, a position for which there is "only" substantial authority, she should not incur risk of penalty. Notwithstanding that, could she expect assistance from her tax adviser, who would risk a tax law penalty since the undisclosed position would fall short of the more likely than not standard? Would such a tax adviser also face professional sanctions? Is that a sensible result? Is there any other situation in which ethical standards penalize a lawyer or other return preparer for assisting a client who engages in entirely lawful conduct?

    5.   How should standards for return preparers relate to their role and the role of the tax return itself in the tax process. The rationale of Formal Opinion 85-352 is based in part on the view that the filing of a tax return may be a step in the adversarial process. It notes that in "many cases a lawyer must realistically anticipate that the filing of the tax return may be the first step in a process that may result in an adversary relationship between the client and the IRS." Given that less than 1 percent of returns are audited, is that view realistic? Another approach would be to treat the tax return like other government filings, such as SEC documents. Accountants likewise view themselves as advocates when advising with respect to tax matters although they also note the preparer's duty to the tax system, and for example, limits on the ability to take a return position to exploit the audit lottery or provide leverage in negotiating with tax authorities. AICPA Statement on Standards for Tax Services No.1 (3), (4).(2000).

4. *Tax Return Accuracy Under the Treasury Department Standard*

Circular 230 historically has required that practitioners exercise due diligence in preparing returns and in other dealings with the Internal Revenue Service, but no more specific standard for practitioner tax return accuracy was provided. In 1994 Treasury amended Circular 230 to provide such a standard — the realistic possibility standard. However, given the changes in May 2007 to the civil penalties standards for tax return preparers under §6694, the Treasury and IRS sought to conform the Circular 230 standards to §6694. Thus, in September 2007, both proposed and final changes to Circular 230 were issued. The final changes were as follows [note that the *standard* for return preparation was not finalized and instead was issued in proposed form, which is provided, following the finalized provisions of §10.34]:

§10.34 Standards with Respect to Tax Return and Documents, Affidavits and Other Papers

(a) [Reserved]

(b) Documents, affidavits and other papers. —

   (1) A practitioner may not advise a client to take a position on a document, affidavit or other paper submitted to the Internal Revenue Service unless the position is not frivolous.

   (2) A practitioner may not advice a client to submit a document, affidavit or other paper to the Internal Revenue Service —

      (i) The purpose of which is to delay or impede the administration of the Federal tax laws;

      (ii) That is frivolous; or

      (iii) That contains or omits information in a manner that demonstrates an intentional disregard of a rule or regulation unless the practitioner also advises the client to submit a document that evidences a good faith challenge to the rule or regulation.

(c)   Advising Clients on potential penalties. —

   (1) A practitioner must inform a client of any penalties that are reasonably likely to apply to the client with respect to —

      (i) A position taken on a tax return if—

         (A) The practitioner advised the client with respect to the position; or

         (B) The practitioner prepared or signed the tax return; and

      (ii) Any document, affidavit or other paper submitted to the Internal Revenue Service.

   (2) The practitioner must also inform the client of any opportunity to avoid any such penalties by disclosure, if relevant, and of the requirements for adequate disclosure.

   (3) This paragraph (c) applies even if the practitioner is not subject to a penalty under the Internal Revenue Code with respect to the position or with respect to the document, affidavit or other paper submitted.

(d) Relying on information furnished by clients.   A practitioner advising a client to take a position on a tax return, document, affidavit or other paper submitted to the Internal Revenue Service, or preparing or signing a tax return as a preparer, generally may rely in good faith without verification upon information furnished by the client. The practitioner may not, however, ignore the implications of information furnished to, or actually know by, the practitioner, and must make reasonable inquiries if the information as furnished appears to be incorrect, inconsistent with an important fact or another factual assumption, or incomplete.

(e) Reserved.

(f) Effective/applicability date. Section 10.34 is applicable to tax returns, documents, affidavits and other papers filed on or after September 26, 2007.

The proposed language for §10.34, issued on September 24, 2007, was:
§10.34

(a) *Tax returns.* A practitioner may not sign a tax return as a preparer unless the practitioner has a reasonable belief that the tax treatment of each position on the return would more likely than not be sustained on its merits (the more likely than not standard), or there is a reasonably basis for each position and each position is adequately disclosed to the Internal Revenue Service. A practitioner may not advise a client to take a position on a tax return, or prepare the portion of a tax return on which a position is taken, unless —

(1) The practitioner has a reasonable belief that the position satisfies the more likely than not standard; or

(2) The position has a reasonably basis and is adequately disclosed to the Internal Revenue Service.

* * * *

(e) Definitions. For purposes of this section —

(1) *More likely than not.* A practitioner is considered to have a reasonable belief that the tax treatment of a position is more likely than not the proper tax treatment if the practitioner analyzes the pertinent facts and authorities, and based on that analysis reasonably concludes in good faith, that there is a greater than fifty-percent likelihood that the tax treatment will be upheld if the IRS challenges it. The authorities described in 26 CFR 1.6662-4(d)(3)(iii), or any successor provision, of the substantial understatement penalty regulations may be taken into account for purposes of this analysis.

(2) *Reasonable basis.* A position is considered to have a reasonable basis if it is reasonably based on one or more of the authorities described in 26 CFR 1.6662-4(d)(3)(iii), or any successor provision, of the substantial understatement penalty regulations. Reasonable basis if a relatively high standard of tax reporting, that is, significantly higher than not frivolous or not patently improper. The reasonable basis standard is not satisfied by a return position that is merely arguable or that is merely a colorable claim. The possibility that a tax return will not be audited, that an issue will not be raised on audit, or that an issue will be settled may not be taken into account.

(3) *Frivolous.* A position is frivolous if it is patently improper.

NOTES

1. The realistic possibility standard adopted in the earlier version Circular 230 conformed closely to that standard as expressed in Opinion 85-352. The proposed revisions would bring Circular 230 in line with the "more likely than not" standard in §6694. Although Opinion 85-352 is important in that it influences the actions of attorneys, as a practical matter, Circular 230 is likely to have a greater operative effect on practitioner conduct. The bar's standard is only mandatory to the extent that it is enforced, and there is no known case where a practitioner was disciplined by an

admitting authority for violating a rule relating to the quality of income tax advice. In contrast, there exists in the service a ready mechanism for alleging and evaluating violations of Circular 230, violations that can result in a range of sanctions.

2.   Consider the implications of the earlier Circular 230 standard that the proposed rules seek to change. The earlier standard (realistic possibility) permits a practitioner to sign a return that includes a position that does not have a realistic possibility of being sustained on the merits if it is not frivolous and is disclosed. If the practitioner did not sign the return, she may advise the taxpayer to take such a position if that position is not frivolous and she advises the client of the opportunity to avoid penalties by disclosing the position. Ordinarily, the client's and the lawyer's interests will not be adverse: The client will want to avoid a penalty and the lawyer will not want to be disciplined. But suppose the client concludes for whatever reason that he does not want to disclose the position. The lawyer, although recognizing that the position is not frivolous, favors disclosure, in part because this will avoid any risk of penalty under §6694 or discipline under Circular 230. If the lawyer knows that the client will not disclose the position, may the lawyer continue to advise it? May the lawyer continue to advise the client if their interests conflict? See Deborah H. Schenk, Conflicts Between the Tax Lawyer and the Client: Vignettes in the Law Office, 20 Cap. U. L. Rev. 387 (1991). The proposed changes to Circular 230 only heighten this pressure because the practitioner requires either a reasonable belief that the position is "more likely than not," or has a reasonable basis for the position and it is disclosed.

Recall also that under §6694 preparer penalties, a taxpayer legitimately can file a return without disclosing under circumstances that would cause a tax preparer to risk a penalty.

C.   The Issue of Amended Returns

If a client has filed a return but subsequently learns that the return contained an error, what are her obligations? Note that the error may have produced an underpayment, in which case an amended return would serve to authorize the assessment of the additional amount due; or, the error may have produced an overpayment, in which case an amended return would serve as a claim for refund of the excess amount paid.

The 2006 edition of IRS Publication 17, Your Federal Income Tax, contains the following rather broad language:

> You should correct your return if, after you have filed it, you find that: (1) You did not report some income, (2) You claimed deductions or credits you should not have claimed, (3) You did not claim deductions or credits you could have claimed, or (4) You should have claimed a different filing status. . . . Use Form 1040X, Amended U.S. Individual Tax Return, to correct a return you have already filed.

There is no corresponding directive in the Code itself, but §6011(a) states that the Secretary of the Treasury need only issue a regulation to impose on taxpayers the obligation to file a return. The regulations issued under §451 (General Rule for Taxable Year of Inclusion) and §461 (General Rule for Taxable Year of Deduction) state that a taxpayer *should* file an amended return if an item of income was improperly excluded or a deduction was improperly claimed in an earlier year. (Emphasis added.) Thus, Reg. §1.451-1(a) provides:

> If a taxpayer ascertains that an item should have been included in gross income in a prior taxable year, he should, if within the period of limitation, file an amended return and pay any additional tax due. Similarly, if a taxpayer ascertains that an item was improperly included in gross income in a prior taxable year, he should, if within the period of limitation, file a claim for credit or refund of any overpayment of tax arising therefrom.

Reg. §1.461-1(a)(3) provides:

> If a taxpayer ascertains that a liability should have been taken into account in a prior taxable year, the taxpayer should, if within the period of limitation, file a claim for credit or refund of any overpayment of tax arising therefrom. Similarly, if a taxpayer ascertains that a liability was improperly taken into account in a prior taxable year, the taxpayer should, if within the period of limitation, file an amended return and pay any additional tax due.

While it is quite possible to infer from these regulations that the taxpayer indeed has an obligation to file an amended return (as well as the right to file a claim for refund) upon discovery of an error in an earlier year, it is notable that the obligation is not expressed in clearly mandatory terms. The Treasury's use of the word "should," and not "shall" or "must," is seen by most tax lawyers as merely hortatory, not directory. Are they right? Should the regulations explicitly *require* the filing of an amended return upon discovery of an error? For an argument in favor of legislation requiring the filing of amended returns to correct prior errors, see Kenneth Harris, On Requiring the Correction of Error Under the Federal Tax Law, 42 Tax Law. 515 (1989); JudsonTemple, Rethinking Imposition of a Legal Duty to Correct Material Tax Return Errors, 67 Neb. L. Rev. 223 (1997). Are there special problems if the filing of an amended return would tend to incriminate the taxpayer? Should any requirement for an amended return be coupled with a voluntary disclosure policy under which there would be no prosecution for voluntarily disclosed tax crimes?

What are the attorney's obligations when he discovers an error on the return? Circular 230, §10.21, provides:

> A practitioner who, having been retained by a client with respect to a matter administered by the Internal Revenue Service, knows that the client has not complied with the revenue laws of the United States or has made an error in or omission from

any return, document, affidavit, or other paper which the client submitted or executed under the revenue laws of the United States, must advise the client promptly of the fact of such noncompliance, error, or omission. The practitioner must advise the client of the consequences as provided under the Code and regulations of such noncompliance, error, or omission.

While a lawyer may not participate in client fraud, Model Rule 1.2(d), a lawyer also may not reveal confidences and secrets of the client, Model Rule 1.6. AICPA Statement on Standards for Tax Services No. 6 (3) requires a CPA to call errors on a return to the attention of the taxpayer and to "recommend the corrective measures to be taken." The CPA "is not obligated to inform the taxing authority, and . . . may not do so without the taxpayer's permission, except when required by law." AICPA Statement No. 6 (3). If the taxpayer client does not correct the error, the CPA should consider "whether to continue a professional or employment relationship with the taxpayer." AICPA Statement No. 6 (4). Does the advisor, whether lawyer or CPA, face a conflict of interest at this point? This subject is explored more fully in Chapter 3.

PROBLEMS

1. If an attorney is about to decline to handle a matter for a client because she feels the activity may subject her to possible penalty under §6694, and the client offers to indemnify the attorney against the penalty, may the lawyer ethically accept the indemnification and go on with the matter? If she does, and a penalty is imposed, is the indemnification agreement enforceable? Should it be? Is the risk of discipline under Circular 230 still present?

2. You are on retainer to a valuable client, a closely held corporation, to provide tax advice and to prepare the tax return. The president of the corporation (who is one of three shareholders) informs you that he has put his father on the payroll as a consultant. The father will attend two meetings a year when he is in town and will be available for consultation. The father, who is a retired school teacher, has no particular expertise in the business. The corporation has made a $10,000 payment to the father and the president indicates that this is a salary expense that the corporation should deduct. May the attorney advise the president that this deduction is appropriate? What else must the attorney advise? If it desires to avoid the risk of penalty, should the corporation disclose the issue in any way other than by including the payment in its total salaries? Could the attorney sign the return with this amount included in the salary deduction? If not, can he continue to represent the corporation with respect to the tax return? With respect to tax matters? With respect to the audit of this tax return?

3. Following the filing of its federal income tax return, a large corporation may discover that literally hundreds of items on the return should be adjusted in some respect. The need for these adjustments may be occasioned by the sheer volume and complexity of transactions rather than a desire to avoid tax liability. You are

consulted by such a corporation, and the question presented is whether it must file an amended return each time that such an item is discovered, or whether it may simply accumulate them in an audit file for disclosure to the IRS agent when the corporate return is audited. Past practice indicates that the IRS audits each year's return of this corporation. How do you respond? See Rev. Proc. 94-69, 1994-2 C.B. 804, in which the Service specifies the circumstances under which a large corporate taxpayer's amended return can avoid the penalties of §6662(b)(1) and (2).

4.   The facts are the same as in Problem 3 except that the volume of potential adjustments is smaller (though still significant), and the corporation's returns are audited only on a sporadic basis. Is your advice the same?

5.   Your client corporation allowed its employees to purchase stock of the corporation under a restricted stock plan at a price of $10 per share. In the hands of the employees, the stock is subject to substantial restrictions that will not lapse for five years. The employees filed elections under §83(b) to have any difference between the price they paid and the value of the stock taxed as income in the year of the stock purchase rather than being taxed on the spread between the price paid and the value of the stock when the restrictions lapse. The IRS audited the year of the stock purchase and established that the value of the stock in the year of purchase was $12 per share and not $10. It increased the income of the employees accordingly. Section 83(h) provides that an employer corporation is entitled to a deduction to the extent that its employees are charged with income. However, Reg. §1.83-6(a)(2) denies this deduction to the employer corporation if it failed to withhold tax on the amount paid to the employee. [Note that the section 83 regulations previously had such a rule.] Your research indicates no statutory support for this regulation. You consider it quite unfair, and you advise your client accordingly. The client desires to file a claim for refund of tax based on a deduction of $2 per share. This position would be directly in conflict with the regulation. What are the considerations that you face as a practitioner?

6.   You are advising a client with respect to a tax return position. The position that the client wishes to take is, in your judgment, aggressive, but you research it carefully. You determine that the U.S. district court in your home district supports your position but that U.S. Courts of Appeal in two other circuits have ruled adversely on the issue. The client wishes to know whether there is substantial authority for the position. How do you advise?

7.   In a situation similar to that in Problem 2, you have advised the client that the presence of substantial authority for the desired position is questionable and that disclosure is thus advisable to avoid any risk of penalty. The client thanks you for your advice, tells you that he believes to disclose such a position would be taken as a signal of weakness, and chooses to go forward without disclosure. You evaluate the situation and conclude that you are not comfortable that the position in question meets the realistic possibility standard. What are your options?

8.   Your client consults you with respect to a tax return position. The position depends upon the construction of a particular statutory provision. There is no informative legislative history, and no regulations have been issued. The client urges a

particular construction that is of benefit to it. You recognize the merits of the client's construction, but you cannot conclude that an alternative construction, unfavorable to your client, might not be equally plausible. Your client asks if substantial authority for its position is present. How do you resolve the question? If you believe the question is a close one, how would you proceed?

9. Your client is a member of a particular industry group. The members of that industry group have been seeking a particular tax result of advantage to them. Five members of the group have secured private letter rulings that confirm the desired result. Your client has not obtained such a ruling, but wishes to take the desired position on its tax return and turns to you for advice. You are surprised that the Service issued the rulings in question and think that they are probably erroneous. How do you advise your client? Reg. §1.6662-4(d)(3)(iii) provides that such determinations are authority, but §6110(k)(3) states that they may not be used or cited as precedent. How do you balance these two sections? Note that the rule of §6110(k)(3) is conditioned by the words, "Unless the Secretary otherwise establishes by regulations . . ."

Chapter 3

Audit and Litigation: Controversy

In this chapter, we consider the situation of the tax lawyer representing a client in a controversy with the IRS. The representation may start at the audit level, continue through an administrative appeal within the Service, into trial and appeal to the circuit court, and finally litigation in the Supreme Court. In this context, the lawyer serves as advocate.

The advocate must always be mindful of two basic obligations to his client, those of loyalty and confidentiality. "Loyalty" tends to be viewed as the avoidance of a "conflict of interest," and this is the first concept we will study in this chapter. Following that, we take up the problem of confidentiality, an ideal the realization of which often involves balancing the client's interest in the preservation of confidences against some competing desire or duty to make disclosure.

The lawyer does, of course, encounter difficulties in meeting his obligations of loyalty and confidentiality in noncontroversial contexts, for example, where he acts as planner and adviser or even preparer, but there the problem is usually less acute than it is in his handling of controversies. Finally, the advocate, like the lawyer in every other role he plays, has a duty under Model Rule 1.1 to "provide competent representation to a client." A breach of that duty, always serious, may be irremediable if it occurs in the course of a trial. Although the duty of competence will not engage us specifically in this chapter, it underlies all that will.

As noted in Chapter 1, the lawyer's duty to the system occasionally trumps or mitigates his duty of loyalty to the client. An example is the lawyer's obligation to bring to the attention of a court the existence of adverse, controlling precedent otherwise unknown to the court.

We conclude this chapter with two other subjects related to controversies in the courts, the issue of the tax lawyer's responsibility to the court concerning the quality of issues presented and the issue of attorney fee awards for prevailing taxpayers in tax cases.

A. Loyalty to the Client — Avoiding Conflict of Interest

1. General

Under the Model Rules, loyalty is considered an essential element of the lawyer-client relationship. Specific rules require the lawyer to exercise independent professional judgment on behalf of his client. A lawyer must decline employment where the representation of that client will be directly adverse to another client or to a third person, or by the lawyer's own interests, Model Rule 1.7(a). Likewise a lawyer should avoid matters in which he or a member of his firm may become a witness, Model Rule 3.7. Similarly a lawyer must ensure that his transactions with his client are fair and reasonable, Model Rule 1.8.

The restriction most commonly encountered, however, is that on the representation of different clients whose interests do or may involve some conflict. Even in this situation, Model Rule 1.7(b) permits the lawyer to proceed with the multiple representation if (1) it is obvious that he can adequately represent the interests of each client, and (2) each client consents to the representation after full disclosure of the possible effect on the lawyer's exercise of independent professional judgment.

> **Rule 1.7**
> *Conflict of Interest: Current Clients —*
>
>   (a) Except as provided in paragraph (b), a lawyer shall not represent a client if the representation involves a concurrent conflict of interest. A concurrent conflict of interest exists if:
>
>   (1) the representation of one client will be directly adverse to another client; or
>
>   (2) there is a significant risk that the representation of one or more clients will be materially limited by the lawyer's responsibilities to another client, a former client or a third person or by a personal interest of the lawyer.
>
>   (b) Notwithstanding the existence of a concurrent conflict of interest under paragraph (a), a lawyer may represent a client if:
>
>   (1) the lawyer reasonably believes that the lawyer will be able to provide competent and diligent representation to each affected client;
>
>   (2) the representation is not prohibited by law;
>
>   (3) the representation does not involve the assertion of a claim by one client against another client represented by the lawyer in the same litigation or other proceeding before a tribunal; and
>
>   (4) each affected client gives informed consent, confirmed in writing.

Circular 230 imposes substantially the same obligation on the tax lawyer. It states in §10.29:

> No attorney, certified public accountant, or enrolled agent shall represent conflicting interests in his practice before the Internal Revenue Service, except

by express consent of all directly interested parties after full disclosure has been made.

See generally Developments in the Law — Conflicts of Interest in the Legal Profession, 94 Harv. L. Rev. 1244 (1981).

Tax Court Rule 24(g), adopted in 1990 (as then Rule 24(f)), provides lawyers appearing before the court with specific guidance concerning their response to conflicts of interest. It provides:

> **(g) Conflict of Interest:** If any counsel of record (1) was involved in planning or promoting a transaction or operating an entity that is connected to any issue in a case, (2) represents more than one person with differing interests with respect to any issue in a case, or (3) is a potential witness in a case, then such counsel must either secure the informed consent of the client (but only as to items (1) and (2)); withdraw from the case; or take whatever other steps are necessary to obviate a conflict of interest or other violation of the ABA Model Rules of Professional Conduct, and particularly Rules 1.7, 1.8, and 3.7 thereof. The Court may inquire into the circumstances of counsel's employment in order to deter such violations. See Rule 201.

Note that Rule 24(g) leaves Model Rule 1.7 as the operative standard that must be satisfied. Since Rule 1.7 already existed and was imported into the Tax Court rules via Rule 201, why was it necessary for the Tax Court to adopt Rule 24(g)?

In the following case, the Tax Court applied *then* Rule 24(f) to disqualify a lawyer who sought to represent both a promoter and the investors in a tax shelter.

Para Technologies Trust v. Commissioner

64 T.C.M. (CCH) 922 (1992)

COHEN, Judge. The issue for decision is whether a conflict of interest exists that requires the disqualification of petitioners' counsel of record. . . .

Nassau Life Insurance Company, Ltd. (Nassau Life), promoted the use of domestic and foreign entities to shelter United States business and investment income from United States Federal income taxation. Nassau Life engaged in this activity through representatives known as "information officers" and through the dissemination of printed materials. From 1982 through 1988, Joe Alfred Izen, Jr. (Izen), was counsel to Nassau Life. In the course of that representation, among other services, he prepared and issued two opinion letters that related to the multiple-entity tax shelter promoted by Nassau Life. In a legal opinion letter dated September 26, 1983, Izen discussed the legal status of "contractual trust companies" that were being promoted by Nassau Life (the 1983 opinion letter).

Ferber [an investor] is a songwriter with a high school education. Anderson [another investor] completed the eighth grade. At the time of the hearing on the pending motions, Ferber was 36 years old and Anderson was 30 years old.

Ferber and Anderson met in India in 1977 and became friends. In late 1984, Anderson began to engage in an electronics business, VideoLab, as a sole proprietor. Because of his limited education, Anderson wanted to adopt a structure for Video-Lab that would minimize the amount of paperwork that was necessary to carry on the business. He discussed his plans with Ferber, who was then employed as an information officer for Nassau Life. Ferber, relying at least partially on the 1983 opinion letter, advised Anderson, who also had access to the 1983 opinion letter, to structure his business as a trust such as those promoted by Nassau Life. . . .

In a legal opinion letter prepared for Nassau Life dated June 20, 1985, Izen discussed the tax aspects of contractual trust companies (the 1985 opinion letter). Among other things, the letter concluded that the grantor trust provisions of the Internal Revenue Code did not apply to "contractual trust companies." Izen's letter failed to discuss decided cases contrary to the positions he was espousing. Anderson and Ferber gained access to the 1985 opinion letter.

Respondent determined deficiencies in petitioners' Federal income taxes for 1987 and 1988. Respondent determined that Para Tech was an association taxable as a corporation for Federal income tax purposes and disallowed its claimed distribution deductions. . . . Respondent determined that Anderson and Ferber were each taxable on an amount equal to the taxable income of Para Tech.

Para Tech, Anderson, and Ferber filed petitions for redetermination with this Court. Izen is counsel of record for petitioners in these cases. Nassau Life is bankrupt. All legal fees are being paid by Para Tech.

The Court is generally reluctant to disqualify counsel of a taxpayer's choice on motion of the adversary. See Alexander v. Superior Court, 685 P.2d 1309, 1317 (Ariz. 1984). In these cases, however, respondent promptly moved for disqualification prior to conducting discovery or engaging in settlement negotiations and before these cases were set for trial. See Duffey v. Commissioner, 91 T.C. 81, 84 (1988).

Rule 201(a) provides that "Practitioners before the Court shall carry on their practice in accordance with the letter and spirit of the Model Rules." This Court, therefore, has the power to compel withdrawal of petitioners' counsel if such representation would violate the Model Rules. Specifically, Rule 24(f)* provides:

> If any counsel of record (1) was involved in planning or promoting a transaction or operating an entity that is connected to any issue in a case, [or] (2) represents more than one person with differing interests with respect to any issue in a case, . . . then such counsel must either secure the informed consent of the client . . . , withdraw from the case, or take whatever other steps are necessary to obviate a conflict of interest or other violation of the ABA Model Rules of Professional Conduct, and particularly [Rule] 1.7. . . .

Petitioners contend that Izen's representation of them does not violate Model Rule 1.7(b) because no potential conflict of interest exists among petitioners.

---

* [Now Rule 24(g). — Eds.]

Petitioners contend that each petitioner is contesting the deficiency and will argue that Para Tech should be recognized as a trust and that Para Tech's Federal income tax returns for 1987 and 1988 were correct.

Respondent contends that Izen's representation of each petitioner may be materially limited by his responsibilities to the other petitioners and by his own interests. Respondent states:

> There are positions which can be advanced on behalf of each Petitioner which, if established, would enable that Petitioner to avoid liability for all or part of the deficiencies and additions to tax determined against that Petitioner, but which cannot be established without irreparably damaging some other Petitioner's case.

... [R]espondent determined that Anderson and Ferber were each taxable on an amount equal to the taxable income of Para Tech. One of respondent's alternative theories is that Para Tech is a grantor trust. Generally, the grantor trust rules apply to a person, such as Anderson, who created the trust. See secs. 671 through 678. Anderson formed the trust and transferred his business to it and is a beneficiary of the trust. Ferber, although serving as a trustee, is less likely to be a grantor. Ferber, and, hypothetically, Para Tech, would avoid taxation if respondent successfully established that the income was taxable to Anderson as the grantor.

Further, respondent has determined that each petitioner is liable for the additions to tax for fraud. In support of that determination, respondent's answer alleges that books and records made available to respondent during the examination of petitioners' returns were false and fraudulent, that petitioners "individually and in concert, refused to cooperate with Respondent's agents and attempted to obstruct Respondent's examination by various means," and that each petitioner understated or failed to report taxable income and tax due from them. In this regard, Anderson and Ferber can each argue that the other was responsible for maintaining the books and records of Para Tech and for preparing its tax returns and that each relied on the other. Each may also claim that he relied on Izen's opinion letters. In addition, Ferber, as trustee of Para Tech, is putatively making decisions for Para Tech, including using its funds to pay for litigation of these cases, while Anderson, not Ferber, has a beneficial interest in Para Tech.

Although it is too early in this litigation to anticipate all of the arguments that will be made, and the foregoing possibilities may not be the positions that petitioners should or will adopt at trial, there is a serious possibility that petitioners' positions may become adverse to each other. See Figueroa-Olmo v. Westinghouse Elec. Corp., 616 F. Supp. 1445, 1451-1454 (D. Puerto Rico 1985); Shadid v. Jackson, 521 F. Supp. 87, 89 (E.D. Tex. 1981).

Izen's personal interests in this case may also conflict with the interests of petitioners. Anderson and Ferber relied, at least partially, on opinion letters that Izen had written. Therefore, Izen has an interest in vindicating the positions he took in the opinion letters in order to maintain his professional reputation and to protect himself from any potential future liability to petitioners. See, e.g., Eisenberg v. Gagnon,

766 F.2d 770, 779780 (3d Cir. 1985) (holding that investors in a tax shelter could recover from an attorney who had misrepresented facts relating to the tax shelter). He would therefore be less likely to advise petitioners disinterestedly with regard to such matters as accepting a settlement offer. See Model Rules Rule 1.7(a) and 1.7 comment (1983) (stating that, "If the probity of a lawyer's own conduct in a transaction is in serious question, it may be difficult or impossible for the lawyer to give a client detached advice."). See also Adams v. Commissioner, 85 T.C. 359, 372-373 (1985). Izen's failure to advise petitioners of the potential adverse defenses or affirmative claims available to them would constitute a breach of his duty of loyalty to them. Figueroa-Olmo v. Westinghouse Elec. Corp., supra at 14531454; Eriks v. Denver, 824 P.2d 1207, 1211-1212 (Wash. 1992) (citing Model Rules Rule 1.7 comment (1984) and holding that as a matter of law there was a conflict of interest between promoters of and investors in a tax shelter). Finally, Izen is potentially a witness with respect to matters set forth in his tax opinion, and testimony on that subject could appropriately be obtained without violation of the attorney-client privilege. See In re Grand Jury Proceedings, 727 F.2d 1352 (4th Cir. 1984); and United States v. Jones, 696 F.2d 1069 (4th Cir. 1982).

Izen and petitioners contend that petitioners have been informed of and waive Izen's conflict of interest. We are not persuaded, however, that the apparent consent of petitioners is informed and voluntary. They testified that they had no intention to sue either Nassau Life or Izen and that they understood that, if a dispute arose between Anderson and Ferber, Izen would have to withdraw. Neither Izen nor petitioners identified any disclosures of the potential adverse positions that might lead to a dispute between Anderson and Ferber. . . . In this regard, Izen's questions and Anderson's responses at the hearing included the following:

Q: As far as Fred [Ferber] is concerned, was there a discussion of any kind with Joe Alfred Izen, Jr., about what would happen if Fred and yourself pointed the finger at each other?

A: Discussion with you or with Fred?

Q: Either one, or both?

A: We had — we had simply discussed the legal possibility that existed but did not see that as a reality or as even a plausible option for us to pursue.

Q: Why wasn't it plausible?

A: We both really have the same interests at heart, I believe, and I don't see what I would get out of, you know, trying to sue Fred. He has as much money as I do, which is almost nothing, so this question is going to come up later anyway, so —

Q: Well, again, though, at the start of the lawsuit and with your discussions with your Attorney Joe Alfred Izen, Jr., did you — were you and Fred Ferber more or less in agreement on the facts of how Para Technologies operated and who got what as far as any benefits or income; that's what I'm trying to ask?

A: Well, yes, of course. I mean, Fred was Trustee and obviously, I needed to be in agreement with what he's directing and have been, through the existence of the Trust.

Q: Right. Was there any expression made that if a conflict between Fred and your-self were to arise based on changing representation of facts, that Joe Alfred Izen, Jr., might have to withdraw?

A: I'm trying to remember the timing of this, of the various issues we had discussed. We had discussed that as a possibility, but I don't recall — I don't recall having the impression at that time that that was very likely to happen.

Q: Do you anticipate in this case any inconsistent defenses by you or Fred Ferber?

A: No.

We are not persuaded that Izen made a full and fair disclosure or that petitioners understood the inherent potential conflicts between them. The backgrounds of the individuals suggest a lack of sophistication in assessing matters such as these, and they relied solely on the advice of Izen in deciding to waive the conflicts of interest. Compare Adams v. Commissioner, 85 T.C. at 372-374 (holding that taxpayers could not be relieved of a settlement agreement based on their attorney's conflict of interest because taxpayers were sophisticated, knew all of the relevant facts, and had been advised by independent counsel before employing the author of an opinion letter). It appears to us that the waiver is not based on informed consent but on the cost of employing independent and separate counsel and having such counsel become familiar with the underlying facts of the cases.

Izen admitted during the hearing on respondent's motion that he had not secured written consents or waivers from petitioners and that he had not con-tacted Nassau Life or other beneficiaries of the Para Tech trust. Under these circumstances, we conclude that it is "more important that unethical conduct be prevented than . . . [that petitioners] have an unfettered right to counsel of . . . [their] choice." Kevlik v. Goldstein, 724 F.2d 844, 849 (1st Cir. 1984). The potential for unfairness to petitioners and damage to the integrity of the judicial process is too serious to permit Izen's representation of petitioners to continue, even in the face of an apparent waiver. Figueroa-Olmo v. Westing-house Elec. Corp., supra at 1451; Shadid v. Jackson, supra at 90; and Model Rules Rule 1.7 comment (1983) (stating that, "when a disinterested lawyer would conclude that the client should not agree to representation under the circumstances, the lawyer involved cannot . . . provide representation on the basis of the client's consent.").

Therefore, Izen must be disqualified from representing petitioners in these cases.

NOTES

1. How far should the principle of Rule 24(g) be carried? If a law firm repre-sents a client in planning a transaction that has tax significance, can that firm rep-resent the client if the tax result is challenged by the IRS on audit? In litigation? If not, why not?

2.   Consider whether a motion by an adversary to disqualify counsel based on an alleged conflict of interest may in reality be a tactical maneuver. For whose protection does the conflict rule exist? The disqualified lawyer's client? The court? The adversary? Should the court, in ruling on a disqualification motion, concern itself with the motivation of the moving party? In the absence of a motion, should the court act on its own motion to forestall representation where there is an apparent conflict?

3.   An attorney who represented both a promoter and investors in a tax shelter without discussing the potential conflict of interest with either party was found to have breached his fiduciary duty and required to disgorge all fees. Eriks v. Denver, 118 Wash. 2d 451 (1992).

In Eisenberg v. Gagnon, 766 F.2d 770 (3rd Cir. 1985), the court found there was sufficient evidence for a jury to find that a promoter was liable for negligence when, in a transaction in which he had a pecuniary interest, he supplied false information for the guidance of third parties. The buyers of tax shelters asserted that the promoter had included information in the offering that he had made no attempt to verify. The court held that "professionals and others with similar access to information must disclose data that calls into question the accuracy of an opinion." Citing *Eisenberg*, the court in In Re Suprema Specialties Inc. Sec. Litig., 438 F.3d 256, 289 (3d Cir. 2006) observed that "[w]hen a professional opinion is issued to the investing public by those in a position to know more than the public, there is an obligation to disclose data indicating that the opinion may be doubtful." Similarly, in Kline v. Arvey, Hodes, Costello & Burman, 24 F.3d 480 (3d Cir. 1994), the same court found that "when a law firm knows or has good reason to know that the factual description of a transaction provided by another is materially different from the actual transaction, it cannot escape liability simply by including in an opinion letter a statement that its opinion is based on provided facts."

If a court fails to deal with an apparent conflict, the consequences, in terms of the use of judicial resources, can be significant. Consider the following case, in which the former husband of the widow of the late Nat King Cole was able to set aside a final judgment of the Tax Court determining substantial tax deficiencies against him.

Devore v. Commissioner

963 F.2d 280 (9th Cir. 1992)

PER CURIAM. Gary Devore appeals from the United States Tax Court's denials of his motions to vacate deficiency judgments for the tax years 1970–1975. Devore contends that dual representation of himself and his ex-wife in the tax proceedings resulted in a conflict of interest that prevented their joint counsel from raising defenses on his behalf. We have jurisdiction under 26 U.S.C. §§7482(a), 7483. We reverse the orders of the tax court and remand for an evidentiary hearing to determine whether Devore was prejudiced by his former counsel's conflict of interest and whether Devore had reasonable grounds for failing to seek independent counsel.

For many years, Maria Cole and her former husband, Nat King Cole, had been represented by attorney Harry Margolis. Margolis continued to represent Maria Cole after Nat King Cole's death. Maria Cole and Gary Devore were married in 1969. For the year 1970, Devore filed an individual return. Joint returns were prepared for all other years during the marriage. Until June 1987, Harry Margolis was the sole counsel of Cole and Devore. Leo Branton Jr. became co-counsel with Margolis in June 1987. Margolis died on or about July 15, 1987 and Branton became the sole counsel of record on behalf of Cole and Devore in connection with the instant actions. The tax proceedings culminated in the entry of two judgments against Devore.

Cole and Devore were separated in 1976, and were divorced in 1978. The tax court did not render judgments in the instant cases until 1989. Despite their divorce, joint counsel continued to represent Cole and Devore throughout the tax proceedings.

After a four day trial, the tax court determined that Devore was individually liable for a federal tax deficiency of $135,302, and for a negligent return penalty of $6,765. The tax court found that Devore failed to carry his burden of proof in establishing that certain checks totaling $210,000 did not constitute reportable income to him. Two checks had been issued to Devore by a company controlled by Margolis. These checks were received by Devore, but were immediately endorsed over to Margolis. Devore alleges that these funds were then used to purchase a home in the name of Maria Cole. The tax court found that the $210,000 represented by the two checks was income attributable to Devore.

In a second judgment entered pursuant to stipulations of settlement, Devore and Cole were held jointly and severally liable for deficiencies totaling over $300,000 for the years 1971–1975.

Devore states that he entered and left his marriage to Cole with a net worth of less than $10,000 and that he lacks the money to satisfy the judgments. He further states that he was unsophisticated in tax matters and that he was continually excluded from the financial affairs of Maria Cole.

Devore moved, through new counsel, to vacate the tax court's deficiency judgments. He asserted that when counsel represented him and Cole jointly, a conflict of interest resulted. This conflict, argues Devore, prevented joint counsel from bringing innocent spouse and agency defenses which would have diminished his tax liability. The tax court denied these motions.

A tax court's decision not to reopen a record for the submission of new evidence "is not subject to review except upon a demonstration of extraordinary circumstances which reveal a clear abuse of discretion." Nor-Cal Adjusters v. Commissioner, 503 F.2d 359, 363, 34 A.F.T.R.2d (P-H) 5834 (9th Cir. 1974).

The facts of Devore's case constitute "extraordinary circumstances." One spouse was in a substantially weaker position with reference to the other. Devore earned a negligible income while his wife controlled a significant sum of money.

Devore was unsophisticated in tax matters and was excluded from the financial affairs of his wife.

Our research uncovered only one case that is directly on point. In Wilson v. Commissioner, 500 F.2d 645, 34 A.F.T.R.2d (P-H) 5677 (2d Cir. 1974), a husband and wife had filed joint tax returns. The husband earned a much larger income than his wife. A deficiency judgment was entered against the couple. Throughout the tax proceedings, they were jointly represented by the same attorney. However, they were also engaged in a simultaneous annulment action. In the annulment action, the husband was represented by the same attorney who represented the couple in the tax proceedings.

The Second Circuit held that it could "reverse a discretionary denial by the Tax Court of post-opinion motions only if there are shown to be 'extraordinary circumstances.'" Wilson, 500 F.2d at 648, quoting Pepi, Inc. v. C.I.R., 448 F.2d 141, 148, 28 A.F.T.R.2d (P-H) 5586 (2d Cir. 1971). The court held that the facts in *Wilson* were sufficiently compelling to constitute "extraordinary circumstances." The attorney could not competently advance the interests of the wife in the tax proceedings while representing the husband in a separate annulment action. It thus reversed the tax court's denial of Mrs. Wilson's post-opinion motions. It remanded the case to the Tax Court, allowing Mrs. Wilson to present evidence explaining her failure to seek the advice of independent counsel and to raise the annulment issue.

The facts supporting Devore's claim of "extraordinary circumstances" are at least as compelling as those of Wilson. In *Wilson*, the attorney represented both the husband and wife in tax proceedings while representing the husband in a simultaneous annulment litigation. However, the couple was still married at the time of the tax proceedings. In the instant case, the parties were separated in 1976 and divorced in 1978. The trial did not take place until 1989. By this time, the marriage was clearly over. Arguably, Devore's interests were compromised by counsel's simultaneous representation of Devore and Cole.

Accordingly, we remand to the tax court for an evidentiary hearing to determine if Devore was prejudiced by his former counsel's conflict of interest and to establish the reasonableness of his failure to retain independent counsel. If Devore satisfies these burdens, he should be granted a new trial at which innocent spouse and agency defenses may be asserted.

NOTES

1. In Toscano v. Commissioner, 441 F.2d 930 (9th Cir. 1971), the court vacated a final judgment of the Tax Court 16 years after it was entered on grounds of fraud on the court.

2. Your firm has represented Client *X* in the tax area for some years, but it has not done work for *X* in other fields of law. *Y* Corporation contacts one of your

partners and asks that he act as counsel in a proposed antitrust action against *X*. May the firm accept the new representation?

3.   Assume, in the previous hypothetical, that your firm has represented both *X* and *Y* for some years, *X* in the tax area and *Y* in general corporate matters. *Y* makes the request previously described. How do you resolve the question?

4.   You are representing *X*, an individual, in a Tax Court case. Corporation *Z*, not a regular client of your firm, asks you to take its tax case, which differs in some material respects from the case for *X*, but you perceive *Z*'s case may require you to argue that an acquisition of stock was a "purchase," not a reorganization. *X*'s case for nonrecognition of gain in a very similar acquisition transaction is predicated on the acquisition's being characterized as a reorganization. How do you proceed? Would your answer differ if *Z* had been a regular client of your firm?

5.   Note 4 presents an "issue conflict." Issue conflicts arise with some frequency, and the question is whether they must be subjected to the same testing as are "interest conflicts" under Model Rule 1.7. Issue conflicts arise when a lawyer on behalf of one client takes a position in a matter that does not directly involve a second client but the result of which might be a precedent not to the liking of the second client. ABA Opinion 93-377 (1993) concludes that, where the matter may produce an unfavorable precedent for the second client, that client's consent to the representation is required.

6.   Closely resembling an issue conflict is the situation where a lawyer, already representing Client *A*, undertakes representation of Client *B* in a matter that does not involve Client *A* and that is unlikely to produce any precedent adverse to Client *A*. However, Clients *A* and *B* are in different industry groups that are historically antagonistic to one another. For example, a tax lawyer engaged in representing tax interests on behalf of a railroad might be approached by a competitor trucking company for tax services unrelated to those being performed for the railroad client. Should the lawyer be precluded from representing Client *B* without Client *A*'s consent? Is this a matter of ethics or of client relations?

2.   *Waiver of Conflict of Interest by the Client*

As you will note from the text of Model Rule 1.7 and Tax Court Rule 24(g), a client may waive most conflicts of interest if the lawyer believes that the representation will not be adversely affected and the client consents. As you saw in *Para Technologies*, the courts require that this consent be an informed one. In the following opinion, the ABA revisits the issue of consent by the client following the 2002 changes to Rule 1.7, which, significantly expanded the circumstances in which consent can be obtained. The opinion deals specifically with a waiver, entered into at the commencement of a representation, that purports to waive all future conflicts that may arise. It is, however, instructive on the entire range of waiver issues.

ABA Formal Opinions 05-436

(2005)

INFORMED CONSENT TO FUTURE CONFLICTS OF INTEREST; WITHDRAWAL OF FORMAL OPINION 93-372

The Model Rules contemplate that a lawyer in appropriate circumstances may obtain the effective informed consent of a client to future conflicts of interest.

General and open-ended consent is more likely to be effective when given by a client that is an experienced user of legal services, particularly if, for example, the client is independently represented by other counsel in giving consent and the consent is limited to future conflicts unrelated to the subject of the representation. Rule 1.7, as amended in February 2002, permits a lawyer to obtain effective informed consent to a wider range of future conflicts than would have been possible under the Model Rules prior to their amendment. Formal Opinion 93-372 (Waiver of Future Conflicts of Interest) [1] therefore is withdrawn.

This opinion applies the ABA Model Rules of Professional Conduct [2] to the subject of a lawyer obtaining a client's informed consent to future conflicts of interest. The Committee concludes, for the reasons discussed below, that ABA Model Rule of Professional Conduct 1.7 permits effective informed consent to a wider range of future conflicts than would have been possible under the Model Rules prior to their amendment.

MODEL RULES 1.7, 1.6, AND 1.9

Rule 1.7 addresses concurrent conflicts of interest and the circumstances in which a lawyer may, with the informed consent of each affected client, represent a client notwithstanding a concurrent conflict. Rule 1.6, regarding confidentiality of information, and Rule 1.9, regarding duties to former clients, are relevant with respect to the confidentiality issues relating to obtaining such consent.

In 1993, when the Committee issued Opinion 93-372, the Model Rules did not expressly address a client's giving informed consent to future conflicts of interest. Moreover, no Rule or Comment [3] provided express guidance as to when an earlier matter for a former client and a later matter for a different client should be considered substantially related. In 2002, that changed in both respects.

---

1. ABA Formal Opinion 93-372 (April 16, 1993), in Formal and Informal Ethics Opinions 1983–1998, 167 (ABA 2000).

2. This opinion is based on the Model Rules of Professional Conduct as amended by the American Bar Association House of Delegates through August 2003. The laws, court rules, regulations, rules of professional conduct, and opinions promulgated in the individual jurisdictions are controlling.

3. "The Comment accompanying each Rule explains and illustrates the meaning and purpose of the Rule. . . . The Comments are intended as guides to interpretations, but the text of each Rule is authoritative." Model Rules of Professional Conduct Preamble: A Lawyer's Responsibilities cmt. 21.

In February 2002, Model Rule 1.7 was restructured and revised. Rule 1.7(a) defines a "concurrent conflict of interest." [4] Rule 1.7(b) addresses the circumstances under which a lawyer may undertake or continue representation of a client in reliance upon the client's informed consent to a conflict:

> Notwithstanding the existence of a concurrent conflict of interest under paragraph (a), a lawyer may represent a client if: (1) the lawyer reasonably believes that the lawyer will be able to provide competent and diligent representation to each affected client; (2) the representation is not prohibited by law; (3) the representation does not involve the assertion of a claim by one client against another client represented by the lawyer in the same litigation or other proceeding before a tribunal; and (4) each affected client gives informed consent, confirmed in writing.

The Comments to Model Rule 1.7 were also revised. New Comment [22] expressly addresses the subject of a client's giving informed consent to future conflicts:

> Whether a lawyer may properly request a client to waive conflicts that might arise in the future is subject to the test of paragraph (b) [of Model Rule 1.7]. The effectiveness of such waivers is generally determined by the extent to which the client reasonably understands the material risks that the waiver entails. The more comprehensive the explanation of the types of future representations that might arise and the actual and reasonably foreseeable adverse consequences of those representations, the greater the likelihood that the client will have the requisite understanding. Thus, if the client agrees to consent to a particular type of conflict with which the client is already familiar, then the consent ordinarily will be effective with regard to that type of conflict. If the consent is general and open-ended, then the consent ordinarily will be ineffective, because it is not reasonably likely that the client will have understood the material risks involved. On the other hand, if the client is an experienced user of the legal services involved and is reasonably informed regarding the risk that a conflict may arise, such consent is more likely to be effective, particularly if, e.g., the client is independently represented by other counsel in giving consent and the consent is limited to future conflicts unrelated to the subject of the representation. In any case, advance consent cannot be effective if the circumstances that materialize in the future are such as would make the conflict nonconsentable under paragraph (b).

The Committee believes that the term "waiver," as used in the first part of Comment [22], is intended to mean the same thing as the term "informed consent," as used in Rule 1.7 and elsewhere in the Comments.

We interpret the meaning of the term "unrelated to the subject of the representation" in Comment [22] by referring to Comment [3] to Model Rule 1.9, also added in February 2002. Comment [3] provides guidance on when an earlier matter for a former client and a later matter for a different client are to be considered

---

4. What constitutes a conflict of interest is beyond the scope of this opinion.

"substantially related." The Comment, which is lengthy, begins with the general principle that "[m]atters are 'substantially related' for purposes of this Rule if they involve the same transaction or legal dispute or if there otherwise is a substantial risk that confidential factual information as would normally have been obtained in the prior representation would materially advance the client's position in the subsequent matter." We are of the opinion, therefore, that the term "unrelated to" as used in Comment [22] should be read as meaning not "substantially related to," as that term is used in Rule 1.9 and its Comment [3], i.e., that the future matters as to which the client's consent to the lawyer's conflicting representation is sought do not involve the same transaction or legal dispute that is the subject of the lawyer's present representation of the consenting client, and are not of such a nature that the disclosure or use by the lawyer of information relating to the representation of the consenting client would materially advance the position of future clients.

As noted above, when the Committee issued Opinion 93-372 no Model Rule or Comment expressly addressed informed consent to future conflicts of interest, and none provided express guidance on when successive matters for different clients are to be considered substantially related. Opinion 93-372 cites Model Rules 1.7 and 1.6, Disciplinary Rule 5-105(c) of the predecessor Model Code of Professional Responsibility, and authorities that predate (with the exception of one decision) the Model Rules. Opinion 93-372 does not cite Model Rule 1.9.

Opinion 93-372 concludes that the effectiveness of a client's "consent after consultation" [5] is generally limited to circumstances in which the lawyer is able to and does identify the potential party or class of parties that may be represented in the future matter(s). Opinion 93-372 also concludes that, in some instances, the lawyer may need to identify the nature of the likely future matter(s). Although Opinion 93-372 acknowledges that clients differ in their level of sophistication, the opinion does not vary its conclusions as to the likely effectiveness of informed consent to future conflicts when the client is an experienced user of legal services or has had the opportunity to be represented by independent counsel in relation to such consent. Also, although Opinion 93-372 is based to a considerable degree on concerns about the possibility of disclosure or use of the client's confidential information against it in a later matter, [6] it does not address those concerns in the context of the

---

5. In 2002, as a result of a recommendation by the ABA Commission on Evaluation of the Rules of Professional Conduct, the term "consent after consultation" was replaced in the Models Rules with the term "informed consent." No change in the meaning of the term as it is used in Rule 1.7 and in other affected Rules was intended by this amendment. See Model Rule 1.0, "Reporter's Explanation of the Changes," P5, available at *http://www.abanet.org/cpr/e2k-rule10rem.html*.

6. Opinion 93-372 stated that consent to waive a future conflict of interest does not have the effect of authorizing the lawyer to reveal or use confidential client information. See Formal and Informal Ethics Opinions 1983–1998 at 171-173. That remains the case. See also Rules 1.6(a) and 1.9(b)(2) and (c)(1). Opinion 93-372's reliance on confidentiality concerns as a basis for limiting the scope of the effectiveness of consent to future conflicts seemed to be based on the risk that the lawyer later may violate Rules 1.6 or 1.9. The Committee does not view the hypothetical risk that the lawyer later might violate the Model Rules as a sufficient basis for proscribing the sort of informed consent to future conflicts contemplated by Rule 1.7 cmt. 22.

lawyer's seeking informed consent that is limited to future matters that are not substantially related to the client's matter. An informed consent that is limited to future matters that are not substantially related should not raise the concerns regarding the disclosure and use of confidential information that were among the central considerations underlying Opinion 93-372, given the criteria, discussed earlier, for determining whether successive matters are substantially related.

Comment [22] supports a lawyer's seeking, and the effectiveness of, a client's informed consent to future conflicts of interest in the circumstances that are acknowledged by Opinion 93-372. The Comment goes further, however, by supporting the likely validity of an "open-ended" informed consent if the client is an experienced user of legal services, particularly if, for example, the client has had the opportunity to be represented by independent counsel in relation to such consent and the consent is limited to matters not substantially related to the subject of the prior representation. Thus, Opinion 93-372 is no longer consistent with the Model Rules. [7]

ADDITIONAL LIMITATIONS AND REQUIREMENTS

The Committee notes the following additional limitations and requirements relating to a client's giving informed consent to a future conflict of interest. First, under Rule 1.7(b)(2) and (3), some conflicts are not consentable. [8] An informed consent to a future conflict (like an informed consent to a current conflict) cannot alter that circumstance. Second, under Rule 1.7(b)(4), the client's informed consent must be confirmed in writing. Third, as noted earlier, a client's informed consent to a future conflict, without more, does not constitute the client's informed consent to the disclosure or use of the client's confidential information against the client. Finally, a lawyer, when considering taking on a later matter covered by an informed consent given in advance, even if the conflict is consentable, still must determine whether accepting the engagement is impermissible for any other reason under Rules 1.7(b) and 1.9, or any other Model Rule. The lawyer also must determine whether informed consent is required from the client who is to be represented in that later matter.

NOTE

Is the shift toward a broader view of acceptable conflict waivers articulated by Opinion 05-436 and Model Rule 1.7 desirable? If your client receives the advice of

---

7. Opinion 93-372's limitation of the scope of effective consent to future conflicts, which is its central conclusion, is inconsistent with the amended Model Rules. Hence, we withdraw Opinion 93-372 in its entirety. The Committee notes that other conclusions in Opinion 93-372 on related points are consistent in whole or in part with the Model Rules as amended; those other conclusions are incorporated in this opinion.

8. See also Model Rule 1.7, cmts. 14 to 17.

other counsel on the subject of granting you a conflict waiver, does that ensure the waiver is valid? Should all such waivers be granted only on the advice of other counsel? As a rule? As a precautionary step?

3. Conflicts Relating to Former Clients

The specter of a disqualifying conflict of interest does not disappear merely because representation ceases. A lawyer may be disqualified from representing a party in litigation if he formerly represented another person in a matter that is substantially related to the pending litigation. Although frequently termed a disqualification by reason of conflict, it may also be regarded as an action necessary to safeguard the former client's expectation of confidentiality, perhaps to assure loyalty, on the part of his former counsel. This procedural disqualification protects the former client in advance of and against a possible future violation of the obligation of confidentiality. See ABA Opinion 346, note 2, infra p. 387.

> **Rule 1.9 Conflict of Interest: Former Client**
> (a) A lawyer who has formerly represented a client in a matter shall not thereafter represent another person in the same or a substantially related matter in which that person's interests are materially adverse to the interests of the former client unless the former client gives informed consent, confirmed in writing.
> (b) A lawyer shall not knowingly represent a person in the same or a substantially related matter in which a firm with which the lawyer formerly was associated had previously represented a client
> > (1) whose interests are materially adverse to that person; and
> > (2) about whom the lawyer had acquired information protected by Rules 1.6 and 1.9(c) that is material to the matter; unless the former client gives informed consent, confirmed in writing.
> (c) A lawyer who has formerly represented a client in a matter or whose present or former firm has formerly represented a client in a matter shall not thereafter:
> > (1) use information relating to the representation to the disadvantage of the former client except as these Rules would permit or require with respect to a client, or when the information has become generally known; or
> > (2) reveal information relating to the representation except as these Rules would permit or require with respect to a client.

With respect to (c) above, Rule 1.6 in this context would generally permit disclosure after the lawyer obtains consent from the former client.

The following case illustrates how the relationships among lawyers and their clients may change, resulting in conflicts with former clients. [Although Rule 1.9 was modified in 2002 after this case, the relevant portions remained the same.] It is an unpublished order by Tax Court Judge James Halpern.

Coleman v. Commissioner

Docket No. 44-86-86 (1991)

This case is calendared for trial at a special trial session commencing July 22, 1991, on the limited issue of petitioner Geraldine Coleman's entitlement to innocent spouse relief from liability for deficiencies in Federal income taxes under section 6013(e) of the Internal Revenue Code of 1954, as amended. Currently pending before the Court is petitioner Philip Coleman's motion to disqualify Richard Kates as counsel for petitioner Geraldine Coleman on the grounds of conflict of interest, pursuant to new Rule 24(f)* and Rule 201 of the Tax Court Rules of Practice and Procedure. In response to the Court's order dated June 24, 1991, Mr. Coleman and Mr. Kates have submitted, for *in camera* examination, various documents, memoranda, and affidavits pertaining to Mr. Kate's current representation of Mrs. Coleman and former representation of Philip Coleman. "Proper disposition of a motion to disqualify requires a careful examination of the allegedly conflicting representations." Hughes v. Paine, Webber, Jackson & Curtis Inc., 565 F.Supp. 663, 664 (N.D. Ill. 1983) (citation omitted). After such examination, the Court concludes that Mr. Coleman's motion to disqualify Mr. Kates should be granted.

In 1983, respondent commenced an audit of Mr. and Mrs. Coleman's 1977 through 1982 taxable years. Initially, the Colemans' accountant represented them in the examination process. In 1984, Mr. Coleman hired attorney Kates to take over representation in connection with the audit, and apparently executed a power of attorney authorizing Mr. Kates to represent both petitioners in that matter. Prior to that time, and continuing through January of 1986, Mr. Kates also represented Mr. Coleman and his business in a commercial litigation and both Mr. and Mrs. Coleman in other personal and business matters. Mr. Kates acquired (from both Mr. Coleman and the accountant) and reviewed a substantial number of both personal and business documents and records in order to respond to respondent's information document requests and to represent the Colemans in the subject tax matters.

In January 1986, when it became apparent that no settlement would be reached, Mr. Coleman hired attorneys from the law firm of Ross & Hardies for the purpose of litigating the matter in this Court and a power of attorney was signed by both Mr. and Mrs. Coleman. Those attorneys filed the petition herein on behalf of both petitioners, which placed in issue, among other items, Geraldine Coleman's entitlement to innocent spouse relief. In 1987, Mr. and Mrs. Coleman were divorced, but made no change in their joint representation. A trial was held in 1988 on the limited issue of whether the statutory period of limitations had expired prior to issuance of the notice of deficiency. A decision was rendered in favor of respondent on that issue and a trial on the merits was scheduled for October 29, 1990. Mr. Coleman subsequently hired special tax counsel to assist in the pending litigation.

---

*[Now Rule 24(g). — Eds.]

Sometime prior to October 1990, Mr. Coleman entered into settlement negotiations with respondent. During the fall of 1990, Mr. Coleman contacted Mrs. Coleman regarding a settlement agreement he had reached with respondent. Mr. Coleman outlined the details of that agreement in a letter to Mr. Kates (who had served as Mrs. Coleman's attorney in various matters subsequent to the divorce) so that he could answer any technical questions Mrs. Coleman might have pertaining to the settlement. Subsequently, Mr. Kates, on behalf of Mrs. Coleman, revoked the Hardies & Ross attorneys' power of attorney to represent Mrs. Coleman and indicated his intention to represent Mrs. Coleman and argue her entitlement to innocent spouse issue in this Court.

In several subsequent letters, Mr. Coleman informed Mr. Kates that he objected strenuously to any representation of Mrs. Coleman in that matter as such representation would be adverse to Mr. Coleman's interests in a matter in which Mr. Kates formerly represented him. Mr. Coleman made no objection to Mrs. Coleman finding independent representation should she refuse to join in the settlement agreement. In return letters, Mr. Kates just as vehemently stated Mrs. Coleman was entitled to her counsel of choice and refused to recuse himself from the proceedings in this court.

Rule 24(f) provides that if any counsel of record represents more than one person with differing interests with respect to any issue in a case, then such counsel must either (1) secure the informed consent of the client; (2) withdraw from the case; or (3) take whatever other steps are necessary to obviate a conflict of interest or other violation of the American Bar Association Model Rules of Professional Conduct (Model Rules). We may inquire into the circumstances of counsel's employment in order to deter such violations. Rule 24(f) became effective on July 1, 1990 and was adopted to ensure the integrity of this Court's decisions and that the bar of this Court disclose or rectify any conflict of interest. Comment to Rule 24(f), 93 T.C. at 858. Further, Rule 201 requires that practitioners before the Court shall carry on their practice in accordance with the letter and spirit of the Model Rules. Thus, we look to the Model Rules, to their counterpart in the State in which Mr. Kates is licensed to practice, and case law interpreting those rules for guidance. We also bear in mind that motions to disqualify must be viewed with caution because of the possibility that they are tactical weapons for the purpose of harassment in the hands of disappointed parties. See Comment to Rule 24(f), supra; Miller v. Norfolk & Western Railway Co., 538 N.E.2d 1293, 1297 (Ill. App. 4 Dist. 1989).

The Model Rules contain an unequivocal prohibition against representation adverse to a former client without consent. [The judge quotes Model Rule 9.1 and 1.6 and discusses their adoption in Illinois.]

Given the acrimonious behavior of the parties to this motion, it is possible that Mr. Coleman may have, in part, filed this motion as a tactical weapon or to embarrass Mr. Kates. Mr. Coleman voiced his objection personally to Mr. Kates, however, prior to trial and submission of his settlement agreement and several months before filing this motion. Moreover, even if such a motive could be attributed to Mr. Coleman, which is not without doubt, its importance here is diminished before the greater purpose served by this Court's Rules and the Rules of Professional

Responsibility. There is no question but that the interests of Mrs. Coleman, who filed a joint return with her ex-husband and now claims entitlement to innocent spouse relief from Federal income tax liabilities, are materially adverse to the interests of Mr. Coleman. If Mrs. Coleman is found to be entitled to relief from all liability for the taxes in issue, the normal rule of joint and several liability does not apply, and respondent may assess only against Mr. Coleman. See sec. 6013(d)(3) and (e). Similarly, there is no question but that the subject matter of Mr. Kates's former representation of Mr. Coleman is the same as that of his adverse representation here. The heart of both representations is, and always has been, who bears liability for deficiencies in income taxes, and to what extent.

Nevertheless, Mr. Kates implicitly argues against disqualification on the grounds that he was never privy to confidential or secret matters pertaining to Mr. Coleman's conduct or finances which could here be used to Mr. Coleman's disadvantage. Thus, he argues, there is no conflict of interest. Outside of his statements, Mr. Kates presented no evidence to show that he never obtained confidential information that could be used to Mr. Coleman's disadvantage here. Based on the record (revealing a long history of representation and review of documents in both personal and business matters and in the very tax matters in issue in this case), we view with skepticism the veracity of such assertions. Because they appear unreasonable or improbable, we are not required to accept Mr. Kates's unsubstantiated self-serving statements. Wood v. Commissioner, 338 F.2d 602, 605 (9th Cir. 1964), affg. 41 T.C. 593 (1964). Moreover, it is the mere potentiality that Mr. Kates might have obtained information that could be used to Mr. Coleman's disadvantage which must be protected against.

> Rule 1.9 is a prophylactic rule to prevent even the potential that a former client's confidences and secrets may be used against him. Without such a rule, clients may be reluctant to confide in attorneys. It is also important for the maintenance of public confidence in the integrity of the bar. [Havens v. State of Indiana, 793 F.2d 143, 145-146 (7th Cir. 1986).]

Further, where, as here, the subject of the former and present representations by the same attorney are substantially related or identical, Illinois courts presume irrebutably that confidential information was disclosed in the earlier representation. Herbes v. Graham, 536 N.E. 2d at 168-169, and cases cited therein. We agree with the reasoning of the Illinois courts; Mr. Kates is presumed to have been the recipient of confidential information which could now be used to Mr. Coleman's disadvantage.

Mr. Kates further argues that Mr. Coleman waived any right to oppose Mr. Kates's representation of Mrs. Coleman on the innocent spouse issue by discussing the possibility of such relief with him during his representation of both Mr. and Mrs. Coleman in the administrative proceedings and because innocent spouse relief was placed in issue in the joint petition. That argument strikes at the heart of the problem of joint representation of husbands and wives in Federal income tax matters. Because of the joint and several liability that attaches when a joint Federal income tax return is filed and the exception for innocent spouse relief, husbands and wives are always potentially adverse in proceedings involving those joint returns. On the other hand, economic and other interests lead many couples, whether presently or formerly married, to seek joint representation in disputes pertaining to tax matters. Thus, it is always incumbent upon counsel to fully disclose to such clients the potential conflict and to obtain the informed consent of both parties to any joint representation. See Model Rule 1.8; Comments to Model Rules 1.6, 1.7, 1.8 & 1.9.

Whether or not Mr. Kates disclosed the conflicts of interest inherent in his former joint representation, however, it may be presumed from this record that, at the time he discussed the innocent spouse issue with Mr. Coleman, Mr. Kates represented Mr. Coleman's interests as well as those of Mrs. Coleman and that a joint representation to the advantage of both clients was intended by all. Mr. Kates was then replaced as counsel for both petitioners and reappeared only when the sole issue remaining was Mrs. Coleman's entitlement to relief from liability. We conclude that the prior discussion and the inclusion of the section 6013(e) issue in the joint petition filed by different counsel are insufficient to constitute a waiver or implied consent to Mr. Kates's representation of Mrs. Coleman in this matter.

At the moment Mr. Kates was dismissed as joint counsel, he assumed an absolute ethical obligation to refrain from representing either Mr. or Mrs. Coleman individually in any proceeding pertaining to their income tax liabilities in which the two were adverse. See Comment to Model Rule 1.7; In the Matter of Hof, 478 N.Y.S.2d 39 (A.D.2d 1984) (prior joint representation precludes present representation of only one client in same matter). Only an explicit waiver or consent given directly to Mr. Kates by Mr. Coleman at the time he undertook his present representation of Mrs. Coleman would suffice to fulfill that obligation. That Mr. Kates did not obtain. Similarly, while it is true that Mr. Coleman did write to Mr. Kates asking him to explain the terms of the proposed settlement of tax liabilities to Mrs. [Coleman], we do not consider that an invitation or implied consent to undertake an adversarial representation. The minute it was clear that Mr. Kates intended to represent Mrs. Coleman here, Mr. Coleman objected strenuously and attempted repeatedly to clarify his objections to Mr. Kates. "[C]ontinued representation under the circumstances would tend to inflame the atmosphere of distrust extant between [petitioners and their counsel], impede the cooperation between their counsel and the free flow of information between them, resulting in the prolongation of the final settlement" of this case. In the Matter of Hof, 478 N.Y.S.2d at 43. Under the circumstances, Mr. Kates should have withdrawn the moment it became clear that Mr. Coleman would not consent to the adverse representation.

NOTES

1.   Note that Rule 1.9 requires that the subject matter of the first representation must be substantially related to the subject matter of the second representation. Does

this mean, for example, that if the attorney represented *A* in a tax matter that he can subsequently represent *B* in a tort claim against *A?* Not necessarily. In Analytica, Inc. v. NPD Research, Inc., 708 F.2d 1263 (7th Cir. 1983), Judge Posner noted that matters are substantially related "if the lawyer could have obtained confidential information in the first representation that would have been relevant in the second." If the attorney representing *A* in the tax matter obtained all of *A*'s financial records, it may be impossible to represent *B* in the tort action competently without using this confidential information from *A*, which he is precluded from doing. Model Rule 1.9(c). If the attorney is disqualified, all partners and associates of his firm would be as well. Model Rule 1.10(a); see also Model Code DR 5-105(D).

2. The *Coleman* case, as well as *Devore*, presented earlier, illustrates the difficulties that arise when a single lawyer seeks to represent husband and wife following marital difficulties. The defense of innocent spouse may be available to one of them and that defense ordinarily will be adverse to the other. See §6015. If the one lawyer representing both spouses fails to assert this defense, the other spouse may seek, years later, as in *Devore*, to have a final decision set aside. Does this prospect place a heavy burden on the court to identify situations in which the innocent spouse defense should be asserted and yet the couple's lawyer is not doing that?

3. Husband and wife *(H* and *W)* file a joint income tax return, and the IRS, after audit, issues a joint notice of deficiency. *H* retains you as counsel for himself and *W*. After consulting with both of them as to their income, deductions, and credits, you file a petition on their behalf in the Tax Court, having taken the precaution of having both *H* and *W* join you in signing the petition. A month before trial, *H* tells you that he and *W* have separated, that each has hired divorce counsel, and that reconciliation is out of the question. What are your obligations to *W?* To *H?* To government counsel? To the court?

4. Note that some forms of disqualification are vicarious, in the sense that the disqualification of one lawyer in a firm means that all lawyers in that firm are likewise disqualified. This is not true where disqualification rests on the status of a lawyer as a witness. Model Rule 3.7(b). It is true of disqualification under Rules 1.7 (present clients) and 1.9 (former clients). Model Rule 1.10. (Note that Model Rule 1.10 (a) does allow a member of a firm to represent a client even though another member of the firm is barred if the "prohibition is based on a personal interest of the prohibited lawyer and does not present a significant risk of materially limiting the representation of the client by the remaining lawyers in the firm.") Special rules exist for lawyers who leave government service to enter private practice, and we will discuss those in Chapter 6.

5. What kinds of problems does vicarious disqualification present? Suppose the tax department of a law firm (Firm *A*) hires an associate who served as a summer associate in the tax department of another firm (Firm *B*) the prior summer. Assume further that the associate became privy to confidential information related to a client of Firm *B* whose interests are directly adverse to the interests of a client of Firm *A*. Does this exposure disqualify Firm *A* from continuing to represent its client? How should firms (and perhaps individual lawyers) act to protect themselves?

4. Disqualification Based on the Lawyer's Status as a Witness

Model Rule 3.7 provides, with certain exceptions, that a lawyer should decline or should withdraw from employment if it is likely that he will be a necessary witness in a trial. One of the exceptions exists where "disqualification of the lawyer would work substantial hardship on the client." This particular form of disqualification is often hotly contested, perhaps because the party seeking disqualification is viewed as simply moving to achieve tactical advantage. In the following tax cases the IRS moved to disqualify opposing counsel on the grounds that such counsel would be called by the government as witness.

United States of America v. Tate & Lyle North American Sugars, Inc.

184 F. Supp. 2d 344 (S.D.N.Y. 2002)

BERMAN, Judge. Plaintiff, the United States of America ("Plaintiff" or the "IRS" or the "Government"), filed this action . . . to recover a $ 1,526.100.60 interest payment it asserts it erroneously made to Defendant. Tate & Lyle North American Sugars, Inc. ("Defendant" or "Tate & Lyle"). On November 26, 2001, Plaintiff moved, pursuant to Federal Rule of Civil Procedure 7, for an order disqualifying the law firm of Burt, Maner & Miller ("BM&M") from representing Defendant at trial. . . .

Since at least 1990 BM&M has represented Tate & Lyle, Inc. and its subsidiaries, including Amstar, in connection with IRS tax audits. . . . On December 14, 1990, Jared Twenty ("Twenty"), the director of taxes for Tate & Lyle, Inc., sent the IRS a letter ("Twenty Letter") concerning a proposed (tax) adjustment and enclosing a remittance of $6,497,710.00 ("December 1990 remittance"). . . . In the letter, Twenty stated that the remittance was for an (anticipated) deficiency in tax, plus interest, resulting from the IRS' adjustment and that "we respectfully request that this deposit be identified as a cash bond in your records." . . . Pursuant to Revenue Procedure 84-58, 1984-2 C.B. at 503, §5.02, the remittance had the effect of stopping interest from accruing on any tax deficiency assessment. . . .

In September 1993, the IRS concluded its audit, determined that Amstar had overpaid its taxes, and sent Amstar $8,240,206.34 for, among other things, the December 1990 remittance (i.e., $6,497,710.00) together with interest thereon in the amount (at issue here) of $1,526,100.60. . . . On January 25, 1996, Rosie Williams ("Williams"), a case manager at the IRS, met with Ann Harris ("Harris"), the Tate & Lyle, Inc. tax director who succeeded Twenty in 1991, and informed her that the IRS had mistakenly paid interest on the "cash bond." . . . By letter dated March 14, 1996, Harris advised the IRS that Defendant would not return the $1,526,100.60 stating, "We did not then, and we do not now, consider the September 1993 refund to be a return of the cash bond paid. . . ."

In the instant motion. Plaintiff asserts that it "expects" to call members of BM&M to testify at trial and the "expected testimony likely will substantially prejudice defendant by contradicting defendant's factual assertions that the December 14, 1990 letter to the [IRS] was simply a cover letter, and that, in any event, Jared Twenty lacked authority to designate the accompanying remittance as a deposit in the nature of a cash bond." Defendant counters that Plaintiff has "failed to show specifically what testimony it will elicit from BM&M witnesses, how that testimony would prejudice Amstar, or why such testimony is strictly necessary."

II. Standard of Review

"Motions to disqualify opposing counsel are viewed with disfavor because they impinge on parties' rights to employ the counsel of their choice." Fulfree v. Manchester, 945 F. Supp. 768, 770 (S.D.N.Y. 1996). "The drastic remedy of disqualification based on the advocate-witness rule is subject to strict scrutiny because of the strong potential for abuse to 'stall and derail the proceedings, redounding to the strategic advantage of one party over another.'" Id. (quoting S&S Hotel Ventures Ltd. Partnership v. 777 S.H. Corp., 508 N.E.2d 647, 650, 508 N.E.2d 647, 515 N.Y.S.2d 735 (N.Y. 1987).) *The party bringing the motion under [Disciplinary Rule 5-102(D)] carries the burden to show both the necessity of the testimony and the substantial likelihood of prejudice.*" Soberman v. Groff Studios Corp., 1999 U.S. Dist. LEXIS 8075, No. 99 Civ. 1005, 1999 WL 349989, at 7 (S.D.N.Y. June 1, 1999) (emphasis added). . . .

III. Analysis

Plaintiff, as noted, seeks to disqualify BM&M because it "expects to call members of that firm to testify" at trial. . . . Plaintiff contends that "BM&M attorneys are the only qualified witnesses who can establish that, through their own silence and failure to take action, at the very least, Twenty's authority and direction were ratified." Defendant argues that Plaintiff has failed to meet its burden of showing the necessity of attorney testimony because, among other things, other evidence is available. See Stratavest Ltd., 903 F. Supp. at 667; Kirshon, Shron, Cornell & Teitelbaum P.C. v. Savarese, 182 A.D.2d 911, 581 N.Y.S.2d 487 (N.Y. App. Div. 1992) (testimony not "necessary" where cumulative of other evidence). . . .

Plaintiff asserts that "this expected testimony will flatly contradict Amstar's factual assertions . . . and thus be prejudicial to Defendant." According to Plaintiff, "all of the expected testimony directly challenges defendant's credibility and undermines its asserted legal position in this case." Defendant contends that the Government "cannot be specific about any BM&M testimony because it did not depose any BM&M witnesses" and has not "demonstrated that a BM&M lawyer's testimony will contradict or impugn a position Amstar takes in this litigation to such an extent that another firm attorney trying the case would be at pains to attack his credibility at trial." . . .

Overall, it does not appear that attorney testimony will add to that which is readily established by, among other things, Defendant's privilege log, the Maner Declaration, deposition testimony of Twenty, Hoyt, Friedman and others, and additional documents produced during discovery. See Rice v. Baron, 456 F. Supp. 1361, 1371-1373 (S.D.N.Y. 1978) (testimony not "sufficiently adverse to the factual assertions or account of events offered on behalf of the client" where it "adds little, if anything, to that which [Plaintiff] has already admitted"). Additionally, the testimony sought appears speculative, and may be subject to the attorney-client privilege. See Frias v. Frias, 155 A.D.2d 585, 547 N.Y.S.2d 652, 653 (N.Y. App. Div. 1989). . . .

In sum, even assuming the issue of prejudice were to be reached, Plaintiff has not shown that the attorney testimony sought would be "sufficiently adverse to the factual assertions or account of events" offered by Defendant. Amalgamated Services and Allied Industries Joint Board, 1996 U.S. Dist. LEXIS 14962, 1996 WL 583351, at 6. Disqualification of BM&M so long after the Complaint was filed and after discovery has ended is unwarranted. . . .

Accordingly, Plaintiff's motion is denied. . . .

NOTES

1.   Should the government be able to both call a taxpayer's lawyer as a witness and also seek to disqualify that lawyer from representing the taxpayer at trial? What are the risks either way?

2.   In Kenosha Auto Transport Corp. v. United States, the Justice Department was notified on January 23, 1973, that plaintiff's witnesses would include members of its counsel's law firm. On January 20, 1975, the Department first raised the question of disqualification. Was it seeking to fashion its sword from plaintiff's shield? Would the court's reaction have been different had the Department raised the disqualification issue immediately upon receiving plaintiff's witness list? How is the situation in *Kenosha Auto Transport* different from *Tate & Lyle*?

3.   The attorney-witness issue frequently arises in tax practice because a client's defense to negligence or fraud penalties may be that he had a "reasonable basis" for a position because he relied on an attorney's advice. The client may waive the attorney-client privilege and testify as to this reliance. The attorney may be called to corroborate this testimony. As discussed in Chapter 2, there also may be a conflict between the attorney and the client if the attorney is subject to penalty.

4.   The disqualification of a lawyer from acting as an advocate because of the likelihood that the lawyer will be called as a witness does not prevent the lawyer's firm from representing the client in the same matter. If, however, the lawyer is required to withdraw because of a conflict of interest under Model Rule 1.7 or 1.9, the entire law firm is disqualified under Model Rule 1.10 (except as noted above on page 153, note 4).

———————

As we saw above, Tax Court Rule 24(g) requires that a lawyer who will be a "potential" witness in a case withdraw or "take whatever other steps are necessary to obviate a conflict of interest or other violation" of the Model Rules, especially Rule 1.7. No option is provided for client waiver in this circumstance. Presumably, the defense of substantial hardship remains available to resist disqualification because it is part of Rule 1.7. In the following case, which arose before the adoption of Rule 24(g), the Tax Court disqualified a lawyer from representing a client where the government identified the lawyer as a necessary witness.

Duffey v. Commissioner

91 T.C. 81 (1988)

KORNER, Judge. This case is now before us on respondent's motion to disqualify petitioners' counsel G. Alohawiwoole Altman (Altman). The basis of respondent's motion is that he intends to call Altman as a witness at the trial of this case.

Rule 201(a) governs the conduct of attorneys before this Court. It provides that attorneys practicing before this Court "shall carry on their practice in accordance with the letter and spirit of the Rules of Professional Conduct of the American Bar Association." Rule 3.7(a) of the American Bar Association Model Rules of Professional Conduct (ABA rule 3.7(a)) limits the circumstances in which an attorney may act as both an advocate and a witness at a trial. . . .

The first step in our analysis is to determine whether Altman is "likely to be a necessary witness" at the trial of this case. If he is, ABA rule 3.7(a) requires him to be disqualified from representing petitioner at trial unless one of that rule's three exceptions applies.

The central issues in this case are whether petitioners received unreported income from the illegal distribution of drugs and, if so, whether their failure to report that income was due to fraud within the meaning of section 6653(b). . . .

Respondent has alleged as part of his fraud case that petitioners utilized various trusts as nominees to hold title to assets derived from their unreported income, and that they failed to maintain complete and accurate records of their income-producing activities.

The stipulated exhibits establish that Altman prepared petitioners' joint Federal income tax returns for two of the three years at issue, and that his firm prepared the return for the remaining year. In addition, the stipulated exhibits establish that Altman was counsel for various trusts in which petitioners held an interest. Whether petitioners concealed the unreported income that they allegedly received from illegal activities from Altman, their tax return preparer, is a fact that is relevant to the issue of fraud. Whether petitioners attempted to conceal unreported income by making false statements to Altman as to the purpose of the trusts and the source of the assets contained in them is similarly a fact that is relevant to the issue of fraud. Altman's position as preparer of petitioners' returns and as counsel to their trusts makes his testimony uniquely valuable, on a principal issue in the case. In these circumstances, we agree with respondent that it would be highly desirable, even necessary, to call

Altman as a witness in order to question him on subjects related to the fraud issue. We accordingly conclude that ABA rule 3.7(a) applies to bar Altman from representing petitioners at trial unless one of the three exceptions applies.

Petitioners argue that [one] of the exceptions [applies], and that Altman is therefore entitled to represent petitioners even if it is likely that he will be called as a necessary witness. . . .

Petitioners' . . . argument is that the disqualification of Altman would cause them substantial hardship. Petitioners argue that Altman has developed a unique familiarity with their financial affairs which has made him irreplaceable as counsel for petitioners. In addition, petitioners argue that Altman is representing them pro bono and that they will be unable to afford to retain another attorney if he is disqualified.

With respect to petitioners' argument that Altman is irreplaceable, we believe that petitioners have ample time to retain another attorney and to allow that attorney to prepare for trial. Respondent properly and commendably brought this matter to the attention of petitioners and this Court well before the case was set for trial. This is therefore not a case in which a disqualification will occur on the eve of a trial so as to make it difficult for petitioners to obtain competent replacement counsel.

With respect to petitioners' argument that they are too destitute to pay for counsel, we are simply unconvinced that that is the case. Petitioners admit in their memorandum in opposition to respondent's motion to disqualify Altman that they have already retained an attorney to serve as Altman's co-counsel and that the attorney bills them on an hourly basis. In sum, we are unconvinced that Altman's disqualification would create a substantial hardship for petitioners.

As we have concluded that Altman is likely to be called as a necessary witness, and as we have been unable to conclude that an exception to disqualification applies, we hold that ABA rule 3.7(a) requires Altman to be disqualified from representing petitioners at trial.

NOTES

1.   In *Duffey*, the Tax Court arrived at the disqualification result without great difficulty by applying Model Rule 1.7. Given that, why was it necessary for the court to adopt a special rule dealing with this situation?

2.   In Coutsoubelis v. Commissioner, 66 TCM (CCH) 934 (1993), the court refused to disqualify a lawyer whom the respondent first proposed to call as a witness three weeks before trial because disqualification "on the eve of this complex and lengthy trial would have caused substantial hardship."

3.   What interests are served by disqualification over the objection of the client? Is the court correct in Ampex v. United States, 211 Ct. Cl. 366 (1976), when it states that the rule is primarily for the benefit of "clients and courts" and not the opposing party? In what respect does the rule benefit courts? Is the avoidance of even the appearance of impropriety involved?

4. In Firestone Tire & Rubber Co. v. Risjord, 449 U.S. 368 (1981), the
Supreme Court held that a trial court's refusal to disqualify opposing counsel may
not be appealed on an interlocutory basis. In Flanagan v. United States, 465 U.S.
259 (1984), the Supreme Court held that the grant of a motion to disqualify in a
criminal case is also not appealable before final judgment. The Court based its
decision on the fact that in criminal cases post-conviction review of a disqualification
order is fully effective.

5. In Richardson-Merrell, Inc. v. Koller, 472 U.S. 424 (1985), the Court held
that an order disqualifying counsel in a civil case is not a collateral order subject to
immediate appeal because it is not a final judgment on the merits for purposes of 28
U.S.C. §1291.

6. For a perceptive article in which the author, a former chairman of the ABA
Tax Section, argues that the lawyer-witness disqualification rule should be elimi-
nated, see James B. Lewis, The Ethical Dilemma of the Testifying Advocate: Fact or
Fancy?, 19 Hous. L. Rev. 75 (1981).

5. Disqualification Arising from Representation of Multiple Parties in an Administrative Investigation

During its investigation of the tax affairs of a particular taxpayer, the Internal Revenue Service may find it desirable to interview or to take statements from friends or
business associates of the taxpayer. Such witnesses may understandably desire representation by counsel in connection with their appearance before the Service. Not
infrequently, they are represented by the lawyer who also represents the taxpayer.

What ethical issues are presented by this dual representation? If the function of
the conflict rules under Model Rule 1.7 is to protect the client, and if both clients
waive any objection to the dual representation, are there nonetheless residual ethical
questions? Are there public policy issues independent of the ethical questions?

Backer v. Commissioner
275 F.2d 141 (5th Cir. 1960)

TUTTLE, Circuit Judge. This action covers a very narrow compass. Appellant is a
Certified Public Accountant who had been employed in connection with preparation of the tax returns of one Walter D. Williams Jr. In the course of investigation of
Williams's tax affairs for five years numerous consultations were had between the
Internal Revenue agents and special agents and appellant. Appellant fully answered
all questions asked, produced all papers requested during the many interviews conducted both with and without the presence of an attorney for taxpayer.

In this posture of affairs, after appellant had disclosed all the information sought
from him touching on Williams's tax affairs, he was subpoenaed to appear and testify

under oath before the Special Agent at a prescribed time and place. He did appear, accompanied by counsel, Cubbedge Snow, Esquire. Mr. Snow had previously filed a power of attorney to represent the taxpayer, Williams, in the investigation of his tax matters. The Special Agent stated that Mr. Snow could not be present at the investigation of appellant, whereupon appellant, on the advice of his counsel, declined to submit to the interrogation; counsel based this action on the provisions of the Administrative Procedure Act which says:

> Any person compelled to appear in person before any agency or representative thereof shall be accorded the right to be accompanied, represented, and advised by counsel. . . . 5 U.S.C.A. §1005.

Thereupon the Commissioner of Internal Revenue filed his petition with the United States District Court to require the attendance of Backer "without the presence of counsel retained by or connected with the said Walter D. Williams Jr."

The trial court expressly found that counsel was employed by Backer at his own expense and without any suggestion from the taxpayer. It also found that both appellant and his counsel were "of unquestioned and unquestionable character" and that neither of them had attempted in any manner to impede the investigation.

Nevertheless, the court held that Backer must appear to give his testimony without being represented by Mr. Snow. The trial court said:

> . . . Whether or not the Commissioner is correct in contending that the mere presence of taxpayer's counsel at the investigation while taxpayer's accountant is being questioned serves as a damper upon the voluntary testimony of taxpayer's accountant, I think the correct solution to this problem was pointed out in United States v. Smith, D.C. Conn. 1949, 87 F. Supp. 293, 294, where the Court said:
>
>> While no harm seems likely from such a situation in this case, since the knowledge of these witnesses is necessarily also the knowledge of the taxpayer, any possibility of prejudice to the investigation should be obviated by requiring that counsel be not connected with, or retained by, the taxpayer.

The Commissioner does not base his right to exclude any particular counsel from such representation of the appellant on any Regulations of the Internal Revenue Service. He acts under a policy established by him prior to the adoption of the Administrative Procedure Act. The policy is stated in a Manual of Instructions for Special Agents, Intelligence Unit, July 10, 1945, which gave a witness the right stated as follows:

> The right to have an attorney present at the time of his questioning for the purpose of advising the witness relevant to his right to refuse to give any answers which might incriminate him under the laws of the United States. Under this policy, however, a third party witness is entitled to the attendance of his own counsel, but not the counsel for taxpayer.

It is clear that the right to counsel guaranteed under the Administrative Procedure Act is much broader than the right to have an attorney to advise him relative to his rights under the Fifth Amendment. The Act says such counsel may accompany, represent and advise the witness, without any limitation. Moreover, it seems quite doubtful that the policy statement itself, even if it were valid under the new act, covers the situation where the counsel is in fact counsel for the witness, even though he is also counsel for the taxpayer. It draws the distinction between counsel for the witness and counsel for the taxpayer. It does not seem to deal with the situation where one lawyer is both.

In any event, we are not here dealing with an attempted limitation on the generality of the right guaranteed under the Administrative Procedure Act by a formally adopted department regulation. We, therefore, do not come to the question whether, if under formal rule-making procedures the Treasury Department had adopted regulations purporting to qualify the right of a witness to be represented by a lawyer who is also counsel for the person under investigation, such regulation would warrant the ruling of the court below. Certain it is that in the absence of any such regulation the Commissioner cannot put limitations on the general authority to have counsel as granted by the statute by saying that the witness's choice cannot include one who also represents the taxpayer.

We recognize that what is in issue here is not the constitutional right to counsel. It is, however, a statutory right. The term "right to counsel" has always been construed to mean counsel of one's choice. See Powell v. State of Alabama, 287 U.S. 45; Chandler v. Fretag, 348 U.S. 3.

We think this is the plain and necessary meaning of this provision of the law. When Congress used the terms "right to be accompanied, represented, and advised by counsel," it must have used the language in the regularly accepted connotation, even though the language of the courts in using it was in connection with the right to counsel guaranteed by the Sixth Amendment to the Constitution.

Nor do we have a case in which the Commissioner is complaining to a trial court that counsel is in fact obstructing the orderly inquiry process by improper conduct or tactics. Cf. Torras v. Stradley, D.C. Ga., 103 F. Supp. 737.

None of the harm which the Commissioner here apprehends will result from letting taxpayer's counsel represent a witness as his own selected counsel will result except upon the failure of counsel to conduct himself in accord with his sworn duty to the court. If he does so fail then is the time for remedial action to be taken. Such action is not permissible when, as here, the trial court and government counsel reject any suggestion that either the witness or counsel will violate either the law or the ethics of their profession in the proposed investigation.

We hold that under the circumstances of this case the action of the District Court was not authorized.

The order of the District Court is reversed and vacated and the case remanded for further proceedings not inconsistent with this opinion.

NOTE

Is the government entitled to exclude the taxpayer when it interrogates a witness in relation to the taxpayer's case? If it is, might not the decision in this case vitiate that right? Should the court have considered the value of that right in reaching its decision? Is the witness' right to counsel of choice so absolute as to compel the result in this case?

United States v. Gopman

531 F.2d 262 (5th Cir. 1976)

TJOFLAT, Circuit Judge. The issue in this appeal is whether the trial judge erred when he disqualified Seymour A. Gopman, Esq., from simultaneously representing certain labor unions and three officials of these unions who had appeared as witnesses before a grand jury. We find no error, and affirm the order of disqualification entered below.

This case arose in the context of a federal grand jury investigation of union activities in the Miami, Florida area. The general emphasis of this investigation was upon possible violations of the Labor-Management Reporting and Disclosure Act (Landrum-Griffin Act), 29 U.S.C. §401 et seq. At the time of the events which led to Gopman's disqualification, the grand jury was considering evidence of alleged embezzlement by union officials, alleged failures by union officials to maintain required records, and the alleged destruction of union records by such officials. There was at that time only one announced "target" of the grand jury investigation. In connection with their probe of the "target" official, the grand jury issued subpoenas to three other union officers ordering them to bring certain records for examination. The three prospective witnesses consulted Gopman, who was their unions' retained counsel, concerning what response should be made to the subpoenas.

It was the practice of Gopman's firm to cease advising union officials once they had become "targets" of a grand jury investigation. In fact, the firm had represented the "target" official himself in the past, but had instructed him to retain separate counsel once he was named as a "target." However, since these three officers were not "targets," Gopman concluded that he could properly advise them as to their appearance before the grand jury. After studying the case, Gopman realized that the officials could be subject to criminal penalties under 29 U.S.C. §439 if they had not maintained the records sought by the grand jury or if they had maintained these records improperly. After being advised by Gopman of these possibilities, and of their right against self-incrimination, all three witnesses elected to invoke the Fifth Amendment before the grand jury; they refused to produce the records or to answer any questions concerning them. The government then contended that Gopman's dual representation of the unions and the individual witnesses was creating a conflict of interest. A motion for disqualification was filed December 13, 1974, and was granted by the court on January 7, 1975. After a dispute arose over the scope of the

Court's order, an amended order of disqualification was filed February 6, 1975. The trial judge ordered Gopman to cease representing the three union officials before the grand jury, and to instruct the witnesses that they should obtain new counsel. Gopman's appeal followed.

It is argued that the government lacked standing to challenge the alleged conflict of interest, and that the trial judge had no jurisdiction to entertain the government's motion for disqualification. We reject these contentions. The substance of the government's motion was that appellant had violated the ethical canons of the American Bar Association, which prohibit a lawyer from representing parties with adverse interests. These ethical canons had been explicitly adopted by the local rules of the district court in which this action arose. When an attorney discovers a possible ethical violation concerning a matter before a court, he is not only authorized but is in fact obligated to bring the problem to that court's attention. See Estates Theatres, Inc. v. Columbia Pictures Industries, Inc., 345 F. Supp. 93, 98 (S.D.N.Y. 1972). Nor is there any reason why this duty should not operate when, as in the present case, a lawyer is directing the court's attention to the conduct of opposing counsel. In fact, a lawyer's adversary will often be in the best position to discover unethical behavior. We also conclude that the trial judge had jurisdiction to act upon this claim of unethical conduct. Local rules whose validity is not challenged expressly incorporate the American Bar Association's ethical canons and expressly give the district court the power to fashion sanctions. Furthermore, it is beyond dispute that lawyers are officers of the court and that the courts have the inherent authority to regulate their professional conduct.

We hold that, as an incident of this supervisory power, a court has jurisdiction to discipline an attorney whose unethical conduct relates to a grand jury proceeding within that court's control. From this conclusion, it naturally follows that an attorney's standing to report ethical problems to the appropriate court extends to the grand jury stage as well.

We are told that the order of disqualification exceeded the trial court's power to regulate the conduct of attorneys practicing before it. The proper standard for our review of a disqualification order is whether the trial judge abused his discretion. See Hull v. Celanese Corp., 513 F.2d 568, 571 (2d Cir. 1975). We also must remember that the court's discretion permits it "to nip any potential conflict of interest in the bud," Tucker v. Shaw, 378 F.2d 304, 307 (2d Cir. 1967). On the record before this Court, it is clear that the possibility of a conflict had become great enough for the trial court to exercise its discretion. The grand jury was investigating possible breaches by union officials of certain fiduciary duties imposed by the Landrum-Griffin Act. As this Court has held, one chief purpose of the Act is to protect union members against possible overreaching by union officials. Therefore, when possible violations of these statutes are under investigation, it is evident that the affected unions' interest will generally be in the fullest possible disclosure of pertinent records. Only if such disclosure is made can the unions be certain that possible problems affecting their rights under the Act are being thoroughly examined. For the same reason, in a normal case union counsel with his clients' interests at heart would tend to favor a complete disclosure of such records. The trial court concluded that appellant could not aggressively and diligently pursue this goal while advising the unions' own officials on whether to produce the records and what testimony, if any, to give regarding them. This conclusion seems entirely reasonable to us, and we find no abuse of discretion on these facts.

Two further constitutional claims warrant a brief discussion. Appellant contends that the disqualification order violated the affected parties' First Amendment freedom of association and the various clients' Sixth Amendment right to obtain counsel of their choice. Certainly, these rights are important ones and will yield only to an overriding public interest. We do not indicate what merit, if any, appellant's arguments might have in a case where the ethical violation is relatively minor. We hold only that the public interest in a properly functioning judicial system must be allowed to prevail in the case presently before us. Appellant had placed himself in a clear conflict situation from which the district court had the duty to rescue both the lawyer and his clients.

NOTES

1.   What justifies the Fifth Circuit's decision in *Gopman* in light of the earlier decision of the same court in *Backer*, supra p. 159?

2.   The courts generally have tended to allow dual representation unless they conclude that the conflict of interest is so apparent that the attorney cannot conclude "that it is obvious that he can adequately represent the interest of each." Compare In re Grand Jury Proceeding, 480 F. Supp. 162 (N.D. Ohio 1979), cert. denied, 449 U.S. 1124 (1981) (lawyer not permitted to represent both "target" and "nontarget" witnesses before grand jury) with United States v. Canessa, 644 F.2d 61 (1st Cir. 1981) (lawyer permitted to represent both target and nontarget witnesses).

3.   In SEC v. Csapo, 533 F.2d 7 (D.C. Cir. 1976), the court held that the agency's sequestration rule, which expressly extended to counsel of witnesses, could not be applied to exclude a lawyer representing multiple witnesses absent "concrete evidence" that his presence would obstruct and impede the investigation.

INTERNAL REVENUE MANUAL

25.5.5.5   Dual Representation (04-30-1999)

1.   Treasury Department Circular 230 (Regulations Governing the Practice of Attorneys, Certified Public Accountants, Enrolled Agents, Enrolled Actuaries, and Appraisers before the Internal Revenue Service) (Rev. 6-2005) provides the following with respect to dual representation:

Section 10.29 Conflicting interests. (a) Except as provided by paragraph (b) of this section, a practitioner shall not represent a client in his or her practice before the Internal Revenue Service if the representation involves a conflict of interest.

2. Paragraph (b) sets several conditions for practice in the case of a practitioner's conflict of interest. These conditions are: 1) the practitioner reasonably believes he or she can provide "competent and diligent representation" to each of the affected clients; 2) the representation is not prohibited by law; and 3) each affected client gives informed consent confirmed in writing.

3. Dual representation exists when a summoned third-party witness is represented by an attorney, certified public accountant, enrolled agent, or other person who also represents the taxpayer or another interested party. It may also occur where an attorney under investigation represents a third-party witness in that investigation or where an attorney-witness seeks to represent another witness in the same investigation. An interested party is one who has a significant pecuniary interest in the testimony of the witness or who, by virtue of the nature of the investigation and the known facts, may be incriminated by the witness. When dual representation exists, notify the Group Manager, and consult Associate Area Counsel, if necessary, to determine the appropriate course of action.

Note: When dual representation is not allowed, continue the summons appearance date to allow time for a resolution of the matter if the attorney witness refuses to testify or produce documents.

4. Except as provided below, the mere existence of a dual representation situation which may potentially have an adverse impact on the investigation will not, without some action by the attorney to impede or obstruct the investigation, provide a sufficient basis for seeking a disqualification. However, where an attorney's representation has substantially prejudiced the questioning of a third-party witness and, as a result, has significantly impaired the progress of the investigation, the Service will request the Department of Justice to seek a court order, as part of the summons enforcement proceeding, to disqualify that attorney as counsel for that witness.

5. In view of the well-established principle granting a person the right to counsel of one's choice, this disqualification procedure will only be used in extreme circumstances, such as where an attorney has taken some action to improperly or unlawfully impede or obstruct the investigation. It is essential that the interviewing officer have sufficient facts to support such allegations.

6. The provisions referring to "attorneys" apply to other representatives (non-attorneys) who represent witnesses or taxpayers.

25.5.5.5.1 INTERVIEWING THE WITNESS (04-30-1999)

1. Upon learning that counsel represents both the taxpayer under investigation (or other interested party) and the summoned witness, the interviewing officer should give consideration to exploring with the attorney, prior to the interview of the witness, whether the attorney realizes that his representation of both the subject of the investigation and the witness may be a conflict of interest.

2.   If, after discussing the potential conflict of interest with the attorney, the question is not resolved, the interviewing officer should ask the witness these questions at the beginning of the interview:

   A. Do you wish the attorney to be present during the questioning?
   B. Did you hire the attorney for this purpose?
   C. Are you paying for the attorney's services, either alone or in conjunction with someone else? If the latter, do you know who?
   D. Do you know that the attorney also represents the taxpayer?
   E. Do you know that the attorney is being paid by the taxpayer (or some other person)?

3.   In those instances where the interviewing officer becomes aware of the potential conflict of interest during the interview, he/she should explore the issue by asking the questions listed. In some situations it may be appropriate for the interviewing officer to tell the witness that in the view of the Service, the interest of the taxpayer under investigation conflicts with that of the witness.

4.   After disclosure of the dual or multiple representation has been made, if the witness unequivocally states that he/she wishes the attorney in question to represent him/her and that he/she is utilizing the services of the attorney in this matter, then the interview should proceed.

5.   However, if the witness states that he/she does not wish to retain that attorney because of the possible conflict of interest, then the witness should be given the opportunity of either proceeding with the interview without an attorney present or adjourning the interview to a specific future date that affords the witness a reasonable amount of time to hire another attorney. The witness should be advised that his/her failure to comply with the summons may result in a recommendation to the Department of Justice that a summons enforcement proceeding be initiated.

25.5.5.5.2   OBSTRUCTION OF INTERVIEW (04-30-1999)

1. If the interviewing officer has reason to anticipate that an attorney will improperly impede or obstruct the questioning of a witness, he/she should consult with Associate Area Counsel prior to the interview with respect to the manner of conducting the questioning.

2. Speculation that the objective of the investigation might be frustrated is insufficient grounds upon which to seek disqualification of an attorney. The fact that the attorney for the summoned witness also represents the taxpayer (or other interested party) does not provide a basis for concluding that the presence of such attorney would obstruct the investigation.

3. Thus, the mere potential for obstruction is generally an insufficient basis to justify a recommendation for disqualification of an attorney. There must be active obstruction by an attorney before disqualification will be sought. A suit to disqualify an attorney for obstruction will be undertaken only where the facts clearly indicate that he/she has actively impeded the investigation.

4.   Unjustifiable obstruction by an attorney may take a variety of forms. It is, therefore, impossible to set forth the precise factual circumstances under which the Government would ask a court to disqualify an attorney as counsel for a third-party witness.

5.   The following is an example of a circumstance which may provide the basis for a recommendation for the institution of litigation to seek the disqualification of an attorney:

> Taxpayer and third-party witness are both represented by the same attorney. The witness is summoned to testify. The attorney refuses to permit the witness to answer questions for other than legitimate reasons or disrupts the questioning by repeatedly making frivolous objections to the questions, or asserts frivolous claims of privilege or defenses on behalf of the witness to delay the investigation, or so disrupts the interview that the interviewing officer, with due diligence and perseverance, is unable to proceed with the interview. [Backer v. Commissioner.] This is not intended to suggest that there is anything inherently wrong in claiming the Fifth Amendment privilege.

A careful distinction must be drawn between situations in which the proper remedy is to compel the witness to answer and those in which the attorney may be disqualified because of this conduct. The latter is an extreme remedy which will only be sought in very unusual circumstances, as courts are reluctant to deprive a person of his/her choice of attorney. Associate Area Counsel, therefore, will make a considered determination on a case-by-case basis prior to seeking disqualification of an attorney.

25.5.5.5.3 SUSPENSION OF INTERVIEW (10-04-2006)

1.   If the interview is suspended because of the attorney's actions, the witness should be given the opportunity to hire another attorney within a reasonable period of time or proceed without an attorney. If the witness declines either to proceed without an attorney or retain a new one within a reasonable period of time, the witness should be informed that a summons enforcement proceeding and an action to disqualify the attorney will be recommended.

2.   After suspending an interview, the interviewing officer will consult with his/her manager. If the manager agrees with the interviewing officer's view that the facts are appropriate for litigation, a request will be made to Associate Area Counsel that they recommend to the Department of Justice that it seek summons enforcement and disqualification of the attorney.

3.   Suspension of an interview should be made judiciously in view of the time delays in the investigation that may be caused by such action.

4.   A record should be made of the circumstances in each instance where an interview is suspended because of dual representation or obstruction by an attorney. The interviewing officer should also have a verbatim transcript of the interview (if possible) so that the factual allegations concerning the attorney's conduct at the interview may be proven.

Note: The Service can have a court reporter present at a summoned interview.

25.5.5.5.4 Procedures for Exclusion of Attorney Prior to Interview of Witness (04-30-1999)

1. Where an individual taxpayer under investigation attempts to appear with a summoned witness as the witness' attorney, the witness should be told that the taxpayer/attorney is the person under investigation and that he/she will not be allowed to be present during the questioning. The witness should be given the opportunity of either proceeding with the interview without the taxpayer present or to adjourn the interview to a specific future date in order to afford the witness an opportunity to secure the services of another attorney. If the witness refuses to either proceed with the interview without the attorney's representations or to adjourn for the purpose of obtaining a new representative, the interview will be terminated and a request will be made to Associate Area Counsel for judicial enforcement of the summons and exclusion of the taxpayer from representing the witness.

2. A witness may appear pursuant to a summons accompanied by an attorney who also represents the taxpayer (or other interested party) where the taxpayer (or other interested party) has already made exculpatory statements to the Service alleging that the witness was criminally responsible for circumstances to be discussed during the interview. In this instance, the witness will be told that the attorney also represents the taxpayer (or other interested party) and that the agent believes that an irreconcilable conflict of interest exists which could prejudice the investigation. The witness should then be given the opportunity of either proceeding with the interview without the attorney present or adjourning the interview to secure the services of another attorney. If the witness insists upon retaining the same attorney despite the assertion of a conflict of interest, the interviewing officer will terminate the interview and a request will be made to Associate Area Counsel for judicial enforcement of the summons and exclusion of the attorney.

3. Refer to IRM 25.5.5.4.8(1) in this handbook for a discussion of other situations involving the exclusion of other persons from an interview.

25.5.5.5.5 Excluding a Taxpayer or a Taxpayer's Representative from the Interview of a Summoned Third Party (10-04-2006)

1. Except as noted below in IRM 25.5.5.5.7(1)-(2), neither the taxpayer under investigation nor his or her representative has a legal right to be present at the summoned interview of a third-party witness, even where a privileged relationship may exist between the taxpayer and the third-party witness. Therefore, the Service may bar those persons from the interview. The only rights a taxpayer and the representative have regarding a third-party summons are to petition to quash the summons under IRC 7609(b)(2) and to intervene in a summons enforcement suit pursuant to IRC 7609(b)(1). Any objections to the summoned information or claims of privilege should be raised in those proceedings.

2.   Where a third-party witness has a fiduciary responsibility or an ethical duty to the taxpayer to assert relevant privileges, such as the attorney-client privilege or tax practitioner privilege under IRC 7525, the Service is not obligated to permit the taxpayer or his counsel to attend the summoned third-party interview.

NOTE

In this instruction to field personnel, the IRS requires that the potential for conflict of interest be brought to the attention of both counsel and the witness (see IRM 25.5.5.5.1 regarding an attorney representing a summoned witness as well as the taxpayer under investigation). The interview is to proceed, however, if neither of them is concerned about that potential. Is the IRS effectively removing itself from a role as arbiter of conflict of interest in these situations, leaving this issue wholly to counsel and the witness? Is this proper? Is the interest of the IRS adequately served so long as the presence of counsel does not "impede or obstruct" the investigation? In what circumstances does this instruction to field personnel *require* termination of an interview. Why the distinction?

6.   *Transactions Between the Lawyer and His Client*

A lawyer must be sure that all transactions with his clients are "fair and reasonable" to the client. Certain situations, however, present inherent conflicts of interest between the lawyer and the client such that Model Rule 1.8 identifies "suspect" transactions that are strictly prohibited or permitted only after satisfying specified requirements. As you study the rule, focus on the situations that might arise in a tax lawyer's practice. For example, could a tax lawyer structure a transaction on behalf of a client and then invest his own money in it? Could he also receive a percentage of the equity in exchange for his services? Later, if the transaction is challenged by the IRS, can he represent both his interests and the interests of his clients in the administrative process? In court? If so, can the clients give him a contingent fee arrangement in payment of his audit and litigation services?

Rule 1.8 Conflict of Interest: Current Clients: Specific Rules
    (a) A lawyer shall not enter into a business transaction with a client or knowingly acquire an ownership, possessory, security or other pecuniary interest adverse to a client unless:
        (1) the transaction and terms on which the lawyer acquires the interest are fair and reasonable to the client and are fully disclosed and transmitted in writing in a manner that can be reasonably understood by the client;
        (2) the client is advised in writing of the desirability of seeking and is given a reasonable opportunity to seek the advice of independent legal counsel on the transaction; and

(3) the client gives informed consent, in a writing signed by the client, to the essential terms of the transaction and the lawyer's role in the transaction, including whether the lawyer is representing the client in the transaction.

(b) A lawyer shall not use information relating to representation of a client to the disadvantage of the client unless the client gives informed consent, except as permitted or required by these Rules.

(c) A lawyer shall not solicit any substantial gift from a client, including a testamentary gift, or prepare on behalf of a client an instrument giving the lawyer or a person related to the lawyer any substantial gift unless the lawyer or other recipient of the gift is related to the client. For purposes of this paragraph, related persons include a spouse, child, grandchild, parent, grandparent or other relative or individual with whom the lawyer or the client maintains a close, familial relationship.

(d) Prior to the conclusion of representation of a client, a lawyer shall not make or negotiate an agreement giving the lawyer literary or media rights to a portrayal or account based in substantial part on information relating to the representation.

(e) A lawyer shall not provide financial assistance to a client in connection with pending or contemplated litigation, except that:

(1) a lawyer may advance court costs and expenses of litigation, the repayment of which may be contingent on the outcome of the matter; and

(2) a lawyer representing an indigent client may pay court costs and expenses of litigation on behalf of the client.

(f) A lawyer shall not accept compensation for representing a client from one other than the client unless:

(1) the client gives informed consent;

(2) there is no interference with the lawyer's independence of professional judgment or with the client-lawyer relationship; and

(3) information relating to representation of a client is protected as required by Rule 1.6.

(g) A lawyer who represents two or more clients shall not participate in making an aggregate settlement of the claims of or against the clients, or in a criminal case an aggregated agreement as to guilty or nolo contendere pleas, unless each client gives informed consent, in a writing signed by the client. The lawyer's disclosure shall include the existence and nature of all the claims or pleas involved and of the participation of each person in the settlement.

(h) A lawyer shall not:

(1) make an agreement prospectively limiting the lawyer's liability to a client for malpractice unless the client is independently represented in making the agreement; or

(2) settle a claim or potential claim for such liability with an unrepresented client or former client unless that person is advised in writing of the desirability of seeking and is given a reasonable opportunity to seek the advice of independent legal counsel in connection therewith.

(i) A lawyer shall not acquire a proprietary interest in the cause of action or subject matter of litigation the lawyer is conducting for a client, except that the lawyer may:

(1) acquire a lien authorized by law to secure the lawyer's fee or expenses; and

(2) contract with a client for a reasonable contingent fee in a civil case.

(j) A lawyer shall not have sexual relations with a client unless a consensual sexual relationship existed between them when the client-lawyer relationship commenced.

(k) While lawyers are associated in a firm, a prohibition in the foregoing paragraphs (a) through (i) that applies to any one of them shall apply to all of them.

NOTES

1.   Circular 230 provides that a practitioner may not charge "an unconscionable fee" for representing a client in a matter before the Internal Revenue Service." §10.27. It does not define unconscionable fee. Model Rule 1.5 prevents a lawyer from charging a fee that is unreasonable. Why is it necessary for Circular 230 to regulate the amount of fees?

2.   In a notice of final rulemaking (September 26, 2007) regarding Circular 230, Treasury repeated its belief that restrictions on contingent fees are necessary to discourage return positions that exploit the audit selection process. Circular 230 provides that a practitioner may not charge a contingent fee for preparing an original return. A contingent arrangement may be entered into, however, for services "in connection with the Service's examination of, or challenge to — (i) an original tax return; or (ii) an amended return or claim for refund or credit where the amended return or claim for refund or credit was filed within 120 days of the taxpayer receiving a written notice of the examination or, or a written challenge to the original tax return." A contingent fee is also permitted regarding "a claim for credit or refund filed solely in connection with the determination of statutory interest or penalties," and for "any judicial proceeding arising under the Internal Revenue Code." §10.27(b). Why would the Service want to regulate contingent fees? For a general discussion of the ethics of contingent fees, see ABA Formal Opinion 94-389 (1994).

3.   Under the AICPA Code of Professional Ethics, a CPA generally may not charge a contingent fee. However, an exception is made for tax matters if the results are "determined based on the results of judicial proceedings or the findings of governmental agencies." AICPA Code of Professional Conduct, Rule 302. This rule does not, however, permit a fee for tax return preparation to depend on the amount of tax "saved." Interpretation under Rule 302(b).

B.   Maintaining the Client's Confidences — Disclosure Problems

1.   General

In considering the issues of confidentiality and disclosure there are three Model Rules that you should carefully consider. Relevant text from these rules is set forth next.

Rule 1.6 Confidentiality of Information

(a) A lawyer shall not reveal information relating to the representation of a client unless the client gives informed consent, the disclosure is impliedly authorized in order to carry out the representation or the disclosure is permitted by paragraph (b).

(b) A lawyer may reveal information relating to the representation of a client to the extent the lawyer reasonably believes necessary:

(1) to prevent reasonably certain death or substantial bodily harm;

(2) to prevent the client from committing a crime or fraud that is reasonably certain to result in substantial injury to the financial interests or property of another and in furtherance of which the client has used or is using the lawyer's services;

(3) to prevent, mitigate or rectify substantial injury to the financial interests or property of another that is reasonably certain to result or has resulted from the client's commission of a crime or fraud in furtherance of which the client has used the lawyer's services;

(4) to secure legal advice about the lawyer's compliance with these Rules;

(5) to establish a claim or defense on behalf of the lawyer in a controversy between the lawyer and the client, to establish a defense to a criminal charge or civil claim against the lawyer based upon conduct in which the client was involved, or to respond to allegations in any proceeding concerning the lawyer's representation of the client; or

(6) to comply with other law or a court order.

The following comment to Model Rule 1.6 explains the current duty to disclose under subsection (b)(1):

> Although the public interest is usually best served by a strict rule requiring lawyers to preserve the confidentiality of information relating to the representation of their clients, the confidentiality rule is subject to limited exceptions. Paragraph (b)(1) recognizes the overriding value of life and physical integrity and permits disclosure reasonably necessary to prevent reasonably certain death or substantial bodily harm. Such harm is reasonably certain to occur if it will be suffered imminently or if there is a present and substantial threat that a person will suffer such harm at a later date if the lawyer fails to take action necessary to eliminate the threat. . . .

With respect to (b)(2), the comment provides:

> Paragraph (b)(2) is a limited exception to the rule of confidentiality that permits the lawyer to reveal information to the extent necessary to enable affected persons or appropriate authorities to prevent the client from committing a crime or fraud, as defined in Rule 1.0(d), that is reasonably certain to result in substantial injury to the financial or property interests of another and in furtherance of which the client has used or is using the lawyer's services. Such a serious abuse of the client-lawyer relationship by the client forfeits the protection of this Rule. The client can, of course, prevent such disclosure by refraining from the wrongful conduct. Although paragraph (b)(2) does not require the lawyer to reveal the client's misconduct, the lawyer may not counsel or assist the client in conduct the lawyer knows is criminal or fraudulent.

See Rule 1.2(d). See also Rule 1.16 with respect to the lawyer's obligation or right to withdraw from the representation of the client in such circumstances, and Rule 1.13(c), which permits the lawyer, where the client is an organization, to reveal information relating to the representation in limited circumstances.

The following comment is also made with respect to disclosure otherwise required or authorized:

Paragraph (b) permits but does not require the disclosure of information relating to a client's representation to accomplish the purposes specified in paragraphs (b)(1) through (b)(6). In exercising the discretion conferred by this Rule, the lawyer may consider such factors as the nature of the lawyer's relationship with the client and with those who might be injured by the client, the lawyer's own involvement in the transaction and factors that may extenuate the conduct in question. A lawyer's decision not to disclose as permitted by paragraph (b) does not violate this Rule. Disclosure may be required, however, by other Rules. Some Rules require disclosure only if such disclosure would be permitted by paragraph (b). See Rules 1.2(d), 4.1(b), 8.1 and 8.3. Rule 3.3, on the other hand, requires disclosure in some circumstances regardless of whether such disclosure is permitted by this Rule. See Rule 3.3(c).

Model Rules 3.3 and 4.1 provide as follows:

Rule 3.3 Candor Toward the Tribunal

(a) A lawyer shall not knowingly:

(1) make a false statement of fact or law to a tribunal or fail to correct a false statement of material fact or law previously made to the tribunal by the lawyer;

(2) fail to disclose to the tribunal legal authority in the controlling jurisdiction known to the lawyer to be directly adverse to the position of the client and not disclosed by opposing counsel; or

(3) offer evidence that the lawyer knows to be false. If a lawyer, the lawyer's client, or a witness called by the lawyer, has offered material evidence and the lawyer comes to know of its falsity, the lawyer shall take reasonable remedial measures, including, if necessary, disclosure to the tribunal. A lawyer may refuse to offer evidence, other than the testimony of a defendant in a criminal matter, that the lawyer reasonably believes is false.

(b) A lawyer who represents a client in an adjudicative proceeding and who knows that a person intends to engage, is engaging or has engaged in criminal or fraudulent conduct related to the proceeding shall take reasonable remedial measures, including, if necessary, disclosure to the tribunal.

(c) The duties stated in paragraphs (a) and (b) continue to the conclusion of the proceeding, and apply even if compliance requires disclosure of information otherwise protected by Rule 1.6.

(d) In an ex parte proceeding, a lawyer shall inform the tribunal of all material facts known to the lawyer that will enable the tribunal to make an informed decision, whether or not the facts are adverse.

Rule 4.1 Truthfulness in Statements to Others

In the course of representing a client a lawyer shall not knowingly:

(a) make a false statement of material fact or law to a third person; or

(b) fail to disclose a material fact to a third person when disclosure is necessary to avoid assisting a criminal or fraudulent act by a client, unless disclosure is prohibited by Rule 1.6.

When the lawyer acts as advocate, she will face situations in which she and her client differ as to the advisability of disclosure of confidences and secrets. In some of these cases, the lawyer may feel quite strongly that disclosure should, and indeed must, be made. If the client disagrees, what course may (must) the lawyer pursue? You will note that Rule 1.6 moves in the direction of requiring confidentiality, while Rules 3.3(a)(3) and 4.1 move in the direction of disclosure. This tension is at the root of the issues we now address.

As we begin this discussion, you should recognize that the ethical obligation of confidentiality is substantially broader than is the evidentiary privilege that protects attorney-client communications from compulsory disclosure. This distinction will be developed more fully below.

When the lawyer deals with a tribunal, Model Rule 3.3(a)(2) imposes a special obligation of disclosure. The application of this principle is illustrated by the following ABA opinion.

ABA Informal Opinion 84-1505

(1984)

DUTY TO DISCLOSE ADVERSE LEGAL AUTHORITY

A lawyer who learns of a controlling court decision which may be interpreted as adverse to his client's position must promptly advise the court, even though the issue is not presently under consideration but may be revived at some later stage in the proceedings.

A trial court has denied defendants' motions to dismiss in a case of first impression interpreting a recently enacted statute. There was considerable analogous case law supporting the conclusion of the trial court. Some months later, during the pendency of the case, an appellate court in another part of the state, not supervisory of the trial court, handed down a decision interpreting the exact statute at issue in the motions to dismiss. The appellate decision, which controls the trial court until its own appellate court passes on the precise question involved, can be interpreted two ways, one of which is directly contrary to the holding of the trial court in denying the motions to dismiss.

Plaintiff's lawyer has learned of the recent decision and asks whether he has a duty to disclose it to the court. He notes that the particular issue is not presently under consideration in the case but may well be revived because the prior ruling was not a final, appealable order. The inquirer asks when, if he has a duty, must he make disclosure to the court. Must he do so immediately or may he await the conclusion of the appeals process in the other case and the revival of the precise issue by the defendants? Finally, the inquirer asks whether disclosure would constitute a concession that there are no reasonable distinctions between the case at bar and the decision of the appeals court.

The committee believes, under the circumstances presented, that plaintiff's lawyer must disclose the newly discovered authority to the court and that he must do so promptly. Of course, he may challenge the soundness of the other decision, attempt to distinguish it from the case at bar, or present other reasons why the court should not follow or even be influenced by it.

Rule 3.3(a)[(2)]* of the Model Rules of Professional Conduct provides "A lawyer shall not knowingly fail to disclose to the tribunal legal authority in the controlling jurisdiction known to the lawyer to be directly adverse to the position of the client and not disclosed by opposing counsel." This provision is virtually identical to its predecessor, DR 7-106(B)(1) of the Model Code of Professional Responsibility. Both provisions continue essentially unchanged the theme of Canon 22 of the Canons of Professional Ethics adopted by the American Bar Association in 1908.

Under Canon 22, this committee issued two opinions bearing on the question presented. In 1935 the committee decided that a lawyer has a duty to tell the court in a pending case of decisions, unknown to his adversary, that are adverse to his client's contentions. We said, "He may, of course, after doing so, challenge the soundness of the decisions or present reasons which he believes would warrant the court in not following them in the pending case." In 1949, the committee, in Formal Opinion 280, first interpreted Opinion 146 to limit the duty of disclosure to only those decisions which were "directly adverse." We then continued:

> We would not confine the Opinion to "controlling authorities" — i.e., those decisive of the pending case — but ... would apply it to a decision directly adverse to any proposition of law on which the lawyer expressly relies, which would reasonably be considered important by the judge sitting on the case.

The committee added: "A case of doubt should obviously be resolved in favor of the disclosure, or by a statement disclaiming the discussion of all conflicting decisions." We felt the duty should be interpreted sensibly so as not to produce absurd results, but concluded that "Where the question is a new or novel one, such as the constitutionality *or construction of a statute, on which there is a dearth of authority*, the lawyer's duty may be broader." (Emphasis added.) We concluded with this test:

> Is the decision which opposing counsel has overlooked one which the court should clearly consider in deciding the case? Would a reasonable judge properly feel that a

---

* [The applicable rule is now Rule 3.3(a)(2). It was previously designated 3.3(a)(3). — Eds.]

lawyer who advanced, as the law, a proposition adverse to the undisclosed decision, was lacking in candor and fairness to him? Might the judge consider himself misled by an implied representation that the lawyer knew of no adverse authority

In the question presented in this inquiry, the recent case is clearly "legal authority in the controlling jurisdiction" and, indeed, is even controlling of the trial court until such time as its own appellate court speaks to the issue. Under one interpretation of the decision, it is clearly "directly adverse to the position of the client." And it involves the "construction of a statute on which there is a dearth of authority."

The committee believes that the court must be advised promptly. Model Rule 3.3[(c)]* provides that the duty of disclosure continues "to the conclusion of the proceeding." This, according to the comment, fixes an outside time limit on the duty: "The conclusion of the proceeding is a reasonably definite point for the termination of the obligation." There is no such precision in the Model Code. DR 7-106(B) fixes the duty on a lawyer "in presenting a matter to a tribunal. . . ." The committee believes the duty continues in the circumstances here presented under either guide, where the same case is still pending in the same court, notwithstanding that the precise issue is not presently being considered by the court.

While there conceivably might be circumstances in which a lawyer might be justified in not drawing the court's attention to the new authority until a later time in the proceedings, here no delay can be sanctioned. The issue is potentially dispositive of the entire litigation. His duty as an officer of the court to assist in the efficient and fair administration of justice compels plaintiff's lawyer to make the disclosure immediately.

In a strikingly similar case, Seidman v. American Express Company, 523 F. Supp. 1107 (E.D. Pa. 1981), the court, applying DR 7-106(B)(1), came to the same conclusion on the duty to disclose as does the committee in this opinion. There a trial court commended defendant's lawyer for calling attention, after oral argument, to a recent case that severely undercut the position defendant had taken at oral argument, and consequently denied defendant's motion for summary judgment. See also Miller v. Aaacon Auto Transport Inc., 447 F. Supp. 1201 (S.D. Fla. 1978); United States v. Slodov, 79-1 USTC ¶9215; vacated and remanded on other grounds, 675 F.2d 808, 82-1 USTC ¶9323 (6th Cir. 1982).

The inquirer should understand that the ABA Model Rules of Professional Conduct may not have been adopted in his jurisdiction, and, accordingly, he should review the professional responsibility code and relevant law in his jurisdiction.

---

* [The applicable rule is now Rule 3.3(c). It was previously designated 3.3(b). — EDS.]

NOTES

1. Under Model Rule 3.3(a)(2), a lawyer must not "fail to disclose to the tribunal legal authority in the controlling jurisdiction known to the lawyer to be directly adverse to the position of the client and not disclosed by opposing counsel." This does not require the lawyer to make a completely "disinterested exposition of the law." It simply requires the advocate to disclose directly adverse authority so that the tribunal can consider all of the legal premises properly applicable to the case. In Stamm International Corp. v. Commissioner, 90 T.C. 315 (1988), the Tax Court upheld a settlement resulting in a $700,000 loss to the Service that apparently resulted from the IRS counsel's lack of knowledge. A court may even grant the lawyer the benefit of the doubt, as in Chew et al. v. KPMG et al., 407 F.Supp. 2d 790, 802 n.13 (2006), in which the court observed:

> the failure of [some of the] defendants to acknowledge the holdings in Bridas [a relevant 5th Circuit case] raises a concern. Under Rule 3.3(a)(3) of the Mississippi Rules of Professional Conduct, "[a] lawyer shall not knowingly . . . fail to disclose to the tribunal legal authority in the controlling jurisdiction known to the lawyer to be directly adverse to the position of the client. . . ." The [defendants] were, or reasonably should have been, on notice of the holdings in Bridas because that case was cited in a slip opinion which was attached as Exhibit "M" to the [defendants'] Memorandum of Law in Support of Renewed Motion to Dismiss the Action and Compel Arbitration. Giving the [defendants] the benefit of the doubt, the Court will assume that the failure to cite Bridas in the briefs was an excusable oversight.

However, sometimes counsel's conduct is determined to clearly cross the line. In Pierotti v. Torian, 96 Cal. Rptr. 2d 553, 563 (2000), the court sanctioned the lawyer and the client each $15,000 where the conduct included "utter failure to discuss the most pertinent legal authority." In addition, the court in *Pierotti* ordered the two lawyers to forward a copy of the opinion, sanctioning them to the State Bar.

When is an omission a mistake that can be "ignored," and when is it a violation? What factors would likely be relevant in making this determination?

2. ABA Opinion 94-386R holds that it is unethical for an attorney to cite an unpublished judicial opinion in a forum court that has a rule prohibiting reference to unpublished opinions. Consider §6110(k)(3), which prohibits the "use" or "citation as precedent" of private letter rulings. (Note that Treas. Reg. §1.6662-4(d) includes letter rulings in its list of sources for "substantial authority.") Practitioners routinely cite letter rulings in ruling requests and briefs and the Supreme Court has even done so. See, for instance, Rowan Companies, Inc. v. Commissioner, 452 U.S. 247 (1981). Is this ethical conduct? For the possible uses of such rulings, see James P. Holden & Michael S. Novey, Legitimate Uses of Letter Rulings Issued to Other Taxpayers, A Reply to Gerald Portnoy, 37 Tax Law. 337 (1984).

3. In response to the corporate scandals of the 1990s and early 2000s, Congress passed Sarbanes-Oxley in 2002, which, along with new Securities and

Exchange Commission regulations increased the burden on lawyers and accountants to police client behavior and report misconduct. The ABA appointed its own task force to:

> examine systemic issues relating to corporate responsibility arising out of the unexpected and traumatic bankruptcy of Enron and other Enron-like situations which have shaken confidence in the effectiveness of the governance and disclosure systems applicable to public companies in the United States. The Task Force will examine the framework of laws and regulations and ethical principles governing the role of lawyers, executive officers, directors, and other key participants. The issues will be studies in the context of the system of checks and balances designed to enhance the public trust in corporate integrity and responsibility. The Task Force will allow the ABA to contribute its perspective to the dialogue now occurring among regulators, legislators, major financial markets and other organizations focusing on legislative and regulatory reform to improve corporate responsibility.

Report of the American Bar Association Task Force on Corporate Responsibility, Part I (March 31, 2003). Ultimately, in August 2003 the ABA amended Rules 1.6 (regarding disclosure) and 1.13 (regarding the organization as client) to enhance and facilitate certain disclosure obligations of the lawyer. For a review of some of the impacts of Sarbanes-Oxley and the related changes to Rules 1.6 and 1.13, see Beverley Earle & Gerald Madek, The New World of Risk for Corporate Attorneys and Their Boards Post-Sarbanes-Oxley: An Assessment of Impact and a Prescription for Action, 2 Berkeley Bus. L. J. 185 (2005).

Specifically, in Rule 1.6 the circumstances under which a lawyer may disclose confidential client information was expanded to cover cases in which disclosure would (1) prevent crime or fraud "that is reasonably certain to result in substantial injury to the financial interests or property of another and in furtherance of which the client has used or is using the lawyer's services," and (2) "prevent, mitigate or rectify substantial injury to the financial interests or property of another that is reasonably certain to result or has resulted from the client's commission of a crime or fraud in furtherance of which the client has used the lawyer's services." See Rule 1.6(b)(2) and (3). Originally Rule 1.6 allowed disclosure only to (1) prevent a criminal act that would likely result in death or substantial bodily harm, (2) allow the lawyer to establish a defense (for the lawyer) in certain contexts. How significant are the expansions in Rule 1.6? How are they related to Sarbanes-Oxley and the role of the lawyer as gatekeeper? Why might these changes be particularly relevant for tax lawyers? How might you expect lawyer-client relations to change in the face of these new rules?

As noted, Rule 1.13 was also amended to reflect the changing role of the lawyer. In particular the question of "who" is the client when the lawyer is retained (or employed) by an organization was clarified to facilitate certain disclosure and gatekeeping duties. The special case of the organization as client is taken up in Chapter 6.

In order to determine whether the disclosure obligation of Model Rule 3.3(a)(2) is applicable in any circumstance, the lawyer must consider whether she is dealing with a tribunal. If a contested matter is pending before the IRS, is the IRS to be viewed as a tribunal? Must adverse authority be disclosed to it? ABA Opinion 314, although superseded insofar as tax return accuracy is concerned, remains effective as guidance in other matters covered in the opinion. Opinion 314 concludes that the IRS "is neither a true tribunal, nor even a quasi-judicial institution." This conclusion serves as the foundation for the opinion's holding that "as an advocate before a Service which itself represents the adversary point of view, where his client's case is fairly arguable, a lawyer is under no duty to disclose its weaknesses, any more than he would be to make such a disclosure to a brother lawyer."

How solid is Opinion 314's conclusion that the IRS is not a tribunal? What would be the consequences of a contrary conclusion? The following article appears to have been written on the premise that the IRS is a tribunal and that there thus exists a duty of disclosure under Model Rule 3.3(a)(3).

In the following excerpt, the author explores the limitations of *general* rules of professional conduct, analyzing problems of disclosure and client confidentiality in a tax setting.

William Popkin, Client-Lawyer Confidentiality*

59 Tex. L. Rev. 755, 775-786 (1981)

The political implications of confidentiality rules are nowhere more apparent than in disputes between the individual and the government, of which tax disputes with the Internal Revenue Service are a good example. A significant body of opinion holds that the relationship between the individual and the government in tax disputes creates a greater obligation of individual disclosure than is required in other types of litigation. The argument, in effect, is that the confidentiality rules should take account of the balance of power between the disputants and tilt it toward the government. If a professional code should not consider such factors, however, then the Model Rules should not make any special provision for tax disputes, but should instead leave the adoption of such provisions to other institutions. I will test this hypothesis first by explaining how the Model Rules would address some typical disclosure problems in tax practice, and then by considering who is competent to adopt special confidentiality rules in tax disputes.

A. PARTICULAR FACT SITUATIONS

1. False Claim on Audit.   A lawyer represents a client who has claimed a deduction for expenses of a two week trip to Europe. After the audit begins, the lawyer discovers that the client spent one of the two weeks on vacation. The law requires an allocation between deductible business and nondeductible personal expenses. The government is challenging the deduction on different grounds, however, arguing that the deduction is improper because of the small amount of time spent on business each day. The government is unaware that one-half of the days were spent on vacation.

Under the Model Rules, the lawyer's obligation to a tribunal prohibits his filing a claim unless there is a reasonable basis for doing so. [Model Rule 3.1] If a misrepresentation occurs while the lawyer is representing the client, the lawyer must disclose the true facts if the client will not. [Model Rule 3.3(a)(3)] In the context of a tax audit, this means that the lawyer cannot argue that an entire expenditure was a deductible travel expense when he knows that a portion was a nondeductible vacation expense; if the lawyer innocently makes this argument, he must upon discovering his error disclose the facts necessary to correct any prior misrepresentation. Even without establishing a greater obligation of disclosure in tax disputes, therefore, the Model Rules require disclosure in this type of situation.

The Model Rules do not explain how a lawyer should deal with a tax obligation unrelated to the claim that is the subject of litigation. For example, suppose that the taxpayer clearly owes tax because entertainment expenses are overstated, but the government's audit is limited to disputed travel expenses. A number of commentators have argued that the claim in dispute is the entire tax obligation, not the issue that is the subject of attention. In this view, denial of an obligation to pay disputed travel expenses is in effect a denial that any taxes are due, at least for that year. Professor Bittker has suggested that a broad obligation of disclosure in this situation would not impose different obligations in tax cases than in other disputes. He analogizes this situation to a lawsuit in which a client who sues for nonpayment after delivery of goods fails to reveal that the goods have not been delivered, when the only defense raised by the defendant is that the goods are defective.

This analogy does not seem particularly apt, however. A suit for payment after delivery of goods necessarily asserts that the goods have been delivered. The more apt analogy is to ask whether a lawyer representing a plaintiff suing for the purchase price of delivered goods must disclose that his client owes the defendant an unrelated debt, even though the defendant has not asserted the debt as a set-off. As long as the lawyer is not required to reveal wrongful acts generally, he should not be required to disclose an error unrelated to the issue in dispute.

Determining what constitutes a "related" issue will admittedly be difficult in some cases. Arguably, the government's claim that the time spent each day on business was negligible is not the same as claiming that some days were spent on exclusively personal pursuits. However, implicit in the lawyer's defending against the government's claim that the time spent each day on business was negligible is the assertion that at least some business transpired daily. The lawyer is not similarly tainted with an assertion of a falsehood if he remains silent about an improper deduction of entertainment expenses not raised by the government auditor.

2. Revealing Facts on Audit.   The government audits a client's tax return and argues that an alleged business trip to Europe was for personal purposes. The lawyer is aware that the taxpayer visited relatives during the trip, a relevant but not dispositive fact that tends to show that the visit was personal.

Under the Final Draft of the Model Rules, the lawyer is not permitted to disclose material facts in this context. [Model Rule 1.6] Unless there is a greater obligation to disclose in tax disputes, the lawyer is under no obligation to disclose material facts tending to support the government's position.

3. Misrepresentations by the Client on Audit.   When the government alleges that a business trip to Europe was for personal purposes, the client denies having visited relatives there. The lawyer knows that the facts are otherwise.

The Model Rules require the disclosure of all facts, whether dispositive or not, [Model Rule 3.3(a), (c)] if they are misrepresented by the client in the course of the lawyer's representation. The Model Rules, therefore, require disclosure even if there is no greater disclosure obligation in tax disputes.

4. False Tax Returns and Revealing Facts on a Tax Return.   When a lawyer prepares a tax return, he may face the same issues that arise in proceedings before a tribunal: false claims, misrepresentations, and disclosure of material facts. The Model Rules prohibit a lawyer from knowingly advancing a false claim or knowingly making a misrepresentation in a return, but they do not require disclosure of material facts in the return. [Model Rule 3.1] What should the lawyer do if he discovers that the client has made a false claim or misrepresentation in a tax return? Must the lawyer disclose that fact, and does the answer to that question depend on whether the lawyer prepared the return or whether the lawyer is now representing the taxpayer on audit?

The principles already discussed essentially provide the answers to these questions. If the lawyer did not prepare the return and an audit has not begun, the question becomes whether the lawyer must disclose a client's prior wrongful act. The Model Rules permit disclosure only to rectify the consequences of a fraudulent act when the lawyer's services have been used in the commission of that act. [Model Rule 3.3] If the lawyer participates in an audit of the return, the Model Rules require disclosure of any false claim or misrepresentation made in the course of the lawyer's representation in the audit, whether or not deliberately wrongful and whether or not the lawyer prepared the return.

These questions also raise a new issue: whether a lawyer's preparation of the return imposes a disclosure obligation under the Model Rules if the lawyer does not represent the taxpayer on audit. The Rules require disclosure only if the return is considered the presentation of evidence to a tribunal. [Model Rule 3.3]

Characterizing a tax return as evidence presented to a tribunal seems farfetched, however. The last thing the taxpayer wants is to begin a dispute requiring resolution by adjudication. The return is best characterized as the culmination of the advice that the lawyer gave to the client. The exception to this characterization is a refund claim.

Such claims, by which the taxpayer affirmatively seeks a determination that the government owes him money, are analogous to commencement of litigation before a tribunal. The Model Rules should be read to require disclosure of false claims and misrepresentations presented in a refund claim prepared by the lawyer if the lawyer subsequently discovers an error.

B. HOW MUCH DISCLOSURE, AND WHO SHOULD DECIDE?

The foregoing discussion can be summarized as follows: Although they expand disclosure, the Model Rules do not clearly require disclosure in several important situations likely to arise in tax disputes. They do not require disclosure of material facts unless a misrepresentation has occurred in the course of an audit in which the lawyer has participated; they do not clearly require disclosure of tax obligations unrelated to the specific issues raised on audit; and they do not clearly require disclosure of false claims or misrepresentations in the absence of an audit when the lawyer has prepared the return. After examining the Model Rules, then, one might argue that lawyers should have greater disclosure obligations in tax disputes than the Rules require.

The argument for a greater disclosure obligation rests on three features of tax disputes. First, the individual's obligation to pay taxes is a special obligation, especially given the importance of citizen honesty in dealing with the government. Second, the volume of returns compared to the small percentage audited makes our tax system dependent upon taxpayer cooperation, especially in view of the taxpayer's control over the facts. Third, government officials who decide disputes are presumably impartial, not adversarial, and allowing taxpayers to play by the adversary rules gives them an unfair advantage.

The opposing view, adopted by an ABA opinion [314], is that the government is not unbiased. Furthermore, if the government needs facts, it can and does ask for them. Any special obligation to pay taxes must therefore yield, just as it does in most adjudication, to the need to protect the individual client.

Whatever the merits of the claim that taxes are a special obligation, the issue is how to adjust the balance of investigatory power between the individual and the agency. We must ask who has an advantage in the struggle between the litigants and whether confidentiality rules should be modified to compensate for any such advantage. The political nature of these questions in the tax context becomes more clear by asking similar questions in the welfare adjudication context. Assume, for example, that the lawyer represents a welfare client who claims that the father of her child has left home and that the family is therefore eligible for Aid to Families with Dependent children (AFDC), or that the lawyer's client argues that she is eligible for disability benefits because she is totally unable to work. Must the lawyer reveal that the father visited the AFDC claimant in her home for two days after the beginning of the father's alleged "continued absence," or that the disabled individual worked for two days after the alleged onset of disability at another job? Neither fact is dispositive, but each is relevant to the government's disposition of the claim. Must the lawyer reveal a clear overpayment of AFDC or disability benefits made prior to the date on which the new claim would be effective, or is the lawyer's obligation limited to the facts and issues relevant to the new claim?

The answers to these questions depend on one's view of the impartiality of the hearing officers in income maintenance disputes, of the importance of professional loyalty for arguably defenseless welfare claimants, and, more generally, of how the power struggle between income maintenance claimants and the government should turn out. After considering these factors, one might favor greater disclosure than that required by a nonpoliticized professional code drafted on the assumption that litigants are more or less equally balanced. Similarly, the desirable amount of disclosure in tax disputes might differ depending on whether one viewed taxpayers as innocents set upon by the government or as schemers who take advantage of the government. The generally strong reactions that people have to the image of a welfare or tax cheater suggests how political these judgments are in both the welfare and tax contexts.

Given the political nature of these issues, it seems doubtful that either the bar or highest court of the state has the procedures or insight to draft specialized confidentiality rules. Their concerns will likely differ from the government's in tax matters because of their members' social backgrounds and client orientation, and because those organizations are unlikely to hold hearings exposing them to the government's concerns. In welfare cases, the organized bar and the government are likely to share a bias against recipients. Confidentiality rules should rest, therefore, on an assumption that the law is a product of more or less balanced political pressures. More politically sensitive institutions should be responsible for deciding whether or not the generally applicable confidentiality rules should apply in specialized areas.

At present, neither Congress nor the Department of Treasury, institutions that presumably are politically sensitive, has shown much interest in controlling tax advisers, much less in dealing with the problem of disclosure. Congress recently imposed penalties for negligent or willful understatement of taxes, and the Treasury proposed regulations controlling tax shelter advice expected to be disseminated to non-client investors. These regulations concern disclosure to a limited extent by requiring the tax shelter opinion to disclose all facts "which bear significantly on each important federal tax aspect" of the transaction. Their major thrust, however, lies in requiring the lawyer to exercise due diligence in determining relevant facts, to state the likely outcome of the transaction, and to issue the opinion only if the bulk of the advantages are more likely than not to be allowable. Outside of the tax shelter area, the Treasury imposes no greater disclosure obligations than does the Code of Professional Responsibility.

Whether greater disclosure could be required by the Treasury without legislative sanction, analogously to the rules recently imposed by the SEC, or only with legislative approval, as the ABA has argued with respect to the SEC rules, depends on how dramatically the proposal departs from generally accepted rules. In the tax context, for example, the more dramatic step of requiring disclosure of relevant facts in the absence of a misrepresentation might require legislative approval. The Treasury might, however, impose a more modest requirement to disclose prior misrepresentations made in a return prepared by a lawyer and tax obligations known to the lawyer but unrelated to the issues specifically in dispute. Agency rules might also deal with highly specialized problems, as in the tax shelter advice proposals. The important point is that those drafting a professional code should not be responsible for adjusting the code to fit the myriad political considerations affecting confidentiality rules in specific areas of practice.

NOTES

1.   Do you agree with Professor Popkin's conclusion that authors of a code of ethics should not attempt to tailor the rules to fit the "myriad political considerations" affecting confidentiality and disclosure in tax practice? Should the authors at least recognize special responsibilities that arise in a particular area of practice? If Congress and the Treasury have not acted up to the present time, can we assume that they will not act in the future?

2.   Should the fact that taxpayers (and sometimes their tax advisers) are pursuing aggressive and often abusive tax schemes support a "tax lawyer duty" to the system? For a discussion of this question following the decline of IRS enforcement activities after the Restructuring and Reform Act of 1998 and the accounting and tax scandals of the past decade, see Camilla E. Watson, Legislating Morality: The Duty to the Tax System Reconsidered, 51 Kan. L. Rev. 1197 (2003) (arguing that past efforts to rely on an "ideological" obligation to the tax system have been unsuccessful and that standards and penalties to be enforced by the IRS are critical).

3.   Why will disclosure to protect victims of client fraud erode client trust, whereas disclosure to facilitate collection of the attorney's fees or to establish his position in litigation with a client will not? Does this imply that as long as a client pays his attorney and does not complain about the competence of the attorney's services, the lawyer must not disclose the client's confidences?

Opinion 314, although denying that the lawyer has a duty to disclose to the IRS the weaknesses in a client's case, nonetheless holds that the lawyer may not mislead the IRS. Does this place the lawyer in a dilemma in some situations? If we assume that the lawyer is fully cognizant of all of the strengths and weaknesses of his client's case, it should be fairly easy for him to avoid both unnecessary disclosure of weaknesses and affirmative and deliberate misleading of the Service. However, life is seldom so well ordered. If the lawyer, honestly relying on facts as he believes them to be, makes his presentation to the Service only to learn later that the facts are significantly weaker than he thought them to be, may he (must he) advise the Service of this weakness? If he does not do so, will he be deliberately and affirmatively misleading the Service? Whose decision is this to make — the client's or the lawyer's Opinion 314 states that, where the client has misled the Service without the lawyer's knowledge or participation, the lawyer must (1) advise the client to correct the situation, and (2) if the client refuses, consider withdrawal, unless that act would itself violate confidentiality. Does this formulation place confidentiality, at least implicitly, in a position of primacy? What effect does the restriction "without the lawyer's . . . participation" have? If the lawyer, as in the previous situation, participated unwittingly in misleading the Service, does some other unexpressed set of rules apply?

Although the previous discussion of confidentiality and disclosure relates to the lawyer's dealings with tribunals and the Service, difficult questions also can arise concerning the disclosure obligation to private parties. What rules apply when a prospective client makes inquiry of a lawyer regarding the latter's availability to handle a particular matter, not knowing that the lawyer already represents an adverse interest? If the inquiring party would be tactically advantaged by the element of surprise, may the lawyer, after declining the proffered representation on grounds of conflict, notify the existing client of the inquiry? This very difficult and not uncommon problem is addressed in Stanley A. Kaplan, Confidential Information on Tender Offers: May It Be Disclosed?, 64 A.B.A. J. 619 (1978).

2.   The Evidentiary Privilege Distinguished

The ethical obligation of confidentiality extends to all confidences and secrets of the client, from whatever source derived. It exists whether or not the client has disclosed the same matter to other persons. It applies whether the lawyer is acting as adviser or advocate. It is thus pervasive and extensive. The attorney-client evidentiary privilege, on the other hand, is a rule of evidence that applies only in the context of controversies and it serves only to limit the information that can be extracted from the lawyer about communications between him and his client. Moreover, it is restricted in scope to those communications treated as confidential by the client.

The ethical obligation of confidentiality precludes only voluntary disclosure by a lawyer. Thus, if a court orders disclosure, the obligation is at an end, and disclosure must occur unless the information is protected by some more durable rule, such as the attorney-client privilege.

This book deals mainly with the ethical principle and the operation of the privilege is of more peripheral concern. Three cases, dealing with the privilege in the context of tax issues, are reproduced below. In the first, the Tenth Circuit holds that the privilege does not protect from disclosure under an IRS summons information concerning fees paid to a lawyer by a particular client. In the second case, the Seventh Circuit holds that §7525 (privilege extended to nonlawyer tax advisors) does not prevent disclosure of names in the context of summonses investigating compliance with tax shelter registration and list-keeping requirement of §6111 and §6112. In the third, the Supreme Court holds that communications from the taxpayer corporation's employees to its counsel, retained to investigate allegedly questionable payments, are not available to the IRS upon summons.

United States v. Hodgson

492 F.2d 1175 (10th Cir. 1974)

BREITENSTEIN, Circuit Judge. Talley, an IRS special agent in the Intelligence Division, was investigating the federal income tax liability of Leroy Dale Hines for the years 1967–1971. On October 16, 1972, he issued a summons to Paul Hodgson, a lawyer, requiring him to produce records of all charges to or in behalf of Hines during the years 1966–1971 for legal services and records of all moneys received from, or credited to, Hines for such services.

Hodgson responded to the summons, declined to produce the records or to testify, and asserted the attorney-client privilege. The United States and the special agent then petitioned for enforcement. See 26 U.S.C. §§7402(b) and 7604(a). Hodgson's answer, supported by his affidavit, admits possession of records reflecting receipts from Hines, and alleges that those records would disclose the general nature of the services rendered. The answer affirmatively says that the special agent was conducting a criminal investigation of Hines for the years in question and asserts the attorney-client privilege as a justification for refusal to respond. After two hearings at which the special agent was the only witness, the district court denied enforcement on the ground that the records and information sought were protected by the claimed privilege.

The question is whether the attorney-client privilege extends to the records and information sought from attorney Hodgson. In the area of federal income tax investigation the claim of privilege is controlled by federal law. Matters relating to receipt of fees from a client are not usually privileged. The reason is that the payment of a fee is not normally a matter of confidence or a communication. Absent confidentiality, the privilege does not apply.

Attorney Hodgson made a blanket claim of the privilege. A general refusal to cooperate is not enough. He must normally raise the privilege as to each record sought and each question asked so that at the enforcement hearing the court can rule with specificity. In the circumstances of the case at bar the records and information sought were not protected by the attorney-client privilege.

NOTES

1. *Hodgson* is useful in demonstrating that, in the face of compulsory legal process, the ethical obligation of confidentiality is not available as a basis for resisting disclosure. The attorney in that case resisted solely on the basis of the attorney-client privilege. Is this the proper relationship between the ethical rule and the evidentiary rule?

2. The privilege ordinarily is not available to resist disclosure of the identity of a lawyer's clients. See, for instance, Colton v. United States, 306 F.2d 633 (1962), cert. denied, 371 U.S. 951 (1963); and Vingelli v. United States, 992 F.2d 449 (2d Cir. 1993). But see In the Matter of Grand Jury Proceeding, Grand Jury 1988-2

Appeal of David Cherney, 898 F.2d 565 (7th Cir. 1990). It may, however, be properly asserted where so much of the substance of the communication has already been disclosed that identifying the client will amount to full disclosure of the communication. See Baird v. Koerner, 279 F.2d 623 (9th Cir. 1960) (identification of client not required where attorney paid back taxes by check for anonymous client); United States v. Liebman, 742 F.2d 807 (3d Cir. 1984) (where an IRS summons seeking names of clients identified lawyer's communication and described its substance, and these allegations were not disputed by lawyer, privilege was available).

3.   The Internal Revenue Service sometimes argues that a taxpayer, by reporting an item on a tax return, has waived the attorney-client privilege with respect to legal advice received with respect to that item. Is this a sound position? For an exposition of the issues, see Bruce Graves, Attorney Client Privilege in Preparation of Income Tax Returns: What Every Attorney-Preparer Should Know, 42 Tax Law. 577 (1989). Mr. Graves concludes that "tax return preparation work, like other legal work performed by a tax lawyer, deserves to be included within the scope of the attorney-client privilege." However, he considers this proposition open to considerable doubt unless the Supreme Court acts to clarify the uncertainties created by the lower courts. Id. at 618. But see Richard Lavoie, Making a List and Checking It Twice: Must Tax Attorneys Divulge Who's Naughty and Nice?, 38 U.C. Davis L. Rev. 141, 191-192 (2004) (concluding that under current law, documents and communications connected to the attorney's return preparation efforts are generally not privileged).

4.   Under §6050I a person who receives, in the course of his business, a cash payment of more than $10,000 must report to the IRS the identity of the payor and certain other information. Assume that a lawyer receives a $10,000 fee in cash for providing tax advice to an organized crime figure. The client does not wish his identity to be disclosed. What must the lawyer do?

There is no question that §6050I applies to lawyers. See Reg. §1.6050I-1(c)(7)(iii) (Ex. 2) (example using a lawyer collecting a fee). Generally, the courts have rejected the argument that the disclosure of the client's identity in response to a summons violates the Fifth or Sixth Amendments or the attorney-client privilege. See, for instance, U.S. v. Leventhal, 961 F.2d 936 (11th Cir. 1992); United States v. Goldberger & Dubin, P.C., 935 F.2d 501, 503 (2d Cir. 1991). A very limited exception, based on Baird v. Koerner, noted above, exists where the fee information represents a "confidential professional communication." This has been applied only in cases where the anonymity of the client was part of the reason the client sought the attorney's services or where disclosure would provide the last link in proving guilt. For example, in United States v. Sindel, 53 F.3d 874 (8th Cir. 1995), the attorney reported cash transactions for two different clients but did not include identifying information. The court concluded (after in camera examination of the attorney) that the attorney could not provide identifying information for one of the clients without divulging the "substance of a confidential communication." However, disclosure was appropriate for the second client because the court concluded that identification of the client would not reveal confidential communications.

Bar associations vigorously lobbied Congress to exempt attorneys from the reporting requirement of §6050I, but were unsuccessful. Should Congress have exempted lawyers? For expressions of the view that §6050I puts the lawyer in an untenable position, see United States v. Ritchie, 15 F.3d 592 (6th Cir. 1994); United States v. Monnat, 853 F. Supp. 1304 (D. Kan. 1994). In each case, however, lawyers were required to comply with §6050I.

Suppose a client suggests paying the lawyer more than $10,000 in cash? Could the lawyer simply accept the cash? Should the lawyer explain §6050I? Could the lawyer properly recommend payment in property, such as highly liquid securities?

What about the impact of other statutory provisions that may require record-keeping and reporting on the part of tax advisors? What impact do such rules have on the government's ability to require disclosure of clients' names? For a consideration of this question in the context of the registration and list-keeping rules for organizers and sellers of "reportable transactions" (i.e., potentially abusive tax shelters) see the Seventh Circuit's analysis in the following case.

United States v. BDO Seidman

337 F.3d 802 (7th Cir. 2003)

RIPPLE, Circuit Judge. Several unnamed clients of BDO Seidman, LLP ("BDO"), a public accounting and consulting firm, appeal from the district court's denial of their motions to intervene in an Internal Revenue Service ("IRS") enforcement action against BDO.

The IRS had issued twenty summonses to BDO as part of its investigation of BDO's compliance with Internal Revenue Code registration and list-keeping requirements for organizers and sellers of potentially abusive tax shelters. See 26 U.S.C. §§6111, 6112. The clients sought to intervene to assert a confidentiality privilege regarding certain documents that BDO intended to produce in response to those summonses. The clients argued that, because these documents reveal their identities as BDO clients who sought advice regarding tax shelters and who subsequently invested in those shelters, disclosure inevitably would violate the statutory privilege protecting confidential communications between a taxpayer and any federally authorized tax practitioner giving tax advice. See 26 U.S.C. §7525. . . .

In September 2000, the IRS received information suggesting that BDO was promoting potentially abusive tax shelters without complying with the registration and listing requirements for organizers and sellers of tax shelters. See 26 U.S.C. §§6111, 6112. . . . Failure to comply with the registration and listing requirements of §6111 and §6112 can lead to the imposition of penalties. See 26 U.S.C. §§6707, 6708. Because the IRS suspected that BDO had violated these statutory provisions by organizing and selling interests in potentially abusive tax shelters without complying with the registration and list-keeping requirements, it issued a series of summonses to BDO, identifying twenty types of tax shelter transactions in which it suspected that BDO's clients had invested.

The summonses command production of documents and testimony relating to the identified transactions, as well as information about BDO clients who invested in the identified tax shelters. For example, the summonses demand documents identifying the investors in the transactions, the date on which those investors acquired an interest, and all tax shelter registrations filed and investor lists prepared with respect to the transactions.

In July 2002, when BDO failed to produce documents as required by the summonses, the IRS petitioned the district court for enforcement. BDO opposed enforcement. . . . BDO . . . claimed that some of the summoned information was protected from disclosure by the attorney-client privilege, the work product doctrine, and the confidentiality privilege of §7525 of the Internal Revenue Code. In October 2002, the district court ruled that the IRS had met its burden of showing that it issued the summonses in good faith, and that BDO had failed to show that enforcement of the summonses would constitute an abuse of process. . . .

Among the responsive documents not previously submitted for the court's *in camera* inspection were records that reveal the identities of the BDO clients who invested in at least one of the 20 types of tax shelters identified in the summonses. BDO informed its clients that it intended to produce these documents to the IRS. In response, two sets of unidentified taxpayers — the John and Jane Does and the Richard and Mary Roes (hereinafter referred to collectively as "the Does") — filed emergency motions to intervene. . . . The Does conceded that, aside from the fact that the documents reveal their identities as BDO clients who invested in at least one of the 20 types of tax shelters described in the summonses, the documents themselves do not contain any otherwise privileged communication. . . . The court concluded that information regarding a client's identity falls outside the scope of the §7525 privilege. . . .

The Does filed timely notices of appeal from the denial of their motions to intervene and requested that this court stay the production of the documents to which they had asserted a privilege in the district court. We granted a temporary stay and remanded the case to the district court for the limited purpose of permitting the district court to enter more extensive findings regarding those documents to which the Does claim a privilege. The remand order directed the district court to perform an *in camera* inspection of the documents at issue and to enter specific findings considering the totality of the circumstances surrounding the Does' privilege claim. . . .

Upon reviewing this subset of documents, the court determined that the identities of at least 55 Does were not subject to privilege under §7525. It noted that many of the confidentiality agreements establish that particular Does engaged BDO's services, in part, for the purpose of preparing income tax returns. In addition, several consulting agreements contained a "No Warranty" provision, which states that "BDO's Services hereunder do not include . . . any legal and/or tax opinions regarding any strategies that may be implemented." . . . This language, the court determined, suggests that the relationship between BDO and the Does was not always that of tax advisor-client and that, in such cases, their communications would not be subject to the §7525 privilege. . . . Furthermore, the court concluded, 28 of the documents were generated for the purpose of preparing tax returns, another unprivileged category of communication. . . .

The primary issue before us is whether the district court erred when it denied the Does' motions to intervene because it believed that they had failed to establish a colorable claim of privilege under §7525. . . . Whether the scope of the §7525 privilege includes protection against the disclosure of client identity is a question of law that this court reviews de novo. . . .

We first consider the regulatory context in which the Does' claim of privilege arises. The Does sought to intervene in proceedings involving the IRS investigation of BDO for potential violations of the tax code, including the provisions requiring organizers of tax shelters to register tax shelters with the IRS, 26 U.S.C. §6111, and organizers and sellers of such shelters to keep lists of the investors, 26 U.S.C. §6112. . . .

Congress, by granting the IRS the broad power to issue summonses to investigate violations of the tax code see 26 U.S.C. §7602, further provides the IRS with great latitude to verify compliance with these tax shelter registration and list-keeping provisions . . . Nevertheless, despite these powerful investigative tools, the IRS' investigatory power is not absolute. If a taxpayer fails to comply with a summons, the IRS must apply to the district court to secure an enforcement order . . .

The IRS' broad power to investigate possible violations of the tax laws is understood to be vial to the efficacy of the federal tax system, "which seeks to assure that taxpayers pay what Congress has mandated and to prevent dishonest persons from escaping taxation thus shifting heavier burdens to honest taxpayers." . . . Because the IRS' investigatory powers are essential to the proper functioning of the tax system, courts are reluctant to restrict the IRS' summons power, absent unambiguous direction from Congress. . . . Nevertheless, a court's power to enforce a summons is not absolute. It is subject to traditional privileges. . . .

The Does' privilege claim rests entirely on §7525, a statute enacted on July 22, 1998, to provide a confidentiality privilege for communications between a taxpayer and a tax practitioner. . . . [T]he §7525 privilege is no broader than that of the attorney-client privilege, and "nothing in [§7525] suggests that . . . nonlawyer practitioners are entitled to privilege when they are doing other than lawyers' work. . . . Because the scope of the tax practitioner-client privilege depends on the scope of the common law protections of confidential attorney-client communications, we must look to the body of common law interpreting the attorney-client privilege to interpret the §7525 privilege.

. . . The purpose of the privilege is to encourage full disclosure and to facilitate open communication between attorneys and their clients. . . . However, because "the privilege has the effect of withholding relevant information," courts construe the privilege to apply only where necessary to achieve its purpose." . . .

The attorney-client privilege protects confidential *communications* made by a client to his lawyer and so ordinarily the identity of a client does not come within the scope of the privilege. . . . However, over the years, a limited exception to this general rule has developed; the identity of a client may be privileged in the rare circumstance when so much of an actual confidential communication has been disclosed already that merely identifying the client will effectively disclose the communication. . . .

. . . In [Tillotson v. Boughner, 350 F. 2d 663 (7th Cir. 1965)] an unidentified taxpayer had determined that he understated his tax liability on previously filed returns and retained an attorney to deliver a cashier's check in the amount of $215,499.95 to the IRS. . . . The IRS sought to enforce a summons it had served on the attorney, demanding that he testify about his client. The attorney asserted the attorney-client privilege and refused to disclose his client's identity. . . . We upheld the invocation of the privilege because "under the peculiar facts of this case, the attorney-client privilege includes, within its scope, the identity of the client." . . . We reasoned that the IRS had become aware of the substantive content of the confidential communication between the unknown taxpayer and his attorney — namely, the taxpayer's tax liability — the moment the cashier's check was delivered. Because revealing the taxpayer's identity would also reveal the context of the confidential communication, the privilege attached. . . .

Relying on these cases, the Does submit that the IRS' summonses set forth such detailed descriptions about suspect types of tax shelters under investigation that any document produced in response that also reveals a client's identity will inevitably reveal that client's *motivation* for seeking tax advice from BDO. The Does define their "motive" for retaining BDO's services as the "desire to engage in financial transactions which the government might later decide to be questionable, or . . . 'potentially abusive.'" . . . Because a client's "motive" for seeking legal advice is considered a confidential communication, the Does contend that the §7525 privilege should protect against the disclosure of their motive for seeking tax advice, a motive that would be known if their identities are revealed.

The Does have not established that a confidential communication will be disclosed if their identities are revealed in response to the summonses. Disclosure of the identities of the Does will disclose to the IRS that the Does participated in one of the 20 types of tax shelters described in its summonses. It is less than clear, however, as to what motive, or other confidential communication of tax advice, can be inferred from that information alone. . . . Moreover, the Does concede that the documents that BDO intends to produce in response to the summonses are not subject to any other independent claim of privilege beyond the Does' assertion of privilege as to identity.

More fundamentally, the Does' participation in potentially abusive tax shelters is information ordinarily subject to full disclosure under the federal tax law. . . . This list-keeping provision precludes the Does from establishing an *expectation of confidentiality* in their communications with BDO, an essential element of the attorney-client privilege and, by extension, the §7525 privilege. . . . Because the Does cannot credibly argue that they expected that their participation in such transactions would not be disclosed, they cannot now establish that the documents responsive to the summonses, which do not contain any tax advice, reveal a *confidential* communication. . . .

BDO's affirmative duty to disclose its clients' participation in potentially abusive tax shelters renders the Does' situation easily distinguishable from the limited circumstances in which we have determined that a client's identity was information subject to the attorney client-privilege. The district court committed no error when it concluded that the Does failed to establish a colorable claim of privilege under §7525.

... For the reasons stated above, the district court's judgements denying the Does' motions for intervention are affirmed.

NOTES

1.   Is the *BDO* case as different from *Tillotson* as the Seventh Circuit contends? What will the IRS likely infer from learning that the Does pursued possible tax shelters with BDO?

2.   How much does the decision in *BDO* turn on the requirements imposed by §6111 and §6112 on organizers and promoters of possible tax shelters? What is the relationship between rules like §6111 (and §6112) and §7525? If Congress requires disclosure of information, does that automatically bar an effective claim by the taxpayer for privilege? Is the Seventh Circuit making that argument?

Upjohn Co. v. United States

449 U.S. 383 (1981)

MR. JUSTICE REHNQUIST delivered the opinion of the Court.

We granted certiorari in this case to address important questions concerning the scope of the attorney-client privilege in the corporate context and the applicability of the work-product doctrine in proceedings to enforce tax summonses.

Petitioner Upjohn manufactures and sells pharmaceuticals here and abroad. In January 1976 independent accountants conducting an audit of one of petitioner's foreign subsidiaries discovered that the subsidiary made payments to or for the benefit of foreign government officials in order to secure government business. The accountants so informed Mr. Gerard Thomas, petitioner's Vice-President, Secretary, and General Counsel. Thomas is a member of the Michigan and New York bars, and has been petitioner's General Counsel for 20 years. He consulted with outside counsel and R.T. Parfet, Jr., petitioner's Chairman of the Board. It was decided that the company would conduct an internal investigation of what were termed "questionable payments." As part of this investigation the attorneys prepared a letter containing a questionnaire which was sent to "all foreign general and area managers" over the Chairman's signature. The letter began by noting recent disclosures that several American companies made "possibly illegal" payments to foreign government officials and emphasized that the management needed full information concerning any such payments made by Upjohn. The letter indicated that the Chairman had asked Thomas, identified as "the company's General Counsel," "to conduct an investigation for the purpose of determining the nature and magnitude of any payments made by the Upjohn Company or any of its subsidiaries to any employee or official of a foreign government." The questionnaire sought detailed information concerning such payments. Managers were instructed to treat the investigation as "highly confidential" and not to discuss it with anyone other than Upjohn employees who might be helpful in providing the requested information. Responses were to be sent directly to Thomas. Thomas and outside counsel also interviewed the recipients of the questionnaire and some 33 other Upjohn officers or employees as part of the investigation.

On March 26, 1976, the company voluntarily submitted a preliminary report to the Securities and Exchange Commission on Form 8-K disclosing certain questionable payments. A copy of the report was simultaneously submitted to the Internal Revenue Service, which immediately began an investigation to determine the tax consequences of the payments. Special agents conducting the investigation were given lists by Upjohn of all those interviewed and all who had responded to the questionnaire. On November 23, 1976, the Service issued a summons pursuant to 26 U.S.C. §7602 demanding production of:

> All files relative to the investigation conducted under the supervision of Gerard Thomas to identify payments to employees of foreign governments and any political contributions made by the Upjohn Company or any of its affiliates since January 1, 1971 and to determine whether any funds of the Upjohn Company had been improperly accounted for on the corporate books during the same period.
>
> The records should include but not be limited to written questionnaires sent to managers of the Upjohn Company's foreign affiliates, and memoranda or notes of the interviews conducted in the United States and abroad with officers and employees of the Upjohn Company and its subsidiaries. App. 17a-18a.

The company declined to produce the documents specified in the second paragraph on the grounds that they were protected from disclosure by the attorney-client privilege and constituted the work product of attorneys prepared in anticipation of litigation. On August 31, 1977, the United States filed a petition seeking enforcement of the summons under 26 U.S.C. §§7402(b) and 7604(a) in the United States District Court for the Western District of Michigan. That court adopted the recommendation of a magistrate who concluded that the summons should be enforced. Petitioner appealed to the Court of Appeals for the Sixth Circuit which rejected the magistrate's finding of a waiver of the attorney-client privilege, 600 F.2d 1223, 1227, n.12, but agreed that the privilege did not apply "to the extent the communications were made by officers and agents not responsible for directing Upjohn's actions in response to legal advice . . . for the simple reason that the communications were not the 'client's.'" Id., at 1225. The court reasoned that accepting petitioner's claim for a broader application of the privilege would encourage upper-echelon management to ignore unpleasant facts and create too broad a "zone of silence." Noting that petitioner's counsel had interviewed officials such as the Chairman and President, the Court of Appeals remanded to the District Court so that a determination of who was within the "control group" could be made. In a concluding footnote the court stated that the work-product doctrine "is not applicable to administrative summonses issued under 26 U.S.C. §7602." Id., at 1228, n.13.

II

Federal Rule of Evidence 501 provides that "the privilege of a witness . . . shall be governed by the principles of the common law as they may be interpreted by the courts of the United States in light of reason and experience." The attorney-client privilege is the oldest of the privileges for confidential communications known to the common law. 8 Wigmore, Evidence §2290 (McNaughton rev. 1961). Its purpose is to encourage full and frank communication between attorneys and their clients and thereby promote broader public interests in the observance of law and administration of justice. The privilege recognizes that sound legal advice or advocacy serves public ends and that such advice or advocacy depends upon the lawyer being fully informed by the client. Admittedly complications in the application of the privilege arise when the client is a corporation, which in theory is an artificial creature of the law, and not an individual; but this court has assumed that the privilege applies when the client is a corporation and the government does not contest the general proposition.

The Court of Appeals, however, considered the application of the privilege in the corporate context to present a "different problem," since the client was an inanimate entity and "only the senior management, guiding and integrating the several operations, . . . can be said to possess an identity analogous to the corporation as a whole."

Such a view, we think, overlooks the fact that the privilege exists to protect not only the giving of professional advice to those who can act on it but also the giving of information to the lawyer to enable him to give sound and informed advice. The first step in the resolution of any legal problem is ascertaining the factual background and sifting through the facts with an eye to the legally relevant. See ABA Code of Professional Responsibility, Ethical Consideration 4-1:

> A lawyer should be fully informed of all the facts of the matter he is handling in order for his client to obtain the full advantage of our legal system. It is for the lawyer in the exercise of his independent professional judgment to separate the relevant and important from the irrelevant and unimportant. The observance of the ethical obligation of a lawyer to hold inviolate the confidences and secrets of his client not only facilitates the full development of facts essential to proper representation of the client but also encourages laymen to seek early legal assistance.

In the case of the individual client the provider of information and the person who acts on the lawyer's advice are one and the same. In the corporate context, however, it will frequently be employees beyond the control group as defined by the court below — "officers and agents . . . responsible for directing [the company's] actions in response to legal advice" — who will possess the information needed by the corporation's lawyers. The control group test adopted by the court below thus frustrates the very purpose of the privilege by discouraging the communication of relevant information by employees of the client to attorneys seeking to render legal advice to the client corporation.

The narrow scope given the attorney-client privilege by the court below not only makes it difficult for corporate attorneys to formulate sound advice when their client is faced with a specific legal problem but also threatens to limit the valuable efforts of corporate counsel to ensure their client's compliance with the law.

The communications at issue were made by Upjohn employees to counsel for Upjohn acting as such, at the direction of corporate superiors in order to secure legal advice from counsel.

The Court of Appeals declined to extend the attorney-client privilege beyond the limits of the control group test for fear that doing so would entail severe burdens on discovery and create a broad "zone of silence" over corporate affairs. Application of the attorney-client privilege to communications such as those involved here, however, puts the adversary in no worse position than if the communications had never taken place. The privilege only protects disclosure of communications; it does not protect disclosure of the underlying facts by those who communicated with the attorney. Here the government was free to question the employees who communicated with Thomas and outside counsel. Upjohn has provided the IRS with a list of such employees, and the IRS has already interviewed some 25 of them. While it would probably be more convenient for the government to secure the results of petitioner's internal investigation by simply subpoenaing the questionnaires and notes taken by petitioner's attorneys, such considerations of convenience do not overcome the policies served by the attorney-client privilege.

[The Court went on to hold that the notes made by counsel concerning interviews with employees were protected from disclosure under the work product doctrine of Hickman v. Taylor, 329 U.S. 495 (1947).]

[The concurring opinion of Burger, C.J., is omitted.]

NOTES

1.   In *Upjohn*, the Supreme Court clarified the scope of the attorney-client privilege by favoring its application to a broad classification of employees. Was this wise? Should the ethical obligation of confidentiality have a similar, or perhaps even broader, scope of application? If a lawyer obtains information from *any* employee of a corporation, is that information subject to Model Rule 1.6? What about the implications of Rule 1.13? Chapter 6 considers in more detail the case in which an organization is the client.

2.   Consider whether the policy that compels recognition of an attorney-client privilege also supports the recognition of an accountant-client privilege. See the material in subpart 5 below relating to tax accrual workpapers.

3.   For an extensive review of the *Upjohn* case and its impact on the policies that justify the attorney-client privilege, see Timothy P. Glynn, Federalizing Privilege, 52 Am. U. L. Rev. 59 (2002); John Sexton, A Post-*Upjohn* Consideration of the Corporate Attorney-Client Privilege, 57 N.Y.U. L. Rev. 443 (1982).

Fu Investment Co., Ltd. v. Commissioner

104 T.C. 408 (1995)

OPINION

DAWSON, Judge. These consolidated cases were assigned to Chief Special Trial Judge Peter J. Panuthos pursuant to the provisions of section 7443A(b)(4) and Rules 180, 181, and 183. The Court agrees with and adopts the opinion of the Chief Special Trial Judge, which is set forth below.

PANUTHOS, Chief Special Trial Judge. This matter is before the Court on petitioners' separate Motions For Protective Order filed December 12, 1994. Petitioners each seek a protective order from the Court precluding respondent from engaging in ex parte communications with petitioners' former employees.

BACKGROUND

Respondent determined that petitioners Fu Investment Co., Ltd., and Coco Palms Investment, Inc., are liable for withholding of income tax at source as follows:

Fu Investment Co., Ltd.		Coco Palms Investment, Inc.	
Year	Amount	Year	Amount
1990	$1,287,375	1990	$483,272
1991	$ 635,642	1991	$238,865

. . . After filing an answer to each of the petitions, respondent mailed letters to three of petitioners' former employees (a former secretary and two accounting supervisors) requesting interviews regarding the matters in dispute in these cases. After being notified of respondent's intentions by one of the former employees, petitioners filed the Motions for Protective Order pending before the Court. Specifically, petitioners request that we preclude respondent from engaging in ex parte contacts with their former employees. Petitioners' counsel requests reasonable advance notice of the name of the former employee, the time and place for the interview, and an opportunity to be present at the interview for the purpose of objecting to questions that might elicit privileged information. . . . [And] that she would suspend her efforts to interview the individuals in question pending the disposition of petitioners' motions.

... Petitioners filed statements with the Court pursuant to Rule 50(c) ... Petitioners' Rule 50(c) statements include declarations submitted by James Murad, a partner with Cooper, White & Cooper, petitioners' general counsel, stating that, while employed by petitioners, each of the former employees in question was privy to confidential attorney-client communications regarding the substantive issues in dispute in these cases.

During the hearing of this matter, counsel for respondent argued that respondent is not obligated to provide advance notice of her intention to interview petitioners' former employees. Counsel for respondent also assured the Court that respondent would attempt to avoid eliciting privileged information from the former employees and, further, would provide petitioners with copies of any notes taken during the interviews.

There is no indication in the record that petitioners' former employees are presently represented by counsel.

DISCUSSION

Petitioners' Motions for Protective Order raise the issue of whether respondent may engage in ex parte communications with the former employees of a taxpayer after the taxpayer has filed a petition for redetermination with this Court. In addition, we must address petitioners' concerns that the former employees in question may disclose matters to respondent that are subject to the attorney-client privilege.

Rule 103 provides that, upon motion by a party or any other affected person, and for good cause shown, the Court may make any order which justice requires to protect a party or other person from annoyance, embarrassment, oppression, or undue burden or expense. We have previously considered the question of the Court's authority to issue a protective order under Rule 103 restricting the use of information obtained through legal procedures that fall outside of the Court's formal discovery procedures. See Ash v. Commissioner, 96 T.C. 459, 469-470 (1991) (interpreting Rule 103 consistently with Fed. R. Civ. P. 26(c) from which the former is derived). Arguably, respondent's efforts to arrange informal witness interviews do not fall within our discovery procedures, and, thus, are not subject to restriction under Rule 103. ...

Nonetheless, it is well settled that courts have inherent powers not derived from any statute to, inter alia, control the conduct of attorneys practicing before them and to regulate their own processes to prevent injustice. See Roadway Express, Inc. v. Piper, 447 U.S. 752, 765 (1980); ... see also Rule 1(a). With these principles in mind, we first turn to the question of whether respondent may engage in ex parte communications with petitioners' former employees.

Rule 201(a) provides that practitioners before the Court shall carry on their practice in accordance with the letter and spirit of the Model Rules of Professional Conduct of the American Bar Association. Duffey v. Commissioner, 91 T.C. 81, 82

(1988). Model Rules of Professional Conduct Rule 4.2 (1992) (hereinafter Model Rule 4.2) states:

> In representing a client, a lawyer shall not communicate about the subject of the representation with a party the lawyer knows to be represented by another lawyer in the matter, unless the lawyer has the consent of the other lawyer or is authorized by law to do so.

In short, Model Rule 4.2 prohibits ex parte communications with a party that the lawyer knows to be represented by another attorney in the matter.

The official comment to Model Rule 4.2 states in pertinent part:

> In the case of an organization, this Rule prohibits communications by a lawyer for one party concerning the matter in representation with persons having a managerial responsibility on behalf of the organization, and with any other person whose act or omission in connection with that matter may be imputed to the organization for purposes of civil or criminal liability or whose statement may constitute an admission on the part of the organization. If an agent or employee of the organization is represented in the matter by his or her own counsel, the consent by that counsel to a communication will be sufficient for purposes of this Rule. Compare Rule 3.4(f).
>
> This Rule also covers any person, whether or not a party to a formal proceeding, who is represented by counsel concerning the matter in question. [Model Rules of Professional Conduct Rule 4.2 cmt. (1992).]

Model Rule 4.2 advances the well-recognized public policy favoring the preservation and protection of the attorney-client relationship. Specifically, by prohibiting ex parte communications with a party represented by counsel, opposing counsel is: (1) Denied the unfair advantage that he would otherwise enjoy over a lay person unfamiliar with the law; and (2) precluded from disturbing an established attorney-client relationship.

. . . Consistent with its official comment, Model Rule 4.2 generally has been interpreted to preclude opposing counsel from engaging in ex parte communications with the present employees of a corporate party. See, e.g., Miano v. AC&R Advertising, Inc., 148 F.R.D. 68, 76-77 (S.D.N.Y. 1993). As indicated, however, we are asked to decide, in a case of first impression in this Court, whether respondent may engage in ex parte communications with the former employees of a corporation/petitioner. The issue to be decided has been addressed by the American Bar Association (ABA) and a substantial number of Federal District Courts.

We begin our review of these authorities with ABA Standing Comm. on Ethics and Professional Responsibility, Formal Op. 91-359 (1991). Focusing on the express language of Model Rule 4.2 and the Rule's official comment, the ABA takes the view that the Rule should not be interpreted to prohibit ex parte contacts with former employees. Formal Op. 91-359 states in pertinent part:

> While the Committee recognizes that persuasive policy arguments can be and have been made for extending the ambit of Model Rule 4.2 to cover some former

corporate employers [sic], the fact remains that the text of the Rule does not do so and the comment gives no basis for concluding that such coverage was intended. Especially where, as here, the effect of the Rule is to inhibit the acquisition of information about one's case, the Committee is loath, given the text of Model Rule 4.2 and its Comment, to expand its coverage to former employees by means of liberal interpretation.

Consistent with ABA Formal Op. 91-359, the majority of jurisdictions considering the issue have held that Model Rule 4.2 generally does not apply to preclude an attorney from engaging in ex parte contacts with the former employees of a corporate party. . . . [S]ee also 2 Hazard & Hodes, The Law of Lawyering: A Handbook on the Model Rules of Professional Conduct, sec. 4.2:107, at 739 (2d ed., 1994 supp.). But cf. Porter v. Arco Metals Co., 642 F.Supp. 1116, 1118 (D. Mont. 1986) (suggesting that Model Rule 4.2 may preclude ex parte contacts with former employees who exercised managerial responsibilities with respect to the matters in litigation).

The courts adopting the majority view . . . have determined that the specific policy considerations underlying Model Rule 4.2 have marginal relevance in the case of a communication between an attorney and former employee of a corporate party. . . .

> Because the former employee no longer works on the organization's behalf, the former employee will not be a party to settlement negotiations. Polycast, 129 F.R.D. at 625; see Hanntz, 766 F.Supp. at 265; Goff, 145 F.R.D. at 354. Furthermore, an attorney-client relationship between former employee and the employer's attorney is unlikely. Accordingly, the risk of jeopardizing an attorney-client relationship is substantially diminished. . . .

We find the majority view described above to be consistent with the literal terms of Model Rule 4.2, as well as the official comment to the Rule. In the first instance, absent extraordinary circumstances, the former employees of an organization such as a corporation are not considered a "party" to corporate matters as that term is used in Model Rule 4.2. Valassis v. Samelson, supra at 122-123. In addition, former employees, by definition, no longer possess managerial responsibilities on behalf of the organization and their statements do not constitute an admission on the part of the organization. Id.; Hanntz v. Shiley, Inc., supra at 266-267; see Fed. R. Evid. 801(d)(2)(D). Further, we are persuaded by, and agree with, the analysis set forth in Polycast Technology Corp. v. Uniroyal, Inc., supra at 626-627, supporting that court's conclusion that former employees do not fall within the class of "any other person" whose act or omission may be imputed to the organization for purposes of civil or criminal liability. [2] But cf., Amarin Plastics, Inc. v. Maryland Cup Corp., 116 F.R.D. 36, 40 (D: Mass. 1987).

2. In Polycast Technology Corp. v. Uniroyal, Inc., 129 F.R.D. 621, 627 (S.D.N.Y. 1990), the court concluded that the language "any other person" in the official comment to Model Rules of Professional Conduct, Rule 4.2 was probably intended to refer to the agents of an organization whose acts might be attributable to the organization but who technically might not be considered employees.

... In the absence of any indication in the record that petitioners' former employees are represented by counsel, we hold that Model Rule 4.2 does not preclude respondent from engaging in ex parte communications with those former employees. Moreover, we observe that the interviews that respondent proposes to conduct are not inconsistent with this Court's approach to pretrial case preparation.

Model Rule 4.2 aside, petitioners assert, in a very general fashion, that the former employees in question were, during their employment with petitioners, in frequent contact with petitioners' counsel regarding the substantive matters in dispute in this case. Thus, petitioners maintain that we should issue a protective order allowing petitioners' counsel to be present at any proposed interview and to object to any question that may elicit information that is subject to the attorney-client privilege.

The attorney-client privilege is the "oldest of the privileges for confidential communications known to the common law." Upjohn Co. v. United States, 449 U.S. 383, 389 (1981); Hartz Mountain Indus., Inc. v. Commissioner, 93 T.C. 521, 524-525 (1989). The Supreme Court ruled that the attorney-client privilege applies when the client is a corporation, summarizing the purpose of the privilege as follows:

> Its purpose is to encourage full and frank communication between attorneys and their clients and thereby promote broader public interests in the observance of law and administration of justice. The privilege recognizes that sound legal advice or advocacy serves public ends and that such advice or advocacy depends upon the lawyer's being fully informed by the client. [Upjohn Co. v. United States, supra at 389.]

In discussing the scope of the attorney-client privilege, the Supreme Court indicated that although the privilege protects "not only the giving of professional advice to those who can act on it but also the giving of information to the lawyer to enable him to give sound and informed advice," id. at 390; "the privilege only protects disclosure of communications; it does not protect disclosure of the underlying facts by those who communicated with the attorney." Id. at 395 ...

Section 7453 provides that the Tax Court is bound by the rules of evidence applicable in trial without a jury in the United States District Court for the District of Columbia. Rule 143(a); Von Tersch v. Commissioner, 47 T.C. 415, 418-419 (1967). The United States District Court for the District of Columbia generally takes the view that all privileges are to be strictly construed. See, e.g., United States v. American Tel. & Tel., 86 F.R.D. 603, 604 (D.D.C. 1979).

The attorney-client privilege existing between a corporate client and its attorneys has been held to extend to both present and former corporate employees. See In re Coordinated PreTrial Proceedings in Petroleum Products Antitrust Litigation, 658 F.2d 1355, 1361 n.7 (9th Cir. 1981); see also Dubois v. Gradco Systems, Inc., 136 F.R.D. at 346-347; Porter v. Arco Metals Co., 642 F. Supp. at 1118; Amarin Plastics, Inc. v. Maryland Cup Corp., supra at 41; Hazard & Hodes, supra, sec. 4.2:107, at 739. The burden of proving that the attorney-client privilege applies rests with the party asserting the privilege. United States v. American Tel. & Tel., supra at 604-605; Hartz Mountain Industries v. Commissioner, supra at 525.

While we hold that respondent may engage in ex parte communications with petitioners' former employees without violating the proscriptions of Model Rule 4.2, we recognize that circumstances may arise where certain precautions (including a narrowly drawn protective order) may be warranted to ensure that such ex parte contacts are not simply a forum for counsel to seek information protected by the attorney-client privilege. Based on the record presented, however, we have no basis for concluding that we should impose specific restrictions on respondent at this time. In short, petitioners' general assertions that the former employees in question were privy to privileged communications are insufficient to allow the Court to issue a meaningful protective order. . . . Absent more specific information regarding the alleged privileged communications, we conclude that petitioners have failed to satisfy their burden of proof justifying a protective order.

Nonetheless, respondent is reminded that the proposed interviews must be conducted within the letter and spirit of the Model Rules of Professional Conduct. Rule 201(a). Of course, nothing we have said herein precludes petitioners' former employees from having counsel (including petitioners' counsel) accompany them to any such interview. In addition, prior to conducting an interview of this nature, respondent must advise each former employee that respondent and petitioners are adverse parties in this proceeding. The agent or attorney conducting the interview likewise must explain his role in the information gathering process. See Model Rule 4.3. [3]

Equally important, during the course of such an interview respondent must limit her questions to factual matters and refrain from eliciting or inducing statements or disclosures by a former employee that involve privileged communications. [4] See Model Rules of Professional Conduct Rule 4.4 (1992) (a lawyer may not use methods of obtaining evidence that violate the legal rights of a third person); see also Valassis v. Samelson, supra at 124-125; Hanntz v. Shiley. Inc., supra at 270-271; Shearson Lehman Bros., Inc. v. Wasatch Bank, 139 F.R.D. at 417-418.

Finally, we expect that respondent will honor the representation made to the Court during the hearing of this matter that she will provide petitioners with copies of any notes taken during the proposed interviews.

To reflect the foregoing,

Orders denying petitioners' Motions for Protective Order will be issued. . . .

---

3. Model Rule of Professional Conduct Rule 4.3 (1992) states:

In dealing on behalf of a client with a person who is not represented by counsel, a lawyer shall not state or imply that the lawyer is disinterested. When the lawyer knows or reasonably should know that the unrepresented person misunderstands the lawyer's role in the matter, the lawyer shall make reasonable efforts to correct the misunderstanding.

4. See ABA Standing Comm. on Ethics and Professional Responsibility, Formal Op. 91-359 (1991), discussed above.

3. Client Fraud: To Disclose or Not to Disclose

A lawyer faces what is perhaps the most difficult of ethical choices when he learns that his client has committed, or will likely commit, fraud upon another person or upon a tribunal or agency. The regulation of the lawyer's conduct in such circumstances has been the focus of significant public debate. The following material provides an historical perspective on the evolution of a lawyer's "duty to disclose" in the context of client fraud.

Under the Model Code, Canon 4 required the lawyer to preserve his client's confidences and secrets.

DR 7-102(B), as originally set forth in the 1969 version of the CPR, provided:

> A lawyer who receives information clearly establishing that
> (1) his client has, in the course of the representation, perpetrated a fraud upon a person or tribunal shall promptly call upon his client to rectify the same, and if his client refuses or is unable to do so, he shall reveal the fraud to the affected person or tribunal.

Soon after adoption of the Code, however, misgivings were expressed by the ABA membership at this apparent overriding of the Canon 4 obligation of confidentiality. As a consequence, in 1974, the following phrase was added to DR 7-102(B): "except when the information is protected as a privileged communication."

Soon thereafter, the bar expressed doubt as to what was meant by the term "privileged communication" as used in the 1974 amendment. Competing interpretations were (1) the narrow view that the term meant only matters within the attorney-client evidentiary privilege, and (2) the broad view that the term extended to all confidences and secrets protected under Canon 4. In Formal Opinion 341, the ABA adopted the broad view.

ABA Formal Opinion 341

(1975)

This opinion is made in response to several inquiries regarding the effect of the February, 1974, amendment to Disciplinary Rule 7-102(B), which presently reads: "(B) A lawyer who receives information clearly establishing that (1) His client has, in the course of the representation, perpetrated a fraud upon a person or tribunal shall promptly call upon his client to rectify the same, and if his client refuses or is unable to do so, he shall reveal the fraud to the affected person or tribunal, *except when the information is protected as a privileged communication.*" [Italicized language added by amendment February, 1974.]

The derivation of D.R. 7-102(B)(1) is informative. The prior American Bar Association Canons of Professional Ethics contained three mandatory revelation rules: Canon 1 (complaint against judge), Canon 29 (exposing dishonest conduct of lawyers and exposing perjury), and Canon 41 (informing injured person of fraud or deception by client). In the Code of Professional Responsibility, D.R. 1-103 contains a duty to reveal knowledge of misconduct by judge or lawyer. But the preliminary draft of the Code of Professional Responsibility (January, 1969) did not contain a disciplinary rule requiring a lawyer to reveal misconduct of a client.

Perhaps the omission was due to the committee's consideration of the high fiduciary duty owed by lawyer to client and consideration of the firm support found in the law of evidence for the attorney-client privilege. The preliminary draft contained a disciplinary rule virtually identical to present D.R. 4-101(C), forbidding a lawyer, with certain exceptions, from knowingly revealing a confidence or secret of his client. Some lawyers objected, however, to the preliminary draft because it did not carry into the Code of Professional Responsibility the substance of prior Canon 41. The result was the addition to the Code of Professional Responsibility, at that time, of D.R. 7-102(B).

When D.R. 7-102(B) was added to the Code of Professional Responsibility prior to its adoption in August, 1969, the full significance of D.R. 4-101(C) apparently was not appreciated, even though the preliminary draft contained a virtually identical provision stating that "[a] lawyer may reveal . . . [c]onfidences or secrets when permitted [under] Disciplinary Rules or required by law or court order." That provision of D.R. 4-101(C), while quite proper in the preliminary draft, had the unacceptable result when combined with new D.R. 7-102(B)(1) of requiring a lawyer in certain instances to reveal privileged communications which he also was duty bound not to reveal according to the law of evidence. The amendment of February, 1974, was necessary in order to relieve lawyers of exposure to such diametrically opposed professional duties.

A similar impasse arising under the prior Canons of Professional Ethics was considered by this committee in Formal Opinion 287 (1953). Then Canon 37 required a lawyer to "preserve his client's confidences," although Canon 29 required a lawyer to reveal perjury to the prosecuting authorities and Canon 41 required a lawyer to inform against his client in certain circumstances in regard to "fraud or deception." The situation in Opinion 287 was that of a client who had committed perjury (which we assume constituted intrinsic fraud upon the tribunal) during the trial of his divorce action. Three months later the client sought advice from the same lawyer who had represented him in the divorce action. The advice was sought in regard to a dispute with his former wife over support money; in connection with this consultation the client told the lawyer that he had given false material testimony in the divorce action in which he had been represented by the same lawyer. Tracing the background of the evidentiary law concerning the attorney-client privilege, this committee held that the duty of the lawyer to preserve his client's confidences prevailed over the duty under Canon 41 to reveal fraud or deception, and over the duty under Canon 29 to bring knowledge of perjury to the attention of others. In Opinion 287 it was said that the lawyer, "despite Canons 29 and 41, should not disclose the facts to the court or to the authorities."

One effect of the 1974 amendment to D.R. 7-102(B)(1) is to reinstate the essence of Opinion 287 which had prevailed from 1953 until 1969. It was as unthinkable then as now that a lawyer should be subject to disciplinary action for failing to reveal information which by law is not to be revealed without the consent of the client, and the lawyer is not now in that untenable position. The lawyer no longer can be confronted with the necessity of either breaching his client's privilege at law or breaching a disciplinary rule.

While the derivation of D.R. 7-102(B)(1) indicates the necessity for the 1974 amendment, the scope of the 1974 amendment can be indicated only by considering the coverage of the basic requirement of D.R. 7102(B)(1) and by examining the interrelation of D.R. 7-102(B)(1) and D.R. 4-101. The conflicting duties to reveal fraud and to preserve confidences have existed side-by-side for some time.

However, it is clear that there has long been an accommodation in favor of preserving confidences either through practice or interpretation. Through the bar's interpretation in practice of its responsibility to preserve confidences and secrets of clients, and through its interpretations like Formal Opinion 287, significant exceptions to any general duty to reveal fraud have been long accepted. Apparently, the exceptions were so broad or the policy underlying the duty to reveal so weak that the earlier drafts of the Code of Professional Responsibility omitted altogether the concept embodied in Canon 41. Nonetheless, D.R. 7-102(B) is a part of the Code of Professional Responsibility and must be given some meaning. Some of the exceptions to a general duty to reveal have been built into the disciplinary rule itself (for example, that the information must "clearly establish" fraud; that it must be received "in the course of representation" and (since 1974) that it must not be information "protected as a privileged communication").

Formal Opinion 287, which dealt with a lawyer's duty to reveal a perjury committed earlier by his client, represents merely one of the exceptions to old Canon 41 (it also pertained to old Canon 29, dealing with revealing perjury to the affected tribunal). We do not think that Formal Opinion 287 was intended to be an *exclusive* exception to old Canon 41. Accordingly, limiting the 1974 amendment to matters of attorney-client privilege covered in Formal Opinion 287 will not necessarily bring D.R. 7-102 into line with past interpretations of a lawyer's duty when a client's confidences and secrets are involved.

The tradition (which is backed by substantial policy considerations) that permits a lawyer to assure a client that information (whether a confidence or a secret) given to him will not be revealed to third parties is so important that it should take precedence, in all the most serious cases, over the duty imposed by D.R. 7-102(B). The many annotations to D.R. 4-101 reflect this policy. Of course, there will be situations where a lawyer may reveal the secrets and confidences of his client. Some of these are recognized in D.R. 4-101(C).

The balancing of the lawyer's duty to preserve confidences and to reveal frauds is best made by interpreting the phrase "privileged communication" in the 1974 amendment to D.R. 7-102(B) as referring to those confidences and secrets that are required to be preserved by D.R. 4-101.

Such an interpretation does not wipe out D.R. 7-102(B), because D.R. 7-102(B) applies to information received from any source, and it is not limited to information gained in the professional relationship as is D.R. 4-101. Under the suggested interpretation, the duty imposed by D.R. 7-102(B) would remain in force if the information clearly establishing a fraud on a person or tribunal and committed by a client in the course of representation were obtained by the lawyer from a third party (but not in connection with his professional relationship with the client), because it would not be a confidence or secret of a client entitled to confidentiality. D.R. 4-102(C) sets out several circumstances under which revelation of a secret or confidence is permissible, and thus in cases where these exceptions apply, D.R. 7-102(B) may make the optional disclosure of information under D.R. 4-101 a mandatory one. For example, when disclosure is required by a law, the "privileged communication" exception of D.R. 7102(B) is not applicable and disclosure may be required.

An interpretation of the 1974 amendment which would limit its scope to the attorney-client privilege as it exists in each jurisdiction and under the Federal Rules of Evidence is undesirable because the lawyer's ethical duty would depend upon the rules of evidence in a particular jurisdiction. There may be significant problems in knowing which jurisdiction's evidentiary rule would be applied in a given case, and the scope of that privilege may vary widely among jurisdictions. Furthermore, limiting the 1974 amendment to the scope of the attorney-client privilege raises problems as to the difference between waiver of privilege by a client and a consent to the lawyer's disclosure of a confidence.

It is not reasonable to put a lawyer at peril of discipline if, after determining that he has information that "clearly" establishes fraud (a difficult task in itself), he must also determine the relevant rule of attorney-client privilege in order to determine whether he must reveal the client's confidences and secrets. Also, we believe that it is inconsistent with the lawyer's confidential relationship with his client to impose at the same time a duty to evaluate the client's confidences to determine whether the level of evidence of "fraud" has been reached that would require disclosure of such confidences. The lawyer's problem is not lessened, in this respect, by interpreting fraud in D.R. 7-102(B), as we do, as being used in the sense of active fraud, with a requirement of *scienter* or intent to deceive.

The interpretation here adopted by the committee, which would preserve confidential information received in connection with the professional relationship, minimizes the problems. The committee believes that this interpretation does not go too far in relieving a lawyer of any responsibility to others because it does not alter the standing sanctions against the lawyer's involvement in a fraud nor alter the lawyer's duty under D.R. 7102(B) when his information is obtained outside the confidential relationship.

NOTES

1.   Does Opinion 341 deprive DR 7-102(B) of all real meaning? In what circumstances might there remain an obligation to disclose? Note that Opinion 341 construes DR 7-102(B) of the old Model Code, which, as the opinion describes,

originally included an obligation of disclosure for client fraud. Model Rule 1.6 succeeds DR 7-102(B). Consider the 2003 expansion of situations in which Rule 1.6 allows disclosure — including those relating to fraud and financial harm. Note though that Rule 1.6 permits but does not require disclosure. Although Model Rule 4.1 calls for disclosure of a fraudulent act of a client, it fences in this obligation by making it subordinate to the confidentiality obligation of Model Rule 1.6. For a critical view of the ABA's ambivalence and clarity on the subject of disclosing client fraud, see Robert Condlin, What's Love Got to Do With It? — It's Not Like They're Your Friends for Christ's Sake: The Complicated Relationship Between Lawyer and Client, 82 Neb. L. Rev. 211 (2003).

2.   The essential issue is the extent to which a lawyer should be required or permitted to reveal information obtained through the lawyer-client relationship that might prevent illegal acts or harm, or rectify past fraud either upon a tribunal or an individual. Historically, the Model Code had imposed upon the attorney an obligation to maintain not only confidences (protected by the attorney-client privilege), but also secrets. Those who supported the traditional view argued that narrowing the scope of confidentiality substantially altered the attorney-client relationship. They were satisfied with the narrow exception that permitted (but did not require) a lawyer to reveal a confidence or secret when necessary to prevent a future crime. Proponents of change wanted to expand the opportunities when an attorney was permitted to "blow the whistle" in order to limit the client's ability to utilize the attorney in committing a fraud and also in order to prevent the harm itself. As discussed previously, with the enactment of Sarbanes-Oxley (and the corporate events that preceded the legislation), the ABA reconsidered its position on the benefit of free communication between the lawyer and the client and expanded disclosure under Rule 1.6.

3.   This problem may vary from jurisdiction to jurisdiction. See, for example, Susan Koniak, Regulating the Lawyers: Past Efforts and Future Possibilities When the Hurlyburly's Done: The Bar's Struggle With the SEC, 103 Colum. L. Rev. 1236 (2003). How much variation in the circumstances requiring, permitting, or forbidding a lawyer's disclosure of client fraud is desirable?

4.   Note that Circular 230, §10.21, states that the tax lawyer who learns that the client has not "complied with the revenue laws" shall promptly advise the client of the noncompliance, although Circular 230 does not appear to require the attorney to call upon the client to rectify the fraud.

4.   Withdrawal

The issue of client fraud and the lawyer's obligation of disclosure has been given attention in two recent ABA opinions. In the first, Opinion 92-366, the ABA considered the ethical obligations of a lawyer who knows or has reason to believe that her services or work product are being used by a client to perpetrate a fraud. In describing the lawyer's proper response to this situation, the Committee on Ethics and Professional Responsibility approved what has become known as the "noisy withdrawal." Reproduced below are the principal conclusions reached in the opinion:

> First, the lawyer must withdraw from any representation of the client that, directly or indirectly, would have the effect of assisting the client's continuing or intended future fraud.
>
> Second, the lawyer may withdraw from all representation of the client, and must withdraw from all representation if the fact of such representation is likely to be known to and relied upon by third persons to whom the continuing fraud is directed, and the representation is therefore likely to assist in the fraud.
>
> Third, the lawyer may disavow any of her work product to prevent its use in the client's continuing or intended future fraud, even though this may have the collateral effect of disclosing inferentially client confidences obtained during the representation. In some circumstances, such a disavowal of work product (commonly referred to as a "noisy" withdrawal) may be necessary in order to effectuate the lawyer's withdrawal from representation of the client.
>
> Fourth and finally, if the fraud is completed, and the lawyer does not know or reasonably believe that the client intends to continue the fraud or commit a future fraud by use of the lawyer's services or work product, the lawyer may withdraw from representation of the client but may not disavow any work product.

In the second opinion, Opinion 93-375, the ABA Committee considered the ethical obligations of a lawyer who represents a bank client in the course of an examination by a federal agency. Borrowing from ABA Opinion 314, the new opinion first determines that the agency, like the IRS, is not a tribunal and that the special disclosure obligations due to tribunals are not operative. We reproduce below those portions of the opinion that deal with particularly difficult issues: false statements by the client in the presence of the lawyer, false statements by the lawyer, and true statements but with material information omitted.

IV. True Statement by Lawyer but Omission of Other Material Information

Our conclusions respecting false statements by the lawyer extend to circumstances in which the lawyer omits mention of Loan 9, if the context is such that she knows the omission is likely to mislead the bank examiners. An omission may in a particular context be tantamount to an affirmative false statement. For example, if the lawyer knows that the examiners are unaware of Loan 9 and/or its implications for the LTOB rule, and if what she says to them affirmatively leads them to conclude that there is no such loan, or that it need not be aggregated, the lawyer may have violated her ethical obligation under Rule 4.1(a) not to mislead a third party. On the other hand, if the lawyer limits her statements to the question whether Loan 8 should be aggregated, and says nothing at all about any other loans, she cannot be faulted for failing to volunteer information about Loan 9 even if the examiners themselves make statements in the lawyer's presence to the effect that there are no other loans that need be aggregated. If Loan 9 has escaped the examiners' notice through no fault of the lawyer, the lawyer has no ethical obligation to dispel their erroneous impression that no such loan exists, and indeed is precluded from doing so by Rule 1.6.

We stress that a lawyer's ethical obligation to disclose in this context depends upon the role she has herself played in creating any misimpression. As noted earlier, if the client does all of the talking during the examination, and the lawyer does not continue her participation in successive meetings with the examiners on these matters, she has no obligation to come forward to divulge the existence of Loan 9. However, as the lawyer's role expands, so does her responsibility for making certain the examiners are not misled. If she is speaking for the client, then her ethical obligations are substantially greater than if she is merely present when the client himself is speaking to the examiners.

Our conclusion here does not depend upon a determination that the lawyer is acting as an "advocate" or as an "agent" for the client; rather, it is based on a purely practical analysis of what the lawyer does or says. We do not believe it helpful to make a lawyer's ethical obligation of disclosure depend upon how she or someone else may abstractly characterize her role in representing a client. Most people, including even lawyers themselves, will doubtless find it easier to decide what responsibility a lawyer had for making or reinforcing a misrepresentation by simply looking at what the lawyer said and did rather than determining what hat the lawyer was wearing when she said or did it.

V. The Lawyer's Written Opinion

If, before becoming aware of Loan 9, the lawyer had written an opinion addressed to the client bank stating that the bank was not in violation of the LTOB rules, and later learned that the client planned to submit the opinion to the regulators, she would have an obligation to see that her opinion (in effect, her services) did not have the effect of assisting the client's fraudulent course of conduct. In ABA Formal Opinion No. 92366, . . . the Committee expressed the view that a lawyer has an affirmative obligation to disaffirm her work product notwithstanding the dictates of Rule 1.6, if failure to do so would have the forbidden effect of lending assistance to the client's continuing or future fraud, even if such disaffirmance would have the collateral effect of inferentially revealing client confidences. However, the obligation to protect client confidences in Rule 1.6 always acts as a counterweight to the lawyer's obligation to disassociate herself from a client's fraud. Thus, before taking any steps to disaffirm the misleading opinion, she should inform the client of her intention to do so, and give the client an opportunity not to use it.

VI. The Regulators' Interpretation of the Law

If the lawyer reasonably believes that Loan 9 need not be aggregated, but also believes that the bank examiners would be of a contrary view, she has no ethical obligation under Rule 4.1 or under any other provision of the rules to bring the loan to the examiners' attention. In deciding what her obligations may be under the ethics rules to disassociate herself from client fraud, the lawyer must be able to rely on her own informed judgment as to whether in fact such a fraud is occurring. If she has a reasonable basis for her legal conclusion, she should not be held liable for an ethical violation simply because the examiners may be of a different view. Nothing in the ethics rules requires a lawyer to bring to the attention of the examiners a violation by a client in which the lawyer has had no role. *A fortiori*, a lawyer has no obligation to bring to the attention of the examiners conduct the lawyer believes is not a violation, even if she has reason to believe that the examiners may be of a contrary view.

Despite the issuance of these opinions by the ABA, the subject of balancing the ethical obligation of confidentiality remains controversial, a controversy that is evidenced by two articles. In Geoffrey C. Hazard, Jr., Lawyers and Client Fraud: They Still Don't Get It, 6 Geo. J. Legal Ethics 701 (1993), Professor Hazard is critical of the conclusions reached in Opinion 92-366. In his view, Rule 1.6 already contemplates a noisy withdrawal in the face of client fraud (see Commentary to the Rule, allowing the withdrawing lawyer to "withdraw or disaffirm any opinion, document, affirmation, or the like"), and he does not believe that an opinion was necessary to establish this point. He also expresses the view that the opinion's broad requirements for mandatory withdrawal are erroneous. Finally, he is of the view that the fact situation chosen by the committee as the framework for the opinion is unrealistic. This article provides valuable insight into the background of the Model Rules relating to client fraud and disclosure obligations.

Two members of the ABA Committee responded to Professor Hazard. Margaret C. Love and Lawrence J. Fox, Letter to Professor Hazard: Maybe Now He'll Get It, 7 Geo. J. Legal Ethics 145 (1993). In their view, the entitlement to make a noisy withdrawal cannot rest in a comment to Rule 1.6 because the Scope note to the Model Rules states that "Comments do not add obligations to the Rules. . . ." They differ with Professor Hazard on the obligation to withdraw and defend the conclusions reached in the opinion. These two articles provide a useful review of an unsettled area of legal ethics, one that may frequently be of concern to the tax lawyer. Does the 2003 expansion of disclosure exceptions in Rule 1.6 lend support to either side of the controversy?

We caution again, however, that resort must be made to the local rules and, where applicable, federal regulatory provisions such as those of the Securities and Exchange Commission, some versions of which explicitly permit (and some mandate) the lawyer to disclose client fraud.

NOTES

1.   Suppose the attorney has been negotiating with the Service over a single issue on a tax return. The lawyer discovers that the client has fraudulently reported another item not at issue. What should the lawyer do? Does it make a difference if the lawyer actually prepared the return?

Recall that Model Rule 1.6 and DR 4-101 generally prohibit a lawyer from revealing confidential information. Several ethics committees have held that an attorney cannot reveal misstatements by the client to the tax authorities unless authorized by the client. See, for instance, Alabama Op. 8389; New York City Op. 81-100. But a lawyer also cannot lie or make a misleading statement. See Circular 230 §10.51(b), which includes within the definition of disreputable conduct "giving false or misleading information or participating in any way in giving false or misleading information."

If the attorney discovers an error, he is obligated to call it to the client's attention. Circular 230 §10.21. Recall the earlier discussion about amended returns. If the client refuses to amend the return, the attorney has no further obligation, although he must avoid misleading the Service. Must the attorney withdraw if the attorney prepared the return?

2.   Clearly, if asked a direct question, a lawyer may not provide false information. For example, if the Service is examining a depreciation deduction, the lawyer may not state that the client purchased a building when, in fact, he purchased nondepreciable land. But suppose the client answers the question, providing the erroneous information and subsequently tells the lawyer that he provided false information. The lawyer of course must remonstrate with the client to reverse the error. But suppose the client refuses? What can the lawyer do?

In this instance, the lawyer has been used to perpetrate the fraud. Nevertheless, in almost all jurisdictions, the lawyer is not free to reveal the information because it is a confidence. The lawyer is free to withdraw and may in fact be required to do so. See ABA Opinion 314. However, the opinion cautions that the duty to disassociate may be tempered if "it is obvious that the very act of disassociation would have the effect of violating" Rule 1.6. Does that concern remain after 2003 with the addition of the language now found in Rule 1.6(b)(2) and (3)? A real issue is how he should go about doing that. Should he communicate the fact of withdrawal to the Service? Opinion 92-366 permits a "noisy withdrawal" where the lawyer has unwittingly assisted in client fraud if the fraud is ongoing and the fact of representation is likely to assist the fraud. Opinion 93-375 notes that the noisy withdrawal option should be interpreted narrowly. Guidelines Second states: "Withdrawal from the engagement must be carefully undertaken so as to balance the desire or obligation to withdraw against the requirements that confidences not be disclosed and the client's interest not be otherwise prejudiced." Is a noisy withdrawal consistent with ABA Opinion 314? What could the attorney possibly say to the IRS that would not trigger suspicion?

Suppose Circular 230 were amended to require that the practitioner must withdraw and take steps to prevent the IRS from relying on the previous false communication. Is that essentially what the Securities and Exchange Commission has done on its behalf? Would the current version of Model Rule 1.6 support such a position on the IRS side if Circular 230 were so amended?

5.   Errors That Favor the Client: To Disclose or Not to Disclose

Closely related to the issue whether client fraud may be disclosed is the question whether the tax lawyer may (must) disclose errors made by her client or by the Service. We assume that such errors favor the client and that the client may not want to have them disclosed. Given the narrow opportunities for disclosure under Model Rule 1.6, it appears that a lawyer who becomes aware of client error generally is not free to disclose that error. Circular 230, §10.21, requires that the tax practitioner who becomes aware of the fact that the client has not complied with the tax law must advise the client of that fact. However, it imposes no disclosure obligation.

Opinion 314 similarly requires no disclosure of client error. AICPA Statement No. 7, reprinted in Appendix H, states that the CPA who discovers an error on a return that is the subject of representation should inform the client promptly but that the "CPA is neither obligated to inform the Internal Revenue Service nor may the CPA do so without the client's permission, except where required by law." Guidelines Second suggest that the practitioner may wish to consider withdrawal, but they do not counsel disclosure.

Circumstances under which a tax practitioner may face this issue are explored in the following notes.

NOTES

1.   Suppose you reach a settlement agreement with the IRS on behalf of your client. When the Service sends a settlement document for you to sign, you discover the Service has made a mathematical mistake in your client's favor. Must you disclose it to the Service? May you disclose it without consulting your client? Model Rule 1.2 provides: "A lawyer shall abide by a client's decisions concerning the objectives of representation . . . and shall consult with the client as to the means by which they are to be pursued." Does this mean that the lawyer must consult with the client? Is consultation sufficient or must the lawyer obtain consent to point out the mistake to the Service? ABA Inf. Op. 86-1518 (1986) held that a lawyer who is aware that his adversary in a negotiation has made a "scrivener's error" in a drafting contract has an ethical obligation to call the error to the adversary's attention without consulting the client. In Guidelines Second, Frederic Corneel likens this to having a cashier return a dollar bill stuck to another one without consulting the store owner. Is this an apt analogy? Presumably the store owner has given the cashier the authority to do this. Has a client automatically given a lawyer the same authority? Two local bar opinions conclude that the client must be consulted and the disclosure may not be made without client consent. Chicago Bar Assn. Op. 864 (1988); Dallas Bar Assn. Op. 1989-4.

2.   Suppose in explaining why a very favorable settlement offer is being made, the appeals officer misstates the law and it is clear she is relying on this erroneous understanding. May you point out the error to the appeals officer? Must you obtain the consent of your client? Is your answer the same if the appeals officer misstates one of the facts?

3.   Does the lawyer have the authority to extend the statute of limitations without client consultation and consent? Suppose an appeals officer sends a settlement offer and asks for a response in two weeks. If you know that the statute of limitations will expire in six days, can you simply wait until the following week to reply? Could you reply on the fourth day without consulting the client?

4.   What if an agent asked the attorney the following: Are you aware of any item in the return that probably would be treated differently by the Service if it knew all the facts? If the attorney knew of an item that was highly problematic (even reasonably problematic), could he answer yes? Could he answer no? See Frederic G. Corneel, The Service and the Private Practitioner: Face to Face and Hand in Hand — A Private Practitioner's View, 11 Am. J. Tax Poly. 343, 348 (1994); Watson, Tax Lawyers, Ethical Obligations, and the Duty to the System, 47 Kan. L. Rev. 847 (1999).

You discover a serious mistake on a client's prior year's return that affects a current matter. You request that the client disclose the mistake and he refuses. You withdraw. A lawyer in a successor firm calls you to ask why the representation was terminated. What can you say?

Most tax practitioners proceed on the assumption that the taxpayer is entitled, as discussed in Chapter 2, to report those tax return positions that satisfy the standards for preassessment litigation in the Tax Court, that is, positions that fall into the reasonable-basis/not-frivolous range. If taxpayers desire assurance against penalty, they will make adequate disclosure of positions for which there is not substantial authority. The assumption is that the Service will challenge those positions with which it disagrees, and that such challenges will result from the Service's examination activity. One unsettled question, however, is whether the Service is entitled to ask a taxpayer very broad questions designed to probe whether the return contains any positions about which the taxpayer may have some doubt.

This kind of self-examination technique was employed by the Service in coordinated examination cases (applicable to large corporate taxpayers) in the early 1980s in the form of the so-called eleven questions. The number of questions was later reduced to five (including: (1) "During the period from __ to __, did the corporation make any loan, donation, or other disbursement, directly or indirectly, to any corporate officer or employee, or any other person, for contributions made or to be made, directly or indirectly, for the benefit of, or for the purpose of opposing, any government or subdivision thereof, political party, political candidate, or political committee, whether domestic or foreign? And (2) During the period from __ to __, did the corporation, or any other person or entity acting on its behalf, maintain a bank account, or any other account of any kind, whether domestic or foreign, which account was not reflected in the corporate books and records, or which account was not listed, titled, or identified in the name of the corporation?"). See Internal Revenue Manual — Audit (CCH) Exhibit 42(11)0-3 (Questionnaire for Use in Coordinated Examinations).

For a discussion critical of the use of this audit technique, see Sherwin P. Simmons, The "Eleven Questions," An Extraordinary New Audit Technique, 30 Tax Law. 23 (1976). Moreover, the authority of the Service to pose such generalized questions has been circumscribed by the courts. See United States v. Richards, 479 F. Supp. 828 (E.D. Va. 1979), aff'd, 631 F.2d 341 (4th Cir. 1980), holding the original eleven questions to be overly broad. Compare United

States v. Wyatt, 637 F.2d 293 (5th Cir. 1981), and United States v. McLain, 84-1 USTC ¶ 9215 (5th Cir. 1984), sustaining the right of the Service to pose its list of questions. In *Wyatt*, the Fifth Circuit held that the issue in a summons enforcement proceeding is one of relevance and not one of the breadth of the questions. See also Barquero v. United States, 18 F.3d 1311 (5th Cir. 1994), in which the court applied the *Wyatt* test of relevance in upholding IRS summonses requiring the production of documents by the taxpayers and various third parties; U.S. v. Bright, 2007 U.S. Dist. LEXIS 67306 (D. HI 2007) (same).

In an analogous area, the Service has, in corporate audits, sought to obtain (1) copies of internal audit reports, (2) copies of audit workpapers held by the corporation's outside auditing firm, and (3) identification of the items that make up the corporation's tax reserve. Instructions to field personnel are reproduced below.

The Internal Revenue Service has extraordinarily broad power to obtain information from taxpayers. Section 7602 permits it to summon "any books, papers, records, or other data . . . as *may* be relevant or material to its inquiry into the correctness of a taxpayer's return." [Emphasis added.] An administrative summons issued by the Service may be enforced in a federal district court under §7604. The courts have indicated a willingness to enforce almost any summons for material of even potential relevance to a return investigation. United States v. Powell, 379 U.S. 48 (1964); United States v. Arthur Young, 465 U.S. 805 (1984).

In one exercise of its summons power to aid in locating errors on tax returns, the Service sought access to the workpapers of the firms that provided accounting and audit services to corporate taxpayers. Specifically the Service sought audit workpapers that detailed the makeup of the company's tax accrual, the account that constituted its estimate of the taxes that it might be required to pay. Under generally accepted accounting principles, the tax liability accrual constituted the company's best assessment of its tax liability, and the Service reasoned that access to this information would lead it to any uncertainties in the reported tax liability. Taxpayers and their accounting firms resisted disclosure of this information, and the Service ultimately issued an Internal Revenue Manual provision directing field personnel to press for this information only in "unusual circumstances" and under prescribed procedures. That manual provision is reproduced below.

Internal Revenue Service Manual: Accountants' Workpapers

AUDIT WORKPAPERS, TAX ACCRUAL WORKPAPERS, AND TAX RECONCILIATION WORKPAPERS DEFINED 4.10.20.2 (07-12-2004)

1.   Audit Workpapers Defined. These are workpapers created by or for the independent auditor. They are retained by the independent auditor and may be shared with the taxpayer. These workpapers include information about the procedures followed, the tests performed, the information obtained, and the conclusions reached pertinent to the independent auditor's review of a taxpayer's financial

statements. Audit workpapers may include work programs, analyses, memoranda, letters of confirmation and representation, abstracts of company documents, and schedules or commentaries prepared or obtained by the auditor. These workpapers provide important support for the independent auditor's opinion as to the fairness of the presentation of the financial statements, in conformity with generally accepted auditing standards and generally accepted accounting principles.

2.   Tax Accrual Workpapers Defined. The term "tax accrual workpapers" refers to those audit workpapers, whether prepared by the taxpayer, the taxpayer's accountant, or the independent auditor, that relate to the tax reserve for current, deferred and potential or contingent tax liabilities, however classified or reported on audited financial statements, and to footnotes disclosing those tax reserves on audited financial statements. These workpapers reflect an estimate of a company's tax liabilities and may also be referred to as the tax pool analysis, tax liability contingency analysis, tax cushion analysis, or tax contingency reserve analysis. The name given the workpapers by the taxpayer, the taxpayer's accountant, or the independent auditor is not determinative.

3.   A. Tax accrual workpapers typically include determinations and related documentation of estimates of potential or contingent tax liabilities related to tax positions taken by the taxpayer on certain transactions. In addition, there may be an audit trail and/or complete explanation of the transactions. There may also be information on whether there was reliance on outside legal advice; an assessment of the taxpayer's position and potential for sustention; references to promotional materials; and comments on unwritten agreements, confidentiality agreements, restitution agreements, contingency fees, expectations, and other material facts surrounding the transactions. The workpapers may include documents written by the taxpayer's employees and officers describing or evaluating the tax strategies. The scope and quality of the workpapers will vary.

B. The total amount of the reserve established on a company's general ledger for all contingent tax liabilities of the company for a specific reporting period is not considered a part of the company's tax accrual workpapers. An examiner may ask a taxpayer about the existence and the total amount of a reserve for all contingent tax liabilities as a matter of routine examination procedure, without a showing of unusual circumstances and without seeking executive approval for the request.

C. A request to reveal the existence or amount of a tax reserve established for any specific known or unknown transaction, however, is the same as asking for a description of a portion of the contents of the tax accrual workpapers. Requests for a description of the contents of the tax accrual workpapers are covered by the same policy of restraint as requests for the actual documents that make up the tax accrual workpapers.

4.   Tax Reconciliation Workpapers Defined. Tax reconciliation workpapers are used in assembling and compiling financial data preparatory to placement on a

tax return. These papers typically include final trial balances for each entity and a schedule of consolidating and adjusting entries. They include information used to trace financial information to the tax return. Any tax return preparation documents that reconcile net income per books or financial statements to taxable income are also tax reconciliation workpapers. Tax reconciliation workpapers do not become tax accrual workpapers when they are used in the preparation of tax accrual workpapers or are attached to tax accrual workpapers. Preexisting documents that a taxpayer, the taxpayer's accountant, or the taxpayer's independent auditor consults, refers to, or relies upon in making evaluations or decisions regarding the tax reserves or in performing an audit are not themselves considered tax accrual workpapers or audit workpapers, even though the taxpayer, the taxpayer's accountant, or independent auditor may store such documents with the tax accrual workpapers or audit workpapers.

SERVICE POLICY FOR REQUESTING WORKPAPERS:
4.10.20.3 (07-12-2004)

1. Tax Reconciliation Workpapers. Tax reconciliation workpapers should be requested as a routine matter at the beginning of an examination. Ordinarily, tax reconciliation workpapers are prepared and provided by the taxpayer. If these workpapers are unavailable from the taxpayer, access will be sought from the taxpayer's accountants.

2. Audit or Tax Accrual Workpapers. The general standard for requests for audit or tax accrual workpapers is the unusual circumstances standard. This standard applies to all requests for audit workpapers, requests for tax accrual workpapers that do not involve a listed transaction as defined in Treas. Reg. §1.6011-4 . . . For the standard for requests for tax accrual workpapers involving a listed transaction for returns filed after February 28, 2000, see IRM 4.10.20.3.2.

UNUSUAL CIRCUMSTANCES STANDARD:
4.10.20.3.1 (07-12-2004)

1. In unusual circumstances (as defined in IRM 4.10.20.3.1(2)), the Service may request audit or tax accrual workpapers. Examiners should keep in mind that the taxpayer's records are the primary source of factual data to support the tax return. Audit or tax accrual workpapers should normally be sought only when such factual data cannot be obtained from the taxpayer's records or from available third parties, and then only as a collateral source for factual data. Audit or tax accrual workpapers should be requested with discretion and not as a matter of standard examining procedure. Such a request should generally be made first to the taxpayer, but may be directed to the taxpayer, the taxpayer's accountant, the independent auditor, or all three, based on the Service's determination as to the location of the workpapers sought. The request should be limited to the portion of the workpapers that is material and relevant to

the examination. Whether an item is considered to be material is based upon the examiner's judgment and an evaluation of the facts and circumstances of the case.

    2.   Unusual circumstances for this purpose exist under the following conditions:

        A. A specific issue has been identified by the examiner for which there exists a need for additional facts;

        B. The examiner has sought from the taxpayer and available third parties all the facts known to them relating to the identified issue; and

        C. The examiner has sought a supplementary analysis (not necessarily contained in the workpapers) of facts relating to the identified issue and the examiner has performed a reconciliation of the taxpayer's Schedule M-1 or M-3 as it pertains to the identified issue.

REQUESTS FOR TAX ACCRUAL WORKPAPERS INVOLVING LISTED TRANSACTIONS: 4.10.20.3.2 (07-12-2004)

    1.   Background. Although the Supreme Court recognized the Service's right to obtain tax accrual workpapers in United States v. Arthur Young & Co., 465 U.S. 805 (1984), the Service announced that it would continue its policy of restraint and would not request tax accrual workpapers as a standard examination technique. Announcement 84-46, 1984-18 I.R.B. 18. In 2002, the Service modified its historical policy of restraint with respect to tax accrual workpapers. In general, the modified policy applies to returns filed by taxpayers claiming benefits from listed transactions. Announcement 2002-63, 2002-2 C.B. 72. A listed transaction is defined in Treas. Reg. §1.6011-4, and subsection (b)(2) defines listed transactions to include substantially similar transactions. The policy governing requests for tax accrual workpapers varies according to when the tax return was filed.

    * * * *

RETURNS FILED ON OR AFTER JULY 1, 2002:
4.10.20.3.2.3 (01-15-2005)

    1.   If a listed transaction was properly disclosed on the return, in the manner prescribed by Treas. Reg. §1.6011-4, the Service will routinely request tax accrual workpapers that pertain only to the listed transaction for the year under examination. In these circumstances, the Service may also request tax accrual workpapers pertaining to the disclosed listed transaction for a year(s) not under examination, if such workpapers may be directly relevant to the Service's audit for the year under examination, such as those described in paragraph (iii).

    2.   If, however, a listed transaction was not timely and properly disclosed in the manner described by Treas. Reg. §1.6011-4, the Service will routinely request all tax accrual workpapers for the year under examination. In these circumstances, the

Service may also request tax accrual workpapers for years not under examination, if such workpapers may be directly relevant to the Service's audit of any known listed transactions for the years under examination.

3. As a discretionary matter, all tax accrual workpapers for the year under examination will be requested if:

    A. The Service determines that the taxpayer claimed tax benefits from multiple listed transactions that were all properly disclosed; or

    B. In connection with the examination of a return claiming tax benefits from a single listed transaction that was disclosed, there are reported financial irregularities with respect to the taxpayer.

Note: In either of these circumstances, the Service may also request tax accrual workpapers pertaining to the known listed transactions or the reported financial irregularities for years not under examination, if such workpapers may be directly relevant to the audit for the years under examination.

4. The term "as a discretionary matter" as used in this section of the IRM denotes the exercise of prudence in executing policies. Wherever that term is used within this section of the IRM, the presumption is that the Service will request all tax accrual workpapers. There may be rare instances in which requesting all workpapers might not be appropriate. For example, if the taxpayer fully concedes all listed transactions, including penalties, and the parties have executed a specific matters closing agreement with respect to the issues conceded by the taxpayer then it may be appropriate not to seek all of the workpapers. If there is an exceptional situation where the examiner believes it is not appropriate to pursue all of the tax accrual workpapers, approval not to request all of the workpapers would be required. . . .

5. If a transaction becomes a listed transaction, within the definition in Treas. Reg. §1.6011-4, subsequent to the filing of a tax return, tax accrual workpapers will be requested, so long as at the time of the request the transaction is a listed transaction. Some listing notices contain effective dates which also should be considered in determining whether a transaction is listed. The examiner should work with Field Counsel to make these determinations.

PROCEDURE FOR REQUESTING AUDIT AND/OR TAX ACCRUAL WORKPAPERS: 4.10.20.4 (07-12-2004)

1. Information Document Requests (IDRs). Upon determining that a request for audit and/or tax accrual workpapers should be made, the examiner will prepare an IDR for the workpapers. . . .

2. Any IDR for audit or tax accrual workpapers should request that, in the event a taxpayer or third party does not produce a document requested by the IDR, the taxpayer or third party should provide the examiner with a description of the document being withheld, including the number of pages contained in the

document, and the specific reason why the document is not being provided in response to the IDR. If a document is not produced based on a claim of privilege, the taxpayer or third party should provide the examiner with a detailed privilege log. However, if the taxpayer or a third party served with an IDR fails to provide (or unreasonably delays providing) the requested descriptions of documents being withheld and/or the requested detailed privilege log for any privilege being claimed, the examiner should promptly issue an appropriate summons, as described in IRM 4.10.20.4.1, Issuance of Summonses, requesting all withheld workpapers.

    3.   Review or Approval. Before an IDR for these workpapers is issued, review or approval must occur. . . .

ISSUANCE OF SUMMONSES: 4.10.20.4.1 (07-12-2004)

    1.   If a taxpayer or third party does not produce audit or tax accrual workpapers in response to an IDR, the examiner must determine whether to issue a summons. The standards and procedures will differ depending upon whether the request for workpapers was made under the unusual circumstances standard (see IRM 4.10.20.3.1) or involved a listed transaction.

    2. Audit or Tax Accrual Workpapers under the Unusual Circumstances Standard.

        A. The examiner should make the decision whether to issue a summons based on all the facts and circumstances surrounding the case. If it is necessary to issue a summons to secure audit or tax accrual workpapers under the unusual circumstances standard, the examiner should ensure that the burden of compliance with the summons will not be unreasonably onerous. The summons should provide a specific and unambiguous description of the records demanded so that the summoned party can reasonably be expected to identify the exact records sought. The summons should also identify the particular taxpayer for which the documents are sought, the period covered, and the nature of the documents. Unless the examiner determines that all of the workpapers are material and relevant, the summons should identify and request only those documents relating to the specific matters under consideration. Finally, the summons should specify whether it seeks audit or tax accrual workpapers, or both.

        B. [Approval]. . . .

        C. [Review]. . . .

        D. Counsel will review the summons to ensure that the summons is appropriately drafted and meets all legal requirements. The summons should be directed to the taxpayer, the taxpayer's accountant, the independent auditor, or all three, based on a determination as to the location of the workpapers.

    3.   Tax Accrual Workpapers Involving Listed Transactions.

        A. The examiner must prepare a summons for workpapers that are not produced in response to an IDR.

B. When the examiner prepares a summons for the workpapers, a statement of the facts and circumstances should also be prepared. The records sought must be described with reasonable certainty. The requirement of reasonable certainty will be satisfied if the description of the records is specific and unambiguous and the summoned party can reasonably be expected to identify the exact records sought. The summons must identify the particular taxpayer for which the documents are sought, the period the documents cover, and the nature of the documents.

C. Executive Review. . . .

D. The examiner will work with Field Counsel to prepare the summons. . . .

E. Counsel will review the summons to ensure that the summons is appropriately drafted and meets all legal requirements. The summons should be directed to the taxpayer, the taxpayer's accountant, the independent auditor, or all three, based on a determination as to the location of the tax accrual workpapers.

ENFORCEMENT OF SUMMONSES: 4.10.20.4.2 (07-12-2004)

1. If the summoned party does not comply with the summons, the examiner will refer the matter to Counsel for enforcement of the summons. . . .

NOTE

Given the breadth of the summons power under §7602, the potential relevance of the information sought, and the willingness of the courts to enforce summonses, why would the Service voluntarily have receded from its earlier, unfettered demands for this kind of information? Was the retreat a tacit admission by the Service that there are some adversarial "rules of the game" in the examination process that must be observed? For example, could the Service include on the Form 1040 a section in which it directed taxpayers to identify all positions that they believe might more likely than not be incorrect? If not, why not? If it did so, what kinds of problems would that create for tax practitioners? Note, however, that the Service has indicated in this most recent version of its policy on workpapers that in the case of "listed transactions" (i.e., potential tax shelters), it is modifying its historic position of restraint. Is there an observable trend among rules and policies governing summonses, confidentiality rules, and regulatory gatekeeping burdens? The rules regarding tax shelters and related issues are explored further in Chapter 4.

Before issuing its more restrictive manual provision, the Service had already engaged various corporate taxpayers and accounting firms in litigation over this issue. Those cases went forward despite the position announced in the manual, and they culminated before the Supreme Court in the following opinion (which was cited above in the IRS Manual excerpt), which was joined in by a unanimous court.

United States v. Arthur Young & Co.

465 U.S. 805 (1984)

Chief Justice BURGER delivered the opinion of the Court.

We granted certiorari to consider whether tax accrual workpapers prepared by a corporation's independent certified public accountant in the course of regular financial audits are protected from disclosure in response to an Internal Revenue Service summons issued under §7602.

I

A

Respondent Arthur Young & Co. is a firm of certified public accountants. As the independent auditor for respondent Amerada Hess Corp., Young is responsible for reviewing the financial statements prepared by Amerada as required by the federal securities laws. In the course of its review of these financial statements, Young verified Amerada's statement of its contingent tax liabilities, and, in so doing, prepared the tax accrual workpapers at issue in this case. Tax accrual workpapers are documents and memoranda relating to Young's evaluation of Amerada's reserves for contingent tax liabilities. Such workpapers sometimes contain information pertaining to Amerada's financial transactions, identify questionable positions Amerada may have taken on its tax returns, and reflect Young's opinions regarding the validity of such positions. . . .

In 1975 the Internal Revenue Service began a routine audit to determine Amerada's corporate income tax liability for the tax years 1972 through 1974. When the audit revealed that Amerada had made questionable payments of $7830 from a "special disbursement account," the IRS instituted a criminal investigation of Amerada's tax returns as well. In that process, pursuant to §7602, the IRS issued an administrative summons to Young, which required Young to make available to the IRS all its Amerada files, including its tax accrual workpapers. Amerada instructed Young not to comply with the summons. . . .

II

Corporate financial statements are one of the primary sources of information available to guide the decisions of the investing public. In an effort to control the accuracy of the financial data available to investors in the securities markets, various provisions of the federal securities laws require publicly held corporations to file their financial statements with the Securities and Exchange Commission. Commission regulations stipulate that these financial reports must be audited by an independent certified public accountant in accordance with generally accepted auditing standards.

By examining the corporation's books and records, the independent auditor determines whether the financial reports of the corporation have been prepared in accordance with generally accepted accounting principles. The auditor then issues an opinion as to whether the financial statements, taken as a whole, fairly present the financial position and operations of the corporation for the relevant period.

An important aspect of the auditor's function is to evaluate the adequacy and reasonableness of the corporation's reserve account for contingent tax liabilities. This reserve account, known as the tax accrual account, the noncurrent tax account, or the tax pool, represents the amount set aside by the corporation to cover adjustments and additions to the corporation's actual tax liability. Additional corporate tax liability may arise from a wide variety of transactions. The presence of a reserve account for such contingent tax liabilities reflects the corporation's awareness of, and preparedness for, the possibility of an assessment of additional taxes.

The independent auditor draws upon many sources in evaluating the sufficiency of the corporation's tax accrual account. Initially, the corporation's books, records, and tax returns must be analyzed in light of the relevant Code provisions, Treasury Regulations, Revenue Rulings, and case law. The auditor will also obtain and assess the opinions, speculations, and projections of management with regard to unclear, aggressive, or questionable tax positions that may have been taken on prior tax returns. In exploring the tax consequences of certain transactions, the auditor often engages in a "worst-case" analysis in order to ensure that the tax accrual account accurately reflects the full extent of the corporation's exposure to additional tax liability. From this conglomeration of data, the auditor is able to estimate the potential cost of each particular contingency, as well as the probability that the additional liability may arise.

The auditor's tax accrual workpapers record this process of examination and analysis. Such workpapers may document the auditor's interviews with corporate personnel, judgments on questions of potential tax liability, and suggestions for alternative treatments of certain transactions for tax purposes. Tax accrual workpapers also contain an overall evaluation of the sufficiency of the corporation's reserve for contingent tax liabilities, including an item-by-item analysis of the corporation's potential exposure to additional liability. In short, tax accrual workpapers pinpoint the "soft spots" on a corporation's tax return by highlighting those areas in which the corporate taxpayer has taken a position that may, at some later date, require the payment of additional taxes.

III

In seeking access to Young's tax accrual workpapers, the IRS exercised the summons power conferred by §7602, which authorizes the Secretary of the Treasury to summon and "examine any books, papers, records, or other data which may be relevant or material" to a particular tax inquiry. The District Court and the Court of Appeals determined that the tax accrual workpapers at issue in this case satisfied the relevance requirement of §7602, because they "might have thrown light upon" the correctness of Amerada's tax return. Because the relevance of tax accrual workpapers is a logical predicate to the question whether such workpapers should be protected by some form of work-product immunity, we turn first to an evaluation of the relevance issue. We agree that such workpapers are relevant within the meaning of §7602.

As the language of §7602 clearly indicates, an IRS summons is not to be judged by the relevance standards used in deciding whether to admit evidence in federal court. Cf. Fed.Rule Evid. 401. The language "may be" reflects Congress' express intention to allow the IRS to obtain items of even *potential* relevance to an ongoing investigation, without reference to its admissibility. The purpose of Congress is obvious: the Service can hardly be expected to know whether such data will in fact be relevant until it is procured and scrutinized. As a tool of discovery, the §7602 summons is critical to the investigative and enforcement functions of the IRS, see United States v. Powell, 379 U.S. 48 (1964); the Service therefore should not be required to establish that the documents it seeks are actually relevant in any technical, evidentiary sense.

That tax accrual workpapers are not actually used in the preparation of tax returns by the taxpayer or its own accountants does not bar a finding of relevance within the meaning of §7602. The filing of a corporate tax return entails much more than filling in the blanks on an IRS form in accordance with undisputed tax principles; more likely than not, the return is a composite interpretation of corporate transactions made by corporate officers in the light most favorable to the taxpayer. It is the responsibility of the IRS to determine whether the corporate taxpayer in completing its return has stretched a particular tax concept beyond what is allowed. Records that illuminate any aspect of the return — such as the tax accrual workpapers at issue in this case — are therefore highly relevant to legitimate IRS inquiry. The Court of Appeals acknowledged this: "It is difficult to say that the assessment by the independent auditor of the correctness of positions taken by the taxpayer in his return would not throw 'light upon' the correctness of the return." 677 F.2d, at 219. We accordingly affirm the Court of Appeals' holding that Young's tax accrual workpapers are relevant to the IRS investigation of Amerada's tax liability.

IV

A

We now turn to consider whether tax accrual workpapers prepared by an independent auditor in the course of a routine review of corporate financial statements should be protected by some form of work-product immunity from disclosure under §7602. Based upon its evaluation of the competing policies of the federal tax and securities laws, the Court of Appeals found it necessary to create a so-called privilege for the independent auditor's workpapers.

Our complex and comprehensive system of federal taxation, relying as it does upon self-assessment and reporting, demands that all taxpayers be forthright in the disclosure of relevant information to the taxing authorities. Without such disclosure, and the concomitant power of the Government to compel disclosure, our national tax burden would not be fairly and equitably distributed. In order to encourage effective tax investigations, Congress has endowed the IRS with expansive information-gathering authority; §7602 is the centerpiece of that congressional design. . . .

While §7602 is "subject to the traditional privileges and limitations," id., at 714, any other restrictions upon the IRS summons power should be avoided "absent unambiguous directions from Congress." United States v. Bisceglia, supra, 420 U.S., at 150. We are unable to discern the sort of "unambiguous directions from Congress" that would justify a judicially created work-product immunity for tax accrual workpapers summoned under §7602. Indeed, the very language of §7602 reflects precisely the opposite: a congressional policy choice *in favor of disclosure* of all information relevant to a legitimate IRS inquiry. In light of this explicit statement by the Legislative Branch, courts should be chary in recognizing exceptions to the broad summons authority of the IRS or in fashioning new privileges that would curtail disclosure under §7602. Cf. Milwaukee v. Illinois, 451 U.S. 304, 315, 68 (1981). If the broad latitude granted to the IRS by §7602 is to be circumscribed, that is a choice for Congress, and not this Court, to make. See United States v. Euge, supra, 444 U.S., at 712.

B

The Court of Appeals nevertheless concluded that "substantial countervailing policies," id., at 711, required the fashioning of a work-product immunity for an independent auditor's tax accrual workpapers. To the extent that the Court of Appeals, in its concern for the "chilling effect" of the disclosure of tax accrual work-papers, sought to facilitate communication between independent auditors and their clients, its remedy more closely resembles a testimonial accountant-client privilege than a work-product immunity for accountants' workpapers. But as this Court stated in Couch v. United States, 409 U.S. 322, 335 (1973), "no confidential accountant-client privilege exists under federal law, and no state-created privilege has been recognized in federal cases." In light of *Couch*, the Court of Appeals' effort to foster candid communication between accountant and client by creating a self-styled work-product privilege was misplaced, and conflicts with what we see as the clear intent of Congress.

Nor do we find persuasive the argument that a work-product immunity for accountants' tax accrual workpapers is a fitting analogue to the attorney work-product doctrine established in Hickman v. Taylor, supra. The *Hickman* work-product doctrine was founded upon the private attorney's role as the client's confidential advisor and advocate, a loyal representative whose duty it is to present the client's case in the most favorable possible light. An independent certified public accountant performs a different role. By certifying the public reports that collectively depict a corporation's financial status, the independent auditor assumes a *public* responsibility transcending any employment relationship with the client. The independent public accountant performing this special function owes ultimate allegiance to the corporation's creditors and stockholders, as well as to investing public. This "public watchdog" function demands that the accountant maintain total independence from the client at all times and requires complete fidelity to the public trust. To insulate from disclosure a certified public accountant's interpretations of the client's financial statements would be to ignore the significance of the accountant's role as a disinterested analyst charged with public obligations. . . .

We also reject respondents' position that fundamental fairness precludes IRS access to accountants' tax accrual workpapers. Respondents urge that the enforcement of an IRS summons for accountants' tax accrual workpapers permits the Government to probe the thought processes of its taxpayer citizens, thereby giving the IRS an unfair advantage in negotiating and litigating tax controversies. But if the SEC itself, or a private plaintiff in securities litigation, sought to obtain the tax accrual workpapers at issue in this case, they would surely be entitled to do so. In light of the broad congressional command of §7602, no sound reason exists for conferring lesser authority upon the IRS than upon a private litigant suing with regard to transactions concerning which the public has no interest. . . .

V

Beyond question it is desirable and in the public interest to encourage full disclosures by corporate clients to their independent accountants; if it is necessary to balance competing interests, however, the need of the Government for full disclosure of all information relevant to tax liability must also weigh in that balance. This kind of policy choice is best left to the Legislative Branch. Accordingly, the judgment of the Court of Appeals is affirmed in part and reversed in part, and the case is remanded for proceedings consistent with this opinion.

NOTES

1. As noted above, prior to the taxpayer's rather disastrous (and probably predictable) loss in *Arthur Young*, the Service had already acted to limit the authority of field personnel to seek access to tax accrual workpapers and related documents. This was probably a result better than might have been obtained in litigation. Given this, why did the litigants permit this case to go as far as it did? Might it have been prudent to limit the damage by settling the ongoing litigation (assuming that the government would have been willing to cooperate toward that end) and avoiding this rather damaging precedent?

2.   Shortly after the decision in *Arthur Young*, the Internal Revenue Service announced that it had no plans to change its administrative policy for seeking tax accrual workpapers:

Summonses for Workpapers

The Service does not plan to change its current procedures for requesting tax accrual workpapers relating to the evaluation of a corporation's reserves for contingent tax liabilities.

In a recent decision, United States v. Arthur Young and Co., the Supreme Court upheld the Service's position that tax accrual workpapers are relevant to an examination and reaffirmed the traditional privileges and limitations upon the Service's summons power.

The Court noted in its decision that the Service has demonstrated administrative sensitivity to the concerns expressed by the accounting profession by tightening its internal controls for the issuance of summonses for workpapers. There are no plans to change the current policy. [Announcement 84-46, 1984-18 I.R.B. 18.]

3.   As the Supreme Court notes, "the Court of Appeals apparently feared that, were the IRS to have access to tax accrual workpapers, a corporation may be tempted to withhold from its auditor" relevant information. Is this concern valid? It assumes that, absent a disclosure obligation to IRS, that taxpayers will freely furnish potentially adverse information to auditors. However, the probable effect of that information (whether or not IRS has access to it) is to require an increase in the tax accrual account and hence a reduction in annual reported earnings. Thus disclosure to an auditor results in lowered earnings. On the other hand, subsequent disclosure to IRS should result in no downward effect on earnings, that provision already having been made through the tax accrual account. Is it thus accurate to assert that possible disclosure to the IRS will inhibit the free flow of information between client and auditor?

4.   Following the *Arthur Young* decision, there were suggestions that taxpayers should engage lawyers, rather than accountants, to review the tax reserve because of the existence of an attorney-client privilege and the absence of an accountant-client privilege. Is this sound advice? Consider the analysis in United States v. Textron, 507 F.Supp.2d 138 (D. R.I. 2007) following the notes below.

5.   If a single accounting firm acts both as auditor of a taxpayer and as tax counselor, is there any internal conflict in light of these roles? The role of auditor requires that the accountant be "independent" but the role of tax advisor does not. See also AICPA Code of Professional Conduct Rules 101 and 102. Obviously an accounting firm may represent a taxpayer either as auditor or tax advisor; the issue is, may it ethically do both?

6.   In *Arthur Young*, the Service chose to proceed against the taxpayer's outside accounting firm rather than to seek the desired information from the taxpayer itself. In United States v. El Paso, 682 F.2d 530 (5th Cir. 1982), cert. denied, 466 U.S. 944 (1984), the Fifth Circuit held that the taxpayer must surrender tax accrual

information in response to an IRS summons. Why would the government not always pursue the taxpayer rather than the taxpayer's auditor? If information as to content of the tax reserve is sought from the taxpayer, as distinguished from the taxpayer's auditor, it is difficult for the taxpayer to resist production — the reserve is, after all, the taxpayer's reserve and not the auditor's — and there is no readily apparent ground for claiming privilege.

7.   When *Arthur Young* was argued before the Supreme Court, the lawyer for Arthur Young was asked by Justice O'Connor whether the information sought by the Internal Revenue Service (tax accrual workpapers relating to a client) would be available to the Securities and Exchange Commission upon request by that agency. Counsel for *Arthur Young* responded that it would be available. Was the game over at that point? Could the taxpayer realistically justify a refusal to produce to the IRS information that it conceded was available to the SEC? Consider the implications of this point as you read United States v. Textron, below.

8.   It has been suggested in some quarters that problems under *Arthur Young* can be avoided simply by having the outside auditors or internal audit personnel retain no explanatory workpapers. Is this realistic? Assume that no papers are retained but that the principal financial officer of the taxpayer corporation is asked under oath to describe all issues considered in creating the tax accrual account. Does he have a basis for refusing to respond?

9.   How should a lawyer advise a client who wants to know if all documents other than those favorable to his position can be destroyed after a transaction has been completed? If an audit has not begun, can the documents be destroyed? See Guidelines to Tax Practice Third, 57 Tax Law. 181 (2003).

Taxpayers have typically sought protection for workpapers under an argument of privilege (e.g. attorney-client, accountant-client). However in the following case, the taxpayer also articulated an independent ground, "work-product," which ultimately was successful. As you read this case, consider the ramifications of its holdings for most large corporate taxpayers under regular audit.

United States v. Textron

507 F. Supp. 2d 138 (2007)

Torres, Judge. . . .

Pursuant to 26 U.S.C. §§7402(b) and 7604, the United States has filed a petition to enforce an Internal Revenue Service (IRS) summons served on Textron Inc. and its subsidiaries ("Textron") in connection with the IRS's examination of Textron's tax liability for tax years 1998–2001. The summons seeks Textron's "tax accrual workpapers" for its 2001 tax year. Textron has refused to produce the requested documents on the grounds that (1) the summons was not issued for a legitimate purpose and (2) the tax accrual workpapers are privileged.

Because this Court finds that the requested documents are protected by the work product privilege, the petition for enforcement is denied.

FACTS

... Textron, Inc. is a publicly traded conglomerate with approximately 190 subsidiaries. One of its subsidiaries is Textron Financial Corporation (TFC), a company that provides commercial lending and financial services. In 2001 and 2002, Textron had six tax attorneys and a number of CPAs in its tax department but TFC's tax department consisted only of CPAs. Consequently, TFC relied on attorneys in Textron's tax department, private law firms, and outside accounting firms for additional assistance and advice regarding tax matters.

Like other large corporations, Textron's federal tax returns are audited periodically at which time the IRS examines the returns for the tax years that are part of the audit cycle. In conducting its audits, the IRS, typically, gathers relevant information by issuing "information document requests" (IDRs) to the taxpayer. If the IRS disagrees with a position taken by the taxpayer on its return, the IRS issues a Notice of Proposed Adjustments to the taxpayer. A taxpayer that disputes the proposed adjustments has several options to resolve the dispute within the agency. Those options range from an informal conference with the IRS team manager to a formal appeal to the IRS Appeals Board. If the dispute is not resolved within the agency, the taxpayer may file suit in federal court. In seven of its past eight audit cycles covering the period between 1980 and the present, Textron appealed disputed matters to the IRS Appeals Board; and three of these disputes resulted in litigation. ...

During the 1998–2001 audit cycle, the IRS learned, from examining Textron's 2001 return, that TFC had engaged in nine "sale-in, lease-out" (SILO) transactions involving telecommunications equipment and rail equipment. The IRS has classified such transactions as "listed transactions" because it considers them to be of a type engaged in for the purpose of tax avoidance. See 26 C.F.R. §1.6011-4(b)(2). The IRS issued more than 500 IDRs in connection with the 1998–2001 audit cycle, and Textron complied with all of them, except for the ones seeking its "tax accrual workpapers."

THE SUMMONS

On June 2, 2005, ... the manager of the IRS team examining Textron's return, issued an administrative summons for "all of the Tax Accrual Workpapers" for Textron's tax year ending on December 29, 2001. The summons defined the "Tax Accrual Workpapers" to include:

[A]ll accrual and other financial workpapers or documents created or assembled by the Taxpayer, an accountant for the Taxpayer, or the Taxpayer's independent auditor relating to any tax reserve for current, deferred, and potential or contingent tax liabilities, however classified or reported on audited financial statements, and to any footnotes disclosing reserves or contingent liabilities on audited financial statements. They include, but are not limited to, any and all analyses, computations,

opinions, notes, summaries, discussions, and other documents relating to such reserves
and any footnotes. . . .

Textron refused to produce its tax accrual workpapers, asserting that they are
privileged and that the summons was issued for an improper purpose.

THE TAX ACCRUAL WORKPAPERS

Because there is no immutable definition of the term "tax accrual workpapers,"
the documents that make up a corporation's "tax accrual workpapers" may vary from
case to case. In this case, the evidence shows that Textron's "tax accrual workpapers"
for the years in question consist, entirely, of:

> 1. A spreadsheet that contains:
> (a) lists of items on Textron's tax returns, which, in the opinion of Textron's
> counsel, involve issues on which the tax laws are unclear, and, therefore, may be
> challenged by the IRS;
> (b) estimates by Textron's counsel expressing, in percentage terms, their judg-
> ments regarding Textron's chances of prevailing in any litigation over those issues (the
> "hazards of litigation percentages"); and
> (c) the dollar amounts reserved to reflect the possibility that Textron might not
> prevail in such litigation (the "tax reserve amounts").
> 2. Backup workpapers consisting of the previous year's spreadsheet and earlier
> drafts of the spreadsheet together with notes and memoranda written by Textron's in-
> house tax attorneys reflecting their opinions as to which items should be included on
> the spreadsheet and the hazard of litigation percentage that should apply to each item.

The evidence shows that while Textron may possess documents, such as leases,
that contain factual information regarding the SILO transactions and other items
that may be listed on the spreadsheet, its tax accrual workpaper files do not include
any such documents. . . .

As stated by Norman Richter, Vice President of Taxes at Textron and Roxanne
Cassidy, Director, Tax Reporting at Textron, Textron's ultimate purpose in preparing the tax accrual workpapers was to ensure that Textron was "adequately
reserved with respect to any potential disputes or litigation that would happen in
the future." It seems reasonable to infer that Textron's desire to establish adequate
reserves also was prompted, in part, by its wish to satisfy an independent auditor that
Textron's reserve for contingent liabilities satisfied the requirements of generally
accepted accounting principles (GAAP) so that a "clean" opinion would be given
with respect to the financial statements filed by Textron with the SEC.

Each year, Textron's tax accrual workpapers are prepared shortly after the corporation's tax return is filed. The first step in preparing the workpapers is that
Textron's accountants circulate to Textron's attorneys a copy of the previous
year's tax accrual workpapers together with recommendations regarding their

proposed changes and/or additions for the current year. Textron's attorneys, then, review those materials, propose further changes to the spreadsheets and hazard litigation percentages which are returned to the accountants who compile the information and perform the mathematical calculations necessary to compute the tax reserve amounts. The attorneys and accountants, then, meet to give their approval so that the accountants may finalize the workpapers.

TFC goes through a similar process in preparing its tax accrual workpapers but, since TFC does not have any in-house attorneys, its accountants rely on tax advice obtained from outside accounting and law firms, before meeting with a Textron tax attorney to finalize the workpapers.

Once the tax reserve amounts for each item on the worksheets are established, those amounts are aggregated with other contingent liabilities and the total is reported as "other liabilities" on Textron's financial statements.

During the course of an audit conducted by Ernst & Young (E&Y), Textron's independent auditor, Textron permitted E&Y to examine the final tax accrual workpapers at issue in this case with the understanding that the information was to be treated as confidential.

ANALYSIS

I.   THE SUMMONS

A.   Scope and Enforceability, in General

. . . .

In this case, Textron does not dispute that the documents sought may be relevant . . . or that the IRS has followed the necessary administrative steps in issuing the summons. Rather, Textron argues that the IRS seeks the documents for the purpose of using them as leverage in settlement negotiations and that the documents are privileged.

B.   The Legitimate Purpose Requirement

Whether the purpose for issuing a summons is legitimate depends on the circumstances. Section 7602(a) makes it clear that "ascertaining the correctness of any return" and "determining the liability of any person for any internal revenue tax" are legitimate purposes for issuing a summons. On the other hand, it is improper to "us[e] a civil summons to gather evidence to be used solely in a criminal prosecution," United States v. Kis, 658 F.2d 526, 535 (7th Cir. 1981), or to issue a summons "to harass the taxpayer or to put pressure on him to settle a collateral dispute, or for any other purpose reflecting on the good faith of the particular investigation." Powell, 379 U.S. at 58.

. . . In short, the IRS has made a prima facie showing that the *Powell* requirements have been satisfied and Textron has failed to rebut that showing.

II.   Applicability of Privilege

Satisfaction of the Powell requirements is not sufficient to warrant enforcement of an IRS summons if the documents sought are privileged. Upjohn Co. v. United States, 449 U.S. 383, 386, 101 S. Ct. 677, 681, 66 L. Ed. 2d 584 (1981) (refusing to enforce IRS summons because documents sought contained communications protected by the attorney-client privilege and also recognizing that "the work-product doctrine does apply in tax summons enforcement proceedings."). . . . In this case, Textron argues that its tax accrual workpapers are protected by the attorney-client privilege, the tax practitioner-client privilege created by 26 U.S.C. §7525, and the work product privilege.

A.   Attorney-Client Privilege

The attorney-client privilege protects confidential communications between an attorney and client relating to legal advice sought from the attorney. . . . Narrow construction of the privilege is especially called for in the case of tax investigations because of "the 'congressional policy choice *in favor of disclosure* of all information relevant to a legitimate IRS inquiry.'" Cavallaro, 284 F.3d at 245 (quoting Arthur Young, 465 U.S. at 816).

Textron's affidavits state that its tax accrual workpapers are privileged because they were prepared by counsel and reflect counsel's legal conclusions in identifying items on Textron's return that may be challenged and assessing Textron's prospects of prevailing in any ensuing litigation. . . . The IRS argues that the workpapers are not privileged because, in preparing them, Textron's attorneys were not providing legal advice but, rather, were performing an accounting function by reconciling the company's tax records and financial statements.

It is true that, generally, the mere preparation of a tax return is viewed as accounting work and a taxpayer may not cloak the documents generated in that process with a privilege simply "by hiring a lawyer to do the work that an accountant, or other tax preparer, or the taxpayer himself . . . normally would do." United States v. Frederick, 182 F.3d 496, 500 (7th Cir. 1999). See E.S. Epstein, The Attorney-Client Privilege and the Work-Product Doctrine 246 (4th ed. 2001). On the other hand, it is equally true that communications containing legal advice provided by an attorney may be privileged even though they are made in connection with the preparation of a return.

Determining the tax consequences of a particular transaction is rooted entirely in the law. . . . [Therefore] [c]ommunications offering tax advice or discussing tax planning . . . are 'legal' communications. U.S. v. Chevron Texaco Corp., 241 F. Supp. 2d 1065, 1076 (N.D. Cal. 2002). . . .

Here, since the tax accrual workpapers of Textron and TFC essentially consist of nothing more than counsel's opinions regarding items that might be challenged because they involve areas in which the law is uncertain and counsel's assessment regarding Textron's chances of prevailing in any ensuing litigation, they are protected by the attorney-client privilege.

The IRS's reliance on Arthur Young is misplaced because, although Arthur Young deemed tax accrual workpapers pinpointing the "soft spots" on a corporation's tax return relevant to examination of the corporation's return, it did not hold the attorney-client privilege inapplicable to legal conclusions of counsel contained in the workpapers. On the contrary, Arthur Young expressly recognized that "§7602 is 'subject to the traditional privileges and limitations.'" Arthur Young, 465 U.S. at 816 (citation omitted). Arthur Young also is distinguishable on the ground that, there, the workpapers had been prepared by the corporation's independent auditor whose "obligation to serve the public interest assures that the integrity of the securities markets will be preserved." Arthur Young, 465 U.S. at 819. By contrast, Textron's workpapers were prepared by its counsel whose function was to provide legal advice to Textron.

B.   Tax Practitioner-Client Privilege — §7525

Section 7525, which created a tax practitioner privilege, was enacted after the Supreme Court's decision in Arthur Young, which declined to create a new "accountant-client privilege" between a corporation and its independent auditor. Arthur Young, 465 U.S. at 817. Section 7525 confers a privilege on tax advice in the form of confidential communications "between a taxpayer and any federally authorized tax practitioner" to the same extent that such communications would be protected between a taxpayer and an attorney. 26 U.S.C. §7525(a)(1).

In the case of a corporation, the privilege does not apply to written communications between the tax practitioner and the corporation "in connection with the promotion of the direct or indirect participation of such corporation in any tax shelter (as defined in section 6662(d)(2)(C)(iii))." 26 U.S.C. §7525(b) (2001). Nor does the privilege extend to a tax practitioner's "work product" in preparing a return or to "communications between a tax practitioner and a client simply for the preparation of a tax return." United States v. KPMG, LLP, 316 F. Supp. 2d 30, 35 (D.D.C. 2004) ("nothing in the statute 'suggests that these nonlawyer practitioners are entitled to privilege when they are doing other than lawyers' work'") (emphasis in original) (citation omitted).

Textron argues that, to the extent that the workpapers in question reflect the advice that TFC received from CPAs in its tax department, they are privileged under §7525. The IRS argues that the opinions of TFC's tax accountants do not qualify for protection under §7525(a); and, even if they did, they fall within the exception contained in §7525(b).

Since TFC's tax accountants participated in advising Textron regarding its tax liability with respect to matters on which the law is uncertain and/or estimating the hazards of litigation percentages, they were performing "lawyers' work." Accordingly, that advice would qualify for the privilege conferred by §7525(a). See 26 U.S.C. 7525(a) (tax advice communications protected "to the extent the communication would be considered a privileged communication if it were between a taxpayer and an attorney").

In support of its argument that the written communications from TFC's tax accountants fall within the "promotion" of a tax shelter exception created by §7525(b), the IRS points out that 26 U.S.C. §6662(d)(2)(C)(ii) defines "tax shelter" to include any arrangement "a significant purpose" of which "is the avoidance or evasion of Federal income tax" and that an IRS notice identifies SILO transactions as a type of tax avoidance arrangement. See 26 C.F.R. §1.6011-4(b)(2); IRS Notice 2005-13 (February 11, 2005), 2005-9 I.R.B. 630. That argument is not persuasive because even if the SILO transactions in which TFC engaged are characterized as "tax avoidance" transactions the communications were not made "in connection with the promotion" of TFC's participation in them. 26 U.S.C. §7525(b) (emphasis added).

Section 7525(b) is aimed at communications by outside tax practitioners attempting to sell tax shelters to a corporate client. See 144 Cong. Rec. S7643-02, S7667 (July 8, 1998) (statement of Sen. Mack) ("[section 7525(b)] was meant to target written promotional and solicitation materials used by the peddlers of corporate tax shelters"). As the Conference Report relating to §7525(b) stated "[t]he Conferees do not understand the promotion of tax shelters to be part of the routine relationship between a tax practitioner and a client. Accordingly, the Conferees do not anticipate that the tax shelter limitation will adversely affect such routine relationships." H.R. Rep. No. 105-599 (Conf. Report to Accompany HR 2676) (June 24, 1998).

Here, TFC's accountants were not "peddlers of corporate tax shelters" or outside promoters soliciting TFC's participation in the SILO transactions. Rather, they were acting as tax advisers and the workpapers reflect their opinions regarding the foreseeable tax consequences of transactions that, already, had taken place, not future transactions they were seeking to promote.

C. The Work Product Privilege

1. The Nature of the Privilege   The work product privilege applies to materials prepared or gathered by an attorney in anticipation of litigation or preparation for trial. The purpose of the privilege is "to preserve a zone of privacy in which a lawyer can prepare and develop legal theories and strategy 'with an eye toward litigation' free from unnecessary intrusion by his adversaries," United States v. Adlman, 134 F.3d 1194, 1196 (2d Cir. 1998) (citing Hickman v. Taylor, 329 U.S. 495, 510-11, 67 S. Ct. 385, 393-94, 91 L. Ed. 451 (1947)), "to prevent a litigant from taking a free ride on the research and thinking of his opponent's lawyer and to avoid the resulting deterrent to a lawyer's committing his thoughts to paper." Frederick, 182 F.3d at 500.

The privilege first was articulated by the Supreme Court in Hickman v. Taylor, 329 U.S. 495, 67 S. Ct. 685, 91 L. Ed. 451 (1947), and, later, was codified in Federal Rule of Civil Procedure 26(b)(3) which provides:

> (3) Trial Preparation Materials. . . . a party may obtain discovery of documents and tangible things otherwise discoverable under subdivision (b)(1) of

this rule and prepared in anticipation of litigation or for trial by or for another party or by or for that other party's representative . . . only upon a showing that the party seeking discovery has substantial need of the materials in the preparation of the party's case and that the party is unable without undue hardship to obtain the substantial equivalent of the materials by other means. In ordering discovery of such materials when the required showing has been made, the court shall protect against disclosure of the mental impressions, conclusions, opinions, or legal theories of an attorney or other representative of a party concerning the litigation.

Fed. R. Civ. P. 26(b)(3)(emphasis added).

As the rule indicates, unlike the attorney-client privilege, the work product privilege is a qualified privilege which may be overcome by a showing of "substantial need." Fed. R. Civ. P. 26(b)(3). The burden of establishing "substantial need" rests on the party seeking to overcome the privilege; and, when "opinion work product" consisting of "mental impressions, conclusions, opinions or legal theories" of attorneys is involved, the burden of establishing "substantial need" is greater than it is with respect to documents that are merely obtained by a party. Upjohn, 449 U.S. at 401-2 ("we think a far stronger showing of necessity and unavailability by other means . . . would be necessary to compel disclosure" of opinion work-product.). Indeed, some courts have accorded "nearly absolute" protection to work product consisting of opinions or theories. In re Grand Jury Subpoena, 220 F.R.D. 130, 145 (D. Mass. 2004) (collecting cases).

In *Upjohn*, the Supreme Court made it clear that the work product privilege may be invoked in response to IRS summonses.

> [T]he obligation imposed by a tax summons remains 'subject to the traditional privileges and limitations.' . . . Nothing in the language of the IRS summons provisions or their legislative history suggests an intent on the part of Congress to preclude application of the work-product doctrine. Rule 26(b)(3) codifies the work-product doctrine, and the Federal Rules of Civil Procedure are made applicable to summons enforcement proceedings by Rule 81(a)(3).

Upjohn, 449 U.S. at 398-99 (citation omitted).

2. The "In Anticipation of Litigation" Requirement   Courts have applied two different tests in determining whether a document was prepared "in anticipation of litigation." Under the "primary purpose" test, documents are held to be prepared in anticipation of litigation "as long as the primary motivating purpose behind the creation of a document was to aid in possible future litigation." El Paso, 682 F.2d at 542. Under the more inclusive "because of" test, the relevant inquiry is whether the document was prepared or obtained "because of" the prospect of litigation. United States v. Adlman, 134 F.3d 1194 (2d Cir. 1998). In Adlman, after making a detailed analysis of the two tests, the Second Circuit found the "because of" test "more consistent with both the literal terms and the purposes of [Rule 26(b)(3)]" and the Court stated:

> In short, the enforceability of the IRS summons for the Memorandum will turn on whether it (or substantially the same document) would have been prepared irrespective of the anticipated litigation and therefore was not prepared because of it.

Adlman, 134 F.3d at 1198, 1205. The First Circuit has adopted the "because of" test articulated in Adlman. Maine v. Dept. of the Interior, 298 F.3d 60, 68 (1st Cir. 2002).

Textron asserts that its tax accrual workpapers were prepared because it anticipated the possibility of litigation with the IRS regarding various items on its return and it points to the hazards of litigation percentages as evidence that the possibility of such litigation was the reason for preparing the workpapers. The IRS asserts that the workpapers were prepared in the ordinary course of business and in order to satisfy the requirements of the securities laws that financial statements filed by publicly traded companies comply with GAAP (which mandate the creation of reserves to meet contingent liabilities). The IRS contends that Textron had to provide its independent auditor with the kind of information contained in the workpapers in order to obtain a "clean" opinion that the reserves satisfy GAAP's requirements.

As the IRS correctly observes, the work product privilege does not apply to "'documents that are prepared in the ordinary course of business or that would have been created in essentially similar form irrespective of the litigation.'" Maine, 298 F.3d at 70 (quoting Adlman, 134 F.3d at 1202). However, it is clear that the opinions of Textron's counsel and accountants regarding items that might be challenged by the IRS, their estimated hazards of litigation percentages and their calculation of tax reserve amounts would not have been prepared at all "but for" the fact that Textron anticipated the possibility of litigation with the IRS. If Textron had not anticipated a dispute with the IRS, there would have been no reason for it to establish any reserve or to prepare the workpapers used to calculate the reserve. Thus, while it may be accurate to say that the workpapers helped Textron determine what amount should be reserved to cover any potential tax liabilities and that the workpapers were useful in obtaining a "clean" opinion from E&Y regarding the adequacy of the reserve amount, there would have been no need to create a reserve in the first place, if Textron had not anticipated a dispute with the IRS that was likely to result in litigation or some other adversarial proceeding.

Nor can there be any doubt that Textron's belief in the likelihood of litigation with the IRS was well-founded. As already noted, the matters identified in the workpapers dealt with issues on which the law was unclear. Moreover, in seven of Textron's eight previous audit cycles, "unagreed" issues had been appealed to the IRS Appeals Board, and three of those issues were litigated in federal court. . . . Moreover, even if the workpapers were needed to satisfy E&Y that Textron's reserves complied with GAAP, that would not alter the fact that the workpapers were prepared "because of" anticipated litigation with the IRS. . . .

III.   WAIVER OR LOSS OF PRIVILEGE

A.   The Attorney-Client and Tax Practitioner-Client Privileges

It is well established that "voluntary disclosure to a third party waives the attorney-client privilege even if the third party agrees not to disclose the communications to anyone else." Westinghouse Elec. Corp. v. Republic of the Philippines, 951 F.2d 1414, 1427 (3d Cir. 1991). That principle has been applied specifically to disclosures made to independent auditors. First Fed. Say. Bank of Hegewisch v. United States, 55 Fed. Cl. 263, 268-69 (Fed. Cl. 2003) (attorney-client privilege was waived when board minutes containing confidential communications between board members and outside counsel were disclosed to outside auditors who were auditing company's financial statements). . . .

Since the tax practitioner privilege created by §7525 mirrors the attorney-client privilege, it, too, may be waived by disclosure to a third party. See United States v. BDO Seidman, 337 F.3d 802, 810 (7th Cir. 2003) ("the §7525 privilege is no broader than that of the attorney-client privilege"); Doe v. KPMG, LLP, 325 F. Supp. 2d 746, 752 (N.D. Tex. 2004) (Court must "look to the law of attorney-client privilege to inform its interpretation of the taxpayer-federally authorized tax practitioner privilege.").

Textron argues that providing the tax accrual workpapers to E&Y did not waive the protection of either privilege and it seeks to distinguish the cases holding that disclosure to an outside auditor waives the attorney-client privilege on the ground that those cases were decided prior to the enactment of §7525. More specifically, Textron argues that, because it occasionally revises its reserves based on the opinions of the independent auditor, the auditor's review of Textron's workpapers should be viewed as performed in connection with providing "tax advice" to Textron and, therefore, it is privileged under §7525. That argument is creative but not persuasive because it ignores reality to describe an independent auditor responsible for reporting to the investing public whether a company's financial statements fairly and accurately reflect its financial condition, as providing "tax advice" to the company when the auditor seeks to determine the adequacy of amounts reserved by the company for contingent tax liabilities.

In short, any attorney-client privilege or tax practitioner privilege that attached under §7525 was waived when Textron provided its workpapers to E&Y.

B.   The Work Product Privilege

1. Waiver   Since the work product privilege serves a purpose different from the attorney-client or tax practitioner privileges, the kind of conduct that waives the privilege also differs.

The purpose of the attorney-client and tax practitioner privileges is to encourage the full and frank discussion necessary for providing the client with sound advice. That purpose is achieved by guaranteeing that confidential communications between the client and the advisor will remain confidential. Since disclosure to a third party is inconsistent with a claim of confidentiality, such disclosure waives the privilege.

By contrast, the purpose of the work product privilege is to prevent a potential adversary from gaining an unfair advantage over a party by obtaining documents prepared by the party or its counsel in anticipation of litigation which may reveal the party's strategy or the party's own assessment of the strengths and weaknesses of its case. Accordingly, only disclosures that are inconsistent with keeping the information from an adversary constitute a waiver of the work product privilege. Gutter, 1998 U.S. Dist. LEXIS 23207, 1988 WL 2017926 *3 (S.D. Fl. 1998). . . .

Most courts considering the question have held that disclosure of information to an independent auditor does not waive the work product privilege because it does not substantially increase the opportunity for potential adversaries to obtain the information. In re JDS Uniphase Corp. Sec. Litig., 2006 U.S. Dist. LEXIS 76169, 2006 WL 2850049 (N. D. Cal. 2006) (work product protection not waived when protected board minutes were disclosed to the independent auditor). . . .

In this case, too, the disclosure of Textron's tax accrual workpapers to E&Y did not substantially increase the IRS's opportunity to obtain the information contained in them. Under AICPA Code of Professional Conduct Section 301 Confidential Client Information, E&Y had a professional obligation "not [to] disclos[e] any confidential client information without the specific consent of the client." Furthermore, E&Y expressly agreed not to provide the information to any other party, and confirms that it has adhered to its promise. (Weston Af. P 3; Raymond Aff. P 20.) Even if the AICPA Code coupled with E&Y's promise did not establish an absolute guarantee of confidentiality, they made it very unlikely that E&Y would provide Textron's "tax accrual workpapers" to the IRS and they negate any inference that Textron waived the work product privilege. . . .

. . . [I]n this case, E&Y was a truly independent auditor that had no obligation to the IRS to determine whether Textron's tax return was correct and no authority to challenge the return. In this instance, E&Y was seeking, only, to determine whether the reserve established by Textron to cover the corporation's contingent tax liabilities satisfied the requirements of GAAP. Since E&Y was not a potential Textron adversary or acting on behalf of a potential adversary, and, since E&Y agreed to treat the workpapers as confidential, disclosure to E&Y did not substantially increase the likelihood that the workpapers would be disclosed to the IRS or other potential Textron adversaries. . . .

2. Overcoming the Privilege As already noted, the work product doctrine creates only a qualified privilege that may be overcome by a showing of (1) "substantial need" for the protected documents, and (2) an inability to otherwise obtain the information contained therein or its substantial equivalent without "undue hardship." Fed. R. Civ. P. 26(b)(3).

While establishing that protected documents relate to a legitimate IRS investigation may satisfy the "relevancy" requirement of §7602, it is insufficient to establish the "substantial need" showing necessary to overcome the work product privilege. See Davis v. Emery Air Freight Corp., 212 F.R.D. 432, 436 (D. Me. 2003) ("the fact that the documents sought might be relevant to [plaintiff's] claims is not enough under Rule 26(b)(3)."). That is especially true in the case of opinion work product, which consists of the "mental impressions, conclusions, opinions or legal theories" of attorneys, where the party seeking the materials must meet a heightened burden. See Upjohn, 449 U.S. at 401-2 ("a far stronger showing of necessity and unavailability by other means . . . would be necessary to compel disclosure" of attorneys' notes and memoranda regarding oral statements of witnesses which "reveal the attorneys' mental processes in evaluating the communications"); see also Fed. R. Civ. P. 26(b)(3) ("In ordering discovery . . . the court shall protect against disclosure of the mental impressions, conclusions, opinions, or legal theories of an attorney or other representative of a party concerning the litigation.").

Here, the IRS has failed to carry the burden of demonstrating a "substantial need" for ordinary work product, let alone the heightened burden applicable to Textron's tax accrual workpapers, which constitute opinion work product. While the opinions and conclusions of Textron's counsel and tax advisers might provide the IRS with insight into Textron's negotiating position and/or litigation strategy, they have little bearing on the determination of Textron's tax liability. . . . The determination of any tax owed by Textron must be based on factual information, none of which is contained in the workpapers and all of which is readily available to the IRS through the issuance of IDRs and by other means. The opinions of Textron's counsel, either favorable or unfavorable, would have little to do with that determination, and forced disclosure of those opinions would put Textron at an unfair disadvantage in any dispute that might arise with the IRS, just as requiring the IRS to disclose the opinions of its counsel regarding areas of uncertainty in the law or the likely outcome of any litigation with Textron would place the IRS at an unfair disadvantage. See e.g. Delaney, Migdail & Young, Chartered v. IRS, 264 U.S. App. D.C. 52, 826 F.2d 124, 127 (D.C. Cir. 1987) (upholding IRS assertion of work product privilege over "IRS memos advis[ing] the agency of the types of legal challenges likely to be mounted against a proposed program, potential defenses available to the agency, and the likely outcome.").

CONCLUSION

For all of the foregoing reasons, the government's petition to enforce the summons is denied.

NOTE

Is it accurate to state that Textron's papers were prepared in anticipation of litigation? What is the relevance of other regulatory demands on the taxpayer? In the case of large corporate taxpayers, could all such material arguably fall into this category? The fact that the SILOs were listed transactions reflects their suspect status as potential tax shelters. Does that enhance the taxpayer's argument that litigation was likely? Would that conclusion create an odd incentive: the more potentially abusive the transaction, the more likely the chance of litigation, hence the more likely the relevant papers are a work product?

PROBLEMS

1. You are engaged to prepare a client's income tax return. The client advises you that his payments to doctors and hospitals for the year in question aggregated $2,500 and you believe him. In fact the correct amount was $1,000. You rely on the client's statement, and his tax liability is accordingly understated. The IRS, upon audit, determines a deficiency, and, in addition, proposes to assess a penalty against you under §6694(b) for negligent or intentional disregard of rules and regulations. You intend to defend yourself by advising the Service that you relied on your client's representations, and you so inform the client. The client objects, asserting that you are obligated under Model Rule 1.6 to maintain his confidences. What course of action would you pursue?

2. You are engaged by a corporate client to handle various problems arising on audit of your client's tax return. In one adjustment, the auditing IRS agent has reduced the depreciation claimed on a building on the ground that the property does not qualify for accelerated depreciation. You are convinced that the agent has overlooked a legal point and that for this reason his conclusion is wrong. In preparing the case, you discover that the company in fact demolished the building several years ago with the expectation of constructing a new building on the site. The inclusion of the demolished building in the depreciation schedule was apparently an oversight, which probably occurred because the new building was never built. You explain the situation to the client's tax manager, who is responsible for retaining your services. He says, "Withdraw our objection to the agent's adjustment. We will simply not protest the agent's position on this issue." What course of action would you take?

6. Disclosure and Third Party Investors

The clear tilt in the ethical rules toward confidentiality and away from disclosure is tempered somewhat when the lawyer's work on behalf of a client may be relied on by third party investors. Although the Model Rules traditionally have favored confidentiality over disclosure as a matter of legal ethics, this may not be consistent with developments concerning the legal obligations of the lawyer, at least insofar as the impact on third persons is concerned — as evidenced by the ABA's changes to the rules following Sarbanes-Oxley. However, attention to the impact of disclosure questions on third parties is not entirely new. SEC v. National Student Marketing Corp., 457 F. Supp. 682 (D.D.C. 1978) provides a good example.

National Student Marketing Corporation (NSMC) agreed to acquire Interstate National Corporation in a statutory merger. When the principals and their counsel met to close the merger transaction, they received an unsigned "comfort letter" from the NSMC auditors. That letter stated that significant unfavorable adjustments would be required in the NSMC financial statements. The closing nonetheless went forward. Subsequently, it developed that the NSMC financial condition was even more serious than disclosed in the letter. The SEC sued the principals as well as their counsel, seeking injunctive sanctions as a result of alleged securities law violations.

SEC v. National Student Marketing Corp.

457 F. Supp. 682 (D.D.C. 1978)

BARRINGTON, District Judge. The major problem arising with regard to the Commission's contention that the attorneys failed to interfere in the closing of the merger is whether inaction or silence constitutes substantial assistance. While there is no definitive answer to this question, courts have been willing to consider inaction as a form of substantial assistance when the accused aider and abettor had a duty to disclose.

Although the duty to disclose in those cases is somewhat distinguishable, in that they contemplate disclosure to an opposing party and not to one's client, they are sufficiently analogous to provide support for a duty here.

Upon receipt of the unsigned comfort letter, it became clear that the merger had been approved by the Interstate shareholders on the basis of materially misleading information. In view of the obvious materiality of the information, especially to attorneys learned in securities law, the attorneys' responsibilities to their corporate client required them to take steps to ensure that the information would be disclosed to the shareholders. However, it is unnecessary to determine the precise extent of their obligations here, since it is undisputed that they took no steps whatsoever to delay the closing pending disclosure to and resolicitation of the Interstate shareholders. But, at the very least, they were required to speak out at the closing concerning the obvious materiality of the information and the concomitant requirement that the merger not be closed until the adjustments were disclosed and approval of the merger was again obtained from the Interstate shareholders. Their silence was not only a breach of this duty to speak, but in addition lent the appearance of legitimacy to the closing.

The combination of these factors clearly provided substantial assistance to the closing of the merger.

Contrary to the attorney defendants' contention, imposition of such a duty will not require lawyers to go beyond their accepted role in securities transactions, nor will it compel them to "err on the side of conservatism, . . . thereby inhibiting clients' business judgments and candid attorney-client communications." Courts will not lightly overrule an attorney's determination of materiality and the need for disclosure. However, where, as here, the significance of the information clearly removes any doubt concerning the materiality of the information, attorneys cannot rest on asserted "business judgments" as justification for their failure to make a legal decision pursuant to their fiduciary responsibilities to client shareholders.

The SEC's contention with regard to counsel's alleged acquiescence in the merger transaction raises significant questions concerning the responsibility of counsel. The basis for the charge appears to be counsel's failure, after the merger, to withdraw their opinion, to demand resolicitation of the shareholders, to advise their clients concerning rights of rescission of the merger, and ultimately, to inform the Interstate shareholders or the SEC of the completion of the merger based on materially false and misleading financial statements. The defendants counter with the argument that their actions following the merger are not subject to the coverage of the securities laws.

The filing of the complaint in this proceeding generated significant interest and an almost overwhelming amount of comment within the legal profession on the scope of a securities lawyer's obligations to his client and to the investing public. The very initiation of this action, therefore, has provided a necessary and worthwhile impetus for the profession's recognition and assessment of its responsibilities in this area. The Court's examination, however, must be more limited. Although the complaint alleges varying instances of misconduct on the part of several attorneys and firms, the Court must narrow its focus to the present defendants and the charges against them.

Meyer, Schauer and Lord, Bissell & Brook are, in essence, here charged with failing to take any action to "undo" the merger. The Court has already concluded that counsel had a duty to the Interstate shareholders to delay the closing of the merger pending disclosure and resolicitation with corrected financials, and that the breach of that duty constituted a violation of the antifraud provisions through aiding and abetting the merger transaction. The Commission's charge, however, concerns the period following that transaction. Even if the attorneys' fiduciary responsibilities to the Interstate shareholders continued beyond the merger, the breach of such a duty would not have the requisite relationship to a securities transaction, since the merger had already been completed. It is equally obvious that such subsequent action or inaction by the attorneys could not substantially assist the merger.

Thus, the Court finds that the attorney defendants aided and abetted the violation of §10(b), Rule 10b-5, and §17(a) through their participation in the closing of the merger. Although the Commission has proved past violations by the defendants, that does not end the Court's inquiry. Proof of a past violation is not a prerequisite to the grant of injunctive relief, nor by itself necessarily sufficient to justify such relief, but it may, in combination with other factors, warrant an inference of future misconduct by the charged party.

The crucial question, though, remains not whether a violation has occurred, but whether there exists a reasonable likelihood of future illegal conduct by the defendant, "something more than the mere possibility which serves to keep the case alive." Thus, the SEC must "go beyond the mere facts of past violations and demonstrate a realistic likelihood of recurrence."

The Commission has not demonstrated that the defendants engaged in the type of repeated and persistent misconduct which usually justifies the issuance of injunctive relief.

Further, it is difficult to characterize the violations presented here as either "willful, blatant, and often completely outrageous," SEC v. Manor Nursing Centers, Inc., 458 F.2d, at 1101, or as the "garden variety fraud" urged by the Commission, SEC Post-Trial Brief, at 129. There is no evidence to suggest that these defendants knew about the comfort letter adjustments prior to the receipt of the unsigned comfort letter at the closing; and after receiving the letter, the defendants were under some pressure to determine a course of action, either to proceed with the transactions as scheduled or to abort both the merger and stock sales. Although it has now been found that they unlawfully and with scienter decided to proceed, their actions in this regard hardly resemble the deliberate and well-planned fraudulent scheme frequently found in securities fraud cases.

Finally, the Commission asserts that an injunction is necessary because the professional occupations of the defendants provide significant opportunities for further involvement in securities transactions. It notes that Brown holds positions as a director and as a consultant with NSMC, and that Meyer, Schauer and LBB continue to be involved in various corporate activities, including securities transactions, as part of their legal practice. While these opportunities distinguish the present defendants from those who, because they completely lack such opportunities, should not be subject to the threat of an injunction, they do not alone justify relief. In fact, various circumstances indicate that this factor is not as one-sided as the commission suggests. Although Brown retains his positions with NSMC, he is in effect virtually retired; the likelihood of his being involved in a securities transaction, other than as an investor, seems quite small.

While the attorney defendants are more likely to be so involved, that fact is countered somewhat by their professional responsibilities as attorneys and officers of the court to conform their conduct to the dictates of the law. The Court is confident that they will take appropriate steps to ensure that their professional conduct in the future comports with the law.

After considering the "totality of circumstances" presented here, the Court concludes that the Securities and Exchange Commission has not fulfilled its statutory obligation to make a "proper showing" that injunctive relief is necessary to prevent further violations by these defendants. Accordingly, judgment will be entered for the defendants and the complaint will be dismissed.

The SEC's complaint in *National Student Marketing Corp.* has spawned a host of commentaries and discussions. See, for instance, Victor H. Kramer, Clients' Frauds and Their Lawyers' Obligations: A Study in Professional Irresponsibility, 67 Geo. L.J. 991 (1979); Samuel H. Gruenbaum, Clients' Frauds and Their Lawyers' Obligations: A Response to Professor Kramer, 68 Geo. L.J. 191 (1979). The district court noted that the filing of the complaint generated "an almost overwhelming amount of comment" dealing with the lawyer's obligation to the client and to the investing public.

The ABA responded in 1975 when its House of Delegates adopted the following statement of policy. Although this statement refers only to the Model Code, it addresses many important ethical issues involving innocent third parties.

ABA House of Delegates, Statement of Policy*

61 A.B.A. J. 1085 (1975)

LAWYERS, CLIENTS AND SECURITIES LAWS

The House adopted a lengthy statement of policy regarding the ethical duties of lawyers who advise clients as to compliance with securities laws administered by the Securities and Exchange Commission. The statement was offered by the Section of Corporation, Banking, and Business Law and adopted as follows:

Be It Resolved. That this Association adopts the following statement of policy regarding responsibilities and liabilities of lawyers in advising with respect to the compliance by clients with laws administered by the Securities and Exchange Commission ("S.E.C."):

1. The confidentiality of lawyer-client consultations and advice and the fiduciary loyalty of the lawyer to the client, as prescribed in the American Bar Association's Code of Professional Responsibility ("C.P.R."), are vital to the basic function of the lawyer as legal counselor because they enable and encourage clients to consult legal counsel freely, with assurance that counsel will respect the confidentiality of the client's communications and will advise independently and in the client's best interest without conflicting loyalties or obligations.

2. This vital confidentiality of consultation and advice would be destroyed or seriously impaired if it is accepted as a general principle that lawyers must inform the S.E.C. or others regarding confidential information received by lawyers from their clients even though such action would not be permitted or required by the C.P.R. Any such compelled disclosure would seriously and adversely affect the lawyers' function as counselor and may seriously and adversely affect the ability of lawyers as advocates to represent and defend their clients' interests.

3.   In light of the foregoing considerations, it must be recognized that the lawyer cannot, consistently with his essential role as legal adviser, be regarded as a source of information concerning possible wrongdoing by clients. Accordingly, any principle of law which, except as permitted or required by the C.P.R., permits or obliges a lawyer to disclose to the S.E.C. otherwise confidential information should be established only by statute after full and careful consideration of the public interests involved and should be resisted unless clearly mandated by law.

4.   Lawyers have an obligation under the C.P.R. to advise clients, to the best of their ability, concerning the need for or advisability of public disclosure of a broad range of events and circumstances, including the obligation of the client to make appropriate disclosures as required by various laws and regulations administered by the S.E.C. In appropriate circumstances, a lawyer may be permitted or required by the disciplinary rules under the C.P.R. to resign his engagement if his advice concerning disclosures is disregarded by the client and, if the conduct of a client clearly establishes his prospective commission of a crime or the past or prospective perpetration of a fraud in the course of the lawyer's representation, even to make the disclosures himself. However, the lawyer has neither the obligation nor the right to make disclosure when any reasonable doubt exists concerning the client's obligation of disclosure, i.e., the client's failure to meet his obligation is not clearly established, except to the extent that the lawyer should consider appropriate action, as required or permitted by the C.P.R., in cases where the lawyer's opinion is expected to be relied on by [third] parties and the opinion is discovered to be not correct, whether because it is based on erroneous information or otherwise.

5.   Fulfillment by attorneys of their obligations to clients under the C.P.R. best serves the public interest of assisting and furthering clients' compliance with legal requirements. Efforts by the government to impose responsibility upon lawyers to assure the quality of their clients' compliance with the law or to compel lawyers to give advice resolving all doubts in favor of regulatory restrictions would evoke serious and far-reaching disruption in the role of the lawyer as counselor, which would be detrimental to the public, clients, and the legal profession. In fulfillment of their responsibility to clients under the C.P.R., lawyers must be free to advise clients as to the full range of their legitimately available courses of action and the relative attendant risks involved. Furthermore, it is often desirable for the lawyer to point out those factors which may suggest a decision that is morally just as well as legally permissible. However, the decision as to the course to be taken should be made by the client. The client's options should not be improperly narrowed through the insistence of an attorney who may, perhaps unconsciously, eliminate available choices from consideration because of his concern over possible personal risks if the position is taken which, though supportable, is subject to uncertainty or contrary to a known, but perhaps erroneous, position of the S.E.C. or a questionable lower court decision. Public policy, we strongly believe, is best served by lawyers acting in conformance with their obligations to their client and others as prescribed under the C.P.R. Accordingly, liability should not be imposed upon lawyers whose conduct is in conformance with the C.P.R.

NOTES

1.   The last paragraph confronts a possible conflict between the lawyer's concern for his own exposure to risk and his duty to maintain his client's confidence. Is this a matter of serious concern? Does the ABA position resolve the issue satisfactorily?

2.   Paragraph 4 states that a lawyer may, if the client's conduct already clearly establishes the past or prospective perpetration of fraud in the course of the representation, be required "to make the disclosures himself." How does this square with ABA Opinion 341, supra p. 202? Note that this language was published in 1975, whereas DR 7-102(B) was amended in 1974. Were the authors of this commentary perhaps unaware of the opinion? If so, which interpretation yields to the other?

3.   The final sentence of paragraph 4 states that the lawyer's obligation of disclosure does not exist when any doubt exists about the client's obligation of disclosure *except* where the lawyer's opinion is to be relied upon by third parties and is discovered to be incorrect. One might expect, in this difficult situation, to find some clear guidance given to the lawyer, but he is told only that he should "consider appropriate action, as required or permitted by the C.P.R." What does this mean?

4.   Suppose that a lawyer, while representing a client in a controversy involving a technical question on his 2007 tax return, is told by the client in the presence of other guests at a cocktail party that he omitted $50,000 of income from his 2005 return and that the IRS is none the wiser. The other guests thought that was terrific. May the lawyer — must he — disclose the client's fraud to the IRS if the client declines to do so when so advised? Should the lawyer continue to handle the 2007 case?

5.   A special rule of nondisclosure affects tax return preparers. Section 7216(a) of the Internal Revenue Code makes it a misdemeanor for a preparer to disclose or use tax return information other than to prepare the return. Does this place the tax lawyer who is a preparer under a more severe restraint as to disclosure than exists generally? Section 7216(b) specifies exceptions for disclosure pursuant to court order or law and authorizes other exemptions through regulations. Reg. §301.7216-2 deals with this subject and permits disclosure in several interesting situations. For example, an accountant preparing a tax return for Company *N* may come across information indicating that a financial statement prepared by his partner for Company *S* is misleading. The regulation concludes that such information may be communicated within the firm and that the firm may notify *S* and the SEC, but without identifying the source of the information. What issue does this raise? What is the situation if the two accountants are not in the same firm but cooperate in representing *S*?

A return preparer may disclose tax information to another return preparer solely for quality or peer review. A lawyer or accountant who prepares a return for a taxpayer may take such information into account and may act upon such information when performing legal or accounting services for another client when the information is necessary for the proper performance of such services. Reg. §301.7216-2(e).

In the context of disclosure to third parties, Model Rule 2.3 appears to recognize that a duty may exist when a lawyer undertakes an evaluation of a matter affecting a client that is intended for the use of someone other than the client. For a discussion of this rule in the context of opinion letters intended for use by third parties, see infra pp. 267-288.

The concern for the well-being of third-party investors extends also to the quality of legal opinions used to promote tax-based investments. We will discuss the particular standards for tax shelter opinions in Chapter 4.

6.   The ABA Statement of Policy on Lawyers, Clients and Securities Laws has not been modified. Is the Statement consistent with the 2003 changes to Rule 1.6? Is any conflict one of substance or one of tone and interpretation?

7.   *The Tax Lawyer's Responsibility to the Court for the Quality of Positions Advanced*

Lawyers who practice before courts bear a responsibility to advance positions that satisfy minimum specified quality levels. ABA Model Rule 3.1, entitled Meritorious Claims and Contentions, provides as follows:

> A lawyer shall not bring or defend a proceeding, or assert or controvert an issue therein, unless there is a basis for doing so that is not frivolous, which includes a good faith argument for an extension, modification or reversal of existing law. A lawyer for the defendant in a criminal proceeding, or the respondent in a proceeding that could result in incarceration, may nevertheless so defend the proceeding as to require that every element of the case be established.

In addition, the courts have adopted specific quality rules, such as Rule 11 of the Federal Rules of Civil Procedure. Rule 11 states that a lawyer's signature on a paper filed with the court indicates that, to the knowledge of the signer after reasonable inquiry, the document "is well grounded in fact and is warranted by existing law or a good faith argument for the extension, modification, or reversal of existing law. . . ." Tax Court Rule 33(b) imposes a similar obligation on lawyers who file documents in that court.

The following case illustrates disciplinary action against a tax lawyer by the Tax Court for violation of Rule 33(b).

Versteeg v. Commissioner
91 T.C. 339 (1988)

PANUTHOS, Special Trial Judge. This matter came before the court on respondent's motion to dismiss for lack of jurisdiction and counsel for petitioners' motion to withdraw. An additional issue raised at the hearing on the aforementioned motions is whether sanctions should be imposed on petitioners' counsel under Rule 33(b).

At the hearing of this matter, respondent requested that we consider the award of counsel fees under Rule 33(b). As a basis for an award of attorney's fees, respondent relies on the fact that counsel for petitioners filed the petition when no notice of deficiency had been issued. Further, even after respondent filed his motion to dismiss for lack of jurisdiction on the ground that no notice of deficiency had been issued, petitioners' counsel did not concede the jurisdictional issue. According to respondent's counsel, counsel for petitioners stated in a telephone conversation that the petition was filed to give petitioners additional time to secure funds to pay the tax liability. Counsel for petitioners did not challenge this statement. Rather, he stated that since the collection division would not negotiate a reduction in taxes, he filed the petition knowing that he could contact the appeals division for a review.

In 1986, Rule 33(b) was amended to allow for an award of attorney's fees in certain circumstances. Amended Rule 33(b) provides as follows:

> The signature of counsel or a party constitutes a certificate by him that he has read the pleading; that, to the best of his knowledge, information, and belief formed after reasonable inquiry, it is well grounded in fact and is warranted by existing law or a good faith argument for the extension, modification, or reversal of existing law, and that it is not interposed for any improper purpose, such as to harass or to cause unnecessary delay or needless increase in the cost of litigation. . . . If a pleading is signed in violation of this Rule, the Court, upon motion or upon its own initiative, may impose upon the person who signed it, a represented party, or both, an appropriate sanction, which may include an order to pay to the other party or parties the amount of the reasonable expenses incurred because of the filing of the pleading, including reasonable counsel's fees. [85 T.C. 1121,1125-1126]

The 1986 amendment to Rule 33(b) parallels the 1983 amendment to rule 11 of the Federal Rules of Civil Procedure. 85 T.C. at 1125-1126. Thus, in any question requiring interpretation of Rule 33(b), the authorities interpreting rule 11, Federal Rules of Civil Procedure, are considered by the Tax Court. Cf. Espinoza v. Commissioner, 78 T.C. 412, 415-416 (1982).

The amendment to Rule 33(b) requires some inquiry into both the facts and law at the time the petition is filed. The level of inquiry is tested against the standard of reasonableness under the circumstances. The Advisory Committee on the amendments to the Federal Rules of Civil Procedure noted as follows with regard to rule 11:

> The court is expected to avoid using the wisdom of hindsight and should test the signer's conduct by inquiring what was reasonable to believe at the time the pleading, motion, or other paper was submitted. Thus, what constitutes a reasonable inquiry may depend on such factors as how much time for investigation was available to the signer; whether he had to rely on a client for information as to the facts underlying the pleading, motion, or other paper; whether the pleading, motion, or other paper was based on a plausible view of the law; or whether he depended on forwarding counsel or another member of the bar. [28 U.S.C.A. 391, Fed. R. Civ. P. 11, advisory committee's note, 1983 amendment (Supp. 1988).]

It does not appear that counsel filed the petition based on faulty facts supplied by petitioners. Nor does it appear that counsel for petitioners relied on another member of the bar in filing the petition. Further, since the petition was filed well within 90 days after the mailing of the collection notice, counsel had ample time to ascertain the pertinent facts.

Thus, the only factor which we find material to our inquiry as to the reasonableness of counsel's action in this case is whether the petition was based on a plausible view of the law. We find that the petition in this case was totally unwarranted by existing law and that no good-faith argument could be made for the extension, modification, or reversal of existing law. In this regard, we find that counsel for petitioners either ignored or failed to make reasonable inquiry into the law before signing the petition. Had counsel made the least bit of inquiry as to the requirements for jurisdiction in this Court, he would have found that our jurisdiction is premised upon the issuance of a notice of deficiency and the timely filing of a petition by the taxpayer.

Instead of conceding the lack of jurisdiction when respondent filed his motion to dismiss, counsel for petitioners first sought additional time to object to respondent's motion, and then, after being granted additional time, attempted to withdraw from the case. Counsel for respondent objected to counsel for petitioners' attempt to withdraw, arguing that it was merely a further attempt to delay. In petitioners' reply to respondent's notice of objection, counsel for petitioners states that "Upon information and belief, a Notice of Deficiency was issued to Petitioners." Thus, while it is apparent that no notice of deficiency was issued to petitioners in this case, counsel for petitioners continued to assert that a notice of deficiency was issued. Counsel for petitioners' response, filed approximately seven months after the jurisdictional issue was raised, further reveals that petitioners' counsel either ignored or failed to make a reasonable inquiry into the facts and law.

Rule 33(b) clearly imposes an affirmative duty on each attorney to conduct a reasonable inquiry into the viability of a pleading before it is signed. See Eastway Construction Corp. v. City of New York. Counsel for petitioners has failed to carry out his responsibility. Accordingly, we will order counsel for petitioners to pay respondent's reasonable expenses, including attorney's fees, under Rule 33(b).

———————

The civil penalty provisions of the Internal Revenue Code also play a role in lawyer responsibility to the Tax Court. Under §6673(a)(2), any attorney admitted to practice before the Tax Court who multiplies the proceedings unreasonably and vexatiously may be held responsible for excess costs, expenses, and attorney's fees reasonably resulting from that conduct. If the offending attorney appears on behalf of the Commissioner, the United States may be held responsible for such costs.

The following case illustrates a situation in which the Tax Court found it appropriate to impose this penalty on a taxpayer's lawyer.

Harper v. Commissioner

99 T.C. 533 (1992)

BEGHE, Judge. . . . This is a case of attorney and taxpayer misconduct. In response to respondent's motions for dismissal and monetary sanctions, we address important questions about the ways in which the Court will deal with attorneys who culpably fail to follow the Court's Rules and orders and with taxpayers who fail properly to prosecute. . . .

The so-called "American Rule" is that a "prevailing litigant is ordinarily not entitled to collect a reasonable attorneys' fee from the loser." Alyeska Pipeline Service Co. v. Wilderness Society, 421 U.S. 240, 247 (1975). However, the rule has exceptions. We have power to assess attorney's fees against counsel for misconduct and abuse of process. These powers are derived from a variety of sources, including the Internal Revenue Code, the Tax Court Rules of Practice and Procedure, and the Federal Rules of Civil Procedure.

Respondent has moved for sanctions against Mr. Feinson under section 6673(a)(2). Because we have not discussed the standards for imposing such sanctions in a reported opinion, we take this occasion to outline the scope and applicability of the statutory provision. . . .

[The court discusses the lack of uniformity of case law interpreting a similar provision of the judicial code. The majority of circuits require a showing of bad faith; a minority of circuits does not. Because the court finds that the petitioner acted in bad faith, it refrains from announcing the standard to be applied as the general rule in §6673(a)(2).]

The Federal courts have sanctioned attorneys under 28 U.S.C. section 1927, the precursor of section 6673(a)(2), in a variety of circumstances. In Apex Oil Co. v. Belcher Co. of New York, 855 F.2d 1009, 1019 (2d Cir. 1988), the Second Circuit affirmed an order of the U.S. District Court for the Eastern District of New York imposing monetary sanctions on an attorney for abuses during pretrial discovery. This case is replete with pretrial discovery abuses. Mr. Feinson failed to comply with the Court's well-known rule which requires the parties to exchange facts, documents, and other data necessary to expedite the case for trial or settlement. When Mr. Feinson told respondent's attorney to come to his office and "roam through the entire file" of some 2,000 documents, he forced respondent's counsel to file a motion to compel production of documents, which we readily granted. . . .

Mr. Feinson's tactic of handing over the documents for copying one item at a time unreasonably and vexatiously multiplied the proceedings. This tactic violated our order compelling document production and prevented discovery from getting off the ground. Mr. Feinson prevented the case from being ready for trial on the last day of the Court's 2-week trial session when he refused to comply with our order of November 15, 1991, after the calendar call, providing, among other things, for production of the remaining documents on November 19, 1991, and setting the case for trial on November 22, 1991.

Inasmuch as one of the principal substantive issues in this case is the substantiation of petitioner's business expenses and itemized deductions, the production of documents was critical to putting the case in shape for a stipulation of agreed facts and, ultimately, for trial.

... Although this case does not appear to be a typical tax protester case, Mr. Feinson advanced frivolous and groundless tax protester-type arguments in petitioner's motion for summary judgment and in his "Reply to the Oral Arguments." Mr. Feinson argued that the notice of deficiency was invalid because it lacked the Commissioner's signature, even though it bore the District Director's signature stamp; he also argued that the Form 872-A extending the period of limitations was invalid because it was not personally signed by the Secretary of the Treasury.

A notice of deficiency is not invalid because it bears a stamped signature. In addition, the 3-year period of limitations had not expired. Mr. Feinson executed the Form 872-A that extended the period of limitations. See sec. 6501(c)(4). The Secretary has properly delegated authority to sign Forms 872 and 872-A to officials of the Internal Revenue Service, including the group manager who signed the Form 872-A in this case.

We also note that Mr. Feinson, in filing his motion for summary judgment, made no attempt to demonstrate the lack of a genuine issue of material fact as required by Rule 121(b). To the contrary, Mr. Feinson stated in his attached memorandum that "The principal issue is a question of fact." Mr. Feinson also refused to comply with other orders of the Court, most notably our standing pretrial order to stipulate facts and to submit a trial memorandum.

Mr. Feinson has been afforded appropriate procedural protections. See Roadway Express, Inc. v. Piper, supra; H. Conf. Rept. 96-1234 (1980). Respondent's motion for sanctions and supplement thereto and our orders gave Mr. Feinson fair notice that he was in danger of sanctions under section 6673(a)(2) and we gave him numerous opportunities to respond to the motion. At the calendar call on November 12, 1991, Mr. Feinson received notice that we were considering imposing sanctions on him under section 6673(a)(2), yet he persisted in his dilatory and obnoxious tactics and made no attempt to remedy the situation. At the second hearing on November 22, 1991, Mr. Feinson had an opportunity to address respondent's motion for sanctions, but did not do so. Our order of February 4, 1992, afforded Mr. Feinson a further opportunity to respond in writing to respondent's motion, but again he chose not to do so.

The record in this case, considered as a whole, demonstrates that petitioner's counsel has displayed a contemptuous disregard for the Rules and orders of this Court, has acted in bad faith, and has knowingly abused the judicial process throughout the course of this proceeding. Mr. Feinson has unreasonably and vexatiously multiplied the proceedings within the meaning of section 6673(a)(2). We will therefore grant respondent's motion for sanctions against Mr. Feinson.

Turning to the amount of the sanction to be imposed on Mr. Feinson, we note that respondent's counsel submitted a claim only for excess attorney's fees. She did not include a claim for excess costs or expenses reasonably incurred during this period, although section 6673(a)(2) expressly encompasses them. Our discussion is therefore limited to respondent's excess attorney's fees.

Attorney's fees awarded under section 6673(a)(2) are to be computed by multiplying the number of excess hours reasonably expended on the litigation by a reasonable hourly rate. The product is known as the "lodestar" amount.

Respondent has submitted an itemized day-by-day accounting of the estimated excess attorney time spent on this case due to Mr. Feinson's misconduct. Respondent's counsel estimates that from February 13, 1991, to December 4, 1991, she and her supervisor spent 98 excess hours working on this case.

Although Mr. Feinson has not objected to the accounting by respondent's counsel, we do not find that all 98 hours of respondent's claimed excess attorney time were caused by Mr. Feinson's misconduct. When we vacated our original dismissal of the case on December 31, 1990, we gave petitioner and his counsel the benefit of the doubt; we attributed petitioner's failure to appear at the December 3, 1990, calendar call to Mr. Feinson's inadvertence, which appeared at that time to constitute nothing more serious than negligence in failing to set up office procedures that would have given him the necessary reminder. Accordingly, after review of respondent's counsel's accounting of excess attorney time, we hold that Mr. Feinson is personally liable for 74 hours of excess attorney time spent by respondent's counsel.

Respondent has requested that we impose a fee of $100 per hour for the excess attorney time. Due to the lack of precedent interpreting section 6673(a)(2) and a dearth of cases applying 28 U.S.C. section 1927 in favor of the Government, we apply the standards used under rule 11 of the Federal Rules of Civil Procedure, which contains language similar to section 6673(a)(2) and 28 U.S.C. section 1927, to determine the rate to charge offending counsel for respondent's expenditure of excess attorney time.

In United States v. Kirksey, 639 F. Supp. 634, 637 (S.D.N.Y. 1986), the District Court held that under rule 11 of the Federal Rules of Civil Procedure:

> The hourly rate properly charged for the time of a government attorney is the "amount to which attorneys of like skill in the area would typically be entitled for a given type of work on the basis of an hourly rate of compensation." City of Detroit v. Grinnell Corp., 495 F.2d 448, 471 (2d Cir. 1974); Spector v. Banner, 80 Civ. 0639, mem. op. at 2-3 (S.D.N.Y., July 15, 1982).

This is also the standard we will use under section 6673(a)(2).

Unlike an application for attorney's fees under section 7430, there is no rate ceiling on attorney's fees imposed under section 6673(a)(2).

To arrive at the lodestar amount, we multiply respondent's 74 excess attorney hours by the hourly rate of $100. There is a strong presumption that the lodestar amount represents a reasonable fee, and we hesitate to adjust it further. Recognizing that our power to impose sanctions under section 6673(a)(2) carries a potential for abuse, we construe the statute narrowly and cautiously so as not to "stifle the enthusiasm or chill the creativity that is the very lifeblood of the law."

We find that $7,400 is a reasonable amount for respondent's excess attorney's fees incurred by reason of Mr. Feinson's unreasonable and vexatious multiplication of these proceedings. We therefore will order that Mr. Feinson personally pay respondent $7,400, that he make payment by means of a certified check, cashier's check, or money order in favor of the Internal Revenue Service, that such payment be delivered to respondent's counsel at the Office of District Counsel in New York City not later than 30 days from the date the order is served.

NOTE

The government lawyer can also be the target of sanctions under section 6673(a)(2), sometimes based on an unjustifiable complaint which itself can backfire. Consider the following case:

Casey v. Commissioner

T.C. Memo 2004-228

THORNTON, Judge: Pursuant to *section 6330(d)*, petitioner seeks review of an Appeals Office determination sustaining respondent's proposed levy to collect his unpaid 1992 Federal income taxes. [After discussing the substantive and procedural issues regarding the collection action against the taxpayer Casey, the court then considered Casey's claim for sanctions against the government lawyer]. . . .

VI.   PETITIONER'S MOTION FOR SANCTIONS AGAINST RESPONDENT

During trial, petitioner orally moved to impose sanctions on counsel for respondent. In support of his motion, petitioner asserted vaguely that "it was my belief that all of his [respondent's counsel's] communications were vexatious and, at that time, tactically not in my favor." He complained broadly that respondent's counsel burdened him with an "inundation of paperwork." Although the Court invited petitioner to address his motion on brief, petitioner failed to file any brief.

Section 6673(a)(2) allows the Tax Court in its discretion to sanction an attorney admitted to practice before the Court if the attorney has "unreasonably or vexatiously multiplied the proceedings." See *Harper v. Commissioner, 99 T.C. 533 (1992)* (imposing sanctions under *section 6673(a)(2)* on the taxpayer's counsel for repeated and egregious conduct during the discovery process that caused significant delay); *Dixon v. Commissioner, T.C. Memo. 2000-116* (imposing sanctions on counsel for the IRS for intentionally misleading the Court).

Petitioner's motion for sanctions is without basis or merit. The record does not suggest that respondent's counsel has engaged in sanctionable conduct. The record does show that petitioner has been uncooperative in complying with respondent's reasonable requests to prepare this case for trial pursuant to this Court's Rules and orders. Petitioner failed to respond to respondent's numerous pretrial letters seeking informal disclosure of information. After respondent implemented formal discovery procedures, petitioner still refused to cooperate and ignored the Court's December 12, 2003, Order that he comply with respondent's motion to compel discovery of documents. Instead of meaningful communication or cooperation in preparing for trial, what respondent received from petitioner, over a period beginning in September 2002, and continuing until shortly before trial, was a series of vexatious cartoon-like messages. [11]

If anyone has engaged in sanctionable conduct in this proceeding, it is petitioner. [12] We strongly caution him against proceeding in bad faith in future litigation before this Court.

Decision will be entered for respondent, and an appropriate order will be issued denying petitioner's motion for sanctions.

C. Attorney's Fee Awards in Tax Cases

Although issues involving attorney's fees do not necessarily involve ethical questions, they are sufficiently related to the fabric of tax practice that we have elected to treat them briefly in this chapter dealing with audit and litigation.

In most civil cases involving the government as a party, a citizen must look to the Equal Access to Justice Act to receive attorney's fees from the government. See 28 U.S.O. §2412(d)(1)(A) (1982). Under the act, the court is to award attorney's fees to a prevailing party unless the "position of the United States was substantially justified or . . . special circumstances make an award unjust." Attorney's fees in civil tax cases are, however, controlled by a different statutory provision. There have been many twists and turns in the trail that leads to §7430, the Code section that now controls the award of attorney's fees in tax controversies.

Under §7430, a taxpayer who prevails or substantially prevails in a court proceeding involving tax issues may recover "reasonable litigation costs" where the

---

11. For instance, on Jan. 23, 2004, respondent's counsel received from petitioner a sheet of paper bearing the handwritten message, "SURRENDER, DANIEL," with a smiley-face voice balloon that says "You mean, I am not the all-powerful Oz?" Days before the scheduled Feb. 2, 2004, trial, respondent's counsel received from petitioner a similar missive that bore the handwritten message, "February 2, 2004: The Day You See The Shadow Of Defeat," with a smiley-face voice balloon that says "Is it Groundhog Day again?"

12. In fact, by Order dated Jan. 16, 2004, this Court sanctioned petitioner for failing to comply with its Dec. 12, 2003, Order to comply with respondent's request for production of documents.

position of the Service "was not substantially justified." Litigation costs may not be awarded unless administrative remedies were exhausted prior to litigation. §7430(b)(1). Litigation costs include a reasonable attorney's fee, generally not to exceed $75 an hour, and in the case of Tax Court litigation, encompass fees paid for the services of any individual who is authorized to practice before that court. §7430(c)(1), (3).

A taxpayer who prevails in an administrative proceeding at the IRS may recover "reasonable administrative costs" where the position of the Service is not substantially justified. §7430(a)(1). Administrative costs include administrative fees and attorneys fees (including fees paid to nonattorneys entitled to practice before the IRS).

The unreasonable government position means a position taken in a judicial proceeding and the position taken in an administrative proceeding as of the earlier of the date of the receipt of the notice by the taxpayer of the decision of the Office of Appeals or the date of the deficiency notice. §7430(d)(7).

Chapter 4

Tax Planning and Advice

Chapters 2 and 3 are concerned with compliance and controversy. Both present the lawyer with past facts and therefore limit the lawyer's function to the effective presentation of these facts and to legal characterization and argument. We now turn to tax planning and advice, a setting in which the facts have yet to be developed. A lawyer who engages in tax planning assists her client in the creation of a transaction and in making the facts. She may also provide her opinion of the tax benefits of a transaction and advise her client about the risks that such benefits will be realized. She may be asked to seek an advance ruling from the Internal Revenue Service on those tax consequences or to provide an opinion to third parties about the tax consequences. How well she performs these roles may determine the ease of her client's later compliance, whether controversy will arise, and, if so, the success of its outcome. The bulk of the tax lawyer's time is spent in tax planning and advice.

When wearing her planning hat, the tax lawyer is an advisor, not an advocate. She is obligated to provide competent advice that sometimes may include telling the client "no" or advising that the transaction be restructured. In this role, the tax lawyer may have a duty to the system that overrides this obligation to serve her client's private interests. The planner is subject to a relatively larger demand on her ethical sensibilities than merely to serve her client zealously and competently. Conduct that would be acceptable for the advocate may be considered off limits for the advisor.

As tax shelters have continued to plague the system, the role of lawyers in devising such shelters and in issuing opinions on their consequences has come under increasing scrutiny. We will consider whether the needs of the system warrant special restraints on the tax lawyer when she deals with so-called abusive tax shelters.

A. The Tax Advisor

The Model Rules do not say a great deal about the lawyer as advisor. There are two Model Rules that deal with the lawyer's role as counselor, Rule 2.1 (Advisor) and Rule 2.3 (Evaluation for Use by Third Parties). We will turn to this latter rule later in the chapter. Model Rule 2.1 requires a lawyer to exercise independent professional judgment and to render candid advice. In doing so, a lawyer "may refer not only to law but to other considerations such as moral, economic, social and political factors that may be relevant to the client's situation." The lawyer is specifically authorized to do more than simply say what the law is or whether a transaction "works." As the comments to the rule note, "purely technical legal advice . . . can sometimes be inadequate." Sophisticated clients will expect the tax lawyer to take into account business, accounting, or securities issues as well as technical tax rules.

The comments to Model Rule 2.1 also recognize that "moral and ethical considerations impinge upon most legal questions and may decisively influence how the law will be applied." Such considerations — perhaps surprisingly — often arise in the tax setting. When consulted for her advice, the tax lawyer may encounter extremely difficult ethical problems. A client may wish to pursue a course of action with large financial stakes and may not understand the lawyer's rejection of that course on ethical grounds. The question, for example, may relate to the client's "business purpose," his state of mind, or the date on which a particular event occurred, all of which may be critically important to a particular tax result. The client may be quite willing to "fuzz" or even misstate the facts. The difficulties faced by the lawyer when this happens are considered in this section.

We will also examine the potential for conflict of interest in tax planning. As discussed earlier, the problems of conflict appear most prominently when the advocate is handling a controversy, but the advisor must face them as well.

1. Fraudulent Conduct

The tax lawyer need have little concern when presented with a clearly fraudulent scheme. If, for example, her client proposes, when acting as church usher, to substitute his check in favor of the church for the cash in the collection plate, and to claim a charitable contribution deduction on the basis of the check, the lawyer is not presented with a difficult choice. This is the "big lie" and must be dealt with accordingly — the lawyer must advise the client that his conduct is fraudulent, and if the client persists in it, she should withdraw from the representation. Model Rule 1.16. The more interesting problems are not big lies but rather are what might be viewed, at least by the client, as little white lies. These arise in situations in which the client perceives very little moral significance in his proposed actions, but the lawyer's perception may be very different.

NOTE

Under Model Rule 1.2(d), the lawyer may not counsel a client to "engage, or assist a client, in conduct that the lawyer knows is criminal or fraudulent." The comment to the rule significantly elaborates upon this general principle: "Paragraph (d) applies whether or not the defrauded party is a party to the transaction. Hence, a lawyer should not participate in a sham transaction; for example, a transaction to effectuate criminal or fraudulent escape of tax liability." Does this imply an affirmative duty to alert third parties such as the government?

2. State of Mind Issues

In many areas of tax law, the taxpayer's purpose or motive is key to the availability of tax benefits or to the applicability of a tax penalty. For example, tax benefits normally available through an acquisition of control of a corporation may be lost if the principal purpose of the acquisition is to secure such benefits. §269. Nonrecognition of gain under the reorganization provisions of the Code may depend on the corporation's "business purpose." The availability of a loss deduction under §165 may depend upon the existence of a profit objective. When these kinds of questions arise, the tax lawyer may know — or have strong reason to believe — that her client's real motivation or purpose is not the one having the more agreeable tax consequences.

The hypothetical set forth below was taken from a perceptive article, Frederic Corneel, Ethical Guidelines for Tax Practice, 28 Tax L. Rev. 1 (1972). At one time gifts made shortly before death were not pulled into a decedent's gross estate so long as they were not made in contemplation of death. Thus, it could become important to demonstrate that although the decedent made transfers shortly before death, such transfers were not *made in contemplation of death* because: (1) there was no reason to believe that the taxpayer would be dying shortly (e.g., no evidence of visits to the doctor; affirmative evidence of plans for the future), and (2) there were other reasons for the transfers made before death. Actual consumption before death also removed assets from the estate. While the legal issue is dated by changes in substantive law, the ethical issues are timeless. [1]

A client has just been advised by his doctor that he only has a limited time to live and the client asks how he can reduce estate taxes on the transfer of his property to his children. The lawyer can properly advise the making of inter vivos gifts, since even gifts made in contemplation of death will save taxes. But can the lawyer ethically say, "Pay your doctor in cash and tell him not to bill you. Buy yourself a new wardrobe. Make arrangements for a cruise around the world next year. Send the checks to your children with a covering letter that you are making the gift in order to let them have some experience in the management of money and to reduce your own time and attention to financial matters, etc."

---

1. The authors are indebted to Mr. Corneel for his early and continued contributions to this subject, on which they have frequently drawn in developing some of the problems used in these materials.

Corneel concludes that, 'The answer to this question is that it is just as unethical to manufacture misleading evidence relative to the client's state of mind as it is unethical, to suggest any other misleading evidence." Id. at 26.

Under the Model Code, E.C. 7-6 stated that a lawyer may "properly assist his client in the development and preservation of evidence of existing motive, intent or desire." But it cautioned that "obviously, he may not do anything furthering the creation or preservation of false evidence." See also DR 7-102(A)(6). A wide area existed between the extreme limits of these principles. And the uncertainty in this area was not helped by EC 7-6 when it continued: "In many cases a lawyer may not be certain as to the state of mind of his client, and in those situations he should resolve reasonable doubts in favor of his client."

Model Rule 3.4(a) provides that a lawyer must not counsel or assist in the unlawful obstruction of "another party's access to evidence or unlawfully alter, destroy or conceal a document or other material having potential evidentiary value." This rule applies to all evidentiary material, not just evidence of motive, intent, or desire. Why do Model Rules not address the special circumstances identified in the Model Code's Ethical Considerations? Is the seeming vagueness desirable?

Circular 230 does not provide additional guidance. It also states that the practitioner may not participate in presenting false or misleading evidence in matters administered by the IRS. §10.51(d).

Where does this leave the lawyer? If the client initiates the discussion by proposing to take action for a specific objective, may the lawyer suggest alternative action that would have better tax results? If she thinks she is "certain" of the client's state of mind, must she refrain from any assistance that would tend to support a contrary presentation? If the client's original objective was formed with no knowledge of the tax consequences, should he be bound by it? Suppose the client's initial question is what actions he might take that would result in favorable consequences?

PROBLEM

X Corp., a manufacturer of electronic products, has never paid a dividend; instead, it has retained its earnings in the business. In 2007 the corporation earned $200 thousand after taxes, and as of December 31, 2007, it has substantial accumulated earnings and profits. A and B, two individuals in the 35 percent bracket, each own one-half of the common stock of X Corp. A serves as president and B as vice president of the firm. The Board of Directors of X Corp. consists of A, B, and C, the treasurer of the corporation.

A and B consult you concerning the corporation's exposure to the accumulated earnings tax under §531. They are unwilling to cause the corporation to pay a substantial dividend. Although they have occasionally discussed the possibility of acquiring an additional plant, they are presently unwilling to commit the corporation to a plan of expansion.

The law provides that a corporation that has unreasonably accumulated its earnings for the purpose of enabling its shareholders to avoid dividend income must pay a "penalty" tax under §531 of as much as 35 percent of its after-tax income. Case law holds that a corporation that has committed itself to a realistic plan for the expansion of its business may accumulate earnings for the purpose of meeting the expansion requirements. Such accumulation is deemed to be a "reasonable" accumulation, giving the corporation a defense under §531.

Query: Would it be proper for you, as attorney, to recommend that the corporation commission an architect to draw plans for expansion and obtain estimates from builders? Should you draft corporate minutes setting forth an intent to expand?

Suppose A simply asks what actions the corporation might take that would indicate a valid purpose for a reasonable accumulation? May you answer the question? Note that the preamble to the ABA Model Rules states that a lawyer, acting as an advisor, "provides a client with an informed understanding of the client's legal rights and obligations and explains their practical implications."

Suppose the corporation commissions the plans, but A confides in you that the corporation has no intention of expanding. Could you prepare a return that does not include a §531 tax?

3.   Issues of Timing

If the occurrence of a particular event on a specific date controls a tax result, what are the lawyer's ethical responsibilities when prodded by a client?

a. Assume, in connection with the last hypothetical, that A and B first consult you on March 16, 2008. After hearing your explanation of the accumulated earnings tax, they conclude that it is best to have X pay a dividend. You point out that March 15, 2008, was the last day for payment of a dividend that would reduce accumulated earnings and profits as of December 31, 2007. See §535(c)(4) and 563(a). A responds that the checks can simply be dated the previous day. He asks you what is likely to happen if that course of action is followed. What do you respond?

b. Assume that A and B had tried to meet with you on the prior day but that you were out of town. On talking with an associate in your office, they were advised to make the dividend payment on March 15. However, they responded that they would rather wait and talk with you. They told your associate that they would draw the checks on March 15 and hold them until you were available on March 16. They now propose to release the checks. What do you advise?

c. Assume that you have prepared a trust instrument for a valued estate planning client. Under it, shares of stock of a publicly held corporation will be placed in trust. The value of the stock on the day of gift will determine your client's gift tax liability. On the basis of insider information, the client thinks that the price of the stock is now higher than it should be and that, over the next month, it will decline, reducing the tax liability. You point out that it may also go up, increasing the liability. The client asks you to wait for 30 days and then date the documents as of the day on which the lowest price occurred. What do you do?

Assume instead that the client says, "Give the documents to me and I will return them to you at the end of 30 days properly signed and dated." What do you do?

4.   *Valuation Issues*

Many tax consequences turn on valuation, and, generally, the lawyer will turn to a qualified appraiser. See Guidelines Second at IV.D. Is it appropriate for the attorney to assist the appraiser? Can the attorney explain to the appraiser that the client will benefit if the appraisal is low? Or high? Suppose the attorney knows that some appraisers are more willing than others to accommodate the client's wishes. Is the attorney free to recommend such an appraiser? Suppose the attorney knows that the Service always assumes that the taxpayer has undervalued a property and, regardless of how honest the valuation, will propose an increase in the reported value? Does this tendency of the Service effectively create a "mendacity premium"? To what extent are your responses affected by the valuation misstatement penalties under §6662 that were discussed in Chapter 2?

5.   *Conflict of Interest: Lawyer as Intermediary*

The principle that a lawyer owes her client undivided loyalty was discussed in Chapter 3 in connection with tax controversies. The tax lawyer must also be aware of this duty when she engages in planning activities. Special problems arise when a lawyer acts as an intermediary in seeking to establish or adjust a relationship between clients [with potentially conflicting interests] on an amicable and mutually advantageous basis." Model Rule 2.2 comment.

A lawyer acts as an intermediary when she (1) organizes a business for two or more client entrepreneurs, (2) reorganizes a business enterprise for two or more clients who have a financial stake in the reorganization, (3) structures a property distribution in an estate, or (4) mediates a disputed issue between two or more interested clients. Model Rule 2.2 comment. Before a lawyer acts as an intermediary, she must satisfy the following requirements.

Rule 2.2 Intermediary
(a) A lawyer may act as intermediary between clients if:

the lawyer consults with each client concerning the implications of the common representation, including the advantages and risks involved, and the effect on the attorney-client privilege, and obtains each client's consent to the common representation; the lawyer reasonably believes that the matter can be resolved on terms compatible with the clients' best interests, that each client will be able to make adequately informed decisions in the matter and that there is little risk of material prejudice to the interests of any of the clients if the contemplated resolution is unsuccessful; and the lawyer reasonably believes that the common representation can be undertaken impartially and without improper effect on other responsibilities the lawyer has to any of the clients.

(b) While acting as intermediary, the lawyer shall consult with each client concerning the decisions to be made and the considerations relevant in making them, so that each client can make adequately informed decisions.

(c) A lawyer shall withdraw as intermediary if any of the clients so requests, or if any of the conditions stated in paragraph (a) is no longer satisfied. Upon withdrawal, the lawyer shall not continue to represent any of the clients in the matter that was the subject of the intermediation.

Compare this rule with Model Rule 1.7, which deals with the problem of multiple client representation. Why was Model Rule 1.7 insufficient protection for the client? Perhaps Model Rule 2.2 expands upon the principles established in Model Rule 1.7 because a lawyer who acts as an intermediary adjusts the relationship between the two parties, while a lawyer representing multiple parties against a third party may have less influence over the relationship between his clients. The comments to these rules fail to explain their interrelationship.

PROBLEMS

1.   Your firm acts as tax counsel to a major corporation. The president of the corporation would like to reduce his current tax liability and asks you to prepare a deferred compensation plan to benefit him. He is not a shareholder. The adoption of the plan has been approved in general terms by the Board of Directors, but the president has ideas about a number of details. Most of his ideas benefit him but you doubt that they are all in the corporation's best interest. What do you do? Would your reaction differ if he were a 25 percent shareholder? 50 percent? 75 percent? 100 percent?

2.   For some years you have represented a closely held corporation. The sole shareholder, *A*, has decided to sell the business and to retire. Two long-time, trusted employees, *X* and *Y*, desire to buy it. *A* asks for an appointment and arrives with *X* and *Y*. They sketch out their plans, stating that they want the most favorable tax consequences. You advise them that their interests may be inconsistent and that each party should have separate counsel. At this, they express great impatience. They point out that there is no disagreement, that they have no desire to make lawyers rich by employing more of them than necessary, and that they strongly desire that you represent all of them. What course of action do you pursue?

6.   The Tax Lawyer as Negotiator

When the tax lawyer acts for his client as negotiator with another party, he broadens his activity as advisor and planner and, to a degree, becomes an advocate as well. As we discussed earlier, the advocate owes his client a duty of zealous representation under the Model Rules. See Preamble: A Lawyer's Responsibilities. To what extent does this duty attach to the negotiator? The Preamble to the Model Rules notes, "As negotiator a lawyer seeks a result advantageous to the client but consistent with requirements of honest dealing with others." Does the negotiator owe any obligation to the plight of the party on the other side? Does it matter whether or not that party is represented by counsel? Is the degree of sophistication of the other party or his counsel relevant? Consider Model Rule 4.3 (Dealing with Unrepresented Person), which provides:

> In dealing on behalf of a client with a person who is not represented by counsel, a lawyer shall not state or imply that the lawyer is disinterested. When the lawyer knows or reasonably should know that the unrepresented person misunderstands the lawyer's role in the matter, the lawyer shall make reasonable efforts to correct the misunderstanding.

Does that provide much guidance when the other party is aware that the lawyer does not represent him but he has no lawyer to represent his interests?

Assume that you are assisting your client in negotiations for the purchase of the assets of a business. The seller is not represented by counsel. It is clear that the seller anticipates paying only a capital gains tax and that he is evaluating the deal on that basis. You recognize that there will be large ordinary income consequences as a result of depreciation recapture. Do you have any obligation to rescue the seller from his folly? In evaluating this question, are you concerned about your client's possible duty to third persons? About your obligation of loyalty to your client? How should a lawyer sort out these issues and resolve the apparent conflict?

In Proulx v. United States, 77-1 USTC ¶ 9194 (Ct Cl. 1977), aff'd, 594 F.2d 832 (Ct. Cl. 1979), the taxpayers, an elderly couple who had sold a motel, giving a covenant not to compete, sought to escape the ordinary income tax consequences to them of the covenant on the ground that their attorney, a local criminal lawyer, had not recognized its tax significance. The court denied relief on the ground that the formulation put on a transaction by the parties is binding absent fraud or duress. From the statement of facts in the case, it appears that the purchasers of the motel were well represented by counsel who fully understood the tax consequences of the covenant. Could that counsel, consistent with his duty of loyalty to the buyers, have saved the elderly, under-represented couple from their error? If counsel had called the problem to the attention of his clients but they had ordered him to proceed, would counsel have had any problem in doing so? Under Model Rule 6.1, could counsel disclose the possibility of adverse tax consequences to the seller if his client will not consent? If the lawyer is troubled by the unfairness to the seller, can he withdraw?

Under Model Rule 4.1(a), a lawyer must not "make a false statement of material fact or law to a third person." The comment to the Rule notes that the determination whether a statement is one of fact depends upon the circumstances. The example provided happens to use a negotiation context:

> Under generally accepted conventions in negotiation, certain types of statements ordinarily are not taken as statements of material fact. Estimates of price or value

placed on the subject of a transaction and a party's intention as to an acceptable settlement of a claim are in this category, and so is the existence of an undisclosed principal except where nondisclosure of the principal would constitute fraud.

Does this comment give an attorney the right to lie or deceive in negotiations when he is making a settlement offer? One can understand why society may not wish to hold a person to the amount offered in settlement as evidence of a value of a claim; however, why do the Model Rules not adopt a "negotiation in good faith" policy?

PROBLEMS

1. As a lawyer/negotiator, you represent a client who is seeking to buy a closely held business. From a remark made by seller's counsel, you gather that he believes the law is as it used to be before the Tax Reform Act of 1986: that the seller can avoid corporate level tax by making the sale during the course of a one-year liquidation of the selling corporation. Seller's counsel is a friend of yours. You would like to tell him of the repeal of the General Utilities doctrine and warn him of his mistake, but you are concerned that the result will be that the seller will try to raise the price to cover at least a part of the unanticipated corporate level tax. May you take any action that will alleviate this problem? What are the limits on your ability to act?

2. *S* is the sole proprietor of a business and is represented by *L* in the possible sale of the business to *P*. At *L*'s suggestion, *S* had the business appraised. *S* believes that the business is worth more than the $2 million appraisal and instructs *L* to inform *P* that "*S* believes the business is worth $3 million and will not accept a penny less." Can *L* do this?

3. Assume in (1) that, in fact, *S* did not obtain an appraisal but instructs *L* to inform *P* that "*S* recently had the business appraised at $3 million." Can *L* do this?

4. Assume in (1) that *S* instructs *L* to inform *P* that all key employees intend to remain under the new management. *L* knows that the head of the IT department has told *S* that he will retire in two months. What should *L* do?

7. Lawyer as Estate Planner

Many tax lawyers are also estate planners because tax considerations play such a major role in planning a client's estate. Estate planners face a number of common ethical problems.

Perhaps the most frequent is a potential conflict of interest. Quite often, a husband and wife approach a lawyer together to ask for assistance in planning their estates. Sometimes the client will be accompanied by a potential beneficiary, such as a child. There are many advantages to coordinating estate planning for all members of a family, but may the lawyer represent the various multiple interests?

There is no per se rule against multiple representation. As we discussed in Chapter 3, Model Rule 1.7(b) provides:

> A lawyer shall not represent a client if the representation of that client may be materially limited by the lawyer's responsibilities to another client or to a third person ... unless (1) the lawyer reasonably believes the representation will not be adversely affected; and (2) the client consents after consultation.

Compare DR 5-105(A) of the Model Code. These rules require that there be informed consent by both parties to the concurrent representation. The key word here is "informed." The lawyer cannot simply say "I assume I have your permission to represent both of you." Rather, as Geoffrey Hazard has pointed out,

> Informed consent by a client requires disclosure to that client of intentions and purposes of the other client that have material significance with respect to the first client's expectations concerning the matter involved in the representation. In estate planning for husband and wife, this ordinarily includes their respective expectations concerning the property of both.

Geoffrey C. Hazard Jr., Conflict of Interest in Estate Planning for Husband and Wife, 20 Prob. Law. 1, 4 (1994). Suppose one client refuses to consent to the disclosure of the necessary information? May the lawyer continue to represent either party? Suppose both clients concur and the wills are drafted. Several years later, the husband contacts the lawyer and reveals a secret that, if known to the wife, would surely cause her to alter her will. May the lawyer tell the wife? Must she tell the wife? Suppose the husband asks the lawyer to draft a new will that decreases the bequest to the wife. Can the lawyer do so?

A similar conflict of interest may arise where a family desires estate planning advice. Suppose a parent and child seek an attorney's assistance. The clients may not have identical interests. What may be desirable from the beneficiary's point of view may not be the most tax efficient. Furthermore, the parent's estate plan may be based on assumptions about the child's marriage or assets that are not warranted. Are there additional considerations if the parent pays the attorney's fee? See Model Rule 1.8(f).

The issues raised in Chapters 2 and 3 regarding return preparation and representation in audits generally are applicable to the estate planner as well. For example, suppose the client informs the lawyer that she previously made substantial gifts, but filed no gift tax returns. If the donor makes a subsequent gift, can the tax be computed on this gift without reference to the earlier gifts?

An estate planner may recommend a particular course of action because it satisfies the client's needs or produces favorable tax consequences. The lawyer's independent judgment in rendering that advice should not be tainted by the lawyer's own financial and personal interests. Model Rule 1.8(a); Model Code DR 5-101(A). Suppose the lawyer recommends the acquisition of life insurance because of favorable tax treatment. If that lawyer is also a licensed insurance broker, may she sell the client the insurance? See N.Y. State 610 (1990).

This is only a sampling of the ethical issues likely to be faced by the estate planner. For an exhaustive analysis of ethical issues encountered in estate planning practice, see Gerald P. Johnston, An Ethical Analysis of Common Estate Planning Practice—Is Good Business Bad Ethics?, 45 Ohio St. L.J. 57 (1984); Jeffrey N. Pennell, Ethics, Professionalism and Malpractice Issues in Estate Planning and Administration, C756 ALI-ABA 393 (1992).

PROBLEMS

1.   You are contacted by the daughter of an elderly woman who has substantial property, no estate plan, and a potential tax liability that is quite large. You are asked by the woman's only child, her daughter, to prepare an estate plan for her mother. The daughter is married to a regular and important client of your firm. You and the daughter reasonably believe she is to be the principal beneficiary of her mother's bounty. Upon talking with the testatrix, however, you discover that she has ideas for the disposition of her property that are not shared by her daughter and son-in-law. How do you proceed?

2.   A lawyer (L) has represented a husband and wife (H and W) for a number of years, both jointly and separately. They consider her their personal lawyer. L has handled business transactions over the years for H and has handled negligence and other routine matters for W. L has drawn wills for both of them, in which H created customary marital deduction and residuary trusts, and W left everything outright to H. H comes to L and explains that he and W have become estranged, but no divorce is contemplated. W has substantial property of her own, and H has a new interest outside the family, a woman whom he wishes to benefit. L explains to H that under the law of the state, since there are two children, W is entitled to one-third of his estate and that this cannot be barred without W's written consent. She suggests, however, that H purchase a single premium life insurance policy on his life, assigning the policy to his friend, and that H give his friend stock. The total gifts will not result in a gift tax liability but will use up his unified credit and therefore deny that amount of credit to his estate. H adopts the plan and instructs L to draw a will leaving all property outright to his two adult children, thus disinheriting W. H states to L that he is quite confident W would not take against the will since it gives all property to her children, and in any event, there will not be much left in his probate estate after the contemplated gifts. H instructs L to keep his will and planning confidential. W, ignorant of the situation, does not change her will. Has L violated any ethical responsibility to H or W?

3. A has been the attorney for a closely held corporation for many years. The majority shareholder, S, is middle-aged and desires estate planning advice. He is interested in having the corporation adopt a buy-sell plan so that his family will not have to sell the shares to an outsider. There are four minority shareholders who are not family members. May A provide estate planning advice to S? If A does so, may he draft the corporate buy-sell agreement? Are S's interests and the corporation's interests identical? Are S's interests and that of the minority shareholders identical?

4.   Yesterday, as part of an estate plan, a major client created an irrevocable trust into which he placed his stock in a closely held corporation that has a subchapter S election in effect. Today, you realize that the trust cannot be an eligible shareholder of an S corporation because the trustee was given a disqualifying power. What can you do? See Sheldon Banoff, Unwinding or Rescinding a Transaction: Good Tax Planning or Tax Fraud?, 62 Taxes 942 (1984); Guidelines Second at VI.C.2.

8.   Rulings Practice

The tax planner often is asked to provide advice to a client with respect to the tax consequences of a proposed transaction. Because of the complexity of the tax law, the practitioner's advice may not be certain. If the client desires greater certainty, he may want to obtain the IRS's view of the tax consequences of the proposed transaction by seeking a ruling. The ruling is a written statement issued to the taxpayers that interprets the law and applies it to a specific set of facts.

When the tax lawyer seeks a ruling on behalf of his client as to a particular proposed transaction, she is generally involved in a phase of tax planning. Often the lawyer will have advised the client with respect to the structure of the transaction, and the request for ruling will reflect her planning advice. In dealing with the Service, does the tax lawyer step beyond her role as advisor and become an advocate? Should she? What is the relationship between the Service, in its rulings activity, and taxpayers (and their lawyers) who seek rulings?

The IRS statement of procedural rules for obtaining rulings is contained in Revenue Procedure 2007-1, 2007 I.R.B. 1. It requires "a complete statement of all of the facts relating to the transaction." Section 7.01 Subpart (9) goes on to say:

> In order to avoid inevitable delay in the ruling process, contrary authorities should be brought to the attention of the Service at the earliest possible opportunity. . . . The taxpayer is strongly encouraged to inform the Service about, and discuss the implications of, any authority believed to be contrary to the position advanced, such as legislation, tax treaties, court decisions, regulations, notices, revenue rulings, revenue procedures, or announcements. If the taxpayer determines that there are no contrary authorities, a statement in the request to this effect would be helpful. If the taxpayer does not furnish either contrary authorities or a statement that none exists, the Service in complex cases or those presenting difficult or novel issues may request submission of contrary authorities or a statement that none exists. Failure to comply with this request may result in the Service's refusal to issue a letter ruling or determination letter.

Compare Model Rule 3.3(a)(3), which requires a lawyer to disclose "legal authority in the controlling jurisdiction known to the lawyer to be directly adverse to the position of the client and not disclosed by opposing counsel." Also compare Model Rule 3.9 comment, imposing a duty to disclose adverse authority upon a lawyer who appears before "administrative agencies acting in a rule-making or policy-making capacity."

Circular 230, §10.22, commands the tax practitioner to exercise "due diligence" in determining the correctness of oral or written representations made to the Service. See also ABA Opinion 314, supra p. 115, which observes, "Nor does the absolute duty not to make false assertions of fact require the disclosure of weaknesses in the client's case." This statement is made in Opinion 314 in the context of tax disputes. Is it applicable also to rulings practice? Is there a difference between an application for a letter ruling (which generally precedes any controversy) and the processing of a technical advice request (which generally arises in the context of an audit)?

PROBLEMS

1.   The taxpayer obtained a favorable ruling after making certain representations in the request. The taxpayer now wants to take additional steps that he represented in the ruling request that he would not take. What should you advise? Suppose the taxpayer does take the additional steps. Is it proper to attach the ruling to the return if the departures are not disclosed? If they are disclosed?

2.   You are advising a client with respect to a proposed "B" reorganization in which your client will be the acquiring corporation. You learn that your client has recently purchased some stock of the target company for cash. Recognizing that the Service would consider the purchase inconsistent with the "solely for stock" requirement of §368(a)(1)(B), you advise the client to avoid the problem by selling the stock on the market prior to the reorganization. Reluctant to part with control over this block of stock, the client proposes to sell it to an investment house but to retain an option to repurchase the stock at a future date. If the reorganization is consummated, and if the investment house exchanges target stock for client stock, no reacquisition would occur. If, however, the reorganization were aborted, the client would repurchase the stock. In preparing the request for ruling, you include these details. The client objects to this disclosure, contending that the stock is no longer owned and that there is no need to refer to it. You are told to remove the description. What do you do?

3.   Suppose that in a prior year a court had held that Corporation's $2000 payment to an individual was a gift, excludable by him under §102. If X seeks a ruling that future payments made under similar circumstances would be deductible by it under §162(a), and not barred by §274(b), must the attorney for X disclose the earlier court decision?

B.   Legal Opinions and Tax Shelters

A legal opinion is typically a lawyer's expression of her professional judgment as to how the legal issues considered by her would be resolved if presented for decision to the appropriate legal forum. Such opinions are a common element in tax planning.

1. Legal Opinions Generally

If a client proposes to enter into a transaction having significant tax consequences, he will probably want a ruling from the Internal Revenue Service, but that may not be feasible for two reasons. First, there may not be sufficient time to process a ruling request. Second, the Service may be known to have a negative view on the tax outcome of the transaction, and if the lawyer disagrees with the IRS view, the client may be willing to take his chances and rely on the lawyer's opinion. Often the client will want the opinion as a means of penalty protection in the case of an audit. Sometimes, the client will distribute the opinion to third parties for use in their tax planning. Are the ethical responsibilities of the tax lawyer the same in either situation, or are they affected by the purpose to which the opinion will be put? Should a lawyer give a written opinion to X if she knows X will use it to persuade Y and Z to enter a particular transaction? Does it matter that the lawyer has not been retained by Y or Z or even met them?

Before we review the specific pronouncements regulating the lawyer's conduct in the tax shelter context, it is useful to examine the general guidelines for a lawyer who provides an opinion. As noted in the previous paragraph, a lawyer may prepare an opinion for third parties as well as for her client. If the opinion is prepared only for the client's eyes, then the lawyer owes the client all of the duties previously discussed in the context of the lawyer's role as an advisor. If the lawyer prepares an opinion for third parties, then she may owe a duty to the third party as well as to the client. The Model Code did not provide the lawyer with specific guidance as to her responsibility to the client or to the third parties who rely on the lawyer's opinion to invest in the transaction. Model Rule 2.3, however, specifically recognizes the lawyer's role in evaluating transactions for the benefit of nonclients:

> A lawyer may provide an evaluation of a matter affecting a client for the use of someone other than the client if the lawyer reasonably believes that making the evaluation is compatible with other aspects of the lawyer's relationship with the client.

The rule, however, refuses to opine whether a legal duty to a third person may or may not arise. "[S]ince such an evaluation involves a departure from the normal client-lawyer relationship, careful analysis of the situation is required." Model Rule 2.3 comment. The compatibility requirement is designed to ensure that the lawyer is able to properly represent the client's interests. The consent requirement is designed to make sure the client understands the inherent conflict of interest in serving as an evaluator and representing the client. The comment to Model Rule 2.3 gives this example: A lawyer may not issue an evaluation on a transaction if she is defending the client against charges of fraud on the same or a related transaction. Even when such a conflict does not exist, the lawyer is required to notify the client of her "responsibilities to third persons and the duty to disseminate the findings." The comment also requires that if the client places a limitation upon the lawyer's freedom and extent of the investigation, she must disclose all limitations that materially affect the evaluation. This requirement of disclosure is an exception to the general rule of confidentiality in Model Rule 1.6. Model Rule 4.1 establishes a duty of truthfulness with respect to communications with third parties.

The comments to Model Rule 2.3 provide that "[w]hen the evaluation is intended for the information or use of a third person, a legal duty may or may not arise . . . [t]hat question is beyond the scope" of the Rules.

2. Best Practices

As part of the amendments to Circular 230 discussed below, a section detailing "best practices" for tax advisors was added. Section 10.33 states that tax advisors "should provide clients with the highest quality representation concerning Federal tax issues" and includes aspirational standards. Because the standards are not mandatory there is no sanction for a violation. The guidelines include the following:

> "Communicating clearly with the client regarding the terms of the engagement. For example, the advisor should determine the client's expected purpose for and use of the advice and should have a clear understanding with the client regarding the form and scope of the advice or assistance to be rendered."
>
> "Establishing the facts, determining which facts are relevant, evaluating the reasonableness of any assumptions or representations, relating the applicable law (including potentially applicable judicial doctrines) to the relevant facts, and arriving at a conclusion supported by the law and facts."
>
> "Advising the client regarding the import of the conclusions reached, including, for example, whether a taxpayer may avoid accuracy-related penalties under the Internal Revenue code if a taxpayer acts in reliance on the advice."
>
> "Acting fairly and with integrity in practice before the Internal Revenue Service."

Section 10.33 also requires that those with responsibility for overseeing a firm's tax practice take steps to ensure that the best practices are followed by everyone in the firm.

3. Tax Shelter Opinions

Tax shelters have been a problem for the government for decades. A key part of tax shelter promotion is the lawyer's opinion, which is used to add a patina of respectability. Even more important, the opinions were thought to provide penalty protection — a purchaser could be assured that no penalties would be asserted if the shelter did not work because the investor had reasonably relied on the opinion of a tax lawyer.

By the late 1970s, abusive tax shelters — transactions designed to generate tax benefits based on exaggerated valuations and mischaracterizations — were a significant problem for the government. Unfortunately, some tax lawyers played an essential role in the promotion of these shelters. Marketing of the shelters often depended on an opinion of tax counsel asserting a "reasonable basis" in support of the claimed tax benefits. [*] Some opinions often did not offer a conclusion as to whether the tax benefits were likely to be realized if challenged by the Service, but third party investors nonetheless relied on the fact that an opinion existed. Other opinions were hypothetical in the sense that they were based on assumed facts rather than the actual facts. As part of the war on tax shelters, and recognizing the important role played by tax practitioners, the Treasury Department proposed amendments to Circular 230, which imposed duties on practitioners who issued tax shelter opinions. 45 Fed. Reg. 58,594 (Sept. 4, 1980). The proposed amendments would have required that a practitioner issuing a tax shelter opinion (1) exercise due diligence to ensure that the opinion made adequate disclosure of the facts, (2) exercise due diligence to ensure that the opinion describes and expresses an opinion on each important federal tax issue, and (3) refrain from issuing any opinion unless the opinion concludes that it is more likely than not that the principal tax benefits will be allowed. This third requirement was the most controversial.

The proposed amendments provoked a response from the tax bar. In 1981 the ABA issued Formal Opinion 346, which defined the duties of a lawyer who issued a tax shelter opinion. As originally issued, Opinion 346 would have prohibited a lawyer from issuing a negative opinion (an opinion in which the practitioner concludes that the material tax benefits were not likely to be allowed if challenged). This provision was subject to severe criticism and the ABA eventually reissued a revised (and more lenient) Opinion 346. Under the revised opinion it is not unethical for a lawyer to provide an opinion to the effect that the contemplated benefits will not be allowed. The opinion relies on another opinion of the ABA, Opinion 335, which is reproduced following Opinion 346.

ABA Formal Opinion 346

(1982)

An opinion by a lawyer analyzing the tax effects of a tax shelter investment is frequently of substantial importance in a tax shelter offering. [1] The promoter of

---

* For discussions of the role the opinions of tax lawyers played in tax shelters, see Joseph Bankman, The New Market in Corporate Tax Shelters, 83 Tax Notes 1775 (1999); Richard Lavoie, Deputizing the Gunslingers, Co-Opting the Tax Bar into Dissuading Corporate Tax Shelters, 21 Va. Tax Rev. 43 (2001); Tanina Rostain, Sheltering Lawyers: The Organized Tax Bar and the Tax Shelter Industry, 23 Yale J. Reg. 77 (2006).

1. A "tax shelter," as the term is used in this opinion, is an investment which has as a significant feature for federal income or excise tax purposes either or both of the following attributes: (1) deductions in excess of income from the investment being available in any year to reduce income from other sources in that year, and (2) credits in excess of the tax attributable to the income from the investment being available in any year to offset taxes on income from other sources in that year. Excluded from the term are investments such as, but not limited to, the following: municipal bonds; annuities; family trusts; qualified retirement plans; individual retirement accounts; stock option plans; securities issued in

the offering may depend upon the recommendations of the lawyer in structuring the venture and often publishes the opinion with the offering materials or uses the lawyer's name in connection with sales promotion efforts. The offerees may be expected to rely upon the tax shelter opinion in determining whether to invest in the venture. It is often uneconomic for the individual offeree to pay for a separate tax analysis of the offering because of the relatively small sum each offeree may invest.

Because the successful marketing of tax shelters frequently involves tax opinions issued by lawyers, concerns have been expressed by the organized bar, regulatory agencies, and others over the need to articulate ethical standards applicable to a lawyer who issues an opinion which the lawyer knows will be included among the tax shelter offering materials and relied upon by offerees. [2]

A responsibility of the committee is to express its opinion on proper professional conduct of lawyers and to do so by a formal opinion where the subject is of widespread interest. A.B.A. Bylaws, Article 30.7; Rules of Procedure of Standing Committee on Ethics and Professional Responsibility, Rules 1 and 3 (August, 1980). Accordingly, the committee expresses its opinion as to the standards applicable to lawyers who issue tax shelter opinions.

A "tax shelter opinion," as the term is used in this opinion, is advice by a lawyer concerning the federal tax law applicable to a tax shelter if the advice is referred to either in offering materials or in connection with sales promotion efforts directed to persons other than the client who engages the lawyer to give the advice. The term includes the tax aspects or tax risks portion of the offering materials prepared by the lawyer whether or not a separate opinion letter is issued. The term does not, however, include rendering advice solely to the offeror or reviewing parts of the offering materials, so long as neither the name of the lawyer nor the fact that a lawyer has rendered advice concerning the tax aspects is referred to at all in the offering materials or in connection with sales promotion efforts. In this case the lawyer has the ethical responsibility of assuring that in the offering materials and in connection with sales promotion efforts there is no reference to the lawyer's name or to the fact that a lawyer has rendered tax

---

a corporate reorganization; mineral development ventures, if the only tax benefit would be percentage depletion; and real estate where it is anticipated that deductions are unlikely to exceed gross income from the investment in any year, and that any tax credits are unlikely to exceed the tax on the income from that source in any year.

2. The U.S. Treasury Department proposed a rule which would require lawyers who provide tax opinions to comply with standards of due diligence, disclosure, and judgmental determinations. Proposed Rule adding to 31 C.F.R., Subtitle A, Part 10, a new Section 10.33 and amending Sections 10.51 and 1.0.52, relating to standards for providing opinions regarding tax shelters, 45 Fed. Reg. 58,594 (1980). See also Sax, Lawyer Responsibility in Tax Shelter Opinions, 34 Tax Law. 5 (1980); Leis, Lawyers' Ethical Responsibilities in Rendering Opinions on Tax Shelter Promotions, Tax Notes (April 13, 1981) at 795. For general discussions of the legal and ethical responsibilities of lawyers who write tax shelter opinions, Lewis, supra; Kennedy, Problems Faced by the Tax Adviser in Registration of Tax Shelter Securities With the SEC, 33 N.Y.U. Tax Inst. 1365, 1389-1395 (1975); Watts, Professional Standards in Tax Practice: Conflicts of Interest, Disclosure Problems under Regulatory Agency Rules, Potential Liabilities, 33 N.Y.U. Tax Inst. 649 (1975).

advice. The term also does not include the case where a small group of investors negotiates the terms of the arrangement directly with the offeror of securities and depends for tax advice concerning the investment entirely upon advisors other than the lawyer engaged to represent the offeror.

DISCIPLINARY STANDARDS

A false opinion is one which ignores or minimizes serious legal risks or misstates the facts or the law, knowingly or through gross incompetence. The lawyer who gives a false opinion, including one which is intentionally or recklessly misleading, violates the disciplinary rules of the Model Code of Professional Responsibility. Quite clearly, the lawyer exceeds the duty to represent the client zealously within the hounds of the law. See D.R. 7-101; E.C. 7-10. Knowingly misstating facts or law violates D.R. 7-102(A)(5) and is "conduct involving dishonesty, fraud, deceit, or misrepresentation," a violation of D.R. 1-102(A)(4). The lawyer also violates D.R. 7-102(A)(7) by counseling or assisting the offeror "in conduct that the lawyer knows to be illegal or fraudulent." In addition, the lawyer's conduct may involve the concealment or knowing nondisclosure of matters which the lawyer is required by law to reveal, a violation of D.R. 7-102(A)(3).

The lawyer who accepts as true the facts which the promoter tells him, when the lawyer should know that a further inquiry would disclose that these facts are untrue, also gives a false opinion. It has been said that lawyers cannot escape criminal liability on a plea of ignorance when they have shut their eyes to what was plainly to be seen." United States v. Benjamin, 328 F. 2d 854, 863 (2d Cir. 1964). Recklessly and consciously disregarding information strongly indicating that material facts expressed in the tax shelter opinion are false or misleading involves dishonesty as does assisting the offeror in conduct the lawyer knows to be fraudulent. Such conduct violates D.R. 1-102(A)(4) and D.R. 7-102(A). We equate the minimum extent of the knowledge required for the lawyer's conduct to have violated these disciplinary rules with the knowledge required to sustain a Rule 10b-5 recovery, see Ernst & Ernst v. Hochfelder, 425 U.S. 185 (1976), rather than the lesser negligence standard. Compare Securities and Exchange Commission v. Coven, 581 F.2d 1020, 1025 (2d Cir. 1978), certiorari denied, 440 U.S. 950, rehearing denied, 441 U.S. 928 (1979); Rolf v. Blyth, Eastman Dillon & Company, 570 F.2d 38, 44-47 (2d Cir.), certiorari denied, 439 U.S. 1039 (1978); Sharp v. Coopers & Lybrand, 457 F. Supp. 879 (E.D. Pa. 1978).

But even if the lawyer lacks the knowledge required to sustain a recovery under the Hochfelder standard, the lawyer's conduct nevertheless may involve gross incompetence, or indifference, inadequate preparation under the circumstances, and consistent failure to perform obligations to the client. If so, the lawyer will have violated D.R. 6-101(A). ABA Informal Opinion 1273 (1973).

ETHICAL CONSIDERATIONS

Beyond the requirements of the disciplinary rules, the lawyer who issues a tax shelter opinion should follow the canons and the ethical considerations of the model code. [3] Although not constituting absolute requirements, the violation of which may result in sanctions, these canons and ethical considerations constitute a body of principles which provide guidance in the application of the lawyer's professional responsibility to specific situations, such as the rendering of tax shelter opinions. The guidelines developed here are to be applied to each specific situation reasonably and in a practical fashion.

Lawyer as Advisor.   E.C. 7-22 says "a litigant or his lawyer may, in good faith and within the framework of the law, take steps to test the correctness of a ruling of a tribunal." See also E.C. 7-25. Principles similar to these are applied where the lawyer represents a client in adversarial proceedings before the Internal Revenue Service. In that case the lawyer has duties not to mislead the service by any misstatement, not to further any misrepresentations made by the client, and to deal candidly and fairly, A.B.A. Formal Opinion 314 (1965); see also Watts, supra note 2, at 651-53.

The lawyer rendering a tax shelter opinion which he knows will be relied upon by third persons, however, functions more as an advisor than as an advocate. See E.C. 7-3, distinguishing these roles. Since the model code was adopted in 1969, the differing functions of the advisor and advocate have become more widely recognized. [4]

The proposed model rules specifically recognize the ethical considerations applicable where a lawyer undertakes an evaluation for the use of third persons other than a client. These third persons have an interest in the integrity of the evaluation. The legal duty of the lawyer therefore "goes beyond the obligations a lawyer normally has to third persons." Proposed model rules, supra note 3, at 117; see also A.B.A. Formal Opinion 335 (1974). Because third persons may rely on the advice of the lawyer who gives a tax shelter opinion, the principles announced in A.B.A. Formal Opinion 314 have little, if any, applicability.

Establishing Lawyers Relationship.   The lawyer should establish the terms of the relationship with the offeror-client at the time the lawyer is engaged to work on

---

3. Canon 1 says "[a] lawyer should assist in maintaining the integrity and competence of the legal profession." Canon 6 says [a] lawyer should represent a client competently." The ethical considerations used to establish the guidelines in this opinion are E.C. 1-5, E.C. 6-1, E.C. 6-4, E.C. 6-5, E.C. 7-1, E.C. 7-3, E.C. 7-5, E.C. 7-6, E.C. 7-8, E.C. 7-10, E.C. 7-22, E.C. 7-25. See also, Model Rules of Professional Conduct (ABA Commission on Evaluation of Professional Standards, Proposed Final Draft, May 30, 1981), Rule 2.3 at 116.

4. See Watts, note 2, at 655-658; Wolfman and Holden, Ethical Problems in Federal Tax Practice (Michie, Bobbs-Merrill 1981) at 1-2, 100-121; see also Proposed Model Rules, supra note 3, Preamble at 1: "As advisor, a lawyer provides a client with an informed understanding of the client's legal rights and obligations and explains their practical implications. As advocate, a lawyer asserts the clients position under the rules of the adversary system."

the tax shelter offering. This includes making it clear that the lawyer requires from the client a full disclosure of the structure and intended operations of the venture and complete access to all relevant information.

Making Factual Inquiry.   A.B.A. Formal Opinion 335 (1974) establishes guidelines which a lawyer should follow when furnishing an assumed facts opinion in connection with the sale of unregistered securities. The same guidelines describe the extent to which a lawyer should verify the facts presented to him as the basis for a tax shelter opinion:

> [T]he lawyer should, in the first instance, make inquiry of his client as to the relevant facts and receive answers. If any of the alleged facts, or the alleged facts taken as a whole, are incomplete in a material respect; or are suspect; or are inconsistent; or either on their face or on the basis of other known facts are open to question, the lawyer should make further inquiry. The extent of this inquiry will depend in each case upon the circumstances; for example, it would be less where the lawyer's past relationship with the client is sufficient to give him a basis for trusting the client's probity than where the client has recently engaged the lawyer, and less where the lawyer's inquiries are answered fully than when there appears a reluctance to disclose information.
>
> Where the lawyer concludes that further inquiry of a reasonable nature would not give him sufficient confidence as to all the relevant facts, or for any other reason he does not make the appropriate further inquiries, he should refuse to give an opinion. However, assuming that the alleged facts are not incomplete in a material respect, or suspect, or in any way inherently inconsistent, or on their face or on the basis of other known facts open to question, the lawyer may properly assume that the facts as related to him by his client, and checked by him by reviewing such appropriate documents as are available, are accurate. . . .
>
> The essence of this opinion . . . is that, while a lawyer should make adequate preparation including inquiry into the relevant facts that is consistent with the above guidelines, and while he should not accept as true that which he should not reasonably believe to be true, he does not have the responsibility to 'audit' the affairs of his client or to assume, without reasonable cause, that a client's statement of the facts cannot be relied upon.

A.B.A. Formal Opinion 335 at 3, 5-6. For instance, where essential underlying information, such as an appraisal or financial projection, makes little common sense, or where the reputation or expertise of the person who has prepared the appraisal or projection is dubious, further inquiry clearly is required. Indeed, failure to make further inquiry may result in a false opinion. See "Disciplinary standards," supra. If further inquiry reveals that the appraisal or projection is reasonably well supported and complete, the lawyer is justified in relying upon the material facts which the underlying information supports.

Relating Law to Facts.   In discussing the legal issues in a tax shelter opinion, the lawyer should relate the law to the actual facts to the extent the facts are ascertainable when the offering materials are being circulated. A lawyer should not issue a tax shelter opinion which declaims responsibility for inquiring as to the accuracy of the facts, fails to analyze the critical facts, or discusses purely hypothetical facts. It is proper, however, to assume facts which are not currently ascertainable, such as the method of conducting future operations of the venture, so long as the factual assumptions are clearly identified as such in the offering materials, and are reasonable and complete.

Nontax Legal Issues. Although the lawyer rendering the tax shelter opinion may not be asked to address the nontax legal issues, the lawyer should make reasonable inquiries to ascertain that a good faith effort has been expended to comply with laws other than tax laws. Tax counsel need not reexamine the conclusions of other counsel rendering opinions in other specialized areas of law, such as the exemption of the transaction or securities from registration or the validity of a patent. Tax counsel, nevertheless, should be satisfied that competent professional advice on these and similar matters has been obtained where relevant to the offering.

Material Tax Issues. A "material" tax issue for purposes of this opinion is any income or excise tax issue relating to the tax shelter that would have a significant effect in sheltering from federal taxes income from other sources by providing deductions in excess of the income from the tax shelter investment in any year or tax credits which will offset tax liabilities in excess of the tax attributable to the tax shelter investment in any year. See definition of "tax shelter," supra note I. The determination of what is material is to be made in good faith by the lawyer based on the information which is available at the time the offering materials are being circulated.

The lawyer should satisfy himself that either he or another competent professional has considered all material tax issues. In addition, the tax shelter opinion should fully and fairly address each material tax issue respecting which there is a reasonable possibility that the Internal Revenue Service will challenge the tax effect proposed in the offering materials. [5]

Where some material tax issues are being considered by other competent professionals, the lawyer should review their written advice and make inquiries of the client and the other professionals to assure that the division of responsibility is clear and to assure reasonably that all material tax issues will he considered, either by the lawyer or by the other tax professional, in accordance with the standards developed in this opinion. If, as a result of review of the written advice of another professional or otherwise, the lawyer believes that there is a reasonable possibility that the Internal Revenue Service will challenge the proposed tax effect respecting any material tax issue considered by the other professional, and the issue is not fully addressed in the

---

5. It is not necessary that these material tax issues be discussed in a separate opinion letter, so long as the issues are fully and fairly addressed in the offering materials in accordance with the standards expressed in this opinion.

offering materials, the lawyer has ethical responsibilities to so advise the client and the other professional and to refuse to provide an opinion unless the matter is addressed adequately in the offering materials. The lawyer also should assure that his own opinion identifies clearly its limited nature, if the lawyer is not retained to consider all of the material tax issues.

Opinion as to Outcome Material Tax Issues. Since the term "opinion" connotes a lawyer's conclusion as to the likely outcome of an issue if challenged and litigated, the lawyer should, if possible, state the lawyer's opinion of the probable outcome on the merits of each material tax issue. [6] However, if the lawyer determines in good faith that it is not possible to make a judgment as to the outcome of a material tax issue the lawyer should so state and give the reasons for this conclusion.

A tax shelter opinion may question the validity of a revenue ruling or the reasoning in a lower court opinion which the lawyer believes is wrong. But there also must be a complete explanation to the offerees, including what position the service is likely to take on the issue and a summary of why this position is considered to be wrong. The opinion also should set forth the risks of an adversarial proceeding if one is likely to occur.

Overall Evaluation of Realization of Tax Benefits. The clear disclosure of the tax risks in the offering materials should include an opinion by the lawyer or by another professional providing an overall evaluation of the extent to which the tax benefits, in the aggregate, which are a significant feature of the investment to the typical investor are likely, to be realized as contemplated by the offering materials. In making this evaluation, the lawyer should state that the significant tax benefits, in the aggregate, probably will not be realized, or that the probabilities of realization and nonrealization of the significant tax benefits are evenly divided.

In rare instances the lawyer may conclude in good faith that it is not possible to make a judgment of the extent to which the significant tax benefits are likely to be realized. This impossibility may occur where, for example, the most significant tax benefits are predicated upon a newly enacted code provision when there are no regulations and the legislative history is obscure. In these circumstances, the lawyer should fully explain why the judgment cannot be made and assure full disclosure in the offering materials of the assumptions and risks which the investors must evaluate.

The committee does not accept the view that it is always ethically improper to issue an opinion which concludes that the significant tax benefits in the aggregate probably will not be realized. However, full disclosure requires that the negative conclusion be clearly stated and prominently noted in the offering materials.

If another professional is providing the overall evaluation, the lawyer should nonetheless satisfy himself that the evaluation meets the standards set forth above.

6. See E.C. 7-3; Sax, supra note 2, at 34, 35; see also Kennedy, supra note 2, at 1383.

Accuracy of Offering Materials. In all cases, the lawyer who issues a tax shelter opinion, especially an opinion which does not contain a prediction of a favorable outcome, should assure that the offerees will not be misled as a result of mischaracterizations of the extent of the opinion in the offering materials or in connection with sales promotion efforts. In addition, the lawyer always should review the offering materials to assure that the standards set forth in this opinion are met and that the offering materials, taken as a whole, make it clear that the lawyer's opinion is not a prediction of a favorable outcome of the tax issues concerning which no favorable prediction is made. The risks and uncertainties of the tax issues should be referred to in a summary statement at the very outset of the opinion or the tax aspects or tax risks section of the offering materials.

If the lawyer disagrees with the client over the extent of disclosure made in the offering materials or over other matters necessary to satisfy the lawyer's ethical responsibilities as expressed in this opinion, and the disagreement cannot be resolved, the lawyer should withdraw from the employment and not issue an opinion. See E.C. 7-8; A.B.A., Formal Opinion 335, supra.

Summary of Ethical Considerations. The general ethical guidelines to be followed by the lawyer who issues a tax shelter opinion are briefly summarized below. However, reference to this summary must not be substituted for a review of the more complete statement of ethical standards contained in this opinion.

1. Establish in the beginning the lawyer's relationship with the offeror-client, making clear that in order to issue the opinion, the lawyer requires from that client a full disclosure of the structure and intended operations of the venture and complete access to all relevant information.
2. Make inquiry as to the relevant facts and, consistent with the standards developed in A.B.A. Formal Opinion 335, be satisfied that the material facts are accurately and completely stated in the offering materials, and that the representations as to intended future activities are dearly identified, reasonable, and complete.
3. Relate the law to the actual facts to the extent ascertainable and, when addressing issues based on future activities, clearly identify what facts are assumed.
4. Make inquiries to ascertain that a good faith effort has been made to address legal issues other than those to be addressed in the tax shelter opinion.
5. Take reasonable steps to assure that all material federal income and excise tax issues have been considered and all of those issues which involve the reasonable possibility of a challenge by the Internal Revenue Service have been fully and fairly addressed in the offering materials.
6. Where possible, provide an opinion as to the likely outcome on the merits of the material tax issues addressed in the offering materials.
7. Where possible, provide an overall evaluation of the extent to which the tax benefits in the aggregate are likely to be realized.

8. Assure that the offering materials correctly represent the nature and extent of the tax shelter opinion.

NOTE

Formal Opinion 346 requires the tax practitioner to exercise a form of due diligence by verifying the facts presented to him as the basis for his tax shelter opinion. First he must "investigate underlying facts to assure accuracy and completeness of the material facts." To assist in defining the scope of this obligation, the opinion refers to the guidelines established in Formal Opinion 335, which deals with the similar obligation to investigate the facts underlying a sale of unregistered securities that is claimed to be exempt from registration requirements.

ABA Formal Opinion 335

(1974)

In writing opinions as the basis for transactions involving sales of unregistered securities, a lawyer should make adequate preparation including inquiry into the relevant facts in a manner consistent with the guidelines set out in this opinion, but, while he should not accept as true that which he does not reasonably believe to be true, he does not have the responsibility to "audit" the affairs of his client or to assume, without reasonable cause, that the client's statement of the facts cannot be relied on.

Release #5168 of the Securities and Exchange Commission (SEC) under the Securities Act of 1933 (Release #9239 under the Securities Exchange Act of 1934) was published on July 7, 1971. It set forth certain basic standards of conduct required of broker-dealers to meet their responsibilities in connection with sales of unregistered securities. In a footnote to the next-to-last paragraph of the Release, dealing with the obligation of a broker-dealer to review the surrounding facts and obtain the opinion of competent disinterested counsel concerning the legality of sales, it referred to Securities Act Release #44445 (Securities Exchange Act Release #6721), published on February 2, 1962, in the following manner:

> In this regard, the Commission has stated that "if an attorney furnishes an opinion based solely on hypothetical facts which he has made no effort to verify, and if he knows that his opinion will be relied upon as the basis for a substantial distribution of unregistered securities, a serious question arises as to the propriety of his professional conduct."

The Commission's repetition of this language led to inquiries of this Committee as to the circumstances under which and the extent to which the Code of

Professional Responsibility might require that a lawyer make some effort to verify or supplement the facts submitted to him as the basis for an opinion that certain sales of securities need not be registered under the Securities Act of 1933. The question is of such importance to so many lawyers that this Committee has issued this Formal Opinion in an effort to clarify the existence' and extent of a lawyer's responsibility in writing such opinions. . . .

Where an exemption is claimed it has been common for the principals to rely on opinions of attorneys who recite the facts, and then say that on the basis of such facts the transaction is entitled to the exemption.

It is, of course, important that the lawyer competently and carefully consider what facts are relevant to the giving of the requested opinion and make a reasonable inquiry to obtain such of those facts as are not within his personal knowledge. Depending upon the circumstances, the lawyer may or may not need to go beyond directing questions to his client and checking the answers by reviewing such appropriate documents as are available. . . .

In any event, the lawyer should, in the first instance, make inquiry of his client as to the relevant facts and receive answers. If any of the alleged facts, or the alleged facts taken as a whole, are incomplete in a material respect; or are suspect; or are inconsistent; or either on their face or on the basis of other known facts are open to question, the lawyer should make further inquiry. The extent of this inquiry will depend in each case upon the circumstances; for example, it would be less where the lawyer's past relationship with the client is sufficient to give him a basis for trusting the client's probity than where the client has recently engaged the lawyer, and less where the lawyer's inquiries are answered fully than when there appears a reluctance to disclose information.

Where the lawyer concludes that further inquiry of a reasonable nature would not give him sufficient confidence as to all the relevant facts, or for any other reason he does not make the appropriate further inquiries, he should refuse to give an opinion. However, assuming that the alleged facts are not incomplete in a material respect, or suspect, or in any way inherently inconsistent, or on their face or on the basis of other known facts open to question, the lawyer may properly assume that the facts as related to him by his client, and checked by him by reviewing such appropriate documents as are available, are accurate.

Preliminarily, we state two examples as a means of defining the extremes of the problem in giving an opinion to a security holder who wishes to sell securities to the public without registration. On the one extreme, if a lawyer is asked to issue an opinion concerning a modest amount of a widely traded security by a responsible client, whose lack of relationship to the issuer is well known to the lawyer, he may ordinarily proceed to issue the opinion with considerable confidence. On the other extreme, if he is asked to prepare an opinion letter covering a substantial block of a little known security, where the client (be it selling shareholder or broker) appears reluctant to disclose exactly where the securities came from or where the surrounding circumstances raise a question as to whether or not the ostensible sellers may be merely intermediaries for controlling persons or statutory underwriters, then searching inquiry is called for. . . .

A properly drafted opinion will recite clearly the sources of the attorney's knowledge of the facts. Where verification is otherwise called for, an attorney should make appropriate verification and should not rely on the use of such phrases as "based upon the facts as you have given them to me" or "apart from what you have told me, I have not inquired as to the facts."

The essence of this opinion . . . is that, while a lawyer should make adequate preparation including inquiry into the relevant facts that is consistent with the above guidelines, and while he should not accept as true that which he should not reasonably believe to be true, he does not have the responsibility to "audit" the affairs of his client or to assume, without reasonable cause, that a client's statement of the facts cannot be relied upon.

The steps reasonably required of the lawyer in making his investigation must be commensurate with the circumstances under which he is called upon to render the opinion, but he must bear in mind that his responsibility is to render to the client his considered, independent opinion whether, having made at least inquiries such as those suggested by the above guidelines, the claimed exemption is or is not available under the law. While the responsibility of the lawyer is to his client, he must not be oblivious of the extent to which others may be affected if he is derelict in fulfilling that responsibility. A good lawyer is a conscientious lawyer who strives to fulfill, not only the obligations imposed by the Code's Disciplinary Rules, but also the higher responsibilities contained in the Code's Ethical Considerations.

NOTE

Compare the obligation of the opinion writer to inquire into facts with the obligation of the return preparer to inquire into his client's representations in certain circumstances. See Rev. Rul. 80-266, 1980-2 C.B. 378, and Reg. §1.6694-1(b)(2).

Although some observers thought that Treasury might not issue amendments to Circular 230 dealing with tax shelters and rely on the organized bar to regulate practice in the tax shelter opinion area, Treasury did amend Circular 230. Treasury, like the drafters of ABA Formal Opinion 346, permitted the issuance of a so-called negative opinion, that is, an opinion that concludes that the principal tax benefits are more likely than not not allowable. Why were negative opinions permitted? If the lawyer honestly believes that the tax benefits will fail, is it improper to say that? On the other hand, why would a tax shelter promoter want such an opinion? For a discussion of the ABA opinion and the penalty regime that followed, see Dennis J. Ventry, Jr., ABA Formal Opinion 346 and a New Statutory Penalty Regime, 111 Tax Notes 1269 (2006).

It was the adoption of section 469 of the Internal Revenue Code dealing with passive losses, rather than any ethical rules with respect to lawyers' opinions, that spelled the end of the tax shelters of the 1970s. Several decades passed when the tax shelter wars appeared to be over. But in the 1990s tax shelters came roaring back. These shelters were quite different. In almost all cases the shelter was based on a literal reading of the statutory language that almost certainly was not what Congress intended. Congress and the IRS responded with new and more stringent penalties, disclosure requirements, and much litigation. See, e.g., §6662A (imposing a 20 percent penalty for understatements resulting from listed transactions and certain other reportable transactions or a 30 percent penalty if the item is not disclosed. At the same time the reasonable cause exception of §6664(d) were strengthened. The penalty is waived only if the relevant facts affecting the tax treatment of the item are adequately disclosed, there is substantial authority for such treatment, and the tax-payer reasonably believed that such treatment was more likely than not the property treatment. A taxpayer may rely on an opinion of a tax advisor in establishing rea-sonable belief; however, the taxpayer may not rely on the opinion of a "disqualified tax advisor" or a "disqualified opinion." A disqualified tax advisor is any advisor who (1) is a "material advisor" and participates in the organization, management, pro-motion or sale of the transaction; (2) is compensated directly or indirectly by a material advisor with respect to the transaction; (3) has a fee arrangement with respect to the transaction that is contingent on all or part of the intended tax benefits being sustained; or (4) has a disqualifying financial interest in the transaction. [*] An opinion is a disqualified opinion if it is based on unreasonable factual or legal assumptions; unreasonably relies on representations, statements, findings, or agree-ments of the taxpayer; does not identify and consider all relevant facts; or fails to meet other requirements imposed by Treasury.

Ultimately, however, Treasury concluded that this was not sufficient. Because the tax benefits were so enormous if the shelter was upheld and the chances of discovering the shelter were low, the only thing that gave the corporate investors pause were the penalties. But most had been led to believe that if they had a legal opinion blessing the shelter, they could avoid penalties. So promoters routinely supplied such an opinion. The investors never had any contact with the lawyers who wrote the opinions; the opinions were supplied by the promoters and sometimes the investors could not even keep them. The opinions were "canned," general opinions that were used over and over again as the promoter sold and resold the shelters. They often were quite general and made significant assumptions, such as the transaction had "economic substance" without backing up the claim.

Treasury responded by proposing amendments to Circular 230 that imposed very stringent limitations on the issuance of certain kinds of tax opinions. The bar unleashed a storm of criticism, but Treasury refused to back down and ultimately

---

* A material advisor is anyone who provides any material aid, assistance, or advice with respect to organizing, managing, promoting, selling, implementing, insuring or carrying out any reportable transaction, and who directly or indirectly derives gross income in excess of $50,000 (or $250,000 if the investors are corporations or partnerships) for such advice or assistance. §6111(b). Material advisors are required to file information returns describing reportable transactions.

finalized in the amendments in 2005. They are summarized in the Note that follows; the text of §10.35 of Circular 230 appears in the Appendix.

NOTE

The most important part of the Circular 230 rules are the standards for "covered opinions." These standards cover all written advice, including e-mails. To determine the practitioner's obligations, the first step is to determine whether the written advice is a covered opinion.

Covered Opinions

The definition of a covered opinion includes advice with respect to three categories of transactions: (1) listed transactions; (2) principal purpose transactions; and (3) significant purpose transactions. Written advice about listed transactions and principal purpose transactions automatically constitutes a covered opinion. For the third category, additional factors must be present.

A listed transaction is a tax avoidance transaction under Treas. Reg. §1.6011-4(b)(2) and identified publicly by the IRS as a "listed transaction." The IRS periodically updates the list of such transactions. This first category of covered opinions includes written advice concerning a transaction that is the same as or substantially similar to a transaction that at the time the advice was rendered has been determined by the IRS to be a tax avoidance transaction.

The second category of covered opinions includes written advice about a partnership or other entity, any investment plan or arrangement, or any other plan or arrangement the principal purpose of which is the avoidance or evasion of any federal tax. To be the "principal" purpose, the tax avoidance purpose must exceed any other purpose. The principal purpose will not be tax evasion, however, if the purpose is to claim tax benefits in a manner consistent with the statute and congressional purpose.

Written advice with respect to a transaction that has a significant purpose of tax avoidance or evasion (but not a principal purpose) is a covered opinion only if it is also (1) a reliance opinion, (2) a marketed opinion, (3) subject to conditions of confidentiality, or (4) subject to contractual protection. A reliance opinion is written advice that "concludes at a confidence level of at least more likely than not (a greater than 50 percent likelihood) that one or more significant Federal tax issues would be resolved in the taxpayer's favor." Note that reliance opinions are not limited to tax shelter opinions. Any "more likely than not" opinion must meet the standards for covered opinions. An issue is "significant" if it is one for which the IRS has a reasonable basis for challenging the position taken by the taxpayer and its resolution could have a significant impact (whether beneficial or adverse) on the tax treatment of the transaction. Thus so long as the IRS has a 20 to 25 percent likelihood of success, the practitioner providing a written "should" or "will" opinion must follow the strict guidelines for covered opinions. There is, however, an important exception. A written opinion (other than advice for a principal purpose or listed transaction) will not be a reliance opinion if the author prominently discloses in the written advice that it was not intended to be used, and cannot be used, by the taxpayer for penalty protection (as a basis under §6664 to avoid the §6662 accuracy-related penalty). This disclaimer must be set forth in a separate section in at least as large a typeface as the rest of the opinion.

A market opinion is written advice if the practitioner knows or has reason to know that it will be used or referred to by a person other than the practitioner (or his firm) in promoting, marketing, or recommending a partnership or other entity or an investment plan or arrangement to a taxpayer. Practitioners are concerned that this broad definition includes many forms of written advice that are not tax shelters. Practitioners can also avoid characterization of written advice as a marketed opinion if they prominently display a disclaimer, which must provide that the advice was not intended and cannot be used for penalty protection, was written to support the promotion or marketing of the transaction, and directs the taxpayer to seek advice based on the taxpayer's particular circumstances from an independent tax advisor.

Written advice is "subject to conditions of confidentiality" if the author imposes on any recipient a limitation of disclosure of the tax treatment or tax structure of the transaction, and that protects the confidentiality of the practitioner's tax strategies, whether or not it is legally binding. Some promoters of abusive tax shelters claim that they have a propriety interest in the shelter and seek to protect that by forbidding the investor to disclose the details or the written advice. Written advice is subject to "contractual protection" if the taxpayer can be at least partially reimbursed for fees if all or part of the intended tax consequences addressed in the written opinion are not sustained or if the fees paid to the practitioner are contingent on the taxpayer's realization of the tax benefits from the transaction.

The definition of covered opinion contains a number of exceptions. First the requirements for covered opinions do not apply to preliminary advice provided to a client where the practitioner reasonably expects to provide subsequent advice satisfying the requirements of §10.35. It is not clear whether the subsequent advice must be a covered opinion or an opt-out opinion (written advice with a disclaimer). The covered opinion standards also do not apply to advice provided to a taxpayer after the taxpayer has filed a return. Since negative advice cannot be used for penalty protection, it also is excluded from the definition of covered opinion. If, however, the advice reaches a conclusion favorable to the taxpayer at any confidence level (such as not frivolous, realistic possibility of success, reasonable basis or substantial authority), the exclusion does not apply. The covered opinion requirements do not apply to in-house advice written by an employee to an employer solely for purposes of determining the tax liability of the employer. This appears to exclude in-house advice about the tax consequences of transactions involving employees (e.g., stock options) or shareholders (use of the company car). Finally the covered opinion requirements do not apply to advice (other than with respect to listed or principal purpose transactions) that concerns a qualified plan, a state or local bond opinion, or advice included in documents filed with the SEC.

Covered Opinion Standards

There are essentially four requirements that a covered opinion must meet: (1) identification of facts, (2) application of law to the facts, (3) evaluation of significant federal tax issues, and (4) overall conclusion. In addition there are other standards that apply to covered opinions. These are discussed below.

The practitioner must make reasonable efforts to identify and ascertain the facts (whether past or future) and determine which facts are relevant. The opinion cannot be based on either unreasonable factual assumptions or unreasonable representations, which the practitioner knows or should know are incorrect or incomplete. For example, the author could not simply accept a representation from the client that the transaction has a business purpose. The practitioner must know what the business purpose is and have evidence as to that purpose. Circular 230 also requires that the opinion have a separate section that identifies all factual representations upon which the practitioner relies. Having determined the facts, the practitioner must relate the applicable law (including applicable judicial doctrines) to the relevant facts. It is not permissible to assume the favorable resolution of any significant federal tax issue, and the practitioner may not base an opinion on unreasonable legal assumptions, representations, or conclusions. The opinion cannot contain internally inconsistent legal analyses or conclusions.

A covered opinion must provide the practitioner's conclusion as to the likelihood that the taxpayer will prevail on the merits with respect to each significant federal tax issue considered in the opinion. [*] If the author cannot reach a conclusion with respect to one or more of those issues, the opinion must state that the practitioner is unable to reach a conclusion with respect to those issues. In addition, the opinion must include the reasons for the conclusions, including the facts and analysis supporting the conclusions, or describe the reasons the practitioner cannot reach a conclusion. If the opinion is a marketed opinion, the written advice, in addition, must provide the practitioner's conclusion that the taxpayer will prevail on the merits at a confidence level of at least more likely than not with respect to each significant tax issues. If she cannot reach a more-likely-than-not conclusion with respect to each significant federal tax issue, the practitioner cannot provide the marketed opinion but may provide written advice with respect to a significant purpose transaction that satisfies the disclosure exception. [**]

In addition to the practitioner's conclusion with respect to each significant federal tax issue, the opinion must provide the practitioner's overall conclusion as to the likelihood that the federal tax treatment of the transaction, or matter that is the subject of the opinion, is the proper treatment and the reasons for that conclusion.

---

* Recall that a significant tax issue is one for which the IRS has a reasonable basis for challenging the position taken by the taxpayer and its resolution could have a significant impact on the tax treatment of the matter.

** Recall that it must state that it was written for marketing purposes, it cannot be relied on to prevent penalties, and it must urge the taxpayer to seek independent advice.

If the practitioner is unable to reach an overall conclusion, the opinion must state that and must describe the reasons for the practitioner's inability. This fact must be prominently disclosed and it must state that with respect to those issues the opinion is not effective for avoiding taxpayer penalties.

There are two general exceptions to these requirements. The first is the so-called limited scope opinion. A practitioner may provide an opinion that considers less than all of the significant federal tax issues if the practitioner and the taxpayer agree that the scope of the opinion and the taxpayer's potential reliance on the opinion for purposes of avoiding penalties are limited to the issues discussed in the opinion. A limited scope opinion must prominently disclose that (1) the opinion is limited to certain issues, (2) that additional issues may exist that could affect the tax treatment of the matter and that the opinion does not discuss them or reach a conclusion with respect to those issues, and (3) that the taxpayer cannot rely on the opinion to avoid penalties with respect to any issues outside the limited scope of the opinion. The second exception applies when the practitioner relies on the opinion of others. Generally a practitioner must be knowledgeable in all aspects of the law on which she is opining. She may rely, however, on the opinion of another practitioner with respect to one or more significant federal tax issues unless she knows that the other practitioner's opinion should not be relied on. If the practitioner relies on the opinion of another, she must identify the opinion and opinion author and set forth the conclusions reached in the other opinion.

In addition a covered opinion must prominently disclose any compensation arrangement, such as a referral fee or a fee-sharing arrangement, between the practitioner (or his firm) and any person (other than the client for whom the opinion is prepared) with respect to promoting, marketing, or recommending the arrangement that is the subject of the opinion. It must also disclose any referral agreement between the practitioner and a promoter who promotes, markets, or recommends the transaction that is the subject of the opinion.

NOTES

1. What is the effect of Circular 230 §10.35 on ABA Formal Opinion 346? That opinion provided that, "where possible," the lawyer should provide an opinion "as to the likely outcome on the merits of material tax issues" and "an overall evaluation of the extent to which the tax benefits in the aggregate are likely to be realized." Can a lawyer still do that? Is the opinion stripped of any effect?

2. Why do you suppose Treasury believed that Opinion 346 was not sufficient to regulate opinion writing with respect to tax shelters? Might it have something to do with the fact that Opinion 346 only applies to lawyers, whereas Circular 230 applies to practitioners? Might it have something to do with the fact that Opinion 346 was based on the aspirational ethical considerations of the Model Code, whereas the Circular 230 rules are mandatory? Might it have something to do with the fact that the two sets of rules are administered by different authorities? Treasury will interpret the Circular 230 rules and punish

those who violate them, whereas state licensing authorities will interpret and discipline lawyers who violate ethical rules.

3.   Is the difference between a "principal purpose" opinion and a "significant purpose" opinion clear? Most practitioners do not believe it is and that this presents serious risks of inconsistent application and inadvertent noncompliance. Recall that written advice with respect to the former is automatically a covered opinion, whereas only certain types of written advice with respect to the latter are. See, e.g., ABA Tax Section, Comments on Proposed Rulemaking, Circular 230, T2004 TNT 58-46; (2004); New York State Bar Association Tax Section Report on Circular 230 Regulations, 2004 TNT 58-46 (2004).

4.   Many firms routinely require that the disclaimer legend be placed on all written communications even if they have nothing to do with tax advice. As a precautionary matter, firms slap the banner on all e-mails, for example, even those inviting a client to lunch. Some lawyers have argued that this degrades the profession. See, e.g., Association of the Bar of the City of New York Comments on Circular 230 Regulations, 2005 TNT 101-26 (May 10, 2005).

What is the effect of a routine disclaimer on such e-mails or on other written advice that could not possibly constitute a reliance opinion?

5.   The definition of a marketed opinion does not include opinions that are mass marketed by the firm that produced the opinion. Law firms and accountants employed this device to market abusive tax shelters in the past. Why are self-marketed opinions excluded from the rules?

6.   Can a covered opinion include alternative theories or rules of law under which the federal tax issue can be resolved favorably? Does it matter if the arguments are dependent on factually inconsistent premises? What if a fact is uncertain? Suppose the value of the property is unclear?

7.   In evaluating the significant federal tax issues addressed in a covered opinion, the practitioner cannot take into account the possibility that a tax return will not be audited, that an issue will not be raised on audit, or that an issue will be resolved through settlement if raised. This is information a client surely would want from his tax advisor. Does this mean that this advice must be provided orally?

8.   The changes to Circular 230 were greeted by howls of protest from lawyers and the organized bar. Many asserted that "law practice as we know it will come to an end." In what ways would you expect tax practice to change? For the better? For the worse?

9.   Treasury has not amended the regulations under §6664, which imply that an opinion would provide penalty protection. Given the strenuous objections to Treasury's efforts to regulate tax practice, why didn't Treasury or Congress simply change the rules for penalty protection? Why should a lawyer's opinion protect a client against penalties if the tax shelter fails? See Deborah H. Schenk, The Circular 230 Amendments: Time to Throw Them Out and Start Over, 110 Tax Notes 1311 (2006).

10.   Many tax lawyers are uncomfortable with tax shelter opinions. Why do they continue to write them? Is it money? Client loyalty? Competitive pressure? See

James P. Holden, Dealing with the Aggressive Tax Shelter Problem, 82 Tax Notes 707 (1999). Is it possible to enlist tax lawyers in solving the shelter problem? Can lawyers help the government without reneging on their duty to their clients? For a thoughtful article offering suggestions how to accomplish this, see David M. Schizer, Enlisting the Tax Bar, 59 Tax L. Rev. 331 (2006).

PROBLEMS

1.   A client asks his usual tax lawyer about a transaction and the lawyer responds by e-mail that there is at least a 50 percent likelihood that the client will obtain the tax benefits of the transaction. The IRS has a reasonable basis for believing that the benefits will not be obtained and asserts a deficiency and an accuracy-related penalty. Suppose you represent the client in the tax deficiency matter. You did not provide the written advice. Can you raise the e-mail as a grounds for a reasonable basis defense under §6664? Could the client argue the following? "Every communication I receive from this lawyer has a disclaimer, even e-mails that have nothing to do with tax. I had no reason to believe that I could not rely on this e-mail." How sympathetic do you think a judge might be to that argument?

2.   You represent two individuals who are organizing an S corporation and intend to locate other investors. You have been asked to provide written tax advice about the tax consequences to the investors if a subchapter S election is made. Your clients intend to show your advice to potential shareholders. In providing your advice, must you comply with the covered opinion rules?

3.   Suppose the client informs you by e-mail that he intends to attend a meeting about a possible investment in a hedge fund. He asks for a brief e-mail opinion about the tax consequences of such an investment. You reply by an e-mail without a disclaimer because you are certain that if the client goes forward he will seek a formal opinion from you. In fact, the client does invest in the fund but never seeks further advice from you. What should you do? What if at the time you wrote the original e-mail, you had serious doubts that the client would invest in the fund?

4.   Your client asks for your advice about the federal tax consequences of a transaction with significant purported tax benefits. You quickly ascertain that this is at least a "significant purpose" transaction, if not a "principal purpose" transaction. You tell the client that a written opinion would cost many thousands of dollars but that you can provide advice orally much more cheaply. What, if anything, must you tell the client about penalties and penalty protection?

4.   Other Written Advice

Circular 230 also imposes standards for written advice that does not rise to the level of a covered opinion. §10.37. These rules apply to all written advice, not just that relating to tax shelters. These standards are written in the negative: A practitioner cannot give written advice concerning federal tax issues if (1) he bases the written advice on unreasonable factual or legal assumptions, (2) unreasonably relies on representations, statements, findings or agreements of the taxpayer or any other person, (3) does not consider all relevant facts that the practitioner knows or should know, or (4) in evaluating a federal tax issue, takes into account the possibility that a tax return will not be audited, that an issue will not be raised on audit, or that an issue will be resolved through settlement. Where the practitioner knows that the opinion will be used or referred to by someone else in promoting or marketing a transaction with a significant purpose of avoiding or evading federal taxes, the determination of whether a practitioner has failed to comply with the standards will be made on the basis of a heightened standard of care because of the greater risk caused by the practitioner's lack of knowledge of the taxpayer's circumstances.

C.   Fee Arrangements for Planning

1.   *The All-Inclusive Fee*

Model Rule 1.5 governs the lawyer's fee arrangement with his client. The rule requires that the fee charged by the lawyer for his services be reasonable. DRs 2-106 and 107 of the Model Code are similar. A lawyer should examine the factors listed in the applicable rule to determine whether his fees are reasonable. These rules also deal with the communication of the fee to the client, the questions of contingency fees, fees that are prohibited, and the division of fees among lawyers not working in the same firm. We discussed the general rules concerning fees in Chapter 3.

The fee charged by a lawyer acting as tax planner may cover not only the planning phase but also representation in connection with any subsequent controversy. The following ABA opinion deals with this issue.

ABA Informal Opinion 1389

(1977)

Lawyers who engage extensively in counseling and advising clients with respect to tax matters are requested from time to time to advise clients on transactions which are largely tax-motivated. If the client-taxpayer's treatment of the transaction is not challenged by the Internal Revenue Service or if any challenge by the IRS is not sustained either on IRS review or by the courts, the transaction may result in a substantial reduction in taxes to the client. If, on the other hand, the transaction is not sustained, the taxpayer will at least be required to pay the tax he hoped to avoid plus interest and possibly a negligence penalty.

You ask whether it is ethically proper for the lawyer, in advising a client on such a transaction with doubtful consequences, to charge the client a fixed fee which includes not only the planning of the transaction but which would also cover representation of the client in the event the client's return is selected for audit, both before the Internal Revenue Service and in possible litigation before the Tax Court. If either the audit or the Tax Court litigation did not ensue, the lawyer would keep the fee.

DR 2-106(A) provides:

> A lawyer shall not enter into an agreement for, charge, or collect an illegal or clearly excessive fee.

DR 2-106(B) provides that a fee is "clearly excessive" when, after a review of the facts, a lawyer of ordinary prudence would be left with a definite and firm conviction that the fee is in excess of a reasonable fee. Factors to be considered as guides in determining the reasonableness of a fee are also set forth in that Disciplinary Rule.

There is nothing improper in a lawyer charging and being paid a fixed fee in advance for legal work on tax matters or litigation before the Tax Court if the client and the lawyer choose to do so and it is fully understood that the fixed fee embraces all work to be done, whether it be relatively simple and of short duration, or complex and protracted.

Also, an attorney can agree with a client on a contingent fee where he is only to be paid if he accomplishes a tax saving for the client. Similarly, an attorney can agree with a client on a fixed fee coupled with a contingency on the outcome of the case providing it is also understood that the fixed fee applies irrespective of the outcome and that the Contingency applies only to the tax saving effected.

An attorney can also agree with a client to charge for legal services on an hourly basis for the time expended by his firm on the matter. If a retainer fee is obtained and the fee is charged on a time-expended basis, it would then be incumbent on the law firm to remit to the client a payment covering any excess, in the event the full amount of the retainer fee was not absorbed in the rendition of the services.

NOTE

Subsequent to this opinion, Circular 230 was amended to deal with contingent fees. §10.27 now provides:

> A practitioner may not charge a contingent fee for preparing an original tax return or for any advice rendered in connection with a position taken or to be taken on an original tax return.

Since the vast majority of tax planning and tax advice involves a position that ultimately will be taken on tax return, does that mean that tax practitioners cannot charge contingent fees for tax advice?

2. *Billing the Proper Party*

If a client requests that services provided to the client be billed instead to another person, for instance, to the clients' controlled corporation, is the lawyer free to honor that request?

ABA Informal Opinion 86-1517

(1986)

BILLING CORPORATIONS FOR PERSONAL LEGAL SERVICES RECONSIDERATION OF INFORMAL OPINION 1494

A lawyer may bill a corporate client for personal non-corporate legal services furnished to an individual shareholder, director, officer or employee client when the corporation and the individual agree and the bill identifies the personal legal services as personal services and the charge for those services. This opinion supersedes Informal Opinion 1494, which is withdrawn.

The Committee has been asked to review ABA Informal Opinion 1494 (July 14, 1982). Opinion 1494 dealt with the propriety of an attorney's complying with a request from a client, the sole shareholder of a corporation, that the lawyer's charges for both corporate legal work and personal legal services be billed directly to the corporation without identifying the personal nature of the legal services included on the bill.

In Opinion 1494, it was noted the lawyer had reason to believe that the shareholder might cause the corporation to deduct the entire fee as a corporate business expense for federal and state income tax purposes. The Committee held, under those circumstances, that the lawyer had a duty to inquire of the client the purpose for requesting the combined billing and, if the lawyer was not satisfied that the client intended to comply with the tax laws, the lawyer should not issue the combined bill unless it adequately described the nature of the services. On further review, the Committee is of the opinion that regardless of the explanation of the reason for the request the lawyer should not comply with the request.

There are two issues presented: first, the propriety of billing the personal services to the corporation; and second, the propriety of including those services on the corporate billing without identifying them as personal services or indicating the amount of the bill applicable to the personal services. There may be many legitimate reasons for billing the personal services to the corporation, such as the existence of a compensation plan providing for payment by the corporation of certain personal legal expenses of employees. Absent any knowledge by the lawyer of facts raising questions about an illegal or fraudulent purpose for the billing to the corporation, it is not ethically improper for the lawyer to bill the corporation for the personal legal services (identifying the services appropriately). [1] The determination of corporate authorization must of course be made in the context of applicable corporate laws. [2]

The request that the lawyer not identify the services on the bill as personal services involves very different considerations. Rule 1.2(d) of the Model Rules of Professional Conduct (1983) provides in part that a lawyer, "shall not counsel a client to engage, or assist a client, in conduct that the lawyer knows is criminal or fraudulent. . . ." Model Rule 8.4(c) states that it is professional misconduct for a lawyer to "engage in conduct involving dishonesty, fraud, deceit or misrepresentation." The predecessor Model Code of Professional Responsibility (1969, revised 1980) contained comparable provisions in DR 7-102(A)(7) and DR 1-102(A)(4). Submission to the corporation of a bill which includes personal services to the shareholder without identifying those services as personal services and the amount of the bill applicable to them may, under these circumstances, constitute assistance to the client in conduct that the lawyer knows is criminal or fraudulent and is at least conduct involving deceit or misrepresentation by the lawyer.

In the absence of knowledge to the contrary, the lawyer normally would assume the reason for the request to be that the shareholder expected to treat the entire fee as a corporate business expense for federal and state income tax purposes. As noted in Opinion 1494, quoting prior opinions, a lawyer cannot avoid a violation of the rules against assisting a client in conduct the lawyer knows to be illegal or fraudulent by disclaiming "knowledge" of illegality or fraud when the lawyer has, without inquiry, recklessly and consciously disregarded information that plainly suggests that a crime or fraud is involved. See, e.g., ABA Formal Opinion 346 (Revised) (January 29, 1982); ABA Informal Opinion 1470 (July 16, 1981). Thus, even though it might be argued the lawyer does not actually "know" that the conduct of the client will be criminal or fraudulent, the facts ordinarily would present a sufficiently clear indication of criminal or fraudulent intent that the billing, without identification of the personal nature of the services and the charge applicable to them, would violate Rule 1.2(d) and DR 7-102(A)(7).

In any event, a bill for legal services addressed to a client, in the absence of a statement to the contrary, clearly implies the services were provided for the client. Thus, billing the corporation for personal legal services for a shareholder without identifying them as personal legal services and indicating the amount applicable to them constitutes conduct involving deceit or misrepresentation in violation of Model Rule 8.4(c) and DR 1-102(A)(4). It could be argued that there is no deceit or misrepresentation because both the corporate and individual clients know the nature of the services billed; however, there could be no reason for the request not to

1. Although the bill should identify the personal services as personal services, it need not include details which would compromise the individual client's right of confidentiality.

2. The lawyer is cautioned to be particularly alert to conflicts of interest that may exist within the corporate structure as they relate to the person receiving the legal services and the person confirming to the lawyer the existence of corporate approval for the billing arrangement. No attempt is made in this opinion to resolve the various conflicts that might exist within the Corporate structure or to address how a corporate entity may indicate its approval for such billing arrangements.

identify the services as personal services on the bill unless the client intended that the services not be so identified by someone entitled to know.

In conclusion, it is the opinion of the Committee that by agreement of a corporate client and an individual client who is a shareholder of the corporate client, a lawyer may bill personal legal services for the individual client to the corporation, but the lawyer must identify the services billed as personal legal services (without necessarily disclosing their nature) and indicate the amount of the bill applicable to them. The Committee believes this opinion applies equally to personal legal services for a director, officer or employee of a corporation which are billed to the corporation. Informal Opinion 1494 is withdrawn.

NOTES

1.   As the informal opinion points out, a lawyer cannot "counsel a client to engage, or assist a client, in conduct that the lawyer knows is criminal or fraudulent." Model Rule 1.2(d). In what circumstances would it be appropriate to send a bill that simply says "for legal services rendered"? Suppose the cost of the lawyer's services should properly be capitalized for tax and accounting purposes. Under ABA Inf. 86-1517, would the submission of a generalized bill for such services be appropriate?

2.   Is it ethical to send a bill in the name of one lawyer when the services were actually provided by another lawyer? In United States v. D'Amato, 39 F.3d 1249 (2d Or. 1994), the court overturned a conviction for mail fraud based on evidence that a partner of Armand D'Amato had submitted bills to a corporation for work D'Amato had done in lobbying his brother, Senator Alphonse D'Amato. The bills had been sent in the name of the law partner to avoid potential unfavorable publicity. Furthermore, the bills requested payment for various reports that were never submitted by the D'Amato firm, in order to hide the true nature of D'Amato's services. The court found this was insufficient evidence of mail fraud. Was either of D'Amato's actions unethical?

3.   Fitting the Work to the Client's Fee Budget

If a tax planning client is interested in knowing whether to invest $10,000 in a proposed transaction, he is not likely to want to pay $3,000 or $4,000 for that advice. Suppose, however, that the tax aspects of the transaction are very complex, and that a lawyer could easily accumulate a charge of that level in order to research the issues thoroughly. May the lawyer accept the assignment subject to a $1,500 fee budget?

The tax law is enormously complex and it may not be economical for the client to purchase absolute certainty with respect to a given issue. Are there ethical limitations on the lawyer's limiting the scope of the representation?

Model Rule 1.1 provides:

A lawyer shall provide competent representation to a client competent representation requires the legal knowledge, skill, thoroughness and preparation reasonably necessary for the representation.

The Comment on thoroughness and preparation adds:

Competent handling of a particular matter includes inquiry into and analysis of the factual and legal elements of the problem, and use of methods and procedures meeting the standards of competent practitioners. It also includes adequate preparation. The required attention and preparation are determined in part by what is at stake; major litigation and complex transactions ordinarily require more elaborate treatment than matters of lesser consequence.

Rule 1.2 provides that a lawyer may limit the objectives of the representation if the client consents after consultation. One of the comments to Rule 1.5 on fees says that an agreement may not be made whose terms "might induce the lawyer improperly to curtail services for the client," and a comment under Rule 1.2 notes that a client may not be asked to limit services in a manner that would violate the lawyer's duty of competence.

Where does this leave a lawyer whose client neither can afford nor wants a complete answer? Is this like any other market transaction? One is free to purchase a Honda rather than a Mercedes. Or is the purchase of professional services different?

If the client cannot afford to pay for a costlier effort, is he entitled to no advice?

In 1990, the ABA Tax Section drafted and sent to the ABA Standing Committee on Ethics and Professional Responsibility a draft opinion that would have addressed this issue and provided lawyers with needed ethical guidance. The concluding paragraph of the draft opinion stated:

In summary, where in the exercise of the lawyer's best legal judgment, based upon relevant experience and a review of appropriate texts and treatises, the lawyer is able to make an informed and intelligent judgment as to a proposed course of conduct, the lawyer freely may counsel with respect thereto, notwithstanding that by agreement with the client the lawyer has not undertaken extensive or complete research, and that research might alter the lawyer's advice. The lawyer is entitled to balance fairly the lawyer's duty of competence and the obligation to do only such work as will command a reasonable fee. The lawyer may limit the extent of the work to be done, by agreement with the client after appropriate discussion, consistent with the lawyer's obligation to provide knowledge, skill, and thoroughness reasonably necessary for the representation, and consistent with the lawyer's duties to the tax system.

Although no opinion on this subject was issued by the ABA Committee, the conclusion of the draft opinion appears to be a reasonable resolution of a difficult question. See Paul J. Sax, When Worlds Collide: Ethics v. Economics, 20 Cap. U.L. Rev. 365 (1991).

Chapter 5
Formulating Tax Policy

Tax policy is primarily the province of Congress and it is reflected in the Internal Revenue Code and other tax-related statutes. The Treasury regulations, published rulings, and court decisions are all supposed to implement that congressionally determined policy, but in the administrative and judicial process, as lacunae are filled and ambiguities resolved, policy is made as well. Policy formulation is therefore the responsibility of members of Congress, Treasury officials, and even judges, but taxpayers and their counsel also actively seek to influence the outcome of the policy formulation process. And lawyers in the Treasury and on the staffs of congressional committees work full time to affect policy choices.

In this chapter we examine the ethical responsibilities of the tax lawyer who seeks to mold or modify tax policy. The lawyer may act in a representative capacity on behalf of a client, or he may act pro bono, expressing either his own convictions or those of a bar association or other professional organization.

When a lawyer acts in a representative capacity, he is required to adhere to particular standards that guide the conduct of advocates. A lawyer acting in the public interest must, in addition, be conscious of the importance of his not representing unduly narrow, particular interests while purporting to act for the more general good. Does a lawyer who has lobbied in the policy area on behalf of a client surrender his freedom to advocate policy objectives "in the public interest" that may not be in the client's direct best interests?

A. The Tax Legislative Process

Before examining ethical issues in this area, it is helpful to gain an understanding of the tax legislative process. The following excerpt describes the process in summary form.

Paul R. McDaniel, Hugh J. Ault, Martin J. McMahon Jr. & Daniel L. Simmons, Federal Income Taxation, Cases and Materials

25-27 (2004)

Tax legislation is a dynamic process. As the history of the income tax demonstrates, the income tax has been continually altered, often from year to year, to meet changing conditions. Since the fiscal policy of the Government must be responsive to current problems, and since the income tax is a vital part of our fiscal policy, this constant change is inevitable and necessary.

Major tax legislation generally originates in response to Presidential recommendations. Occasionally, however, Congress takes the initiative. Because under the Constitution revenue legislation must originate in the House of Representatives, historically, the first Congressional step, whatever the impulse, usually was the holding of a public hearing by the Committee on Ways and Means of the House of Representatives. In recent years, however, hearings have been perfunctory, if they have been held at all. Usually the hearing is against a background of these general Presidential or Congressional proposals, but sometimes a particular bill is before the Committee. The first witness is generally either a member of Congress who has proposed particular tax legislation, or if a proposal originates with the Administration, the Secretary of the Treasury. The principal technical official of the Treasury Department who assists the Secretary in this regard and who is responsible for the direct supervision of tax legislation in the Executive branch is the Assistant Secretary for Tax Policy.

The Secretary of the Treasury may be followed by other Administration witnesses, such as the Chair of the Council of Economic Advisors or the Director of the Office of Management and Budget, depending on the nature of the proposals. Then come representatives of various private interests concerned with the proposed legislation. These range from spokespersons for trade associations, business interests, labor unions, and farm organizations, to attorneys representing particular taxpayers and even taxpayers themselves. The testimony before the Committee is published under the title of Hearings on Tax Reform, or some similar title.

After the public hearings, the Ways and Means Committee meets to make its decisions. All committee meetings are presumptively open to the public and a separate roll call vote is required to close any committee meeting. The Committee in these "mark up" deliberations determines the main outlines of the bill it desires to report. Its policy decisions are then translated into statutory form by members of the Office of the House Legislative Counsel, an office of expert legal drafters responsible for the drafting of almost all of the important legislation originating in the House. Generally, the same representatives of this Office work on tax legislation from year to year, so that continuity is preserved. They are assisted in the drafting by technical representatives from the Treasury, the Internal Revenue Service, and the Staff of the Joint Committee on Taxation. A report to accompany the bill, containing material justifying its policies and explaining its provisions, known as a Committee Report, is also prepared by this group. The bill and Committee Report are then considered by the

Committee and, when approved, are reported to the full House. The bill is generally debated and voted on in the House under a "closed rule" procedure, which permits amendments to be offered only by the Committee (or perhaps a few amendments approved for consideration by the House Rules Committee), so that the bill as reported by the Committee is generally the bill as passed by the House. The debate, which often touches on the interpretation of particular language in the bill in addition to the general policy, is contained verbatim in the Congressional Record.

A similar procedure then starts in the Committee on Finance of the Senate. The cast of characters, with Senators replacing Representatives, is much the same. The Senate Finance Committee makes its policy decisions, which may range from minor differences from the House bill to a completely different bill. [17] It then reports a bill, with an accompanying Senate Finance Committee Report. The debate on the Senate floor is without restriction, and any Senator may propose an amendment dealing with any tax matter. Consequently, those interests desiring changes in the bill endeavor to secure the cooperation of a Senator or Senators in agreement with their objectives and thereby to change the bill on the floor of the Senate.

The House and Senate bills then go to a Committee of Conference of the House and Senate, composed of the ranking members, by parties, of the House Ways and Means Committee and the Senate Finance Committee. The House and Senate conferees adjust the differences between the two bodies, generally through compromises on the main issues. The two bills may have little resemblance and the Conference Committee picks and chooses among the provisions of the different bills. In some instances, the Conference Committee adds provisions that were in neither the House nor the Senate bills. Often the Conference Report produced in Conference is the first time some provisions have seen the light of day and they are enacted without the benefit [of] critical examination in hearings and committee deliberations. The Conference action is then set forth in a Conference Report which states the action on each Senate amendment and contains the language of Conference changes. The Report also contains a Joint Explanatory Statement of the Conference Committee by the Managers on the part of the House and the Senate that explains the actions taken, thus performing the function of a Committee Report. [18] The House and Senate act on the Conference Report, and almost always approve it. The final legislation then is sent to the President for action. While revenue bills are usually approved, some have been vetoed with the veto in turn sometimes overridden, and others have become law without signature.

The legislative tools for the tax technician — the sources of legislative history — are evident from this procedure: Presidential messages, Committee hearings, the successive stages of the bill and its amendments, Committee and Conference

17. As in the House, committee meetings of the Senate are open to the public and a committee meeting may be closed only on a vote of the committee in order to discuss certain specified matters.

18. The Committee Reports through 1938 are contained in 1939-1 Cum.Bull., Part 2. Subsequent Committee reports are contained in the Cumulative Bulletin for the year of the legislation involved. All tax legislation is also reprinted in these Bulletins, issued by the Internal Revenue Service.

Reports, the Congressional debates, a message accompanying the President's action on the bill. Reports of Subcommittees, Treasury Department Statements, material prepared by the Staff of the Joint Committee on Taxation, and press conferences held by Committee Chairpersons also provide interpretive material.

NOTE

A number of sources chronicle the relationship between politics and taxation. For an historical overview of tax history in the United States, see W. Elliot Brownlee, *Federal Taxation in America: A Short History* (2004); for a thoughtful description of the tax legislative process, with emphasis on the politics of tax reform, see Thomas Reese, *The Politics of Taxation* (Quorum Books 1980), and Daniel Shaviro, "Beyond Public Choice and Public Interest: A Study of the Legislative Process as Illustrated by Tax Legislation in the 1980s," 139 Penn. L. Rev. 1 (1990); for a fascinating look at the highly politically charged debate and legislative action surrounding the estate tax, see Michael Graetz & Ian Shapiro, *Death by a Thousand Cuts: The Fight Over Taxing Inherited Wealth* (2005).

B. The Tax Lawyer Serving a Client: Client Interest Versus Public Interest

Citizens are entitled to petition their government for changes in tax policy, and many of them exercise this right. Moreover, they are free to, and often do, engage the assistance of counsel in pursuing their policy goals. Accordingly, the practice of many tax lawyers includes the representation of clients who seek or resist change in tax policy.

Generally, a lawyer representing a client before a legislative or administrative body attempts to persuade the tribunal to favor the client's particular interest. This class of advocacy, like others, obligates the lawyer to observe his customary duties of competence, loyalty, and confidentiality, as discussed in Chapter 3. Model Rule 3.9 further provides that a lawyer who represents a client before a legislative body or administrative tribunal in a nonadjudicative proceeding must disclose that he appears in a representative capacity. A lawyer appearing in a representative capacity must deal with the tribunal honestly and in conformity with its applicable rules of procedure. The Model Code's requirement was slightly more stringent. EC 7-16 directed the lawyer to identify himself and his client, if the identity of his client was not "privileged." Why did the authors of the Model Rules remove the requirement that the attorney disclose the client's identity? Can a legislative or administrative body require that a lawyer disclose the identity of his client? If so, may a lawyer properly invoke the evidentiary privilege to refuse such disclosure?

When a client pursues a particular tax policy objective, that objective may or may not be consistent with the public interest as perceived by a lawyer. May that lawyer nonetheless represent the client as an advocate in that matter? Ethical Consideration 8-4 of the Model Code provided:

> A lawyer may advocate such changes on behalf of a client even though he does not agree with them. But when a lawyer purports to act on behalf of the public, he should espouse only those changes which he conscientiously believes to be in the public interest.

Although the Model Rules do not explicitly address the issues involving a lawyer's personal agreement with positions that he advocates before a legislative or administrative body, one rule may apply by analogy.

Under Model Rule 1.2(b), a lawyer who represents a client may advocate positions that he does not agree with, because such representation "does not constitute an endorsement of the client's political, economic, social, or moral views or activities." Should this general principle change when a lawyer represents a client's interest before a legislative or administrative body? One possible difference is that a lawyer who accepts an engagement before a legislative tribunal may have to argue that his client's position is "in the public interest." Should he do so if he does not believe in his client's position personally? Is this problem more pronounced in the tax field where the public interest involves both the Treasury and the interest of other taxpayers? Nothing in the Model Rules indicates whether a lawyer purporting to act in the public interest must believe that what he proposes to do is in fact in the public interest. Why was the statement in EC 84 omitted from the Model Rules? Was it too difficult to enforce? Or is it in fact implied in the lawyer's actions when he acts "in the public interest"? Or does the omission negate that implication?

Under the Model Code, the lawyer had an express ethical dispensation to act on behalf of his client in seeking legislative or administrative changes even though the lawyer did not, in his personal or private capacity, agree with those changes. The point of the Model Code's position was made somewhat more forcefully than in EC 8-4 by Louis Eisenstein, a respected tax scholar and practitioner, in the following passage. In fact Eisenstein's argument really moves to the broader question of a tax lawyer's "duty" to the system, which permeates much discussion of professional ethics in taxation. The following excerpt from Eisenstein's 1962 speech entitled Ethics in Tax Practice — The Lawyer's Approach, was quoted in M. Carr Ferguson, The Legacy of Louis Eisenstein, 22 Tax L. Rev. 7, 28 (1966).

> The ethical obligations of tax lawyers do not seem particularly different from the ethical obligations of other lawyers. The same standards are merely applied to the practice of tax law.
>
> Recently, however, a new theory of moral responsibility has been advanced for tax lawyers — and for accountants, too. I will not mention names — except to say that they are rather respectable. It is argued that tax advisers are subject to special ethical limitations which do not generally apply to other practitioners. This argument usually rests

on a combination of five grounds. The first ground is that our tax system rests on honest self-assessment. Therefore, a tax lawyer is particularly obliged to see that a client fully declares his income or fully alerts the Service on all debatable items. The second ground is that the other party involved is the Treasury of the United States. The Treasury, it is said, should not be treated like an ordinary private adversary. The third ground is that the Treasury labors under grave disadvantages. It cannot audit every return thoroughly, and must largely rely on information supplied by the taxpayer. The fourth ground is that a tax lawyer has special responsibilities to the Treasury because he is a member of the Treasury bar. The fifth ground goes much further. We are told that a tax lawyer has a special social obligation to his country and his countrymen to assist in the fair enforcement of the tax laws. He should not help a client avoid his proper share of the common burden.

It is hard to say what all these observations come down to. Those who make them, whether in or out of the Government, usually drift off into clichés and ambiguities. But I gather that they are trying to say two things. The first is that tax lawyers should actively discourage tax avoidance by their clients. The second is that tax lawyers should affirmatively help the Treasury to collect taxes. Frankly, I regard all this talk as confused nonsense. Under our legal system a tax lawyer represents his client, not the Treasury. His one and only function is to look out for his client's interests within the ethical standards that generally apply to all lawyers. Indeed, it would be downright unethical for a lawyer to attempt to serve both his client and the Treasury. When a client retains me, he is paying me for my services as a tax lawyer, not for my wisdom as a tax philosopher. A lawyer who fails to distinguish between the two when he is representing a client has no business representing him.

Has much changed in the intervening 45 years since this speech? The tensions identified and the competing visions offered for the tax lawyer's role remain prominent today. Is that a sign of failure? A sign of intractable and inherent conflicts?

How should we think about the tax lawyer's role in influencing and shaping legislation? Should concerns about the general tax system constrain advocacy and representation on the legislative side? Consider the following excerpt from a report by a committee of the Association of the Bar of the City of New York.

Sidney I. Roberts, Wilbur H. Friedman, Martin D. Ginsburg, Carter T. Louthan, Donald C. Lubick, Milton Young & George E. Zeitlin, A Report on Complexity and the Income Tax

27 Tax L. Rev. 325, 368 (1972)

The practitioner's required devotion to the client's interests does not terminate at the level of advice, consultation and the planning of transactions to minimize or avoid tax. The litigator who develops a novel theory or a neat distinction that benefits his client but compounds confusion of the tax law has performed a proper function when he persuades a court to adopt it. When the situation requires legislative solution, the attorney who formulates and secures that legislation has performed a proper function even though his success may engraft upon the Code an anomaly of no significance to any other taxpayer or, worse, a more generally applicable monument to confusion and complexity. Thus, if the attorney believes a legislative solution is more likely to be obtained through an amendment to the Code rather than through the route of a private relief bill, the concern that he should have for the integrity of the system will not sway him from the former course.

Nonetheless, the dominant imperative of our jurisprudence, that the lawyer represents the client, does not mandate total unconcern with irrationality and complexity, even at the level of practice. Client representation and a sensible revenue system are not mutually exclusive concepts and to the extent they can be harmonized there is profit to all sides.

NOTES

1.   As noted above, a lawyer who attempts to influence a legislative or administrative body must comply with its rules. One source of applicable laws governing conduct before Congress is the Lobbying Disclosure Act originally enacted in 1995, 2 U.S.C. §§1601-1612. The rules of both Houses are located in the Ethics Manual for Members and Employees of the United States House of Representatives and the corresponding Senate Manual.

2.   What is the meaning of the reservation in the second paragraph of the City Bar report? How are client representation and a sensible revenue system to be harmonized? If the client's objectives are consistent with the latter, that is indeed a happy situation for the lawyer. But what if they are not? Is the reservation any more than an observation that it is nice (in the policy area, as in other areas) when a cause that the lawyer advocates on behalf of his client coincides with the lawyer's perception of the public interest?

3.   Are there any ethical limits on the lawyer's right to pursue lawful policy objectives on behalf of a client? Should there be? Model Rule 1.7(a)(2) states that a lawyer shall not represent a client if the representation would be materially limited "a personal interest of the lawyer." Would such "interests" include the lawyer's strong personal convictions that a particular policy objective is contrary to public interest? Consider these questions as you review the following problems.

4.   Can a lawyer on behalf of one client urge a policy change that would be directly adverse to another client? See Model Rule 1.7(a)(1). Does it matter that the lawyer is providing tax advice on an entirely different subject and has not been asked to lobby by the second client? Recall the discussion of issue conflicts in Chapter 3, p. 143.

5.   Is it ethical for a lawyer to represent different clients with respect to the same legislation? Suppose the attorney has been hired by a consortium of law firms and accounting firms to fight a proposal to put service industries on the cash method. What if a compromise proposal is offered that would affect each profession differently?

PROBLEMS

Assume that you are asked to represent a client with respect to one or more of the following issues. What considerations would you take into account in deciding whether to accept the representation?

a. A trade association representing the auto industry desires a Code amendment to allow a 10 percent tax credit upon the purchase of all domestic automobiles. The purpose is to stimulate lagging sales of domestic automobiles and thus bolster the economy.

b. An association of private secondary schools desires a Code amendment to allow a deduction for the full cost of private school tuition. The objective is to reduce the cost of education in private institutions. Are the considerations any different if enrollment in member schools is limited to children with learning disabilities?

c. An association of those who rent rather than own their dwellings desires legislation to permit renters to deduct that portion of the rent that is reasonably related to interest and taxes on the rented property. The argument is that it is unfair to subsidize home owners by allowing deductions for interest and taxes while denying similar deductions to renters.

d. An association of retired persons desires legislation to expand the existing standard deduction additions for old age and blindness. They observe that the existing levels fall far short of the realistic financial needs of the elderly.

e. A major university seeks to convince the Treasury that its tuition remission plan for children of faculty should not be classified as a taxable benefit, regardless of the manner in which other fringe benefits are classified and taxed. The position is that this benefit is taken into account in establishing the university's salary structure and to tax it would unbalance that structure and require levels of compensation higher than it can bear. Furthermore, university faculty are notoriously underpaid — as all law professors will affirm. Does your decision whether to take the representation depend on whether your client will be a particular university, the American Association of University Professors, or a 45-year-old professor of Latin whose husband deserted her and their five children a few years ago?

f. An organization dedicated to racial integration in education desires to support IRS efforts to enforce denial of tax exempt status to private schools that do not meet prescribed antidiscrimination guidelines. It also desires to attack vigorously the notion that Congress can or should restrain administrative action in this area by legislative proscription.

g. An organization dedicated to all-white schools desires legislation requiring the IRS to restrict itself to the constitutional minimum in ferreting out racial discrimination in order to deny or revoke tax exemption for private schools.

h. A major oil company wants to convince the Internal Revenue Service and the Treasury not to issue substantially more restrictive regulations interpreting the foreign tax credit, especially as applicable to extractive industries. If that effort appears likely to fail, the representation would include an appeal to Congress to head off the restrictive regulations through a rider on an appropriation bill.

i. A client desired to convert to Subchapter S status, which requires the filing of an election under §1362 by March 15 in order to be effective for the current year. The election was timely prepared, consented to by the shareholders, and delivered to the accountant for mailing. The accountant misplaced it and it was not discovered until six months later. She promptly filed it with an explanatory letter. The auditing agent expresses great sympathy but points out that the Service has no discretion to allow the late filing and he assesses a $250,000 deficiency for the unpaid corporate tax. You have concluded there is no basis for successful litigation. The client now desires that you persuade Congress to pass legislation specifically permitting the late filing in this case.

j. A client with foreign operations cannot qualify for the foreign tax credit in a particular country under existing regulations. The client is aware that the U.S. tax treaty with the country is being renegotiated and desires that the treaty specially allow the credit for payments made to the foreign government in the course of its particular operations.

C. The Tax Lawyer Serving the "Public Interest"

Part B of this chapter just explored the question of whether any broad public policies concerns (or personal beliefs of the lawyer) can or should impact the lawyer's decision to advocate on behalf of a client, especially outside of the litigation context. This part takes on what could be viewed as the opposite question. When, if at all, should a lawyer be constrained in serving the public interest on the grounds that the changes advocated by that lawyer may not be in the interests of some (or all) of the lawyer's clients? The Model Rules encourage lawyers to participate in activities to improve the law, the legal system, and the legal profession. See Model Rule 6.1(b)(3) (a lawyer should "participat[e] in activities for improving the law, the legal system or the legal profession"); Preamble to the Model Rules ("As a public citizen, a lawyer should seek improvement of the law. . . . As a member of a learned profession, a lawyer should cultivate knowledge of the law beyond its use for clients, employ that knowledge in reform of the law and work to strengthen legal education. . . ."). To encourage such participation, Model Rule 6.4 provides:

> A lawyer may serve as a director, officer or member of an organization involved in reform of the law or its administration notwithstanding that the reform may affect the interests of a client of the lawyer. When the lawyer knows that the interests of a client may be materially benefited by a decision in which the lawyer participates, the lawyer shall disclose that fact but need not identify the client.

If the tax lawyer concludes that existing provisions of law are not in the public interest and she wishes to exercise her responsibility under Model Rule 6.1 to improve the system, to what extent is she constrained by the interests of her clients?

If the change favored by the lawyer would clearly be disadvantageous to an existing client, is she nonetheless free to proceed? Are there any qualifications on the seemingly very strong statement of Model Rule 6.4 allowing lawyers to press for such reform despite its impact on clients? The comment to Model Rule 6.4 states "In determining the nature and scope of participation in such activities, a lawyer should be mindful of obligations to clients under other Rules, particularly Rule 1.7 [conflict of interest]."

In a 1950 article, Erwin Griswold, former dean of the Harvard Law School, asserted that lawyers "should sell their services to their clients . . . but not their souls." Erwin Griswold, The Blessings of Taxation, 36 A.B.A. J. 999 (1950). While all may readily agree with these words, what do they mean?

If we accept the notion that the lawyer, by accepting a client, sells her services and not her soul, that she retains her right to speak out in the public interest, how is she to reconcile her duty of loyalty to her client with her sense of fidelity to her conscience and the public interest? If she chooses to pursue the public interest and, in a particular situation, the adverse impact on the client is severe, is there a conflict of interest under the Model Rules that requires her to withdraw from representation of the client? If so, would the lawyer have been justified in the first instance in accepting the public interest role? Is the severity of the impact on the client a relevant test? Is the immediacy of impact relevant? Would the lawyer in any event be required to disclose to her client her intention to take a public interest stance that may differ from the client's personal interest?

If the lawyer does not believe withdrawal is necessary, does she have any obligation to disclose to her client that she intends to advocate a position that is contrary to the client's interests? Must she seek consent?

When the lawyer acts not for a client, or not merely for a client, but rather *pro bono publico*, do his responsibilities differ? EC 8-4, supra p. 299, requires that he "conscientiously believe" that his proposals are in the public interest. Is this a heavier burden than that borne by the lawyer serving only a private interest, in light of the fact that the same Ethical Consideration absolves the private lawyer from any need to believe in his cause? Should the burdens be different? Conversely, what can and will a *client* do in the face of a lawyer so serving in the "public interest"? The following excerpt renders these questions very real.

Ronald D. Rotunda, Alleged Conflicts of Interest Because of the Appearance of Impropriety*

33 Hofstra L. Rev. 1141 (2005)

Consider on of the earliest cases of the modern trend [of allegations of appearance of impropriety against lawyers working on broader policy matters potential against

*Reprinted with the permission of the Hofstra Law Review Association.

client interests] — the case of John Erlenborn. President George H. W. Bush appointed Erlenborn, a former member of Congress to the Board of the Legal Services Corporation ("LSC"). Erlenborn was also a partner in a major law firm that represented growers in disputes over farm workers' conditions; the farm workers were often represented by LSC-funded lawyers. The American Farm Bureau Federation, a private lobbying group representing agricultural interests, began a campaign to persuade the firm's agricultural clients (the Farm Bureau was not one of the firm's clients) to object to what the Farm Bureau characterized as Erlenborn's conflict of interest, for example, he took a position as an LSC board member, that the Farm Bureau claims was harmful to farm interests.

Erlenborn offered to recuse himself from any decision of the LSC board the directly involved reform legislation that the Farm Bureau supported, or that involved agricultural activities that could have an impact on this firm's clients, but the Farm Bureau's objections (including its objection to Erlenborn's proposed congressional testimony on the reform legislation) continued until Erlenborn resigned from the LSC board. The then ABA President-elect said that there was no conflict of interest that required Erlenborn's resignation. Rules 6.3 and 6.4 of the ABA Model Rules, dealing with law reform activities that affect private clients, make that clear. Nothing ethically required Erlenborn to resign from the LSC board; it is understandable that his firm wanted to please some of its clients. The consequence of this charge [of the appearance of impropriety], too freely made, is that it may have tarred a person's reputation, cost the government the benefit of the former Congressman's advice, and increased the cost of future pro bono work (measured by attacks one must be willing to suffer). . . .

Is it really an appearance of impropriety for a lawyer to take a position in one case while having a friendship with a lawyer on the other side, or for the lawyer to take a personal position on a legal issue that is adverse to a position that one of the lawyer's clients favors? May a lawyer, for example, represent a tobacco or alcohol company and still personally oppose smoking or drinking?

There is a fair amount of law on this topic and it does not favor those who loosely bandy about the charge of an "appearance of impropriety."

Consider, for example, the situation where a lawyer openly takes a public position on a controversial issue that is contrary to the views of some or all of that lawyer's clients. The American Law Institute's Restatement (Third) of the Law Governing Lawyers concludes that there is no conflict and that "consent of the lawyer's clients is not required." Lawyers bring to each of their clients "professional detachment." For example, "if tax lawyers advocating positions about tax reform were obliged to advocate only positions that would serve the positions of their present clients, the public would lose the objective contributions to policy making of some persons most able to help." (citations omitted.)

Perhaps it is bad business for the lawyer to advocate tax reform that may not be consistent with the interests of one or more clients, but that does not make the lawyer's pro bono advocacy unethical. It is one thing for a client to charge that the lawyer is making a mistake; it is quite another for the client to charge that the lawyer is acting unethically. The client can always fire the lawyer, but lawyers are not fungible (at least, good ones are not).

The ALI reflects the long-held view of the ABA, most recently expressed in the ABA's Model Rules of Professional Conduct, Rule 6.4, which provides that the lawyer need not secure client consent to participate in a decision that hurts a client, but she should disclose to the legal reform group that the decision will help a present client (although she need not identify the name of the private client). Similarly, the fact that a lawyer represents a client, whether pro bono or fee-based, implies nothing about what the lawyer's personal beliefs are. (citations omitted.)

Let us assume that the lawyer represents Alpha Corporation in negotiations with the Internal Revenue Service. The lawyer wants the IRS to permit Alpha Corporation to employ accelerated depreciation methods for machinery purchased in a prior tax year. While the lawyer is negotiating, she personally believes that the accelerated depreciation laws for manufacturing equipment are unwise public policy. Because of her beliefs, she is also working with a bar association committee to develop a policy statement against the accelerated depreciation allowance. Indeed, let us further assume that the committee chair has requested this lawyer to testify before Congress in support of the report and its proposal to repeal all depreciation allowances. This new legislation (like typical tax enactments) would apply only for current and future tax years, thus not directly affecting Alpha Corporation's case before the IRS. Even though the proposed legislation is against Alpha's economic interests, the ALI advises that the lawyer, without Alpha's consent, may continue to represent Alpha while simultaneously working to repeal the accelerated depreciation allowance. (citations omitted.)

NOTE

Lawyers have long maintained concerns about the impact of "public service" work on their client relations. Tackling this question 50 years ago, Randolph Paul observed:

> I know that many tax advisers and economists would like nothing better than to spend a substantial part of their time working for a better tax system and a more intelligent fiscal policy. But they leave the job to others because they honestly think that they cannot afford the luxury of promoting the public interest. If they are tax lawyers, they have accepted the doctrine that they can attract and hold tax business only if they remain completely conventional, and exhibit agreement with the political and social views of their clients. . . . They believe that silence is golden when measures objectively looking to the improvement of our tax system and the development of a better fiscal policy are being canvassed. . . .
>
> I wish I could confidently say that there is no rational foundation for this attitude. But I cannot make this statement. The most I can say is that I do not think surrender needs to be unconditional. And I do suspect that the thinking of some tax advisers exaggerates the objections clients have to activities on behalf of improvement in the tax system. I have known clients who do not always know what is good for them, and there

is a sense in which what is good for the United States is good for clients. I know tax advisers who accomplish the double job of ably representing their clients and faithfully working for the tax system taxpayers deserve. . . . At the bread and butter level there is no evidence that these tax advisers and economists suffer excessively. At another level I venture the opinion that they lead a more comfortable life than do many of their colleagues. Of one thing I am very sure — that both taxpayers and the government need many more of these independent advisers.

Randolph Paul, Taxation in the United States: The Responsibilities of Tax Experts 771-774 (Harv. U. Press 1954).

As suggested above, a major problem in the tax policy area is the absence of assigned, effective champions of the public viewpoint. The following commentary highlights the problem. Though 50 years have passed since the late Professor Surrey wrote these words, the situation has not changed significantly.

Stanley S. Surrey, The Congress and the Tax Lobbyist — How Special Tax Provisions Get Enacted*

70 Harv. L. Rev. 1145, 1170-1179 (1957)

The lack of any pressure-group allies for the Treasury in its representation of the tax-paying public could have been remedied in part by effective aid from the tax bar. Yet for a good many years the vocal tax bar not only withheld any aid but very often conducted itself as an ally of the special pressure groups. Many a lawyer representing a client seeking a special provision could without much difficulty obtain American Bar Association or local-bar-association endorsement for his proposal. He could then appear before Congress and solemnly exhibit the blessing of the legal profession. In fact, the activity of the Bar Association in this respect became so obvious that it seemingly boomeranged — many a congressman began instinctively to smell mischief when presented with a Bar Association tax proposal or endorsement.

The pendulum is beginning to swing, however, and there is some hope for a more objective attitude on the part of the bar. The Council and the committees of the Tax Section of the American Bar Association are becoming far more appreciative of the public interest. The signs of a growing maturity in the Tax Section on these matters are constantly increasing. But so far this change in attitude has been negative and limited to self-restraint and refusal to join with the proponents of special tax provisions. The change has not carried the Tax Section to the point of appearing affirmatively before Congress to oppose the particular proposals of special-interest groups or to urge the elimination of existing provisions. The Tax Section is becoming less and less a protagonist against the Treasury Department, especially on the more extreme proposals, but it has not yet become a vocal ally of the Treasury in defending the integrity of the tax system before the tax committees. In this respect it appears to be lagging behind the other chief professional group in the tax field, the accountants. Over one-third of the items in the 1955 statement of tax proposals of the American Institute of Accountants are recommendations urging the elimination of tax provisions which it considers to constitute unjustified favoritism for special groups. Yet one can scan report after report from the American Bar Association without finding a single similar recommendation.

This does not mean that the bar will not some day provide objective guidance to the Congress in these matters. In this regard the corporate provisions of the House version of the 1954 Code may be a harbinger. For perhaps the first time we find bar associations going before Congress and pointing out that proposed legislation will open up unjustified tax loopholes. True, the bar, and also the accountants, were not opposing other special groups, but they were seeking to save the Congress from the weaknesses of the particular measures. The bar in this instance deserves much credit for its affirmative guidance on the side of intelligent and fair tax legislation.

There are obvious obstacles to affirmative action by the legal profession in opposing special tax provisions. The Council of the Tax Section of the American Bar Association can speak publicly only on matters which have been approved by votes at annual meetings held in different geographical areas. The absence of a continuous group, with the consequence of shifting viewpoints and the lack of opportunity for sustained and informed consideration over the years, injects considerable instability and fortuitous results into the formal actions of the Tax Section. For, as discussed later, lawyers as a group need considerable discussion and education on these matters before objectivity replaces biases. Further, matters approved by the Tax Section must in turn be approved by the House of Delegates. A body that has regularly approved a proposed constitutional amendment to limit income-tax rates to twenty-five percent is not likely to understand the problems of special tax provisions. The Council of the Tax Section, whatever its inclinations might be, is thus largely circumscribed by the institutional framework of the American Bar Association. The accountants, on the other hand, are able to speak through their Committee on Federal Taxation of the American Institute of Accountants, a group free from corresponding institutional forces. This may well account for the more aggressive stand against special tax provisions taken by that Committee.

One of the chief problems here is that most tax lawyers have hardly any conception of what is involved in approaching a tax issue from the overall legislative standpoint. They can readily perceive the adverse effect of the tax laws upon a particular client or transaction. They can then phrase the legislative solution they think necessary to remove the claimed tax obstacle or burden. But they are usually quite incapable of standing off from the problem and their proposed solution and viewing both from the perspective of the general public interest. The difficulty is largely one of lack of experience, not lack of judgment or moral values.

Moreover, policy insights in the tax field are hard to come by. Here a large responsibility rests upon the Treasury. Unless its technical tax staffs are charged with utilizing their experience and information by engaging in research on current tax issues, and unless that research is made public, those interested in tax issues face great difficulties in obtaining the full picture. The government tax experts, both in the Treasury and in the Congress, must also be encouraged to write for the professional journals and to make available the insights they have reached through experience. The papers and hearings presented recently by the Subcommittee on Tax Policy of the Joint Committee on the Economic Report are another excellent illustration of what can be done to increase understanding of tax issues. The professors of tax law and the tax economists in the universities also bear a responsibility here, for they have more freedom from the pressures of time and situation which the bar faces. There is significance in the fact that when the Subcommittee on Tax Policy of the Joint Committee on the Economic Report desired objective analyses of various tax issues it went for the most part to the economists and law professors in the universities.

After all, most members of our tax bar are really opposed to "special privileges." They have a respect for the tools of their trade. They know that in the long run the pendulum may swing and that a "loophole" may be closed with a vigor that pushes the cure too far. Even when their legal business requires them to lobby directly for a special tax favor for their clients, I doubt that most lawyers relish the task. The door may open for them, but it may open wider for the next attorney, and who knows where the game will end? Hence a bar association's advocacy of any particular special tax provision is in most cases traceable to the lawyer's sympathy for the welfare of his clients and to a lack of understanding of the basic tax issues involved. If the lawyer is exposed to those issues and if he is not acting simply as an outright advocate for a particular client—that is, as a tax lobbyist on the particular measure—he will generally emerge with the correct answer. Hence the importance of forcing a bar association to see the issues and face up to them.

Tradition also plays a role. Lawyers as a profession are deeply conscious of a duty of loyalty to their clients. In his day-to-day relations with other lawyers and with the business world a lawyer does not act contrary to his clients' interests. These attitudes of loyalty and protection are ingrained in the profession; their roots lie deep in the past. Can they be reconciled with speaking out in the public interest against special tax provisions? The problem is of course more acute as the particular provision comes closer to the client's situation. But it must have been presented in one way or another to almost every lawyer who has considered the situation. The same problem arises in a different form when a client asks his lawyer to seek a legislative change in favor of the client. Should the lawyer apply different standards to his client's case in deciding whether to represent him before a tax committee than he does in deciding whether to represent him in litigation? Must a lawyer seeking a legislative change believe the change to be in the public interest? And if he does not, should he still represent his client before the legislature? Or need the lawyer as legislative advocate have no more belief in the fairness of his client's cause than when the matter is in litigation? In short, how does a lawyer adjust the considerations of private interest and public interest in the area of legislation? Clearly, these matters are difficult. Some lawyers manage to find a way through the difficulties and speak openly and positively against special provisions. Others write, or speak in bar-association meetings. Others meet the situation by neither publicly opposing special provisions nor seeking them on behalf of clients; in effect, they turn away from the problems entirely and simply practice law. And others act as legislative advocates, with varying degrees of belief in the proposals they present and with stress on the view that a person is entitled to have his case presented to the legislature just as he is entitled to his day in court.

Given these problems, it is hard to say whether the tax bar can take a position of leadership in this area. Yet here also there is room for development. The work of the American Law Institute in its Tax Project has had a significant effect in educating a number of tax lawyers to the many facets that must be examined in the legislative exploration of a tax proposal. Further, its drafts of proposed solutions to technical tax problems stand as a benchmark against which to measure other proposals. It is significant that much of the criticism of the corporate provisions of the House bill in 1954 was based upon the inadequacy of those provisions when measured against the standards hammered out in the work of the Institute. Moreover, the close cooperation between the Institute and the American Bar Association Tax Section has had an important effect on the content of tax legislation in a number of areas, for it represents a genuine working merger of the criteria of tax fairness and practical sense. The most significant consequence of the Institute's Tax Project is the demonstration that lawyers working under procedures such as those of the Institute can on most technical tax matters develop constructive proposals which balance fairly the interests of the "government" and the "taxpayer." Some of these special provisions represent simply private-relief claims for the particular individual benefited. While phrased as amendments to the tax law, they are only money claims against the government based on the equities asserted to exist. Thus, it is said of a senator skilled in congressional ways that he would ask the legislative draftsman preparing the draft of a particular tax provision to make the amendment as general in language and as specific in application as was possible. The tax committees and the Treasury have not solved the problem of how to handle these special bills. Curiously enough, some tax situations do come through the judiciary committees as private-relief bills along with other private-relief bills involving claims against the government. These bills may involve, for example, a removal of the barrier of the statute of limitations in cases thought equitable, or the recovery of funds spent for revenue stamps lost in some fashion. Here they are subject to the criteria developed over the decades by those committees in the handling of private-claims bills. These criteria are reasonably strict, and few of the bills pass the Congress. Of those that do succeed, a number are vetoed, and a veto is customarily regarded as a final disposition of the bill.

Many situations come before the tax committees that are quite comparable, in that the tax proposal is equivalent to a money claim against the government, equal to the tax to be saved, sought for a specific taxpayer on equitable grounds. This is especially true in the case of proposals of a retroactive character. In the tax committees these special proposals tend to take on the coloration of an amendment to the tax code of the same character as all the various substantive tax matters before these committees. In essence, all amendments to the tax laws that private groups push on their own behalf are designed to lower taxes for the proponents and thereby relieve them from a tax burden to which they are subject. The special proposals thus become simply one more amendment in the long list of changes to be considered. The proponents of these special proposals are thereby able to cloak the fact that they are presenting private-relief claims against the government. This is especially so when the proposal is considered as merely one more item in a general revenue bill. Here it is also protected from the threat — and fate — of a presidential veto. Even when the proposal is considered as a separate bill, the fact that it is merely one of the bills before a tax committee that is considering a great many substantive bills involving amendments to the tax code generally produces the same result. The committee will tend to focus on the proposal as curing a substantive defect in the law and lose sight of the fact that the special proposal is essentially a private-relief bill.

The tax laws are not perfect and cannot be. They will affect some taxpayers more seriously than others, and hardships and inequities will certainly occur. But every hardship and every inequity cannot be corrected; and this is even dearer when the correction must be retroactive. Some standards must be evolved against which a claim for relief may be judged, or chaos will result. Tax lobbying will grow by leaps and bounds — it is already doing that. But what standards may be formulated, what procedures should be adopted, what institutional changes may be necessary — these are still unstudied topics.

———

Organizations that seek to represent the public interest include established professional organizations such as the ABA Section of Taxation, the AICPA Federal Tax Division, and, also in recent years, organizations that are specifically dedicated to affecting tax policy. The Tax Section of the New York State Bar Association has been actively involved in analyzing tax legislation and tax proposals for many years. The reports prepared by the NYSBA Tax Section have generally garnered particular respect and the attention of government policy makers. What factors might contribute to a Tax Section's advice and analysis receiving such respect?

The ABA Section of Taxation regards the improvement of the tax system as part of its mission. Section 1.1 of its Guide to Committee Operations (2007–2009) provides:

Mission Statement Goals. To lead and serve the members of the ABA Section of Taxation, the legal profession, and the public to achieve an equitable and efficient tax system.

Goals:

I.   To serve as the national representative of the legal profession with regard to the tax system.
II. To improve public understanding of, confidence in, and respect for the tax system.
III. To provide leadership in simplifying and improving the tax system.
IV. To provide unbiased, thoughtful and timely input into the legislative and administrative process.
V.   To promote and maintain an active, vigorous, growing and interested Section membership.

VI. To provide programs and services of unique quality which promote professionalism, competence and ethical conduct.
VII. To provide a national forum for communication among Section members and interchange between the public and private sectors.

Why would bar organizations be reluctant to adopt positions that have a high policy content? Because they really dislike policy issues? Or because they find it difficult to develop a consensus on issues that have a high policy content? The ABA Section of Taxation policy on fundamental tax issues is as follows (Section 1.3, Guide to Committee Operations (2007–2009)):

> *Tax Policy Issues.* It is the policy of the Section to confine its recommendations, comments, and testimony to its areas of professional expertise. The simplicity, enforceability, fairness and probable effect of the tax system on economic, business and personal behavior are all within the area in which the Section believes it is expert. The need for a tax cut to stimulate the economy or the need for a shift in tax burdens between income classes illustrates economic and political questions on which the Section does not believe it is expert. Many issues of fundamental tax policy involve both the legal, technical and tax system policy issues on which the Section is expert. It is the policy of the Section, in considering such issues, to confine its comments to the aspects of the issue on which the Section is expert; such comments are explicitly subject to the effect of the remaining aspects of the issue on which the Section is not expert.

Under Model Rule 3.9, a lawyer who represents a client in proceeding before a legislative body has a duty to disclose that he appears in representative capacity. By analogy, a lawyer who represents a client in pursuit of policy objectives and who is also active in bar organizations that address the same policies has an ethical responsibility to disclose that he acts in a representative capacity and not as an individual professional. Moreover, bar organizations have a legitimate interest in requiring their members to observe this precept, to the end that the organization does not become a vehicle for advancing client interest rather than the public interest. The ABA Section of Taxation has long had a policy requiring disclosure of client interest and, in appropriate cases, recusal. Its current policy statement is as follows (Section 1.2, Guide to Committee Operations (2007–2009)):

> **Conflicts of Interest.** Members of the Section of Taxation should always be mindful of their dual capacity; *no member should permit the interest of a client to cause him or her to support or oppose within the Section a proposal that he or she would otherwise not support or oppose within the Section.* This is not only a matter of ethical responsibility, but is also a matter of enhancing the effectiveness and credibility of the Section. Members of the Section should be mindful of ABA Model Rule 6.4, which provides that, "[w]hen the lawyer knows that the interests of a client may be materially benefited by a decision [of a law reform organization] in which the lawyer participates, the lawyer shall disclose that fact but need not identify the client." See also, to the same effect, ABA Model

Code EC 8-4. Accordingly, when actively supporting or opposing a position within the Section, a member should determine that he or she acts out of personal conviction rather than client interest and should make disclosure where a client may benefit materially as a consequence of such support or opposition. . . .

If a member (or the member's firm to the member's actual knowledge) has been engaged by a client to influence a government decision or policy determination on an issue that is also under consideration within the Section, such member shall not participate in the preparation of Section materials intended to be submitted to governmental personnel with respect to that issue. The member may, after disclosure as provided [above], supply information or analysis related to the decision or determination for consideration by Section members who are preparing Section material. In applying this paragraph, good judgment is called for in identifying the scope of an issue and the member's consequent disqualification. Some issues may be fundamental to the project, thus requiring complete disqualification. Some issues may be narrow, warranting only limited preclusion. . . .

This policy applies to all Section projects, including, without limitation, comments on proposed or existing legislation, regulations, rulings, or governmental policies. It is the special responsibility of the officers of each Committee, in staffing a project, to give particular thought to the matter of actual or apparent conflicts of interest, not only to avoid potential criticism, but also to encourage the formulation in the produce of a balanced view.

NOTES

1. The organization to which a lawyer belongs may occasionally take positions that are not in the best interests of her client. The comment to Model Rule 6.4 notes that, although membership in an organization does not create an attorney-client relationship, "[i]n determining the nature and scope of participation in such activities, a lawyer should be mindful of obligations to clients under other Rules, particularly Rule 1.7." Why does this Model Rule refer to the Model Rule dealing with conflicts of interest if there is no second "client"? Would the attorney have to obtain the client's consent to belong to the organization? To represent the organization in supporting a position adverse to the client?

2. Suppose you wish to support publicly a repeal of §1014, which provides for a basis step-up at death? Would you need the consent of all your clients?

3. Does it matter if the lawyer's expertise has been gained entirely from work performed for a client who would be adversely affected?

What about the government actors involved in the tax legislative process? What are their roles, skills, constraints, incentives, and limitations? Certainly public interest may be represented in the formulation of tax policy by the government, by concerned organizations, or by individual lawyers. The government's role is described in the following excerpt.

Joseph Pechman, Federal Tax Policy [*]

54-57 (Brookings Institution, 5th ed., 1987)

IMPROVING THE PROCESS

The tax legislative process has been examined by numerous congressional committees, political scientists, students of taxation, citizen and professional committees, and other groups. Opinion is generally critical: tax laws are unnecessarily detailed and complicated and divert attention from the major policy issues; the committees and other members of Congress are said to be unnecessarily influenced by special interest groups who do not speak in the national interest; and there is no systematic way to consider revisions of the structure of the tax system. However, revised procedures for congressional consideration of the budget were enacted in 1974 and 1985. The revisions have helped to coordinate overall tax and expenditure policies and have had considerable effect on tax legislation.

SIMPLIFYING THE TAX LAW

Almost every bill dealing with the structure of the tax system contains a mass of detailed amendments to the internal revenue code that deal with complicated, sometimes esoteric matters and are written in language that few people can understand. The committee reports on such bills, which provide a legislative history and explain the intent of Congress to the Internal Revenue Service and the courts, are also lengthy and difficult to understand. For example, the report of the Senate Finance Committee on the 1986 tax reform bill consisted of 1,124 closely packed pages of technical language. For anyone but the expert it is virtually impossible to distinguish the major issues from the minor in such a report, let alone to decide how they should be resolved.

When tax bills are finally brought to the floor of the House or Senate, few representatives or senators are familiar enough with the fine points to understand the implications of the legislation and to debate them with the committee chairmen, who have expert staff assistance to help them cope with the technicalities. Fewer still have the necessary skill and experience to introduce amendments on their own and to persuade the House or the Senate to overrule their tax committees. The emphasis on detail obscures the major policy issues, conceals large tax benefits that are introduced by influential committee members on behalf of special interest groups, and slows down the pace of congressional action on tax reform.

The practice of legislating every detail of the tax structure arose partly because Congress has not been willing to leave the details of the tax law to the interpretation of tax administrators and partly because the courts have not consistently construed the code on the basis of underlying theme and congressional purpose. To break this

*Reprinted with permission of the Brookings Institution.

practice, Congress would have to declare its intention to make general tax policy and leave the details to be worked out by the Treasury Department through its regulations. The specific language of the regulations would be subject to comments by the staff of the Joint Taxation Committee, but for constitutional reasons the final decisions on the regulations would have to be made by the Treasury. When there are differences of opinion, the issues might be brought to the attention of the joint committee itself, which could consider remedial legislation if it concluded that the proposed regulations would not carry out the congressional intent. Many tax experts believe that the tax legislative and administrative process would be much more effective and less vulnerable to the influence of lobbyists under such a procedure. However, shifting the focus of lobbying from the legislature to the executive, where groups might be equally influential but less visible, would not necessarily improve the tax process. Moreover, the likelihood that Congress would give up its tax legislative authority is small.

REPRESENTATION OF THE PUBLIC INTEREST

Individuals who appear before the two tax committees hardly represent a cross section of opinion on tax matters. The committees generally permit representatives of organized groups to testify and even allow individuals to testify on behalf of their own views; expert testimony comes only from administration officials and, on occasion, a few invited economists and tax lawyers. The result is that, day after day, the committees are subject to a drumfire of complaints against the tax system, arguments against the elimination of special tax advantages, and reasons for additional preferences.

In such an atmosphere, the secretary of the treasury and, to a lesser extent, the chairmen of the tax committees assume the role of defenders of the national interest. They spend much of their time fighting off new tax advantages and are only moderately successful in eliminating old ones. Whether taxes are to be raised or lowered, most of the witnesses find good reasons for favoring the groups or individuals they represent. The secretary and the chairmen take a broader, national view and try to strike a balance among competing claims. Since the stakes are high and there are no generally accepted criteria for evaluating questions of tax policy, their decisions may be regarded as arbitrary or contrary to the public interest by some groups and vigorously opposed in open hearings or in behind-the-scenes lobbying. Occasionally, they are supported by some of the national citizens' organizations, but testimony from them — although more frequent in recent years — is still the exception rather than the rule.

Fortunately, the committee members are not neophytes in the legislative process. Most of them have the capacity to detect self-serving witnesses. Furthermore, they have an excellent opportunity to check the merits of the public testimony in markup sessions or in private with the staffs of the Joint Taxation Committee, the Congressional Budget Office, and the Treasury and outside experts. When the issues are particularly significant and complicated, the staffs prepare summaries of the pros and cons of the various positions. (In 1985, fourteen pamphlets on specific issues were prepared for the Ways and Means Committee.) Through such methods, individual committee members familiarize themselves with the major issues and evaluate the mass of information hurled at them.

It would nevertheless be helpful to give the public, committee members, and other congressmen easier access to impartial analysis and expert opinion on tax matters. Two things can be done to improve consideration of tax legislation, particularly matters relating to tax structure.

First, the Joint Taxation Committee or the two separate committees might provide background material before a tax issue is put on the legislative calendar. It should be possible to divide the entire field of taxation into several categories and to hold periodic hearings on each category to keep the subject continually under review and to solicit new ideas. The procedures might follow the pattern set by the hearings on the Ways and Means Committee's famous 1959 Tax Revision Compendium, a three-volume collection of articles by leading tax experts, which influenced professional and legislative views on tax policy for many years.

Second, the joint committee might organize expert commissions or task forces once every five years to review the major problems in taxation and to make recommendations for legislative action. This type of advisory council was set up by the Social Security Act to consider social security matters once every four years, and a special commission was appointed in 1981 to deal with the imbalance of social security benefits and receipts. These advisory groups have had a significant impact on the development of the social security system, particularly the 1981 commission, whose proposals, transmitted in January 1983, were enacted by the Congress and approved by the president virtually intact in April of the same year.

But procedural changes by themselves will not greatly improve the results of the tax legislative process. Powerful forces are arrayed against major changes in the tax loopholes, while there is rarely an effective lobby for the general public. The key may be to reform the campaign financing laws so that congressmen will not be dependent on the financial support of powerful lobbies for their election. Until the people elect representatives and senators who are able to resist pressure from special interest groups, progress in reforming the tax system will continue to be slow.

_____

PROBLEMS

1. You represent a client who packages and sells financial derivatives. At any one time you may be providing advice as to the tax consequences of several derivatives. Although the sale of the instruments is wholly lawful and your participation meets the relevant professional standards, you believe that, as a tax policy matter, the tax treatment of the instruments is erroneous. Yet, the marketing of your client's products depends upon that tax treatment and your client's business is founded on that treatment. The administration proposes to amend the law so as

to tax more accurately the income from the derivatives. As a leader of the tax bar, you are asked to testify in support of the legislation. What considerations do you weigh in responding, and what do you conclude? If you decline this invitation, and your client asks you to testify in opposition to the legislation, what are the considerations?

2. You have a regular client with large-scale foreign operations. The client makes extensive use of the foreign tax credit. Your representation of the client spans all areas of the tax law, including the foreign tax credit. The administration proposes regulations that would significantly restrict the availability of the foreign tax credit in operations such as those conducted by your client. This result is perceived by your client as very detrimental to its interests. Would it be appropriate for you, appearing in your individual capacity as a concerned member of the tax bar, to testify in support of the proposed regulations?

3. You have successfully represented a client in securing enactment of a particular piece of tax legislation of major benefit to the client. Although you effectively represented the client, you did not personally believe that the legislation constituted sound tax policy. That representation is now at an end. May you actively support repeal of the legislation as a member of the ABA Section of Taxation in its committees? By publishing an article urging repeal? By appearing as a witness before Congress?

NOTE

The ethical problems of the government lawyer are the subject of the next chapter, but consider now whether she should be more or less free than the private lawyer to express her own views of proper tax policy when they differ from those of the "client" for which she works or used to work. If she thinks her agency is wrong, may she work on behalf of its position by day and write articles by night espousing the opposite view? If there is an obligation to seek to improve the law, how does that obligation affect the government lawyer or a lawyer working full-time as inside tax counsel for a large corporation?

Chapter 6

Tax Lawyer for the Entity: Government and Corporation

When a tax lawyer's client is an entity rather than an individual, special questions arise about the identity of the client. In the lawyer's usual relationship to an individual client, the lawyer knows that she owes to that individual the duties that we have previously identified — loyalty, confidentiality, and competence. Presumably, those same duties are owed to the client that is an entity. That much is evident. What is less evident is the personification of the client. Most entities are represented by various officers and employees. How does the lawyer determine who among these representatives is entitled to those special claims on the allegiance of the lawyer. Put more simply, who is the client?

If the lawyer works for a government agency, is the client her supervisor? The individual who is the head of the agency? The agency itself, as distinguished from any of its representatives? The larger department of which the agency may be a subunit? The entire executive branch? The President? The government as a whole? The broader public interest? Where the lawyer is employed by a corporation, similar questions arise concerning the locus of the lawyer's responsibilities.

Questions like these have occupied the attention of thoughtful practitioners and bar representatives for many years, and the answers are not yet altogether clear. However, there has been much exploration of the questions, and we now turn to a review of the prior work. We deal first with the issue in the context of the government lawyer, and we then turn to the situation of the corporate lawyer.

A. Lawyer for the Government

1. Who Is the Government Lawyer's Client?

Does the lawyer working for the government represent his client with the same obligations and the same freedoms as a private practice lawyer representing an individual or corporate client? The identity of the client is, of course, important in determining to whom the duties of loyalty, confidentiality, and competence are owed. If the government lawyer believes strongly that his superiors are resolving a case or a policy issue in an erroneous way, what may or must he do? If the lawyer believes that a coworker has engaged in misconduct, but that the disclosure of the misconduct will harm the agency, what are his options?

Although a government lawyer performs many of the same advocate and advisor roles common to a private practice lawyer, the special question of the identity of the government lawyer's client shapes the focal point of his duties. Moreover, the government lawyer's relationship to his employer demands that he act not only in compliance with the normal ethical rules but also in accordance with certain special rules and restraints that are set out for government lawyers. Included among these special restraints are general ethical standards and also statutes that subject certain transgressions to criminal penalties. Beyond these restraints on the active government lawyer, other statutory and ethical limitations will follow the former government lawyer into private practice.

Model Rule 1.13 represents the most recent attempt to define a lawyer's duty to the organizational client. The category of organizational client includes both the government as client and the corporation as client. This chapter considers both cases and some of the special questions they raise.

Rule 1.13 Organization as Client

(a) A lawyer employed or retained by an organization represents the organization acting through its duly authorized constituents.

(b) If a lawyer for an organization knows that an officer, employee or other person associated with the organization is engaged in action, intends to act or refuses to act in a matter related to the representation that is a violation of a legal obligation to the organization, or a violation of law that reasonably might be imputed to the organization, and is likely to result in substantial injury to the organization, then the lawyer shall proceed as is reasonably necessary in the best interest of the organization. Unless the lawyer reasonably believes that it is not necessary in the best interest of the organization to do so, the lawyer shall refer the matter to higher authority in the organization, including, if warranted by the circumstances to the highest authority that can act on behalf of the organization as determined by applicable law.

(c) Except as provided in paragraph (d), if

(1) despite the lawyer's efforts in accordance with paragraph (b) the highest authority that can act on behalf of the organization insists upon or fails to address in a timely and appropriate manner an action, or a refusal to act, that is clearly a violation of law, and

(2) the lawyer reasonably believes that the violation is reasonably certain to result in substantial injury to the organization,

Then the lawyer may reveal information relating to the representation whether or not Rule 1.6 permits such disclosure, but only if and to the extent the lawyer reasonably believes necessary to prevent substantially injury to the organization.

(d) Paragraph (c) shall not apply with respect to information relating to a lawyer's representation of an organization to investigate an alleged violation of law, or to defend the organization or an officer, employee or other constituent associated with the organization against a claim arising out of an alleged violation of law.

(e) A lawyer who reasonably believes that he or she has been discharged because of the lawyer's actions taken pursuant to paragraphs (b) or (c), or who withdraws under circumstances that require or permit the lawyer to take action under either of those paragraphs, shall proceed as the lawyer reasonably believes necessary to assure that the organization's highest authority is informed of the lawyer's discharge or withdrawal.

(f) In dealing with an organization's directors, officers, employees, members, shareholders or other constituents, a lawyer shall explain the identity of the client when the lawyer knows or reasonably should know that the organization's interests are adverse to those of the constituents with whom the lawyer is dealing.

(g) A lawyer representing an organization may also represent any of its directors, officers, employees, members, shareholders or other constituents, subject to the provisions of Rule 1.7. If the organization's consent to the dual representation is required by Rule 1.7, the consent shall be given by an appropriate official of the organization other than the individual who is to be represented, or by the shareholders.

Comment 9 to Model Rule 1.13 states that, "when the client is a governmental organization, a different balance may be appropriate between maintaining confidentiality and assuring that the wrongful act is prevented or rectified, for public business is involved." The comment notes that this question may be especially difficult in the governmental context because the identity of the client is often unclear, and various statutes and regulations prescribe the government lawyer's conduct:

Although in some circumstances the client may be a specific agency, it may also be a branch of government, such as the executive branch, or the government as a whole. For example, if the action or failure to act involves the head of a bureau, either the department of which the bureau is a part or the relevant branch of government may be the client for purpose of this Rule. Moreover, in a matter involving the conduct of government officials, a government lawyer may have authority under applicable law to question such conduct more extensively than that of a lawyer for a private organization in similar circumstances.

After the Model Code became effective on January 1, 1970, a committee of the Federal Bar Association analyzed the new ethical guidelines and concluded that the government lawyer needed additional guidance in his practice. In September 1970, the National Council of the Federal Bar Association commissioned a comprehensive study of the unique problems of the government lawyer under the Model Code. The study produced ethical considerations and disciplinary rules specifically for the government lawyer. During 1973, the Federal Bar Association adopted these special rules as a supplement to the general guidelines of the Model Code. Even with the American Bar Association's enactment of the Model Rules, [*] the Federal Bar Association's ethical considerations remain a valuable source of guidance for the

*A comment to the Model Rules provides that a government lawyer, whether employed or specifically retained by the government, is subject to the Model Rules. Model Rule 1.11 comment.

government lawyer, and continues to be referenced by those analyzing the ethical questions facing the government lawyer. Those special provisions are described in the following article.

Normand C. Poirier, The Federal Government Lawyer and Professional Ethics*

60 A.B.A. J. 1541 (1974)

There are some eleven thousand lawyers who hold appointments to civilian attorney positions in the executive agencies of the federal government and some five thousand lawyers in uniform serving as judge advocates in the military departments or as law specialists with the coast guard. There are several hundred lawyers employed as legal counsel in the legislative branch of the government.

Federal government lawyers are all subject to the Code of Professional Responsibility of the American Bar Association, made applicable to their professional conduct in one or more ways. First, their agency or department may make their professional conduct subject to the code by administrative direction or regulation. The code may also be made to govern each federal government lawyer's professional conduct by the bar of the state in which he is admitted.

FEDERAL ETHICAL CONSIDERATIONS ADOPTED

The federal ethical considerations presented in this article represent a first step at providing specific guidance under the Code of Professional Responsibility to the federal government lawyer. Several more steps can be taken to refine and develop what already is contained in the code with respect to the practice of law by lawyers representing the federal government, either in the form of ethical considerations or disciplinary rules.

Federal government lawyers essentially practice in specialized areas. The diversity of responsibilities exercised by them ranges from participation in highly sophisticated international security negotiations, such as the Strategic Arms Limitations Talks or the Conference of the Committee on Disarmament, to the provision of legal advice regarding social and rehabilitative services offered to the poor; from the drafting of complicated tax regulations to making legal determinations regarding veterans' benefits; from frequent appearance in trial or appellate courts to exhaustive legal research in support of proposed federal legislation. Circumstances of the federal government lawyer's practice do indeed differ from those affecting lawyers in private practice. The differences in practice extend also to client relationships.

A number of federal statutes impose obligations on federal lawyers that directly affect their professional duties. For example, under Canon 2 and Ethical

Consideration 2-25 of the code, lawyers should assist in making legal counsel available to the poor. However, because of the conflict of interest provisions of the United States Code (18 U.S.C. §205), federal government lawyers may not be appointed to represent an indigent person accused of a crime under federal law and, because of the unique status of the District of Columbia, a person accused of a crime under the District of Columbia Code. Within the District the prohibition extends to the provision of legal counsel in civil matters if the lawyer would be required to represent his client before an agency of the government of the District.

No discussion of the federal ethical considerations would be complete without a few words concerning Opinion 73-1 of the Committee on Professional Ethics of the Federal Bar Association. The opinion, which is referenced in Federal Ethical Consideration 1-1 and which was published in 32 Fed. B. J. 71 (1973), deals with important issues involving the government client and confidentiality. It represents *inter alia* the first extensive published treatment of the identity of the federal government lawyer's "client."

On this subject the opinion, after considering the special status of the federal lawyer designated to represent another in government service against whom proceedings are brought of a disciplinary, administrative, or personnel character, including a court-martial, states:

> The more usual situation of the federally employed lawyer, however, is that of the lawyer who is a principal legal officer of a department, agency or other legal entity of the Government, or a member of the legal staff of the department, agency, or entity. This lawyer assumes a public trust, for the government, overall and in each of its parts, is responsible to the people in our democracy with its representative form of government. Each part of the government has the obligation of carrying out, in the public interest, its assigned responsibility in a manner consistent with the Constitution, and the applicable laws and regulations. In contrast, the private practitioner represents the client's personal or private interest. In pointing out that the federally employed lawyer thus is engaged professionally in the furtherance of a particular governmental responsibility, we do not suggest, however, that the public is the client as the client concept is usually understood. It is to say that the lawyer's employment requires him to observe in the performance of his professional responsibility the public interest sought to be served by the governmental organization of which he is a part.
>
> Proceeding upon the foregoing background, the client of the federally employed lawyer, using the term in the sense of where lies his immediate professional obligation and responsibility, is the agency where he is employed, including those charged with its administration insofar as they are engaged in the conduct of the public business. The relationship is a confidential one, an attribute of the lawyer's profession which accompanies him in his government service.

TEXT OF FEDERAL ETHICAL CONSIDERATIONS

The following are the supplemental ethical considerations under the nine canons of the American Bar Association Code of Professional Responsibility which take into account the particular circumstances faced by the federal lawyer in his legal work. The symbol "F. E.C." denotes "Federal Ethical Consideration."

CANON 1. A LAWYER SHOULD ASSIST IN MAINTAINING THE INTEGRITY AND COMPETENCE OF THE LEGAL PROFESSION

F.E.C.-1-1.   This canon, as well as all others, is fully applicable to the federal lawyer. Better to comply with it he should acquaint himself with the regulations especially applicable to his department or other agency of his employment. In that connection attention is directed to 5 C.F.R. §735.210, 28 U.S.C. §535, House Concurrent Resolution No. 175 of July 11, 1958, 72 Stat. B12, and Chapter 11 of 18 U.S.C. concerned *inter alia* with conflicts of interests.

(Note: Reference is also made to Opinion 73-1 of March 15, 1973, of the Professional Ethics Committee of the Federal Bar Association, published in the Fed. B. J., 32 F.B.J. 71-75 [Winter, 1973]. The opinion, however, has status only as an opinion of the Professional Ethics Committee. Problems may arise as to the application of the opinion. Their solution would depend upon the particular circumstances. These supplemental ethical considerations do not purport to cover the range of diverse circumstances not now presented in specific terms.)

CANON 2. A LAWYER SHOULD ASSIST THE LEGAL PROFESSION IN FULFILLING ITS DUTY TO MAKE LEGAL COUNSEL AVAILABLE

F.E.C.-2-1.   The federal lawyer, within the limitations of statute, of agency regulations, and of general conflict-of-interest laws and principles, bears a professional responsibility to make legal counsel available to all in need.

    A. The offering of his services is on his own time and not at the expense of the government except where statutory or regulatory provision is made for the rendering of such services at government expense.

    B. Within the limitations above referred to he should be receptive to representing the poor in matters referred to him by local legal aid and community action societies.

F.E.C.-2-2.   The federal lawyer is encouraged, where his position permits, to undertake review from time to time of agency or departmental regulations or policy with the view of enabling citizens unable to pay for needed services to obtain the help of the federal lawyer insofar as may be done within the limitations applicable to his position and consistently with his primary obligation to the government service.

F.E.C.-2-3.   The federal lawyer who notes that a person with whom he is dealing is in need of legal counsel would be well advised to recommend that he obtain counsel.

CANON 3. A LAWYER SHOULD ASSIST IN PREVENTING THE UNAUTHORIZED PRACTICE OF LAW

F.E.C.-3-1. This canon is fully applicable to the federal lawyer.

CANON 4. A LAWYER SHOULD PRESERVE THE CONFIDENCES AND SECRETS OF A CLIENT

F.E.C.-4-1. If, in the conduct of official business of his department or agency, it appears that a fellow employee of the department or agency is revealing or about to reveal information concerning his own illegal or unethical conduct to a federal lawyer acting in his official capacity the lawyer should inform the employee that a federal lawyer is responsible to the department or agency concerned and not the individual employee and, therefore, the information being discussed is not privileged.

F.E.C.-4-2. If a fellow employee volunteers information concerning himself which appears to involve illegal or unethical conduct or is violative of department or agency rules and regulations which would be pertinent to that department's or agency's consideration of disciplinary action, the federal lawyer should inform the individual that the lawyer is responsible to the department or agency concerned and not the individual employee.

F.E.C.-4-3. The federal lawyer has the ethical responsibility to disclose to his supervisor or other appropriate departmental or agency official any unprivileged information of the type discussed above in F.E.C.-4-1 and 2.

F.E.C.-4-4. The federal lawyer who has been duly designated to act as an attorney for a fellow employee who is the subject of disciplinary, loyalty, or other personnel administration proceedings or as defense counsel for court-martial matters or for civil legal assistance to military personnel and their dependents is for those purposes acting as an attorney for a client and communications between them shall be secret and privileged. In respects not applicable to the private practitioner the federal lawyer is under obligation to the public to assist his department or agency in complying with the Freedom of Information Act 5 U.S.C. §552 (1970), and regulations and authoritative decisions thereunder.

CANON 5. A LAWYER SHOULD EXERCISE INDEPENDENT PROFESSIONAL JUDGMENT ON BEHALF OF A CLIENT

F.E.C.-5-1. The immediate professional responsibility of the federal lawyer is to the department or agency in which he is employed, to be performed in light of the particular public interest function of the department or agency. He is required to exercise independent professional judgment which transcends his personal interests, giving consideration, however, to the reasoned views of others engaged with him in the conduct of the business of the government.

Canon 6. A Lawyer Should Represent a Client Competently

F.E.C.-6-1.   In performing the duties of his particular employment this obligation is fully applicable to the federal lawyer, to be fulfilled with special regard to the public interest. When designated to represent a fellow employee or a member of the armed services in matters referred to in F.E.C.-4-4, the public interest is not inconsistent with the assumption of the traditional attorney-client relationship with the individual represented.

Canon 7. A Lawyer Should Represent a Client Zealously Within the Bounds of the Law

F.E.C.-7-1.   The obligation stated in this canon is fully applicable to the responsibility of the federal lawyer when representing an individual in the circumstances referred to in F.E.C.-4-4 and F.E.C.-6-1. In the performance of the obligations of his position in other respects he is well and faithfully to discharge the duties of his office as prescribed by his oath of office. Of special application to the federal lawyer are the American Bar Association Ethical Considerations 7-13 and 7-14, the former respecting the responsibility of a public prosecutor, and the latter the government lawyer who has discretionary power relative to litigation.

F.E.C.-7-2.   The federal lawyer is under the professional obligation faithfully to apply his professional talents to the promotion under law and applicable regulations of the public interest entrusted to the department, agency or other governmental agency of his employment.

Canon 8. A Lawyer Should Assist in Improving the Legal System

F.E.C.-8-1.   The general obligation to assist in improving the legal system applies to federal lawyers. In such situations he may have a higher obligation than lawyers generally. Since his duties include responsibility for the application of law to the resolution of problems incident to his employment there is a continuing obligation to seek improvement. This may be accomplished by the application of legal considerations to the day-to-day decisional process. Moreover it may eventuate that a federal lawyer by reason of his particular tasks may have insight which enhances his ability to initiate reforms, thus giving rise to a special obligation under Canon 8. In all these matters paramount consideration is due the public interest.

F.E.C.-8-2.   The situation of the federal lawyer which may give rise to special considerations, not applicable to lawyers generally, include certain limitations on complete freedom of action in matters relating to Canon 8. For example, a lawyer in the Office of the Chief Counsel of the Internal Revenue Service may reasonably be expected to abide, without public criticism, with certain policies or rulings closely allied to his sphere of responsibility even if he disagrees with the position taken by the agency. But even if involved personally in the process of formulating policy or ruling there may be rare occasions when his conscience compels him publicly to attack a decision which is contrary to his professional, ethical or moral judgment. In that event, however, he should be prepared to resign before doing so, and he is not free to abuse professional confidences reposed in him in the process leading to the decision.

F.E.C.-8-3. The method of discharging the obligations imposed by Canon 8 may vary depending upon the circumstances. The federal lawyer is free to seek reform through the processes of his agency even if the agency has no formal procedure for receiving and acting upon suggestions from lawyers employed by it. Such intra-agency activities may be the only appropriate course for him to follow if he is not prepared to leave the agency's employment. However, there may be situations in which he could appropriately bring intra-agency problems to the attention of other federal officials (such as those in the Office of Management and Budget or Department of Justice) with responsibility and authority to correct the allegedly improper activities of the employing agency. Furthermore, it may be possible for the lawyer to participate in bar association or other activities designed to improve the legal system within his agency without being involved in a public attack on the agency's practices, so long as the requirement to protect confidences is observed.

Sound policy favors encouraging government officials to invite and consider the views of counsel. This tends to prevent the adoption of illegal policies. Even where there are choices between legal alternatives, the lawyer's viewpoint may be valuable in affecting the choice. Lawyers in federal service accordingly should conduct themselves so as to encourage utilization of their advice within the agencies, retaining at all times an obligation to exercise independent professional judgment, even though their conclusions may not always be warmly embraced. The failure of lawyers to respect official and proper confidences discourages this desirable resort to them.

F.E.C.-8-4. Federal lawyers facing questions concerning the propriety of pursuing efforts to improve the legal system because of their official position or responsibilities, or confidences enjoyed as a result thereof, would be well advised to explore with senior legal officials of their agency, or in some cases of other agencies, better to assure that all relevant ethical factors are considered before determining the course to adopt.

CANON 9. A LAWYER SHOULD AVOW EVEN THE APPEARANCE OF PROFESSIONAL IMPROPRIETY

F.E.C.-9-1. This canon No. 9 and the American Bar Association ethical and disciplinary considerations with respect thereto should be observed by the federal lawyer.

F.E.C.-9-2. While a federal lawyer may appropriately represent on appointment an indigent accused of crime in the circumstances set forth in these federal ethical considerations, see F.E.C.-2-1, he may not do so, other than in the proper discharge of his official duties, in federal criminal cases or otherwise as proscribed by 18 U.S.C. §205, entitled "Activities of officers and employees in claims against and other matters affecting the government."

————

Later, in 1990, the Federal Bar Association issued model rules addressing federal lawyers and lawyers practicing before government agencies. These rules repeated the Federal Bar Association's characterization of the lawyer's *agency* as the client.

Poirier cites the issuance of Opinion 73-1 of the Committee on Professional Ethics of the Federal Bar Association, noting that it represents the first extensive published treatment of the identity of the federal government lawyer's client. FBA Opinion 73-1, which was cited in In re Lindsey, 158 F.3d 1263 (D.Ct. D.C. 1998), is reproduced below.

Professional Ethics Committee of the Federal Bar Association, Opinion 73-1

32 Fed. B.J. 71 (1973)

1. Under what circumstances may a federally employed lawyer disclose information concerning a government official of any rank which would reveal corrupt, illegal, or grossly negligent conduct?
2. If disclosure may be properly made, to whom may it be made?
3. Who is the client of a government attorney in the Executive or Legislative branches of government?

A few remarks as to terminology are in order. Thus, the "federally employed lawyer," for purposes of this opinion, is considered to be the lawyer employed by the federal government in a legal capacity. This opinion may at times refer to him as the government lawyer, or simply as the lawyer or attorney, without repetition that he is "federally employed." In defining the terms "corrupt, illegal or grossly negligent" conduct, as used in the opinion, and in judging whether particular conduct comes within those terms, special care is required. The "corrupt" conduct referred to in the request for an opinion was construed to be venal conduct in violation of law and duty, engaged in for personal gain or the gain of another, the gain ordinarily being of a pecuniary or other valuable nature which is measurable. Defining "illegal" conduct was not so easy for such conduct is often subject to reasonable differences of opinion as to its legality. The profession as well as the courts are constantly troubled and at odds about whether particular conduct is legal or not. For purposes of this opinion "illegal" conduct is divided into two general categories. One consists of the willful or knowing disregard of or breach of law, other than of a corrupt character, the latter type of illegal conduct having been separately defined. The second category of illegal conduct was considered to be that about which the lawyer may hold a firm position as to its illegality but which he nevertheless recognizes is in an area subject to reasonable differences of professional opinion as to its legality. Conduct which is "grossly negligent" would seem not to lend itself to greater clarification than those words themselves indicate.

One further general comment seems desirable. The federally employed lawyer in reaching a conclusion that the type of conduct referred to has occurred must be fully aware of the circumstances and exercise care commensurate with his own professional nature and responsibility, with a consciousness of the need always to avoid an unjust or mistaken derogatory characterization of the conduct of another.

Assuming the described conduct to have occurred, answers to the three questions can be more clearly developed by considering first the question posed as to who is the client of the federally employed lawyer in the executive and legislative branches of the government. Problems of disclosure involved in the other questions should be considered in light of the answer to the client question.

The client problem also divides according to the duties involved. There is the government lawyer who is designated to represent another in government service against whom proceedings are brought of a disciplinary, administrative or personnel character, including a court-martial. The answer to the client question in these situations seems clear. The person the lawyer is designated to represent is the client. The usual attorney-client relationship arises, with its privilege and professional responsibility to protect and defend the interest of the one represented.

The more usual situation of the federally employed lawyer, however, is that of the lawyer who is a principal legal officer of a department, agency or other legal entity of the government, or a member of the legal staff of the department, agency, or entity. This lawyer assumes a public trust, for the government, overall and in each of its parts, is responsible to the people in our democracy with its representative form of government. Each part of the government has the obligation of carrying out, in the public interest, its assigned responsibility in a manner consistent with the Constitution, and the applicable laws and regulations. In contrast, the private practitioner represents the client's personal or private interest. In pointing out that the federally employed lawyer thus is engaged professionally in the furtherance of a particular governmental responsibility we do not suggest, however, that the public is the client as the client concept is usually understood. It is to say that the lawyer's employment requires him to observe in the performance of his professional responsibility the public interest sought to be served by the governmental organization of which he is a part.

Proceeding upon the foregoing background, the client of the federally employed lawyer, using the term in the sense of where lies his immediate professional obligation and responsibility, is the agency where he is employed, including those charged with its administration insofar as they are engaged in the conduct of the public business. The relationship is a confidential one, an attribute of the lawyer's profession which accompanies him in his government service. This confidential relationship is usually essential to the decision-making process to which the lawyer brings his professional talents. Moreover, it encourages resort to him for consultation and advice in the ongoing operations of the agency.

The relationship above described gives rise to the question whether or to what degree the attorney-client privilege known to private practice attaches with respect to those to whom the government lawyer is professionally obligated in the conduct of the public business. No all-inclusive answer to the problem of the privilege is attempted herein, not only because no concrete factual situation has been posed, but also because the questions as submitted call for consideration of the privilege only as it bears upon the problem of disclosure. In that context the following is submitted.

The Committee does not believe there are any circumstances in which corrupt conduct may not be disclosed by the federally employed lawyer, apart from those situations to which we have referred in which the lawyer has been designated to defend an individual in a proceeding against him with respect to a personal problem.

In other instances of corruption the ethical aspect of the answer merges with the legal. Section 535 of Tide 28 of the United States Code provides:

> (b) Any information, allegation, or complaint received in a department or agency of the executive branch of the government relating to violations of Title 18 [the federal criminal code] involving government officers and employees shall be expeditiously reported to the Attorney General by the head of the department or agency, unless —
>
>   (1) the responsibility to perform an investigation with respect thereto is specifically assigned otherwise by another provision of law; or
>
>   (2) as to any department or agency of the government, the Attorney General directs otherwise with respect to a specified class of information, allegation, or complaint.
>
> (c) This section does not limit —
>
>   (1) The authority of the military departments to investigate persons or offenses over which the armed forces have jurisdiction under the Uniform Code of Military Justice (chapter 47 of Title 10); or
>
>   (2) The primary authority of the Postmaster General to investigate postal offenses.

In addition to this statute, there is House Concurrent Resolution No. 175 of July 11, 1958, 72 Stat. B12, entitled "Code of Ethics for Government Service." Its provisions have been made applicable to the entire Executive branch by Regulations of the Civil Service Commission, 5 C.F.R. §735.10. The Resolution provides: "Any person in the Government service should: 9. Expose corruption wherever discovered." . . .

Reading section 535 of Tide 28 of the United States Code with Joint Resolution and the Civil Service Commission Regulations, corrupt conduct and other illegal conduct of a criminal character, that is, the willful or knowing disregard of or breach of law, in either the Legislative or Executive branch may be disclosed by the federally employed lawyer, that is, reported to the "head of the department or agency" or other governmental entity, who shall report it to the Attorney General. If the head officer referred to is involved, the report in our opinion may be made directly to the Attorney General, or other appropriate official of the Department of Justice.

With respect to the second category of illegal conduct, conduct about which there may be reasonable differences of opinion as to its legality, and grossly negligent conduct, the Committee considers the problem to be different. Ordinarily there is no need of disclosure of such conduct beyond the personnel of the agency where it arises. Differences of opinion as to the legality of action are often unavoidable in the process of arriving at a course of action to be recommended or adopted. The lawyer may not deem the decision reached or the action taken to be legally sound, but in the situations in which the question arises it may not be misconduct at all. Moreover, when we turn particularly to the grossly negligent category, one must consider that the particular conduct may be accidental by a person ordinarily careful. There should usually be an adequate remedy in the public interest calling for no disclosure beyond the immediate persons involved, including if need be other members of the agency. In all of these matters there may be regulations of the agency pointing to the course which should be followed. These should be observed unless for some very good reason the lawyer deems them inapplicable. In any event, the opportunity to correct these matters should first be within the agency itself.

Something more needs to be said. The confidential relationship of the lawyer with those entitled to consult with and be advised by him varies in degree according to the subject matter. It is one thing in the area of national security or the conduct of foreign affairs, for example, and quite another if there is involved, for example, a dispute over the validity of a particular order of the National Labor Relations Board. The diversity of situations is almost innumerable. It is to be borne in mind throughout that ours is an open society insofar as compatible with the orderly and effective conduct of government. This follows from the nature of the relationship of our government with the people, and it has been given legislative recognition in recent years by the Freedom of Information Act, with its limited exemptions from the obligation of disclosure. Moreover, the government lawyer cannot be a refuge for the corrupt or looked upon as a secret repository for illegal or grossly negligent conduct of the business of the government. There is a dividing line between conduct which falls in the area of strict confidentiality and that which falls within the area of appropriate public knowledge. This line cannot accurately be drawn except upon consideration of a particular factual situation, and even then not always easily or accurately drawn, certainly not to the satisfaction of all. Accordingly, the Committee feels obliged to limit its answer respecting disclosure to acceptance of the principle that disclosure beyond the confines of the agency or other law enforcing or disciplinary authorities of the government is warranted only in the case when the lawyer, as a reasonable and prudent man, conscious of his professional obligation of care, confidentiality and responsibility, concludes that these authorities have without good cause failed in the performance of their own obligation to take remedial measures required in the public interest. In the absence of a concrete situation upon which to pass judgment as to the ethical course which should be followed we go no further than to adopt the above stated ethical principle. We think it appropriate for us to affirm the position that honesty and faithfulness is the prevailing rule in the government service, and we warn against applying the principle we have stated to any situation without that care and sense of responsibility which is the hallmark of the legal profession at its best. Such care would call for resort by the lawyer himself to a trustworthy advisor as to the course to be followed. The ultimate decision, however, remains with him.

———

As you will note from Opinion 73-1, the Federal Bar committee concluded that the government lawyer's client, "using the term in the sense of where lies his immediate professional obligation and responsibility, is the agency where he is employed." This opinion provided the government lawyer with a framework from which to apply general ethical standards in a government context. If the client was the agency, it was the agency to which the tripartite duties of loyalty, confidentiality, and competence were owed.

However, this was not the end of inquiry into this subject. Fifteen years later, a special committee appointed by the District of Columbia Bar issued a report on the application of the Model Rules (as adopted in D.C.) to the government lawyer. Given the dominant role of government legal service within the District of Columbia, the work of the D.C. Bar in this respect deserves careful attention. Relevant excerpts from the D.C. Bar committee's report are set forth below, followed by a discussion of the debate in which it has become a representative position.

Report by the District of Columbia Bar Special Committee on Government Lawyers and the Model Rules of Professional Conduct*

3 The Wash. Law. (Sept./Oct. 1988)

. . . The Model Rules proposed by the ABA contained a number of specific provisions and references to government lawyers. Based on their review, the Model Rules Committee and the Board of Governors concluded, for the most part, that the special concerns of government lawyers had not been sufficiently evaluated. With the exception of Rule 3.8, which was extensively modified, the Model Rules Committee deleted most references to government lawyers, and suggested that a special committee be appointed to review the Model Rules from the perspective of government lawyers. The Board of Governors agreed and this Special Committee was appointed.

B.   The Special Committee's Works

The Special Committee, comprised of a broad mix of lawyers engaged in various forms of practice in the District of Columbia, held its initial meeting on June 3, 1987. The Special Committee's charge was to consider in what ways, if any, the

*© 1988 District of Columbia Bar. Reprinted with permission.

proposed Rules recommended by the Board of Governors to the District of Columbia Court of Appeals should be modified to apply to government lawyers.

Over the course of the next year, the Special Committee met ten times to discuss the proposed Rules and their application to government lawyers. Subcommittees were formed to study each Rule and its Comment more closely and to make recommendations to the Special Committee as a whole. Various sources of practical and legal information were investigated, and the Special Committee received suggestions and comments from a number of interested individuals and agencies. As a result of these efforts, the Special Committee has unanimously adopted this Report and the recommendations included herein.

The Report contains [two] segments. [They] discuss the role of the government lawyer and the process by which the lawyer identifies the client to which he or she is directly responsible. . . .

I. THE ROLE OF THE GOVERNMENT LAWYER

The decision of the Model Rules Committee to delete references in the proposed Rules relating to additional special ethical rules for government lawyers, and the subsequent conclusion by the Board of Governors that a Special Committee be appointed to consider whether there should be such additional rules, reflected those bodies' recognition that the government lawyer must address ethical issues in a different environment from the lawyer in private practice. Because of their status as government employees, government lawyers are subject to a wide range of statutes and regulations governing their conduct that are not applicable to lawyers in private practice. In addition, the private lawyer, whether employed by a single employer or by a multitude of clients, generally has a clear understanding of who his or her client is and what his or her obligations are to that client. While there are circumstances in which ambiguities can arise for the private lawyer, practical necessities and ethical requirements generally point in the same, relatively clear direction.

The government lawyer faces a more complex environment. Many people believe that government service — *public* service — requires a recognition of a duty to the "public interest," however that may be defined. Since elected and appointed officials are generally transients reflecting the flux of political administrations, some believe there is a higher obligation than to the individual who currently commands a government agency or department. Who really is the client of the government lawyer? This question, generally a given in private practice, is a critical first step in understanding the ethical obligations of every lawyer employed by a governmental body, for the identity of the client will determine the outcome of conflict questions, the appropriateness of disclosure of confidential information, and even the amount of discretion the government lawyer can exercise in handling litigation.

Based on its review and discussion, the Special Committee concluded that the critical ethical issue facing the government lawyer was determining the identity of his or her client. If, as Judge Charles Fahy concluded in a 1950 lecture at Columbia University School of Law, "the Government is a composite of the people and

Government counsel therefore has as a client the people as a whole," significant confidentiality and conflict issues may arise. If, on the other hand, the "client of the [government] lawyer, using the term in the sense of where lies his immediate professional obligation and responsibility, is the agency where he is employed . . . , as the Professional Ethics Committee of the Federal Bar Association concluded in its Opinion 73-1 (1973), different confidentiality and conflict issues may be presented.

After considerable discussion, the Special Committee concluded that the employing agency should in normal circumstances be considered the client of the government lawyer. The explanation of how this decision was reached serves as a useful description of the general thrust of the Special Committee's proposed recommendations for changes to the proposed Rules as adopted by the Board of Governors.

II.   THE AGENCY AS CLIENT: THE CRITICAL BUILDING BLOCK OF THE PROPOSED RULES

The ultimate source of authority for government under our constitutional system is, as the Constitution recognizes: "We, the people. . . ." For any governmental employee, therefore, there must be some sense of obligation to the public interest, however abstract that concept may be. There are some who argue strenuously that a government lawyer's ultimate obligation must be to the public interest as he or she sees it. For example, one commentator, after criticizing the purported assumption in the Code of Professional Responsibility that the lawyer's client is a readily identifiable human being, concluded that the government lawyer's obligations must be to "justice" and "fairness."

As a general proposition, however, the notion of the "public interest" as the ultimate standard of performance, professional or otherwise, is an anarchic one, and is not the model upon which our governmental bodies function today. While there are various procedural and substantive limitations throughout the range of governmental entities in this country, all are organized to allow command and response employment structures, and all have one or more individuals (generally elected) who have ultimate responsibility for governmental action. Government in this country is consensual, but the form of government is hierarchical.

This fact permeates our government structures. Notwithstanding the fact that government is the people's business, all governmental bodies make and implement policy decisions, where necessary, through direction of employees who may or may not agree with the particular policy they are asked to implement. Thus, a budget analyst or a legislative aide must respond to instructions by superiors or face dismissal, even if that individual's conception of the "public interest" differs from that of his superiors.

It could be argued that government *lawyers* should be different. To some, government lawyers represent the independent conscience of government. Because of the lawyer's duty to serve his client's interests above all others, save for extraordinary circumstances, some believe the government lawyer is *required* to look beyond the individuals who are his superiors and the agency he serves and address the interest of his ultimate client—the public. As one commentator has written, the government lawyer should look to statutes and applicable constitutional provisions in determining the interests of his client, rather than "the whims of persons momentarily in the executive branch."

The Special Committee recognized the importance of this concept as an abstract principle. Most, if not all, government lawyers are drawn to government service by a sincere desire to serve the public interest. The Special Committee concluded, however, that "the public interest" was an unworkable ethical guideline, and indeed was inconsistent with the underlying rationale of many significant ethical concepts. If a lawyer is to function effectively as counselor and adviser to elected and appointed officials, those officials must not view the lawyer as some independent actor, liable at any time to arrive at some individualistic perception of the "public interest" and act accordingly. The governmental client, to be encouraged to use lawyers, must believe that the lawyer will represent the legitimate interests the governmental client seeks to advance, and not be influenced by some unique and personal vision of the "public interest." Just like a private client, the governmental client must have a reasonable belief in the confidentiality of his or her communications to a lawyer in order to encourage free and full communications. In the governmental context, in short, a lawyer must be the same kind of professional servant of the client that is required by ethical rules in the private sector.

Taking these factors into account, the Special Committee concluded that the "public interest" was too amorphous a standard to have practical utility in regulating lawyer conduct or in providing ethical guidance. The Special Committee then considered, as an alternative, that the particular government as a whole (e.g., the United States government or the District of Columbia) should appropriately be considered the government lawyer's client. Three possible justifications were raised in support of this proposition. First, it could be argued that the attorney-client relationship in the context of the government lawyer is too complicated to make more specific rules that can be effectively applied. By defining the client as the government as a whole, government lawyers are effectively removed from the strictures of many of the ethical rules. This is not a problem, arguably, because there are sufficient internal controls within the government, such as statutes, regulations, and agency or departmental codes of ethics, to regulate the conduct of the government lawyer. Finally, this definition would recognize that external regulation of government lawyers may be preempted in some situations by the government's internal controls.

Notwithstanding the provocative issues raised by these arguments, the Special Committee concluded that the "entire government as client" standard was also not an appropriate decisional foundation for ethical rules. First, this approach could arguably remove members of the D.C. Bar from the Bar's disciplinary jurisdiction simply because they were employed by a governmental body. Consistent with the conclusion of the Board of Governors that a government lawyer who violates ethical rules should not be immune from discipline by the body that has admitted that lawyer to practice, the Special Committee rejected any general exemption from the proposed Rules based solely on the fact of government employment.

Rejection of the "entire government as client" approach was also consistent with the various changes to the ABA's Model Rules that have been adopted by the Board of Governors. The changes, taken as a whole, emphasize the primacy of client interests and control, and the corresponding obligation of lawyers to determine and follow the client's decision unless inconsistent with law or ethical regulation.

It is simply not consistent with this primary thrust of these proposed Rules to permit a government lawyer, in effect, to define the lawyer's client merely by reference to the attorney's personal perception of the public interest. The identification of one's client as the entire government would raise serious questions regarding client control and confidentiality. For example, without some focus of responsibility, each government lawyer would be free to perform as he or she saw fit, subject only to the practical constraint of internal agency discipline. The Board of Governors rejected this concept in calling for the appointment of this Special Committee, and it would be inconsistent with both this Committee's charge and the generic values represented by the proposed Rules to accept a concept of client that eliminated any realistic possibility of ethical discipline. The Special Committee concluded that defining the client of the government lawyer as the government as a whole, or even as the particular branch of government in which the lawyer functions, suffered from the same essential deficiencies as the public interest approach.

This analysis inevitably led to the conclusion that the employing agency should normally be regarded as the client of the government lawyer. In most cases, the employing agency will be a discrete entity, clearly definable and the source of identifiable lines of authority. The lawyer's duties typically will be directed by the head of the agency or his delegate; the lawyer's explicit responsibilities will be limited to those assigned by the agency; and agency regulations provide a clear benchmark for assessing attorney conduct. These factors provide bounds and give concrete meaning to the lawyer-client relationship in the government context.

This identification of the client with the employing agency permits a lawyer seeking guidance from the Rules, in the vast majority of situations, to determine clearly his or her duties and obligations, both in advancing the interests of the client and protecting its confidences and secrets. It permits those in the agency to rely on the lawyer in the same way that a private client can rely on its private lawyer. And finally, the rules so interpreted can be effectively enforced by a disciplinary body.

The Special Committee's conclusion is consistent with the conclusions reached by a number of commentators and ethical bodies. One article, after discussing the issue of the identity of the client of the government lawyer, noted that "[i]n this article, we use the term 'client' in its more conventional sense to mean the government agency." As previously mentioned, the Professional Ethics Committee of the Federal Bar Association reached the same conclusion in its Opinion 73-1 (1973): "The client of the federally employed lawyer . . . is the agency where he is employed."

With respect to conflicts between clients, the Committee on Professional Ethics of the New York State Bar Association ruled in its Opinion 501 (1979) that "[w]hen a governmental body is organized into a number of separate departments or agencies, such department or agency, and not the parent governmental unit, should be treated as the client for purposes of the rule which forbids the concurrent representation of one client against another."

Obviously, the conclusion that the government lawyer's client is the lawyer's employing agency does not answer every ethical question. After all, there are many situations in government where lawyers are asked to represent diverse client interests: several different agencies, for example, or perhaps individuals and agencies simultaneously. In these situations, a careful analysis will be required to determine the lawyer's obligations. But these problems are inherent in the legal profession, and are faced by nongovernmental lawyers every day. Lawyers employed by a corporation, for example, occasionally confront issues in which the interests of the corporation's officers, directors, and shareholders are not necessarily in harmony. In such circumstances, the lawyer's first task is to identify with precision the client he or she represents. While the lawyer in private practice may have more control over the decision to represent specific clients, he or she faces the same analytical issues and ethical obligations.

The "employing agency as client" approach also recognizes that government bodies have the ability to establish different attorney-client obligations in particular circumstances. If an agency or branch of government wants a specific lawyer to have a lawyer-client relationship with an agency or entity other than the employing agency, it can establish such a different responsibility by executive or court order, regulation or statute. If it is thought desirable to allow government lawyers to disclose outside the employing agency what would otherwise be confidential client information, such disclosure can be authorized by the client or compelled by proper order, regulation or statute, just as is the case with a private lawyer-client relationship.

In effect, what the Special Committee is recommending is a rule of thumb — a benchmark from which deviations can be made as appropriate. But absent special circumstances or exceptions, the government lawyer is entitled to know what the D.C. Bar believes are the lawyer's obligations to his or her clients, and ascertainment of these obligations must begin with an identification of the client.

Establishing a definitional benchmark for government lawyers employed in the judicial and legislative branches of government may appear somewhat more complicated but, after due consideration, the Special Committee concluded that those who are in fact employed and functioning as lawyers in the judicial and legislative branches should be governed by the same Rules as executive branch lawyers. Finally, it must be noted that some members of the D.C. Bar employed as government lawyers are employed by state or local governments (including, most importantly, the District of Columbia) rather than the federal government. In certain instances, particularly at the local level, the government lawyer might be employed by a municipal corporation, which may constitute a single legal entity. Notwithstanding this legal difference, the Special Committee concluded that the same generic Rules should apply, with the municipal corporation or other entity of course free to modify by regulation, statute, or ordinance the obligations imposed by the Rules to meet any particular needs.

As you will note from its report, the D.C. committee followed the course of the Federal Bar committee by concluding that the government lawyer's client is the employing agency. This resolution, however, has attracted some opposition, as discussed in the excerpt from following article.

George C. Harris, The Rule of Law and the War on Terror: The Professional Responsibility of Executive Branch Lawyers in the Wake of 9/11*

1 J. Nat'l Security L. & Pol'y 409 (2005)

I.   EXISTING GUIDANCE FOR THE GOVERNMENT LAWYER

A.   GENERAL STANDARDS

The legal profession's standards of conduct offer surprisingly little guidance specifically for lawyers who advise the government on legal issues. What guidance there is tends to treat the government as a special variety of organizational client, with differing views as to how or under what circumstances the government differs from a private, organizational client. The relevant rules and commentary also vary in their answers to the foundational question: who is the "entity" client to which the government lawyer owes her duties? While these authorities would, in most circumstances, focus on the agency or department of the government that employs the lawyer, not the "public interest" or the "American people" in a more general sense, there are differing views about what role the "public interest" should play in guiding the government lawyer's conduct. The ABA Model Rules of Professional Conduct devote a rule to the "Special Responsibilities of a Prosecutor" (Rule 3.8) and one to "Special Conflicts of Interest for Former and Current Government Officers and Employees" (Rule 1.11), but they mention a lawyer's duties to a government client only as a comment to Rule 1.13 ("Organization as Client"). That comment advises that the duty defined in Rule 1.13 "applies to government organizations." It warns, however, that "defining precisely the identity of the client and prescribing the resulting obligations of such lawyers may be more difficult in the government context and is a matter beyond the scope of these Rules."

---

*Reprinted with permission. © 2005 University of the Pacific, Mc George School of Law.

Rule 1.13 provides generally that a lawyer for an organization represents the entity — "the organization acting through its duly authorized constituents" — rather than any constituent of the organization. A comment notes that for the government lawyer "in some circumstances the client may be a specific agency, [but] it may also be a branch of government, such as the executive branch, or the government as a whole." With apparent reference to the lawyer's "reporting up" duties and "reporting out" discretion under Rule 1.13 in the case of wrongful conduct by a constituent acting on behalf of the organization, the comment also suggests that whistle-blowing may more often be appropriate for the government lawyer than for her private counterpart, since the public interest is at stake.

Some provisions of the Model Rules that are not specific to representation of the government apply to a lawyer who advises any client about what the law allows or prohibits. Model Rule 2.1, which pertains specifically to a lawyer's duties as an "Advisor," provides, "In representing a client, a lawyer shall exercise independent professional judgment and render candid advice. In rendering advice, a lawyer may refer not only to law but to other considerations such as moral, economic, social and political factors, that may be relevant to the client's situation." The official comments to Rule 2.1 emphasize the need for candor and "honest assessment," even when the advice may be unwelcome to the client, and they stress the need in some circumstances to go beyond "purely technical legal advice" to include "moral and ethical considerations in giving advice."

Model Rule 1.2(d) addresses the limits of the role that a lawyer may play in advising a client on legal prohibitions. It provides that "[a] lawyer shall not counsel a client to engage, or assist a client, in conduct that the lawyer knows is criminal or fraudulent, but a lawyer may discuss the legal consequences of any proposed course of conduct with a client and may counsel or assist a client to make a good faith effort to determine the validity, scope, meaning or application of the law." The comments to Rule 1.2 provide that a lawyer may "[give] an honest opinion about the actual consequences that appear likely to result from a client's conduct," emphasizing the distinction between "presenting an analysis of legal aspects of questionable conduct," which is permissible, and "recommending the means by which a crime or fraud might be committed with impunity," which is not.

The predecessor to the Model Rules, the ABA Model Code of Professional Responsibility, also contains minimal direct guidance to the lawyer for the government. Recognizing that "the lawyer in the federal government faces ethical problems not dealt with by the ethical considerations of the Code of Professional Responsibility," the Federal Bar Association in 1973 adopted "Federal Ethical Considerations" to supplement the Code's Ethical Considerations and promulgated a related formal opinion (Opinion 73-1 of the Committee on Professional Ethics of the Federal Bar Association). These Federal Ethical Considerations provide, among other things, that "the immediate professional responsibility of the federal lawyer is to the department or agency in which he is employed, to be performed in light of the particular public interest function of the department or agency." They direct the government lawyer's duty of zealous representation not to the agency or department itself, however, but to "the public interest entrusted to the department, agency or other governmental agency of his employment." As analyzed by one commentator, the Federal Bar Association's ethical considerations and opinion, at least in the disclosure context, located the government lawyer's duties of client loyalty as much or more with the lawyer's view of the public interest as with the agency that employs her.

In 1988, a special committee of the District of Columbia Bar issued a report on government lawyers and their duties under the Model Rules. It concluded that the agency, not the public interest, should be considered the government lawyer's client. It reasoned that government officials "must believe that the lawyer will represent the legitimate interests the governmental client seeks to advance, and not be influenced by some unique and personal vision of the "public interest.'"

The ALI Restatement of the Law Governing Lawyers, adopted in 1998, concludes that "no universal definition of the client of a governmental lawyer is possible." While noting that "the goals of a governmental client necessarily include pursuit of the public interest," it advises that "for many purposes, the preferable approach . . . is to regard the respective agencies as the clients and to regard the lawyers working for the agencies as subject to the direction of those officers authorized to act in the matter involved in the representation."

Commentators have split between the "agency loyalty" and "public interest" approaches to government lawyering. Many agree with the Restatement that there is no universal answer to the question of who is the government lawyer's client and that the question can only be answered when placed in specific context. As Professor Wolfram has observed, "the question, which seems straightforward, in fact disguises complexities that arise in very different settings, in many of which it should be given different answers."

In addition to the agency and public interest approaches, there is a third approach, based on the work of William Simon and others, which takes a critical legal studies perspective on the client-lawyer relationship. A recent Harvard Law Review note applies this "critical model" to the role of government lawyers. From the perspective of the critical model, "the government lawyer's primary responsibility is to help the agency develop its position in a way that is consistent with democratic values." The lawyer should not only determine whether the agency's proposed objectives comply with established understandings of the law, but "should also consider whether the objectives are consistent with the underlying purposes of the law; whether they comport with executive and congressional policy; whether they can be justified in terms of commonly accepted values; and whether they treat the affected parties justly." The lawyer's goal is to "develop the agency's position with reference to the public interest" and, through a process of communication with other members of the agency and the public, "to help the agency understand and realize [its] objectives."

As the previous article notes, some commentators have urged the view that the client of the government lawyer is the public interest. Below, the author makes the case for this perspective.

Keith W. Donahoe, The Model Rules and the Government Lawyer, a Sword or Shield? A Response to the D.C. Bar Special Committee on Government Lawyers and the Model Rules of Professional Conduct [*]

2 Geo. J. Legal Ethics 987 (1989)

The D.C. Bar's Special Committee on Government Lawyers and the Federal Bar Association's Professional Ethics Committee both decided that the government lawyer's client should be the agency for which he works. However, these committees sacrificed the high ideals of the Model Rules for a practical solution. To consider the agency for which the lawyer works as his client is a neat and tidy solution. Unfortunately, this definition undermines the purpose for which the Model Rules were written.

The Model Rules were promulgated to guide an attorney confronted with a situation which pricks his conscience, and to hold him responsible to the general consensus of the profession if he has a conscience which never seems to be bothered. The Model Rules were written for the unusual situation, not the average one. They were not written, for example, for an attorney retained by a man for the purpose of preparing a general will, but rather for an attorney retained by a ninety-year-old friend-of-the-family for the purpose of writing his will with the attorney as sole beneficiary. The Model Rules exist to help the attorney avoid this situation and to hold him accountable if he does not.

The D.C. Bar Committee established a general rule of thumb to provide guidance to the government lawyer as to who his client is when applying the Model Rules. It also noted the unique nature of the government lawyer's attorney-client relationship and the presence of various constraints upon the government attorney independent of the bar's disciplinary authority. It maintained that a general rule which gave guidance to the attorney in his daily routine was necessary and exceptions could be made for any unusual occurrences. This, however, is contrary to the previously stated purpose of the Model Rules.

Just as the human condition often attempts to force general rules across wide areas of application where they do not apply, commentators and committees too often ignore or minimize the unique position of the government attorney when attempting to apply the Model Rules to his situation. The government lawyer is very different from his corporate cousin. In 1910, Justice Brandeis pointed out the uniqueness of government service during the investigation into possible wrongdoing involving Secretary Ballinger. After Secretary Ballinger complained of the disloyalty of men in his department, Brandeis asked him:

> Well, now, did it ever occur to you, Mr. Secretary, that this supposed lack of loyalty, or, putting it another way, that the personal loyalty of one in public service to a superior or to an associate might involve disloyalty to 99,000,000 people?

One has only to read the accounts written by attorneys who have spent substantial portions of their careers in state attorney's offices or among one of the many legal positions in the federal government to comprehend these vast differences.

One such account expressed the point more vividly than the rest. The Honorable Jack B. Weinstein, Chief Judge of the United States District Court for the Eastern District of New York, was a former County Attorney for Nassau County, New York. Shortly after becoming County Attorney, he was presented with a proposed settlement in a condemnation case. It was an offer which represented about one-third of the appraised value of the land involved. Now, if Judge Weinstein, as a County Attorney, was simply representing the interests of the county, his job would be to get the lowest possible settlement for the land. The privately retained attorney of the condemnees, on the other hand, would be attempting to get the highest possible settlement from the county. This is how the system is supposed to work, or is it?

After further inquiry, Judge Weinstein discovered that the condemnees were not represented by an attorney. He called them and learned they were an elderly couple who had held the land for many years and had no idea of its true value. He found himself faced with a dilemma. As a County Attorney his job was to negotiate for the lowest possible settlement; however, he felt it was wrong to pay the couple less than the land was worth. He felt his obligations to the county did not include taking advantage of the couple's ignorance. Most attorneys would agree that Judge Weinstein had an obligation to work for a just result even if that meant convincing the couple of the real value of their property to the detriment of the county. However, do the Model Rules require this result? Under the D.C. Bar Committee's finding, Judge Weinstein's client would be the county. Thus, he would have been required to do no more than reach a settlement acceptable to the county. This is an instance where Judge Fahy's remark that the government attorney is the "conscience of the Government" comes alive.

What possible good can come of a government that puts its interests above those of its people? For if the Nassau County government is a servant of its people, then so is Judge Weinstein, and his obligations should run not to the county, but to the people. Thus, for the purposes of the Model Rules, his client should be the public interest. That is the only way the Model Rules will reflect the true consensus of the profession's conscience.

Another glaring example of the unsoundness of the D.C. Bar Committee's findings is in its applicability to the Justice Department. For the same reasons that a Nassau County attorney owes his allegiance to the people of the county and not the County government, the lawyers of the Justice Department have a duty to represent the interests of the people and not merely the concerns of the government. This duty has been recognized and practiced for many years by the Solicitor General's practice of "confessing error" before the Supreme Court. If, in representing the United States before the Supreme Court, the Solicitor General believes the position taken by the United States in the lower courts was in error, then he can "confess error," or in other words, state his belief to the Court that the decisions of the lower courts, although in the government's favor were incorrect. This practice virtually guarantees that the judgment will be against the United States. If the Solicitor General merely represented the interests of the United States government, this practice would never occur. It is obvious from its use that many Solicitor Generals have felt they owe a higher allegiance to the public interest and justice. Therefore in their eyes, their true client was the public interest and not merely the interests of the United States government. This was certainly the view of former Solicitor General Erwin Griswold who said:

> The Solicitor General's client in a particular case cannot be properly represented before the Supreme Court except from a broad point of view, taking into account all of the factors which affect sound government and the proper formulation and development of the law. In providing for the Solicitor General . . . to attend to the "interests of the United States" in litigation, the statutes have always been understood to mean the long-range interests of the United States, not simply in terms of its fisc, or its success in the particular litigation, but as a government, as a people.

The D.C. Bar Association should reflect this belief by holding the client of the government lawyer to be the public interest. To hold otherwise would emphasize the interests of the government over those of the people.

This point can be shown by the following hypothetical situation. Assume Mr. Smith is the senior legal advisor on the White House Counsel staff. An assistant to the head of the President's National Security Council, Mr. Myers, comes to see him. Mr. Myers explains that he was told in the interest of national security, and under the direct order of the President, to put together a team of experts who could break into an office and gather information without being discovered. He did as requested. He learned later that the real purpose of the break-ins was not to protect national security, but rather to gain damaging information about the managing editors of the New York Times and the Washington Post. The information was used to blackmail the papers from printing information implicating the administration in a monumental scandal. Mr. Myers believes the break-ins occurred over a month ago. It is his impression that the whole cabinet was involved. He is scared and wants Mr. Smith to tell him what to do.

Mr. Smith tried to convince Mr. Myers to release the story to the public. However, Mr. Myers was horrified at the suggestion. He tells Mr. Smith that he came to him only for legal advice, believing his story was protected by the attorney-client privilege. Mr. Smith has a difficult decision to make. What guidance will the Model Rules provide him?

If the D.C. Bar Association considered the agency which employed Mr. Smith to be his client under the Model Rules, then he could not disclose the story without violating the attorney-client privilege. Thus, the Model Rules would prove to be no help if he wished to expose the wrongdoing. They would, however, provide him with a very substantial defense if he decided to do nothing. Who could expect him to violate the attorney-client privilege? If the D.C. Bar considered the whole government to be his client under the Model Rules, then he could go to the Attorney General or the F.B.I. However, since Mr. Myers had led him to believe the whole cabinet was involved, the Model Rules would prove to be no great impetus in exposing the scandal. If the D.C. Bar considered his client to be the people of the United States or the "public interest," he would be given clear, unambiguous guidance that his obligations run to the people and the "public interest." He would be given the unobstructed opportunity to expose the scandal, and if he failed to do so, the Model Rules would not provide him with a shield to hide behind.

The legal profession must not forget that fifteen years ago it was publicly disgraced by the participation of many of its members in the Watergate affair. It was the public perception of the time that the Model Code had been designed to allow lawyers to hide behind it. An article in the New York Magazine used this as a headline for one of its stories:

> The point about lawyers . . . is that they are free to commit outrages against common morality and sense behind hallowed and intricate shields, cannons, and jargon.

The legal profession cannot afford to foster this opinion. If the profession claims that a government lawyer's client is the agency for whom he works, it provides him with a shield to hide behind if he fails to expose governmental wrongdoing. If the profession provides him with such a shield, after the next Watergate affair Congress may not be so generous when it writes the Model Rules itself.

Finally, the same reasons which the D.C. Bar Committee used to support its conclusion that the agency should be considered the client of the government attorney can be utilized to support the opposite conclusion. That the agency is usually a discrete entity with clearly identifiable lines of authority, and that the attorney's duties are usually defined by the agency and directed by the agency head are factors that show that the attorney does not need any further external constraints upon his daily routine. The internal constraints present in the agency's structure, and contained in various statutes and agency regulations are enough to constrain the day to day duties of the government attorney. It is the unusual case involving gross misconduct or acts of illegality in which the government attorney needs guidance. It is in such a case that the Committee's recommendations fail to provide any assistance.

Since the agency as client will not provide the guidance which the Model Rules require, the only other possible candidate besides the public interest is the government as a whole. The government as client is an attractive alternative for many of the same reasons as the agency. It is a discrete entity with clearly identifiable lines of authority. The attorney would be subject to the authority of his superiors, including those of all three branches. His duties and responsibilities would be defined and regulated by the government and through delegated authority by the agency for which he works. However, the government as client suffers from many of the same problems as that of the agency. It offers a practical solution to the problem by providing guidance to the attorney in his daily routine which is already provided by the internal controls inherent in the structure of government and various statutes and agency regulations. It gives the attorney more freedom in reporting wrongdoing within his agency, but it still leaves the attorney's ultimate responsibility misguided. His allegiance should not be to the government, but to the people.

V. Conclusion

The client of the government lawyer should be the public interest. That is the only way the true purpose of the Model Rules will be served. The government attorney will be constrained in his day to day actions by the internal structure of government and the presence of statutes and regulations guiding his conduct. A government attorney does not need the Model Rules to govern his daily routine. On any given day he does not consider violating the confidence of his superiors. In this practical sense, his daily client is his superior. However, it is not the purpose of the Model Rules to recognize the practical necessities of daily living. Their purpose is to uphold an ideal while providing a baseline from which to judge the actions of an attorney.

To allow the government attorney to claim that his immediate superior is his client would be to allow him to hide behind the Model Rules when confronted with an ethical violation. He would have been following his client's directions, and the Model Rules would have prevented any disclosure. If the public interest was considered the government lawyer's client, he would not have an affirmative obligation to report an ethical violation, but at least the Model Rules would permit him to do so. The D.C. Bar Committee concluded this would subject every superior in the government to the individual ethical beliefs of their lawyers, thereby destroying their trust in, and ability to use, the services of their attorneys.

Practical necessity should have shown the committee that this would not occur. An attorney is not going to run to the press because he disagrees with his superior on a policy matter. If he did, he would not be working in the government for long. His superior's authority to fire him is a sufficient constraint upon the attorney from acting too quickly. Before a government attorney takes a matter to the public, he will have to balance the gravity of the wrongdoing against the risk of being fired for crying wolf. Even the Federal Bar Association's Opinion requires him to do this. Defining the government attorney's client as the public interest would allow an attorney with knowledge of gross misconduct or illegalities to bring them to the attention of the proper authorities or the press. Congress has expressed its desire to facilitate the exposition of governmental wrongdoings; the legal profession should not do otherwise under the guise of legal ethics.

The Model Rules should be interpreted to apply where they are needed the most—in cases of corruption or clear illegality. To accomplish this without making specific exceptions to unenforced general rules is to consider the client of the government lawyer to be the public interest. The holdings of the D.C. Bar Committee and the Federal Bar Committee do not go far enough. If the government attorney's client were the public interest, the Model Rules would permit him to take an issue beyond his immediate superiors when he felt it was necessary. To interpret the Model Rules otherwise will restrain the attorney from defending the public interest while protecting him if he fails to expose the illegality. If the Model Rules are an attempt by the legal profession to achieve greater overall justice, as they in fact should be, then they must be used as a sword and not as a shield.

The question of who is the government lawyer's client takes on a new dimension in the context of intragovernmental debate, particularly that of an independent counsel. The following excerpt considers who has an attorney-client privilege with the government lawyer.

Michael Stokes Paulsen, Who "Owns" the Government Attorney-Client Privilege? [*]

83 Minn. L. Rev. 473 (1998)

. . . My thesis in this article is that the United States government possesses, as a matter of common law, the same attorney-client privilege that exists for a corporation or other organizational entity. That privilege extends to communications made by subordinate officers or employees of the government to the government attorney, for purposes of enabling the attorney to give legal advice to the government, as an organization. It is, however, the entity—the United States government—and not the individual making the communication, that is the client. Joint representation of the government as an organization and the individual government officer is, and should be, strongly disfavored on conflict-of-interest grounds. Typically, in the corporate context, present management controls the decision whether to invoke or waive the privilege, and the same should hold true with respect to the government's (that is, the executive's) attorney-client privilege. Under Article II of the Constitution, the President is the Chief Executive Officer of USA, Inc., and thus, ordinarily, controls the privilege.

But the issue becomes more problematic in the context of assertion of the privilege against an Independent Counsel investigating executive branch officials. We live today in a legal and political regime under which one or more Independent Counsel frequently exercise a portion of the control over the law-execution function of the United States government. Since *Morrison v. Olson*—and, arguably, ever

*Reprinted with permission. © Minnesota Law Review 1998.

since *United States v. Nixon*—the executive branch of the United States government has, from time to time, been subjected to divided executive management.

... In 1997, the United States Court of Appeals for the Eighth Circuit, in the innocuously-titled but hugely important case of In re Grand Jury Subpoena Duces Tecum (denied review under the more provocative, divided-executive caption of *Office of the President v. Office of Independent Counsel*), considered a claim by the Clinton White House of attorney-client privilege against a grand jury subpoena issued in connection with the investigation of Whitewater Independent Counsel Kenneth Starr. The subpoena and the claim of privilege concerned notes taken by attorneys in the Office of Counsel to the President (popularly known as "White House Counsel") of meetings with the President's wife, Hillary Rodham Clinton, and her privately-retained personal counsel during breaks at Mrs. Clinton's grand jury testimony concerning the mysterious disappearance and reappearance of Rose Law Firm billing records from the White House residence. The grand jury subpoena also sought White House Counsel notes of conversations with Mrs. Clinton concerning her actions following the suicide of White House Deputy Counsel Vincent Foster in 1993. The White House abandoned an earlier claim of "executive privilege" with respect to the notes. The Eighth Circuit's controversial opinion rejected, by vote of 2-1, the claim of executive branch attorney-client privilege as against an Independent Counsel conducting a federal criminal investigation, on the ground that the privilege simply does not exist in such a context.

In 1998, in a dramatic series of events, the D.C. Circuit considered essentially the same issue in a slightly different factual context. In re Lindsey initially involved claims by Deputy White House Counsel Bruce Lindsey of both executive privilege and governmental attorney-client privilege as the basis for refusing to answer grand jury inquiries about his conversations with President Bill Clinton and others, concerning President Clinton's possible unlawful conduct, and the White House's responses to legal proceedings investigating such conduct, on a wide range of matters—most notoriously, the possibility that President Clinton committed perjury and obstruction of justice in connection with the Paula Jones sexual harassment civil litigation, in which Clinton was a defendant.

... Like the Eighth Circuit before it, a divided panel of the D.C. Circuit held that considerations of public policy did not warrant recognition of a governmental attorney-client privilege as against a federal grand jury's criminal inquiry conducted by an Independent Counsel. ... The D.C. Circuit's decision in *Lindsey*, combined with the decision of another panel of the D.C. Circuit just weeks earlier, denying the Clinton administration's claim of a Secret Service "protective functions" testimonial privilege as against a federal criminal investigation and the refusal of Chief Justice Rehnquist to grant a stay in either case, was a contributing proximate cause of Clinton's being forced to acknowledge (in part) having publicly lied for over seven months about the conduct under investigation, and of having (at least) given deceptive testimony in his deposition in the Jones lawsuit. It is no exaggeration to say that the D.C. Circuit's rejection of a governmental attorney-client privilege that would permit Lindsey to refuse to answer questions before a grand jury concerning Lindsey's conversations with President Clinton, was a significant factor in the series of events leading to exposure of presidential misconduct in office — exposure that, as this article goes to press, may lead to President Clinton's impeachment or resignation. In re Grand Jury Subpoena Duces Tecum and In re Lindsey provide useful and important vehicles for considering the question of who controls — who "owns" — the government's attorney-client privilege, both generally and in the special context of an Independent Counsel investigation. . . . The D.C. Circuit's judgment, like the Eighth Circuit's, ultimately rests on the debatable policy judgment that the government's attorney-client privilege ought not to apply intra-government, against federal criminal grand jury proceedings, and that the chilling effect of its absence in that context would not have serious detrimental effects on legitimate governmental deliberations involving the need for legal counsel (or, at least, would have no more serious detrimental effects than does the absence of executive privilege, under *Nixon*).

Despite weaknesses in analysis, both courts' conclusions are nonetheless correct, not for mere "policy" reasons, but because of the unique situation of federal Independent Counsel investigations in a post-*Morrison* constitutional world. Control of the attorney-client privilege of USA, Inc. is greatly affected by the "corporate" governance structure of USA, Inc., which in turn is a function of the constitutional law of Article II. In a post-*Morrison* world, the issue presented by assertions of "executive attorney-client privilege" as against an Independent Counsel acting within the sphere of his assigned jurisdiction, is analogous to the privilege issue presented when management of a corporation has passed into the hands of a trustee or successor, or when a shareholder's derivative suit makes a threshold showing of "good cause" to believe that management has violated a duty to the corporation. In the former case, control of the corporation — and thus control of the privilege — has passed into the hands of new management, and former management's claims of privilege on behalf of the corporation are without effect. In the latter case, a corporate constituent or beneficiary that has made a sufficient showing of a likely violation by present management of a fiduciary obligation to the corporation, is provided with access to information that would otherwise fall within the corporation's attorney-client privilege, for the limited purposes of the litigation challenging present management's conduct. Application of these doctrines, well-accepted in the corporate context, to the analogous situation of an Independent Counsel investigation of possible federal criminal wrongdoing involving executive branch officials, friends, and intimate associates, yields the conclusion that, in the context of such an investigation, the Independent Counsel, not the President of the United States, controls the decision to invoke or waive the United States government's attorney-client privilege.

. . . The constitutional principles of a unitary executive and of presidential executive supremacy are set forth clearly — one would think unmistakably — in the text of Article II of the Constitution. Article II of the Constitution vests the executive power, in its entirety, in "a President of the United States." . . . Unfortunately, the principle of presidential executive supremacy within a unitary executive branch was badly wounded in *United States v. Nixon*, was mugged and left for dead in *Morrison v. Olson*, and, as a consequence, probably will not rise again.

Taken together, *Nixon* and *Morrison* stand for the proposition that the President of the United States is not constitutionally entitled to the final word as to the interest of the executive branch concerning issues arising in a federal criminal prosecution within the jurisdiction of an independent counsel; and that such a limitation on presidential executive supremacy does not violate Article II of the Constitution, as construed by the Supreme Court. . . . Rather, in the context of an Independent Counsel investigation, the Article II "executive power" — the management of the United States Government — is divided, uneasily and awkwardly from a constitutional standpoint, between the elected Chief Executive of the United States (CEO) and an independent ombudsman/trustee/investigator who possesses her own jurisdiction and who is not accountable to the CEO for her exercise of the executive power within that jurisdiction (except under the narrowest of circumstances). She is subject to the supervision only of the panel of "outside directors" (the special three-judge panel of the D.C. Circuit) who appointed her (once the President, through the Attorney General, acquiesces in the need for an appointment to be made).

. . . How does this constitutional restructuring of the Article II branch of government affect an executive branch attorney's duties of confidentiality toward his governmental "client"? How does it affect the attorney-client privilege of the United States of America (that is, the executive branch)?

Part of the answer to these questions lies in answering the question of just who is the "client" of a governmental attorney in the first place. In the In re Grand Jury Subpoena Duces Tecum case, the Eighth Circuit spoke at length about the issue of whether "The White House" possesses an attorney-client privilege, apparently assuming that "The White House" is a distinct legal entity with the capability of being a "client" with its own attorney-client relationship separate and apart from that of the United States government as a whole, and likewise capable of possessing an attorney-client privilege of its own — separate and apart from (and therefore, implicitly, assertable against) — the United States government as a whole, or some other agency or separable "entity" within it.

Such an implication is badly misleading. Nomenclature matters to clear-headed analysis, especially in identifying exactly who is "the client" of an attorney representing a corporate or other institutional entity in an organizational capacity, or in some other "triangular" legal relationship. The Eighth Circuit's sloppiness on this score affects its whole opinion, and it is worth pausing to get this point right. (The D.C. Circuit, as I explain below, did get this point right.)

Does an attorney working in the White House Counsel's office represent (a) Bill Clinton, personally; (b) the President of the United States (POTUS); (c) "the White House" (that is, as an agency within the executive branch); (d) the United States of America, or "USA, Inc." (that is, the United States government, as embodied in its executive branch); or (e) "We the People of the United States" in some rarified meta-institutional sense?

The answer that seems most appropriate, as a matter of constitutional law — that is, as a matter of the constitutive law of the legal entity in question — is "(d)": an attorney working for an agency within the executive branch represents the government of the United States of America (that is, the executive branch).

The chief executive officer of the entity is the President of the United States, but the attorney plainly does not represent the purely personal, individual interests of the present occupant of the office of President of the United States (so answer "(a)" is clearly wrong). Nor does the attorney represent "the White House" as a legal personage or as an "agency" with a distinctive legal identity in its own right. It is clear, as a matter of constitutional structure, that "the White House" is not an agency or entity separate and apart from the United States government. The "unitary executive" principle continues to hold true as the organizing structure of Article II to the extent not impaired by judicially-validated departures from that structure in specific instances (like the Independent Counsel), so that an attorney for one agency or division within the Executive Branch ultimately has as his or her client the Executive Branch of the U.S. government.

The fact that an attorney's *job responsibilities* may concern only a particular agency does not alter the fact that the attorney's client is the United States of America, not the agency, and that it is to that ultimate client that the attorney's duties and obligations run, just as an attorney working within a particular department of a corporation probably (depending on the corporation's charter, bylaws and procedures) has as his or her client the corporation as a whole, and not the department or division that is the focus of the attorney's legal work for the corporation. Thus, a government lawyer in the Treasury Department has, as his or her client, not the Treasury Department or the Secretary of the Treasury, but the executive branch of the United States government — which remains a unitary executive, except to the extent altered by *Morrison*. Answer "(c)" — "the White House" — the Eighth Circuit's apparent conception, is thus plainly wrong. The D.C. Circuit's opinion in In re Lindsey avoids the Eighth Circuit's conceptual sloppiness about whom the government attorney represents. From the outset, the D.C. Circuit's opinion notes that posing the question presented properly — may a federal government attorney refuse to answer questions in a federal grand jury investigation concerning possible criminal conduct by federal officials? — leads unavoidably to a negative answer, for the simple reason that "the Office of the President is a part of the federal government, consisting of government employees doing government business."

That is the key first step. The government lawyer's client is not an individual or a subcomponent office within the government. The client is the United States government — that is, the executive branch. Under Article II of the Constitution, one can almost say that the President is the executive branch, making "(b)" — White House Counsel lawyers represent the President of the United States (POTUS) — the least-wrong wrong answer. More precisely, though, the President possesses the entirety of the constitutional power of the executive branch under Article II, and thus determines and speaks for the interests of the United States government as an entity (subject, of course, to the exceptions carved out of Article II by the Supreme

Court in *Morrison*). In corporate terms, the President is a CEO who is not answerable to a separate Board of Directors, and who serves a term of years by virtue of his election. He is removable only by the process of impeachment, a decision that lies within the province of an entirely separate branch of government that otherwise is constitutionally forbidden from exercising direct control of the executive management of the United States government. By virtue of separation of powers, and the checks and balances that result from the interaction of the in independent and shared powers of each branch, Congress possesses important practical and political checks on the President's manner of exercise of the executive power; but Congress cannot itself acquire or subsume the executive power.

. . . The constitutional analysis frames the question of who controls the government's attorney-client privilege, but it does not itself answer the question. To say that the President does not have exclusive control over the executive power of the United States in an Independent Counsel proceeding is not to say that the Independent Counsel does have exclusive control in such matters, and that such control extends to control of the privilege. Such a claim would be too strong, in light of the holding in *United States v. Nixon*. *Nixon* did not hold that the President had transferred to the special prosecutor the power to decide whether executive privilege should apply in a particular instance; it held that the special prosecutor, by virtue of the assignment to him of executive prosecutorial power within a prescribed sphere, could contest the President's assertion of a privilege (and that such a contest over whose claimed interest better represented the interests of the United States government in this matter was a "justiciable controversy" susceptible of judicial resolution, within the traditional context of a motion to enforce a subpoena). The question framed by In re Grand Jury Subpoena Duces Tecum and In re Lindsey is similar: who speaks for the interests of the United States in asserting or waiving governmental attorney-client privilege, in the context of a federal grand jury investigation of high executive branch officials conducted by an Independent Counsel?

. . . Institutional attorney-client privilege is a distinct claim, having rather little to do with the fact that the particular institution in question is the United States government. (That fact is relevant to the question of the particular "corporate officer" who controls the decision whether to invoke the privilege, but not the question of whether the privilege exists and what it covers.) It is, rather, the corporate analogy of the *Upjohn* case that is the correct one. *Upjohn* involved the claim by a corporation, responding to an IRS summons, to attorney-client privilege with respect to communications made by subordinate officers or employees (including persons outside the management or "control group" of the company) to corporate counsel, at the direction of management, in order to enable corporate counsel to give legal advice to the corporation. The United States Supreme Court recognized the privilege as embracing such communications, and denied enforcement of the IRS summons.

. . . [T]he D.C. Circuit in In re Lindsey embraced the Upjohn corporate privilege analogy in the course of rejecting President Clinton's claim of governmental attorney-client privilege with respect to his conversations with his Deputy White House Counsel (and long-time confidant) Bruce Lindsey. The D.C. Circuit's opinion, however, addressed the corporate analogy only obliquely, as part of its policy balancing of the costs and benefits of recognizing the privilege in the context of a federal criminal investigation of federal officials, not as a point central to the analysis. The D.C. Circuit's opinion, while avoiding some of the problems with the Eighth Circuit's analysis, likewise focused primarily on whether "reason and experience" — that is, policy — support recognition of the common law attorney-client privilege in this distinctive context.

. . . Like the Eighth Circuit, the D.C. Circuit in In re Lindsey conceived of the question as whether government attorney-client privilege should exist in the first place, in this particular context. The difference is subtle, but potentially important, for while the D.C. Circuit's ultimate conclusion is sound, to the extent its holding rests on questions of policy and judgment rather than on the executive branch governance structure that exists as a matter of law in a post-*Morrison* constitutional world, the holding is vulnerable. Reasonable minds can differ as to the policy question of whether government officials should possess an attorney-client privilege covering communications to government lawyers for purposes of obtaining (presumably) legitimate legal advice, as against a federal grand jury inquiry (just as private parties consulting with private lawyers do). But the question of control over the privilege — the power to waive or override it — is a question not of judgment but of analysis and application of the corporate bylaws and statutes of USA, Inc., to ascertain how the lines of authority are drawn concerning this matter.

. . . Under *Upjohn*, the attorney-client privilege of a corporation extends not only to communications between corporate officers and corporate counsel, for purposes of obtaining legal advice for the corporation, but also to communications from lower echelon employees to counsel for the corporation made for such purpose, concerning matters within the scope of the employee's duties for the entity. Clearly, communications from President Clinton, as CEO of USA, Inc., to legal counsel for the United States (be it White House Counsel, the Attorney General, or another government lawyer), are covered by the *Upjohn* formulation. Although Hillary Clinton is technically neither an "officer" nor an "employee" of the executive branch (at least not for all purposes), as a factual matter she probably has the type of quasi-agency relationship to the United States government that nonetheless brings her statements to "corporate" counsel for the government within the ambit of *Upjohn*. If the *Upjohn* privilege applies in the government context, Mrs. Clinton's statements concerning incidents involving herself and federal personnel occurring in the federal workplace are likely covered by the government's attorney-client privilege.

Upjohn might initially appear to be a strong case for the White House, for it is well accepted that present management of the corporation "owns" the privilege and thus possesses the prerogative to invoke or waive the privilege. In the governmental context, President Clinton and subordinate executive branch officials subject to his direction and control constitute the present management of USA, Inc. . . . Thus (the argument might go), if *Upjohn* applies to the federal government, the White House need not produce the notes (in the Hillary Clinton case) or the witness (in the *Lindsey* subpoena matter). Only if the requisites of the absolute privilege are not satisfied, or if the privilege has been waived, or if the communications are prima facie shown to have been made for the purpose of and in furtherance of the client's crime or fraud, would the privilege not apply to defeat the subpoenas.

Each of these premises appears to be correct. But the conclusion is still wrong, because the argument fails to take into account an additional well-recognized "exception" to the privilege in the organizational client context: the so-called Garner doctrine, named for the leading Fifth Circuit decision in *Garner v. Wolfinbarger*. As noted above, *Garner* addressed the problem that exists when a shareholder's derivative suit, brought (in theory) on behalf of the interests of the corporation, alleges a violation by present management of duties owed to the corporation as an entity. What happens in such a situation when present management asserts the attorney-client privilege of the entity against another constituent of the entity, as a defense to discovery or testimony concerning certain communications or documents?

The Fifth Circuit, observing that "when all is said and done management is not managing for itself," held that the principles that govern assertion of the corporation's privilege as against corporate outsiders do not necessarily govern with respect to shareholders to whom management owes a fiduciary duty. The court held that, while the corporation retained the privilege, the availability of the privilege to present management is "subject to the right of the stockholders to show cause why it should not be invoked in the particular instance." . . . The Fifth Circuit noted that traditional means of balancing such interests, including protective orders imposing confidentiality requirements on the shareholders, or in camera inspections, are available to trial judges considering such claims.

. . . The Garner doctrine is entirely distinct from the crime-fraud exception to the privilege (though they cover some of the same ground and thus might both be applicable in a given case). The crime-fraud exception, where it applies, negates the existence of the privilege. The Garner doctrine negates the exclusivity of present management's control of the privilege, as against other constituents of the entity who possess a legitimate claim to represent the interests of the entity. As one leading scholarly treatment explains it, the crime-fraud exception "may be too narrow for the purposes envisioned by Garner, which seeks to ensure the attorney-client privilege is asserted in the best interests of the organization rather than for the benefit of management. Garner is concerned with bad faith in asserting the privilege, not bad faith in communicating with counsel for an illegal purpose."

The distinction can be critical: the entity's attorney-client privilege is not forfeited under the crime-fraud exception just because the officer communicating with counsel for the entity sought or made use of the legal advice for an illegal purpose. Here is where the Eighth Circuit's awkward insight that "the White House" cannot commit a crime arguably comes in. An entity's attorney-client privilege is almost never lost because the officers who actually engaged in discussions with counsel did so for fraudulent or criminal purposes. The entity still possesses the privilege. It is up to present (or successor) management whether to waive the privilege (and hang the officer, so to speak) or to invoke it (to protect the officer). The decision to do the latter does not itself mean a crime or fraud is being committed by the entity, but it may well constitute a situation in which those invoking the privilege are not acting in the best interests of the entity.

... It follows, I submit, that within the context of an Independent Counsel investigation of members of present management of the United States government, including the President, it should almost always be the case that the Independent Counsel — not the President — that properly controls the decision of the United States whether to assert the attorney-client privilege of the United States as a limitation on the information available to a federal criminal investigation. Present management of the United States may not assert the governmental attorney-client privilege of the United States against a subpoena or other request for information submitted by a duly-appointed Independent Counsel acting within the scope of her jurisdiction on behalf of the United States.

... As long as *Nixon* and *Morrison* remain good law, the law of attorney-client privilege in the governmental context must accommodate the constitutional reality that the executive power of the United States — and thus control of the attorney-client privilege of the United States — is partially divested from the President of the United States. One needs new wineskins to hold the new wine. ...

———

Another setting in which the identity of the client is important involves government lawyers engaging in whistleblowing. The author of the following excerpt was herself a whistleblower while employed by the Department of Justice.

Jesselyn Radack, The Government Attorney-Whistleblower and the Rule of Confidentiality[*]

17 Geo. J. Legal Ethics 125 (2003)

The ethical dilemmas facing government attorneys ... who blow the whistle are confusing, complex and potentially perilous. On the one hand, statutes like the Whistleblower Protection Act ("WPA"), which will be a focus of this Article, encourage government employees, including lawyers, to "serve the public interest by assisting in the elimination of fraud, waste, abuse, and unnecessary Government expenditures." On the other hand, the American Bar Association ("ABA") *Model Rules of Professional Conduct ("Model Rules")*, until recently, forbade lawyers from revealing confidential information acquired during the course of representing a client, which could include the attorney's "supervisor in the department or agency, the agency itself, the statutory mission of the agency, the entire government of which that agency is part, and the public interest."

The government attorney who wanted to blow the whistle faced a seemingly impossible ethical dilemma between the competing considerations of keeping

*Reprinted with permission of the publisher, Georgetown Journal of Legal Ethics, © 2003.

inviolate the client's confidences and protecting society's interests in avoiding the substantial consequences of crime, mismanagement, fraud, waste, abuse, and danger to public health or safety. This dilemma, in which a lawyer must balance the needs of the client with her devotion to truth and justice, has been referred to variously as a "legal paradox," a "Hobson's choice," and a "Catch-22."

Recent scholarship on the restrictive Model Rule 1.6 has focused on the plight of securities lawyers, environmental lawyers, health lawyers and transactional lawyers, but not government attorney-whistleblowers. The seminal article on confidentiality and the government lawyer, Professor Roger Cramton's *The Lawyer as Whistleblower*, while required reading for any attorney-whistleblower, appeared in the *Georgetown Journal of Legal Ethics* more than a decade ago. There since has been a major overhaul of the *Model Rules* and amendments to the WPA that merit re-examination.

This Article submits that the ABA's new Ethics 2000 version of Model Rule 1.6, which broadens the exceptions to confidentiality, is a giant step towards easing the dilemma for government attorney-whistleblowers. . . . Finally, the Article argues that states should, at a minimum, adopt the new Rule 1.6, and bar committees should construe paragraph (b)(4) as applying to whistleblowers. Finally, the Article predicts that whistleblowing by government attorneys will increase as a result.

I.   A BRIEF HISTORY OF THE DUTY OF CONFIDENTIALITY

. . . In recent years, the standards for confidentiality have varied significantly, and sometimes contradictorily, from state to state. Forty-two states and the District of Columbia adopted some variation of the *Model Rules,* but only a handful of these have adhered to Model Rule 1.6 verbatim. "The modifications adopted by [the other] states range from dramatic rejections to minor adjustments." Six states still followed the old confidentiality exceptions of the predecessor Model Code DR 4-101, which was somewhat more expansive than the *Model Rules.*

Thirty-seven states allowed a lawyer to disclose confidential information to prevent a crime or fraud, but of those states, three allowed disclosure for criminal fraud only. Twenty-five states allowed disclosure for any crime, including criminal fraud. Six states allowed disclosure for both criminal and non-criminal fraud, while three allowed disclosure to prevent any crime, including criminal and non-criminal fraud. Four states actually *required* attorneys to report criminal fraud. Suffice it to say, Rule 1.6 was all over the map, literally and metaphorically, with the vast majority of states adopting confidentiality standards that were broader than what was permitted by the categorical prohibition of Rule 1.6.

In addition to the lack of uniformity in how states adopted Rule 1.6, there existed a general feeling that Rule 1.6 at best was "lagging behind changes in the profession and society generally," and at worst, was "radically out of step with the realities of the modern world." Finally, "Model Rule 1.6 reflects a strict interpretation of confidentiality that does not give an attorney much leverage when deciding when to disclose client information."

... In mid-1997, the ABA responded to the "hodgepodge assortment of state rules that will bewilder the most sophisticated and experienced multi-jurisdictional law practitioner" by appointing the "Ethics 2000 Commission" to review and propose revisions to the *Model Rules.*

... The new *Model Rules* now include the Ethics 2000 changes made in February 2002, as well as the Multijurisdictional Practice Commission and Ethics Committee changes from August 2002, which have been sent to the states for adoption into their professional codes.

... The most radical recommendations proposed by the Ethics 2000 Commission with regard to Rule 1.6 — the additions of an exception in order to prevent client crimes or frauds reasonably certain to cause substantial economic injury and an exception in order to rectify any injury that has already been caused by client behavior — ended up on the ABA House of Delegates' cutting room floor. It should be noted, however, that on August 12, 2003, although these two provisions did not make it into the Ethics 2000 Rule 1.6, the ABA House of Delegates, at the urging of the ABA Task Force on Corporate Responsibility, adopted them in order to complement the Sarbanes-Oxley Act of 2002 and new SEC rules.

... The changes broadened significantly the right to disclose client confidences.

... As revised, Rule 1.6 explicitly permits, but does not require, disclosure where it is required by law. By moving from a categorical mandate of silence to a more normative standard, the Rule is friendlier to attorney-whistleblowers. ...

III. WHISTLEBLOWER PROTECTION LAWS

"The guiding principle behind [whistleblower protection] law is the logic of disclosure. Without measures to ensure disclosure ... unless rights are provided and protected under the law, potential whistleblowers will often choose to remain silent." To the extent that the narrow disclosure restrictions of Rule 1.6 have been expanded, it should alleviate, in large part, most whistleblowers' fears about their ethical obligations concerning client confidentiality.

The WPA provides protection to federal government employees who blow the whistle on fraud, waste and abuse. Section 2302(b)(8) prohibits an agency official from taking an adverse personnel action against an employee as a reprisal for:

(A) any disclosure of information by an employee ... which the employee ... reasonably believes evidences —

(i) a violation of any law, rule, or regulation, or

(ii) gross mismanagement, a gross waste of funds, an abuse of authority, or a substantial and specific danger to public health or safety ...

... The confidentiality exceptions to the old Rule 1.6 posed an irreconcilable conflict for government attorney-whistleblowers because the exceptions were much stricter and permitted disclosure only for self-defense or "to prevent the client from committing a criminal act ... likely to result in imminent death or substantial bodily harm." The whistleblower protections covered a broader category of disclosure for health and safety dangers; unlawful behavior; and fraud, waste and abuse. This created unpalatable choices for conscientious government attorneys between discipline for insubordination if they refused to go along with the wrongdoing, potential liability for knowingly sanctioning violations of the law if they acquiesced, or possible violation of the ethics rules, which could end not only their job, but their entire legal career, by blowing the whistle.

There is nothing in the WPA that excludes attorneys from whistleblower protection. "While government employees are protected from on-the-job retaliation for reporting wrongdoing under the whistleblower laws, these laws do not shield government attorneys from discipline and potential loss of their license for violating client confidentiality in order to protect the public from harm." If a government lawyer knows that the agency has violated the law or endangered the public, does he or she breach attorney-client confidentiality by disclosing the matter? If so, does such breach fall within an exception to Rule 1.6? Because Rule 1.6 undercuts the effectiveness of the WPA, legal scholars often fell back on the compelling moral arguments. "Even if revealing the information would violate a state's ethical rules, would a state bar committee discipline a lawyer for [blowing the whistle]?" As Professor Cramton, the leading authority on this issue, noted:

> since no statute directly addresses the issue of public disclosures on the part of *lawyers* employed by the federal government, agency regulations requiring lawyer confidentiality appear to be overridden by the whistleblower protection provisions. That is, a covered lawyer who makes a public disclosure of information protected by the whistleblower provisions may not be subjected to retaliatory employment actions. The prohibition surely includes any effort by a federal agency to discipline a lawyer for a violation of professional duties of confidentiality. Although the whistleblower provisions deal expressly only with retaliatory actions of the employing agency, the application of professional discipline by a state disciplinary board is likely to be precluded.

Despite the logic and obvious moral appeal of broadening the scope of permissible disclosure under Rule 1.6 to be more compatible with laws like the WPA, government agencies and some state bar associations have behaved otherwise.

V. A Proposal

In most state bar codes, the government lawyer is treated the same as the lawyer in private practice. However, case law has long recognized that government attorneys face ethical obligations not shared by other lawyers. The classic and most frequently cited description of the "special" role of government lawyers comes from *Berger v. United States*. A government lawyer:

> is the representative not of an ordinary party to a controversy, but of a sovereignty [the United States] whose obligation to govern impartially is as compelling as its obligation to govern at all; and whose interest, therefore, in a criminal prosecution is not that it shall win a case, but that justice shall be done. As such, he is in a peculiar

and very definite sense the servant of the law, the twofold aim of which is that guilt shall not escape or innocence suffer.

The notion that government lawyers owe a higher duty to the public is not limited to the criminal context.

While the Supreme Court was speaking of government prosecutors in *Berger*, courts have suggested that the same principle applies with equal force to the government's civil lawyers.

. . . States should be encouraged to adopt the new Rule 1.6, and bar ethics committees should be encouraged to construe paragraph (b)(4) as applying to whistleblowers. Additionally, state bar codes should treat government lawyers differently from private counsel. Deciding to blow the whistle can be the single most important decision a lawyer ever makes. It should not be an ethical nightmare to serve the public good. It should not be a question of *whether* to blow the whistle, but of *how loudly* to blow it. Government lawyers who want to blow the whistle should no longer have to choose between their conscience and their career.

NOTE

The above excerpt considers the real life ramifications for a government lawyer who engages in "whistleblowing" and reveals potential client confidences. The author urges a broad interpretation of Rule 1.6 (b) and its application to government lawyers, in part calling upon the importance of protecting the public good. Could this whistleblowing "problem" for government lawyers be resolved by a different or more precise understanding of who is the client? The following excerpt from the classic article by Roger Cramton on whistleblowing and government lawyers (cited above by Radack) considers the client angle to this issue. Although Cramton's article is directed at protections available to the government lawyer who becomes a whistleblower, a necessary predicate to that discussion is the identity of the lawyer's client.

Roger C. Cramton, The Lawyer as Whistleblower: Confidentiality and the Government Lawyer [*]

5 Geo. J. Legal Ethics 291 (1989)

. . . In this unusual world, who is the government lawyer's client? The question has vexed decision-makers and commentators for many years. The possibilities include: (1) the public (2) the government as a whole (3) the branch of government in which the lawyer is employed (4) the particular agency or department in which the lawyer works and (5) the responsible officers who make decisions for the agency.

---

*Reprinted with permission of the publisher, Georgetown Journal of Legal Ethics, © 1991.

Although a scattering of support can be found for each possibility, the dispute has been primarily between a broader loyalty to "the public interest" or the government as a whole, on the one hand, and a more restricted vision of the government lawyer as the employee of a particular agency, on the other. With rare exceptions, the discussion has not taken full account of the array of constitutional and statutory obligations that override the simple issue of "who is the client?" The remainder of this part considers this question apart from the possible application of the whistleblower protections enacted in 1978 and expanded in 1989.

Normally, the identification of a lawyer-client relationship is a predicate to determining the lawyer's duties. Once a person is determined to be a lawyer's client, then the fiduciary and other obligations of a lawyer to that person attach: competence, confidentiality, diligence, loyalty (avoidance of conflict of interest), zeal and the like. However, the simplicity of this approach, in which duties flow inexorably from the existence of the lawyer-client relationship, belies the complexity of actual practice even in the case of private lawyers. A lawyer may owe certain duties to a person who is consulting the lawyer, even though both lawyer and prospective client are considering whether or not to establish the relationship. When the lawyer renders services that are intended to benefit or influence third persons with whom the client has a relationship, the third persons may be treated as client equivalents for certain purposes. When a lawyer represents a person with respect to a matter in which that person owes duties to a second person, such as when a lawyer represents a trustee, executor, or guardian, the lawyer may also have duties to those to whom the fiduciary is obligated. The lawyer's duty to avoid conflicts of interest may flow to persons who are not clients in any ordinary sense of the word. Thus the answer to whether or not a person or organization will be treated as a client depends on the purpose for which the inquiry is made.

Other factors must be borne in mind when considering who is the client of the government lawyer. Even more so than the lawyer who represents a large, publicly held corporation, the government lawyer must deal with a wide range of interests, constituencies and competing values. "A government lawyer serves the interests of many different entities: his supervisor in the department or agency, the agency itself, the statutory mission of the agency, the entire government of which that agency is part, and the public interest." These interests are not inchoate but are expressed in constitutional structure and duties, statutory command and regulatory obligations. The professional rules are drafted on the assumption that the normal case is one in which a lawyer is representing an individual client or an uncomplicated organization. Only in recent years has specific attention been given to the special problems that arise when a lawyer represents a complex organization.

For day-to-day operating purposes, the government lawyer may properly view as his or her client the particular agency by which the lawyer is employed. The Federal Bar Association proposed this rule of thumb in 1973, but immediately qualified it to include "those charged with [the agency's] administration insofar as they are engaged in the conduct of the public business." The inquiry then turns to when the responsible officers are no longer "engaged in the conduct of the public business." Fifteen years later, a special committee of the District of Columbia Bar reached a similar conclusion. An analysis of the public interest versus agency approach demonstrates the good sense of their conclusions.

A.   The Public Interest Approach

Some years ago, Judge Fahy argued that "because the government is a composite of the people[,] government counsel therefore has as a client the people as a whole." Under this approach, the government lawyer becomes "the maker of the conscience of the government." This approach has several serious drawbacks. First, the public interest approach would interfere with the government lawyer's ability to function effectively as counselor and adviser to government officials. Second, conceptions of the "public interest" vary significantly from one person to the next. Third, the public interest approach raises separation of powers concerns. In short, defining the government lawyer's client as the public interest would fail to provide any real guidance in regulating lawyers' conduct.

The public interest approach distances the government lawyer from the officials that must rely on the lawyer's legal advice. The D.C. Committee summarized the problems inherent in this aspect of the public interest approach:

> If a lawyer is to function effectively as a counselor and advisor to elected and appointed officials, those officials must not view the lawyer as some independent actor, liable at any time to arrive at some individualistic perception of the "public interest" and act accordingly. The governmental client, to be encouraged to use lawyers, must believe that the lawyer will represent the legitimate interests the governmental client seeks to advance, and not be influenced by some unique and personal vision of the "public interest."

Other commentators share the D.C. Committee's concern for preserving the efficacy of the relationship between agency officials and government lawyers. For example, Bruce Fein stated that "[n]either the Constitution nor the electorate has entrusted the government attorney with an independence to determine what policies are enlightened or advance the cause of justice, and to dedicate his legal talents to furthering his personal public policy desires." The underlying problem in the public interest approach derives from the government lawyer's discretion to fashion a personal and subjective notion of the public good.

The D.C. Committee also concluded that "the 'public interest' was too amorphous a standard to have practical utility in regulating lawyer conduct." As Professor Geoffrey Miller observed, "there are as many ideas of the 'public interest' as there are people who think about the subject." This aspect of the public interest approach simply has no place in a representative democracy. In effect, the public interest approach invites each government lawyer to analyze and define the public interest, a task that no individual lawyer can hope to perform on his own. Furthermore, a government lawyer who attempts to define the public interest "is not a lawyer representing a client but a lawyer representing herself."

Separation of powers concerns also weigh against adoption of the public interest approach. Suppose, for example, that a government lawyer refuses to participate in the creation of a program on the grounds that it violates Supreme Court precedent and lacks congressional authorization. He bases his refusal on a belief that he represents the government as a whole, and that his participation in such a program would disserve the judicial and legislative branches of government. The government lawyer's assumption, however, fails to take into account the fact that he operates "within a system of separation of powers and checks and balances." In such a system, "it is not the responsibility of an agency attorney to represent the interests of Congress or the Court." Instead, the constitutional system places a premium on "the institutional loyalty of its lawyers." The public interest approach threatens the separation of powers and fails to adequately protect this constitutional system.

B.   The Agency Approach

The Professional Ethics Committee of the Federal Bar Association and the D.C. Committee both endorsed the "agency as client" approach. The D.C. Committee emphasized that the agency approach would "provide bounds and give concrete meaning to the lawyer-client relationship in the government context." The D.C. Committee asserted that "identification of the client with the employing agency" fulfilled three purposes. First, it allowed a government lawyer, in the vast majority of situations, to clearly determine his or her duties and obligations. Second, it permitted agency officials to rely on the government lawyer "in the same way that a private client can rely on its private lawyer." Third, it allowed the D.C. Bar to subject all its members, no matter how employed, to its disciplinary rules. Adoption of the public interest approach, on the other hand, would not fulfill any of these purposes.

The D.C. Committee did not contend that the agency approach would answer every ethical question. It did suggest, however, that the agency approach provided a rule of thumb to guide the ethical conduct of government lawyers. The Federal Ethical Considerations (F.E.C.) adopted by the National Council of the Federal Bar Association in 1973 also support the agency approach. For example, F.E.C.-5-1 states, "[t]he immediate professional responsibility of the federal lawyer is to the department or agency in which he is employed, to be performed in light of the particular public interest function of the department or agency." Although F.E.C.-5-1 refers to the "public interest," it does not suggest that the government lawyer must defer to the "public interest function" of the agency. Any other conclusion would "lead to a government of lawyers, not of laws, a result as objectionable as a government of people, not of law."

C.   A Structural Approach

The simple rule of thumb that "the employing agency should in normal circumstances be considered the client of the government lawyer" offers useful guidance to government attorneys. For most day-to-day purposes, a government lawyer properly may consider the employing agency as the client. Responsible officials of that agency hire the lawyer, provide instructions and supervision, and make decisions concerning change or termination of employment. But the agency approach does not reflect the complex web of institutional arrangements, regulations, statutes, and constitutional commands that shape the government lawyer's actions in those situations in which they come into play. On some occasions, the general litigating authority of the Department of Justice may alter the responsibilities of the agency lawyer. Obligations to report wrongdoing to officials within and without the agency may override normal duties of confidentiality owed to the agency and its responsible officials. If the particular activity is subject to the direction of the President, and the President chooses to exercise authority, the head of the executive branch displaces the agency head as the authoritative architect of government policy. Discussion of some illustrative situations will clarify these points.

Assume that Charles Hughes works on the legal staff of a federal agency that administers a major federal program subsidizing private activity. In the course of providing legal advice on subsidy applications, he learns from the head of the agency that a particular application was approved ahead of many others because the applicant had plied the official with special favors, including an all-expenses paid trip to last year's Super Bowl.

Do duties of confidentiality prevent Hughes from disclosing this information to an appropriate law enforcement official within or outside his agency? The intuition that tells one that the answer must be "no" is correct. But reflect a minute on some potential difficulties in reaching this conclusion. If Hughes was a lawyer in private practice and an individual client, in seeking legal advice from him, had revealed information indicating the commission of a past crime, Hughes could not disclose the information without violating his professional obligations. A voluntary disclosure would violate the professional duty of confidentiality, and the attorney-client privilege would prevent the forced disclosure of the information by a tribunal authorized to summon evidence. If Hughes represented a private client who had bribed an official (other than the tribunal before whom the lawyer is representing the client), and this information was communicated to the lawyer during the course of representation, one of the stronger cases for confidentiality would forever seal the lawyer's lips (except to the extent that disclosure was in the client's interest and with the client's consent). Why is the situation different when Hughes receives the information as a government lawyer?

The short answer, of course, is that Hughes doesn't represent the officer in the latter's individual capacity. True, he may have been hired by the officer and be supervised by and somewhat dependent upon the officer. Yet Hughes works for an agency of the executive branch of the Government of the United States, not for an individual who temporarily occupies one of its offices. The officer should understand that; if he does not, Hughes should take early steps to relieve the officer of the false impression that Hughes is his personal lawyer. The situation is not unlike that of in-house counsel for a public corporation who learns from an officer of the corporation that the officer has violated duties owed to the corporation. The lawyer should take steps to protect the interest of the corporation, including disclosure to the highest authority within the organization, usually the board of directors, even though there is much personal loyalty and a longstanding relationship with the officer. The information or privilege is that of the corporation, not the officer, and the corporation's highest authorities may ultimately decide to disclose the information that Hughes has received.

As a federal lawyer, Hughes has statutory duties to report criminal misconduct to the head of his agency, and, if the agency head is involved, to the Attorney General. These duties would preempt the District of Columbia professional code if the latter purported to prohibit Hughes from disclosing the communication outside the agency in which he is employed (assuming that Hughes practices in the Washington, D.C., headquarters of his agency). There is no conflict, however, if the executive branch is viewed as the client when corrupt official behavior is involved. The duty of disclosure inside the organization does not stop at the boundaries of the agency. Federal law requires that illegality be reported to appropriate law enforcement officials, who are ultimately subject to presidential authority as head of the executive branch. Under this view, however, disclosure other than to appropriate law enforcement officers would not be professionally appropriate.

Consider, however, a second scenario. In this one Hughes is asked to assist the responsible agency officials in a course of action suggested or determined by a new administration. The proposed action — it could be promulgation of a legislative rule, a change of position in ongoing or frequent litigation or the major alteration or abandonment of a current federal program — is politically sensitive and raises substantial legal issues. At one end of the spectrum, the proposed action, in Hughes's view, is clearly illegal: unauthorized by statute, directly contrary to controlling court decisions or violative of well-established constitutional rights. At midpoint on the spectrum, it is of uncertain legality, but plausible legal arguments can be made on its behalf. Toward the other end of the spectrum, it is a legal option available to the agency, but strong policy arguments can be made against it. Should Hughes, who shares the policy objections against the proposed action, do legal work on the proposal? May he seek to mobilize political support against the proposal by disclosing the agency's plans or its legal strategy?

If an individual client asked Hughes to do legal work under these varying circumstances, Hughes's professional obligations would be fairly clear. Hughes could exercise his choice as to whether to undertake the representation, and his dislike for the cause could be an important or controlling factor in his decision. If the proposed action was clearly illegal (one end of the spectrum), or the lawsuit involved a frivolous claim or defense and the client did not have a good faith basis for arguing for a change in the law, Hughes would be required to refuse assistance. If the proposal is not clearly illegal, however, Hughes would be free to undertake representation. Having done so, he would be required to put his personal feelings aside except as they might be brought to bear to persuade the client to alter the goals of representation or to assist in achieving the client's goals.

What difference does it make that Hughes is a full-time staff attorney for the agency undertaking the proposed action? Unless the agency accommodates a request to be assigned to other work, a request that in itself may have adverse effects on Hughes's future, Hughes is faced with a starker choice. If ordered to proceed, he must do so or resign. Even if the case for illegality is strong, the proposal was unlikely to be advanced unless there was something to be said for its legality. The reinterpretation of old law and the development of new law often flow from executive initiative founded on an electoral mandate. The leeway of a new President, armed with a victory at the polls, to argue for a change in the law, either by a reinterpretation of a statute or the distinguishing or overruling of prior court decisions, is substantial. American history is studded with instances in which Presidents attempted, often successfully, to move the law in a new direction.

If Hughes does undertake to work on the matter, to whom does he owe loyalty and confidentiality? Normally, unless the action is clearly illegal, Hughes is obliged to advance the goals of the agency and the executive branch. Only in the extreme case, where the proposal is indisputably illegal, do the professional rules and statutory obligations prohibit Hughes from providing legal assistance. Lawyers, as well as other federal employees, are obligated to uphold the Constitution and the laws of the United States. In addition, as a lawyer, Hughes may not assist in pursuing frivolous claims or defenses in litigation or assist in carrying out a crime or fraud. If clear illegality is involved, he may neither undertake representation nor continue after it is discovered. But a legal rule or litigation posture for which a good faith argument exists, even though there is some likelihood that it will be found to be illegal, is not a crime or fraud. And there are strong arguments in support of the position that the appropriate government policy-maker, not Hughes, should make the decision whether to test the legitimacy of the proposed action. We are a process-oriented society that has reached a high degree of agreement on the procedures and institutions by which political controversy should be resolved. The decision should be made by officials who are elected and appointed for that purpose rather than by staff lawyers.

More detail is needed about the particular problem and agency before a confident response can be given as to who is the appropriate decision maker. If rule-making or litigating authority has been delegated to an independent agency or to an officer who is substantially immunized from executive branch control, the agency or officer is Hughes's client. In the more usual situation in which ultimate policy in the executive branch is determined by the President, disclosure beyond the agency for which Hughes works should not be a problem. Assuming the (unlikely) situation in which an agency is secretly working against the policy approach of the President, disclosure of the agency's position to the White House is appropriate. Another variant of the same problem is a case in which the Attorney General has statutory authority over the litigation, but several agencies or departments have strong and divergent interests. The Department of Justice, for example, may represent the Environmental Protection Administration (EPA) in the action, but the responsibilities of the Departments of Energy and Transportation are affected and they take positions contrary to that of EPA. Lawyers in the Environmental Division of Justice who are working on the case should be free to communicate with each of the three agencies in an effort to formulate a common policy, obtain information or improve the government's overall litigating position. If the policy disagreement is a major political issue, the President may properly seek to make the decision. Any notion that a lawyer working for EPA would breach confidentiality by communicating facts, work product or litigating strategy to officials in any of the agencies or officials involved in the matter is unfounded. Only disclosure beyond the Executive Branch, or out of proper channels, would be violative of the professional duty of confidentiality. In this type of situation, and for this purpose, the executive branch, headed by the President, is best viewed as the lawyer's client.

NOTES

1.   Who is to enforce the federal bar disciplinary rules? Do these federal rules have only aspirational significance? Remember that the ABA's ethical rules have no legal force except as they may be adopted by the courts that admit lawyers to practice. Could federal agencies adopt special rules for agency lawyers? What if they conflict with the rules adopted by states in which the lawyers are admitted to the bar?

2.   Canon 5 of the Federal Ethical Considerations says: "The immediate professional responsibility of the federal lawyer is to the department or agency in which he is employed." Does that make it clear who is the client of a lawyer employed by the IRS? Is it the people of the United States? The President? The agency, such as the Treasury Department? A sub-agency, such as the Internal Revenue Service? The Secretary of the Treasury? The Commissioner of Internal Revenue? The Chief Counsel? The lawyer's immediate supervisor? It may be that the identity of the client depends on the position the lawyer occupies and the reason for asking the question. If the lawyer is a litigator working for District Counsel, she is much like any prosecutor. If the lawyer reports to an official with policymaking power, such as an attorney-advisor at the Treasury Department, she is like a lawyer in private practice providing counsel to a client.

3.   Another case study that starkly raises the issue "who is the client" revolved around the Reagan administration's decision to reverse its support for the authority of the IRS to deny tax-exempt status to racially segregated schools. The IRS had previously withdrawn the tax exemption of Bob Jones University on the ground that it practiced racial discrimination, a decision challenged by the University. Subsequently, the Attorney General, the Assistant Attorney General in charge of the Civil Rights Division, the Deputy Treasury Secretary, and, ultimately, the President approved a reversal in the government's position over the objection of the Commissioner and Chief Counsel of the IRS. Suppose the lawyer in the Solicitor General's office who is asked to sign the "Confession of Error" prefers not to do so? Is it relevant that she previously had filed documents with the Supreme Court stating a different position? Is it relevant that the IRS continues to believe in the legality of its

position? Are the lawyer's personal beliefs relevant (either as to the legal correctness of the IRS position or as to tax exemption for segregated schools generally)? Can the government lawyer simply "withdraw" from the matter? If the lawyer believes there is no merit to the government's revised position, is she free nevertheless to argue it in court? Is it appropriate for any of the lawyers involved to take policy or political considerations into account? The decision in the case is reported at 461 U.S. 574 (1983). A full report of the events is found in Administration's Change in Federal Policy Regarding the Tax Status of Racially Discriminatory Private Schools, 97th Cong., 2d Sess. (1982).

———

As the Poirier article noted, government lawyers are all subject to the ethical rules of the state in which they are admitted. Sometimes these rules are also imposed by agency directive. For example, the Internal Revenue Manual states that attorneys in the Office of Chief Counsel are required to be admitted to practice to a bar. Internal Revenue Manual 30.4.1.3.2.1. These attorneys are "bound by the professional codes of the states where they are admitted to the bar. Internal Revenue Manual 39.1.1.3 (08-11-2004). Moreover, Chief Counsel attorneys "must adhere to the letter and the spirit of the Tax Court Rules of Practice and Procedure, the ABA Model Rules of Professional Conduct, the Office of Government Ethics Standards of Ethical Conduct for Employees of the Executive Branch, the Department of Treasury Employee Rules of Conduct, and Supplemental Standards of Ethical Conduct for Employees of the Department of Treasury." Internal Revenue Manual 39.1.1.2 (08-11-2004). However, the manual also notes that the "Office of Chief Counsel will not discipline an attorney for a violation of these codes except to the extent a violation of same is also a violation of the [specified Treasury and other government employee handbooks, regulations and rules]. A violation of a professional code could likewise be a violation of the applicable ethics authorities if the violation of the code brought discredit upon the Service or the Treasury Department. Bringing discredit upon the Service or the Treasury Department could subject the attorney to discipline by the Office of Chief Counsel." Internal Revenue Service Manual 39.1.1.2 (08-11-2004).

Where the government lawyer is a prosecutor in a criminal case, there are additional responsibilities. Model Rule 3.8 provides:

Rule 3.8 Special Responsibilities of a Prosecutor
The prosecutor in a criminal case shall:

(a) refrain from prosecuting a charge that the prosecutor knows is not supported by probable cause;

(b) make reasonable efforts to assure that the accused has been advised of the right to, and the procedure for obtaining, counsel and has been given reasonable opportunity to obtain counsel;

(c) not seek to obtain from an unrepresented accused a waiver of important pretrial rights, such as the right to a preliminary hearing;

(d) make timely disclosure to the defense of all evidence or information known to the prosecutor that tends to negate the guilt of the accused or mitigates the offense, and, in connection with sentencing, disclose to the defense and to the tribunal all unprivileged mitigating information known to the prosecutor, except when the prosecutor is relieved of this responsibility by a protective order of the tribunal; and

(e) not subpoena a lawyer in a grand jury or other criminal proceeding to present evidence about a past or present client unless the prosecutor reasonably believes:

(1) the information sought is not protected from disclosure by any applicable privilege;

(2) the evidence sought is essential to the successful completion of an ongoing investigation or prosecution; and

(3) there is no other feasible alternative to obtain the information;

(f) except for statements that are necessary to inform the public of the nature and extent of the prosecutor's action and that serve a legitimate law enforcement purpose, refrain from making extrajudicial comments that have a substantial likelihood of heightening public condemnation of the accused and exercise reasonable care to prevent investigators, law enforcement personnel, employees or other persons assisting or associated with the prosecutor in a criminal case from making an extrajudicial statement that the prosecutor would be prohibited from making under Rule 3.6 or this Rule.

These responsibilities emerge from the prosecutor's role as a "minister of justice" and not simply as an advocate. Why should these duties apply only to the government prosecutor in a criminal case? Should similar responsibilities be placed on all government lawyers "to see that the [individual taxpayer] is accorded procedural justice" when he deals with the government?

2. Quality Standards for Positions Adopted by Government Lawyers

Recall that in Chapter 2, we discussed the statutory and ethical limits on positions that a taxpayer's lawyer may take on a tax return and in litigation. Are there any limitations on positions the government may take in a tax controversy? May the government take a position for which it does not have a reasonable basis? May the government take a position for which it believes there is less than a one-in-three chance it will prevail?

In Rev. Proc. 64-22, 1964-1 C.B. 689 (which continues to be cited by the government, see, e.g., Chief Counsel Notice 2000 CCN Lexis 52 (Oct. 25, 2000), the Service indicates it will not assert "a strained construction." Is this more or less helpful than "reasonable basis" or "realistic possibility of success"? In the tax context, if the government lawyer concludes that the taxpayer's position is correct, it is then his duty to bring that to the attention of his supervisors. If, however, the lawyer believes that the IRS position is meritorious, it is not only ethical but mandatory that he use the legal process to the fullest extent possible to advance the government's position. Presumably the "government," through its lawyers often decides not to use the available legal process to its fullest extent possible. When is that an appropriate decision on the part of the government lawyer? When would that decision breach the government lawyer's duty to the government client? May a government tax lawyer yield on part of a clearly meritorious position in order to induce a taxpayer to settle an unrelated tax issue on which the government's position is weaker?

An Invitational Conference on Professionalism held under the auspices of the American College of Tax Counsel, the ABA Tax Section, the AICPA, and other tax professional organizations considered standards applicable to the IRS. See Report on the Invitational Conference on Professionalism in Tax Practice, 11 Am. J. Tax Pol'y 369 (1994). Among the subjects discussed by the panelists at this conference was the minimum quality standard for litigation positions of the Service. The report states:

> A private practitioner panelist inquired what standard for the possibility of prevailing should apply to the Service's decision to litigate, presumably assuming that the issue fell above the meritorious-issue line necessary for a revenue agent to put the matter in play in the first instance.
>
> A Service panelist suggested there might be three responses. First, since the Service has the nuisance rule — it will not litigate a case with only nuisance value — if there is only a "minuscule" chance the Service can prevail it should not pursue the case. Second, cases that involve fact-sensitive issues, or mixed questions of fact and law, are inherently difficult to be tested by a standard because they require a judgment about the taxpayer's ability to carry its burden of proof, which may not be readily ascertainable in advance of trial. But third, where the question is one of law the Service should have a "reasonable basis . . . to believe that we have a chance of prevailing." Thus, the Service's attorney "should feel reasonably confident that [the] position is correct, and that [the Service has] a pretty good chance of prevailing."
>
> Admittedly, the Service panelist said in relation to the third case, it is very difficult to quantify that test but as a general proposition the panelist ventured "I don't think we have to have better than 50 percent . . . [W]e have to feel we have a pretty good shot at winning."

The Service panelist appears to place the minimum quality standard for government positions at a more-likely-than-not level, using "pretty good shot" as a description for that level of probability. However, the report indicates otherwise at a later point:

> One substantive matter that appeared to capture the attention of commentators was the discussion by some of the Service panelists of the standard employed by the Service for asserting positions in tax controversies: the pretty-good-shot standard. Some saw that as an example of comparative professionalism in the public and the private sector. Thus, one view was that the pretty-good-shot standard plainly stands above the private practitioners' standard for asserting a position, measured by non-frivolous or reasonable-basis tests, and is probably equivalent to the realistic possibility of success standard in the formal rules for both attorneys and CPAs.
>
> Another commentator, however, questioned whether the Service's pretty-good-shot standard did not amount to giving away the farm. Is it not the Service's acute

responsibility, he wondered, to assert positions in order to establish, refine, or clarify tax law doctrine in the proper process of forming tax policy through the judicial process? In his view, it is not enough to accept the Service as "stepping out ahead" on occasion; rather that should be accepted and encouraged as one of its prime responsibilities.

A third view was to the effect that the degree of the probability of success of prevailing, standing alone, is too general and therefore an inadequate test. Instead, the question for the Service in determining whether to proffer an issue should depend on the nature of the issue (fact, law, or mixed), the impact of the determination of the issue (establish precedent, resolve inconsistent positions, or important only as to a single taxpayer), and the level at which the determination is made (examining agent, National Office).

But the minimally defensible position question is one faced by each side. That is, from the side of the private practitioner, is it permissible to take a minimally defensible position merely to serve the client's immediate interest in tax deferral. Or, from the side of the Service, is it permissible to undertake a minimally defensible challenge only to move an item of income from the future to the nearby, or to downstream a deduction, when the thing at stake is only the time value of the money at issue. Does the possibility of interest on the item alone justify the minimal position?

At this point, the report seems to indicate that the "pretty good shot" quality standard is lower, perhaps equivalent to the realistic possibility standard, which, as discussed earlier, is generally construed at a one-in-three level. The one conclusion that the student may safely draw from this is that there exists today no real consensus on a minimum quality standard for government positions.

Does a government lawyer have any special responsibilities in using discovery and other potentially expensive and burdensome pretrial procedures? A comment to Model Rule 3.1 provides: "The advocate has a duty to use legal procedure for the fullest benefit of the client's cause, but also a duty not to abuse legal procedure." In the case of a federal agency, the cause or goal is to obtain the correct result under the substantive law, whether or not that includes winning the case. Can that goal ever permit a tactic designed to discourage the taxpayer from pursuing a meritorious claim?

PROBLEMS

A perceptive article on the nature of the ethical obligations of the government lawyer raises some interesting problems. Catherine J. Lanctot, The Duty of Zealous Advocacy and the Ethics of the Federal Government Lawyer: The Three Hardest Questions, 64 S. Cal. L. Rev. 951 (1991). The three situations posed by Professor Lanctot are set forth below. Although they are set in terms of the Social Security system, the issues are equally applicable to tax practice.

(1) A lawyer employed by the United States Department of Justice is assigned to handle a case filed in a federal district court against the Social Security Administration

("SSA"). Plaintiff is a widow who claims that the SSA has unlawfully denied her Social Security benefits. In her complaint, she asserts that the benefits are her only source of income and that without them she will be destitute. Upon reviewing the case, the government lawyer determines that the agency violated its own regulations in handling the claim and that, under its regulations, the plaintiff would have been entitled to Social Security benefits. The government lawyer also determines, however, that the statute of limitations has run and that the claim is time barred. May the government lawyer ethically assert the statute of limitations defense?

(2) The government lawyer then does further research and learns that some obscure quirk in the Social Security Act renders the statute of limitations inapplicable in this case. The government lawyer therefore does not raise the defense in the agency's joint motion for dismissal or, in the alternative, for summary judgment. Nevertheless, in ruling on the government's motions, the district court raises the statute of limitations sua sponte and erroneously dismisses the case. The government lawyer knows that the opposing counsel is extremely inexperienced in federal litigation and is unlikely to detect the error. Is the government lawyer ethically required to call the court's attention to its erroneous ruling?

(3) Assume the same facts, but without the issue of the statute of limitations. In her complaint, plaintiff has challenged not only the erroneous administrative decision denying her benefits, but also the constitutionality of the regulations upon which the decision was based, claiming a violation of her due process rights. The leading United States Supreme Court case on this issue virtually forecloses a successful defense on the merits, although the government lawyer determines that one could advance a non-frivolous argument attempting to distinguish the adverse precedent. The government lawyer recommends to agency officials that the SSA abandon its defense of these regulations because defeat on the constitutional issue is almost certain. The agency, however, is determined to press its defense of this important policy matter regardless of the chances of success. May the government lawyer ethically defend this case?

3.   Criminal Statutes of Concern to the Government Lawyer

Congress has imposed minimum standards of conduct on wide classes of government employees and has made a violation of these standards a crime. Several provisions that directly affect the government lawyer are reproduced below.

Compensation to Members of Congress, Officers, and Others in Matters Affecting the Government

18 U.S.C. §203 (2007)

(a) Whoever, otherwise than as provided by law for the proper discharge of official duties, directly or indirectly

(1) demands, seeks, receives, accepts, or agrees to receive or accept any compensation for any representational services, as agent or attorney, or otherwise, rendered or to be rendered either personally or by another

(A) at a time when such person is a Member of Congress, Member of Congress Elect, Delegate, Delegate Elect, Resident Commissioner, or Resident Commissioner Elect; or

(B) at a time when such person is an officer or employee or Federal judge of the United States in the executive, legislative, or judicial branch of the government, or in any agency of the United States, in relation to any proceeding, application, request for a ruling or other determination, contract, claim, controversy, charge, accusation arrest or other particular matter in which the United States is a party or has a direct and substantial interest, before any department, agency court, court-martial, officer, or any civil, military, or naval commission; or

(2) knowingly gives, promises, or offers any compensation for any such representational services rendered or to be rendered at a time when the person to whom the compensation is given, promised or offered, is or was such a Member, Member Elect, Delegate, Delegate Elect, Commissioner, Commissioner Elect, Federal judge, officer, or employee; shall be subject to the penalties set forth in section 216 of this title.

(b) Whoever, otherwise than as provided by law for the proper discharge of official duties, directly or indirectly

(1) demands, seeks, receives, accepts, or agrees to receive or accept any compensation for any representational services, as agent or attorney or otherwise, rendered or to be rendered either personally or by another at a time when such person is an officer or employee of the District of Columbia, in relation to any proceeding, application, request for a ruling or other determination, contract, claim, controversy, charge, accusation, arrest, or other particular matter in which the District of Columbia is a party or has a direct and substantial interest, before any department, agency, court, officer, or commissioner; or

(2) knowingly gives, promises, or offers any compensation for any such representation services rendered or to be rendered at a time when the person to whom the compensation is given, promised, or offered, is or was an officer of the District of Columbia, shall be subject to the penalties set forth in section 216 of this title.

(c) A special Government employee shall be subject to subsections (a) and (b) only in relation to a particular matter involving a specific party or parties

(1) in which such employee has at any time participated personally and substantially as a Government employee or as a special Government employee through decision, approval, disapproval, recommendation, the rendering of advice, investigation or otherwise; or

(2) which is pending in the department or agency of the Government in which such employee is serving except that paragraph (2) of this subsection shall not apply in the case of a special Government employee who has served in such department or agency no more than sixty days during the immediately preceding period of three hundred and sixty-five consecutive days.

NOTE

A "special government employee" includes a consultant (such as a law school professor). Why does subsection (c) lift the stricture of subsection (b) from a not-more-than-sixty-day consultant?

Activities of Officers and Employees in Claims Against and Other Matters Affecting the Government

18 U.S.C. §205 (2007)

(a) Whoever, being an officer or employee of the United States in the executive, legislative, or judicial branch of the government or in any agency of the United States, other than in the proper discharge of his official duties

(1) acts as agent or attorney for prosecuting any claim against the United States, or receives any gratuity, or any share of or interest in any such claim, in consideration of assistance in the prosecution of such claim; or

(2) acts as agent or attorney for anyone before any department, agency, court, court-martial, officer, or civil, military, or naval commission in connection with any covered matter in which the United States is a party or has a direct and substantial interest; shall be subject to the penalties set forth in section 216 of this title.

(b) Whoever, being an officer or employee of the District of Columbia or an officer or employee of the Office of the United States Attorney for the District of Columbia, otherwise than in the proper discharge of official duties

(1) acts as agent or attorney for prosecuting any claim against the District of Columbia, or receives any gratuity, or any share of or interest in any such claim in consideration of assistance in the prosecution of such claim; or

(2) acts as agent or attorney for anyone before any department, agency, court, officer, or commission in connection with any covered matter in which the District of Columbia is a party or has a direct and substantial interest; shall be subject to the penalties set forth in section 216 of this title.

(c) A special Government employee shall be subject to subsections (a) and (b) only in relation to a covered matter involving a specific party or parties

(1) in which he has at any time participated personally and substantially as a Government employee or special Government employee through decision, approval, disapproval, recommendation, the rendering of advice, investigation, or otherwise; or

(2) which is pending in the department or agency of the government in which he is serving.

Paragraph (2) shall not apply in the case of a special Government employee who has served in such department or agency no more than sixty days during the immediately preceding period of three hundred and sixty-five consecutive days. . . .

(h) For the purpose of this section, the term "covered matter" means any judicial or other proceeding, application, request for a ruling or other determination, contract, claim, controversy, investigation, charge, accusation, arrest, or other particular matter.

NOTE

Once again the not-more-than-sixty-day consultant is permitted greater latitude than the longer-term special government employee. Is that sound policy?

Acts Affecting a Personal Financial Interest
18 U.S.C. §208 (2007)

(a) Except as permitted by subsection (b) hereof, whoever, being an officer or employee of the executive branch of the United States Government, or of any independent agency of the United States, a Federal Reserve bank director, officer, or employee, or an officer or employee of the District of Columbia, including a special Government employee, participates personally and substantially as a Government officer or employee, through decision, approval, disapproval, recommendation, the rendering of advice, investigation, or otherwise, in a judicial or other proceeding, application, request for a ruling or other determination, contract, claim, controversy, charge, accusation, arrest, or other particular matter in which, to his knowledge, he, his spouse, minor child, general partner, organization in which he is serving as officer, director, trustee, general partner or employee, or any person or organization with whom he is negotiating or has any arrangement concerning prospective employment, has a financial interest — Shall be subject to the penalties set forth in section 216 of this title.

(b) Subsection (a) shall not apply —

(1) if the officer or employee first advises the Government official responsible for appointment to his or her position of the nature and circumstances of the judicial or other proceeding, application, request for a ruling or other determination, contract, claim, controversy, charge, accusation, arrest, or other particular matter and makes full disclosure of the financial interest and receives in advance a written determination made by such official that the interest is not so substantial as to be deemed likely to affect the integrity of the services which the Government may expect from such officer or employee;

(2) if, by regulation issued by the Director of the Office of Government Ethics, applicable to all or a portion of all officers and employees covered by this section, and published in the Federal Register, the financial interest has been exempted from the requirements of subsection (a) as being too remote or

too inconsequential to affect the integrity of the services of the Government officers or employees to which such regulation applies:

(3) in the case of a special Government employee serving on an advisory committee within the meaning of the Federal Advisory Committee Act (including an individual being considered for an appointment to such a position), the official responsible for the employee's appointment, after review of the financial disclosure report filed by the individual pursuant to the Ethics in Government Act of 1978, certifies in writing that the need for the individual's services outweighs the potential for a conflict of interest created by the financial interest involved . . .

PROBLEMS

1.   If an IRS attorney handling a matter relating to a particular corporate taxpayer, for instance, a request for a ruling, were to discuss the possibility of future employment with that corporation, would he violate 18 U.S.C. §208? Would he violate the section if he discussed employment with the law firm representing the taxpayer? See also Circular 230 §10.25, discussed below.

2.   An IRS attorney is consulted by field examination personnel who are considering an adjustment against a publicly held corporation. The adjustment would have a major impact on the financial condition of the company. The attorney advises those who consult him and his superiors that he owns stock in that company and that he is recusing himself from participation in the matter. In fact, the investment that he has is a substantial one, constituting the college fund for his three teenage daughters. Having learned of the potential impact of the IRS action on this company and the possible loss in value of its stock, can he now sell the stock before any adverse news becomes public? Would this be a violation of 18 U.S.C. §208? If not, are there any other considerations?

4.   *Ethical Restraints on the Former Government Lawyer Who Has Entered Private Practice*

When a government attorney leaves his public employment and moves into private practice, he is not free, as a matter of ethics or law, to represent a client in a matter in which he had substantial responsibility as a government lawyer. This is analogous, of course, to the standards considered in Chapter 3, relating to the lawyer's duties of loyalty and confidentiality to his client, duties that do not terminate at the end of the representation. The Model Code's ethical rule applicable to government lawyers is expressed in EC 9-3 and in DR 9-101(B). Model Rule 1.11(a) has generally adopted the prior standard of conduct. The legal rule is expressed in the form of a criminal sanction imposed by 18 U.S.C. §207. Circular 230 also addresses practice before the IRS by former government employees, their partners and associates.

The cornerstone federal statute dealing with disqualification of former government attorneys is 18 U.S.C. §207 (2007) (first enacted in 1962). As you read this section, keep in mind that it is a criminal statute, to be distinguished in that respect from the ethical rules, which follow, on the same subject.

Disqualification of Former Officers and Employees; Disqualification of Partners of Current Officers and Employees

18 U.S.C. §207 (2007)

(a) Restrictions on all officers and employees of the executive branch and certain other agencies.

(1) Permanent restrictions on representation on particular matters. — Any person who is an officer or employee (including any special Government employee) of the executive branch of the United States (including any independent agency of the United States), or of the District of Columbia, and who, after the termination of his or her service or employment with the United States or the District of Columbia, knowingly makes, with the intent to influence, any communication to or appearance before any officer or employee of any department, agency, court, or court-martial of the United States or the District of Columbia, on behalf of any other person (except the United States or the District of Columbia) in connection with a particular matter —

(A) in which the United States or the District of Columbia is a party or has a direct and substantial interest,

(B) in which the person participated personally and substantially as such officer or employee, and

(C) which involved a specific party or specific parties at the time of such participation, shall be punished as provided in section 216 of this title.

(2) Two-year restrictions concerning particular matters under official responsibility — Any person subject to the restrictions contained in paragraph (1) who, within two years after the termination of his or her service or employment with the United States or the District of Columbia, knowingly makes, with the intent to influence, any communication to or appearance before any officer or employee of any department, agency, court, or court-martial of the United States or the District of Columbia, on behalf of any other person (except the United States or the District of Columbia), in connection with a particular matter —

(A) in which the United States or the District of Columbia is a party or has a direct and substantial interest,

(B) which such person knows or reasonably should know was actually pending under his or her official responsibility as such officer or employee within a period of one year before the termination of his or her service or employment with the United States or the District of Columbia, and

(C) which involved a specific party or specific parties at the time it was so pending, shall be punished as provided in section 216 of this title.

(3) Clarification of restrictions — The restrictions contained in paragraphs (1) and (2) shall apply —

(A) in the case of an officer or employee of the executive branch of the United States (including any independent agency), only with respect to communications to or appearances before any officer or employee of any department, agency, court, or court-martial of the United States on behalf of any other person (except the United States), and only with respect to a matter in which the United States is a party or has a direct and substantial interest; and

(B) in the case of an officer or employee of the District of Columbia, only with respect to communications to or appearances before any officer or employee of any department, agency, or court of the District of Columbia on behalf of any other person (except the District of Columbia), and only with respect to a matter in which the District of Columbia is a party or has a direct and substantial interest.

(b) One-year restrictions on aiding or advising.

(1) In general. Any person who is a former officer or employee of the executive branch of the United States (including any independent agency) and is subject to the restrictions contained in subsection (a)(1), or any person who is a former officer or employee of the legislative branch or a former Member of Congress, who personally and substantially participated in any ongoing trade or treaty negotiation on behalf of the United States within the one-year period preceding the date on which his or her service or employment with the United States terminated, and who had access to information concerning such trade or treaty negotiation which is exempt from disclosure under section 552 of title 5, which is so designated by the appropriate department or agency, and which the person knew or should have known was so designated, shall not, on the basis of that information, knowingly represent, aid, or advise any other person (except the United States) concerning such ongoing trade or treaty negotiation for a period of one year after his or her service or employment with the United States terminates. Any person who violates this subsection shall be punished as provided in section 216 of this title. . . .

(c) One-year restrictions on certain senior personnel of the executive branch and independent agencies.

(1) Restrictions — In addition to the restrictions set forth in subsections (a) and (b), any person who is an officer or employee (including any special Government employee) of the executive branch of the United States (including an independent agency), who is referred to in paragraph (2), and who, within one year after the termination of his or her service or employment as such officer or employee, knowingly makes, with the intent to influence, any communication to or appearance before any officer or employee of the department or agency in which such person served within one year before such termination, on behalf of any other person (except the United States), in connection with any matter on which such person seeks official action by any officer or employee of such department or agency, shall be punished as provided in section 216 of this title.

(2) Persons to whom restrictions apply—

(A) Paragraph (1) shall apply to a person (other than a person subject to the restrictions of subsection (d))—

(i) employed at a rate of pay specified in or fixed according to subchapter II of chapter 53 of title 5,

(ii) employed in a position which is not referred to in clause (i) and for which that person is paid at a basic rate of pay which is equal to or greater than 86.5 percent of the rate of basic pay for level II of the Executive Schedule . . . ,

(iii) appointed by the President to a position under section 105(a)(2)(B) of title 3 or by the Vice President to a position under section 106(a)(1)(B) of title 3, or

(iv) employed in a position which is held by an active duty commissioned officer of the uniformed services who is serving in a grade or rank for which the pay grade (as specified in section 201 of title 37) is pay grade 0–7 or above. . . .

(B) Paragraph (1) shall not apply to a special Government employee who serves less than 60 days in the one-year period before his or her service or employment as such employee terminates.

(C) At the request of a department or agency, the Director of the Office of Government Ethics may waive the restrictions contained in paragraph (1) with respect to any position, or category of positions, referred to in clause (ii) or (iv) of subparagraph (A), in such department or agency if the Director determines that—

(i) the imposition of the restrictions with respect to such position or positions would create an undue hardship on the department or agency in obtaining qualified personnel to fill such position or positions, and

(ii) granting the waiver would not create the potential for use of undue influence or unfair advantage.

(d) Restrictions on very senior personnel of the executive branch and independent agencies.

(1) Restrictions—In addition to the restrictions set forth in subsections (a) and (b), any person who—

(A) serves in the position of Vice President of the United States,

(B) is employed in a position in the executive branch of the United States (including any independent agency) at a rate of pay payable for level I of the Executive Schedule or employed in a position in the Executive Office of the President at a rate of pay payable for level II of the Executive Schedule, or

(C) is appointed by the President to a position under section 105(a)(2)(A) of title 3 or by the Vice President to a position under section 106(a)(1)(A) of title 3, and who, within one year after the termination of that person's service in that position, knowingly makes, with the intent to influence, any communication to or appearance before any person described in paragraph (2), on behalf of any other person (except the United States), in connection with any matter on which such person seeks official action by any officer or employee of the executive branch of the United States, shall be punished as provided in section 216 of this title.

(2) Persons who may not be contacted—The persons referred to in paragraph (1) with respect to appearances or communications by a person in a position described in subparagraph (A), (B), or (C) of paragraph (1) are—

(A) any officer or employee of any department or agency in which such person served in such position within a period of 1 year before such person's service or employment with the United States government terminated, and

(B) any person appointed to a position in the executive branch which is listed in sections 5312, 5313, 5314, 5315, or 5316 of title 5.

(e) Restrictions on members of Congress and officers and employees of the legislative branch—

(1) Members of Congress and elected officers—

(A) Any person who is a Member of Congress or an elected officer of either House of Congress and who, within one year after that person leaves office, knowingly makes, with the intent to influence, any communication to or appearance before any of the persons described in subparagraph (B) or (C), on behalf of any other person (except the United States) in connection with any matter on which such former Member of Congress or elected officer seeks action by a Member, officer, or employee of either House of Congress, in his or her official capacity, shall be punished as provided in section 216 of this title.

(B) The persons referred to in subparagraph (A) with respect to appearances or communications by a former Member of Congress are any Member, officer, or employee of either House of Congress, and any employee of any other legislative office of the Congress.

(C) The persons referred to in subparagraph (A) with respect to appearances or communications by a former elected officer are any Member, officer, or employee of the House of Congress in which the elected officer served.

(2) Personal staff—

(A) Any person who is an employee of a Senator or an employee of a Member of the House of Representatives and who, within one year after the termination of that employment, knowingly makes, with the intent to influence, any communication to or appearance before any of the persons described in subparagraph (B), on behalf of any other person (except the United States) in connection with any matter on which such former employee seeks action by a Member, officer, or employee of either House of Congress, in his or her official capacity, shall be punished as provided in section 216 of this title.

(B) The persons referred to in subparagraph (A) with respect to appearances or communications by a person who is a former employee are the following:

(i) the Senator or Member of the House of Representatives for whom that person was an employee; and

(ii) any employee of that Senator or Member of the House of Representatives.

(3) Committee staff—Any person who is an employee of a committee of Congress and who, within one year after the termination of that person's employment on such committee, knowingly makes, with the intent to influence, any communication to or appearance before any person who is a member or an employee of that committee or who was a member of the committee in the year immediately prior to the termination of such person's employment by the committee, on behalf of any other person (except the United States) in connection with any matter on which such former employee seeks action by a Member, officer, or employee of either House of Congress, in his or her official capacity, shall be punished as provided in section 216 of this title.

(4) Leadership staff—

(A) Any person who is an employee on the leadership staff of the House of Representatives or an employee on the leadership staff of the Senate and who, within one year after the termination of that person's employment on such staff, knowingly makes, with the intent to influence, any communication to or appearance before any of the persons described in subparagraph (B), on behalf of any other person (except the United States) in connection with any matter on which such former employee seeks action by a member, officer, or employee of either House of Congress, in his or her official capacity, shall be punished as provided in section 216 of this title.

(B) The persons referred to in subparagraph (A) with respect to appearances or communications by a former employee are the following:

(i) in the case of a former employee on the leadership staff of the House of Representatives, those persons are any member of the leadership of the House of Representatives and any employee on the leadership staff of the House of Representatives; and

(ii) in the case of a former employee on the leadership staff of the Senate, those persons are any Member of the leadership of the Senate and any employee on the leadership staff of the Senate.

(5) Other legislative offices—

(A) Any person who is an employee of any other legislative office of the Congress and who, within one year after the termination of that person's employment in such office, knowingly makes, with the intent to influence, any communication to or appearance before any of the persons described in subparagraph (B), on behalf of any other person (except the United States) in connection with any matter on which such former employee seeks action by any officer or employee of such office, in his or her official capacity, shall be punished as provided in section 216 of this title.

(B) The persons referred to in subparagraph (A) with respect to appearances or communications by a former employee are the employees and officers of the former legislative office of the Congress of the former employee.

(6) Limitation on restrictions—

(A) The restrictions contained in paragraphs (2), (3), and (4) apply only to acts by a former employee who, for at least 60 days, in the aggregate, during the one-year period before that former employee's service as such employee terminated, was paid a rate of basic pay equal to or greater than an amount which is 75 percent of the basic rate of pay payable for a Member of the House of Congress in which such employee was employed.

(B) The restrictions contained in paragraph (5) apply only to acts by a former employee who, for at least 60 days, in the aggregate, during the one-year period before that former employee's service as such employee terminated, was employed in a position for which the rate of basic pay, exclusive of any locality-based pay adjustment under section 5302 of title 5 (or any comparable adjustment pursuant to interim authority of the President), is equal to or greater than the basic rate of pay payable for level 5 of the Executive Schedule. . . .

(i) Definitions. For purposes of this section—

(1) the term "officer or employee," when used to describe the person to whom a communication is made or before whom an appearance is made, with the intent to influence, shall include—

(A) in subsections (a), (c), and (d), the President and the Vice President; and

(B) in subsection (f), the President, the Vice President, and Members of Congress;

(2) the term "participated" means an action taken as an officer or employee through decision, approval, disapproval, recommendation, the rendering of advice, investigation, or other such action; and

(3) the term "particular matter" includes any investigation, application, request for a ruling or determination, rulemaking, contract, controversy, claim, charge, accusation, arrest, or judicial or other proceeding. . . .

(j) . . .

(6) Exception for testimony. Nothing in this section shall prevent an individual from giving testimony under oath, or from making statements required to be made under penalty of perjury. Notwithstanding the preceding sentence—

(A) a former officer or employee of the executive branch of the United States (including any independent agency) who is subject to the restrictions contained in subsection (a)(1) with respect to a particular matter may not, except pursuant to court order, serve as an expert witness for any other person (except the United States) in that matter; and

(B) a former officer or employee of the District of Columbia who is subject to the restrictions contained in subsection (a)(1) with respect to a particular matter may not, except pursuant to court order, serve as an expert witness for any other person (except the District of Columbia) in that matter.

(k)
(1)
(A) The President may grant a waiver of a restriction imposed by this section to any officer or employee described in paragraph (2) if the President determines and certifies in writing that it is in the public interest to grant the waiver and that the services of the officer or employee are critically needed for the benefit of the federal government. Not more than 25 officers and employees currently employed by the federal government at any one time may have been granted waivers under this paragraph.

(B)(i) A waiver granted under this paragraph to any person shall apply only with respect to activities engaged in by that person after that person's federal government employment is terminated and only to that person's employment at a government-owned, contractor-operated entity with which the person served as an officer or employee immediately before the person's federal government employment began . . .

———

The Model Rules impose ethical limitations on a government attorney who subsequently enters private practice:

Model Rule 1.11 Special Conflicts of Interest for Former and Current Government Officers and Employees

(a) Except as law may otherwise expressly permit, a lawyer who has formerly served as a public officer or employee of the government:

(1) Is subject to Rule 1.9(c); and

(2) shall not otherwise represent a client in connection with a matter in which the lawyer participated personally and substantially as a public officer or employee, unless the appropriate government agency gives its informed consent, confirmed in writing, to the representation.

(b) When a lawyer is disqualified from representation under paragraph (a), no lawyer in a firm with which that lawyer is associated may knowingly undertake or continue representation in such matter unless:

(1) the disqualified lawyer is timely screened from any participation in the matter and is apportioned no part of the fee therefrom; and

(2) written notice is promptly given to the appropriate government agency to enable it to ascertain compliance with the provisions of this rule.

(c) Except as law may otherwise expressly permit, a lawyer having information that the lawyer knows is confidential government information about a person acquired when the lawyer was a public officer or employee, may not represent a private client whose interests are adverse to that person in a matter in which the information could be used to the material disadvantage of that person. As used in this Rule, the term "confidential government information" means information that has been obtained under governmental authority and which, at the time this Rule is applied, the government is prohibited by law from disclosing to the public or has a legal privilege not to disclose, and which is not otherwise available to the public. A firm with which that lawyer is associated may undertake or continue representation in the matter only if the disqualified lawyer is timely screened from any participation in the matter and is apportioned no part of the fee therefrom.

(d) Except as law may otherwise expressly permit, a lawyer serving as a public officer or employee:

(1) is subject to Rules 1.7 and 1.9; and

(2) shall not:

(i) participate in a matter in which the lawyer participated personally and substantially while in private practice or nongovernmental employment, unless the appropriate government agency gives its informed consent, confirmed in writing; or

(ii) negotiate for private employment with any person who is involved as a party or as lawyer for a party in a matter in which the lawyer is participating personally and substantially, except that a lawyer serving as a law clerk to a judge, other adjudicative officer or arbitrator may negotiate for private employment as permitted by Rule 1.12(b) and subject to the conditions state in Rule 1.12(b).

(e) As used in this Rule, the term "matter" includes:

(1) any judicial or other proceeding, application, request for a ruling or other determination, contract, claim, controversy, investigation, charge, accusation, arrest or other particular matter involving a specific party or parties, and

(2) any other matter covered by the conflict of interest rules of the appropriate government agency.

Comment:

[1] A lawyer who has served or is currently serving as a public officer or employee is personally subject to the Rules of Professional Conduct, including the prohibition against concurrent conflicts of interest stated in Rule 1.7. In addition, such a lawyer may be subject to statutes and government regulations regarding conflict of interest. Such statutes and regulations may circumscribe the extent to which the government agency may give consent under this Rule. See Rule 1.0(e) for the definition of informed consent.

[2] Paragraphs (a)(1), (a)(2) and (d)(1) restate the obligations of an individual lawyer who has served or is currently serving as an officer or employee of the government toward a former government or private client. Rule 1.10 is not applicable to the conflicts of interest addressed by this Rule. Rather, paragraph (b) sets forth a special imputation rule for former government lawyers that provides for screening and notice. Because of the special problems raised by imputation within a government agency, paragraph (d) does not impute the conflicts of a lawyer currently serving as an officer or employee of the government to other associated government officers or employees, although ordinarily it will be prudent to screen such lawyers.

[3] Paragraphs (a)(2) and (d)(2) apply regardless of whether a lawyer is adverse to a former client and are thus designed not only to protect the former client, but also to prevent a lawyer from exploiting public office for the advantage of another client. For example, a lawyer who has pursued a claim on behalf of the government may not pursue the same claim on behalf of a later private client after the lawyer has left government service, except when authorized to do so by the government agency under paragraph (a). Similarly, a lawyer who has pursued a claim on behalf of a private client may not pursue the claim on behalf of the government, except when authorized to do so by paragraph (d). As with paragraphs (a)(1) and (d)(1), Rule 1.10 is not applicable to the conflicts of interest addressed by these paragraphs.

[4] This Rule represents a balancing of interests. On the one hand, where the successive clients are a government agency and another client, public or private, the risk exists that power or discretion vested in that agency might be used for the special benefit of the other client. A lawyer should not be in a position where benefit to the other client might affect performance of the lawyer's professional functions on behalf of the government. Also, unfair advantage could accrue to the other client by reason of access to confidential government information about the client's adversary obtainable only through the lawyer's government service. On the other hand, the rules governing lawyers presently or formerly employed by a government agency should not be so restrictive as to inhibit transfer of employment to and from the government. The government has a legitimate need to attract qualified lawyers as well as to maintain high ethical standards. Thus a former government lawyer is disqualified only from particular matters in which the lawyer participated personally and substantially. The provisions for screening and waiver in paragraph (b) are necessary to prevent the disqualification rule from imposing too severe a deterrent against entering public service. The limitation of disqualification in paragraphs (a)(2) and (d)(2) to matters involving a specific party or parties, rather than extending disqualification to all substantive issues on which the lawyer worked, serves a similar function.

[5] When a lawyer has been employed by one government agency and then moves to a second government agency, it may be appropriate to treat that second agency as another client for purposes of this Rule, as when a lawyer is employed by a city and subsequently is employed by a federal agency. However, because the conflict of interest is governed by paragraph (d), the latter agency is not required to screen the lawyer as paragraph (b) requires a law firm to do. The question of whether two government agencies should be regarded as the same or different clients for conflict of interest purposes is beyond the scope of these Rules. See Rule 1.13 Comment [9].

[6] Paragraphs (b) and (c) contemplate a screening arrangement. See Rule 1.0(k) (requirements for screening procedures). These paragraphs do not prohibit a lawyer from receiving a salary or partnership share established by prior independent agreement, but that lawyer may not receive compensation directly relating the lawyer's compensation to the fee in the matter in which the lawyer is disqualified.

[7] Notice, including a description of the screened lawyer's prior representation and of the screening procedures employed, generally should be given as soon as practicable after the need for screening becomes apparent.

[8] Paragraph (c) operates only when the lawyer in question has knowledge of the information, which means actual knowledge; it does not operate with respect to information that merely could be imputed to the lawyer.

[9] Paragraphs (a) and (d) do not prohibit a lawyer from jointly representing a private party and a government agency when doing so is permitted by Rule 1.7 and is not otherwise prohibited by law.

[10] For purposes of paragraph (e) of this Rule, a "matter" may continue in another form. In determining whether two particular matters are the same, the lawyer should consider the extent to which the matters involve the same basic facts, the same or related parties, and the time elapsed.

Tax practitioners who practice before the Treasury Department and previously were government employees are subject to yet another set of rules. Circular 230 §10.25 provides:

(b) *General rules.*

(1) No former Government employee may, subsequent to Government employment, represent anyone in any matter administered by the Internal Revenue Service if the representation would violate 18 U.S.C. 207 or any other laws of the United States.

(2) No former Government employee who personally and substantially participated in a particular matter involving specific parties may, subsequent to Government employment, represent or knowingly assist, in that particular matter, any person who is or was a specific party to that particular matter.

(3) A former Government employee who within a period of one year prior to the termination of Government employment had official responsibility for a particular matter involving specific parties may not, within two years after Government employment is ended, represent in that particular matter any person who is or was a specific party to that particular matter.

(4) No former Government employee may, within one year after Government employment is ended, communicate with or appear before, any employee of the Treasury Department in connection with the publication, withdrawal, amendment, modification, or interpretation of a rule in the development of which the former Government employee participated in, or for which, within a period of one year prior to the termination of Government employment, the former government employee had official responsibility. This paragraph (b)(4) does not, however, preclude any former employee from appearing on one's own behalf or from representing a taxpayer before the Internal Revenue Service in connection with a particular matter involving specific parties involving the application or interpretation of a rule with respect to that particular matter, provided that the representation is otherwise consistent with the other provisions of this section and the former employee does not utilize or disclose any confidential information acquired by the former employee in the development of the rule.

(c) *Firm representation.*

(1) No member of a firm of which a former Government employee is a member may represent or knowingly assist a person who was or is a specific party in any particular matter with respect to which the restrictions of paragraph (b)(2) of this section apply to the former Government employee, in that particular matter, unless the firm isolates the former Government employee in such a way to ensure that the former Government employee cannot assist in the representation.

(2) When isolation of the former Government employee is required under paragraph (c)(1) of this section, a statement affirming the fact of such isolation must be executed under oath by the former Government employee and by another member of the firm acting on behalf of the firm. The statement must clearly identify the firm, the former Government employee, and the particular matter(s) requiring isolation. The statement must be retained by the firm and, upon request, provided to the Director of the Office of Professional Responsibility.

     (d) *Pending representation.* The provisions of this regulation will govern practice by former Government employees, their partners and associates with respect to representation in particular matters involving specific parties where actual representation commenced before the effective date of this regulations.

As the following case illustrates, the ethical and the legal may overlap.

United States v. Trafficante

328 F.2d 117 (5th Cir. 1964)

JONES, Circuit Judge. During the period between April 20, 1955, and April 20, 1959, Roger L. Davis was employed as an attorney in the office of the Regional Counsel of the Internal Revenue Service at Jacksonville, Florida. While so employed he handled income tax claims for the years 1945, 1946, and 1947 against Santo Trafficante, Jr. and Sam Trafficante. During the employment of Mr. Davis these claims were settled and stipulated decisions were entered in the Tax Court. On January 11, 1962, the United States brought suit against the Messrs. Trafficante above named and others for the foreclosure of liens for federal taxes, including the income taxes for 1945, 1946, and 1947. A liability for wagering taxes, penalties and interest was also asserted. The Government's complaint set forth certain payment credits upon the 1945, 1946, and 1947 income tax assessments and specified balances owing by each of the Messrs. Trafficante. The Government also set forth the details of its claim for wagering taxes of the Messrs. Trafficante and of its tax claims against other defendants.

     On January 24, 1962, Roger L. Davis wrote one of the attorneys in the Department of Justice requesting advice as to the propriety of his representing the Messrs. Trafficante in the action then pending. A reply from an Assistant Attorney General advised that "While the statutory provisions regarding conflict of interests probably do not cover this case, it is believed that professional ethics would dictate your not representing the defendant." On January 22, 1962, prior to his inquiry, Davis had been employed to represent the Messrs. Trafficante and the other taxpayer defendants in the pending action. On February 15, 1962, Davis replied to the Department of Justice, saying that he deemed the matter in suit to be entirely unrelated to work performed during his Government employment, and that he had accepted employment.

     On March 5, 1962, Davis filed, on behalf of the taxpayer defendants, including the Messrs. Trafficante, an answer in which the correctness of the payment credits and balances on the 1945, 1946, and 1947 income tax liabilities, as pleaded by the United States, was denied. The United States filed a motion seeking the disqualification and removal of Roger L. Davis as attorney in the action on the ground that his participation would be in violation of the Canons of Ethics of the American Bar

Association and of the Florida Bar. The motion was denied. From the order denying the motion, the Government has appealed.

Both the Government and the appellees, in their briefs, state the question presented as being whether 18 U.S.C.A. §207(a) disqualified Mr. Davis from representing the defendants Trafficante in the pending suit. But, we think, the appeal must be decided on the record. There was no application made to disqualify Mr. Davis by reason of any violation of Section 207(a). The Government's motion, which presented the issue decided by the district court, asserted violations of those provisions of the Code of Ethics of the Florida Bar designated as Canons 6, 36, and 37.

But whether the question be one which involves the Canons of Professional Ethics or Section 207(a), it is our view that the conduct of Mr. Davis constitutes a violation which disqualifies him from the representation which he has undertaken in this case. The test is not, as appellees urge, whether the attorney represented the adverse party, here the United States, with respect to the specific issues in the pending litigation. Prichec v. Tecon Corporation, Fla. App., 139 So. 2d 712; 5 Am. Jur. 296-297, 299300, Attorneys at Law §§64, 69. The prohibition of Canon 36 is against acceptance of employment "in connection with any matter which he has investigated or passed upon while in such [public] office or employ." The collection of a tax is "in connection with" the determination or assessment of the tax. We do not think Section 207(a) permits any less rigid standard of conduct or prescribes any less exacting test. The statutory interdiction includes acting adversely to the United States in connection with a claim of the United States in which the attorney participated personally and substantially. Mr. Davis "handled" income tax "claims" of the Government against some of the Trafficantes. The handling by Mr. Davis resulted in the assessment of a tax which the United States here seeks to collect. The assessment and the collection are in connection with the same claim. It is not necessary, in order that disqualification result from a prior employment, that it be shown that the attorney acquired knowledge while representing the prior client which could operate to his disadvantage in the subsequent adverse representation. 5 Am. Jur. 297-298, Attorneys at Law §66.

The Preamble to the Canons of Ethics admonishes the members of the bar that their conduct should be such as to merit the approval of all good men. That conduct should not be weighed with hair-splitting nicety. We have found no exceptions to the exhortation to "abstain from all appearance of evil." 1 Thessalonians 5:22.

We do not say, and the record is free from any intimation, that Mr. Davis has been guilty of any intentional wrong, nor has his conduct been such as to suggest any turpitude. We do hold that a case has been made out for the disqualification of Mr. Davis to represent those appellees who have retained him in this case.

NOTES

1.   In a similar case, a former IRS attorney was disqualified from representing investors in a tax shelter because he previously had litigated against other investors in

the same tax shelter. When he was with the Service, he was substantially involved in the same matter and had formulated and implemented the Service's litigation and settlement position for cases against other investors. Kosby v. Commissioner, 64 TCM (CCH) 733 (1992).

2. Disqualification under Model Rule 1.11 and 18 U.S.C. §207 (2007) occurs only with reference to "matters." What is a "matter"? Model Rule 1.11 defines a matter to include a situation "involving a specific party or parties" and "any other matter covered by the conflict of interest rules of the appropriate government agency." Section 207 similarly requires that a "matter" involve a specific party or parties. Does this exclude the former government lawyer's participation in rulemaking? Should it? Interpretative regulations containing helpful examples have been issued under 18 U.S.C. §207 (2007) by the Office of Personnel Management. See 31 C.F.R. 15.737 (2007). Relevant portions of these regulations are reproduced as Appendix G. Should these examples be used to interpret "matter" in Model Rule 1.11? Note that until September 26, 2007, Circular 230 used the terms "transaction" and "rule" rather than "matter," and it differentiated between them. §10.25 (a). The regulations finalized on September 26, 2007, replaced the term "transaction" with "matter." Why? Separately, note that §10.25 distinguishes between situations involving participation by the former government employee and those merely under his "official responsibility."

ABA Formal Opinion 342 (1975) defines "matter":

> [T]he term seems to contemplate a discrete and isolatable transaction or set of transactions between identifiable parties. . . . The same lawsuit or litigation is the same matter. The same issue of fact involving the same parties and the same situation or conduct is the same matter. By contrast, work as a government employee in drafting, enforcing or interpreting government or agency procedures, regulations, or laws, or in briefing abstract principles of law, does not disqualify the lawyer under DR 9-101(3) from subsequent private employment involving the same regulations, procedures, or points of law; the same "matter" is not involved because there is lacking the discrete, identifiable transactions or conduct involving a particular situation and specific parties.

Other ethics committees disagree with the ABA determination as to rulemaking. For example, New York City Bar Association Opinion No. 889 (1976) includes within the definition of matter a case "where a lawyer has specifically analyzed and passed upon the validity of a regulation and after leaving government service is faced with the question of accepting employment in a matter which may involve an attack upon the validity of that very regulation." Would either the Model Rules or Circular 230 prevent an attorney from writing an article in which he either criticized or revealed loopholes in regulations he had drafted?

3. In Opinion 342, the ABA defined "substantial responsibility" as:

> As used in DR 9-101(B), "substantial responsibility" envisages a much closer and more direct relationship than that of a mere perfunctory approval or disapproval of the

matter in question. It contemplates a responsibility requiring the official to become personally involved to an important, material degree, in the investigative or deliberative processes regarding the transactions or facts in question. Thus, being the chief official in some vast office or organization does not ipso facto give that government official or employee the "substantial responsibility" contemplated by the rule in regard to all the minutiae of facts lodged within that office. Yet it is not necessary that the public employee or official shall have personally and in a substantial manner investigated or passed upon the particular matter, for it is sufficient that he had such a heavy responsibility for the matter in question that it is unlikely he did not become personally and substantially involved in the investigative or deliberative processes regarding that matter. With a responsibility so strong and compelling that he probably became involved in the investigative or decisional processes, a lawyer upon leaving the government service should not represent another in regard to that matter. To do so would be akin to switching sides, might jeopardize confidential government information, and gives the appearance of professional impropriety in that accepting subsequent employment regarding that same matter creates a suspicion that the lawyer conducted his governmental work in a way to facilitate his own future employment in that matter.

4.   Under Model Rule 1.11, a former government lawyer may represent a private client in a matter in which the lawyer participated if the appropriate government agency consents. Would it ever be appropriate for the lawyer to "switch sides" in a litigated matter? Suppose an attorney, while employed by the IRS, drafted a revenue ruling. A client now wants to hire the lawyer to litigate a case in which taxpayer would take a position directly opposed to the ruling. Could the lawyer accept the representation? Assuming this is in connection with the same "matter," who could give consent? Is it possible that the government official who might give consent could himself be conflicted because he will also return to private practice in the future?

Note that consent will not cure the conflict where the departing attorney has confidential government information about a person that might be used in the representation of a private client whose interests are adverse to that person. A classic example would be information gleaned from a tax return. Suppose the former government attorney acquired confidential information about *A*'s tax return. He could not now represent *B* in a matter against *A* where the information about *A* could be used to *B*'s disadvantage.

5.   Revolving door issues affect not only a former government lawyer who enters private practice but also the partners and associates of his or her new firm. Model Rule 1.11 permits partners and associates to accept employment so long as the former government lawyer is screened and notice is given to the government agency. The Model Code, by contrast, had called for vicarious disqualification in all cases. DR 9-101(B); DR 5-105(D). That harsh rule was subject to criticism. For example, the ABA Committee on Ethics and Professional Responsibility issued Formal Opinion 342, 62 A.B.A. J. 517 (1976), expressing the view that weighty policy considerations precluded a literal interpretation of DR 5-105(D) so as automatically

to impute the individual lawyer's disqualification to his firm. The committee expressed these policy issues:

> [T]he ability of government to recruit young professionals and competent lawyers should not be interfered with by imposition of harsh restraints upon future practice nor should too great a sacrifice be demanded of the lawyers willing to enter government service; the rule serves no worthwhile public interest if it becomes a mere tool enabling a litigant to improve his prospects by depriving his opponent of competent counsel; and the rule should not be permitted to interfere needlessly with the right of litigants to obtain competent counsel of their own choosing, particularly in specialized areas requiring special technical training and experience.

Several states subsequently adopted amendments to the Code that provided for screening. They formed the basis for Model Rule 1.11.

Several courts have addressed Opinion 342's screening approach in the context of imputed disqualification of an entire law firm. In Kesselhaut v. United States, 555 F.2d 791 (Ct. Cl. 1977), the Court of Claims reviewed a trial judge's order disqualifying an entire law firm because one member of the firm, a former government attorney, was individually disqualified. The Court of Claims reversed the order and embraced Opinion 342. It further held that a government agency could not arbitrarily refuse to waive the imputed disqualification rule. See also Sierra Vista Hosp. v. United States, 639 F.2d 749 (Ct. Cl. 1981).

Courts have not universally accepted Opinion 342's screening approach. In Armstrong v. McAlpin, 606 F.2d 28 (2d Cir. 1979), the court reversed a district court's refusal to disqualify an entire firm. The potential for harm was considered to be too significant to allow screening as an option to firm disqualification. An en banc panel of the Second Circuit reversed the original appellate opinion on the grounds that a district court's refusal to disqualify was not immediately appealable. Armstrong v. McAlpin, 625 F.2d 433 (2d Cir. 1980). The en banc opinion also reached the merits of the imputed disqualification issue and found that the screening alternative should not be automatically rejected because of any possible appearance of impropriety. The court held that no threat of a possible taint to the trial existed in the case. These Second Circuit opinions are interesting and potentially important (and continue to be cited by the Second Circuit itself, see Hempstead v. Inc. Vill. of Valley Stream, 409 F.3d 127 (2d Cir. 2005)) even though the Supreme Court vacated them because a refusal to disqualify counsel was not immediately appealable under the holding in Firestone Tire & Rubber Co. v. Risjord, 449 U.S. 368 (1981).

5. *Ethical Restraints on the Former Private Lawyer Who Has Entered Government Service*

The revolving door spins in both directions. Model Rule 1.11 also has limitations on a government lawyer who moves from private practice. The lawyer may not participate in a "matter in which the lawyer participated personally and substantially while in private practice or nongovernmental employment." The Model Rules do not require disqualification of the entire office or agency, although courts often require screening.

PROBLEMS

1.   The former Chief Counsel of the IRS, Tom Tax, left government on June 30, 2007, having held his position since January 15, 2005. On August 1, 2007, a request for technical advice, pending in the office of the Assistant (Technical) Commissioner up to that time, moved to the office of the Chief Counsel. Prior to that point, neither the Chief Counsel nor any of his staff had been involved in the matter. On July 1, 2008, the taxpayer, unhappy with the slow pace, asks his attorney to employ Mr. Tax as co-counsel and to ask Mr. Tax to urge the current Chief Counsel to move the case rapidly and favorably. May Tom Tax accept the representation? If the answer is negative or doubtful, may his partners do so?

2.   Nine months after leaving the Service, Tom Tax is asked by a client to attack the validity of a Treasury Department regulation. While at the Service, Mr. Tax participated personally and substantially in the development of this particular regulation. Can he appear before the Service in connection with it? If not, can he help the client prepare a strategy for the client to present to the Service, assuming Tom Tax is not present at the meeting? Can his partners work on it?

3.   Three years after leaving the Service, Tom Tax is asked by a client to represent it by resisting revocation of a previously issued, favorable letter ruling on a reorganization transaction. The Service contends that critical facts were omitted from or misstated in the request for ruling. While at the Service, Mr. Tax participated personally and substantially in issuing this ruling. May he accept the representation? May his partners? Would either answer be different if the representation involved litigation over the tax aspects of the transaction (following revocation of the letter ruling) rather than the issue of revocation itself?

B.   Tax Lawyer for the Corporation

1.   Introduction

Many corporations employ both in-house lawyers and outside counsel, depending upon the particular matter that must be performed and the relative financial burden to the corporation. Are the responsibilities and duties of in-house lawyers the same as those of outside counsel? Potential differences exist in resolving the identity of the client, multiple client representation, corporate misconduct, and lawyer-client privilege. Before delving into them, it will be useful to read the following article on the role that the modern in-house counsel is expected to play.

Sarah Helene Duggin, The Pivotal Role of the General Counsel in Promoting Corporate Integrity and Professional Responsibility*

51 St. Louis. L. J. 989 (2007)

In the complex, highly regulated world in which business corporations operate, corporate general counsel play a key role in promoting organizational integrity and ethical lawyering. The fiduciary and professional responsibilities of the general counsel — or chief legal office — are explicit in the rules adopted by the Securities and Exchange Commission (SEC) pursuant to section 307 of the Sarbanes-Oxley Act of 2002. They are also implicit in the August 2003 amendments to Model Rule of Professional Responsibility 1.13. . . . As advisors and liaisons to senior corporate officers, directors, boards, and board committees, general counsel have a great deal to do with the way business managers perceive both their particular legal obligations and corporate responsibility in general. General counsel are ideally situated to serve as leaders in the struggle to define the parameters of corporate conscience.

. . . As former Chief Justice Rehnquist observed in Upjohn Co. v. United States, "corporations, unlike most individuals, 'constantly [needed to] go to lawyers to find out how to obey the law'"; by the early 1980s, corporate legal compliance was "hardly an instinctive matter." At the time of the *Upjohn* decision, SEC and Internal Revenue Service (IRS) [were pursuing] enforcement initiatives pursuant to the Foreign Corrupt Practices Act n29. . . .

The following discussion . . . illustrate[s] both the wide variety of the roles of contemporary general counsel and the many stages on which they play them. . . . While the formal tasks constitute the official responsibilities of general counsel, the ways in which general counsel operate informally — i.e., behind the scenes — can exert a great deal of influence on the attitudes of managers and employees toward lawyers and legal obligations.

1. FORMAL FUNCTIONS

. . . Many aspects of a general counsel's work are those traditionally expected of lawyers. Others, described here as "quasi-legal" roles, encompass less traditional tasks — e.g., compliance monitoring. These functions are often assigned to or undertaken by general counsel in response to evolving demands generated by regulation, litigation, and other changes in the milieu in which corporations operate. . . .

A. TRADITIONAL LAWYERING ROLES

I. Legal Advisor

Perhaps the most widely recognized and far-reaching duty of contemporary general counsel is to provide legal advice to officers, directors, and other constituents acting on behalf of entities . . . [on] a broad spectrum of issues ranging from internal matters such as corporate governance, to external affairs such as transactions, litigation, and regulatory issues. . . . General counsel are often the first lawyers to hear of matters requiring legal input and the last to sign off before proposed actions become a reality. In providing advice to the client, a general counsel "must be a futurist, a seer . . . using . . . legal foresight to discern trends in the law and to predict how those trends will impact the company's business over time."

In the course of their advice work, general counsel necessarily develop direct working relationships with senior managers. The quality of these relationships almost certainly affects the influence a general counsel exerts over an entity and its business managers. At the same time, there is an inherent danger that relationships that become too close may compromise the ability of general counsel to give objective legal advice, particularly when the advice appears to raise barriers to the accomplishment of business objectives. There is evidence, however, that business managers realize the importance of seeking out candid legal advice in the post-Sarbanes-Oxley environment. A number of businesses have hired former prosecutors and even judges for their top legal positions in efforts to achieve better legal compliance.

Part of the complexity of the role of legal advisor arises out of the general counsel's obligation to provide advice to directors as well as to officers. . . . [T]he general counsel is still the primary provider of legal advice to corporate boards and board committees as well as to the CEO and other senior corporate officers. This dual reporting responsibility can create tensions in situations that require general counsel to advise against actions recommended by senior managers, or to report troublesome acts or omissions by officers. The general counsel's ultimate responsibility, however, is always to the client, and the highest authority capable of speaking on behalf of a corporate client is ordinarily its board of directors.

One of the principal areas in which general counsel provide advice is the corporate governance arena. While they are not "gatekeepers" in the same sense as accountants who perform audits, general counsel often have the practical ability to change an entity's direction by raising objections to a planned course of action. Even in the pre-Enron era, it took an unusually determined group of directors to vote to consummate a major transaction or proceed on other key matters when confronted with directly contrary advice by a company's general counsel — particularly in situations in which the general counsel was instrumental in structuring a major transaction or obtaining the legal opinions necessary for it to proceed. As Delaware's former Chief Justice E. Norman Veasey notes, "The finest service that the corporate lawyer can perform for the board is to guide it toward the adoption and consistent implementation of best practices that consistently ensure loyalty, good faith and due care" on the part of all constituents.

II.   Educator

. . . General counsel serve as educators. . . . As the principal in-house legal advisor for the client, a general counsel has the responsibility to find ways to inform business managers and constituents throughout the company about what they can and cannot lawfully do as they pursue business objectives. This function is particularly important when major new legal obligations — e.g., those created by Sarbanes-Oxley — come into existence.

... [I]n-house lawyers are particularly well suited to acquire "back channel" information. Access to such information not only creates unique challenges, it offers important opportunities to engage proactively in identifying potential legal problems and educating constituents about relevant legal obligations. In these and other circumstances, general counsel and staff members aware of potential problems arising in the conduct of daily corporate business and alert to out-of-the-ordinary events can engage in the kind of on-the-spot client education that can prevent major legal problems. ...

III.   Transactions Facilitator

The daily life of a modern business includes mergers, acquisitions, sales of assets, spin-off businesses, joint ventures, acquisition and transfer of intellectual property, real estate deals, procurement of goods and services, and a host of other transactions. These transactions often entail complex business structures and highly sophisticated financing arrangements with extensive legal consequences. "As key advisers to senior management [general counsel] usually participate in the negotiation, structuring and documentation of the corporation's significant business transactions." As chief legal officers, they are responsible for managing inside lawyers and outside counsel working on transactions. It is also the general counsel's role to advise directors whether shareholder approval is needed and, if so, what mechanisms will suffice to obtain the requisite approval.

The existence of corporate law departments should promote early legal involvement in proposed transactions. While most business lawyers undoubtedly would like to be involved in significant transactions from their inception, simply having lawyers on hand does not necessarily produce this result. Even within an entity, the extent to which lawyers have access to business planning information is a function of both corporate culture and the degree of trust managers have in the capabilities of their in-house lawyers. However, the ready availability of in-house counsel at least puts these lawyers in position to get involved at earlier stages of transactions than outside lawyers.

IV.   Advocate

When it comes to advocacy work, general counsel captain both the defensive and offensive teams for their client entities and marshal the resources to respond to legal actions ranging from routine civil claims to criminal investigations. To do so effectively, a general counsel must make predictions about the outcome of litigation and regulatory proceedings in many different jurisdictions. The general counsel must safeguard the entity's interests and take steps to ensure that its lawyers adopt coherent and consistent stances in tribunals across the nation and throughout the world, while simultaneously managing the costs of advocacy responsibly from an institutional point of view. In these endeavors, a general counsel bears responsibility for overseeing the ethical propriety of litigation on the entity's behalf and for requiring responsible, professional behavior on the part of the lawyers who represent the company.

A general counsel's advocacy function also includes the role of liaison with governmental authorities. . . . Participation of counsel is critical in those situations in which government actions may result in significant sanctions, especially when criminal proceedings are a risk.

V. Investigator

. . . When suspicions of significant problems with potentially serious legal consequences arise within organizations it is often the general counsel who persuades corporate constituents of the need to pursue the matter and initiates an internal investigation. The general counsel determines whether the inquiry will be handled in-house or by an outside law firm, a decision that is far more nuanced than is often appreciated. Key factors include ability to access information, an understanding of its significance in the context of the corporation's business and operations, and preservation of attorney-client privilege and work product protections. Even choosing among outside law firms requires thoughtful consideration. Thorough investigation and candid advice are essential, but some investigators pursue their charges so aggressively that they are more likely to destroy a company than cure its ills. It is ordinarily the role of the general counsel to strike the necessary balance.

When lawyers conduct internal investigations for the purpose of providing legal advice and preparing for anticipated litigation, corporations and other entities have an opportunity to invoke attorney-client privilege and work product protections to safeguard the confidentiality of investigative findings. The United States Supreme Court confirmed the availability of these protections to corporations in *Upjohn Co. v. United States* in adjudicating a dispute over the confidentiality of the fruits of an internal investigation of potential Foreign Corrupt Practices Act violations by Upjohn's general counsel. Since then, the subject of corporate attorney-client and work product protections has sparked tremendous controversy, particularly in the context of federal prosecution of business entities and other organizations. Nevertheless, because of the special skills lawyers bring to bear in investigating potential legal violations and the concomitant availability of attorney-client and work product protections, the role of initiating and supervising internal investigations has become a recognized responsibility of general counsel.

VI. Client Representative

In addition to doing the kinds of work lawyers find most familiar on behalf of corporations, general counsel often sit on the other side of the table as the embodiment of their organizational client. The role of client is not a part lawyers generally play. Like any other role it presents a unique set of challenges. As the client representative, a general counsel must focus on business objectives and other organizational goals, manage the costs of outside legal services in relation to their benefits, and ensure that the many different individual lawyers and law firms who represent the corporate client utilize strategies that make sense in terms of overall client objectives rather than focusing solely on particular cases or transactions.

B. QUASI-LEGAL ROLES

In recent years many general counsel have taken on new formal responsibilities consonant with the evolution of the legal environment in which corporations and other entities operate. These tasks require a combination of skills, including both legal acumen and managerial ability. Two significant examples — compliance and ethics roles — are discussed below.

I. Compliance Officer

. . . In response [to events of the prior decades], the SEC and the IRS, followed by the Department of Justice and several other federal agencies, began to pursue civil sanctions against corporations and other entities. Criminal prosecutions soon followed. In 1991, the United States Sentencing Commission's publication of its Organizational Guidelines made it quite clear that corporations and other entities were likely to be scrutinized by law enforcement officials and subjected to criminal sanctions where appropriate.

. . . A number of factors have contributed to the prominent place corporate compliance programs now occupy in corporate practice. First and foremost, of course, is the opportunity to deter and, if deterrence fails, discover wrongdoing. Perhaps even more significant is the impact of the dramatic increase in civil enforcement actions and criminal prosecutions against corporations and their constituents that began in the late 1970s, and the importance of institutional compliance programs in persuading law enforcement officials not to prosecute, as well as the potential mitigating impact pursuant to the Organizational Guidelines.

In many corporations, the general counsel serves as chief compliance officer. In others, the compliance function is separate from the law department, and the role of the general counsel ranges from providing legal advice pertaining to compliance functions to hiring compliance officers and briefing senior managers and directors on compliance matters. Whether or not the formal corporate compliance function reports directly to the general counsel, the general counsel and other in-house lawyers play a major role in ensuring legal compliance throughout the entity. The "conception of the lawyer as a promoter of corporate compliance with law emanates from the basic values of the legal profession," and it is a vital responsibility of contemporary general counsel.

II.   Corporate Ethics Officer

Many general counsel also have primary responsibility for resolving ethics issues relevant to corporate policies that go beyond legal compliance. For example, general counsel are often key contributors to the development of business conduct codes and other corporate ethics standards — e.g., rules governing the acceptance of gifts and gratuities or use of corporate vehicles and other resources. Codes of conduct and business ethics policies require proactive education if they are to be effective. Employees must be informed about ethical requirements relevant to their jobs, including internal grievance procedures, limitations on personal matters such as financial investments, nepotism issues, and rules pertaining to interactions with people and entities outside the company. In many corporations, the general counsel sets up a process for responding to ethics inquiries; acts as the ultimate arbiter of conflict-of-interest matters, questions involving business, and other ethics issues; and establishes procedures for notifying the company of ethics violations and disciplining errant constituents. Even when another official performs this function with respect to employees, because of their stature within the entity general counsel often handle issues pertaining to directors and senior managers.

C.   MANAGEMENT AND OTHER EXTRA-LEGAL BUSINESS ROLES

The third category of duties often formally assigned to general counsel encompasses managerial responsibilities and extra-legal business roles. Examples of these kinds of functions are described below.

I.   Manager of Law Department and Related Functions

. . . [V]irtually all general counsel serve as senior managers of corporate legal departments. They supervise financial and administrative functions and, most importantly, oversee the hiring and training of the in-house legal staff. It is the general counsel who sets the tone for the law department and who is ultimately responsible for setting the standards that govern how in-house lawyers represent the corporate client and deal with its constituents. As a department manager, the general counsel often has considerable leeway in establishing compensation and benefit packages for subordinate lawyers. He or she is the principal advocate for lawyers and other law department personnel within the corporation, and his or her willingness to support staff inevitably has a major impact on the respect other constituents accord to members of the law department and the extent to which they value their input. From an ethical standpoint, the general counsel is a supervisory attorney within the meaning of the SEC's Part 205 rules and Model Rule 5.1. . . .

Depending on the structure of the particular organization, the functions a general counsel supervises may include document retention, equal employment opportunity, disciplinary proceedings, intellectual property management, risk management, and a host of other matters related to quasi-legal organizational functions. In many organizations the role of the law department is to oversee the provision of advice in these areas, but in other entities these functions report directly to the general counsel. In recent years, the position of law department manager also has included encouraging and supporting pro bono work and bar activities by corporate counsel.

II. Manager of Outside Legal Resources

As the organization's chief legal officer, the general counsel oversees the retention and management of the outside lawyers and law firms engaged to represent the entity or to assist in legal matters. ... General counsel establish policies and practices that directly impact the terms and conditions of engagements, interactions with in-house lawyers and client constituents, billing practices, and many other aspects of the relationship of outside counsel to the client entity and its constituents. These policy-making and oversight functions are particularly important in an era when few law firm lawyers are intimately familiar with client corporations. As Professor DeMott observes, "The diffusion of corporate work among multiple law firms limits the breadth of any one firm's knowledge of the client, empowering general counsel in dealings with firms but reducing the capacity of any one firm to bring judgment to bear when more comprehensive insight into the corporation may be desirable."

III. Corporate Officer

Many, perhaps most, general counsel are corporate officers. Titles such as "vice president and general counsel" or "vice president, legal affairs" are common. A high percentage of general counsel also hold the office of corporate secretary. As vice presidents and secretaries, in addition to their professional obligations, general counsel owe fiduciary allegiance to the corporation as officers. In the performance of their duties, however, they may well be held to the ethical standards of conduct applicable to lawyers.

IV. Management Committee Member

General counsel routinely sit on corporate management or executive committees. In this capacity, they are part of an elite group whose members guide both significant day-to-day management decisions and long-range planning. [They] learn about the operational issues and financial questions critical to client corporations ... have the stature to gain access to the Chief Executive Officer (CEO), Chief Financial Officer (CFO) and other members of a company's senior management team. Consequently, this role offers the opportunity to influence significant corporate decisions as they are formulated and implemented.

V. Strategic Planner

For public corporations the strategic planning process necessarily involves consideration of legal issues. Corporate initiatives may rise or fall on legal questions, and profits may depend heavily on tax consequences and other legal aspects of particular ventures or financing structures. . . . Both legal feasibility and risk levels are critical factors in the calculus of whether or not to proceed with new projects or redesign existing programs. Involvement in the strategic planning process therefore affords general counsel and the in-house lawyers they supervise a chance to help shape business initiatives to meet legal requirements.

VI. Director

Some general counsel serve as corporate directors for the entities that employ them. Service as a director of a client corporation, however, is "among the most controversial of the legal/business activities that U.S. lawyers undertake" because lawyer-directors must navigate an ethical minefield. A general counsel can bring a great deal of insight to a corporate board as a result of his or her intimate familiarity with the organization and sensitivity to the legal ramifications of business matters. At the same time, a general counsel who serves as a director risks losing the independent judgment that makes counsel valuable to the entity and becoming entangled in conflicts between the role of legal advisor and corporate decision maker. The ability of the board to invoke the attorney-client privilege in seeking legal advice from the general counsel is also imperiled when the general counsel is a director. In a 1998 formal opinion pertaining to the dual role of counsel and director, the ABA declined to prohibit lawyers from serving on the boards of client corporations. The opinion, however, cautioned of the hazards of this role and the potential need to resign from the board and/or withdraw from the representation in the event of a conflict of interest. General counsel are especially vulnerable to these ethical traps because their primary responsibility is to serve as their corporations' chief legal officers.

2. INFORMAL ROLES OF GENERAL COUNSEL

One of the reasons that general counsel can be so influential in organizations is that, in addition to fulfilling their formal or official duties, they frequently play a variety of informal parts that have a less visible but sometimes even more powerful impact on client corporations and the way constituents view the corporation's lawyers. The following discussion focuses on these kinds of informal roles — those that do not appear in any job description but often comprise an important part of what a general counsel does and account for much of his or her influence.

A. LEGAL SERVICES MARKETER

As Carl Liggio, former General Counsel of Ernst & Young and a founder of the Association of Corporate Counsel, has observed, "Within the corporate hierarchy, the legal department is a cost center, not a profit center." This is one reason lawyers are not always popular with corporate constituents. Many business managers — even those who hold to the highest standards of personal and corporate integrity — resent the cost of legal services and too often perceive lawyers as creators of obstacles rather than facilitators of business objectives. Yet lawyers cannot successfully represent clients who do not seek their services and willingly confide in them. Consequently, to function effectively within a corporate structure, general counsel must persuade senior managers and others within their organizations that it makes sense to seek legal services early and often. This task has evolved into an internal marketing function that necessitates both educating managers as to why early legal input makes sense and demonstrating the ability of lawyers to "add value" in business contexts. While the sobering revelations of the corporate debacles of recent years should heighten awareness of the need for good legal counsel in business matters, internal marketing of legal services still remains an important component of in-house lawyers' responsibility, particularly for general counsel.

B. AD HOC PLANNING ADVISOR

. . . As in-house lawyers have earned respect for their ability to offer perceptive insights on a variety of subjects important to the business planning process, constituents have come to consult their in-house lawyers early in the course of corporate initiatives, often seeking their advice before a new project is formally proposed. The exchanges that make these kinds of preliminary contacts possible arise out of a shared working environment that involves contacts in company meetings and social events, as well as chance encounters "at the water cooler."

C. ETHICS COUNSELOR

Whether or not a general counsel serves as the official ethics officer for his or her company, as in the informal planning context, general counsel often serve as trustworthy advisors or "wise counselors" when thorny issues arise. Many ethical dilemmas have legal ramifications, but, even in corporate settings, not all ethical issues involve legal questions. It is not at all uncommon for others to turn to a general counsel seeking moral or ethical guidance because of respect for his or her personal integrity and ability to think clearly. As Professor Russell observes, "Lawyers are routinely called upon to exercise moral judgment in advising clients. In the corporate setting, lawyers often become trusted advisers not only for their legal knowledge, but also for the practical wisdom they offer."

D. CRISIS MANAGER

From industrial accidents to security breaches, from insider trading to workplace violence, every organization has crises that range along a continuum from minor incidents to financial debacles to terrible human tragedy. . . . For public companies, media attention frequently creates adverse publicity, and adverse publicity often impacts stock prices. Depending on the nature of the underlying event, government investigators may arrive before it is even possible to sort out exactly what has happened. Customers and employees may require immediate assistance, and psychological, as well as physical, needs must be addressed. At times, human lives may be in danger, and the very survival of the entity may be at issue.

In crisis situations, while operations managers deal with physical events and financial personnel assess the extent of monetary harm, immediate steps must be taken to obtain accurate information, inform directors, employees, and other key stakeholders, coordinate media statements, deal with government authorities, investigate what happened, and take steps to mitigate damage to the entity's interests. Each of these steps has significant legal ramifications. In light of their legal expertise and leadership skills, general counsel are usually found in the midst of the fray, identifying what must be done and marshalling the resources necessary to do it.

E.   ARBITRATOR

. . . While many different people may serve [as arbitrator] within an organization, lawyers often have a skill set uniquely suited to identifying the issues at the core of internecine disputes and negotiating workable resolutions. As chief legal officers, general counsel are ideally situated to appreciate the impact of factionalization and the damage that it can do, particularly when disgruntled employees fairly or unfairly believe that their rights have been violated or that another group within the entity has engaged in inappropriate behavior. As lawyers trained in the art of negotiation, general counsel also have skills that often prove invaluable in resolving intracorporate disputes among business units or administrative departments.

NOTE

Considering the wide range of functions served by the corporate law department, what tensions can you envision arising? The above article identifies some — what others can you anticipate? Are the Model Rules, as discussed in the article, more supportive today of an in-house lawyer seeking to provide good legal advice and ethical guidance? What does the article suggest about the identity of the general counsel's client?

2.   Client Identity

Does the corporation's lawyer represent the corporation or the shareholders, directors, officers, or other employees of the corporation? Does he — can he — represent all of them? Is the client the same for the in-house lawyer and the outside counsel?

Under Model Rule 1.13(a), "A lawyer employed or retained by an organization represents the organization acting through its duly authorized constituents."

The comment to the rule explains that Rule 1.13 applies to "unincorporated associations" and, therefore, the word "constituents" embraces the association's members, management, and employees.

While the language of Model Rule 1.13(a) defining the lawyer's client appears to be direct and explicit, it does not resolve specific ethical dilemmas. The Model Rules emphasize the relationship between the lawyer and the client. The corporation's lawyer, whether in-house or independent, cannot deal with the "entity" as an abstract client. He must interact with those who have specific authority to act on behalf of the corporation. When conflicting views arise among individual officers or board members of the corporation, the lawyer must determine who represents the interests of the "client."

Under Model Rule 1.13(f), "if the organization's interests are adverse to those of the constituents with whom the lawyer is dealing," the lawyer must make clear to those "constituents" that he is representing the entity as such and not them. What should the lawyer do if one of the "constituents" urges the lawyer to view the corporation's best interests as she sees them, not as they are seen by the corporate officer who retained the lawyer or by the lawyer himself? Does the answer depend on who in the corporate hierarchy retained the lawyer or on whether he is an in-house lawyer?

NOTES

1. As noted above, Model Rule 1.13 applies equally to in-house lawyers and to outside counsel. Should it? Does the in-house lawyer have more information to determine whether a particular act is adverse to the client? Or is the outside counsel more objective in his evaluation of the agent's position? What is the effect of organizational hierarchy on in-house counsel?

2. Suppose you are a tax lawyer employed in-house by a major corporation. Who should dictate the client's tax strategy? Should you listen to the president who urges you to adopt aggressive positions or to the board of directors who wish to adopt more conservative positions to protect the image of the corporation? Does your answer change if you are outside tax counsel? If so, why? Some argue that the lawyer should listen to the individual or group that retains the power to speak authoritatively for the corporation, normally the board of directors. See, for instance, Stanley A. Kaplan, Some Ruminations on the Role of Counsel for a Corporation, 56 Notre Dame L. Rev. 873, 874 (1981). Should you look to the chief operating officer or to the board, or do you do nothing until the board and the officers resolve their conflict?

3. Under Model Rule 1.13(g), a lawyer may represent both the organization and one of its constituents as long as the normal rules against conflict of interest are satisfied. See Model Rule 1.7, discussed supra 134. Could a tax lawyer represent both the corporation and a major shareholder in an IRS challenge to a corporate deduction and imputed dividend case?

4. When a lawyer represents a partnership, who is the client? ABA Opinion 91-361 opines that the lawyer represents the partnership but that the lawyer

normally may not withhold information from the partners. If the lawyer has been consulted to provide tax advice about the treatment of an item that will flow through to the partners, with whom should the lawyer consult? Does it matter that the entity, for instance, the partnership, has no economic stake in the tax treatment?

5.　The Model Rules identify the entity as the client and reject other conflicting theories. One theory would require that the lawyer represent all of the constituents' interests. Once the interests of one group of constituents diverged from the interests of another group, separate representation would become necessary. See Developments in the Law-Conflicts of Interest in the Legal Profession, 94 Harv L. Rev. 1244, 1335 (1981). The second theory would require that the lawyer serve as "'counsel for the situation' with a mandate to act, like a mediator, in the interests of justice and the good of all." Sarah Weddington, A Fresh Approach to Preserving Independent Judgment, 11 Ariz. L. Rev. 31, 35-36 (1969). Why did the authors of the Model Rules reject these theories?

3.　Corporate Misconduct

Under Model Rule 1.13(b), a lawyer who determines

> that an officer, employee or other person associated with the organization is engaged in action, intends to act or refuses to act in a matter related to the representation that is a violation of a legal obligation to the organization, or a violation of law that reasonably might be imputed to the organization, and that is likely to result in substantial injury to the organization, then the lawyer shall proceed as is reasonably necessary in the best interest of the organization. Unless the lawyer reasonably believes that it is not necessary in the best interest of the organization to do so, the lawyer shall refer the matter to higher authority in the organization, including, if warranted by the circumstances to the highest authority that can act on behalf of the organization as determined by applicable law.

The comment to the rule indicates that, ordinarily, the lawyer should not question policy judgments of corporate management. However, if the comment continues: "the lawyer knows that the organization is likely to be substantially injured by action of an officer or other constituent that violates a legal obligation to the organization or is in violation of law that might be imputed to the organization, the lawyer must proceed as is reasonably necessary in the best interest of the organization."

Under the earlier version of Model Rule 1.13(c), if a lawyer attempted unsuccessfully to have the corporation avoid unlawful and potentially harmful conduct to the corporation, he could resign or withdraw if the action would violate the law and would likely result in substantial injury to the corporation. Was this a viable option for an in-house lawyer? Less so than for an outside counsel? The *current* version of Rule 1.13(c) provides that if the lawyer cannot persuade the highest authority within the organization to respond appropriately, and the lawyer reasonably believes that the violation is reasonably certain to result in substantial injury to the organization, then the lawyer may reveal information relating to the representation whether or not Rule 1.6 permits such disclosure, but only if and to the extent the lawyer reasonably believes necessary to prevent substantial injury to the organization.

Certain caveats apply to disclosure of information regarding the "lawyer's representation of an organization to investigate an alleged violation of law, or to defend the organization or an officer, employee or other constituent associated with the organization against a claim arising out of an alleged violation of law." Rule 1.13(d). How much flexibility does the new version of Rule 1.13 offer the corporate counsel? Must the counsel act? Consider the impact of these Model Rule changes in light of some of the reporting obligations required of lawyers under the securities regulations as described in the articles in the next section.

NOTES

1.   A lawyer may have a legal duty to do what he can to have a corporation's employees comply with the securities laws, and if compliance is not assured, he may have a duty to disclose this fact to the board of directors. See SEC v. National Student Marketing, 457 F. Supp. 682 (D.D.C. 1978), discussed supra pp. 238-245. Also consider the new duties for lawyers imposed by Sarbanes-Oxley as discussed in the following articles.

2.   Does an in-house tax lawyer have a greater obligation to uncover the facts, motive, or intent underlying a transaction than an outside tax counsel? If so, might this encourage corporations to use only outside counsel?

3.   What if an in-house tax lawyer discovers that an officer of the corporation is using his company car primarily as a personal vehicle? Should he inform the officer that the personal use of the car must be reported as income? Should he attempt to change corporate procedures to require compliance with contemporaneous reporting requirements of the tax laws? What steps can (must) he take if he knows that the corporation is ignoring the personal use in filing its tax return or the employee's W-2?

4.   Suppose in-house tax counsel discovers that a corporate accumulation of earnings designed to avoid a dividend to the majority shareholder is likely to subject the corporation to a tax under §531? Should he — may he — disclose that fact to the board? To the public? Minority shareholders? In what order? On what grounds?

4.   Lawyer-Client Privilege in the Corporate Context

In Chapter 3, supra p. 192-196, we reviewed Upjohn v. United States, 449 U.S. 383 (1981). It held that the lawyer-client privilege covered all confidential communications to counsel by corporate employees, when the communications relate to the counsel's effort to formulate legal advice.

Upjohn applies to communications to outside counsel as well as to the in-house lawyer. The only potential difference is that in-house lawyers may be engaged in many legal corporate activities that would not be protected under the privilege. That would be much less likely in the case of outside counsel. See In re International Sys. & Controls Ling., 91 F.R.D. 552, 557 (S.D. Tex. 1981), vacated on other grounds, 693 F.2d 1235 (5th Cir. 1982).

To what extent can and has federal law overridden some traditional dimensions of client privilege? What is at stake on both sides with these rules (in particular the recent securities regulations discussed below)?

Lisa H. Nicholson, Sarbox 370's Impact on Subordinate In-House Counsel: Between a Rock and Hard Place [*]

2004 Mich. St. L. Rev. 559 (2004)

What is now referred to as the Sarbanes-Oxley Act of 2002 . . . was pushed through Congress at a rapid pace in an attempt to assuage investors as their losses mounted in the wake of financial fraud at some of the nation's largest companies. . . . The corporate scandal epidemic began most notably with the October 2001 public announcement that energy-trading giant, Enron Corporation (Enron), would restate its earnings downward by $586 million. Enron subsequently was forced to seek bankruptcy protection two months later as details of its financial affairs, including off-balance-sheet financings involving affiliated partnerships, began surfacing. The reported result? A $67 billion loss to investors. Enron, however, only proved to be the tip of the iceberg. . . .

Many argued that the breakdown in corporate accountability at these public companies occurred when the "lawyers, internal and external auditors, corporate boards, Wall Street security analysts, ratings agencies, and large institutional investors all failed for one reason or another to detect and blow the whistle on those who breached the level of trust essential to well-functioning markets." Some attributed the breakdown by these so-called market gatekeepers to the fact that they put the needs of corporate officers and directors before the interests of the shareholders. Indeed, numerous commentators opined that lawyers have impermissibly treated the corporate managers as their clients rather than the corporate entity.

. . . [T]he Act . . . is aimed primarily at auditing and corporate reform, it also greatly expands the authority of the U.S. Securities and Exchange Commission (the SEC or Commission) to regulate previously unregulated entities. In particular, Congress — in one of its more controversial moves — gave the Commission authority to federalize standards of professional conduct for securities lawyers. . . .

*Reprinted with permission of the author.

[Following the enactment of Sarbanes-Oxley], the SEC proposed its "Standards of Professional Conduct for Attorneys Appearing and Practicing before the Commission" (Part 205 Rules). . . . Lawyers, whether retained as outside counsel or employed in-house by public companies, must be familiar with the obligations imposed by the final Part 205 Rules. The core rules that were initially proposed and expressly mandated by Congress have not changed. All lawyers "appearing and practicing before the Commission" must report "evidence of a material violation," determined according to an objective standard, "up-the-ladder" within the issuer to the CLO, or the CEO of the company, or the equivalent. Moreover, the reporting attorney may make the report directly to the audit committee or the independent committee, or the issuer's board of directors, as appropriate, if he or she reasonably believes that it would be futile to report first to the CLO or CEO. . . .

C. The ABA Leadership's Response to Corporate Fraud

Although the Part 205 Rules establish the standard of professional conduct for those lawyers who "appear and practice" before the Commission, they still must abide by the ethical standards of the jurisdictions in which they are admitted and practice. Because no pre-emptive intent is indicated by the statute itself, these "securities lawyers" remain subject to state disciplinary proceedings that are not inconsistent with the rules of professional conduct adopted by the SEC. In fact, the SEC's adoption of final Part 205 Rules does not preclude any state's ability from imposing more rigorous obligations on lawyers than the SEC does, so long as the state rules are not inconsistent with the new SEC rules. Section 307 of the Act and the core reporting requirements of the Part 205 Rules promulgated thereunder are loosely premised on ABA Model Rule 1.13. The pre-SarbOx version of Model Rule 1.13 included a similar but narrower reporting requirement for lawyers representing organizations, applicable only when the lawyer "knows" that a violation is occurring or going to occur that is likely to result in substantial injury to the organization. There was no requirement of "up-the-ladder" reporting in the version of Model Rule 1.13 then existing. Lawyers were only required to "proceed as is reasonably necessary in the best interest of the organization." Up-the-ladder reporting was only a suggested possibility. No specific course of action was mandated, however.

Not to be overshadowed by the SEC's mandated response to this corporate fund, the ABA Task Force issued an eighty-nine-page Final Report of its findings and recommendations to the ABA's Board of Governors on April 29, 2003. Chief among its recommendations was the need to amend ABA Model Rules 1.6 and 1.13. . . .

[The proposed and ultimate approved] Model Rule 1.13 . . . would contain a supplemental exception to Model Rule 1.6's confidentiality requirement that would allow lawyers to report outside the company, rather than merely to withdraw, where corporate officials are clearly violating the law and serious harm to the company is reasonably certain. Indeed, where the organization's highest authority fails or refuses to act, and the lawyer reasonably believes that the violation is reasonably certain to result in substantial injury to the organization, the lawyer may reveal information relating to the representation, but only if and to the extent necessary to prevent substantial injury to the organization. . . .

II.   THE ALL-POWERFUL IN-HOUSE COUNSEL: A PARADOX

A.   The Governmental Perspective

The corporate accountability spotlight shifted to lawyers in the wake of the scandal-ridden, post-Enron period that reached a boiling point in June of 2002. Congress (and subsequently, the SEC) seized the opportunity to zero in on lawyer professional conduct standards during that summer. . . .

Senator John Edwards subsequently jumped on the "lawyer as accountable gatekeeper" bandwagon when he and his co-sponsors introduced the "Edwards Amendment" to the then-pending Sarbanes Bill that addressed corporate responsibility and accountability. He opened discussion on the Senate bill by noting that:

> Managers and accountants are the focus of the [pending Senate bill], and they are critical to us doing what needs to be done to correct this problem [of corporate misconduct] and to restore the public confidence. The truth is that executives and accountants do not work alone. Anybody who works in corporate America knows that wherever you see corporate executives and accountants working, lawyers are virtually always there looking over their shoulder. If executives and or accountants are breaking the law, you can be sure that part of the problem is that the lawyers who are there and involved are not doing their jobs.

Senator Michael Enzi, another co-sponsor of the Edwards Amendment, added:

> As we beat up on accountants a little bit, one of the thoughts that occurred to me was that probably in almost every transaction there was a lawyer who drew up the documents involved in that procedure. . . . It seemed only right that there ought to be some kind of an ethical standard put in place for the attorneys as well [as accountants].

The Senate adopted what has become section 307 of the Sarbanes-Oxley Act on the basis of comments such as these, and the SEC promulgated the Part 205 Rules thereunder — noting that lawyers "play an important and expanding role in the internal processes and governance of issuers, ensuring compliance with applicable reporting and disclosure requirements (including, inter alia, requirements mandated by the federal securities laws)." . . .

One is led to wonder, however, whether this "one size fits all" legislation applicable to all lawyers who appear and practice before the Commission can be applied to the very diverse group of individuals who are the public company in-house counsel. Not only are there several types of in-house counsel in any one legal department (e.g., the subordinate attorneys and the supervising attorneys, all of who may be led by the general counsel) performing various functions, but there are also numerous ways in which to organize an in-house legal department. The comments made in connection with legislating federal professional conduct standards beg the question of whether Congress and the SEC either correctly understand the role of in-house corporate counsel, or aptly appreciates the ability of each and every in-house counsel to effect change within his or her organization.

B.   The Reality of the Role of In-House Corporate Counsel

. . . [N]ot all corporate legal departments are the same. Much depends upon the organizational make up and the size of the in-house legal department; the level of decentralization; and how the general counsel (as chief legal officer) views his or her role within the organization as well as the level of experience of the corporate legal staff. Each of these factors will impact the ability of every in-house counsel (and subordinate in-house counsel in particular) to effect change with the corporate entity.

. . . The consequences for in-house counsel who endeavor to maintain ethical standards while earning a satisfactory living can be quite severe. Indeed, some lawyers who pursue misconduct to the highest levels of the organization may confront the choice of resignation or termination, as well as the risks of becoming a pariah in the industry. Although it may not be easy for any in-house counsel to bring situations where the company's senior management is failing to take appropriate actions to the attention of the company's board of directors, the general counsel typically will be better positioned to make the report — their close relationship with the CEO and other top management should give the general counsel an opportunity to assure good behavior; particularly where the vast majority of them report directly to the chief executive officer, and to have a path to the company's board of directors if management ignores such counsel. Subordinate in-house lawyers, conversely, may not have been able to forge relationships in the same manner or to the same extent as the general counsel so as to have the ability to effect change in management's behavior, or the corporate culture. However, armed with hindsight and the memory of the 21A report issued in the Salomon Brothers case, in-house counsel are aware that the non-reports, in the long run, can adversely affect one's reputation and career. As a result, subordinate in-house lawyers may find themselves in a tighter squeeze between a rock and a hard place. Of course, giving all in-house counsel recourse against former employers for blowing the whistle on corporate misconduct may help ensure his or her independence. In the meantime, a "one-size fits all" view of in-house counsel clearly is inaccurate and any legislation aimed at addressing corporate misconduct based on this misconception may disparately impact in-house lawyers generally, and some subordinate in-house lawyers in particular.

III.   SUBORDINATE IN-HOUSE COUNSEL: THE "HEADS THEY WIN, TAILS YOU LOSE" DILEMMA

The practice of spreading fragments of the business around to different outside law firms and different lawyers internally makes it easier for corporate managers to shop around for compliant lawyers who will approve complex transactions with little more than verbal assurances from the managers. But for the existence of a legal department, where all information flows through the general counsel, rarely will there be one individual or entity that either is fully informed or equipped with the overall knowledge of the business strategy and the resulting impact that any legal advice would have on the company's business practices. . . . Enron reportedly had a perfect example of the dysfunctional legal department.

The Enron corporate legal department was decentralized, fragmented and multi-layered. In fact, James Derrick, Enron's former executive vice president and general counsel, reportedly had no means of controlling or supervising all of the legal advice the company had been receiving because the different business divisions all had their own in-house legal staff as well as outside firms. Enron's lawyers also were unable to obtain information about a particular transaction's purpose or its underlying facts from their discussions with the corporate managers before the lawyers were asked to certify its legality. If Enron's mid-level employees, including subordinate in-house counsel, had questions about some of the deals, they reportedly were discouraged from delving deeper for answers. In Enron's case, it did not mean that those questions were not raised, however.

A.   Enron: Did It Matter That Someone in Legal Was Watching?

Years before Enron's accounting scandal became public, in-house lawyer Stuart R. Zisman reportedly wrote a memo in which he warned that one of the partnership deals orchestrated by chief financial officer, Andrew Fastow, ran a high risk of being seen as balance-sheet manipulation. He wrote in September 2000 that a close review of the transactions "might lead one to believe that the financial books at Enron are being manipulated in order to eliminate the drag on earnings that would otherwise [and in fact did] occur." Zisman was subsequently reprimanded by his superiors and asked to tone down his memo. Earlier that same year, an Enron corporate manager also uncovered the transactions that would eventually trigger Enron's financial collapse. Jeff McMahon, who worked as Enron Global Finance Group treasurer, was supervised by Fastow until March 2000 when he voiced concern about potential conflicts of interest posed by the off-the-books partnerships that masked Enron's debt. Three days later, McMahon was reassigned to the new job at Enron which he had previously rejected.

Red flags were waved again almost a year later following Jordan Mintz's transfer to the Enron Global Finance Group to serve as vice president and general counsel from October 2000 through November 2001. In early 2002 Mintz testified before the House Energy and Commerce Committee of his unsuccessful attempts to warn upper management during 2001 that some of the financial operations of Enron Global Finance Group appeared questionable. He testified that he had several conversations with Derrick; that when he reported to Derrick "what was going on [with the Global Finance Group on the twentieth floor]" beginning sometime in March 2001, Mintz believed his concerns had fallen on "deaf ears"; and that Derrick could not appreciate the "dysfunctionality" of the Global Finance Group. Mintz also testified of his numerous attempts through May 2001 to get Enron chief executive officer Skilling to sign off on the so-called "related party transactions," involving Enron personnel (as was required by the board of directors when it waived the conflicts of interest), to no avail despite his countless attempts to get on Skilling's calendar to discuss the fairness of such transactions between Enron and the partnerships.

Mintz also subsequently voiced his concern to his two non-lawyer Enron superiors: chief risk officer, Richard Buy, and chief accounting officer, Richard Causey. Afterwards, Buy told him, "I wouldn't stick my neck out;" that Skilling "was very fond of Andy Fastow." Mintz further testified that after his failed attempts to obtain approval for the deals from Skilling, he again notified his (non-lawyer) superiors, Buy and Causey, who said, "You tried, . . . so leave it at that." After failing to obtain a satisfactory response from any of his superiors, Mintz hired an outside law firm to investigate and evaluate the propriety of the related-party transactions in May 2001. Mintz, however, never went any further in-house — and never contacted the board of directors. When asked by Congress why he had not, Mintz stated, "In an organization like Enron, I try to work within the system and report to people who are senior to me who I felt had the direct responsibilities with the board."

Whether the recently adopted Part 205 Rules would have changed the outcome at Enron is debatable. Some Enron employees, including in-house counsel, clearly did speak up, but their worries were almost always dismissed or assuaged. While Mintz did not go to the board with his suspicions, he did at least bring the matter to the CLO's attention. That the board was aware of the possibility of a conflict of interest when it approved Enron's use of related-party transactions may have affected Mintz's decision not to advise them of the questionable nature of the transactions. Nevertheless, if liability for responding to reports of evidence of wrongdoing were made to lie with the general counsel, Derrick may have tried harder to understand Mintz's concerns and may have intervened sooner to unearth the corporate fraud. It is difficult to imagine under similar circumstances, Mintz or any subordinate in-house counsel bypassing both his or her lawyer and non-lawyer supervisors, as well as the general counsel — even if so required by law — to continually sound the alarms that fall on deaf ears. Arguably the board would not have responded to Mintz's report had it been made to them. Even to its last days, Enron at its highest levels either overlooked, or tried to brush under the rug reported evidence of misconduct. . . .

Beverly Earle & Gerald Madek, The New World of Risk for Corporate Attorneys and Their Boards Post-Sarbanes-Oxley: An Assessment of Impact and a Prescription for Action [*]

2 Berkeley Bus. L. J. 185 (2005)

From the legal profession's point of view, the central issue raised by the SEC's adoption of 17 C.F.R. §205 [the regulations implementing the Sarbanes-Oxley's call for professional conduct standards for lawyers] is the potential conflict between the importance of encouraging clients to be honest with attorneys as recognized public policy and part 205's mandate that attorneys function as gatekeepers who, in some situations, must reveal client confidences. The SEC insists that imposing a monitoring duty on securities attorneys also serves an important public policy consideration — protecting investors in public companies — and as a result, protecting the health of the U.S. economy.

. . . In an attempt to prevent the SEC from enacting [certain] proposals, the ABA has modified its suggested Model Rules of Professional Conduct to outline what this organization views as gatekeeping requirements that do not gut the concept of attorney-client privilege. . . . An examination of these ABA rule changes reveals an organization that is attempting to be responsive to the SEC's vision of the securities attorney's role in protecting investors, while asserting its own right to protect its internal vision of attorney loyalty to a client. This is a balancing act that requires nuance and compromise, both of which can be found in the ABA's proposed rule changes.

The ABA's response to part 205 clearly represents a loosening of traditional strictures against revealing confidential information. The changes to the Model Rules were recommended by a Task Force charged with examining the ethical principles which should govern lawyers in the post-Enron world and were approved by the ABA House of Delegates. The recommended changes involve two ABA Model Rules: Rule 1.6 and Rule 1.13. In framing these rule changes, the ABA immediately concedes some ground on attorney-client privilege. By emphasizing that lawyers have personal consciences and that moral considerations play a role in an attorney's decision to report corporate misdeeds, the ABA implies that securities attorneys have a moral duty to consider economic, social, and political factors which might adversely affect investors, rather than simply deferring to a traditional view of attorney-client privilege. However, while giving ground, the ABA also defends its own past stewardship of attorneys' ethics by emphasizing that, prior to these revisions, other Model Rules already required attorneys to act to protect the investor. Specifically, Model Rule 1.2(d) prohibits an attorney from assisting a client in committing a fraudulent act. In the face of a client who refuses to desist from the illegal activity, this rule requires the attorney to withdraw his representation of the client and even mandates "noisy withdrawal" in certain circumstances. Additionally, Rule 4.1 states that an attorney must not "fail to disclose a material fact when disclosure is necessary to avoid assisting a criminal or fraudulent act by a client." Nevertheless, notwithstanding these original rules, the rule changes described below clearly shift the slant of the ABA Model Rules from protection of the corporate constituents with whom the attorney deals to protection of the corporation itself and its investors.

A.   Model Rule 1.6

Rule 1.6 mandates that an attorney keep information which is relevant to that attorney's representation of a client strictly confidential. This rule, as originally written, allowed breach of confidentiality only in two very specific circumstances: (1) to prevent a client from committing a crime which the lawyer felt was likely to result in death or injury, and (2) to establish a defense for the lawyer himself in a criminal or civil matter. . . .

While the original rule allowed attorneys to breach confidences only to prevent physical harm, revised Rule 1.6 also allows an attorney to breach client confidence to prevent or mitigate financial harm and prohibits an attorney from allowing his services to be used in furtherance of such crimes. Permission to reveal confidences after a crime has been committed when the damage to be mitigated is financial and not physical represents substantial loosening of traditional strictures against revealing client confidences. This change, which circumscribes attorney-client privilege more tightly, clearly represents the ABA's concession that securities attorneys must sometimes function as gatekeepers, responsible in part for preventing future corporate financial misconduct. . . . By modifying its stance on attorney-client privilege to allow attorneys to take a more active role in preventing future Enrons, the ABA is outlining what it considers to be tolerable modifications to the concept of attorney-client privilege.

B. Model Rule 1.13

In revising Rule 1.13, the ABA further expands what it views as the permissible context within which attorneys may function as gatekeepers. As with Rule 1.6, however, this revision appears meant to stave off the ultimate SEC demand for "noisy withdrawal." Rule 1.13 establishes that the organization, not the officers or other constituents with whom securities attorneys deal are, in fact, the clients of securities attorneys. Establishing this fact allows the ABA to permit securities attorneys to divulge limited information in carefully defined situations without compromising attorney-client privilege. If the organization, not the constituent, is the attorney's client, then the traditionally protected attorney loyalty is owed to the organization, not to the constituents. The recent changes to this rule eliminated wording which seemed to discourage reporting suspicions of financial crimes up the ladder. . . . [R]evised Rule 1.13 outlines a reporting scheme which actually requires securities attorneys to report up the ladder within a company and further allows them to report out to the SEC in specifically defined circumstances, but stops short of requiring external reporting as was required by the SEC's originally proposed "noisy withdrawal" requirement.

In matters relating to an attorney's representation of an organization, revised Rule 1.13 requires that the attorney shall report up the ladder as far as the highest authority within a company when an officer or other employee of the company "is engaged in action, [or] intends to act or refuses to act in a manner . . . [which] is a violation of a legal obligation to the organization . . . , and is likely to result in substantial injury to the organization." . . . By emphasizing that the attorney's ultimate loyalty is to the company, these revisions illuminate the ABA's shift from protecting the corporate constituent to protecting the company and its stockholders. . . . Thus, the revised rules move the ABA much closer to the SEC on the gatekeeping issue. However, revised Rule 1.13 clearly leaves the final decision about whether to report out to the attorney. This revised rule also emphasizes that permission to breach attorney-client privilege is still strictly limited to attorneys functioning in specific roles.

By modifying Rule 1.6 and 1.13 to require that securities attorneys report up the ladder within client organizations and in certain instances report out, the ABA is accepting the SOX mandate that securities attorneys act as internal gatekeepers. These changes constitute acquiescence to the wishes of Congress and an attempt on the part of the ABA to compromise with the SEC. The ABA rules do not, however, sanction mandatory "noisy withdrawal." That is, the changes to the Model Rules do not require an attorney to withdraw and inform the SEC although they do permit him to do so. Thus, the ABA makes significant concessions while attempting to preserve attorney independence and its own prerogative to police the legal profession. If the SEC, on the other hand, decides to adopt its pending proposal on "noisy withdrawal," a face-off with the ABA is likely.

C. Criticism of ABA Action

. . . While [the Model Rule] changes do accept that securities attorneys should perform some gatekeeping functions, some detractors have found that these changes are not as extensive as they would like, while other critics are displeased because they have found that the revisions breach the integrity of attorney-client privilege more than they would prefer. In effect, this carefully balanced ABA response may illustrate why the ABA may not be the appropriate body to craft rules to mandate attorney's compliance with SOX. In effect, the ABA is a private, guild-like organization whose allegiance is clearly to the legal profession. In effect, this reality creates a conflict of interest which perhaps compromises protection of the public interest against massive corporate fraud. To complicate this matter, each individual state bar association sets its own rules of conduct which may or may not conform to the ABA's Model Rules. While auditors and analysts are both regulated by independent organizations that are external to the profession and whose sole duty is to protect the public interest, attorneys are not regulated by any such board. Thus, critics point out that SEC regulation, which is arguably more objective than ABA regulation, may be more necessary in the case of attorneys than of auditors and analysts.

Critics of the ABA's protective stance feel that securities attorney is synonymous with gatekeeper. Thus, a more objective body, like the SEC, might, absent political pressures, diminish the emphasis on an attorney's independent judgment and impose more restrictive requirements on securities lawyers. These critics would argue this more objective agency would more explicitly acknowledge that standards for securities attorneys should be very different from standards for litigators because securities attorneys act in many ways like auditors, at minimum reviewing financial disclosure on which investors rely. These standards might, in fact, include "noisy withdrawal" and the review of attorney certification of financial results.

On the other hand, others within the legal profession clearly intend to protect attorney-client privilege regardless of the effect on the public interest. These critics feel that the ABA has done undesirable damage to attorney-client privilege in its attempt to protect the public interest. Thus, the President of the New York State Bar Association states that the revised Model Rules strike at "one of the 'core values' of the legal profession — lawyer-client confidentiality." Predictably, such critics emphasize that trust is essential to the attorney-client relationship and that expanding the situations where this trust can be breached is intolerable and unnecessary. These critics also object to the attorney's increased license to report up and out under the revised Model Rules. . . . Whether the ABA or the challengers of its prerogatives are correct about the degree to which the public interest should supersede attorney-client privilege turns on how much compromise of this sacred legal tradition is actually necessary to protect the public interest.

NOTES

1.   What do Sarbanes-Oxley and Rule 1.13 assume (or expect) of the corporation lawyer? Is this realistic? Have these rules struck the appropriate balance between client confidentiality and the gatekeeping role? Is the burden on the corporation lawyer too heavy? Is strong enforcement of Sarbanes-Oxley and related SEC regulations necessary to achieve the changes sought, and perhaps give the corporation lawyers both the incentive and the strength to fully live up to the expectations?

2.   How much were Sarbanes-Oxley and the modifications to Rule 1.13 driven by a changing vision of who is the client for the corporation lawyer?

3.   The above articles raise the question of how to address the reality that many corporate law departments function in very different ways, and that as a result, a single set of rules may not best achieve our goals. However, the range of variety is even greater, when you consider that there are many small, closely held entities whose counsel will at least be subject to Model Rule 1.13. How well does Model Rule 1.13, reprinted supra 320, work with closely held entities? Suppose there are only three shareholders, each of whom is a corporate officer and director, and they disagree? Who are the corporation's "duly authorized constituents"? Whose directions should the attorney follow?

What if two of the three disagree about the treatment of an item on the corporation's tax return? Would it make any difference if the corporation had a subchapter S election in effect and the issue was one that only affected the shareholders?

Chapter 7

The Business of the Profession

Although the practice of law has long been characterized as a "profession" it is also a business, and the intersection of the two generates practical and ethical problems. Four commons arenas in which these questions arise are: (1) advertising, (2) solicitation, (3) specialization, and (4) the obligation to provide legal services to those who cannot afford to pay. This chapter examines the rules, guidelines, and case law addressing these issues.

A. Advertising

Businesses accept advertising as a commonplace aspect of their daily activity. So does the public. Yet, for years the legal and medical professions severely limited the right of their members to advertise. The Supreme Court has held that many of these barriers are unconstitutional and has protected the profession's right to advertise. A closely related issue is solicitation of business, both in person and by direct mail. Whether lawyers should be entitled to hold themselves out as specialists in a particular field is an issue of great concern to tax lawyers. Taxation is often given as the classic example of a specialty. There are serious questions as to whether specialization and certification are good ideas.

The rules regarding the propriety of lawyer advertising have changed dramatically over the last several decades. Beginning with Bates v. State Bar of Arizona, 433 U.S. 350 (1977), in which the Supreme Court held that the First Amendment bars a state-enforced general ban on lawyer advertising, the Court has continued to knock down many state restrictions. Model Rule 7.1 now limits a lawyer's ability to advertise only by prohibiting the lawyer from making a "false or misleading communication." Many states, however, have been reluctant to relinquish their traditional ban on lawyer advertising, and thus strictly interpret "false or misleading." The following case is illustrative.

Ibanez v. Florida Department of Business and Professional Regulation, Board of Accountancy

512 U.S. 136 (1994)

Justice GINSBURG delivered the opinion of the Court.

Petitioner Silvia Safille Ibanez, a member of the Florida Bar since 1983, practices law in Winter Haven, Florida. She is also a Certified Public Accountant (CPA), licensed by Respondent Florida Board of Accountancy (Board) to "practice public accounting." In addition, she is authorized by the Certified Financial Planner Board of Standards, a private organization, to use the trademarked designation "Certified Financial Planner" (CFP).

Ibanez referred to these credentials in her advertising and other communication with the public. She placed CPA and CFP next to her name in her yellow pages listing (under "Attorneys") and on her business card. She also used those designations at the left side of her "Law Offices" stationery. Notwithstanding the apparently truthful nature of her communication—it is undisputed that neither her CPA license nor her CFP certification has been revoked—the Board reprimanded her for engaging in "false, deceptive, and misleading" advertising.

The record reveals that the Board has not shouldered the burden it must carry in matters of this order. It has not demonstrated with sufficient specificity that any member of the public could have been misled by Ibanez's constitutionally protected speech or that any harm could have resulted from allowing that speech to reach the public's eyes. We therefore hold that the Board's decision censuring Ibanez is incompatible with First Amendment restraints on official action. . . .

The Board learned of Ibanez's use of the designations CPA and CFP when a copy of Ibanez's Yellow Pages listing was mailed, anonymously, to the Board's offices; it thereupon commenced an investigation and, subsequently, issued a complaint against her. The Board charged Ibanez with . . . using a "specialty designation"—CFP—that had not been approved by the Board . . . and appending the CPA designation after her name, thereby "implying that she abides by the provisions of [the Public Accountancy Act]," in violation of Rule 24.001(1)'s ban on "fraudulent, false, deceptive, or misleading" advertising. . . .

The Board correctly acknowledged that Ibanez's use of the CPA and CFP designations was "commercial speech." Because "disclosure of truthful, relevant information is more likely to make a positive contribution to decision making than is concealment of such information," Peel v. Attorney Registration and Disciplinary Comm'n of Ill., 496 U.S. 91, 108, 110 L. Ed. 2d 83, 110 S. Ct. 2281 (1990), only false, deceptive, or misleading commercial speech may be banned. Zauderer v. Office of Disciplinary Counsel of Supreme Court of Ohio, 471 U.S. 626, 638, 85 L. Ed. 2d 652, 105 S. Ct. 2265 (1985), citing Friedman v. Rogers, 440 U.S. 1, 59 L. Ed. 2d 100, 99 S. Ct. 887 (1979); see also In re R.M.J., 455 U.S. 191, 203, 71 L. Ed. 2d 64, 102 S. Ct. 929 (1982) ("Truthful advertising related to lawful activities is entitled to the protections of the First Amendment. . . . Misleading advertising may be prohibited entirely.").

Commercial speech that is not false, deceptive, or misleading can be restricted, but only if the State shows that the restriction directly and materially advances a substantial State interest in a manner no more extensive than necessary to serve that interest. Central Hudson Gas & Electric Corp. v. Public Service Comm'n of N.Y., 447 U.S. 557, 566, 65 L. Ed. 2d 341, 100 S. Ct. 2343 (1980); see also id., at 564 (regulation will not be sustained if it "provides only ineffective or remote support for the government's purpose"); Edenfield v. Fane, 507 U.S. —, — (1993) (slip op., at 5-6) (regulation must advance substantial state interest in a "direct and material way" and be in "reasonable proportion to the interests served"); In re R.M.J., supra, at 203 (State can regulate commercial speech if it shows that it has "a substantial interest" and that the interference with speech is "in proportion to the interest served").

The State's burden is not slight; the "free flow of commercial information is valuable enough to justify imposing on would-be regulators the costs of distinguishing the truthful from the false, the helpful from the misleading, and the harmless from the harmful." Zauderer, supra, at 646. "Mere speculation or conjecture" will not suffice; rather the State "must demonstrate that the harms it recites are real and that its restriction will in fact alleviate them to a material degree." Edenfield, supra, at —; see also Zauderer, supra, at 648-649 (State's "unsupported assertions" insufficient to justify prohibition on attorney advertising; "broad prophylactic rules may not be so lightly justified if the protections afforded commercial speech are to retain their force"). Measured against these standards, the order reprimanding Ibanez cannot stand.

We turn first to Ibanez's use of the CPA designation in her commercial communications. On that matter, the Board's position is entirely insubstantial. To reiterate, Ibanez holds a currently active CPA license which the Board has never sought to revoke. The Board asserts that her truthful communication is nonetheless misleading because it "[tells] the public that she is subject to the provisions of [the Accountancy Act], and the jurisdiction of the Board of Accountancy when she believes and acts as though she is not. . . ."

Nor can the Board rest on a bare assertion that Ibanez is "unwilling to comply" with its regulation. To survive constitutional review, the Board must build its case on specific evidence of noncompliance. Ibanez has neither been charged with, nor found guilty of, any professional activity or practice out of compliance with the governing statutory or regulatory standards. And as long as Ibanez holds an active CPA license from the Board we cannot imagine how consumers can be misled by her truthful representation to that effect.

The Board's justifications for disciplining Ibanez for using the CFP designation are scarcely more persuasive. The Board concluded that the words used in the designation — particularly, the word "certified" — so closely resemble "the terms protected by state licensure itself, that their use, when not approved by the Board, inherently misleads the public into believing that state approval and recognition exists." This conclusion is difficult to maintain in light of Peel. We held in Peel that an attorney's use of the designation "Certified Civil Trial Specialist By the National Board of Trial Advocacy" was neither actually nor inherently misleading.

The Board offers nothing to support a different conclusion with respect to the CFP designation. Given "the complete absence of any evidence of deception," the Board's "concern about the possibility of deception in hypothetical cases is not sufficient to rebut the constitutional presumption favoring disclosure over concealment."

The Board alternatively contends that Ibanez's use of the CFP designation is "potentially misleading," entitling the Board to "enact measures short of a total ban to prevent deception or confusion." If the "protections afforded commercial speech are to retain their force," Zauderer, 471 U.S., at 648-649, we cannot allow rote invocation of the words "potentially misleading" to supplant the Board's burden to "demonstrate that the harms it recites are real and that its restriction will in fact alleviate them to a material degree." Edenfield, 507 U.S., at (slip op., at 9).

The Board points to Rule 24.001(1)(j), Fla. Admin. Code §61H1-24.001(1)(j) (1994), which prohibits use of any "specialist" designation unless accompanied by a disclaimer, made "in the immediate proximity of the statement that implies formal recognition as a specialist"; the disclaimer must "state that the recognizing agency is not affiliated with or sanctioned by the state or federal government," and it must set out the recognizing agency's "requirements for recognition, including, but not limited to, educational, experience[,] and testing." See Brief for Respondent 33-35. Given the state of this record — the failure of the Board to point to any harm that is potentially real, not purely hypothetical — we are satisfied that the Board's action is unjustified. We express no opinion whether, in other situations or on a different record, the Board's insistence on a disclaimer might serve as an appropriately tailored check against deception or confusion, rather than one imposing "unduly burdensome disclosure requirements [that] offend the First Amendment." Zauderer, supra, at 651. This much is plain, however: The detail required in the disclaimer currently described by the Board effectively rules out notation of the "specialist" designation on a business card or letterhead, or in a yellow pages listing.

The concurring Justices in Peel, on whom the Board relies, did indeed find the "[NBTA] Certified Civil Trial Specialist" statement on a lawyer's letterhead "potentially misleading," but they stated no categorical rule applicable to all specialty designations. Thus, they recognized that "the potential for misunderstanding might be less if the NBTA were a commonly recognized organization and the public had a general understanding of its requirements." Peel, supra, at 115. In this regard, we stress again the failure of the Board to back up its alleged concern that the designation CFP would mislead rather than inform.

The Board never adverted to the prospect that the public potentially in need of a civil trial specialist, see Peel, supra, is wider, and perhaps less sophisticated, than the public with financial resources warranting the services of a planner. Noteworthy in this connection, "Certified Financial Planner" and "CFP" are well-established, protected federal trademarks that have been described as "the most recognized designations in the planning field." Financial Planners: Report of Staff of United States Securities and Exchange Commission to the House Committee on Energy and Commerce's Subcommittee on Telecommunications and Finance 53 (1988), reprinted in Financial Planners and Investment Advisors, Hearing before the

Subcommittee on Consumer Affairs of the Senate Committee on Banking, Housing and Urban Affairs, 100th Cong., 2d Sess., 78 (1988). Approximately 27,000 persons have qualified for the designation nationwide. Brief for Certified Financial Planner Board of Standards, Inc., et al. as Amici Curiae 3. Over 50 accredited universities and colleges have established courses of study in financial planning approved by the Certified Financial Planner Board of Standards, and standards for licensure include satisfaction of certain core educational requirements, a passing score on a certification examination "similar in concept to the Bar or CPA examinations," completion of a planning-related work experience requirement, agreement to abide by the CFP Code of Ethics and Professional Responsibility, and an annual continuing education requirement. Id., at 10-15.

Ibanez, it bears emphasis, is engaged in the practice of law and so represents her offices to the public. Indeed, she performs work reserved for lawyers but nothing that only CPAs may do. It is therefore significant that her use of the designation CFP is considered in all respects appropriate by the Florida Bar.

Beyond question, this case does not fall within the caveat noted in *Peel* covering certifications issued by organizations that "had made no inquiry into petitioner's fitness," or had "issued certificates indiscriminately for a price"; statements made in such certifications, "even if true, could be misleading." *Peel,* 496 U.S., at 102. We have never sustained restrictions on constitutionally protected speech based on a record so bare as the one on which the Board relies here. To approve the Board's reprimand of Ibanez would be to risk toleration of commercial speech restraints "in the service of . . . objectives that could not themselves justify a burden on commercial expression."

NOTES

1. ABA Informal Opinion 1131 (1970) held that it was improper for an attorney who held an LL.M. (in taxation) degree from New York University Law School to include the parenthetical reference when referring to his degree. Is this opinion still valid?

2. Circular 230 prohibits advertising containing "a false, fraudulent, coercive statement or claim; or a misleading or deceptive statement or claim." §10.30. What is a "coercive statement"?

3. In May 2007, the Pennsylvania Bar Association issued a comprehensive report on lawyer advertising. The Pennsylvania Report was preceded by a study based on telephone polling that sought to assess the public perception of lawyers in the state. Among their conclusions: "Nearly three in five respondents (56%) agreed, 'attorneys/lawyers who advertise gave the legal profession a bad name.'" Report of the Pennsylvania Bar Association Task Force on Lawyer Advertising (May 2007) (quoting the 2005 Bar polling study).

The 2007 Report, prompted in part by the work of the New York State Bar Association on this topic, reviewed the backdrop to efforts to regulate attorney advertising: the First Amendment and antitrust rules. The Report made a number of recommendations seeking, among other measures, clarification of certain standards and terms, and "more effective regulations or monitoring of the content of lawyer Web site and Internet advertising and solicitation."

4.   The First Amendment continues to be a battleground for challenges to state bar association efforts to regulate lawyer advertising. In July 2007, a federal district court judge barred enforcement of several (but not all) New York disciplinary rules on advertising that took effect February 1, 2007. Alexander v. Cahill, 5:07-CV-117 (FJS/GHL) (July 20, 2007).

B.   Solicitation

Solicitation generally refers to direct personal communication, whether by mail, telephone, or in person. The Supreme Court held unconstitutional a ban on targeting mailing to those known to be in need of legal services. Shapero v. Kentucky Bar Assn., 486 U.S. 466 (1988). In response, the Model Rules were amended to permit written and recorded forms of solicitation unless (1) the prospective client has made known to the lawyer a desire not to be solicited by the lawyer, or (2) the solicitation involves coercion, duress, or harassment. Model Rule 7.3(b). The Model Rules also require that such a solicitation be labeled as "advertising material."

Circular 230 contains similar limitations. It permits targeted mailings so long as they are clearly marked as such. Furthermore, the letter must identify the source of the information used in choosing the recipient. §10.30(a)(2).

The Supreme Court has upheld a ban on in-person solicitation, Ohralik v. Ohio State Bar Assn., 436 U.S. 447 (1978), and the Model Rules and Circular 230 follow suit. Model Rule 7.3(a) states: "A lawyer shall not by in-person, live telephone or realtime electronic contact solicit professional employment from a prospective client when a significant motive for the lawyer's doing so is the lawyer's pecuniary gain, unless the person contacted (1) is a lawyer; or (2) has a family, close personal, or prior professional relationship with the lawyer." Circular 230 similarly prohibits in-person and telephone solicitation. §10.30(a)(2). It does, however, permit "non-coercive in-person solicitation" by employees, members, or officers of a tax-exempt organization. The Supreme Court extended greater protection to political, rather than commercial speech, and held that an attorney for a nonprofit entity who offered free legal assistance for the purpose of advancing civil liberties, could not be disciplined. In re Primus, 436 U.S. 412 (1978).

The Supreme Court has struck down a ban on CPA solicitation because there was no evidence that suggested "personal solicitation . . . creates the dangers" that the state claimed to fear. Edenfield v. Fane, 567 U.S. 761 (1993). Does it make sense that a CPA could personally solicit a client's business in preparing a tax return or in giving tax advice, but a lawyer could not?

Model Rule 8.4 prohibits a lawyer from attempting to violate an ethical rule through the acts of another. See also DR 1-102(A). Several state bar ethics committees have held that it would be ethically impermissible for lawyers to solicit legal clients from a second line of business. See, for example, N.Y. State 206 (1971). Suppose a lawyer/CPA is hired to perform an audit of the client's business. Can the lawyer solicit the client to provide legal services? As noted above, Model Rule 7.3(a)(2) carves out an exception from the solicitation ban where a prior professional relationship exists. Would this cover the accounting relationship?

What about the negative public image of the legal profession? Recall the findings of the 2005 Pennsylvania Bar Association Survey discussed above. Can regulation of solicitation be defended on the grounds that it is necessary to address "the public's perception of, and confidence in, its system of justice and those who administer it"? See Florida Bar v. Went For It, Inc., 515 U.S. 618 (1995) (Supreme Court upheld a Florida Bar Association rule that barred a lawyer from sending a direct-mail solicitation for personal injury/wrongful death to victims and/or the families within 30 days of the underlying event).

C.   Specialization

The ethical rules in most jurisdictions permit a lawyer to communicate that he does or does not practice in a particular field of law, but he may not state that he is a "specialist" unless the state in which he practices has certification programs for specialists (for example, Florida, California, Ohio, and Louisiana offer certification in tax law). Model Rule 7.4(d); DR 2-105(A). In Peel v. Illinois Attorney Registration and Disciplinary Commn., 496 U.S. 91 (1990), however, the Supreme Court held that Illinois, which had no certification program, could not ban statements of specialization that are only potentially, rather than inherently, misleading since such a ban is "broader than reasonably necessary to prevent the perceived evil." The Court overturned the discipline of an attorney who identified himself on his letterhead as a "certified trial specialist by the National Board of Trial Advocacy." The court found that there was little possibility that the public would confuse certification as a specialist by a national organization with formal state recognition.

The court in *Peel* noted:

> We do not ignore the possibility that some unscrupulous attorneys may hold themselves out as certified specialists when there is no qualified organization to stand behind that certification. A lawyer's truthful statement that "*XYZ* certification Board" has "certified" him as a "specialist in admiralty law" would not necessarily be entitled to First Amendment protection if the certification were a sham. States can require an attorney who advertises "*XYZ* certification" to demonstrate that such certification is available to all lawyers who meet objective and consistently applied standards relevant to practice in a particular area of the law.

Suppose the Tax Section of the American Bar Association proposed to certify tax lawyers as "tax specialists" provided they had "practiced tax law" for ten years and had ten hours of continuing legal education in tax law each year. Could a state ban the use of the title?

Lawyers have long advertised that their practice is limited to a particular area of the law. Lawyers may make other truthful statements that convey the same message. For example, a lawyer may indicate that he has an LL.M. in taxation or previously served as a lawyer for the IRS. It is the word "specialist" that triggers concern. Is a consumer likely to be any more misled by a lawyer's statement that she "specializes in federal tax law" than a statement that her "practice is limited to federal taxation"? Does either phrase have any defined content? As an ABA Report noted,

> A lawyer who calls himself a tax specialist, for instance, may mean that he concentrates his practice on tax matters more than he concentrates on estate planning, even though he may spend no more than 15 percent of his time on any field of law, or that he limits his practice to federal tax questions, or that he has special knowledge or education in state and local taxes, or that he is a litigator before the Tax Court.

ABA Standing Committee on Specialization Report to the House of Delegates, Info. Bull. #4 (1978). Given the increased complexity of tax law, a lawyer who "specializes" in tax may know nothing about pension plans or state tax or estate and gift tax. Is that misleading?

D.   Availability of Service to the Nonaffluent

Tax lawyers generally serve clients whose incomes are well above the poverty line. Taxpayers with modest incomes, however, may have real difficulty in filing a tax return and may fail to satisfy their obligation to file. Worse, they may forgo benefits to which they are otherwise entitled. Who should help these taxpayers? The IRS? Accountants? The tax bar? Or does the answer lie in eliminating the complexity facing average filers? Taxpayers also may have tax disputes that do not involve enough money in controversy to warrant a tax lawyer's taking the case. Yet, a $300 deficiency may loom large in the eyes and pocketbook of a blue-collar worker. Typically, legal aid and legal service organizations are not available to help such a taxpayer. Is this a problem for the tax bar, for the legal profession generally, for the government, or should it be left to market forces to resolve?

Society has granted a kind of monopoly to the elite — the legal profession — and within that group there is the tax bar. We look here at its perquisites and its special obligations and ask why it has been so favored.

In recent years, lawyers have recognized the need, indeed the obligation, to ensure that legal services are available to the nonaffluent. In 1993, the ABA

House of Delegates, in a controversial decision, amended Model Rule 6.1 to provide that a "lawyer should aspire to render at least (50) hours of pro bono public legal services per year." The Rule also directs lawyers to provide services to "persons of limited means" or to charitable and nonprofit organizations "which are designed primarily to address the needs of persons of limited means." Additional service to "organizations seeking to secure or protect civil rights, civil liberties or public rights, or charitably religious, civic, community, governmental and educational organizations" is also encouraged. This is an aspirational rule only. The comment indicates that it is not to be enforced through the disciplinary process.

This hortatory Model Rule represents something of a compromise. Traditionally, the responsibility has been that of the individual lawyers. EC 2-25 of the ABA Model Code provided that the "basic responsibility for providing legal services for those unable to pay ultimately rests upon the individual lawyer. . . . Every lawyer, regardless of professional prominence or professional work load, should find time to participate in serving the disadvantaged." EC 8-3 stated that "Whose persons unable to pay for legal services should be provided needed services." In the recent past, however, there has been a push for a mandatory pro bono obligation to be enforced by the courts or bar associations. See, for instance, Thomas Ehrlich, Rationing Justice, 34 Record 729 (1979). Others, however, believe that while the argument for the ethical obligation to provide pro bono service is quite strong, the obligation cannot be imposed or enforced. See, for example, David Shapiro, The Enigma of the Lawyer's Duty to Serve, 55 N.Y.U. L. Rev. 735 (1980). In part, this is due to practical issues that have confounded states that have considered mandatory pro bono programs. For example, should lawyers be able to buy their way out of the obligation by making contributions to charitable organizations or by paying someone else to perform the services? Should solo practitioners be required to participate even though they risk destroying their practices to take on pro bono representations? Should tax lawyers or securities fraud lawyers be required to take on landlord-tenant or criminal matters?

Courts are split on whether requiring an attorney to perform legal services for no compensation is constitutional. Compare United States v. Dillon, 346 F.2d 633 (9th Cir. 1965) (finding that court order requiring counsel to represent indigent defendant was not a "taking" under Fifth Amendment), cert. denied, 382 U.S. 978 (1966), with DeLisio v. Alaska Superior Court, 740 P.2d 437 (Ak. 1987) (attorney cannot be required to represent defendant without just compensation).

Another trend that has resulted in increased provision of legal services to the nonaffluent has been the development of prepaid legal service programs. These are essentially insurance programs in which either groups or individuals may participate. In return for the payment of a "premium," the participant receives a certain level of legal services. These plans often enable individuals to spread and control costs, to monitor quality, and perhaps to increase the use of legal services because of an ability to anticipate costs. Nevertheless, they are more likely to provide legal services to middle-income than to indigent individuals.

In the tax area, nonaffluent taxpayers often need assistance in discharging their legal obligations to file tax returns and pay taxes. How should this responsibility be allocated between the government and tax practitioners? Many taxpayers are unwilling to seek assistance from the IRS, particularly where the Service might take a position contrary to the taxpayer. Low-income taxpayers can seek free assistance from the Voluntary Income Taxpayer Assistance program, which, although supported by the Service, uses nongovernment volunteers to help prepare tax returns. Many law schools have VITA programs, sponsored by the ABA's Tax Section and Law Student Division. In some cities, private groups of attorneys and accountants also provide such a service.

Low-income taxpayers may also need assistance in responding to notices from the IRS, or in participating in an audit, or even in litigation. Should the government establish an agency independent of the IRS to provide nonaffluent taxpayers with representation during audits and for administrative appeals? In court as well? Code §7463 authorizes a special Tax Court procedure for handling small cases (generally less than $50,000) that is available at the option of the taxpayers. Tax Court rules provide for simpler pleadings and more informal trials than in regular cases, but there is no possibility of appeal.

Some law schools sponsor student clinical programs that permit students, under a faculty member's supervision, to assist taxpayers in administrative proceedings with the Service and in court. In California, for example, members of the Tax Section of the State Bar Association contact those who have filed pro se petitions in Tax Court, offering free assistance. What additional steps might be taken to secure adequate legal representation for nonaffluent taxpayers? What about anecdotal evidence that tax practitioners may engage in less pro bono activities than other lawyers? Why might that be? See Bruce Kayle, Pro Bono Tax Matters (Not A Contradiction in Terms): A Primer, 108 Tax Notes 777 (Aug. 15, 2005) (suggesting that much of the assistance needed by pro bono clients involves complex detailed matters, such as the earned income tax credit, child tax credit, and innocent spouse relief, that are not familiar to tax lawyers regularly engaging in corporate practice). Note that despite acknowledging the gap between the corporate tax lawyers' practice and the needs of the pro bono tax clients, Kayle urges tax lawyers to become active in pro bono work, and offers his report as an overview of these important pro bono tax issues.

5 U.S.C. §500 (2000)

SUBCHAPTER I. GENERAL PROVISIONS

§500. ADMINISTRATIVE PRACTICE; GENERAL PROVISIONS

(a) For the purpose of this section—

(1) "agency" has the meaning given it by section 551 of this title; and

(2) "State" means a State, a territory or possession of the United States including a Commonwealth, or the District of Columbia.

(b) An individual who is a member in good standing of the bar of the highest court of a State may represent a person before an agency on filing with the agency a written declaration that he is currently qualified as provided by this subsection and is authorized to represent the particular person in whose behalf he acts.

(c) An individual who is duly qualified to practice as a certified public accountant in a State may represent a person before the Internal Revenue Service of the Treasury Department on filing with that agency a written declaration that he is currently qualified as provided by this subsection and is authorized to represent the particular person in whose behalf he acts.

(d) This section does not—

(1) grant or deny to an individual who is not qualified as provided by subsection (b) or (c) of this section the right to appear for or represent a person before an agency or in an agency proceeding;

(2) authorize or limit the discipline, including disbarment, of individuals who appear in a representative capacity before an agency;

(3) authorize an individual who is a former employee of an agency to represent a person before an agency when the representation is prohibited by statute or regulation; or

(4) prevent an agency from requiring a power of attorney as a condition to the settlement of a controversy involving the payment of money.

(e) Subsections (b)-(d) of this section do not apply to practice before the United States Patent and Trademark Office with respect to patent matters that continue to be covered by chapter 3 (sections 31-33) of title 35.

(f) When a participant in a matter before an agency is represented by an individual qualified under subsection (b) or (c) of this section, a notice or other written communication required or permitted to be given the participant in the matter shall be given to the representative in addition to any other service specifically required by statute. When a participant is represented by more than one such qualified representative, service on any one of the representatives is sufficient.

31 U.S.C. §330 (2006)

§330. PRACTICE BEFORE THE DEPARTMENT

(a) Subject to section 500 of title 5, the Secretary of the Treasury may—

(1) regulate the practice of representatives of persons before the Department of the Treasury; and

(2) before admitting a representative to practice, require that the representative demonstrate—

(A) good character;

(B) good reputation;

(C) necessary qualifications to enable the representative to provide to persons valuable service; and

(D) competency to advise and assist persons in presenting their cases.

(b) After notice and opportunity for a proceeding, the Secretary may suspend or disbar from practice before the Department, or censure, a representative who—

(1) is incompetent;

(2) is disreputable;

(3) violates regulations prescribed under this section; or

(4) with intent to defraud, willfully and knowingly misleads or threatens the person being represented or a prospective person to be represented.

The Secretary may impose a monetary penalty on any representative described in the preceding sentence. If the representative was acting on behalf of an employer or any firm or other entity in connection with the conduct giving rise to such penalty, the Secretary may impose a monetary penalty on such employer, firm, or entity if it knew, or reasonably should have known, of such conduct. Such penalty shall not exceed the gross income derived (or to be derived) from the conduct giving rise to the penalty and may be in addition to, or in lieu of, any suspension, disbarment, or censure of the representative.

(c) After notice and opportunity for a hearing to any appraiser, the Secretary may—

(1) provide that appraisals by such appraiser shall not have any probative effect in any administrative proceeding before the Department of the Treasury or the Internal Revenue Service, and

(2) bar such appraiser from presenting evidence or testimony in any such proceeding.

(d) Nothing in this section or in any other provision of law shall be construed to limit the authority of the Secretary of the Treasury to impose standards applicable to the rendering of written advice with respect to any entity, transaction plan or arrangement, or other plan or arrangement, which is of a type which the Secretary determines as having a potential for tax avoidance or evasion.

Appendix C

Treasury Department Circular 230

§10.1 Director of the Office of Professional Responsibility

(a) *Establishment of office.* The Office of Professional Responsibility is established in the Internal Revenue Service. The Director of the Office of Professional Responsibility is appointed by the Secretary of the Treasury, or delegate.

(b) *Duties.* The Director of the Office of Professional Responsibility acts on applications for enrollment to practice before the Internal Revenue Service; makes inquiries with respect to matters under the Director's jurisdiction; institutes and provides for the conduct of disciplinary proceedings relating to practitioners (and employers, firms or other entities if applicable) and appraisers; and performs other duties as are necessary or appropriate to carry out the functions under this part or as are prescribed by the Secretary of the Treasury, or delegate.

(c) *Acting Director of the Office of Professional Responsibility.* The Secretary of the Treasury, or delegate, will designate an officer or employee of the Treasury Department to act as Director of the Office of Professional Responsibility in the absence of the Director or during a vacancy in that office.

(d) *Effective/applicability date.* This section is applicable on September 26, 2007.

§10.2 Definitions

(a) As used in this part, except where the text provides otherwise—

(1) *Attorney* means any person who is a member in good standing of the bar of the highest court of any state, territory, or possession of the United States, including a Commonwealth, or the District of Columbia.

(2) *Certified public accountant* means any person who is duly qualified to practice as a certified public accountant in any state, territory, or possession of the United States, including a Commonwealth, or the District of Columbia.

(3) *Commissioner* refers to the Commissioner of Internal Revenue.

(4) *Practice before the Internal Revenue Service* comprehends all matters connected with a presentation to the Internal Revenue Service or any of its officers or employees relating to a taxpayer's rights, privileges, or liabilities under laws or regulations administered by the Internal Revenue Service. Such presentations

include, but are not limited to, preparing and filing documents, corresponding and communicating with the Internal Revenue Service, rendering written advice with respect to any entity, transaction, plan or arrangement, or other plan or arrangement having a potential for tax avoidance or evasion, and representing a client at conferences, hearings and meetings.

(5) *Practitioner* means any individual described in paragraphs (a), (b), (c), (d) or (e) of §10.3.

(6) A *tax return* includes an amended tax return and a claim for refund.

(7) *Service* means the Internal Revenue Service.

(b) *Effective/applicability date.* This section is applicable on September 26, 2007.

§10.3   WHO MAY PRACTICE

(a) *Attorneys.* Any attorney who is not currently under suspension or disbarment from practice before the Internal Revenue Service may practice before the Internal Revenue Service by filing with the Internal Revenue Service a written declaration that the attorney is currently qualified as an attorney and is authorized to represent the party or parties. Notwithstanding the preceding sentence, attorneys who are not currently under suspension or disbarment from practice before the Internal Revenue Service are not required to file a written declaration with the IRS before rendering written advice covered under §10.35 or §10.37, but their rendering of this advice is practice before the Internal Revenue Service.

(b) *Certified public accountants.* Any certified public accountant who is not currently under suspension or disbarment from practice before the Internal Revenue Service may practice before the Internal Revenue Service by filing with the Internal Revenue Service a written declaration that the certified public accountant is currently qualified as a certified public accountant and is authorized to represent the party or parties. Notwithstanding the preceding sentence, certified public accountants who are not currently under suspension or disbarment from practice before the Internal Revenue Service are not required to file a written declaration with the IRS before rendering written advice covered under §10.35 or §10.37, but their rendering of this advice is practice before the Internal Revenue Service.

(c) *Enrolled agents.* Any individual enrolled as an agent pursuant to this part who is not currently under suspension or disbarment from practice before the Internal Revenue Service may practice before the Internal Revenue Service.

(d) *Enrolled actuaries—*

(1) Any individual who is enrolled as an actuary by the Joint Board for the Enrollment of Actuaries pursuant to 29 U.S.C. 1242 who is not currently under suspension or disbarment from practice before the Internal Revenue Service may practice before the Internal Revenue Service by filing with the Internal Revenue Service a written declaration stating that he or she is currently qualified as an enrolled actuary and is authorized to represent the party or parties on whose behalf he or she acts. Practice as an enrolled actuary is limited to representation with respect to issues involving the following statutory provisions

Internal Revenue Code (Title 26 U.S.C.) sections: 401 (relating to qualification of employee plans), 403(a) (relating to whether an annuity plan meets the requirements of section 404(a) (2)), 404 (relating to deductibility of employer contributions), 405 (relating to qualification of bond purchase plans), 412 (relating to funding requirements for certain employee plans), 413 (relating to application of qualification requirements to collectively bargained plans and to plans maintained by more than one employer), 414 (relating to definitions and special rules with respect to the employee plan area), 419 (relating to treatment of funded welfare benefits), 419A (relating to qualified asset accounts), 420 (relating to transfers of excess pension assets to retiree health accounts), 4971 (relating to excise taxes payable as a result of an accumulated funding deficiency under section 412), 4972 (relating to tax on nondeductible contributions to qualified employer plans), 4976 (relating to taxes with respect to funded welfare benefit plans), 4980 (relating to tax on reversion of qualified plan assets to employer), 6057 (relating to annual registration of plans), 6058 (relating to information required in connection with certain plans of deferred compensation), 6059 (relating to periodic report of actuary), 6652(e) (relating to the failure to file annual registration and other notifications by pension plan), 6652(f) (relating to the failure to file information required in connection with certain plans of deferred compensation), 6692 (relating to the failure to file actuarial report), 7805(b) (relating to the extent to which an Internal Revenue Service ruling or determination letter coming under the statutory provisions listed here will be applied without retroactive effect); and 29 U.S.C. 1083 (relating to the waiver of funding for nonqualified plans).

(2) An individual who practices before the Internal Revenue Service pursuant to paragraph (d)(1) of this section is subject to the provisions of this part in the same manner as attorneys, certified public accountants and enrolled agents.

(e) *Enrolled Retirement Plan Agents—*

(1) Any individual enrolled as a retirement plan agent pursuant to this part who is not currently under suspension or disbarment from practice before the Internal Revenue Service may practice before the Internal Revenue Service.

(2) Practice as an enrolled retirement plan agent is limited to representation with respect to issues involving the following programs: Employee Plans Determination Letter program; Employee Plans Compliance Resolution System; and Employee Plans Master and Prototype and Volume Submitter program. In addition, enrolled retirement plan agents are generally permitted to represent taxpayers with respect to IRS forms under the 5300 and 5500 series which are filed by retirement plans and plan sponsors, but not with respect to actuarial forms or schedules.

(3) An individual who practices before the Internal Revenue Service pursuant to paragraph (e)(1) of this section is subject to the provisions of this part in the same manner as attorneys, certified public accountants and enrolled agents.

(f) *Others.* Any individual qualifying under paragraph (d) of §10.5 or §10.7 is eligible to practice before the Internal Revenue Service to the extent provided in those sections.

(g) *Government officers and employees, and others.* An individual, who is an officer or employee of the executive, legislative, or judicial branch of the United States Government; an officer or employee of the District of Columbia; a Member of Congress; or a Resident Commissioner may not practice before the Internal Revenue Service if such practice violates 18 U.S.C. 203 or 205.

(h) *State officers and employees.* No officer or employee of any State, or subdivision of any State, whose duties require him or her to pass upon, investigate, or deal with tax matters for such State or subdivision, may practice before the Internal Revenue Service, if such employment may disclose facts or information applicable to Federal tax matters.

(i) *Effective/applicability date.* This section is applicable on September 26, 2007.

§10.4   Eligibility for Enrollment

(a) *Enrollment as an enrolled agent upon examination.* The Director of the Office of Professional Responsibility may grant enrollment as an enrolled agent to an applicant who demonstrates special competence in tax matters by written examination administered by, or administered under the oversight of, the Director of the Office of Professional Responsibility and who has not engaged in any conduct that would justify the censure, suspension, or disbarment of any practitioner under the provisions of this part.

(b) *Enrollment as a retirement plan agent upon examination.* The Director of the Office of Professional Responsibility may grant enrollment as an enrolled retirement plan agent to an applicant who demonstrates special competence in qualified retirement plan matters by written examination administered by, or administered under the oversight of, the Director of the Office of Professional Responsibility and who has not engaged in any conduct that would justify the censure, suspension, or disbarment of any practitioner under the provisions of this part.

(c) *Enrollment of former Internal Revenue Service employees.* The Director of the Office of Professional Responsibility may grant enrollment as an enrolled agent or enrolled retirement plan agent to an applicant who, by virtue of past service and technical experience in the Internal Revenue Service, has qualified for such enrollment and who has not engaged in any conduct that would justify the censure, suspension, or disbarment of any practitioner under the provisions of this part, under the following circumstances—

(1) The former employee applies for enrollment to the Director of the Office of Professional Responsibility on a form supplied by the Director of the Office of Professional Responsibility and supplies the information requested on the form and such other information regarding the experience and training of the applicant as may be relevant.

(2) An appropriate office of the Internal Revenue Service, at the request of the Director of the Office of Professional Responsibility, will provide the Director of the Office of Professional Responsibility with a detailed report of the nature and rating of the applicant's work while employed by the Internal Revenue Service and

a recommendation whether such employment qualifies the applicant technically or otherwise for the desired authorization.

(3) Enrollment as an enrolled agent based on an applicant's former employment with the Internal Revenue Service may be of unlimited scope or it may be limited to permit the presentation of matters only of the particular class or only before the particular unit or division of the Internal Revenue Service for which the applicant's former employment has qualified the applicant. Enrollment as an enrolled retirement plan agent based on an applicant's former employment with the Internal Revenue Service will be limited to permit the presentation of matters only with respect to qualified retirement plan matters.

(4) Application for enrollment as an enrolled agent or enrolled retirement plan agent based on an applicant's former employment with the Internal Revenue Service must be made within 3 years from the date of separation from such employment.

(5) An applicant for enrollment as an enrolled agent who is requesting such enrollment based on former employment with the Internal Revenue Service must have had a minimum of 5 years continuous employment with the Internal Revenue Service during which the applicant must have been regularly engaged in applying and interpreting the provisions of the Internal Revenue Code and the regulations relating to income, estate, gift, employment, or excise taxes.

(6) An applicant for enrollment as an enrolled retirement plan agent who is requesting such enrollment based on former employment with the Internal Revenue Service must have had a minimum of 5 years continuous employment with the Internal Revenue Service during which the applicant must have been regularly engaged in applying and interpreting the provisions of the Internal Revenue Code and the regulations relating to qualified retirement plan matters.

(7) For the purposes of paragraphs (b)(5) and (b)(6) of this section, an aggregate of 10 or more years of employment in positions involving the application and interpretation of the provisions of the Internal Revenue Code, at least 3 of which occurred within the 5 years preceding the date of application, is the equivalent of 5 years continuous employment.

(d) *Natural persons.* Enrollment to practice may be granted only to natural persons.

(e) *Effective/applicability date.* This section is applicable on September 26, 2007.

§10.5   APPLICATION FOR ENROLLMENT AS AN ENROLLED AGENT OR ENROLLED RETIREMENT PLAN AGENT

(a) *Form; address.* An applicant for enrollment as an enrolled agent or enrolled retirement plan agent must apply as required by forms or procedures established and published by the Office of Professional Responsibility, including proper execution of required forms under oath or affirmation. The address on the application will be the address under which a successful applicant is enrolled and is the address to which all correspondence concerning enrollment will be sent.

(b) *Fee.* A reasonable nonrefundable fee will be charged for each application for enrollment as an enrolled agent filed with the Director of the Office of Professional Responsibility in accordance with 26 CFR 300.5. A reasonable nonrefundable fee will be charged for each application for enrollment as an enrolled retirement plan agent filed with the Director of the Office of Professional Responsibility.

(c) *Additional information; examination.* The Director of Practice, as a condition to consideration of an application for enrollment, may require the applicant to file additional information and to submit to any written or oral examination under oath or otherwise. The Director of Practice will, on written request filed by an applicant, afford such applicant the opportunity to be heard with respect to his or her application for enrollment.

(d) *Temporary recognition.* On receipt of a properly executed application, the Director of Practice may grant the applicant temporary recognition to practice pending a determination as to whether enrollment to practice should be granted. Temporary recognition will be granted only in unusual circumstances and it will not be granted, in any circumstance, if the application is not regular on its face, if the information stated in the application, if true, is not sufficient to warrant enrollment to practice, or if there is any information before the Director of Practice indicating that the statements in the application are untrue or that the applicant would not otherwise qualify for enrollment. Issuance of temporary recognition does not constitute enrollment to practice or a finding of eligibility for enrollment, and the temporary recognition may be withdrawn at any time by the Director of Practice.

(e) *Appeal from denial of application.* The Director of Practice must inform the applicant as to the reason(s) for any denial of an application for enrollment. The applicant may, within 30 days after receipt of the notice of denial of enrollment, file a written appeal of the denial of enrollment with the Secretary of the Treasury or his or her delegate. A decision on the appeal will be rendered by the Secretary of the Treasury, or his or her delegate, as soon as practicable.

(f) *Effective/applicability date.* This section is applicable to enrollment applications received on or after September 26, 2007.

§10.6   ENROLLMENT AS AN ENROLLED AGENT OR ENROLLED RETIREMENT PLAN AGENT

(a) *Term of enrollment.* Each individual enrolled to practice before the Internal Revenue Service will be accorded active enrollment status subject to his or her renewal of enrollment as provided in this part.

(b) *Enrollment card.* The Director of the Office of Professional Responsibility will issue an enrollment card to each individual whose application for enrollment to practice before the Internal Revenue Service is approved after July 26, 2002. Each enrollment card will be valid for the period stated on the enrollment card. An individual is not eligible to practice before the Internal Revenue Service if his or her enrollment card is not valid.

(c) *Change of address.* An enrolled agent or enrolled retirement plan agent must send notification of any change of address to the address specified by the Director of the Office of Professional Responsibility. This notification must include the enrolled agent's or enrolled retirement plan agent's name, prior address, new address, social security number or tax identification number and the date.

(d) *Renewal of enrollment.* To maintain active enrollment to practice before the Internal Revenue Service, each individual is required to have the enrollment renewed. Failure to receive notification from the Director of the Office of Professional Responsibility of the renewal requirement will not be justification for the individual's failure to satisfy this requirement.

(1) All individuals licensed to practice before the Internal Revenue Service who have a social security number or tax identification number that ends with the numbers 0, 1, 2, or 3, except for those individuals who received their initial enrollment after November 1, 2003, must apply for renewal between November 1, 2003, and January 31, 2004. The renewal will be effective April 1, 2004.

(2) All individuals licensed to practice before the Internal Revenue Service who have a social security number or tax identification number that ends with the numbers 4, 5, or 6, except for those individuals who received their initial enrollment after November 1, 2004, must apply for renewal between November 1, 2004, and January 31, 2005. The renewal will be effective April 1, 2005.

(3) All individuals licensed to practice before the Internal Revenue Service who have a social security number or tax identification number that ends with the numbers 7, 8, or 9, except for those individuals who received their initial enrollment after November 1, 2005, must apply for renewal between November 1, 2005, and January 31, 2006. The renewal will be effective April 1, 2006.

(4) Thereafter, applications for renewal as an enrolled agent will be required between November 1 and January 31 of every subsequent third year as specified in paragraph (d)(1), (2) or (3) of this section according to the last number of the individual's social security number or tax identification number. Those individuals who receive initial enrollment as an enrolled agent after November 1 and before April 2 of the applicable renewal period will not be required to renew their enrollment before the first full renewal period following the receipt of their initial enrollment. Applications for renewal as an enrolled retirement plan agent will be required of all enrolled retirement plan agents between April 1 and June 30 of every third year period subsequent to their initial enrollment.

(5) The Director of the Office of Professional Responsibility will notify the individual of the renewal of enrollment and will issue the individual a card evidencing enrollment.

(6) A reasonable nonrefundable fee will be charged for each application for renewal of enrollment as an enrolled agent filed with the Director of the Office of Professional Responsibility in accordance with 26 CFR 300.6. A reasonable nonrefundable fee will be charged for each application for renewal of enrollment as an enrolled retirement plan agent filed with the Director of the Office of Professional Responsibility.

(7) Forms required for renewal may be obtained by sending a written request to the Director of the Office of Professional Responsibility, Internal Revenue Service, 1111 Constitution Avenue, N.W., Washington, D.C. 20224 or from such other source as the Director of the Office of Professional Responsibility will publish in the Internal Revenue Bulletin (see 26 CFR 601.601(d)(2)(ii)(b)) and on the Internal Revenue Service Web page (http://www.irs.gov).

(e) *Condition for renewal: Continuing professional education.* In order to qualify for renewal of enrollment, an individual enrolled to practice before the Internal Revenue Service must certify, on the application for renewal form prescribed by the Director of the Office of Professional Responsibility, that he or she has satisfied the following continuing professional education requirements.

(1) *Definitions.* For purposes of this section—

(i) *Enrollment year* means January 1 to December 31 of each year of an enrollment cycle.

(ii) *Enrollment cycle* means the three successive enrollment years preceding the effective date of renewal.

(iii) The *effective date of renewal* is the first day of the fourth month following the close of the period for renewal described in paragraph (d) of this section.

(2) *For renewed enrollment effective after December 31, 2006—*

(i) *Requirements for enrollment cycle.* A minimum of 72 hours of continuing education credit must be completed during each enrollment cycle.

(ii) *Requirements for enrollment year.* A minimum of 16 hours of continuing education credit, including 2 hours of ethics or professional conduct, must be completed during each enrollment year of an enrollment cycle.

(iii) *Enrollment during enrollment cycle—*

(A) *In general.* Subject to paragraph (e)(2)(iii)(B) of this section, an individual who receives initial enrollment during an enrollment cycle must complete 2 hours of qualifying continuing education credit for each month enrolled during the enrollment cycle. Enrollment for any part of a month is considered enrollment for the entire month.

(B) *Ethics.* An individual who receives initial enrollment during an enrollment cycle must complete 2 hours of ethics or professional conduct for each enrollment year during the enrollment cycle. Enrollment for any part of an enrollment year is considered enrollment for the entire year.

(f) *Qualifying continuing education—*

(1) *General—*

(i) *Enrolled agents.* To qualify for continuing education credit for an enrolled agent, a course of learning must—

(A) Be a qualifying program designed to enhance professional knowledge in Federal taxation or Federal tax related matters (programs comprised of current subject matter in Federal taxation or Federal tax related matters, including accounting, tax preparation software and taxation or ethics);

(B) Be a qualifying program consistent with the Internal Revenue Code and effective tax administration; and

(C) Be sponsored by a qualifying sponsor.

(ii) *Enrolled retirement plan agents.* To qualify for continuing education credit for an enrolled retirement plan agent, a course of learning must—

(A) Be a qualifying program designed to enhance professional knowledge in qualified retirement plan matters;

(B) Be a qualifying program consistent with the Internal Revenue Code and effective tax administration; and

(C) Be sponsored by a qualifying sponsor.

(2) *Qualifying programs—*

(i) *Formal programs.* A formal program qualifies as continuing education programs if it—

(A) Requires attendance. Additionally, the program sponsor must provide each attendee with a certificate of attendance; and

(B) Requires that the program be conducted by a qualified instructor, discussion leader, or speaker, i.e., a person whose background, training, education and experience is appropriate for instructing or leading a discussion on the subject matter of the particular program; and

(C) Provides or requires a written outline, textbook, or suitable electronic educational materials.

(ii) *Correspondence or individual study programs (including taped programs).* Qualifying continuing education programs include correspondence or individual study programs that are conducted by qualifying sponsors and completed on an individual basis by the enrolled individual. The allowable credit hours for such programs will be measured on a basis comparable to the measurement of a seminar or course for credit in an accredited educational institution. Such programs qualify as continuing education programs if they—

(A) Require registration of the participants by the sponsor;

(B) Provide a means for measuring completion by the participants (e.g., a written examination), including the issuance of a certificate of completion by the sponsor; and

(C) Provide a written outline, textbook, or suitable electronic educational materials.

(iii) *Serving as an instructor, discussion leader or speaker.*

(A) One hour of continuing education credit will be awarded for each contact hour completed as an instructor, discussion leader, or speaker at an educational program that meets the continuing education requirements of paragraph (f) of this section.

(B) Two hours of continuing education credit will be awarded for actual subject preparation time for each contact hour completed as an instructor, discussion leader, or speaker at such programs. It is the responsibility of the individual claiming such credit to maintain records to verify preparation time.

(C) The maximum credit for instruction and preparation may not exceed 50 percent of the continuing education requirement for an enrollment cycle.

(D) An instructor, discussion leader, or speaker who makes more than one presentation on the same subject matter during an enrollment cycle, will receive continuing education credit for only one such presentation for the enrollment cycle.

(iv) *Credit for published articles, books, etc.*

(A) For enrolled agents, continuing education credit will be awarded for publications on Federal taxation or Federal tax related matters, including accounting, tax preparation software, and taxation or ethics, provided the content of such publications is current and designed for the enhancement of the professional knowledge of an individual enrolled to practice before the Internal Revenue Service. The publication must be consistent with the Internal Revenue Code and effective tax administration. For enrolled retirement plan agents, continuing education credit will be awarded for publications on qualified retirement plan matters, provided the content of such publications is current and designed for the enhancement of the professional knowledge of an individual enrolled to practice as an enrolled retirement plan agent before the Internal Revenue Service. The publication must be consistent with the Internal Revenue Code and effective tax administration.

(B) The credit allowed will be on the basis of one credit hour for each hour of preparation time for the material. It is the responsibility of the person claiming the credit to maintain records to verify preparation time.

(C) The maximum credit for publications may not exceed 25 percent of the continuing education requirement of any enrollment cycle.

(3) *Periodic examination.*

(i) Individuals may establish eligibility for renewal of enrollment for any enrollment cycle by—

(A) Achieving a passing score on each part of the Special Enrollment Examination administered under this part during the three year period prior to renewal; and

(B) Completing a minimum of 16 hours of qualifying continuing education during the last year of an enrollment cycle.

(ii) Courses designed to help an applicant prepare for the examination specified in paragraph (a) of §10.4 are considered basic in nature and are not qualifying continuing education.

(g) *Sponsors.*

(1) Sponsors are those responsible for presenting programs.

(2) To qualify as a sponsor, a program presenter must—

(i) Be an accredited educational institution;

(ii) Be recognized for continuing education purposes by the licensing body of any State, territory, or possession of the United States, including a Commonwealth, or the District of Columbia.

(iii) Be recognized by the Director of the Office of Professional Responsibility as a professional organization or society whose programs include offering continuing professional education opportunities in subject matters within the scope of paragraph (f)(1)(i) of this section; or

(iv) File a sponsor agreement with the Director of the Office of Professional Responsibility and obtain approval of the program as a qualified continuing education program.

(3) A qualifying sponsor must ensure the program complies with the following requirements—

(i) Programs must be developed by individual(s) qualified in the subject matter;

(ii) Program subject matter must be current;

(iii) Instructors, discussion leaders, and speakers must be qualified with respect to program content;

(iv) Programs must include some means for evaluation of technical content and presentation;

(v) Certificates of completion must be provided to the participants who successfully complete the program; and

(vi) Records must be maintained by the sponsor to verify the participants who attended and completed the program for a period of three years following completion of the program. In the case of continuous conferences, conventions, and the like, records must be maintained to verify completion of the program and attendance by each participant at each segment of the program.

(4) Professional organizations or societies wishing to be considered as qualified sponsors must request this status from the Director of the Office of Professional Responsibility and furnish information in support of the request together with any further information deemed necessary by the Director of the Office of Professional Responsibility.

(5) *Sponsor renewal*—

(i) *In general.* A sponsor maintains its status as a qualified sponsor during the sponsor enrollment cycle.

(ii) *Renewal period.* Each sponsor must file an application to renew its status as a qualified sponsor between May 1 and July 31, 2008. Thereafter, applications for renewal will be required between May 1 and July 31 of every subsequent third year.

(iii) *Effective date of renewal.* The effective date of renewal is the first day of the third month following the close of the renewal period.

(iv) *Sponsor enrollment cycle.* The sponsor enrollment cycle is the three successive calendar years preceding the effective date of renewal.

(h) *Measurement of continuing education coursework.*

(1) All continuing education programs will be measured in terms of contact hours. The shortest recognized program will be one contact hour.

(2) A contact hour is 50 minutes of continuous participation in a program. Credit is granted only for a full contact hour, i.e., 50 minutes or multiples thereof.

For example, a program lasting more than 50 minutes but less than 100 minutes will count as one contact hour.

(3) Individual segments at continuous conferences, conventions and the like will be considered one total program. For example, two 90-minute segments (180 minutes) at a continuous conference will count as three contact hours.

(4) For university or college courses, each semester hour credit will equal 15 contact hours and a quarter hour credit will equal 10 contact hours.

(i) *Recordkeeping requirements.*

(1) Each individual applying for renewal must retain for a period of three years following the date of renewal of enrollment the information required with regard to qualifying continuing professional education credit hours. Such information includes—

(i) The name of the sponsoring organization;

(ii) The location of the program;

(iii) The title of the program and description of its content;

(iv) Written outlines, course syllabi, textbook, and/or electronic materials provided or required for the course;

(v) The dates attended;

(vi) The credit hours claimed;

(vii) The name(s) of the instructor(s), discussion leader(s), or speaker(s), if appropriate; and

(viii) The certificate of completion and/or signed statement of the hours of attendance obtained from the sponsor.

(2) To receive continuing education credit for service completed as an instructor, discussion leader, or speaker, the following information must be maintained for a period of three years following the date of renewal of enrollment—

(i) The name of the sponsoring organization;

(ii) The location of the program;

(iii) The title of the program and description of its content;

(iv) The dates of the program; and

(v) The credit hours claimed.

(3) To receive continuing education credit for publications, the following information must be maintained for a period of three years following the date of renewal of enrollment—

(i) The publisher;

(ii) The title of the publication;

(iii) A copy of the publication;

(iv) The date of publication; and

(v) Records that substantiate the hours worked on the publication.

(j) *Waivers.*

(1) Waiver from the continuing education requirements for a given period may be granted by the Director of the Office of Professional Responsibility for the following reasons—

(i) Health, which prevented compliance with the continuing education requirements;

(ii) Extended active military duty;

(iii) Absence from the United States for an extended period of time due to employment or other reasons, provided the individual does not practice before the Internal Revenue Service during such absence; and

(iv) Other compelling reasons, which will be considered on a case-by-case basis.

(2) A request for waiver must be accompanied by appropriate documentation. The individual is required to furnish any additional documentation or explanation deemed necessary by the Director of the Office of Professional Responsibility. Examples of appropriate documentation could be a medical certificate or military orders.

(3) A request for waiver must be filed no later than the last day of the renewal application period.

(4) If a request for waiver is not approved, the individual will be placed in inactive status, so notified by the Director of the Office of Professional Responsibility, and placed on a roster of inactive enrolled individuals.

(5) If a request for waiver is approved, the individual will be notified and issued a card evidencing renewal.

(6) Those who are granted waivers are required to file timely applications for renewal of enrollment.

(k) *Failure to comply.*

(1) Compliance by an individual with the requirements of this part is determined by the Director of the Office of Professional Responsibility. An individual who fails to meet the requirements of eligibility for renewal of enrollment will be notified by the Director of the Office of Professional Responsibility at his or her enrollment address by first-class mail. The notice will state the basis for the determination of noncompliance and will provide the individual an opportunity to furnish information in writing relating to the matter within 60 days of the date of the notice. Such information will be considered by the Director of the Office of Professional Responsibility in making a final determination as to eligibility for renewal of enrollment.

(2) The Director of the Office of Professional Responsibility may require any individual, by notice sent by first-class mail to his or her enrollment address, to provide copies of any records required to be maintained under this part. The Director of the Office of Professional Responsibility may disallow any continuing professional education hours claimed if the individual fails to comply with this requirement.

(3) An individual who has not filed a timely application for renewal of enrollment, who has not made a timely response to the notice of noncompliance with the renewal requirements, or who has not satisfied the requirements of eligibility for renewal will be placed on a roster of inactive enrolled individuals. During this time, the individual will be ineligible to practice before the Internal Revenue Service.

(4) Individuals placed in inactive enrollment status and individuals ineligible to practice before the Internal Revenue Service may not state or imply that they

are enrolled to practice before the Internal Revenue Service, or use the terms enrolled agent or enrolled retirement plan agent, the designations "EA" or "ERPA" or other form of reference to eligibility to practice before the Internal Revenue Service.

(5) An individual placed in an inactive status may be reinstated to an active enrollment status by filing an application for renewal of enrollment and providing evidence of the completion of all required continuing professional education hours for the enrollment cycle. Continuing education credit under this paragraph (k)(5) may not be used to satisfy the requirements of the enrollment cycle in which the individual has been placed back on the active roster.

(6) An individual placed in an inactive status must file an application for renewal of enrollment and satisfy the requirements for renewal as set forth in this section within three years of being placed in an inactive status. The name of such individual otherwise will be removed from the inactive enrollment roster and his or her enrollment will terminate. Eligibility for enrollment must then be reestablished by the individual as provided in this section.

(7) Inactive enrollment status is not available to an individual who is the subject of a disciplinary matter in the Office of Professional Responsibility.

(l) *Inactive retirement status.* An individual who no longer practices before the Internal Revenue Service may request being placed in an inactive retirement status at any time and such individual will be placed in an inactive retirement status. The individual will be ineligible to practice before the Internal Revenue Service. Such individual must file a timely application for renewal of enrollment at each applicable renewal or enrollment period as provided in this section. An individual who is placed in an inactive retirement status may be reinstated to an active enrollment status by filing an application for renewal of enrollment and providing evidence of the completion of the required continuing professional education hours for the enrollment cycle. Inactive retirement status is not available to an individual who is the subject of a disciplinary matter in the Office of Professional Responsibility.

(m) *Renewal while under suspension or disbarment.* An individual who is ineligible to practice before the Internal Revenue Service by virtue of disciplinary action is required to be in conformance with the requirements for renewal of enrollment before his or her eligibility is restored.

(n) *Verification.* The Director of the Office of Professional Responsibility may review the continuing education records of an enrolled individual and/or qualified sponsor in a manner deemed appropriate to determine compliance with the requirements and standards for renewal of enrollment as provided in paragraph (f) of this section.

(o) *Enrolled actuaries.* The enrollment and the renewal of enrollment of actuaries authorized to practice under paragraph (d) of §10.3 are governed by the regulations of the Joint Board for the Enrollment of Actuaries at 20 CFR 901.1 through 901.71.

(p) *Effective/applicability date.* This section is applicable to enrollment effective on or after September 26, 2007.

§10.7   Representing Oneself; Participating in Rulemaking;
Limited Practice; Special Appearances; and Return Preparation

(a) *Representing oneself.* Individuals may appear on their own behalf before the Internal Revenue Service provided they present satisfactory identification.

(b) *Participating in rulemaking.* Individuals may participate in rulemaking as provided by the Administrative Procedure Act. See 5 U.S.C. 553.

(c) *Limited practice*—

(1) *In general.* Subject to the limitations in paragraph (c)(2) of this section, an individual who is not a practitioner may represent a taxpayer before the Internal Revenue Service in the circumstances described in this paragraph (c)(1), even if the taxpayer is not present, provided the individual presents satisfactory identification and proof of his or her authority to represent the taxpayer. The circumstances described in this paragraph (c)(1) are as follows:

(i) An individual may represent a member of his or her immediate family.

(ii) A regular full-time employee of an individual employer may represent the employer.

(iii) A general partner or a regular full-time employee of a partnership may represent the partnership.

(iv) A bona fide officer or a regular full-time employee of a corporation (including a parent, subsidiary, or other affiliated corporation), association, or organized group may represent the corporation, association, or organized group.

(v) A regular full-time employee of a trust, receivership, guardianship, or estate may represent the trust, receivership, guardianship, or estate.

(vi) An officer or a regular employee of a governmental unit, agency, or authority may represent the governmental unit, agency, or authority in the course of his or her official duties.

(vii) An individual may represent any individual or entity, who is outside the United States, before personnel of the Internal Revenue Service when such representation takes place outside the United States.

(viii) An individual who prepares and signs a taxpayer's tax return as the preparer, or who prepares a tax return but is not required (by the instructions to the tax return or regulations) to sign the tax return, may represent the taxpayer before revenue agents, customer service representatives or similar officers and employees of the Internal Revenue Service during an examination of the taxable year or period covered by that tax return, but, unless otherwise prescribed by regulation or notice, this right does not permit such individual to represent the taxpayer, regardless of the circumstances requiring representation, before appeals officers, revenue officers, Counsel or similar officers or employees of the Internal Revenue Service or the Department of Treasury.

(2) *Limitations.*

(i) An individual who is under suspension or disbarment from practice before the Internal Revenue Service may not engage in limited practice before the Internal Revenue Service under paragraph (c)(1) of this section.

(ii) The Director, after notice and opportunity for a conference, may deny eligibility to engage in limited practice before the Internal Revenue Service under paragraph (c)(1) of this section to any individual who has engaged in conduct that would justify a sanction under §10.50.

(iii) An individual who represents a taxpayer under the authority of paragraph (c)(1) of this section is subject, to the extent of his or her authority, to such rules of general applicability regarding standards of conduct and other matters as the Director of Practice prescribes.

(d) *Special appearances.* The Director of Practice may, subject to such conditions as he or she deems appropriate, authorize an individual who is not otherwise eligible to practice before the Internal Revenue Service to represent another person in a particular matter.

(e) *Preparing tax returns and furnishing information.* Any individual may prepare a tax return, appear as a witness for the taxpayer before the Internal Revenue Service, or furnish information at the request of the Internal Revenue Service or any of its officers or employees.

(f) *Fiduciaries.* For purposes of this part, a fiduciary (i.e., a trustee, receiver, guardian, personal representative, administrator, or executor) is considered to be the taxpayer and not a representative of the taxpayer.

(g) *Effective/applicablity date.* This section is applicable on September 26, 2007.

§10.8   CUSTOMHOUSE BROKERS

Nothing contained in the regulations in this part will affect or limit the right of a customhouse broker, licensed as such by the Commissioner of Customs in accordance with the regulations prescribed therefore, in any customs district in which he or she is so licensed, at a relevant local office of the Internal Revenue Service or before the National Office of the Internal Revenue Service, to act as a representative in respect to any matters relating specifically to the importation or exportation of merchandise under the customs or internal revenue laws, for any person for whom he or she has acted as a customhouse broker.

SUBPART B—DUTIES AND RESTRICTIONS RELATING TO PRACTICE BEFORE THE INTERNAL REVENUE SERVICE

§10.20   INFORMATION TO BE FURNISHED

(a) *To the Internal Revenue Service*

(1) A practitioner must, on a proper and lawful request by a duly authorized officer or employee of the Internal Revenue Service, promptly submit records or

information in any matter before the Internal Revenue Service unless the practitioner believes in good faith and on reasonable grounds that the records or information are privileged.

(2) Where the requested records or information are not in the possession of, or subject to the control of, the practitioner or the practitioner's client, the practitioner must promptly notify the requesting Internal Revenue Service officer or employee and the practitioner must provide any information that the practitioner has regarding the identity of any person who the practitioner believes may have possession or control of the requested records or information. The practitioner must make reasonable inquiry of his or her client regarding the identity of any person who may have possession or control of the requested records or information, but the practitioner is not required to make inquiry of any other person or independently verify any information provided by the practitioner's client regarding the identity of such persons.

(b) *To the Director of Practice*. When a proper and lawful request is made by the Director of Practice, a practitioner must provide the Director of Practice with any information the practitioner has concerning an inquiry by the Director of Practice into an alleged violation of the regulations in this part by any person, and to testify regarding this information in any proceeding instituted under this part, unless the practitioner believes in good faith and on reasonable grounds that the information is privileged.

(c) *Interference with a proper and lawful request for records or information*. A practitioner may not interfere, or attempt to interfere, with any proper and lawful effort by the Internal Revenue Service, its officers or employees, or the Director of Practice, or his or her employees, to obtain any record or information unless the practitioner believes in good faith and on reasonable grounds that the record or information is privileged.

§10.21 Knowledge of Client's Omission

A practitioner who, having been retained by a client with respect to a matter administered by the Internal Revenue Service, knows that the client has not complied with the revenue laws of the United States or has made an error in or omission from any return, document, affidavit, or other paper which the client submitted or executed under the revenue laws of the United States, must advise the client promptly of the fact of such noncompliance, error, or omission. The practitioner must advise the client of the consequences as provided under the Code and regulations of such noncompliance, error, or omission.

§10.22 Diligence as to Accuracy

(a) *In general*. A practitioner must exercise due diligence—

(1) In preparing or assisting in the preparation of, approving, and filing tax returns, documents, affidavits, and other papers relating to Internal Revenue Service matters;

(2) In determining the correctness of oral or written representations made by the practitioner to the Department of the Treasury; and

(3) In determining the correctness of oral or written representations made by the practitioner to clients with reference to any matter administered by the Internal Revenue Service.

(b) *Reliance on others.* Except as provided in §§10.34, 10.35 and 10.37, a practitioner will be presumed to have exercised due diligence for purposes of this section if the practitioner relies on the work product of another person and the practitioner used reasonable care in engaging, supervising, training, and evaluating the person, taking proper account of the nature of the relationship between the practitioner and the person.

(c) *Effective/applicability date.* This section is applicable on September 26, 2007.

§10.23   PROMPT DISPOSITION OF PENDING MATTERS

A practitioner may not unreasonably delay the prompt disposition of any matter before the Internal Revenue Service.

§10.24   ASSISTANCE FROM OR TO DISBARRED OR SUSPENDED PERSONS AND
FORMER INTERNAL REVENUE SERVICE EMPLOYEES

A practitioner may not, knowingly and directly or indirectly:

(a) Accept assistance from or assist any person who is under disbarment or suspension from practice before the Internal Revenue Service if the assistance relates to a matter or matters constituting practice before the Internal Revenue Service.

(b) Accept assistance from any former government employee where the provisions of §10.25 or any Federal law would be violated.

§10.25   PRACTICE BY FORMER GOVERNMENT EMPLOYEES, THEIR PARTNERS
AND THEIR ASSOCIATES

(a) *Definitions.* For purposes of this section—

(1) *Assist* means to act in such a way as to advise, furnish information to, or otherwise aid another person, directly, or indirectly.

(2) *Government employee* is an officer or employee of the United States or any agency of the United States, including a special Government employee as defined in 18 U.S.C. 202(a), or of the District of Columbia, or of any State, or a member of Congress or of any State legislature.

(3) *Member of a firm* is a sole practitioner or an employee or associate thereof, or a partner, stockholder, associate, affiliate or employee of a partnership, joint venture, corporation, professional association or other affiliation of two or more practitioners who represent nongovernmental parties.

(4) *Particular matter involving specific parties* is defined at 5 CFR 2637.201(c) or superseding post-employment regulations issued by the U.S. Office of Government Ethics.

(5) Rule includes Treasury regulations, whether issued or under preparation for issuance as notices of proposed rulemaking or as Treasury decisions, revenue rulings, and revenue procedures published in the Internal Revenue Bulletin (see 26 CFR 601.601(d)(2)(ii)(b)).

(b) *General rules*—

(1) No former Government employee may, subsequent to Government employment, represent anyone in any matter administered by the Internal Revenue Service if the representation would violate 18 U.S.C. 207 or any other laws of the United States.

(2) No former Government employee who personally and substantially participated in a particular matter involving specific parties may, subsequent to Government employment, represent or knowingly assist, in that particular matter, any person who is or was a specific party to that particular matter.

(3) A former Government employee who within a period of one year prior to the termination of Government employment had official responsibility for a particular matter involving specific parties may not, within two years after Government employment is ended, represent in that particular matter any person who is or was a specific party to that particular matter.

(4) No former Government employee may, within one year after Government employment is ended, communicate with or appear before, with the intent to influence, any employee of the Treasury Department in connection with the publication, withdrawal, amendment, modification, or interpretation of a rule the development of which the former Government employee participated in, or for which, within a period of one year prior to the termination of Government employment, the former government employee had official responsibility. This paragraph (b)(4) does not, however, preclude any former employee from appearing on one's own behalf or from representing a taxpayer before the Internal Revenue Service in connection with a particular matter involving specific parties involving the application or interpretation of a rule with respect to that particular matter, provided that the representation is otherwise consistent with the other provisions of this section and the former employee does not utilize or disclose any confidential information acquired by the former employee in the development of the rule.

(c) *Firm representation*—

(1) No member of a firm of which a former Government employee is a member may represent or knowingly assist a person who was or is a specific party in any particular matter with respect to which the restrictions of paragraph (b)(2) of this section apply to the former Government employee, in that particular matter, unless the firm isolates the former Government employee in such a way to ensure that the former Government employee cannot assist in the representation.

(2) When isolation of a former Government employee is required under paragraph (c)(1) of this section, a statement affirming the fact of such isolation must be executed under oath by the former Government employee and by another member of the firm acting on behalf of the firm. The statement must clearly

identify the firm, the former Government employee, and the particular matter(s) requiring isolation. The statement must be retained by the firm and, upon request, provided to the Director of the Office of Professional Responsibility.

(d) *Pending representation.* The provisions of this regulation will govern practice by former Government employees, their partners and associates with respect to representation in particular matters involving specific parties where actual representation commenced before the effective date of this regulation.

(e) *Effective/applicability date.* This section is applicable on September 26, 2007.

§10.26   NOTARIES

A practitioner may not take acknowledgments, administer oaths, certify papers, or perform any official act as a notary public with respect to any matter administered by the Internal Revenue Service and for which he or she is employed as counsel, attorney, or agent, or in which he or she may be in any way interested.

§10.27   FEES

(a) *In general.* A practitioner may not charge an unconscionable fee in connection with any matter before the Internal Revenue Service.

(b) *Contingent fees—*

(1) Except as provided in paragraphs (b)(2), (3), and (4) of this section, a practitioner may not charge a contingent fee for services rendered in connection with any matter before the Internal Revenue Service.

(2) A practitioner may charge a contingent fee for services rendered in connection with the Service's examination of, or challenge to—

(i) An original tax return; or

(ii) An amended return or claim for refund or credit where the amended return or claim for refund or credit was filed within 120 days of the taxpayer receiving a written notice of the examination of, or a written challenge to the original tax return.

(3) A practitioner may charge a contingent fee for services rendered in connection with a claim for credit or refund filed solely in connection with the determination of statutory interest or penalties assessed by the Internal Revenue Service.

(4) A practitioner may charge a contingent fee for services rendered in connection with any judicial proceeding arising under the Internal Revenue Code.

(c) *Definitions.* For purposes of this section—

(1) *Contingent fee* is any fee that is based, in whole or in part, on whether or not a position taken on a tax return or other filing avoids challenge by the Internal Revenue Service or is sustained either by the Internal Revenue Service or in litigation. A contingent fee includes a fee that is based on a percentage of the refund reported on a return, that is based on a percentage of the taxes saved, or that otherwise depends on the specific result attained. A contingent fee also

includes any fee arrangement in which the practitioner will reimburse the client for all or a portion of the client's fee in the event that a position taken on a tax return or other filing is challenged by the Internal Revenue Service or is not sustained, whether pursuant to an indemnity agreement, a guarantee, rescission rights, or any other arrangement with a similar effect.

(2) *Matter before the Internal Revenue Service* includes tax planning and advice, preparing or filing or assisting in preparing or filing returns or claims for refund or credit, and all matters connected with a presentation to the Internal Revenue Service or any of its officers or employees relating to a taxpayer's rights, privileges, or liabilities under laws or regulations administered by the Internal Revenue Service. Such presentations include, but are not limited to, preparing and filing documents, corresponding and communicating with the Internal Revenue Service, rendering written advice with respect to any entity, transaction, plan or arrangement, and representing a client at conferences, hearings, and meetings.

(d) *Effective/applicability date.* This section is applicable for fee arrangements entered into after March 26, 2008.

§10.28   Return of Client's Records

(a) In general, a practitioner must, at the request of a client, promptly return any and all records of the client that are necessary for the client to comply with his or her Federal tax obligations. The practitioner may retain copies of the records returned to a client. The existence of a dispute over fees generally does not relieve the practitioner of his or her responsibility under this section.

Nevertheless, if applicable state law allows or permits the retention of a client's records by a practitioner in the case of a dispute over fees for services rendered, the practitioner need only return those records that must be attached to the taxpayer's return. The practitioner, however, must provide the client with reasonable access to review and copy any additional records of the client retained by the practitioner under state law that are necessary for the client to comply with his or her Federal tax obligations.

(b) For purposes of this section—*Records of the client* include all documents or written or electronic materials provided to the practitioner, or obtained by the practitioner in the course of the practitioner's representation of the client, that preexisted the retention of the practitioner by the client. The term also includes materials that were prepared by the client or a third party (not including an employee or agent of the practitioner) at any time and provided to the practitioner with respect to the subject matter of the representation. The term also includes any return, claim for refund, schedule, affidavit, appraisal or any other document prepared by the practitioner, or his or her employee or agent, that was presented to the client with respect to a prior representation if such document is necessary for the taxpayer to comply with his or her current Federal tax obligations. The term does not include any return, claim for refund, schedule, affidavit, appraisal or any other document prepared by the practitioner or the practitioner's firm, employees or agents if the practitioner is withholding such document pending the client's performance of its contractual obligation to pay fees with respect to such document.

§10.29   Conflicting Interests

(a) Except as provided by paragraph (b) of this section, a practitioner shall not represent a client before the Internal Revenue Service if the representation involves a conflict of interest. A conflict of interest exists if—

(1) The representation of one client will be directly adverse to another client; or

(2) There is a significant risk that the representation of one or more clients will be materially limited by the practitioner's responsibilities to another client, a former client or a third person, or by a personal interest of the practitioner.

(b) Notwithstanding the existence of a conflict of interest under paragraph (a) of this section, the practitioner may represent a client if—

(1) The practitioner reasonably believes that the practitioner will be able to provide competent and diligent representation to each affected client;

(2) The representation is not prohibited by law; and

(3) Each affected client waives the conflict of interest and gives informed consent, confirmed in writing by each affected client, at the time the existence of the conflict of interest is known by the practitioner. The confirmation may be made within a reasonable period after the informed consent, but in no event later than 30 days.

(c) Copies of the written consents must be retained by the practitioner for at least 36 months from the date of the conclusion of the representation of the affected clients, and the written consents must be provided to any officer or employee of the Internal Revenue Service on request.

(d) *Effective/applicability date.* This section is applicable on September 26, 2007.

§10.30   Solicitation

(a) *Advertising and solicitation restrictions.*

(1) A practitioner may not, with respect to any Internal Revenue Service matter, in any way use or participate in the use of any form or public communication or private solicitation containing a false, fraudulent, or coercive statement or claim; or a misleading or deceptive statement or claim. Enrolled agents or enrolled retirement plan agents, in describing their professional designation, may not utilize the term of art "certified" or imply an employer/employee relationship with the Internal Revenue Service. Examples of acceptable descriptions for enrolled agents are "enrolled to represent taxpayers before the Internal Revenue Service," "enrolled to practice before the Internal Revenue Service," and "admitted to practice before the Internal Revenue Service." Similarly, examples of acceptable descriptions for enrolled retirement plan agents are "enrolled to represent taxpayers before the Internal Revenue Service as a retirement plan agent"

and "enrolled to practice before the Internal Revenue Service as a retirement plan agent."

(2) A practitioner may not make, directly or indirectly, an uninvited written or oral solicitation of employment in matters related to the Internal Revenue Service if the solicitation violates Federal or State law or other applicable rule, e.g., attorneys are precluded from making a solicitation that is prohibited by conduct rules applicable to all attorneys in their State(s) of licensure. Any lawful solicitation made by or on behalf of a practitioner eligible to practice before the Internal Revenue Service must, nevertheless, clearly identify the solicitation as such and, if applicable, identify the source of the information used in choosing the recipient.

(b) *Fee information.*

(1)

(i) A practitioner may publish the availability of a written schedule of fees and disseminate the following fee information—

(A) Fixed fees for specific routine services.

(B) Hourly rates.

(C) Range of fees for particular services.

(D) Fee charged for an initial consultation.

(ii) Any statement of fee information concerning matters in which costs may be incurred must include a statement disclosing whether clients will be responsible for such costs.

(2) A practitioner may charge no more than the rate(s) published under paragraph (b)(1) of this section for at least 30 calendar days after the last date on which the schedule of fees was published.

(c) *Communication of fee information.* Fee information may be communicated in professional lists, telephone directories, print media, mailings, electronic mail, facsimile, hand delivered flyers, radio, television, and any other method. The method chosen, however, must not cause the communication to become untruthful, deceptive, or otherwise in violation of this part. A practitioner may not persist in attempting to contact a prospective client if the prospective client has made it known to the practitioner that he or she does not desire to be solicited. In the case of radio and television broadcasting, the broadcast must be recorded and the practitioner must retain a recording of the actual transmission. In the case of direct mail and e-commerce communications, the practitioner must retain a copy of the actual communication, along with a list or other description of persons to whom the communication was mailed or otherwise distributed. The copy must be retained by the practitioner for a period of at least 36 months from the date of the last transmission or use.

(d) *Improper associations.* A practitioner may not, in matters related to the Internal Revenue Service, assist, or accept assistance from, any person or entity who, to the knowledge of the practitioner, obtains clients or otherwise practices in a manner forbidden under this section.

(e) *Effective/applicability date.* This section is applicable on September 26, 2007.

§10.31   Negotiation of Taxpayer Checks

A practitioner who prepares tax returns may not endorse or otherwise negotiate any check issued to a client by the government in respect of a Federal tax liability.

§10.32   Practice of Law

Nothing in the regulations in this part may be construed as authorizing persons not members of the bar to practice law.

§10.33   Best Practices for Tax Advisors

(a) *Best practices.* Tax advisors should provide clients with the highest quality representation concerning Federal tax issues by adhering to best practices in providing advice and in preparing or assisting in the preparation of a submission to the Internal Revenue Service. In addition to compliance with the standards of practice provided elsewhere in this part, best practices include the following:

(1) Communicating clearly with the client regarding the terms of the engagement. For example, the advisor should determine the client's expected purpose for and use of the advice and should have a clear understanding with the client regarding the form and scope of the advice or assistance to be rendered.

(2) Establishing the facts, determining which facts are relevant, evaluating the reasonableness of any assumptions or representations, relating the applicable law (including potentially applicable judicial doctrines) to the relevant facts, and arriving at a conclusion supported by the law and the facts.

(3) Advising the client regarding the import of the conclusions reached, including, for example, whether a taxpayer may avoid accuracy-related penalties under the Internal Revenue Code if a taxpayer acts in reliance on the advice.

(4) Acting fairly and with integrity in practice before the Internal Revenue Service.

(b) *Procedures to ensure best practices for tax advisors.* Tax advisors with responsibility for overseeing a firm's practice of providing advice concerning Federal tax issues or of preparing or assisting in the preparation of submissions to the Internal Revenue Service should take reasonable steps to ensure that the firm's procedures for all members, associates, and employees are consistent with the best practices set forth in paragraph (a) of this section.

(c) *Applicability date.* This section is effective after June 20, 2005.

§10.34   Standards for Advising with Respect to Tax Return Positions and for Preparing or Signing Returns

(a) *[Reserved].*

(b) *Documents, affidavits and other papers—*

(1) A practitioner may not advise a client to take a position on a document, affidavit or other paper submitted to the Internal Revenue Service unless the position is not frivolous.

(2) A practitioner may not advise a client to submit a document, affidavit or other paper to the Internal Revenue Service—

(i) The purpose of which is to delay or impede the administration of the Federal tax laws;

(ii) That is frivolous; or

(iii) That contains or omits information in a manner that demonstrates an intentional disregard of a rule or regulation unless the practitioner also advises the client to submit a document that evidences a good faith challenge to the rule or regulation.

(c) *Advising clients on potential penalties*—

(1) A practitioner must inform a client of any penalties that are reasonably likely to apply to the client with respect to—

(i) A position taken on a tax return if—

(A) The practitioner advised the client with respect to the position; or

(B) The practitioner prepared or signed the tax return; and

(ii) Any document, affidavit or other paper submitted to the Internal Revenue Service.

(2) The practitioner also must inform the client of any opportunity to avoid any such penalties by disclosure, if relevant, and of the requirements for adequate disclosure.

(3) This paragraph (c) applies even if the practitioner is not subject to a penalty under the Internal Revenue Code with respect to the position or with respect to the document, affidavit or other paper submitted.

(d) *Relying on information furnished by clients.* A practitioner advising a client to take a position on a tax return, document, affidavit or other paper submitted to the Internal Revenue Service, or preparing or signing a tax return as a preparer, generally may rely in good faith without verification upon information furnished by the client. The practitioner may not, however, ignore the implications of information furnished to, or actually known by, the practitioner, and must make reasonable inquiries if the information as furnished appears to be incorrect, inconsistent with an important fact or another factual assumption, or incomplete.

(e) [*Reserved*].

(f) *Effective/applicability date.* Section 10.34 is applicable to tax returns, documents, affidavits and other papers filed on or after September 26, 2007.

§10.35 Requirements for Covered Opinions

(a) A practitioner who provides a covered opinion shall comply with the standards of practice in this section.

(b) *Definitions.* For purposes of this subpart—

(1) A *practitioner* includes any individual described in §10.2(a)(5).

(2) *Covered opinion*—

(i) *In general.* A covered opinion is written advice (including electronic communications) by a practitioner concerning one or more Federal tax issues arising from—

(A) A transaction that is the same as or substantially similar to a transaction that, at the time the advice is rendered, the Internal Revenue Service has determined to be a tax avoidance transaction and identified by published guidance as a listed transaction under 26 CFR 1.6011-4(b)(2);

(B) Any partnership or other entity, any investment plan or arrangement, or any other plan or arrangement, the principal purpose of which is the avoidance or evasion of any tax imposed by the Internal Revenue Code; or

(C) Any partnership or other entity, any investment plan or arrangement, or any other plan or arrangement, a significant purpose of which is the avoidance or evasion of any tax imposed by the Internal Revenue Code if the written advice—

(1) Is a reliance opinion;

(2) Is a marketed opinion;

(3) Is subject to conditions of confidentiality; or

(4) Is subject to contractual protection.

(ii) *Excluded advice.* A covered opinion does not include—

(A) Written advice provided to a client during the course of an engagement if a practitioner is reasonably expected to provide subsequent written advice to the client that satisfies the requirements of this section;

(B) Written advice, other than advice described in paragraph (b)(2)(i)(A) of this section (concerning listed transactions) or paragraph (b)(2)(i)(B) of this section (concerning the principal purpose of avoidance or evasion) that—

(1) Concerns the qualification of a qualified plan;

(2) Is a State or local bond opinion; or

(3) Is included in documents required to be filed with the Securities and Exchange Commission.

(C) Written advice prepared for and provided to a taxpayer, solely for use by that taxpayer, after the taxpayer has filed a tax return with the Internal Revenue Service reflecting the tax benefits of the transaction. The preceding sentence does not apply if the practitioner knows or has reason to know that the written advice will be relied upon by the taxpayer to take a position on a tax return (including for these purposes an amended return that claims tax benefits not reported on a previously filed return) filed after the date on which the advice is provided to the taxpayer;

(D) Written advice provided to an employer by a practitioner in that practitioner's capacity as an employee of that employer solely for purposes of determining the tax liability of the employer; or

(E) Written advice that does not resolve a Federal tax issue in the taxpayer's favor, unless the advice reaches a conclusion favorable to the taxpayer at any confidence level (e.g., not frivolous, realistic possibility of success, reasonable basis or substantial authority) with respect to that issue. If written advice concerns more than one Federal tax issue, the advice must comply with the requirements of paragraph (c) of this section with respect to any Federal tax issue not described in the preceding sentence.

(3) A Federal tax issue is a question concerning the Federal tax treatment of an item of income, gain, loss, deduction, or credit, the existence or absence of a taxable transfer of property, or the value of property for Federal tax purposes.

For purposes of this subpart, a Federal tax issue is significant if the Internal Revenue Service has a reasonable basis for a successful challenge and its resolution could have a significant impact, whether beneficial or adverse and under any reasonably foreseeable circumstance, on the overall Federal tax treatment of the transaction(s) or matter(s) addressed in the opinion.

(4) *Reliance opinion*—

(i) Written advice is a reliance opinion if the advice concludes at a confidence level of at least more likely than not a greater than 50 percent likelihood that one or more significant Federal tax issues would be resolved in the taxpayer's favor.

(ii) For purposes of this section, written advice, other than advice described in paragraph (b)(2)(i)(A) of this section (concerning listed transactions) or paragraph (b)(2)(i)(B) of this section (concerning the principal purpose of avoidance or evasion), is not treated as a reliance opinion if the practitioner prominently discloses in the written advice that it was not intended or written by the practitioner to be used, and that it cannot be used by the taxpayer, for the purpose of avoiding penalties that may be imposed on the taxpayer.

(5) *Marketed opinion*—

(i) Written advice is a marketed opinion if the practitioner knows or has reason to know that the written advice will be used or referred to by a person other than the practitioner (or a person who is a member of, associated with, or employed by the practitioner's firm) in promoting, marketing or recommending a partnership or other entity, investment plan or arrangement to one or more taxpayer(s).

(ii) For purposes of this section, written advice, other than advice described in paragraph (b)(2)(i)(A) of this section (concerning listed transactions) or paragraph (b)(2)(i)(B) of this section (concerning the principal purpose of avoidance or evasion), is not treated as a marketed opinion if the practitioner prominently discloses in the written advice that—

(A) The advice was not intended or written by the practitioner to be used, and that it cannot be used by any taxpayer, for the purpose of avoiding penalties that may be imposed on the taxpayer;

(B) The advice was written to support the promotion or marketing of the transaction(s) or matter(s) addressed by the written advice; and

(C) The taxpayer should seek advice based on the taxpayer's particular circumstances from an independent tax advisor.

(6) *Conditions of confidentiality.* Written advice is subject to conditions of confidentiality if the practitioner imposes on one or more recipients of the written advice a limitation on disclosure of the tax treatment or tax structure of the transaction and the limitation on disclosure protects the confidentiality of that practitioner's tax strategies, regardless of whether the limitation on disclosure is

legally binding. A claim that a transaction is proprietary or exclusive is not a limitation on disclosure if the practitioner confirms to all recipients of the written advice that there is no limitation on disclosure of the tax treatment or tax structure of the transaction that is the subject of the written advice.

(7) *Contractual protection.* Written advice is subject to contractual protection if the taxpayer has the right to a full or partial refund of fees paid to the practitioner (or a person who is a member of, associated with, or employed by the practitioner's firm) if all or a part of the intended tax consequences from the matters addressed in the written advice are not sustained, or if the fees paid to the practitioner (or a person who is a member of, associated with, or employed by the practitioner's firm) are contingent on the taxpayer's realization of tax benefits from the transaction. All the facts and circumstances relating to the matters addressed in the written advice will be considered when determining whether a fee is refundable or contingent, including the right to reimbursements of amounts that the parties to a transaction have not designated as fees or any agreement to provide services without reasonable compensation.

(8) *Prominently disclosed.* An item is prominently disclosed if it is readily apparent to a reader of the written advice. Whether an item is readily apparent will depend on the facts and circumstances surrounding the written advice including, but not limited to, the sophistication of the taxpayer and the length of the written advice. At a minimum, to be prominently disclosed an item must be set forth in a separate section (and not in a footnote) in a typeface that is the same size or larger than the typeface of any discussion of the facts or law in the written advice.

(9) *State or local bond opinion.* A State or local bond opinion is written advice with respect to a Federal tax issue included in any materials delivered to a purchaser of a State or local bond in connection with the issuance of the bond in a public or private offering, including an official statement (if one is prepared), that concerns only the excludability of interest on a State or local bond from gross income under section 103 of the Internal Revenue Code, the application of section 55 of the Internal Revenue Code to a State or local bond, the status of a State or local bond as a qualified tax-exempt obligation under section 265 (b)(3) of the Internal Revenue Code, the status of a State or local bond as a qualified zone academy bond under section 1397E of the Internal Revenue Code, or any combination of the above.

(10) *The principal purpose.* For purposes of this section, the principal purpose of a partnership or other entity, investment plan or arrangement, or other plan or arrangement is the avoidance or evasion of any tax imposed by the Internal Revenue Code if that purpose exceeds any other purpose. The principal purpose of a partnership or other entity, investment plan or arrangement, or other plan or arrangement is not to avoid or evade Federal tax if that partnership, entity, plan or arrangement has as its purpose the claiming of tax benefits in a manner consistent with the statute and Congressional purpose. A partnership, entity, plan or arrangement may have a significant purpose of avoidance or evasion even though

it does not have the principal purpose of avoidance or evasion under this paragraph (b)(10).

(c) *Requirements for covered opinions.* A practitioner providing a covered opinion must comply with each of the following requirements.

(1) *Factual matters.*

(i) The practitioner must use reasonable efforts to identify and ascertain the facts, which may relate to future events if a transaction is prospective or proposed, and to determine which facts are relevant. The opinion must identify and consider all facts that the practitioner determines to be relevant.

(ii) The practitioner must not base the opinion on any unreasonable factual assumptions (including assumptions as to future events). An unreasonable factual assumption includes a factual assumption that the practitioner knows or should know is incorrect or incomplete. For example, it is unreasonable to assume that a transaction has a business purpose or that a transaction is potentially profitable apart from tax benefits. A factual assumption includes reliance on a projection, financial forecast or appraisal. It is unreasonable for a practitioner to rely on a projection, financial forecast or appraisal if the practitioner knows or should know that the projection, financial forecast or appraisal is incorrect or incomplete or was prepared by a person lacking the skills or qualifications necessary to prepare such projection, financial forecast or appraisal. The opinion must identify in a separate section all factual assumptions relied upon by the practitioner.

(iii) The practitioner must not base the opinion on any unreasonable factual representations, statements or findings or of the taxpayer or any other person. An unreasonable factual representation includes a factual representation that the practitioner knows or should know is incorrect or incomplete. For example, a practitioner may not rely on a factual representation that a transaction has a business purpose if the representation does not include a specific description of the business purpose or the practitioner knows or should know that the representation is incorrect or incomplete.

The opinion must identify in a separate section all factual representations, statements or finds of the taxpayer relied upon by the practitioner.

(2) *Relate law to facts.*

(i) The opinion must relate the applicable law (including potentially applicable judicial doctrines) to the relevant facts.

(ii) The practitioner must not assume the favorable resolution of any significant Federal tax issue except as provided in paragraphs (c)(3)(v) and (d) of this section, or otherwise base an opinion on any unreasonable legal assumptions, representations, or conclusions.

(iii) The opinion must not contain internally inconsistent legal analyses or conclusions.

(3) *Evaluation of significant Federal tax issues—*

(i) *In general.* The opinion must consider all significant Federal tax issues except as provided in paragraphs (c)(3)(v) and (d) of this section.

(ii) *Conclusion as to each significant Federal tax issues.* The opinion must provide the practitioner's conclusion as to the likelihood that the taxpayer will prevail on the merits with respect to each significant Federal tax issue considered in the opinion. If the practitioner is unable to reach a conclusion with respect to one or more of those issues, the opinion must state that the practitioner is unable to reach a conclusion with respect to those issues. The opinion must describe the reasons for the conclusions, including the facts and analysis supporting the conclusions, or describe the reasons that the practitioner is unable to reach a conclusion as to one or more issues. If the practitioner fails to reach a conclusion at the confidence level of at least more likely than not with respect to one or more significant Federal tax issues considered, the opinion must include the appropriate disclosure(s) required under paragraph (e) of this section.

(iii) *Evaluation based on chances of success on the merits.* In evaluating the significant Federal tax issues addressed in the opinion, the practitioner must not take into account the possibility that a tax return will not be audited, that an issue will not be raised on audit, or that an issue will be resolved through settlement if raised.

(iv) *Marketed opinions.* In the case of a marketed opinion, the opinion must provide the practitioner's conclusion that the taxpayer will prevail on the merits at a confidence level of at least more likely than not with respect to each significant Federal tax issue. If the practitioner is unable to reach a more likely than not conclusion with respect to each significant Federal tax issue, the practitioner must not provide the marketed opinion, but may provide written advice that satisfies the requirements in paragraph (b)(5)(ii) of this section.

(v) *Limited scope opinions.*

(A) The practitioner may provide an opinion that considers less than all of the significant Federal tax issues if—

(1) The practitioner and the taxpayer agree that the scope of the opinion and the taxpayer's potential reliance on the opinion for purposes of avoiding penalties that may be imposed on the taxpayer are limited to the Federal tax issue(s) addressed in the opinion;

(2) The opinion is not advice described in paragraph (b)(2)(i)(A) of this section (concerning listed transactions), paragraph (b)(2)(i)(B) of this section (concerning the principal purpose of avoidance or evasion) or paragraph (b)(5) of this section (a marketed opinion); and

(3) The opinion includes the appropriate disclosure(s) required under paragraph (e) of this section.

(B) A practitioner may make reasonable assumptions regarding the favorable resolution of a Federal tax issue (as assumed issue) for purposes of providing an opinion on less than all of the significant Federal tax issues as provided in this paragraph (c)(3)(v).

The opinion must identify in a separate section all issues for which the practitioner assumed a favorable resolution.

(4) *Overall conclusion.*

(i) The opinion must provide the practitioner's overall conclusion as to the likelihood that the Federal tax treatment of the transaction or matter that is the subject of the opinion is the proper treatment and the reasons for that conclusion. If the practitioner is unable to reach an overall conclusion, the opinion must state that the practitioner is unable to reach and overall conclusion and describe the reasons for the practitioner's inability to reach a conclusion.

(ii) In the case of a marketed opinion, the opinion must provide the practitioner's overall conclusion that the Federal tax treatment of the transaction or matter that is the subject of the opinion is the proper treatment at a confidence level of at least more likely than not.

(d) *Competence to provide opinion; reliance on opinions of others.*

(1) The practitioner must be knowledgeable in all of the aspects of Federal tax law relevant to the opinion being rendered, except that the practitioner may rely on the opinion of another practitioner with respect to one or more significant Federal tax issues, unless the practitioner knows or should know that the opinion of the other practitioner should not be relied on. If a practitioner relies on the opinion of another practitioner, the relying practitioner's opinion must identify the other opinion and set forth the conclusions reached in the other opinion.

(2) The practitioner must be satisfied that the combined analysis of the opinions, taken as a whole, and the overall conclusion, if any, satisfy the requirements of this section.

(e) *Required disclosures.* A covered opinion must contain all of the following disclosures that apply—

(1) Relationship between promoter and practitioner. An opinion must prominently disclose the existence of—

(i) Any compensation arrangement, such as a referral fee or a fee-sharing arrangement, between the practitioner (or the practitioner's firm or any person who is a member of, associated with, or employed by the practitioner's firm) and any person (other than the client for whom the opinion is prepared) with respect to promoting, marketing or recommending the entity, plan, or arrangement (or a substantially similar arrangement) that is the subject of the opinion; or

(ii) Any referral agreement between the practitioner (or the practitioner's firm or any person who is a member of, associated with, or employed by the practitioner's firm) and a person (other than the client for whom the opinion is prepared) engaged in promoting, marketing or recommending the entity, plan, or arrangement (or a substantially similar arrangement) that is the subject of the opinion.

(2) *Marketed opinions.* A marketed opinion must prominently disclose that—

(i) The opinion was written to support the promotion or marketing of the transaction(s) or matter(s) addressed in the opinion; and

(ii) The taxpayer should seek advice based on the taxpayer's particular circumstances from an independent tax advisor.

(3) *Limited scope opinions.* A limited scope opinion must prominently disclose that—

(i) The opinion is limited to the one or more Federal tax issues addressed in the opinion;

(ii) Additional issues may exist that could affect the Federal tax treatment of the transaction or matter that is the subject of the opinion and the opinion does not consider or provide a conclusion with respect to any additional issues; and

(iii) With respect to any significant Federal tax issues outside the limited scope of the opinion, the opinion was not written, and cannot be used by the taxpayer, for the purpose of avoiding penalties that may be imposed on the taxpayer.

(4) *Opinions that fail to reach a more likely than not conclusion.* An opinion that does not reach a conclusion at a confidence level of at least more likely than not with respect to a significant Federal tax issue must prominently disclose that—

(i) The opinion does not reach a conclusion at a confidence level of at least more likely than not with respect to one or more significant Federal tax issues addressed by the opinion; and

(ii) With respect to those significant Federal tax issues, the opinion was not written, and cannot be used by the taxpayer, for the purpose of avoiding penalties that may be imposed on the taxpayer.

(5) *Advice regarding required disclosures.* In the case of any disclosure required under this section, the practitioner may not provide advice to any person that is contrary to or inconsistent with the required disclosure.

(f) *Effect of opinion that meets these standards—*

(1) *In general.* An opinion that meets the requirements of this section satisfies the practitioner's responsibilities under this section, but the persuasiveness of the opinion with regard to the tax issues in question and the taxpayer's good faith reliance on the opinion will be determined separately under applicable provisions of the law and regulations.

(2) *Standards for other written advice.* A practitioner who provides written advice that is not a covered opinion for purposes of this section is subject to the requirements of §10.37.

(g) *Effective date.* This section applies to written advice that is rendered after June 20, 2005.

§10.36   PROCEDURES TO ENSURE COMPLIANCE

(a) *Requirements for covered opinions.* Any practitioner who has (or practitioners who have or share) principal authority and responsibility for overseeing a firm's practice of providing advice concerning Federal tax issues must take reasonable steps to ensure that the firm has adequate procedures in effect for all members, associates, and employees for purposes of complying with §10.35. Any such practitioner will be subject to discipline for failing to comply with the requirements of this paragraph if—

(1) The practitioner through willfulness, recklessness, or gross incompetence does not take reasonable steps to ensure that the firm has adequate procedures to comply with §10.35, and one or more individuals who are members of, associated with, or employed by, the firm are, or have engaged in a pattern or practice, in connection with their practice with the firm, of failing to comply with §10.35; or

(2) The practitioner knows or should know that one or more individuals who are members of, associated with, or employed by, the firm are, or have, engaged in a pattern or practice, in connection with their practice with the firm, that does not comply with §10.35 and the practitioner, through willfulness, recklessness, or gross incompetence, fails to take prompt action to correct the noncompliance.

(b) *Effective date.* This section is applicable after June 20, 2005.

§10.37 Requirements for Other Written Advice

(a) *Requirements.* A practitioner must not give written advice (including electronic communications) concerning one or more Federal tax issues if the practitioner bases the written advice on unreasonable factual or legal assumptions (including assumptions as to future events), unreasonably relies upon representations, statements, findings or agreements of the taxpayer or any other person, does not consider all relevant facts that the practitioner knows or should know, or, in evaluating a Federal tax issue, takes into account the possibility that a tax return will not be audited, that an issue will not be raised on audit, or that an issue will be resolved through settlement if raised. All facts and circumstances, including the scope of the engagement and the type and specificity of the advice sought by the client will be considered in determining whether a practitioner has failed to comply with this section. In the case of an opinion the practitioner knows or has reason to know will be used or referred to by a person other than the practitioner (or a person who is a member of, associated with, or employed by the practitioner's firm) in promoting, marketing or recommending to one or more taxpayers a partnership or other entity, investment plan or arrangement a significant purpose of which is the avoidance or evasion of any tax imposed by the Internal Revenue Code, the determination of whether a practitioner has failed to comply with this section will be made on the basis of a heightened standard of care because of the greater risk caused by the practitioner's lack of knowledge of the taxpayer's particular circumstances.

(b) *Effective date.* This section applies to written advice that is rendered after June 20, 2005.

§10.38 Establishment of Advisory Committees

(a) *Advisory committees.* To promote and maintain the public's confidence in tax advisors, the Director of the Office of Professional Responsibility is authorized to establish one or more advisory committees composed of at least five individuals authorized to practice before the Internal Revenue Service. The Director should ensure that membership of an advisory committee is balanced among those who practice as attorneys, accountants, and enrolled agents. Under procedures prescribed by the Director, an advisory committee may review and make general recommendations regarding professional standards or best practices for tax advisors, including whether hypothetical conduct would give rise to a violation of §§10.35 or 10.36.

(b) *Effective date.* This section applies after December 20, 2004.

SUBPART C—SANCTIONS FOR VIOLATION OF THE REGULATIONS

§10.50   SANCTIONS

(a) *Authority to censure, suspend, or disbar.* The Secretary of the Treasury, or delegate, after notice and an opportunity for a proceeding, may censure, suspend, or disbar any practitioner from practice before the Internal Revenue Service if the practitioner is shown to be incompetent or disreputable (within the meaning of §10.51), fails to comply with any regulation in this part (under the prohibited conduct standards of §10.52), or with intent to defraud, willfully and knowingly misleads or threatens a client or prospective client. Censure is a public reprimand.

(b) *Authority to disqualify.* The Secretary of the Treasury, or delegate, after due notice and opportunity for hearing, may disqualify any appraiser for a violation of these rules as applicable to appraisers.

(1) If any appraiser is disqualified pursuant to this subpart C, the appraiser is barred from presenting evidence or testimony in any administrative proceeding before the Department of the Treasury or the Internal Revenue Service, unless and until authorized to do so by the Director of the Office of Professional Responsibility pursuant to §10.81, regardless of whether the evidence or testimony would pertain to an appraisal made prior to or after the effective date of disqualification.

(2) Any appraisal made by a disqualified appraiser after the effective date of disqualification will not have any probative effect in any administrative proceeding before the Department of the Treasury or the Internal Revenue Service. An appraisal otherwise barred from admission into evidence pursuant to this section may be admitted into evidence solely for the purpose of determining the taxpayer's reliance in good faith on such appraisal.

(c) Authority to impose monetary penalty—

(1) In *general.*

(i) The Secretary of the Treasury, or delegate, after notice and an opportunity for a proceeding, may impose a monetary penalty on any practitioner who engages in conduct subject to sanction under paragraph (a) of this section.

(ii) If the practitioner described in paragraph (c)(1)(i) of this section was acting on behalf of an employer or any firm or other entity in connection with the conduct giving rise to the penalty, the Secretary of the Treasury, or delegate, may impose a monetary penalty on the employer, firm, or entity if it knew, or reasonably should have known, of such conduct.

(2) *Amount of penalty.* The amount of the penalty shall not exceed the gross income derived (or to be derived) from the conduct giving rise to the penalty.

(3) *Coordination with other sanctions.* Subject to paragraph (c)(2) of this section—

(i) Any monetary penalty imposed on a practitioner under this paragraph (c) may be in addition to or in lieu of any suspension, disbarment or censure and may be in addition to a penalty imposed on an employer, firm or other entity under paragraph (c)(1)(ii) of this section.

(ii) Any monetary penalty imposed on an employer, firm or other entity may be in addition to or in lieu of penalties imposed under paragraph (c)(1)(i) of this section.

(d) *Sanctions to be imposed.* The sanctions imposed by this section shall take into account all relevant facts and circumstances.

(e) *Effective/applicability date.* This section is applicable to conduct occurring on or after September 26, 2007, except paragraph (c) which applies to prohibited conduct that occurs after October 22, 2004.

§10.51 INCOMPETENCE AND DISREPUTABLE CONDUCT

(a) *Incompetence and disreputable conduct.* Incompetence and disreputable conduct for which a practitioner may be sanctioned under §10.50 includes, but is not limited to—

(1) Conviction of any criminal offense under the Federal tax laws.

(2) Conviction of any criminal offense involving dishonesty or breach of trust.

(3) Conviction of any felony under Federal or State law for which the conduct involved renders the practitioner unfit to practice before the Internal Revenue Service.

(4) Giving false or misleading information, or participating in any way in the giving of false or misleading information to the Department of the Treasury or any officer or employee thereof, or to any tribunal authorized to pass upon Federal tax matters, in connection with any matter pending or likely to be pending before them, knowing the information to be false or misleading. Facts or other matters contained in testimony, Federal tax returns, financial statements, applications for enrollment, affidavits, declarations, and any other document or statement, written or oral, are included in the term "information."

(5) Solicitation of employment as prohibited under §10.30, the use of false or misleading representations with intent to deceive a client or prospective client in order to procure employment, or intimating that the practitioner is able improperly to obtain special consideration or action from the Internal Revenue Service or any officer or employee thereof.

(6) Willfully failing to make a Federal tax return in violation of the Federal tax laws, or willfully evading, attempting to evade, or participating in any way in evading or attempting to evade any assessment or payment of any Federal tax.

(7) Willfully assisting, counseling, encouraging a client or prospective client in violating, or suggesting to a client or prospective client to violate, any Federal tax law, or knowingly counseling or suggesting to a client or prospective client an illegal plan to evade Federal taxes or payment thereof.

(8) Misappropriation of, or failure properly or promptly to remit, funds received from a client for the purpose of payment of taxes or other obligations due the United States.

(9) Directly or indirectly attempting to influence, or offering or agreeing to attempt to influence, the official action of any officer or employee of the Internal Revenue Service by the use of threats, false accusations, duress or coercion, by the offer of any special inducement or promise of an advantage, or by the bestowing of any gift, favor or thing of value.

(10) Disbarment or suspension from practice as an attorney, certified public accountant, public accountant or actuary by any duly constituted authority of any State, territory, or possession of the United States, including a Commonwealth, or the District of Columbia, any Federal court of record or any Federal agency, body or board.

(11) Knowingly aiding and abetting another person to practice before the Internal Revenue Service during a period of suspension, disbarment or ineligibility of such other person.

(12) Contemptuous conduct in connection with practice before the Internal Revenue Service, including the use of abusive language, making false accusations or statements, knowing them to be false or circulating or publishing malicious or libelous matter.

(13) Giving a false opinion, knowingly, recklessly, or through gross incompetence, including an opinion which is intentionally or recklessly misleading, or engaging in a pattern of providing incompetent opinions on questions arising under the Federal tax laws. False opinions described in this paragraph (a)(13) include those which reflect or result from a knowing misstatement of fact or law, from an assertion of a position known to be unwarranted under existing law, from counseling or assisting in conduct known to be illegal or fraudulent, from concealing matters required by law to be revealed, or from consciously disregarding information indicating that material facts expressed in the opinion or offering material are false or misleading. For purposes of this paragraph (a)(13), reckless conduct is a highly unreasonable omission or misrepresentation involving an extreme departure from the standards of ordinary care that a practitioner should observe under the circumstances. A pattern of conduct is a factor that will be taken into account in determining whether a practitioner acted knowingly, recklessly, or through gross incompetence. Gross incompetence includes conduct that reflects gross indifference, preparation which is grossly inadequate under the circumstances, and a consistent failure to perform obligations to the client.

(14) Willfully failing to sign a tax return prepared by the practitioner when the practitioner's signature is required by the Federal tax laws unless the failure is due to reasonable cause and not due to willful neglect.

(15) Willfully disclosing or otherwise using a tax return or tax return information in a manner not authorized by the Internal Revenue Code, contrary to the order of a court of competent jurisdiction, or contrary to the order of an administrative law judge in a proceeding instituted under §10.60.

(b) *Effective/applicability date*. This section is applicable to conduct occurring on or after September 26, 2007.

§10.52   Violations Subject to Sanction

(a) A practitioner may be sanctioned under §10.50 if the practitioner:

(1) Willfully violates any of the regulations (other than §10.33) contained in this part; or

(2) Recklessly or through gross incompetence (within the meaning of §10.51(a)(13)) violates §§10.34, 10.35, 10.36 or 10.37.

(b) *Effective/applicability date*. This section is applicable to conduct occurring on or after September 26, 2007.

§10.53   Receipt of Information Concerning Practitioner

(a) *Officer or employee of the Internal Revenue Service*. If an officer or employee of the Internal Revenue Service has reason to believe that a practitioner has violated any provision of this part, the officer or employee will promptly make a written report to the Director of the Office of Professional Responsibility of the suspected violation. The report will explain the facts and reasons upon which the officer's or employee's belief rests.

(b) *Other persons*. Any person other than an officer or employee of the Internal Revenue Service having information of a violation of any provision of this part may make an oral or written report of the alleged violation to the Director of the Office of Professional Responsibility or any officer or employee of the Internal Revenue Service. If the report is made to an officer or employee of the Internal Revenue Service, the officer or employee will make a written report of the suspected violation to the Director of the Office of Professional Responsibility.

(c) *Destruction of report*. No report made under paragraph (a) or (b) of this section shall be maintained by the Director of the Office of Professional Responsibility unless retention of the report is permissible under the applicable records control schedule as approved by the National Archives and Records Administration and designated in the Internal Revenue Manual. The Director of the Office of Professional Responsibility must destroy the reports as soon as permissible under the applicable records control schedule.

(d) *Effect on proceedings under subpart D*. The destruction of any report will not bar any proceeding under subpart D of this part, but will preclude the Director of the Office of Professional Responsibility's use of a copy of the report in a proceeding under subpart D of this part.

(e) *Effective/applicability date*. This section is applicable on September 26, 2007.

SUBPART D—RULES APPLICABLE TO DISCIPLINARY PROCEEDINGS

§10.60   INSTITUTION OF PROCEEDING

(a) Whenever the Director of the Office of Professional Responsibility determines that a practitioner (or employer, firm or other entity, if applicable) violated any provision of the laws governing practice before the Internal Revenue Service or the regulations in this part, the Director of the Office of Professional Responsibility may reprimand the practitioner or, in accordance with §10.62, institute a proceeding for sanction described in §10.50. A proceeding is instituted by the filing of a complaint, the contents of which are more fully described in §10.62.

(b) Whenever the Director of Practice is advised or becomes aware that a penalty has been assessed against an appraiser under section 6701(a) of the Internal Revenue Code, the Director of Practice may reprimand the appraiser or, in accordance with §10.62, institute a proceeding for disqualification of the appraiser. A proceeding for disqualification of an appraiser is instituted by the filing of a complaint, the contents of which are more fully described in §10.62.

(c) Except as provided in §10.82, a proceeding will not be instituted under this section unless the proposed respondent previously has been advised in writing of the law, facts and conduct warranting such action and has been accorded an opportunity to dispute facts, assert additional facts, and make arguments (including an explanation or description of mitigating circumstances).

(d) *Effective/Applicability date.* This section is applicable on September 26, 2007.

§10.61   CONFERENCES

(a) *In general.* The Director of the Office of Professional Responsibility may confer with a practitioner, employer, firm or other entity, or an appraiser concerning allegations of misconduct irrespective of whether a proceeding has been instituted. If the conference results in a stipulation in connection with an ongoing proceeding in which the practitioner, employer, firm or other entity, or appraiser is the respondent, the stipulation may be entered in the record by either party to the proceeding.

(b) *Voluntary sanction—*

(1) *In general.* In lieu of a proceeding being instituted or continued under §10.60(a), a practitioner or appraiser (or employer, firm or other entity, if applicable) may offer a consent to be sanctioned under §10.50.

(2) *Discretion; acceptance or declination.* The Director of the Office of Professional Responsibility may, in his or her discretion, accept or decline the offer described in paragraph (b)(1) of this section. In any declination, the Director of the Office of Professional Responsibility may state that he or she would accept the offer described in paragraph (b)(1) of this section if it contained different terms. The Director of the Office of Professional Responsibility may, in his or her

discretion, accept or reject a revised offer submitted in response to the declination or may counteroffer and act upon any accepted counteroffer.

(c) *Effective/applicability date.* This section is applicable on September 26, 2007.

§10.62   CONTENTS OF COMPLAINT

(a) *Charges.* A complaint must name the respondent, provide a clear and concise description of the facts and law that constitute the basis for the proceeding, and be signed by the Director of the Office of Professional Responsibility or a person representing the Director of the Office of Professional Responsibility under §10.69(a)(1). A complaint is sufficient if it fairly informs the respondent of the charges brought so that the respondent is able to prepare a defense.

(b) *Specification of sanction.* The complaint must specify the sanction sought by the Director of the Office of Professional Responsibility against the practitioner or appraiser. If the sanction sought is a suspension, the duration of the suspension sought must be specified.

(c) *Demand for answer.* The Director of the Office of Professional Responsibility must, in the complaint or in a separate paper attached to the complaint, notify the respondent of the time for answering the complaint, which may not be less than 30 days from the date of service of the complaint, the name and address of the Administrative Law Judge with whom the answer must be filed, the name and address of the person representing the Director of the Office of Professional Responsibility to whom a copy of the answer must be served, and that a decision by default may be rendered against the respondent in the event an answer is not filed as required.

(d) *Effective/applicability date.* This section is applicable to complaints brought on or after September 26, 2007.

§10.63   SERVICE OF COMPLAINT; SERVICE AND FILING OF OTHER PAPERS

(a) *Service of complaint.*

(1) *In general.* The complaint or a copy of the complaint must be served on the respondent by any manner described in paragraphs (a) (2) or (3) of this section.

(2) *Service by certified or first class mail.*

(i) Service of the complaint may be made on the respondent by mailing the complaint by certified mail to the last known address (as determined under section 6212 of the Internal Revenue Code and the regulations thereunder) of the respondent. Where service is by certified mail, the returned post office receipt duly signed by the respondent will be proof of service.

(ii) If the certified mail is not claimed or accepted by the respondent, or is returned undelivered, service may be made on the respondent, by mailing the complaint to the respondent by first-class mail. Service by this method will be considered complete upon mailing, provided the complaint is addressed to the respondent at the respondent's last known address as determined under section 6212 of the Internal Revenue Code and the regulations thereunder.

(3) *Service by other than certified or first-class mail.*

(i) Service of the complaint may be made on the respondent by delivery by a private delivery service designated pursuant to section 7502(f) of the Internal Revenue Code to the last known address (as determined under section 6212 of the Internal Revenue Code and the regulations there under) of the respondent. Service by this method will be considered complete, provided the complaint is addressed to the respondent at the respondent's last known address as determined under section 6212 of the Internal Revenue Code and the regulations thereunder.

(ii) Service of the complaint may be made in person on, or by leaving the complaint at the office or place of business of, the respondent. Service by this method will be considered complete and proof of service will be a written statement, sworn or affirmed by the person who served the complaint, identifying the manner of service, including the recipient, relationship of recipient to respondent, place, date and time of service.

(iii) Service may be made by any other means agreed to by the respondent. Proof of service will be a written statement, sworn or affirmed by the person who served the complaint, identifying the manner of service, including the recipient, relationship of recipient to respondent, place, date and time of service.

(4) For purposes of this paragraph (a) "respondent" means the practitioner or appraiser named in the complaint or any other person having the authority to accept mail on behalf of the practitioner or appraiser.

(b) *Service of papers other than complaint.* Any paper other than the complaint may be served on the respondent, or his or her authorized representative under §10.69(a)(2) by:

(1) mailing the paper by first-class mail to the last known address (as determined under section 6212 of the Internal Revenue Code and the regulations thereunder) of the respondent or the respondent's authorized representative,

(2) delivery by a private delivery service designated pursuant to section 7502(f) of the Internal Revenue Code to the last known address (as determined under section 6212 of the Internal Revenue Code and the regulations thereunder) of the respondent or the respondent's authorized representative, or

(3) as provided in paragraphs (a)(3)(ii) and (a)(3)(iii) of this section.

(c) *Service of papers on the Director of Practice.* Whenever a paper is required or permitted to be served on the Director of Practice in connection with a proceeding under this part, the paper will be served on the Director of Practice's authorized representative under §10.69(a)(1) at the address designated in the complaint, or at an address provided in a notice of appearance. If no address is designated in the complaint or provided in a notice of appearance, service will be made on the Director of Practice, Internal Revenue Service, 1111 Constitution Avenue, N.W., Washington, D.C. 20224.

(d) *Service of evidence in support of complaint.* Within 10 days of serving the complaint, copies of the evidence in support of the complaint must be served on the respondent in any manner described in paragraphs (a)(2) and (3) of this section.

(e) *Filing of papers.* Whenever the filing of a paper is required or permitted in connection with a proceeding under this part, the original paper, plus one additional copy, must be filed with the Administrative Law Judge at the address specified in the complaint or at an address otherwise specified by the Administrative Law Judge. All papers filed in connection with a proceeding under this part must be served on the other party, unless the Administrative Law Judge directs otherwise. A certificate evidencing such must be attached to the original paper filed with the Administrative Law Judge.

(f) *Effective/applicability date.* This section is applicable to complaints brought on or after September 26, 2007.

§10.64   Answer; Default

(a) *Filing.* The respondent's answer must be filed with the Administrative Law Judge, and served on the Director of Practice, within the time specified in the complaint unless, on request or application of the respondent, the time is extended by the Administrative Law Judge.

(b) *Contents.* The answer must be written and contain a statement of facts that constitute the respondent's grounds of defense. General denials are not permitted. The respondent must specifically admit or deny each allegation set forth in the complaint, except that the respondent may state that the respondent is without sufficient information to admit or deny a specific allegation. The respondent, nevertheless, may not deny a material allegation in the complaint that the respondent knows to be true, or state that the respondent is without sufficient information to form a belief, when the respondent possesses the required information. The respondent also must state affirmatively any special matters of defense on which he or she relies.

(c) *Failure to deny or answer allegations in the complaint.* Every allegation in the complaint that is not denied in the answer is deemed admitted and will be considered proved; no further evidence in respect of such allegation need be adduced at a hearing.

(d) *Default.* Failure to file an answer within the time prescribed (or within the time for answer as extended by the Administrative Law Judge), constitutes an admission of the allegations of the complaint and a waiver of hearing, and the Administrative Law Judge may make the decision by default without a hearing or further procedure. A decision by default constitutes a decision under §10.76.

(e) *Signature.* The answer must be signed by the respondent or the respondent's authorized representative under §10.69(a)(2) and must include a statement directly above the signature acknowledging that the statements made in the answer are true and correct and that knowing and willful false statements may be punishable under 18 U.S.C. 1001.

§10.65   Supplemental Charges

(a) *In general.* The Director of the Office of Professional Responsibility may file supplemental charges, by amending the complaint with the permission of the Administrative Law Judge, against the respondent, if, for example—

(1) It appears that the respondent, in the answer, falsely and in bad faith, denies a material allegation of fact in the complaint or states that the respondent has insufficient knowledge to form a belief, when the respondent possesses such information; or

(2) It appears that the respondent has knowingly introduced false testimony during the proceedings against the respondent.

(b) *Hearing.* The supplemental charges may be heard with other charges in the case, provided the respondent is given due notice of the charges and is afforded a reasonable opportunity to prepare a defense to the supplemental charges.

(c) *Effective/applicability date.* This section is applicable on September 26, 2007.

§10.66   Reply to Answer

The Director of Practice may file a reply to the respondent's answer, but unless otherwise ordered by the Administrative Law Judge, no reply to the respondent's answer is required. If a reply is not filed, new matter in the answer is deemed denied.

§10.67   Proof; Variance; Amendment of Pleadings

In the case of a variance between the allegations in pleadings and the evidence adduced in support of the pleadings, the Administrative Law Judge, at any time before decision, may order or authorize amendment of the pleadings to conform to the evidence. The party who would otherwise be prejudiced by the amendment must be given a reasonable opportunity to address the allegations of the pleadings as amended and the Administrative Law Judge must make findings on any issue presented by the pleadings as amended.

§10.68   Motions and Requests

(a) *Motions—*

(1) *In general.* At any time after the filing of the complaint, any party may file a motion with the Administrative Law Judge. Unless otherwise ordered by the Administrative Law Judge, motions must be in writing and must be served on the opposing party as provided in §10.63(b). A motion must concisely specify its grounds and the relief sought, and, if appropriate, must contain a memorandum of facts and law in support.

(2) *Summary adjudication.* Either party may move for a summary adjudication upon all or any part of the legal issues in controversy. If the nonmoving party opposes summary adjudication in the moving party's favor, the nonmoving party

must file a written response within 30 days unless ordered otherwise by the Administrative Law Judge.

(3) *Good faith.* A party filing a motion for extension of time, a motion for postponement of a hearing, or any other non-dispositive or procedural motion must first contact the other party to determine whether there is any objection to the motion, and must state in the motion whether the other party has an objection.

(b) *Response.* Unless otherwise ordered by the Administrative Law Judge, the nonmoving party is not required to file a response to a motion. If the Administrative Law Judge does not order the nonmoving party to file a response, and the nonmoving party files no response, the nonmoving party is deemed to oppose the motion. If a nonmoving party does not respond within 30 days of the filing of a motion for decision by default for failure to file a timely answer or for failure to prosecute, the nonmoving party is deemed not to oppose the motion.

(c) *Oral motions; oral argument—*

(1) The Administrative Law Judge may, for good cause and with notice to the parties, permit oral motions and oral opposition to motions.

(2) The Administrative Law Judge may, within his or her discretion, permit oral argument on any motion.

(d) *Orders.* The Administrative Law Judge should issue written orders disposing of any motion or request and any response thereto.

(e) *Effective/applicability date.* This section is applicable on September 26, 2007.

§10.69   Representation; Ex Parte Communication

(a) *Representation.*

(1) The Director of Practice may be represented in proceedings under this part by an attorney or other employee of the Internal Revenue Service. An attorney or an employee of the Internal Revenue Service representing the Director of Practice in a proceeding under this part may sign the complaint or any document required to be filed in the proceeding on behalf of the Director of Practice.

(2) A respondent may appear in person, be represented by a practitioner, or be represented by an attorney who has not filed a declaration with the Internal Revenue Service pursuant to §10.3. A practitioner or an attorney representing a respondent or proposed respondent may sign the answer or any document required to be filed in the proceeding on behalf of the respondent.

(b) *Ex parte communication.* The Director of Practice, the respondent, and any representatives of either party, may not attempt to initiate or participate in ex parte discussions concerning a proceeding or potential proceeding with the Administrative Law Judge (or any person who is likely to advise the Administrative Law Judge on a ruling or decision) in the proceeding before or during the pendency of the proceeding. Any memorandum, letter or other communication concerning the merits of the proceeding, addressed to the Administrative Law Judge, by or on behalf of any party shall be regarded as an argument in the proceeding and shall be served on the other party.

§10.70   Administrative Law Judge

(a) *Appointment.* Proceedings on complaints for the sanction (as described in §10.50) of a practitioner, employer, firm or other entity, or appraiser will be conducted by an Administrative Law Judge appointed as provided by 5 U.S.C. 3105.

(b) *Powers of the Administrative Law Judge.* The Administrative Law Judge, among other powers, has the authority, in connection with any proceeding under §10.60 assigned or referred to him or her, to do the following:

(1) Administer oaths and affirmations;

(2) Make rulings on motions and requests, which rulings may not be appealed prior to the close of a hearing except in extraordinary circumstances and at the discretion of the Administrative Law Judge;

(3) Determine the time and place of hearing and regulate its course and conduct;

(4) Adopt rules of procedure and modify the same from time to time as needed for the orderly disposition of proceedings;

(5) Rule on offers of proof, receive relevant evidence, and examine witnesses;

(6) Take or authorize the taking of depositions or answers to requests for admission;

(7) Receive and consider oral or written argument on facts or law;

(8) Hold or provide for the holding of conferences for the settlement or simplification of the issues with the consent of the parties;

(9) Perform such acts and take such measures as are necessary or appropriate to the efficient conduct of any proceeding; and

(10) Make decisions.

(c) *Effective/applicability date.* This section is applicable on September 26, 2007.

§10.71   Discovery

(a) *In general.* Discovery may be permitted, at the discretion of the Administrative Law Judge, only upon written motion demonstrating the relevance, materiality and reasonableness of the requested discovery and subject to the requirements of §10.72(d)(2) and (3). Within 10 days of receipt of the answer, the Administrative Law Judge will notify the parties of the right to request discovery and the timeframes for filing a request. A request for discovery, and objections, must be filed in accordance with §10.68. In response to a request for discovery, the Administrative Law Judge may order—

(1) Depositions upon oral examination; or

(2) Answers to requests for admission.

(b) *Depositions upon oral examination—*

(1) A deposition must be taken before an officer duly authorized to administer an oath for general purposes or before an officer or employee of the Internal Revenue Service who is authorized to administer an oath in Federal tax law matters.

(2) In ordering a deposition, the Administrative Law Judge will require reasonable notice to the opposing party as to the time and place of the deposition. The opposing party, if attending, will be provided the opportunity for full examination and cross-examination of any witness.

(3) Expenses in the reporting of depositions shall be borne by the party at whose instance the deposition is taken. Travel expenses of the deponent shall be borne by the party requesting the deposition, unless otherwise authorized by Federal law or regulation.

(c) *Requests for admission.* Any party may serve on any other party a written request for admission of the truth of any matters which are not privileged and are relevant to the subject matter of this proceeding. Requests for admission shall not exceed a total of 30 (including any subparts within a specific request) without the approval from the Administrative Law Judge.

(d) *Limitations.* Discovery shall not be authorized if—

(1) The request fails to meet any requirement set forth in paragraph (a) of this section;

(2) It will unduly delay the proceeding;

(3) It will place an undue burden on the party required to produce the discovery sought;

(4) It is frivolous or abusive;

(5) It is cumulative or duplicative;

(6) The material sought is privileged or otherwise protected from disclosure by law;

(7) The material sought relates to mental impressions, conclusions, or legal theories of any party, attorney, or other representative, of a party prepared in anticipation of a proceeding; or

(8) The material sought is available generally to the public, equally to the parties, or to the party seeking the discovery through another source.

(e) *Failure to comply.* Where a party fails to comply with an order of the Administrative Law Judge under this section, the Administrative Law Judge may, among other things, infer that the information would be adverse to the party failing to provide it, exclude the information from evidence or issue a decision by default.

(f) *Other discovery.* No discovery other than that specifically provided for in this section is permitted.

(g) *Effective/applicability date.* This section is applicable to proceedings initiated on or after September 26, 2007.

§10.72   Hearings

(a) *In general—*

(1) *Presiding officer.* An Administrative Law Judge will preside at the hearing on a complaint filed under §10.60 for the sanction of a practitioner, employer, firm or other entity, or appraiser.

(2) *Time for hearing.* Absent a determination by the Administrative Law Judge that, in the interest of justice, a hearing must be held at a later time, the Administrative Law Judge should, on notice sufficient to allow proper preparation, schedule the hearing to occur no later than 180 days after the time for filing the answer.

(3) *Procedural requirements.*

(i) Hearings will be stenographically recorded and transcribed and the testimony of witnesses will be taken under oath or affirmation.

(ii) Hearings will be conducted pursuant to 5 U.S.C. 556.

(iii) A hearing in a proceeding requested under §10.82(g) will be conducted de novo.

(iv) An evidentiary hearing must be held in all proceedings prior to the issuance of a decision by the Administrative Law Judge unless—

(A) The Director of the Office of Professional Responsibility withdraws the complaint;

(B) A decision is issued by default pursuant to §10.64(d);

(C) A decision is issued under §10.82(e);

(D) The respondent requests a decision on the written record without a hearing; or

(E) The Administrative Law Judge issues a decision under §10.68(d) or rules on another motion that disposes of the case prior to the hearing.

(b) *Cross-examination.* A party is entitled to present his or her case or defense by oral or documentary evidence, to submit rebuttal evidence, and to conduct cross-examination, in the presence of the Administrative Law Judge, as may be required for a full and true disclosure of the facts. This paragraph (b) does not limit a party from presenting evidence contained within a deposition when the Administrative Law Judge determines that the deposition has been obtained in compliance with the rules of this subpart D.

(c) *Prehearing memorandum.* Unless otherwise ordered by the Administrative Law Judge, each party shall file, and serve on the opposing party or the opposing party's representative, prior to any hearing, a prehearing memorandum containing—

(1) A list (together with a copy) of all proposed exhibits to be used in the party's case in chief;

(2) A list of proposed witnesses, including a synopsis of their expected testimony, or a statement that no witnesses will be called;

(3) Identification of any proposed expert witnesses, including a synopsis of their expected testimony and a copy of any report prepared by the expert or at his or her direction; and

(4) A list of undisputed facts.

(d) *Publicity*—

(1) *In general.* All reports and decisions of the Secretary of the Treasury, or delegate, including any reports and decisions of the Administrative Law Judge, under this subpart D are, subject to the protective measures in paragraph (d)(4) of

this section, public and open to inspection within 30 days after the agency's decision becomes final.

(2) *Request for additional publicity.* The Administrative Law Judge may grant a request by a practitioner or appraiser that all the pleadings and evidence of the disciplinary proceeding be made available for inspection where the parties stipulate in advance to adopt the protective measures in paragraph (d)(4) of this section.

(3) *Returns and return information—*

(i) *Disclosure to practitioner or appraiser.* Pursuant to section 6103(l)(4) of the Internal Revenue Code, the Secretary of the Treasury, or delegate, may disclose returns and return information to any practitioner or appraiser, or to the authorized representative of the practitioner or appraiser, whose rights are or may be affected by an administrative action or proceeding under this subpart D, but solely for use in the action or proceeding and only to the extent that the Secretary of the Treasury, or delegate, determines that the returns or return information are or may be relevant and material to the action or proceeding.

(ii) *Disclosure to officers and employees of the Department of the Treasury.* Pursuant to section 6103(l)(4) of the Internal Revenue Code, the Secretary of the Treasury, or delegate, may disclose returns and return information to officers and employees of the Department of the Treasury for use in any action or proceeding under this subpart D, to the extent necessary to advance or protect the interests of the United States.

(iii) *Use of returns and return information.* Recipients of returns and return information under this paragraph (d)(3) may use the returns or return information solely in the action or proceeding, or in preparation for the action or proceeding, with respect to which the disclosure was made.

(iv) *Procedures for disclosure of returns and return information.* When providing returns or return information to the practitioner or appraiser, or authorized representative, the Secretary of the Treasury, or delegate, will—

(A) Redact identifying information of any third party taxpayers and replace it with a code;

(B) Provide a key to the coded information; and

(C) Notify the practitioner or appraiser, or authorized representative, of the restrictions on the use and disclosure of the returns and return information, the applicable damages remedy under section 7431 of the Internal Revenue Code, and that unauthorized disclosure of information provided by the Internal Revenue Service under this paragraph (d)(3) is also a violation of this part.

(4) *Protective measures—*

(i) *Mandatory protective order.* If redaction of names, addresses, and other identifying information of third party taxpayers may still permit indirect identification of any third party taxpayer, the Administrative Law Judge will issue a protective order to ensure that the identifying information is available to the parties and the Administrative Law Judge for purposes of the proceeding, but is not disclosed to, or open to inspection by, the public.

(ii) *Authorized orders.*

(A) Upon motion by a party or any other affected person, and for good cause shown, the Administrative Law Judge may make any order which justice requires to protect any person in the event disclosure of information is prohibited by law, privileged, confidential, or sensitive in some other way, including, but not limited to, one or more of the following—

(1) That disclosure of information be made only on specified terms and conditions, including a designation of the time or place;

(2) That a trade secret or other information not be disclosed, or be disclosed only in a designated way.

(iii) *Denials.* If a motion for a protective order is denied in whole or in part, the Administrative Law Judge may, on such terms or conditions as the Administrative Law Judge deems just, order any party or person to comply with, or respond in accordance with, the procedure involved.

(iv) *Public inspection of documents.* The Secretary of the Treasury, or delegate, shall ensure that all names, addresses or other identifying details of third party taxpayers are redacted and replaced with the code assigned to the corresponding taxpayer in all documents prior to public inspection of such documents.

(e) *Location.* The location of the hearing will be determined by the agreement of the parties with the approval of the Administrative Law Judge, but, in the absence of such agreement and approval, the hearing will be held in Washington, D.C.

(f) *Failure to appear.* If either party to the proceeding fails to appear at the hearing, after notice of the proceeding has been sent to him or her, the party will be deemed to have waived the right to a hearing and the Administrative Law Judge may make his or her decision against the absent party by default.

(g) *Effective/applicability date.* This section is applicable on September 26, 2007.

§10.73   EVIDENCE

(a) *In general.* The rules of evidence prevailing in courts of law and equity are not controlling in hearings or proceedings conducted under this part. The Administrative Law Judge may, however, exclude evidence that is irrelevant, immaterial, or unduly repetitious.

(b) *Depositions.* The deposition of any witness taken pursuant to §10.71 may be admitted into evidence in any proceeding instituted under §10.60.

(c) *Requests for admission.* Any matter admitted in response to a request for admission under §10.71 is conclusively established unless the Administrative Law Judge on motion permits withdrawal or modification of the admission. Any admission made by a party is for the purposes of the pending action only and is not an admission by a party for any other purpose, nor may it be used against a party in any other proceeding.

(d) *Proof of documents.* Official documents, records, and papers of the Internal Revenue Service and the Office of Professional Responsibility are admissible in evidence without the production of an officer or employee to authenticate them. Any documents, records, and papers may be evidenced by a copy attested to or identified by an officer or employee of the Internal Revenue Service or the Treasury Department, as the case may be.

(e) *Withdrawal of exhibits.* If any document, record, or other paper is introduced in evidence as an exhibit, the Administrative Law Judge may authorize the withdrawal of the exhibit subject to any conditions that he or she deems proper.

(f) *Objections.* Objections to evidence are to be made in short form, stating the grounds for the objection. Except as ordered by the Administrative Law Judge, argument on objections will not be recorded or transcribed. Rulings on objections are to be a part of the record, but no exception to a ruling is necessary to preserve the rights of the parties.

(g) *Effective/applicability date.* This section is applicable on September 26, 2007.

§10.74 TRANSCRIPT

In cases where the hearing is stenographically reported by a Government contract reporter, copies of the transcript may be obtained from the reporter at rates not to exceed the maximum rates fixed by contract between the Government and the reporter. Where the hearing is stenographically reported by a regular employee of the Internal Revenue Service, a copy will be supplied to the respondent either without charge or upon the payment of a reasonable fee. Copies of exhibits introduced at the hearing or at the taking of depositions will be supplied to the parties upon the payment of a reasonable fee (Sec. 501, Public Law 82-137)(65 Stat. 290)(31 U.S.C. 483a).

§10.75 PROPOSED FINDINGS AND CONCLUSIONS

Except in cases where the respondent has failed to answer the complaint or where a party has failed to appear at the hearing, the parties must be afforded a reasonable opportunity to submit proposed findings and conclusions and their supporting reasons to the Administrative Law Judge.

§10.76 DECISION OF ADMINISTRATIVE LAW JUDGE

(a) *In general—*

(1) *Hearings.* Within 180 days after the conclusion of a hearing and the receipt of any proposed findings and conclusions timely submitted by the parties, the Administrative Law Judge should enter a decision in the case. The decision must include a statement of findings and conclusions, as well as the reasons or basis for making such findings and conclusions, and an order of censure, suspension, disbarment, monetary penalty, disqualification, or dismissal of the complaint.

(2) *Summary adjudication.* In the event that a motion for summary adjudication is filed, the Administrative Law Judge should rule on the motion for

summary adjudication within 60 days after the party in opposition files a written response, or if no written response is filed, within 90 days after the motion for summary adjudication is filed. A decision shall thereafter be rendered if the pleadings, depositions, admissions, and any other admissible evidence show that there is no genuine issue of material fact and that a decision may be rendered as a matter of law. The decision must include a statement of conclusions, as well as the reasons or basis for making such conclusions, and an order of censure, suspension, disbarment, monetary penalty, disqualification, or dismissal of the complaint.

(3) *Returns and return information.* In the decision, the Administrative Law Judge should use the code assigned to third party taxpayers (described in §10.72(d)).

(b) *Standard of proof.* If the sanction is censure or a suspension of less than six months' duration, the Administrative Law Judge, in rendering findings and conclusions, will consider an allegation of fact to be proven if it is established by the party who is alleging the fact by a preponderance of the evidence in the record. If the sanction is a monetary penalty, disbarment or a suspension of six months or longer duration, an allegation of fact that is necessary for a finding against the practitioner must be proven by clear and convincing evidence in the record. An allegation of fact that is necessary for a finding of disqualification against an appraiser must be proven by clear and convincing evidence in the record.

(c) *Copy of decision.* The Administrative Law Judge will provide the decision to the Director of the Office of Professional Responsibility, with a copy to the Director's authorized representative, and a copy of the decision to the respondent or the respondent's authorized representative.

(d) *When final.* In the absence of an appeal to the Secretary of the Treasury or delegate, the decision of the Administrative Law Judge will, without further proceedings, become the decision of the agency 30 days after the date of the Administrative Law Judge's decision.

(e) *Effective/applicability date.* This section is applicable to proceedings initiated on or after September 26, 2007.

§10.77 Appeal of Decision of Administrative Law Judge

(a) *Appeal.* Any party to the proceeding under this subpart D may file an appeal of the decision of the Administrative Law Judge with the Secretary of the Treasury, or delegate. The appeal must include a brief that states exceptions to the decision of the Administrative Law Judge and supporting reasons for such exceptions.

(b) *Time and place for filing of appeal.* The appeal and brief must be filed, in duplicate, with the Director of the Office of Professional Responsibility within 30 days of the date that the decision of the Administrative Law Judge is served on the parties. The Director of the Office of Professional Responsibility will immediately furnish a copy of the appeal to the Secretary of the Treasury or delegate who decides appeals. A copy of the appeal for review must be sent to any non-appealing party. If the Director of the Office of Professional Responsibility files an appeal, he or she will provide a copy of the appeal and certify to the respondent that the appeal has been filed.

(c) *Effective/applicability date*. This section is applicable on September 26, 2007.

§10.78   DECISION ON REVIEW

(a) *Decision on review*. On appeal from or review of the decision of the Administrative Law Judge, the Secretary of the Treasury, or delegate, will make the agency decision. The Secretary of the Treasury, or delegate, should make the agency decision within 180 days after receipt of the appeal.

(b) *Standard of review*. The decision of the Administrative Law Judge will not be reversed unless the appellant establishes that the decision is clearly erroneous in light of the evidence in the record and applicable law. Issues that are exclusively matters of law will be reviewed de novo. In the event that the Secretary of the Treasury, or delegate, determines that there are unresolved issues raised by the record, the case may be remanded to the Administrative Law Judge to elicit additional testimony or evidence.

(c) *Copy of decision on review*. The Secretary of the Treasury, or delegate, will provide copies of the agency decision to the Director of the Office of Professional Responsibility and the respondent or the respondent's authorized representative.

(d) *Effective/applicability date*. This section is applicable on September 26, 2007.

§10.79   EFFECT OF DISBARMENT, SUSPENSION, OR CENSURE

(a) *Disbarment*. When the final decision in a case is against the respondent (or the respondent has offered his or her consent and such consent has been accepted by the Director of Practice) and such decision is for disbarment, the respondent will not be permitted to practice before the Internal Revenue Service unless and until authorized to do so by the Director of Practice pursuant to §10.81.

(b) *Suspension*. When the final decision in a case is against the respondent (or the respondent has offered his or her consent and such consent has been accepted by the Director of Practice) and such decision is for suspension, the respondent will not be permitted to practice before the Internal Revenue Service during the period of suspension. For periods after the suspension, the practitioner's future representations may be subject to conditions as authorized by paragraph (d) of this section.

(c) *Censure*. When the final decision in the case is against the respondent (or the respondent has offered his or her consent and such consent has been accepted by the Director of Practice) and such decision is for censure, the respondent will be permitted to practice before the Internal Revenue Service, but the respondent's future representations may be subject to conditions as authorized by paragraph (d) of this section.

(d) *Conditions*. After being subject to the sanction of either suspension or censure, the future representations of a practitioner so sanctioned shall be subject to conditions prescribed by the Director of Practice designed to promote high standards of conduct. These conditions can be imposed for a reasonable period in light of the gravity of the practitioner's violations. For example, where a practitioner is censured because he or she failed to advise his or her clients about a potential conflict of interest or failed to obtain the clients' written consents, the Director of Practice may require the practitioner to provide the Director of Practice or another Internal Revenue Service official with a copy of all consents obtained by the practitioner for an appropriate period following censure, whether or not such consents are specifically requested.

§10.80   Notice of Disbarment, Suspension, Censure, or Disqualification

On the issuance of a final order censuring, suspending, or disbarring a practitioner or a final order disqualifying an appraiser, the Director of Practice may give notice of the censure, suspension, disbarment, or disqualification to appropriate officers and employees of the Internal Revenue Service and to interested departments and agencies of the Federal government. The Director of Practice may determine the manner of giving notice to the proper authorities of the State by which the censured, suspended, or disbarred person was licensed to practice.

§10.81   Petition for Reinstatement

The Director of Practice may entertain a petition for reinstatement from any person disbarred from practice before the Internal Revenue Service or any disqualified appraiser after the expiration of 5 years following such disbarment or disqualification. Reinstatement may not be granted unless the Director of Practice is satisfied that the petitioner, thereafter, is not likely to conduct himself contrary to the regulations in this part, and that granting such reinstatement would not be contrary to the public interest.

§10.82   Expedited Suspension upon Criminal Conviction or Loss of License for Cause

(a) *When applicable*. Whenever the Director of the Office of Professional Responsibility determines that a practitioner is described in paragraph (b) of this section, the Director of the Office of Professional Responsibility may institute a proceeding under this section to suspend the practitioner from practice before the Internal Revenue Service.

(b) *To whom applicable*. This section applies to any practitioner who, within five years of the date a complaint instituting a proceeding under this section is served:

(1) Has had a license to practice as an attorney, certified public accountant, or actuary suspended or revoked for cause (not including failure to pay a professional licensing fee) by any authority or court, agency, body, or board described in §10.51(a)(10).

(2) Has, irrespective of whether an appeal has been taken, been convicted of any crime under title 26 of the United States Code, any crime involving dishonesty or breach of trust, or any felony for which the conduct involved renders the practitioner unfit to practice before the Internal Revenue Service.

(3) Has violated conditions imposed on the practitioner pursuant to §10.79(d).

(4) Has been sanctioned by a court of competent jurisdiction, whether in a civil or criminal proceeding (including suits for injunctive relief), relating to any taxpayer's tax liability or relating to the practitioner's own tax liability, for—

(i) Instituting or maintaining proceedings primarily for delay;

(ii) Advancing frivolous or groundless arguments; or

(iii) Failing to pursue available administrative remedies.

(c) *Instituting a proceeding.* A proceeding under this section will be instituted by a complaint that names the respondent, is signed by the Director of the Office of Professional Responsibility or a person representing the Director of the Office of Professional Responsibility under §10.69(a)(1), is filed in the Director of the Office of Professional Responsibility's office, and is served according to the rules set forth in paragraph (a) of §10.63. The complaint must give a plain and concise description of the allegations that constitute the basis for the proceeding. The complaint must notify the respondent—

(1) Of the place and due date for filing an answer;

(2) That a decision by default may be rendered if the respondent fails to file an answer as required;

(3) That the respondent may request a conference with the Director of the Office of Professional Responsibility to address the merits of the complaint and that any such request must be made in the answer; and

(4) That the respondent may be suspended either immediately following the expiration of the period within which an answer must be filed or, if a conference is requested, immediately following the conference.

(d) *Answer.* The answer to a complaint described in this section must be filed no later than 30 calendar days following the date the complaint is served, unless the Director of the Office of Professional Responsibility extends the time for filing. The answer must be filed in accordance with the rules set forth in §10.64, except as otherwise provided in this section. A respondent is entitled to a conference with the Director of the Office of Professional Responsibility only if the conference is requested in a timely filed answer. If a request for a conference is not made in the answer or the answer is not timely filed, the respondent will be deemed to have waived his or her right to a conference and the Director of the Office of Professional Responsibility may suspend such respondent at any time following the date on which the answer was due.

(e) *Conference.* The Director of the Office of Professional Responsibility or his or her designee will preside at a conference described in this section. The conference will be held at a place and time selected by the Director of the Office of Professional Responsibility, but no sooner than 14 calendar days after the date by which the answer must be filed with the Director of the Office of Professional Responsibility, unless the respondent agrees to an earlier date. An authorized representative may represent the respondent at the conference. Following the conference, upon a finding that the respondent is described in paragraph (b) of this section, or upon the respondent's failure to appear at the conference either personally or through an authorized representative, the Director of the Office of Professional Responsibility may immediately suspend the respondent from practice before the Internal Revenue Service.

(f) *Duration of suspension.* A suspension under this section will commence on the date that written notice of the suspension is issued. A practitioner's suspension will remain effective until the earlier of the following—

(1) The Director of the Office of Professional Responsibility lifts the suspension after determining that the practitioner is no longer described in paragraph (b) of this section or for any other reason; or

(2) The suspension is lifted by an Administrative Law Judge or the Secretary of the Treasury in a proceeding referred to in paragraph (g) of this section and instituted under §10.60.

(g) *Proceeding instituted under §10.60.* If the Director of the Office of Professional Responsibility suspends a practitioner under this section, the practitioner may ask the Director of the Office of Professional Responsibility to issue a complaint under §10.60. The request must be made in writing within 2 years from the date on which the practitioner's suspension commences. The Director of the Office of Professional Responsibility must issue a complaint requested under this paragraph within 30 calendar days of receiving the request.

(h) *Effective/applicability date.* This section is applicable on September 26, 2007.

SUBPART E—GENERAL PROVISIONS

§10.90   RECORDS

(a) *Roster.* The Director of the Office of Professional Responsibility will maintain, and may make available for public inspection in the time and manner prescribed by the Secretary of the Treasury, or delegate, rosters of—

(1) Enrolled agents, including individuals—

(i) Granted active enrollment to practice;

(ii) Whose enrollment has been placed in inactive status for failure to meet the requirements for renewal of enrollment;

(iii) Whose enrollment has been placed in inactive retirement status; and

(iv) Whose offer of consent to resign from enrollment has been accepted by the Director of the Office of Professional Responsibility under §10.61.

(2) Individuals (and employers, firms or other entities, if applicable) censured, suspended, or disbarred from practice before the Internal Revenue Service or upon whom a monetary penalty was imposed;

(3) Disqualified appraisers; and

(4) Enrolled retirement plan agents, including individuals—

(i) Granted active enrollment to practice;

(ii) Whose enrollment has been placed in inactive status for failure to meet the requirements for renewal of enrollment;

(iii) Whose enrollment has been placed in inactive retirement status; and

(iv) Whose offer of consent to resign from enrollment has been accepted by the Director of the Office of Professional Responsibility under §10.61.

(b) *Other records.* Other records of the Director of the Office of Professional Responsibility may be disclosed upon specific request, in accordance with the applicable law.

(b) [sic] *Effective/applicability date.* This section is applicable on September 26, 2007.

§10.91   SAVING PROVISION

Any proceeding instituted under this part prior to July 26, 2002, for which a final decision has not been reached or for which judicial review is still available will not be affected by these revisions. Any proceeding under this part based on conduct engaged in prior to September 26, 2007, which is instituted after that date, will apply subpart D and E or this part as revised, but the conduct engaged in prior to the effective date of these revisions will be judged by the regulations in effect at the time the conduct occurred.

§10.92   SPECIAL ORDERS

The Secretary of the Treasury reserves the power to issue such special orders as he or she deems proper in any cases within the purview of this part.

§10.93   EFFECTIVE DATE

Except as otherwise provided in each section and Subject to §10.91, Part 10 is applicable on July 26, 2002.

Appendix D

United States Tax Court Rules of Practice

RULE 200. ADMISSION TO PRACTICE AND PERIODIC REGISTRATION FEES

(a) Qualifications.

(1) General. An applicant for admission to practice before the Court must establish to the satisfaction of the Court that the applicant is of good moral and professional character and possesses the requisite qualifications to provide competent representation before the Court. In addition, the applicant must satisfy the other requirements of this Rule. If the applicant fails to satisfy the requirements of this Rule, then the Court may deny such applicant admission to practice before the Court.

(2) Attorney Applicants. An applicant who is an attorney at law must, as a condition of being admitted to practice, file with the Admissions Clerk at the address listed in Rule 200(b) a completed application accompanied by a fee to be established by the Court, see Appendix II, and a current certificate from the Clerk of the appropriate court, showing that the applicant has been admitted to practice before and is a member in good standing of the Bar of the Supreme Court of the United States, or of the highest or appropriate court of any State or of the District of Columbia, or any commonwealth, territory, or possession of the United States. A current court certificate is one executed within 90 calendar days preceding the date of the filing of the application.

(3) Nonattorney Applicants. An applicant who is not an attorney at law must, as a condition of being admitted to practice, file with the Admissions Clerk at the address listed in Rule 200(b), a completed application accompanied by a fee to be established by the Court. See Appendix II. In addition, such an applicant must, as a condition of being admitted to practice, satisfy the Court, by means of a written examination given by the Court, that the applicant possesses the requisite qualifications to provide competent representation before the Court. Written examinations for applicants who are not attorneys at law will be held no less often than every two years. By public announcement at least six months prior to the date of each examination, the Court will announce the date and the time of such examination. The Court will notify each applicant, whose application for admission is in order, of the time and the place at which the applicant is to be present for such

examination, and the applicant must present that notice to the examiner as authority for taking such examination.

(b) Applications for Admission. An application for admission to practice before the Court must be on the form provided by the Court. Application forms and other necessary information will be furnished upon request addressed to the Admissions Clerk, United States Tax Court, 400 Second St., N.W., Washington, D.C. 20217. As to forms of payment for application fees, see Rule 11.

(c) Sponsorship. An applicant for admission by examination must be sponsored by at least two persons theretofore admitted to practice before this Court, and each sponsor must send a letter of recommendation directly to the Admissions Clerk at the address listed in Rule 200(b), where it will be treated as a confidential communication. The sponsor shall send this letter promptly after the applicant has been notified that he or she has passed the written examination required by paragraph (a)(3). The sponsor shall state fully and frankly the extent of the sponsor's acquaintance with the applicant, the sponsor's opinion of the moral character and repute of the applicant, and the sponsor's opinion of the qualifications of the applicant to practice before this Court. The Court may in its discretion accept such an applicant with less than two such sponsors.

(d) Admission. Upon the Court's approval of an application for admission in which an applicant has subscribed to the oath or affirmation and upon an applicant's satisfaction of the other applicable requirements of this Rule, such applicant will be admitted to practice before the Court and be entitled to a certificate of admission.

(e) Change of Address. Each person admitted to practice before the Court shall promptly notify the Admissions Clerk at the address listed in Rule 200(b) of any change in office address for mailing purposes. See also Rule 21(b)(4) regarding the filing of a separate notice of change of address for each docket number in which such person has entered an appearance.

(f) Corporations and Firms Not Eligible. Corporations and firms will not be admitted to practice or recognized before the Court.

(g) Periodic Registration Fees.

(1) Each person admitted to practice before the Court shall pay a periodic registration fee. The frequency and the amount of such fee shall be determined by the Court, except that such amount shall not exceed $30 per calendar year. The Clerk shall maintain an Ineligible List containing the names of all persons admitted to practice before the Court who have failed to comply with the provisions of this Rule 200(g)(1). No such person shall be permitted to commence a case in the Court or enter an appearance in a pending case while on the Ineligible List. The name of any person appearing on the Ineligible List shall not be removed from the List until the currently due registration fee has been paid and arrearages have been made current. Each person admitted to practice before the Court, whether or not engaged in private practice, must pay the periodic registration fee. As to forms of payment, see Rule 11.

(2) The fees described in Rule 200(g)(1) shall be used by the Court to compensate independent counsel appointed by the Court to assist it with respect to disciplinary matters. See Rule 202(f).

RULE 201.   CONDUCT OF PRACTICE BEFORE THE COURT

(a) General. Practitioners before the Court shall carry on their practice in accordance with the letter and spirit of the Model Rules of Professional Conduct of the American Bar Association.

(b) Statement of Employment. The Court may require any practitioner before it to furnish a statement, under oath, of the terms and circumstances of his or her employment in any case.

RULE 202.   DISCIPLINARY MATTERS

(a) General. A member of the Bar of this Court may be disciplined by this Court as a result of:

(1) Conviction in any court of the United States, or of the District of Columbia, or of any state, territory, commonwealth, or possession of the United States of any felony or of any lesser crime involving false swearing, misrepresentation, fraud, criminal violation of any provision of the Internal Revenue Code, bribery, extortion, misappropriation, theft, or moral turpitude;

(2) Imposition of discipline by any other court of whose bar an attorney is a member, or an attorney's disbarment or suspension by consent or resignation from the bar of such court while an investigation into allegations of misconduct is pending;

(3) Conduct with respect to the Court which violates the letter and spirit of the Model Rules of Professional Conduct of the American Bar Association, the Rules of the Court, or orders or other instructions of the Court; or

(4) Any other conduct unbecoming a member of the Bar of the Court.

(b) Disciplinary Actions. Discipline may consist of disbarment, suspension from practice before the Court, reprimand, admonition, or any other sanction that the Court may deem appropriate. The Court may, in the exercise of its discretion, immediately suspend a practitioner from practice before the Court until further order of the Court. However, no person shall be suspended for more than 60 days or disbarred until such person has been afforded an opportunity to be heard. A Judge of the Court may immediately suspend any person for not more than 60 days for contempt or misconduct during the course of any trial or hearing.

(c) Disciplinary Proceedings. Upon the occurrence or allegation of any event described in Rule 202(a)(1) through (a)(4), except for any suspension imposed for 60 days or less pursuant to Rule 202(b), the Court shall issue to the practitioner an order to show cause why the practitioner should not be disciplined or shall otherwise take appropriate action. The order to show cause shall direct that a written response be filed within such period as the Court may direct and shall set a prompt hearing on the matter before one or more Judges of the Court. If the disciplinary proceeding is predicated upon the complaint of a Judge of the Court, the hearing shall be conducted before a panel of three other Judges of the Court.

(d) Reinstatement.

(1) A practitioner suspended for 60 days or less pursuant to Rule 202(b) shall be automatically reinstated at the end of the period of suspension.

(2) A practitioner suspended for more than 60 days or disbarred pursuant to Rule 202 may not resume practice before the Court until reinstated by order of the Court.

(A) A disbarred practitioner or a practitioner suspended for more than 60 days who wishes to be reinstated to practice before the Court must file a petition for reinstatement. Upon receipt of the petition for reinstatement, the Court may set the matter for prompt hearing before one or more Judges of the Court. If the disbarment or suspension for more than 60 days was predicated upon the complaint of a Judge of the Court, any such hearing shall be conducted before a panel of three other Judges of the Court.

(B) In order to be reinstated before the Court, the practitioner must demonstrate by clear and convincing evidence in the petition for reinstatement and at any hearing that such practitioner's reinstatement will not be detrimental to the integrity and standing of the Court's Bar or to the administration of justice, or subversive of the public interest.

(C) No petition for reinstatement under this Rule shall be filed within 1 year following an adverse decision upon a petition for reinstatement filed by or on behalf of the same person.

(e) Right to Counsel. In all proceedings conducted under the provisions of this Rule, the practitioner shall have the right to be represented by counsel.

(f) Appointment of Court Counsel. The Court, in its discretion, may appoint counsel to the Court to assist it with respect to any disciplinary matters.

(g) Jurisdiction. Nothing contained in this Rule shall be construed to deny to the Court such powers as are necessary for the Court to maintain control over proceedings conducted before it, such as proceedings for contempt under Code Section 7456 or for costs under Code Section 6673(a)(2).

Preparer Rules

IRC §6694. UNDERSTATEMENT OF TAXPAYER'S LIABILITY BY TAX RETURN PREPARER

(a) Understatement due to unreasonable positions.—

(1) In general.—Any tax return preparer who prepares any return or claim for refund with respect to which any part of an understatement of liability is due to a position described in paragraph (2) shall pay a penalty with respect to each such return or claim in an amount equal to the greater of—

(A) $1,000, or

(B) 50 percent of the income derived (or to be derived) by the tax return preparer with respect to the return or claim.

(2) Unreasonable position.—A position is described in this paragraph if—

(A) the tax return preparer knew (or reasonably should have known) of the position,

(B) there was not a reasonable belief that the position would more likely than not be sustained on its merits, and

(C)

(i) the position was not disclosed as provided in section 6662(d)(2)(B)(ii), or

(ii) there was no reasonable basis for the position.

(3) Reasonable cause exception.—No penalty shall be imposed under this subsection if it is shown that there is reasonable cause for the understatement and the tax return preparer acted in good faith.

(b) Understatement due to willful or reckless conduct.—

(1) In general.—Any tax return preparer who prepares any return or claim for refund with respect to which any part of an understatement of liability is due to a conduct described in paragraph (2) shall pay a penalty with respect to each such return or claim in an amount equal to the greater of—

(A) $5,000, or

(B) 50 percent of the income derived (or to be derived) by the tax return preparer with respect to the return or claim.

(2) Willful or reckless conduct.—Conduct described in this paragraph is conduct by the tax return preparer which is—

(A) a willful attempt in any manner to understate the liability for tax on the return or claim, or

(B) a reckless or intentional disregard of rules or regulations.

(3) Reduction in penalty.—The amount of any penalty payable by any person by reason of this subsection for any return or claim for refund shall be reduced by the amount of the penalty paid by such person by reason of subsection (a).

(c) Extension of period of collection where preparer pays 15 percent of penalty.—

(1) In general.—If, within 30 days after the day on which notice and demand of any penalty under subsection (a) or (b) is made against any person who is a tax return preparer, such person pays an amount which is not less than 15 percent of the amount of such penalty and files a claim for refund of the amount so paid, no levy or proceeding in court for the collection of the remainder of such penalty shall be made, begun, or prosecuted until the final resolution of a proceeding begun as provided in paragraph (2). Notwithstanding the provisions of section 7421(a), the beginning of such proceeding or levy during the time such prohibition is in force may be enjoined by a proceeding in the proper court. Nothing in this paragraph shall be construed to prohibit any counterclaim for the remainder of such penalty in a proceeding begun as provided in paragraph (2).

(2) Preparer must bring suit in district court to determine his liability for penalty.—If, within 30 days after the day on which his claim for refund of any partial payment of any penalty under subsection (a) or (b) is denied (or, if earlier, within 30 days after the expiration of 6 months after the day on which he filed the claim for refund), the tax return preparer fails to begin a proceeding in the appropriate United States district court for the determination of his liability for such penalty, paragraph (1) shall cease to apply with respect to such penalty, effective on the day following the close of the applicable 30-day period referred to in this paragraph.

(3) Suspension of running of period of limitations on collection.—The running of the period of limitations provided in section 6502 on the collection by levy or by a proceeding in court in respect of any penalty described in paragraph (1) shall be suspended for the period during which the Secretary is prohibited from collecting by levy or a proceeding in court.

(d) Abatement of penalty where taxpayer's liability not understated.—If at any time there is a final administrative determination or a final judicial decision that there was no understatement of liability in the case of any return or claim for refund with respect to which a penalty under subsection (a) or (b) has been assessed, such assessment shall be abated, and if any portion of such penalty has been paid the amount so paid shall be refunded to the person who made such payment as an overpayment of tax without regard to any period of limitations which, but for this subsection, would apply to the making of such refund.

(e) Understatement of liability defined.—For purposes of this section, the term "understatement of liability" means any understatement of the net amount payable with respect to any tax imposed by this title or any overstatement of the net amount creditable or refundable with respect to any such tax. Except as otherwise provided in subsection (d), the determination of whether or not there is an understatement of liability shall be made without regard to any administrative or judicial action involving the taxpayer.

(f) Cross reference.—

For definition of tax return preparer, see section 7701(a)(36).

IRC   §6695.   OTHER ASSESSABLE PENALTIES WITH RESPECT TO THE PREPARATION OF TAX RETURNS FOR OTHER PERSONS (OMITTING SUBSECTION b-g)

(a) Failure to furnish copy to taxpayer.—Any person who is a tax return preparer with respect to any return or claim for refund who fails to comply with section 6107(a) with respect to such return or claim shall pay a penalty of $50 for such failure, unless it is shown that such failure is due to reasonable cause and not due to willful neglect. The maximum penalty imposed under this subsection on any person with respect to documents filed during any calendar year shall not exceed $25,000.

IRC   §7701.   DEFINITIONS §7701(A)(36)

(a) When used in this title, where not otherwise distinctly expressed or manifestly incompatible with the intent thereof—

(36) Tax return preparer.—

(A) In general.—The term "tax return preparer" means any person who prepares for compensation, or who employs one or more persons to prepare for compensation, any return of tax imposed by this title or any claim for refund of tax imposed by this title. For purposes of the preceding sentence, the preparation of a substantial portion of a return or claim for refund shall be treated as if it were the preparation of such return or claim for refund.

(B) Exceptions.—A person shall not be an "tax return preparer" merely because such person—

(i) furnishes typing, reproducing, or other mechanical assistance,

(ii) prepares a return or claim for refund of the employer (or of an officer or employee of the employer) by whom he is regularly and continuously employed,

(iii) prepares as a fiduciary a return or claim for refund for any person, or

(iv) prepares a claim for refund for a taxpayer in response to any notice of deficiency issued to such taxpayer or in response to any waiver of restriction after the commencement of an audit of such taxpayer or another taxpayer if a determination in such audit of such other taxpayer directly or indirectly affects the tax liability of such taxpayer.

REGULATIONS

§1.6694-1   Section 6694 Penalties Applicable to Income Tax Return Preparer

(a) Overview. Section 6694(a) and section 6694(b) impose penalties on income tax return preparers for certain understatements of liability on a return or claim for refund. The section 6694(a) penalty is imposed for an understatement of liability with respect to tax imposed by subtitle A of the Internal Revenue Code that is due to a position for which there was not a realistic possibility of being sustained on its merits. The section 6694(b) penalty is imposed for an understatement of liability with respect to tax imposed by subtitle A of the Internal Revenue Code that is due to a willful attempt to understate tax liability or that is due to reckless or intentional disregard of rules or regulations. See §1.6694-2 for rules relating to the penalty under section 6694(a). See §1.6694-3 for rules relating to the penalty under section 6694(b).

(b) Income tax return preparer—

(1) In general. Solely for purposes of the regulations under section 6694, the term "income tax return preparer" ("preparer") means any person who is an income tax return preparer within the meaning of section 7701(a)(36) and §301.7701-15 of this Chapter, except that no more than one individual associated with a firm (for example, as a partner or employee) is treated as a preparer with respect to the same return or claim for refund. If a signing preparer is associated with a firm, that individual, and no other individual associated with the firm, is a preparer with respect to the return or claim for purposes of section 6694. If two or more individuals associated with a firm are income tax return preparers with respect to a return or claim for refund, within the meaning of section 7701(a)(36) and §301.7701-15 of this Chapter, and none of them is the signing preparer, only one of the individuals is a preparer (i.e., nonsigning preparer) with respect to that return or claim for purposes of section 6694. In such a case, ordinarily, the individual who is a preparer for purposes of section 6694 is the individual with overall supervisory responsibility for the advice given by the firm with respect to the return or claim. To the extent provided in §1.6694-2(a)(2) and §1.6694-3(a)(2), an individual and the firm with which the individual is associated may both be subject to penalty under section 6694 with respect to the same return or claim for refund. If an individual (other than the sole proprietor) who is associated with a sole proprietorship is subject to penalty under section 6694, the sole proprietorship is considered a "firm" for purposes of this paragraph.

(2) Signing and nonsigning preparers. A "signing preparer" is any preparer who signs a return of tax or claim for refund as a preparer. A "nonsigning preparer" is any preparer who is not a signing preparer. Examples of nonsigning preparers are preparers who provide advice (written or oral) to a taxpayer or to a

preparer who is not associated with the same firm as the preparer who provides the advice.

(3) Example. The provisions of paragraph (b) of this section are illustrated by the following example:

Example.   Attorney *A* provides advice to Client *C* concerning the proper treatment of a significant item on *C*'s income tax return. The advice constitutes preparation of a substantial portion of the return. In preparation for providing that advice, *A* discusses the matter with Attorney *B*, who is associated with the same firm as *A*, but *A* is the attorney with overall supervisory responsibility for the advice. Neither Attorney *A* nor any other attorney associated with *A*'s firm signs *C*'s return as a preparer. For purposes of the regulations under section 6694, *A* is a preparer with respect to *C*'s return and is subject to penalty under section 6694 with respect to *C*'s return. *B* is not a preparer with respect to *C*'s return and, therefore, is not subject to penalty under section 6694 with respect to a position taken on *C*'s return. This would be true even if *B* recommends that *A* advise *C* to take an undisclosed position that did not satisfy the realistic possibility standard. In addition, since *B* is not a preparer for purposes of the regulations under section 6694, *A* may not avoid a penalty under section 6694 with respect to *C*'s return by claiming he relied on the advice of *B*. See §1.6694- 2(d)(5).

(c) Understatement of liability. For purposes of the regulations under section 6694, an "understatement of liability" exists if, viewing the return or claim for refund as a whole, there is an understatement of the net amount payable with respect to any tax imposed by subtitle A of the Internal Revenue Code, or an overstatement of the net amount creditable or refundable with respect to any tax imposed by subtitle A of the Internal Revenue Code. The net amount payable in a taxable year with respect to the return for which the preparer engaged in conduct proscribed by section 6694 is not reduced by any carryback. Tax imposed by subtitle A of the Internal Revenue Code does not include additions to the tax provided by section 6654 and section 6655 (relating to underpayments of estimated tax). Except as provided in paragraph (d) of this section, the determination of whether an understatement of liability exists may be made in a proceeding involving the preparer apart from any proceeding involving the taxpayer.

(d) Abatement of penalty where taxpayer's liability not understated. If a penalty under section 6694(a) or section 6694(b) concerning a return or claim for refund has been assessed against one or more preparers, and if it is established at any time in a final administrative determination or a final judicial decision that there was no understatement of liability relating to the return or claim for refund, then—

(1) The assessment must be abated; and

(2) If any amount of the penalty was paid, that amount must be refunded to the person or persons who so paid, as if the payment were an overpayment of tax, without consideration of any period of limitations.

(e) Verification of information furnished by taxpayer—

(1) In general. For purposes of section 6694(a) and section 6694(b), the preparer generally may rely in good faith without verification upon information furnished by the taxpayer. Thus, the preparer is not required to audit, examine or review books and records, business operations, or documents or other evidence in order to verify independently the taxpayer's information. However, the preparer may not ignore the implications of information furnished to the preparer or actually known by the preparer. The preparer must make reasonable inquiries if the information as furnished appears to be incorrect or incomplete. Additionally, some provisions of the Code or regulations require that specific facts and circumstances exist—for example, that the taxpayer maintain specific documents, before a deduction may be claimed. The preparer must make appropriate inquiries to determine the existence of facts and circumstances required by a Code section or regulation as a condition to the claiming of a deduction.

(2) Example. The provisions of paragraph (e) of this section are illustrated by the following example:

Example.   A taxpayer, during an interview conducted by the preparer, stated that he had paid $6,500 in doctor bills and $5,000 in deductible travel and entertainment expenses during the tax year, when in fact he had paid smaller amounts. On the basis of this information, the preparer properly calculated deductions for medical expenses and for travel and entertainment expenses which resulted in an understatement of liability for tax. The preparer had no reason to believe that the medical expense and travel and entertainment expense information presented was incorrect or incomplete. The preparer did not ask for underlying documentation of the medical expenses but inquired about the existence of travel and entertainment expense records. The preparer was reasonably satisfied by the taxpayer's representations that the taxpayer had adequate records (or other sufficient corroborative evidence) for the deduction of $5,000 for travel and entertainment expenses. The preparer is not subject to a penalty under section 6694.

(f) Effective date. Sections 1.6694-1 through 1.6694-3 are generally effective for documents prepared and advice given after December 31, 1991. However, §1.6694-3(c)(3) (which provides that a preparer is not considered to have recklessly or intentionally disregarded a revenue ruling or notice if the position contrary to the ruling or notice has a realistic possibility of being sustained on its merits) is effective for documents prepared and advice given after December 31, 1989. Except as provided in the preceding sentence, section 6694 and the existing rules and regulations thereunder (to the extent not inconsistent with the statute as amended by the Omnibus Budget Reconciliation Act of 1989), and Notice 90-20, 1990-1 C.B. 328, apply to documents prepared and advice given on or before December 31, 1991. For the effective date of §1.6694-4, see §1.6694-4(d).

§301.7701-15 Income Tax Return Preparer

(a) In general. An income tax return preparer is any person who prepares for compensation, or who employs (or engages) one or more persons to prepare for compensation, other than for the person, all or a substantial portion of any return of tax under subtitle A of the Internal Revenue Code of 1954 or of any claim for refund of tax under subtitle A of the Internal Revenue Code of 1954.

(1) A person who furnishes to a taxpayer or other preparer sufficient information and advice so that completion of the return or claim for refund is largely a mechanical or clerical matter is considered an income tax return preparer, even though that person does not actually place or review placement of information on the return or claim for refund. See also paragraph (b) of this section.

(2) A person who only gives advice on specific issues of law shall not be considered an income tax return preparer, unless—

(i) The advice is given with respect to events which have occurred at the time the advice is rendered and is not given with respect to the consequences of contemplated actions; and

(ii) The advice is directly relevant to the determination of the existence, characterization, or amount of an entry on a return or claim for refund. For example, if a lawyer gives an opinion on a transaction which a corporation has consummated, solely to satisfy an accountant (not at the time a preparer of the corporation's return) who is attempting to determine whether the reserve for taxes set forth in the corporation's financial statement is reasonable, the lawyer shall not be considered a tax return preparer solely by reason of rendering such opinion.

(3) A person may be an income tax return preparer without regard to educational qualifications and professional status requirements.

(4) A person must prepare a return or claim for refund for compensation to be an income tax return preparer. A person who prepares a return or claim for refund for a taxpayer with no explicit or implicit agreement for compensation is not a preparer, even though the person receives a gift or return service or favor.

(5) A person who prepares a return or claim for refund outside the United States is an income tax return preparer, regardless of his nationality, residence, or the locations of his places of business, if the person otherwise satisfies the definition of income tax return preparer. Notwithstanding the provisions of §301.6109-1(g), the person shall secure an employer identification number if he is an employer of another preparer, is a partnership in which one or more of the general partners is a preparer, or is an individual not employed (or engaged) by another preparer. The person shall comply with the provisions of section 1203 of the Tax Reform Act of 1976 and the regulations thereunder.

(6) An official or employee of the Internal Revenue Service performing his official duties is not an income tax return preparer.

(7) The following persons are not income tax return preparers:

(i) Any individual who provides tax assistance under a Volunteer Income Tax Assistance (VITA) program established by the Internal Revenue Service;

(ii) Any organization sponsoring or administering a Volunteer Income Tax Assistance (VITA) program established by the Internal Revenue Service, but only with respect to that sponsorship or administration;

(iii) Any individual who provides tax counseling for the elderly under a program established pursuant to section 163 of the Revenue Act of 1978;

(iv) Any organization sponsoring or administering a program to provide tax counseling for the elderly established pursuant to section 163 of the Revenue Act of 1978, but only with respect to that sponsorship or administration;

(v) Any individual who provides tax assistance as part of a qualified Low-Income Taxpayer Clinic (LITC), as defined by section 7526, subject to the requirements of paragraphs (a)(7)(vii) and (viii) of this section; and

(vi) Any organization that is a qualified Low-Income Taxpayer Clinic (LITC), as defined by section 7526, subject to the requirements of paragraphs (a)(7)(vii) and (viii) of this section.

(vii) Paragraphs (a)(7)(v) and (vi) of this section apply only if any assistance with a return of tax or claim for refund under subtitle A is directly related to a controversy with the Internal Revenue Service for which the qualified LITC is providing assistance, or is an ancillary part of an LITC program to inform individuals for whom English is a second language about their rights and responsibilities under the Internal Revenue Code.

(viii) Notwithstanding paragraph (a)(7)(vii) of this section, paragraphs (a)(7)(v) and (vi) of this section do not apply if an LITC charges a separate fee or varies a fee based on whether the LITC provides assistance with a return of tax or claim for refund under subtitle A, or if the LITC charges more than a nominal fee for its services.

(b) Substantial preparation.

(1) Only a person (or persons acting in concert) who prepares all or a substantial portion of a return or claim for refund shall be considered to be a preparer (or preparers) of the return or claim for refund. A person who renders advice which is directly relevant to the determination of the existence, characterization, or amount of an entry on a return or claim for refund, will be regarded as having prepared that entry. Whether a schedule, entry, or other portion of a return or claim for refund is a substantial portion is determined by comparing the length and complexity of, and the tax liability or refund involved in, that portion to the length and complexity of, and tax liability or refund involved in, the return or claim for refund as a whole.

(2) For purposes of applying the rule of paragraph (b)(1) of this section, if the schedule, entry, or other portion of the return or claim for refund involves amounts of gross income, amounts of deductions, or amounts on the basis of which credits are determined which are—

(i) Less than $2,000; or

(ii) Less than $100,000, and also less than 20 percent of the gross income (or adjusted gross income if the taxpayer is an individual) as shown on the return or claim for refund, then the schedule or other portion is not considered to be a substantial portion. If more than one schedule, entry or other portion is involved, they shall be aggregated in applying the rule of this paragraph (b)(2). Thus, if a person, for an individual taxpayer's return, prepares a schedule for dividend income which totals $1,500 and gives advice making him a preparer of a schedule of medical expenses which results in a deduction for medical expenses of $1,500, the person is not a preparer if the taxpayer's adjusted gross income shown on the return is more than $15,000. This paragraph shall not apply to a person who prepares all of a return or claim for refund.

(3) A preparer of a return is not considered to be a preparer of another return merely because an entry or entries reported on the return may affect an entry reported on the other return, unless the entry or entries reported on the prepared return are directly reflected on the other return and constitute a substantial portion of the other return. For example, the sole preparer of a partnership return of income or a small business corporation income tax return is considered a preparer of a partner's or a shareholder's return if the entry or entries on the partnership or small business corporation return reportable on the partner's or shareholder's return constitute a substantial portion of the partner's or shareholder's return.

(c) Return and claim for refund—

(1) Return. A return of tax under subtitle A is a return filed by or on behalf of a taxpayer reporting the liability of the taxpayer for tax under subtitle A. A return of tax under subtitle A also includes an information return filed by or on behalf of a person or entity that is not a taxable entity and which reports information which is or may be reported on the return of a taxpayer of tax under subtitle A.

(i) A return of tax under subtitle A includes an individual or corporation income tax return, a fiduciary income tax return (for a trust or estate), a regulated investment company undistributed capital gains tax return, a return of a charitable remainder trust, a return by a transferor of stock or securities to a foreign corporation, foreign trust, or foreign partnership, a partnership return of income, a small business corporation income tax return, and a DISC return.

(ii) A return of tax under subtitle A does not include an estate tax return, a gift tax return, any other return of excise taxes or income taxes collected at source on wages, an individual or corporation declaration of estimated tax, an application for an extension of time to file an individual or corporation income tax return, or an information statement on Form 990, any Form 1099, or similar form.

(2) Claim for refund. A claim for refund of tax under subtitle A includes a claim for credit against any tax under subtitle A.

(d) Persons who are not preparers. A person shall not be considered to be a preparer of a return or claim for refund if the person performs only one or more of the following services:

(1) Typing, reproduction, or other mechanical assistance in the preparation of a return or claim for refund.

(2) Preparation of a return or claim for refund of a person, or an officer, a general partner, or employee of a person, by whom the individual is regularly and continuously employed or in which the individual is a general partner.

(3) Preparation of a return or claim for refund for a trust or estate of which the person either is a fiduciary or is an officer, general partner, or employee of the fiduciary.

(4) Preparation of a claim for refund for a taxpayer in response to—

(i) A notice of deficiency issued to the taxpayer; or

(ii) A waiver of restriction after initiation of an audit of the taxpayer or another taxpayer if a determination in the audit of the other taxpayer affects, directly or indirectly, the liability of the taxpayer for tax under subtitle A.

For purposes of paragraph (d)(2) of this section, the employee of a corporation owning more than 50 percent of the voting power of another corporation, or the employee of a corporation more than 50 percent of the voting power of which is owned by another corporation, is considered the employee of the other corporation as well. For purposes of paragraph (d)(3) of this section, an estate, guardianship, conservatorship, committee, and any similar arrangement for a taxpayer under a legal disability (such as a minor, an incompetent, or an infirm individual) is considered a trust or estate.

31 C.F.R. §§737-1 to 737-2828 (2007)

SUBPART A—GENERAL PROVISIONS

§15.737-1 SCOPE

This part contains rules governing discipline of a former officer or employee of the Department of the Treasury because of a post employment conflict of interest. Such discipline may include prohibition from practice before the Department or a separate statutory agency thereof as those terms are defined in this part.

§15.737-2 DEFINITIONS

For the purpose of this part—

(a) The term "Department" means the Department of the Treasury and includes the separate statutory agencies thereof.

(b) The term "Director" means the Director of Practice.

(c) The term "General Counsel" means the General Counsel of the Department.

(d) The term "practice" means any informal or formal appearance before, or, with the intent to influence, any oral or written communication to the Department or, where applicable, to a separate statutory agency thereof on a pending matter of business on behalf of any other person (except the United States).

(e) The term "separate statutory agency thereof" means an agency or bureau within the Department designated by rule by the Director, Office of Government Ethics, as a separate agency or bureau. The Internal Revenue Service, Bureau of Alcohol, Tobacco and Firearms, United States Secret Service, Bureau of the Mint, United States Customs Service, Bureau of Engraving and Printing, and Comptroller of the Currency were so designated effective July 1, 1979.

§15.737-3 DIRECTOR OF PRACTICE

There is, in the Office of the Secretary of the Treasury, the Office of Director of Practice. The Director shall institute and provide for the conduct of disciplinary proceedings involving former employees of the Department as authorized by

18 U.S.C. 207(j), and perform such other duties as are necessary or appropriate to carry out his/her functions under this part.

§15.737-4   OTHER DISCIPLINE

For activity alleged to violate 18 U.S.C. 207 (a), (b) or (c), the Director may also bring a disciplinary proceeding pursuant to the regulations governing practice before the Bureau of Alcohol, Tobacco and Firearms or the Internal Revenue Service as found in 31 CFR Part 8 and 31 CFR Part 10, respectively. Such proceeding may be consolidated with any proceeding brought pursuant to this part.

§15.737-5   RECORDS

There are made available to public inspection at the Office of Director of Practice the roster of all persons prohibited from practice before the Department. Other records may be disclosed upon specific request, in accordance with appropriate disclosure regulations of the Department.

SUBPART B. RULES APPLICABLE TO POST EMPLOYMENT PRACTICE BY OFFICERS AND EMPLOYEES OF THE DEPARTMENT

§15.737-6   INTERPRETATIVE STANDARDS

A determination that a former officer or employee of the Department violated 18 U.S.C. 207 (a), (b) or (c) will be made in conformance with the standards established in the interpretative regulations promulgated by the Office of Government Ethics and published at 5 CFR Part 737.

SUBPART C. ADMINISTRATIVE ENFORCEMENT PROCEEDINGS

§15.737-7   AUTHORITY TO PROHIBIT PRACTICE

Pursuant to 18 U.S.C. 207(j), if the General Counsel finds, after notice and opportunity for a hearing, that a former officer or employee of the Department violated 18 U.S.C. 207 (a), (b) or (c), the General Counsel in his/her discretion may prohibit that person from engaging in practice before the Department or a separate statutory agency thereof for a period not to exceed five years, or may take other appropriate disciplinary action.

§15.737-8   SPECIAL ORDERS

The General Counsel may issue special orders as he/she may consider proper in any case within the purview of this part.

§15.737-9   Receipt of Information Concerning Former Treasury Employee

If an officer or employee of the Department has reason to believe that a former officer or employee of the Department has violated 18 U.S.C. 207 (a), (b) or (c), or if any such officer or employee receives information to that effect, he/she shall promptly make a written report thereof, which report or a copy thereof shall be forwarded to the Inspector General, Department of the Treasury. If any other person has information of such violations, he/she may make a report thereof to the Inspector General or to any officer or employee of the Department. The Inspector General shall refer any information he/she deems warranted to the Director.

§15.737-10   Conferences

(a) *In general.* The Director may confer with a former officer or employee concerning allegations of misconduct irrespective of whether an administrative disciplinary proceeding has been instituted against him/her. If such conference results in a stipulation in connection with a proceeding in which such person is the respondent, the stipulation may be entered in the record at the instance of either party to the proceeding.

(b) *Voluntary suspension.* A former officer or employee, in order to avoid the institution or conclusion of a proceeding, may offer his/her consent to suspension from practice before the Department or a separate statutory agency thereof. The Director in his/her discretion, may suspend a former officer or employee in accordance with the consent offered.

§15.737-11   Institution of Proceeding

(a) Whenever the Director has reason to believe that any former officer or employee of the Department has violated 18 U.S.C. 207 (a), (b) or (c), he/she may reprimand such person or institute an administrative disciplinary proceeding for that person's suspension from practice before the Department or a separate statutory agency thereof. The proceeding shall be instituted by a complaint which names the respondent and is signed by the Director and filed in his/her office. Except in cases of willfulness, or where time, the nature of the proceeding, or the public interest does not permit, a proceeding will not be instituted under this section until facts or conduct which may warrant such action have been called to the attention of the proposed respondent in writing and he/she has been accorded the opportunity to provide his/her position on the matter.

(b) The Director shall coordinate proceedings under this part with the Department of Justice in cases where it initiates criminal prosecution.

§15.737-12   CONTENTS OF COMPLAINT

(a) *Charges.* A complaint shall give a plain and concise description of the allegations which constitute the basis for the proceeding. A complaint shall be deemed sufficient if it fairly informs the respondent of the charges against him/her so that the respondent is able to prepare a defense.

(b) *Demand for answer.* In the complaint, or in a separate paper attached to the complaint, notification shall be given of the place and time within which the respondent shall file his/her answer, which time shall not be less than 15 days from the date of service of the complaint, and notice shall be given that a decision by default may be rendered against the respondent in the event he/she fails to file an answer as required.

§15.737-13   SERVICE OF COMPLAINT AND OTHER PAPERS

(a) *Complaint.* The complaint or a copy thereof may be served upon the respondent by certified mail, or first-class mail as hereinafter provided; by delivering it to the respondent or his/her attorney or agent of record either in person or by leaving it at the office or place of business of the respondent, attorney or agent; or in any other manner which has been agreed to by the respondent. Where the service is by certified mail, the return post office receipt duly signed by or on behalf of the respondent shall be proof of service. If the certified mail is not claimed or accepted by the respondent and is returned undelivered, complete service may be made upon the respondent by mailing the complaint to him/her by first-class mail, addressed to him/her at the last address known to the Director. If service is made upon the respondent or his/her attorney or agent of record in person or by leaving the complaint at the office or place of business of the respondent, attorney or agent, the verified return by the person making service, setting forth the manner of service, shall be proof of such service.

(b) *Service of papers other than complaint.* Any paper other than the complaint may be served upon a respondent as provided in paragraph (a) of this section or by mailing the paper by first-class mail to the respondent at the last address known to the Director, or by mailing the paper by first-class mail to the respondent's attorney or agent of record. Such mailing shall constitute complete service. Notices may be served upon the respondent or his/her attorney or agent of record by telegraph.

(c) *Filing of papers.* Whenever the filing of a paper is required or permitted in connection with a proceeding, and the place of filing is not specified by this subpart or by rule or order of the Administrative Law Judge, the paper shall be filed with the Director of Practice, Department of the Treasury, Washington, D.C. 20220. All papers shall be filed in duplicate.

§15.737-14   ANSWER

(a) *Filing.* The respondent's answer shall be filed in writing within the time specified in the complaint, unless on application the time is extended by the Director or the Administrative Law Judge. The answer shall be filed in duplicate with the Director.

(b) *Contents.* The answer shall contain a statement of facts which constitute the grounds of defense, and it shall specifically admit or deny each allegation set forth in the complaint, except that the respondent shall not deny a material allegation in the complaint which he/she knows to be true, or state that he/she is without sufficient information to form a belief when in fact he/she possesses such information. The respondent may also state affirmatively special matters of defense.

(c) *Failure to deny or answer allegations in the complaint.* Every allegation in the complaint which is not denied in the answer shall be deemed to be admitted and may be considered as proved, and no further evidence in respect of such allegation need be adduced at a hearing. Failure to file an answer within the time prescribed in the notice to the respondent, except as the time for answer is extended by the Director or the Administrative Law Judge, shall constitute an admission of the allegations of the complaint and a waiver of hearing, and the Administrative Law Judge may make his/her decision by default without a hearing or further procedure.

§15.737-15   REPLY TO ANSWER

No reply to the respondent's answer shall be required, and new matter in the answer shall be deemed to be denied, but the Director may file a reply in his/her discretion or at the request of the Administrative Law Judge.

§15.737-16   PROOF; VARIANCE; AMENDMENT OF PLEADINGS

In the case of a variance between the allegations in a pleading and the evidence adduced in support of the pleading, the Administrative Law Judge may order or authorize amendment of the pleading to conform to the evidence: *Provided,* That the party who would otherwise be prejudiced by the amendment is given reasonable opportunity to meet the allegations of the pleading as amended; and the Administrative Law Judge shall make findings on any issue presented by the pleadings as so amended.

§15.737-17   MOTIONS AND REQUESTS

Motions and requests may be filed with the Director or with the Administrative Law Judge.

§15.737-18   REPRESENTATION

A respondent or proposed respondent may appear in person or he/she may be represented by counsel or other representative. The Director may be represented by an attorney or other employee of the Department.

§15.737-19   Administrative Law Judge

(a) *Appointment.* An Administrative Law Judge appointed as provided by 5 U.S.C. 3105 (1966), shall conduct proceedings upon complaints for the administrative disciplinary proceedings under this part.

(b) *Power of Administrative Law Judge.* Among other powers, the Administrative Law Judge shall have authority, in connection with any proceeding assigned or referred to him/her, to do the following:

(1) Administer oaths and affirmations;

(2) Make rulings upon motions and requests, which rulings may not be appealed from prior to the close of a hearing except, at the discretion of the Administrative Law Judge, in extraordinary circumstances;

(3) Determine the time and place of hearing and regulate its course and conduct;

(4) Adopt rules of procedure and modify the same from time to time as occasion requires for the orderly disposition of proceedings;

(5) Rule upon offers of proof, receive relevant evidence, and examine witnesses;

(6) Take or authorize the taking of depositions;

(7) Receive and consider oral or written argument on facts or law;

(8) Hold or provide for the holding of conferences for the settlement or simplification of the issues by consent of the parties;

(9) Assess the responsible party extraordinary costs attributable to the location of a hearing;

(10) Perform such acts and take such measures as are necessary or appropriate to the efficient conduct of any proceeding; and

(11) Make initial decisions.

§15.737-20   Hearings

(a) *In general.* The Administrative Law Judge shall preside at the hearing on a complaint for the suspension of a former officer or employee from practice before the Department. Hearings shall be stenographically recorded and transcribed and the testimony of witnesses shall be taken under oath or affirmation. Hearings will be conducted pursuant to 5 U.S.C. 556.

(b) *Public access to hearings.* Hearings will be closed unless an open hearing is requested by the respondent, except that if classified information or protected information of third parties (such as tax information) is likely to be adduced at the hearing, it will remain closed. A request for an open hearing must be included in the answer to be considered.

(c) *Failure to appear.* If either party to the proceeding fails to appear at the hearing, after due notice thereof has been sent to him/her, he/she shall be deemed to have waived the right to a hearing and the Administrative Law Judge may make a decision against the absent party by default.

§15.737-21   Evidence

(a) *In general.* The rules of evidence prevailing in courts of law and equity are not controlling in hearings on complaints for the suspension of a former officer or employee from practice before the Department. However, the Administrative Law Judge shall exclude evidence which is irrelevant, immaterial, or unduly repetitious.

(b) *Depositions.* The deposition of any witness taken pursuant to §15.737-22 of this part may be admitted.

(c) *Proof of documents.* Official documents, records and papers of the Department shall be admissible in evidence without the production of an officer or employee to authenticate them. Any such documents, records, and papers may be evidenced by a copy attested or identified by an officer or employee of the Department.

(d) *Exhibits.* If any document, record, or other paper is introduced in evidence as an exhibit, the Administrative Law Judge may authorize the withdrawal of the exhibit subject to any conditions which he/she deems proper.

(e) *Objections.* Objections to evidence shall be in short form, stating the grounds of objection relied upon, and the record shall not include argument thereon, except as ordered by the Administrative Law Judge. Rulings on such objections shall be a part of the record. No exception to the ruling is necessary to preserve the rights of the parties.

§15.737-22   Depositions

Depositions for use at a hearing may, with the consent of the parties in writing or the written approval of the Administrative Law Judge, be taken by either the Director or the respondent or their duly authorized representatives. Depositions may be taken upon oral or written interrogatories, upon not less than 10 days' written notice to the other party before any officer duly authorized to administer an oath for general purposes or before an officer or employee of the Department who is authorized to administer an oath. Such notice shall state the names of the witnesses and the time and place where the depositions are to be taken. The requirement of 10 days' notice may be waived by the parties in writing, and depositions may then be taken from the persons and at the times and places mutually agreed to by the parties. When a deposition is taken upon written interrogatories, any cross-examination shall be upon written interrogatories. Copies of such written interrogatories shall be served upon the other party with the notice, and copies of any written cross-interrogation shall be mailed or delivered to the opposing party at least 5 days before the date of taking the depositions, unless the parties mutually agree otherwise. A party upon whose behalf a deposition is taken must file it with the Administrative Law Judge and serve one copy upon the opposing party. Expenses in the reporting of depositions shall be borne by the party at whose instance the deposition is taken.

§15.737-23　Transcript

In cases where the hearing is stenographically reported by a Government contract reporter, copies of the transcript may be obtained from the reporter at rates not to exceed the maximum rates fixed by contract between the Government and the reporter or from the Department at actual cost of duplication. Where the hearing is stenographically reported by a regular employee of the Department, a copy thereof will be supplied to the respondent either without charge or upon payment of a reasonable fee. Copies of exhibits introduced at the hearing or at the taking of depositions will be supplied to the parties upon the payment of a reasonable fee (Sec. 501, Pub.L. 82-137, 65 Stat. 290 (31 U.S.C. 483a)).

§15.737-24　Proposed Findings and Conclusions

Except in cases where the respondent has failed to answer the complaint or where a party has failed to appear at the hearing, the Administrative Law Judge prior to making his/her decision, shall afford the parties a reasonable opportunity to submit proposed findings and conclusions and supporting reasons therefor.

§15.737-25　Decision of the Administrative Law Judge

As soon as practicable after the conclusion of a hearing and the receipt of any proposed findings and conclusions timely submitted by the parties, the Administrative Law Judge shall make the initial decision in the case. The decision shall include (a) a statement of findings and conclusions, as well as the reasons or basis therefor, upon all the material issues of fact, law, or discretion presented on the record, and (b) an order of suspension from practice before the Department or separate statutory agency thereof or other appropriate disciplinary action, or an order of dismissal of the complaint. The Administrative Law Judge shall file the decision with the Director and shall transmit a copy thereof to the respondent or his/her attorney of record. In the absence of an appeal to the General Counsel or review of the decision upon motion of the General Counsel, the decision of the Administrative Law Judge shall without further proceedings become the decision of the General Counsel 30 days from the date of the Administrative Law Judge's decision.

§15.737-26　Appeal to the General Counsel

Within 30 days from the date of the Administrative Law Judge's decision, either party may appeal to the General Counsel. The appeal shall be filed with the Director in duplicate and shall include exceptions to the decision of the Administrative Law Judge and supporting reasons for such exceptions. If an appeal is filed by the Director, he/she shall transmit a copy thereof to the respondent. Within 30 days after receipt of an appeal or copy thereof, the other party may file a reply brief in duplicate with the Director. If the reply brief is filed by the Director, he/she shall transmit a copy of it to the respondent. Upon the filing of an appeal and a reply brief, if any, the Director shall transmit the entire record to the General Counsel.

§15.737-27   DECISION OF THE GENERAL COUNSEL

On appeal from or review of the initial decision of the Administrative Law Judge, the General Counsel will make the agency decision. In making his/her decision, the General Counsel will review the record or such portions thereof as may be cited by the parties to permit limiting of the issues. A copy of the General Counsel's decision shall be transmitted to the respondent by the Director.

§15.737-28   NOTICE OF DISCIPLINARY ACTION

(a) Upon the issuance of a final order suspending a former officer or employee from practice before the Department or a separate statutory agency thereof, the Director shall give notice thereof to appropriate officers and employees of the Department. Officers and employees of the Department shall refuse to participate in any appearance by such former officer or employee or to accept any communication which constitutes the prohibited practice before the Department or separate statutory agency thereof during the period of suspension.

(b) The Director shall take other appropriate disciplinary action as may be required by the final order.

Appendix G

AICPA Statements on Standards for Tax Services (2000)

STATEMENT ON STANDARDS FOR TAX SERVICES NO. 1, TAX RETURN POSITIONS*

Introduction

1. This Statement sets forth the applicable standards for members when recommending tax return positions and preparing or signing tax returns (including amended returns, claims for refund, and information returns) filed with any taxing authority. For purposes of these standards, a tax return position is (a) a position reflected on the tax return as to which the taxpayer has been specifically advised by a member or (b) a position about which a member has knowledge of all material facts and, on the basis of those facts, has concluded whether the position is appropriate. For purposes of these standards, a taxpayer is a client, a member's employer, or any other third-party recipient of tax services.

Statement

2. The following standards apply to a member when providing professional services that involve tax return positions:

   a. A member should not recommend that a tax return position be taken with respect to any item unless the member has a good-faith belief that the position has a realistic possibility of being sustained administratively or judicially on its merits if challenged.

   b. A member should not prepare or sign a return that the member is aware takes a position that the member may not recommend under the standard expressed in paragraph 2a.

c. Notwithstanding paragraph 2a, a member may recommend a tax return position that the member concludes is not frivolous as long as the member advises the taxpayer to appropriately disclose. Notwithstanding paragraph 2b, the member may prepare or sign a return that reflects a position that the member concludes is not frivolous as long as the position is appropriately disclosed.

d. When recommending tax return positions and when preparing or signing a return on which a tax return position is taken, a member should, when relevant, advise the taxpayer regarding potential Tax Return Positions penalty consequences of such tax return position and the opportunity, if any, to avoid such penalties through disclosure.

3. A member should not recommend a tax return position or prepare or sign a return reflecting a position that the member knows—

a. Exploits the audit selection process of a taxing authority.

b. Serves as a mere arguing position advanced solely to obtain leverage in the bargaining process of settlement negotiation with a taxing authority.

4. When recommending a tax return position, a member has both the right and responsibility to be an advocate for the taxpayer with respect to any position satisfying the aforementioned standards.

Explanation

5. Our self-assessment tax system can function effectively only if taxpayers file tax returns that are true, correct, and complete. A tax return is primarily a taxpayer's representation of facts, and the taxpayer has the final responsibility for positions taken on the return.

6. In addition to a duty to the taxpayer, a member has a duty to the tax system. However, it is well established that the taxpayer has no obligation to pay more taxes than are legally owed, and a member has a duty to the taxpayer to assist in achieving that result. The standards contained in paragraphs 2, 3, and 4 recognize the members' responsibilities to both taxpayers and to the tax system.

7. In order to meet the standards contained in paragraph 2, a member should in good faith believe that the tax return position is warranted in existing law or can be supported by a good-faith argument for an extension, modification, or reversal of existing law. For example, in reaching such a conclusion, a member may consider a well-reasoned construction of the applicable statute, well-reasoned articles or treatises, or pronouncements issued by the applicable taxing authority, regardless of whether such sources would be treated as authority under Internal Revenue Code section 6662 and the regulations thereunder. A position would not fail to meet these standards merely because it is later abandoned for practical or procedural considerations during an administrative hearing or in the litigation process.

8. If a member has a good-faith belief that more than one tax return position meets the standards set forth in paragraph 2, a member's advice concerning alternative acceptable positions may include a discussion of the likelihood that each such position might or might not cause the taxpayer's tax return to be examined

and whether the position would be challenged in an examination. In such circumstances, such advice is not a violation of paragraph 3a.

9. In some cases, a member may conclude that a tax return position is not warranted under the standard set forth in paragraph 2a. A taxpayer may, however, still wish to take such a position. Under such circumstances, the taxpayer should have the opportunity to take such a position, and the member may prepare and sign the return provided the position is appropriately disclosed on the return or claim for refund and the position is not frivolous. A frivolous position is one that is knowingly advanced in bad faith and is patently improper.

10. A member's determination of whether information is appropriately disclosed by the taxpayer should be based on the facts and circumstances of the particular case and the authorities regarding disclosure in the applicable taxing jurisdiction. If a member recommending a position, but not engaged to prepare or sign the related tax return, advises the taxpayer concerning appropriate disclosure of the position, then the member shall be deemed to meet these standards.

11. If particular facts and circumstances lead a member to believe that a taxpayer penalty might be asserted, the member should so advise the taxpayer and should discuss with the taxpayer the opportunity to avoid such penalty by disclosing the position on the tax return. Although a member should advise the taxpayer with respect to disclosure, it is the taxpayer's responsibility to decide whether and how to disclose.

12. For purposes of this Statement, preparation of a tax return includes giving advice on events that have occurred at the time the advice is given if the advice is directly relevant to determining the existence, character, or amount of a schedule, entry, or other portion of a tax return.

INTERPRETATION NO. 1-1, "REALISTIC POSSIBILITY STANDARD" OF STATEMENT ON STANDARDS FOR TAX SERVICES NO. 1, TAX RETURN POSITIONS

Background

1. Statement on Standards for Tax Services (SSTS) No. 1, Tax Return Positions, contains the standards a member should follow in recommending tax return positions and in preparing or signing tax returns. In general, a member should have a good-faith belief that the tax return position being recommended has a realistic possibility of being sustained administratively or judicially on its merits, if challenged. The standard contained in SSTS No. 1, paragraph 2a, is referred to here as the realistic possibility standard. If a member concludes that a tax return position does not meet the realistic possibility standard: a. The member may still recommend the position to the taxpayer if the position is not frivolous, and the member recommends appropriate disclosure of the position; or b. The member may still prepare or sign a tax return containing the position, if the position is not frivolous, and the position is appropriately disclosed.

2. A frivolous position is one that is knowingly advanced in bad faith and is patently improper (see SSTS No. 1, paragraph 9). A member's determination of whether information is appropriately disclosed on a tax return or claim for refund is based on the facts and circumstances of the particular case and the authorities regarding disclosure in the applicable jurisdiction (see SSTS No. 1, paragraph 10).

3. If a member believes there is a possibility that a tax return position might result in penalties being asserted against a taxpayer, the member should so advise the taxpayer and should discuss with the taxpayer the opportunity, if any, of avoiding such penalties through disclosure (see SSTS No. 1, paragraph 11). Such advice may be given orally.

General Interpretation

4. To meet the realistic possibility standard, a member should have a good-faith belief that the position is warranted by existing law or can be supported by a good-faith argument for an extension, modification, or reversal of the existing law through the administrative or judicial process. Such a belief should be based on reasonable interpretations of the tax law. A member should not take into account the likelihood of audit or detection when determining whether this standard has been met (see SSTS No. 1, paragraphs 3a and 8).

5. The realistic possibility standard is less stringent than the substantial authority standard and the more likely than not standards that apply under the Internal Revenue Code (IRC) to substantial understatements of liability by taxpayers. The realistic possibility standard is stricter than the reasonable basis standard that is in the IRC.

6. In determining whether a tax return position meets the realistic possibility standard, a member may rely on authorities in addition to those evaluated when determining whether substantial authority exists under IRC section 6662. Accordingly, a member may rely on well-reasoned treatises, articles in recognized professional tax publications, and other reference tools and sources of tax analyses commonly used by tax advisers and preparers of returns.

7. In determining whether a realistic possibility exists, a member should do all of the following:

- Establish relevant background facts
- Distill the appropriate questions from those facts
- Search for authoritative answers to those questions
- Resolve the questions by weighing the authorities uncovered by that search
- Arrive at a conclusion supported by the authorities.

8. A member should consider the weight of each authority to conclude whether a position meets the realistic possibility standard. In determining the weight of an authority, a member should consider its persuasiveness, relevance, and source. Thus, the type of authority is a significant factor. Other important factors include whether

the facts stated by the authority are distinguishable from those of the taxpayer and whether the authority contains an analysis of the issue or merely states a conclusion.

9. The realistic possibility standard may be met despite the absence of certain types of authority. For example, a member may conclude that the realistic possibility standard has been met when the position is supported only by a well-reasoned construction of the applicable statutory provision.

10. In determining whether the realistic possibility standard has been met, the extent of research required is left to the professional judgment of the member with respect to all the facts and circumstances known to the member. A member may conclude that more than one position meets the realistic possibility standard.

Specific Illustrations

11. The following illustrations deal with general fact patterns. Accordingly, the application of the guidance discussed in the General Interpretation section to variations in such general facts or to particular facts or circumstances may lead to different conclusions. In each illustration there is no authority other than that indicated.

12. Illustration 1. A taxpayer has engaged in a transaction that is adversely affected by a new statutory provision. Prior law supports a position favorable to the taxpayer. The taxpayer believes, and the member concurs, that the new statute is inequitable as applied to the taxpayer's situation. The statute is constitutional, clearly drafted, and unambiguous. The legislative history discussing the new statute contains general comments that do not specifically address the taxpayer's situation.

13. Conclusion. The member should recommend the return position supported by the new statute. A position contrary to a constitutional, clear, and unambiguous statute would ordinarily be considered a frivolous position.

14. Illustration 2. The facts are the same as in illustration 1 except that the legislative history discussing the new statute specifically addresses the taxpayer's situation and supports a position favorable to the taxpayer.

15. Conclusion. In a case where the statute is clearly and unambiguously against the taxpayer's position but a contrary position exists based on legislative history specifically addressing the taxpayer's situation, a return position based either on the statutory language or on the legislative history satisfies the realistic possibility standard.

16. Illustration 3. The facts are the same as in illustration 1 except that the legislative history can be interpreted to provide some evidence or authority in support of the taxpayer's position; however, the legislative history does not specifically address the situation.

17. Conclusion. In a case where the statute is clear and unambiguous, a contrary position based on an interpretation of the legislative history that does not explicitly address the taxpayer's situation does not meet the realistic possibility standard. However, because the legislative history provides some support or evidence for the taxpayer's position, such a return position is not frivolous. A member may recommend the position to the taxpayer if the member also recommends appropriate disclosure.

18. Illustration 4. A taxpayer is faced with an issue involving the interpretation of a new statute. Following its passage, the statute was widely recognized to contain a drafting error, and a technical correction proposal has been introduced. The taxing authority issues a pronouncement indicating how it will administer the provision. The pronouncement interprets the statute in accordance with the proposed technical correction.

19. Conclusion. Return positions based on either the existing statutory language or the taxing authority pronouncement satisfy the realistic possibility standard.

20. Illustration 5. The facts are the same as in illustration 4 except that no taxing authority pronouncement has been issued.

21. Conclusion. In the absence of a taxing authority pronouncement interpreting the statute in accordance with the technical correction, only a return position based on the existing statutory language will meet the realistic possibility standard. A return position based on the proposed technical correction may be recommended if it is appropriately disclosed, since it is not frivolous.

22. Illustration 6. A taxpayer is seeking advice from a member regarding a recently amended statute. The member has reviewed the statute, the legislative history that specifically addresses the issue, and a recently published notice issued by the taxing authority. The member has concluded in good faith that, based on the statute and the legislative history, the taxing authority's position as stated in the notice does not reflect legislative intent.

23. Conclusion. The member may recommend the position supported by the statute and the legislative history because it meets the realistic possibility standard.

24. Illustration 7. The facts are the same as in illustration 6 except that the taxing authority pronouncement is a temporary regulation.

25. Conclusion. In determining whether the position meets the realistic possibility standard, a member should determine the weight to be given the regulation by analyzing factors such as whether the regulation is legislative or interpretative, or if it is inconsistent with the statute. If a member concludes that the position does not meet the realistic possibility standard, because it is not frivolous, the position may nevertheless be recommended if the member also recommends appropriate disclosure.

26. Illustration 8. A tax form published by a taxing authority is incorrect, but completion of the form as published provides a benefit to the taxpayer. The member knows that the taxing authority has published an announcement acknowledging the error.

27. Conclusion. In these circumstances, a return position in accordance with the published form is a frivolous position.

28. Illustration 9. A taxpayer wants to take a position that a member has concluded is frivolous. The taxpayer maintains that even if the taxing authority examines the return, the issue will not be raised.

29. Conclusion. The member should not consider the likelihood of audit or detection when determining whether the realistic possibility standard has been met.

The member should not prepare or sign a return that contains a frivolous position even if it is disclosed.

30. Illustration 10. A statute is passed requiring the capitalization of certain expenditures. The taxpayer believes, and the member concurs, that to comply fully, the taxpayer will need to acquire new computer hardware and software and implement a number of new accounting procedures. The taxpayer and member agree that the costs of full compliance will be significantly greater than the resulting increase in tax due under the new provision. Because of these cost considerations, the taxpayer makes no effort to comply. The taxpayer wants the member to prepare and sign a return on which the new requirement is simply ignored.

31. Conclusion. The return position desired by the taxpayer is frivolous, and the member should neither prepare nor sign the return.

32. Illustration 11. The facts are the same as in illustration 10 except that a taxpayer has made a good-faith effort to comply with the law by calculating an estimate of expenditures to be capitalized under the new provision.

33. Conclusion. In this situation, the realistic possibility standard has been met. When using estimates in the preparation of a return, a member should refer to SSTS No. 4, Use of Estimates.

34. Illustration 12. On a given issue, a member has located and weighed two authorities concerning the treatment of a particular expenditure. A taxing authority has issued an administrative ruling that required the expenditure to be capitalized and amortized over several years. On the other hand, a court opinion permitted the current deduction of the expenditure. The member has concluded that these are the relevant authorities, considered the source of both authorities, and concluded that both are persuasive and relevant.

35. Conclusion. The realistic possibility standard is met by either position.

36. Illustration 13. A tax statute is silent on the treatment of an item under the statute. However, the legislative history explaining the statute directs the taxing authority to issue regulations that will require a specific treatment of the item. No regulations have been issued at the time the member must recommend a position on the tax treatment of the item.

37. Conclusion. The member may recommend the position supported by the legislative history because it meets the realistic possibility standard.

38. Illustration 14. A taxpayer wants to take a position that a member concludes meets the realistic possibility standard based on an assumption regarding an underlying nontax legal issue. The member recommends that the taxpayer seek advice from its legal counsel, and the taxpayer's attorney gives an opinion on the nontax legal issue.

39. Conclusion. A member may in general rely on a legal opinion on a nontax legal issue. A member should, however, use professional judgment when relying on a legal opinion. If, on its face, the opinion of the taxpayer's attorney appears to be unreasonable, unsubstantiated, or unwarranted, a member should consult his or her attorney before relying on the opinion.

40. Illustration 15. A taxpayer has obtained from its attorney an opinion on the tax treatment of an item and requests that a member rely on the opinion.

41. Conclusion. The authorities on which a member may rely include well-reasoned sources of tax analysis. If a member is satisfied about the source, relevance, and persuasiveness of the legal opinion, a member may rely on that opinion when determining whether the realistic possibility standard has been met.

STATEMENT ON STANDARDS FOR TAX SERVICES NO. 2, ANSWERS TO QUESTIONS ON RETURNS

Introduction

1. This Statement sets forth the applicable standards for members when signing the preparer's declaration on a tax return if one or more questions on the return have not been answered. The term "questions" includes requests for information on the return, in the instructions, or in the regulations, whether or not stated in the form of a question.

Statement

2. A member should make a reasonable effort to obtain from the taxpayer the information necessary to provide appropriate answers to all questions on a tax return before signing as preparer.

Explanation

3. It is recognized that the questions on tax returns are not of uniform importance, and often they are not applicable to the particular taxpayer. Nevertheless, there are at least two reasons why a member should be satisfied that a reasonable effort has been made to obtain information to provide appropriate answers to the questions on the return that are applicable to a taxpayer.

a. A question may be of importance in determining taxable income or loss, or the tax liability shown on the return, in which circumstance an omission may detract from the quality of the return.

b. A member often must sign a preparer's declaration stating that the return is true, correct, and complete.

4. Reasonable grounds may exist for omitting an answer to a question applicable to a taxpayer. For example, reasonable grounds may include the following:

a. The information is not readily available and the answer is not significant in terms of taxable income or loss, or the tax liability shown on the return.

b. Genuine uncertainty exists regarding the meaning of the question in relation to the particular return.

c. The answer to the question is voluminous; in such cases, a statement should be made on the return that the data will be supplied upon examination.

5. A member should not omit an answer merely because it might prove disadvantageous to a taxpayer.

6. If reasonable grounds exist for omission of an answer to an applicable question, a taxpayer is not required to provide on the return an explanation of the reason for the omission. In this connection, a member should consider whether the omission of an answer to a question may cause the return to be deemed incomplete.

STATEMENT ON STANDARDS FOR TAX SERVICES NO. 3, CERTAIN PROCEDURAL ASPECTS OF PREPARING RETURNS

Introduction

1. This Statement sets forth the applicable standards for members concerning the obligation to examine or verify certain supporting data or to consider information related to another taxpayer when preparing a taxpayer's tax return.

Statement

2. In preparing or signing a return, a member may in good faith rely, without verification, on information furnished by the taxpayer or by third parties. However, a member should not ignore the implications of information furnished and should make reasonable inquiries if the information furnished appears to be incorrect, incomplete, or inconsistent either on its face or on the basis of other facts known to a member. Further, a member should refer to the taxpayer's returns for one or more prior years whenever feasible.

3. If the tax law or regulations impose a condition with respect to deductibility or other tax treatment of an item, such as taxpayer maintenance of books and records or substantiating documentation to support the reported deduction or tax treatment, a member should make appropriate inquiries to determine to the member's satisfaction whether such condition has been met.

4. When preparing a tax return, a member should consider information actually known to that member from the tax return of another taxpayer if the information is relevant to that tax return and its consideration is necessary to properly prepare that tax return. In using such information, a member should consider any limitations imposed by any law or rule relating to confidentiality.

Explanation

5. The preparer's declaration on a tax return often states that the information contained therein is true, correct, and complete to the best of the preparer's knowledge and belief based on all information known by the preparer. This type of reference should be understood to include information furnished by the taxpayer or by third parties to a member in connection with the preparation of the return.

6. The preparer's declaration does not require a member to examine or verify supporting data. However, a distinction should be made between (a) the need either

to determine by inquiry that a specifically required condition, such as maintaining books and records or substantiating documentation, has been satisfied or to obtain information when the material furnished appears to be incorrect or incomplete, and (b) the need for a member to examine underlying information. In fulfilling his or her obligation to exercise due diligence in preparing a return, a member may rely on information furnished by the taxpayer unless it appears to be incorrect, incomplete, or inconsistent. Although a member has certain responsibilities in exercising due diligence in preparing a return, the taxpayer has the ultimate responsibility for the contents of the return. Thus, if the taxpayer presents unsupported data in the form of lists of tax information, such as dividends and interest received, charitable contributions, and medical expenses, such information may be used in the preparation of a tax return without verification unless it appears to be incorrect, incomplete, or inconsistent either on its face or on the basis of other facts known to a member.

7. Even though there is no requirement to examine underlying documentation, a member should encourage the taxpayer to provide supporting data where appropriate. For example, a member should encourage the taxpayer to submit underlying documents for use in tax return preparation to permit full consideration of income and deductions arising from security transactions and from pass-through entities, such as estates, trusts, partnerships, and S corporations.

8. The source of information provided to a member by a taxpayer for use in preparing the return is often a pass-through entity, such as a limited partnership, in which the taxpayer has an interest but is not involved in management. A member may accept the information provided by the pass-through entity without further inquiry, unless there is reason to believe it is incorrect, incomplete, or inconsistent, either on its face or on the basis of other facts known to the member. In some instances, it may be appropriate for a member to advise the taxpayer to ascertain the nature and amount of possible exposure to tax deficiencies, interest, and penalties, by contact with management of the pass-through entity.

9. A member should make use of a taxpayer's returns for one or more prior years in preparing the current return whenever feasible. Reference to prior returns and discussion of prior-year tax determinations with the taxpayer should provide information to determine the taxpayer's general tax status, avoid the omission or duplication of items, and afford a basis for the treatment of similar or related transactions. As with the examination of information supplied for the current year's return, the extent of comparison of the details of income and deduction between years depends on the particular circumstances.

STATEMENT ON STANDARDS FOR TAX SERVICES NO. 4, USE OF ESTIMATES

Introduction

1. This Statement sets forth the applicable standards for members when using the taxpayer's estimates in the preparation of a tax return. A member may advise on

estimates used in the preparation of a tax return, but the taxpayer has the responsibility to provide the estimated data. Appraisals or valuations are not considered estimates for purposes of this Statement.

Statement

2. Unless prohibited by statute or by rule, a member may use the taxpayer's estimates in the preparation of a tax return if it is not practical to obtain exact data and if the member determines that the estimates are reasonable based on the facts and circumstances known to the member. If the taxpayer's estimates are used, they should be presented in a manner that does not imply greater accuracy than exists.

Explanation

3. Accounting requires the exercise of professional judgment and, in many instances, the use of approximations based on judgment. The application of such accounting judgments, as long as not in conflict with methods set forth by a taxing authority, is acceptable. These judgments are not estimates within the purview of this Statement. For example, a federal income tax regulation provides that if all other conditions for accrual are met, the exact amount of income or expense need not be known or ascertained at year end if the amount can be determined with reasonable accuracy.

4. When the taxpayer's records do not accurately reflect information related to small expenditures, accuracy in recording some data may be difficult to achieve. Therefore, the use of estimates by a taxpayer in determining the amount to be deducted for such items may be appropriate.

5. When records are missing or precise information about a transaction is not available at the time the return must be filed, a member may prepare a tax return using a taxpayer's estimates of the missing data.

6. Estimated amounts should not be presented in a manner that provides a misleading impression about the degree of factual accuracy.

7. Specific disclosure that an estimate is used for an item in the return is not generally required; however, such disclosure should be made in unusual circumstances where nondisclosure might mislead the taxing authority regarding the degree of accuracy of the return as a whole. Some examples of unusual circumstances include the following:

a. A taxpayer has died or is ill at the time the return must be filed.

b. A taxpayer has not received a Schedule K-1 for a pass-through entity at the time the tax return is to be filed.

c. There is litigation pending (for example, a bankruptcy proceeding) that bears on the return.

d. Fire or computer failure has destroyed the relevant records.

STATEMENT ON STANDARDS FOR TAX SERVICES NO. 5, DEPARTURE FROM A POSITION PREVIOUSLY CONCLUDED IN AN ADMINISTRATIVE PROCEEDING OR COURT DECISION

Introduction

1. This Statement sets forth the applicable standards for members in recommending a tax return position that departs from the position determined in an administrative proceeding or in a court decision with respect to the taxpayer's prior return.

2. For purposes of this Statement, administrative proceeding also includes an examination by a taxing authority or an appeals conference relating to a return or a claim for refund.

3. For purposes of this Statement, court decision means a decision by any court having jurisdiction over tax matters.

Statement

4. The tax return position with respect to an item as determined in an administrative proceeding or court decision does not restrict a member from recommending a different tax position in a later year's return, unless the taxpayer is bound to a specified treatment in the later year, such as by a formal closing agreement. Therefore, as provided in Statement on Standards for Tax Services (SSTS) No. 1, Tax Return Positions, the member may recommend a tax return position or prepare or sign a tax return that departs from the treatment of an item as concluded in an administrative proceeding or court decision with respect to a prior return of the taxpayer.

Explanation

5. If an administrative proceeding or court decision has resulted in a determination concerning a specific tax treatment of an item in a prior year's return, a member will usually recommend this same tax treatment in subsequent years. However, departures from consistent treatment may be justified under such circumstances as the following:

a. Taxing authorities tend to act consistently in the disposition of an item that was the subject of a prior administrative proceeding but generally are not bound to do so. Similarly, a taxpayer is not bound to follow the tax treatment of an item as consented to in an earlier administrative proceeding.

b. The determination in the administrative proceeding or the court's decision may have been caused by a lack of documentation. Supporting data for the later year may be appropriate.

c. A taxpayer may have yielded in the administrative proceeding for settlement purposes or not appealed the court decision, even though the position met the standards in SSTS No. 1.

d. Court decisions, rulings, or other authorities that are more favorable to a taxpayer's current position may have developed since the prior administrative proceeding was concluded or the prior court decision was rendered.

6. The consent in an earlier administrative proceeding and the existence of an unfavorable court decision are factors that the member should consider in evaluating whether the standards in SSTS No. 1 are met.

STATEMENT ON STANDARDS FOR TAX SERVICES NO. 6, KNOWLEDGE OF ERROR: RETURN PREPARATION

Introduction

1. This Statement sets forth the applicable standards for a member who becomes aware of an error in a taxpayer's previously filed tax return or of a taxpayer's failure to file a required tax return. As used herein, the term "error" includes any position, omission, or method of accounting that, at the time the return is filed, fails to meet the standards set out in Statement on Standards for Tax Services (SSTS) No. 1, Tax Return Positions. The term "error" also includes a position taken on a prior year's return that no longer meets these standards due to legislation, judicial decisions, or administrative pronouncements having retroactive effect. However, an error does not include an item that has an insignificant effect on the taxpayer's tax liability.

2. This Statement applies whether or not the member prepared or signed the return that contains the error.

Statement

3. A member should inform the taxpayer promptly upon becoming aware of an error in a previously filed return or upon becoming aware of a taxpayer's failure to file a required return. A member should recommend the corrective measures to be taken. Such recommendation may be given orally. The member is not obligated to inform the taxing authority, and a member may not do so without the taxpayer's permission, except when required by law.

4. If a member is requested to prepare the current year's return and the taxpayer has not taken appropriate action to correct an error in a prior year's return, the member should consider whether to withdraw from preparing the return and whether to continue a professional or employment relationship with the taxpayer. If the member does prepare such current year's return, the member should take reasonable steps to ensure that the error is not repeated.

Explanation

5. While performing services for a taxpayer, a member may become aware of an error in a previously filed return or may become aware that the taxpayer failed to file a required return. The member should advise the taxpayer of the error and the measures to be taken. Such recommendation may be given orally. If the member believes that the taxpayer could be charged with fraud or other criminal misconduct, the taxpayer should be advised to consult legal counsel before taking any action.

6. It is the taxpayer's responsibility to decide whether to correct the error. If the taxpayer does not correct an error, a member should consider whether to continue a professional or employment relationship with the taxpayer. While recognizing that the taxpayer may not be required by statute to correct an error by filing an amended return, a member should consider whether a taxpayer's decision not to file an amended return may predict future behavior that might require termination of the relationship. The potential for violating Code of Professional Conduct rule 301 (relating to the member's confidential client relationship), the tax law and regulations, or laws on privileged communications, and other considerations may create a conflict between the member's interests and those of the taxpayer. Therefore, a member should consider consulting with his or her own legal counsel before deciding upon recommendations to the taxpayer and whether to continue a professional or employment relationship with the taxpayer.

7. If a member decides to continue a professional or employment relationship with the taxpayer and is requested to prepare a tax return for a year subsequent to that in which the error occurred, the member should take reasonable steps to ensure that the error is not repeated. If the subsequent year's tax return cannot be prepared without perpetuating the error, the member should consider withdrawal from the return preparation. If a member learns that the taxpayer is using an erroneous method of accounting and it is past the due date to request permission to change to a method meeting the standards of SSTS No. 1, the member may sign a tax return for the current year, providing the tax return includes appropriate disclosure of the use of the erroneous method.

8. Whether an error has no more than an insignificant effect on the taxpayer's tax liability is left to the professional judgment of the member based on all the facts and circumstances known to the member. In judging whether an erroneous method of accounting has more than an insignificant effect, a member should consider the method's cumulative effect and its effect on the current year's tax return.

9. If a member becomes aware of the error while performing services for a taxpayer that do not involve tax return preparation, the member's responsibility is to advise the taxpayer of the existence of the error and to recommend that the error be discussed with the taxpayer's tax return preparer. Such recommendation may be given orally.

STATEMENT ON STANDARDS FOR TAX SERVICES NO. 7, KNOWLEDGE OF ERROR: ADMINISTRATIVE PROCEEDINGS

Introduction

1. This Statement sets forth the applicable standard for a member who becomes aware of an error in a return that is the subject of an administrative proceeding, such as an examination by a taxing authority or an appeals conference. The term "administrative proceeding" does not include a criminal proceeding. As used herein, the term "error" includes any position, omission, or method of accounting that, at the time the return is filed, fails to meet the standards set out in Statement on Standards for Tax Services (SSTS) No.1, Tax Return Positions. The term "error" also includes a position taken on a prior year's return that no longer meets these standards due to legislation, judicial decisions, or administrative pronouncements having retroactive effect. However, an error does not include an item that has an insignificant effect on the taxpayer's tax liability.

2. This Statement applies whether or not the member prepared or signed the return that contains the error. Special considerations may apply when a member has been engaged by legal counsel to provide assistance in a matter relating to the counsel's client.

Statement

3. If a member is representing a taxpayer in an administrative proceeding with respect to a return that contains an error of which the member is aware, the member should inform the taxpayer promptly upon becoming aware of the error. The member should recommend the corrective measures to be taken. Such recommendation may be given orally. A member is neither obligated to inform the taxing authority nor allowed to do so without the taxpayer's permission, except where required by law.

4. A member should request the taxpayer's agreement to disclose the error to the taxing authority. Lacking such agreement, the member should consider whether to withdraw from representing the taxpayer in the administrative proceeding and whether to continue a professional or employment relationship with the taxpayer.

Explanation

5. When the member is engaged to represent the taxpayer before a taxing authority in an administrative proceeding with respect to a return containing an error of which the member is aware, the member should advise the taxpayer to disclose the error to the taxing authority. Such recommendation may be given orally. If the member believes that the taxpayer could be charged with fraud or other

criminal misconduct, the taxpayer should be advised to consult legal counsel before taking any action.

6. It is the taxpayer's responsibility to decide whether to correct the error. If the taxpayer does not correct an error, a member should consider whether to withdraw from representing the taxpayer in the administrative proceeding and whether to continue a professional or employment relationship with the taxpayer. While recognizing that the taxpayer may not be required by statute to correct an error by filing an amended return, a member should consider whether a taxpayer's decision not to file an amended return may predict future behavior that might require termination of the relationship. Moreover, a member should consider consulting with his or her own legal counsel before deciding on recommendations to the taxpayer and whether to continue a professional or employment relationship with the taxpayer. The potential for violating Code of Professional Conduct rule 301 (relating to the member's confidential client relationship), the tax law and regulations, laws on privileged communications, potential adverse impact on a taxpayer of a member's withdrawal, and other considerations may create a conflict between the member's interests and those of the taxpayer.

7. Once disclosure is agreed on, it should not be delayed to such a degree that the taxpayer or member might be considered to have failed to act in good faith or to have, in effect, provided misleading information. In any event, disclosure should be made before the conclusion of the administrative proceeding.

8. Whether an error has an insignificant effect on the taxpayer's tax liability is left to the professional judgment of the member based on all the facts and circumstances known to the member. In judging whether an erroneous method of accounting has more than an insignificant effect, a member should consider the method's cumulative effect and its effect on the return that is the subject of the administrative proceeding.

STATEMENT ON STANDARDS FOR TAX SERVICES NO. 8, FORM AND CONTENT OF ADVICE TO TAXPAYERS

Introduction

1. This Statement sets forth the applicable standards for members concerning certain aspects of providing advice to a taxpayer and considers the circumstances in which a member has a responsibility to communicate with a taxpayer when subsequent developments affect advice previously provided. The Statement does not, however, cover a member's responsibilities when the expectation is that the advice rendered is likely to be relied on by parties other than the taxpayer.

Statement

2. A member should use judgment to ensure that tax advice provided to a taxpayer reflects professional competence and appropriately serves the taxpayer's

needs. A member is not required to follow a standard format or guidelines in communicating written or oral advice to a taxpayer.

3. A member should assume that tax advice provided to a taxpayer will affect the manner in which the matters or transactions considered would be reported on the taxpayer's tax returns. Thus, for all tax advice given to a taxpayer, a member should follow the standards in Statement on Standards for Tax Services (SSTS) No. 1, Tax Return Positions.

4. A member has no obligation to communicate with a taxpayer when subsequent developments affect advice previously provided with respect to significant matters, except while assisting a taxpayer in implementing procedures or plans associated with the advice provided or when a member undertakes this obligation by specific agreement.

Explanation

5. Tax advice is recognized as a valuable service provided by members. The form of advice may be oral or written and the subject matter may range from routine to complex. Because the range of advice is so extensive and because advice should meet the specific needs of a taxpayer, neither a standard format nor guidelines for communicating or documenting advice to the taxpayer can be established to cover all situations.

6. Although oral advice may serve a taxpayer's needs appropriately in routine matters or in well-defined areas, written communications are recommended in important, unusual, or complicated transactions. The member may use professional judgment about whether, subsequently, to document oral advice in writing.

7. In deciding on the form of advice provided to a taxpayer, a member should exercise professional judgment and should consider such factors as the following:

a. The importance of the transaction and amounts involved
b. The specific or general nature of the taxpayer's inquiry
c. The time available for development and submission of the advice
d. The technical complications presented
e. The existence of authorities and precedents
f. The tax sophistication of the taxpayer
g. The need to seek other professional advice

8. A member may assist a taxpayer in implementing procedures or plans associated with the advice offered. When providing such assistance, the member should review and revise such advice as warranted by new developments and factors affecting the transaction.

9. Sometimes a member is requested to provide tax advice but does not assist in implementing the plans adopted. Although such developments as legislative or administrative changes or future judicial interpretations may affect the advice previously provided, a member cannot be expected to communicate subsequent developments that affect such advice unless the member undertakes this obligation by specific agreement with the taxpayer.

10. Taxpayers should be informed that advice reflects professional judgment based on an existing situation and that subsequent developments could affect previous professional advice. Members may use precautionary language to the effect that their advice is based on facts as stated and authorities that are subject to change.

11. In providing tax advice, a member should be cognizant of applicable confidentiality privileges.

Table of Cases

Table of Rules, Codes, and Regulations

Index